Oracle Database Programming with Visual Basic.NET

Oracle Database Programming with Visual Basic.NET

Concepts, Designs, and Implementations

Ying Bai
Department of Computer Science and Engineering
Johnson C. Smith University
Charlotte, North Carolina

IEEE PRESS
WILEY

Published by John Wiley & Sons, Inc., Hoboken, New Jersey.
Published simultaneously in Canada.

For general information on our other products and services or for technical support, please contact our Customer Care Department within the United States at (800) 762-2974, outside the United States at (317) 572-3993 or fax (317) 572-4002.

Wiley also publishes its books in a variety of electronic formats. Some content that appears in print may not be available in electronic formats. For more information about Wiley products, visit our web site at www.wiley.com.

Library of Congress Cataloging-in-Publication Data applied for:

ISBN: 9781119734390

Cover design by Wiley
Cover image: © metamorworks/iStock/Getty Images

Set in 9.5/12.5pt STIXTwoText by SPi Global, Pondicherry, India

10 9 8 7 6 5 4 3 2 1

This book is dedicated to my wife, Yan Wang, and my daughter, Susan (Xue) Bai.

Contents

About the Author

Dr. YING BAI is a Professor in the Department of Computer Science and Engineering at Johnson C. Smith University. His special interests include: artificial intelligences, soft computing, mixed-language programming, fuzzy logic and deep learning, robotic controls, robots calibrations, and database programming.

His industry experience includes positions as software engineer and senior software engineer at companies such as Motorola MMS, Schlumberger ATE Technology, Immix TeleCom, and Lam Research.

Since 2003, Dr. Bai has published sixteen (16) books with publishers such as Prentice Hall, CRC Press LLC, Springer, Cambridge University Press, and Wiley IEEE Press. The Russian translation of his first book titled *Applications Interface Programming Using Multiple Languages* was published by Prentice Hall in 2005. The Chinese translation of his eighth book titled *Practical Database Programming with Visual C#.NET* was published by Tsinghua University Press in China in 2011. Most books are about software programming, serial port programming, fuzzy logic controls in industrial applications, microcontroller controls and programming as well as classical and modern controls on microcontrollers.

During recent years, Dr. Bai has also published more than sixty (60) academic research papers in IEEE Trans. Journals and International conferences.

Preface

Databases have become an integral part of our modern-day life. We are an information-driven society. Database technology has a direct impact on our daily lives. Decisions are routinely made by organizations based on the information collected and stored in the databases. A record company may decide to market certain albums in selected regions based on the music preference of teenagers. Grocery stores display more popular items at the eye level and reorders are based on the inventories taken at regular intervals. Other examples include patients' records in hospitals, customers' account information in banks, book orders by the libraries, club memberships, auto part orders, and winter cloth stock by department stores, and many others.

In addition to database management systems, in order to effectively apply and implement databases in real industrial or commercial systems, a good Graphic User Interface (GUI) is needed to allow users to access and manipulate their records or data in databases. Visual Basic.NET is an ideal candidate to be selected to provide this GUI functionality. Unlike other programming languages, Visual Basic.NET is a kind of language that has advantages such as easy-to-learn and easy-to-be-understood with little learning curves. In the beginning of Visual Studio.NET 2005, Microsoft integrated a few programming languages such as Visual C++, Visual Basic, C#, and Visual J# into a dynamic model called .NET Framework that makes Internet and Web programming easy and simple, and any language integrated in this model can be used to develop professional and efficient Web applications that can be used to communicate with others via Internet. ADO.NET and ASP. NET are two important submodels of .NET Framework. The former provides all components, including the Data Providers, DataSet, and DataTable, to access and manipulate data against different databases. The latter provides support to develop Web applications and Web services in ASP. NET environment to allow users to exchange information between clients and servers easily and conveniently.

This book is mainly designed for college students and software programmers who want to develop practical and commercial database programming with Visual Basic.NET and relational database such as Oracle XE 18c. The book provides a detailed description about the practical considerations and applications in database programming with Visual Basic.NET 2019 with authentic examples and detailed explanations. More important, a new writing style is developed and implemented in this book, combined with real examples, to provide readers with a clear picture as how to handle the database programming issues in Visual Basic.NET 2019 environment.

The outstanding features of this book include, but no limited to:

1) A novel writing style is adopted to try to attract students' or beginning programmers' interest in learning and developing practical database programs and to avoid the headache caused by using huge blocks of codes in the traditional database programming books.

2) Updated database programming tools and components are covered in the book, such as .NET Framework 4.7, LINQ, ADO.NET 4.6, and ASP.NET 4.6, to enable readers to easily and quickly learn and master advanced techniques in database programming and develop professional and practical database applications.

3) A real completed sample Oracle XE 18c database CSE_DEPT is provided and used for the entire book. Step by step, a detailed illustration and description about how to design and build a practical relational database are provided.

4) Covered both fundamental and advanced database-programming techniques to the convenience of both beginning students and experienced programmers.

5) All projects can be run in Microsoft Visual Studio.NET 2019 with Oracle XE 18c database.

6) Good textbook for college students, good reference book for programmers, software engineers, and academic researchers.

I sincerely hope that this book can provide useful and practical help and guide to all readers or users who adopted this book, and I will be more than happy to know that you guys can develop and build professional and practical database applications with the help of this book.

Ying Bai

Acknowledgments

First, a special thanks to my wife, Yan Wang, for I could not have finished this book without her sincere encouragement and support.

Special thanks also to Dr. Satish Bhalla, a specialist in database programming and management, especially in SQL Server, Oracle, and DB2, who spent a lot of time preparing materials for Chapter 2.

Many thanks to the Senior Editor, Mary Hatcher, who made this book available to the public, without whose perseverance and hard work this book would not be available in the market. Thanks should also go to the entire editorial team for all their contributions which made it possible to publish this book.

Thanks are extended to the following book reviewers for their valuable suggestions and inputs:

- Dr. Jiang (Linda) Xie, Professor, Department of Electrical and Computer Engineering, University of North Carolina at Charlotte.
- Dr. Dali Wang, Professor, Department of Physics and Computer Science, Christopher Newport University.
- Dr. Daoxi Xiu, Application Analyst Programmer, North Carolina Administrative Office of the Courts.

Finally, but not the least, I would like to express my gratitude to all the people who supported me in completing this book.

About the Companion Website

This book is accompanied by a companion website:

www.wiley.com/go/bai-VB-Oracle

The book companion website includes:

1) Instructor materials (accessible only by Instructors)

   a) HW DB Project Solutions
   b) HW Question Solutions
   c) Images
   d) Sample Database
   e) Teaching-PPT

2) Student materials

   a) Class DB Projects
   b) Images
   c) Sample Database
   d) VB Forms

1

Introduction

For many years during my teaching Visual Basic.NET programming and database-related programming courses in my college, I found that it is not easy to find a good textbook for this topic and I had to combine a few different professional books together as references to teach these courses. Most of those books are specially designed for programmers or software engineers, which cover a lot of programming strategies and huge blocks of codes, which is a terrible headache to the college students or beginning programmers who are new to the Visual Basic.NET and database programming. I have to prepare my class presentations and figure out all home works and exercises for my students. I dream that one day I could find a good textbook that is suitable for the college students or beginning programmers and could be used to help them to learn and master the database programming with Visual Basic.NET easily and conveniently. Finally, I decided that I need to do something for this dream myself after a long time waiting.

Another reason for me to have this idea is the job market. As you know, most industrial and commercial companies in US belong to database application businesses such as manufactures, banks, hospitals, and retails. Majority of them need professional people to develop and build database-related applications but not database management and design systems. To enable our students to become good candidates for those companies, we need to create a book like this one.

Unlike most of database programming books in the current market, which discuss and present the database programming techniques with huge blocks of programming codes from the first page to the last page, this book tries to use a new writing style to show readers, especially to the college students, how to develop professional and practical database programs with Visual Basic.NET by using Visual Studio.NET Design Tools and Wizards related to ADO.NET and to apply codes that are auto-generated by various Wizards. By using this new style, the over headache caused by using huge blocks of programming codes can be removed; instead, a simple and easy way to create database programs using the Design Tools can be taken to attract students' learning interest and furthermore to enable students to build professional and practical database programming in more efficient and interesting ways.

There are so many different database-programming books available on the market, but rarely can you find a book like this one, which implemented a novel writing style to attract the students' learning interests in this topic. To meet the needs of some experienced or advanced students or software engineers, the book contains two programming methods: the interesting and easy-to-learn fundamental database programming method – Visual Studio.NET Design Tools and

Oracle Database Programming with Visual Basic.NET: Concepts, Designs, and Implementations, First Edition. Ying Bai.
© 2021 The Institute of Electrical and Electronics Engineers, Inc. Published 2021 by John Wiley & Sons, Inc.
Companion website: www.wiley.com/go/bai-VB-Oracle

Wizards – and the advanced database programming method – runtime object method. In the second method, all database-related objects are created and applied during or when your project is running by utilizing quite a few blocks of codes.

1.1 Outstanding Features About This Book

1) All programming projects can be run in Microsoft Visual Studio.NET 2019 with Oracle XE 18c databases.
2) A novel writing style is adopted to try to attract students' or beginning programmers' interests in learning and developing practical database programs and to avoid the headache caused by using huge blocks of codes in the traditional database programming books.
3) Updated database programming tools and components are covered in the book, such as .NET Framework 4.7, LINQ, ADO.NET 4.6, and ASP.NET 4.7, to enable readers to easily and quickly learn and master advanced techniques in database programming and develop professional and practical database applications.
4) A real completed sample database `CSE_DEPT` with Oracle XE 18c database engine is provided and used for the entire book. Step by step, a detailed illustration and description about how to design and build a practical relational database are provided.
5) Covered both fundamental and advanced database programming techniques to convenience both beginning students and experienced programmers.
6) Provides homework and exercises for students and teaching materials for instructors, and these enable students to understand what they learned better by doing something themselves and allow instructors to organize and prepare their courses easily and rapidly.
7) Good textbook for college students, good reference book for programmers, software engineers, and academic researchers.

1.2 Who This Book Is For

This book is designed for college students and software programmers who want to develop practical and commercial database programming with Visual Basic.NET and relational databases such as Oracle XE 18c. Fundamental knowledge and understanding on Visual Basic.NET and Visual Studio.NET IDE is assumed.

1.3 What This Book Covered

Nine (9) chapters are included in this book. The contents of each chapter can be summarized as below.

- Chapter 1 provides an introduction and summarization to the whole book.
- Chapter 2 provides detailed discussions and analyses of the structure and components about relational databases. Some key technologies in developing and designing database are also given and discussed in this part. The procedure and components used to develop a practical relational database with Oracle XE 18c are analyzed in detailed with some real data tables in our sample database `CSE_DEPT`.

- Chapter 3 provides an introduction to the ADO.NET, which includes the architectures, organizations, and components of the ADO.NET. Detailed discussions and descriptions are provided in this chapter to give readers both fundamental and practical ideas and pictures in how to use components in ADO.NET to develop professional data-driven applications. Two ADO.NET architectures are discussed to enable users to follow the directions to design and build their preferred projects based on the different organizations of the ADO.NET. Four popular data providers, such as OleDb, ODBC, SQL Server, and Oracle, are discussed. The basic ideas and implementation examples of DataTable and DataSet are also analyzed and described with some real coding examples.

- Chapter 4 provides detailed discussions and analyses about the Language-Integrated Query (LINQ), which includes LINQ to Objects, LINQ to DataSet, LINQ to Entities, and LINQ to XML. An introduction to LINQ general programming guide is provided in the first part of this chapter. Some popular interfaces widely used in LINQ, such as IEnumerable, IEnumerable(Of T), IQueryable and IQueryable(Of T), and Standard Query Operators (SQO) including the deferred and non-deferred SQO, are also discussed in that part. An introduction to LINQ Query is given in the second section of this chapter. Following this introduction, a detailed discussion and analysis about the LINQ queries that are implemented for different data sources is provided in detail with quite a few example projects.

- Starting from Chapter 5, the real database programming techniques with Visual Basic.NET such as data selection queries are provided and discussed. Two parts are covered in this chapter: Part I contains the detailed descriptions in how to develop professional data-driven applications with the help of the Visual Studio.NET design tools and wizards with some real projects. This part contains a lot of hiding codes that are created by Visual Basic.NET automatically when using those design tools and wizards. Therefore, the coding job for this part is very simple and easy. Part II covers an advanced technique, the runtime object method, in developing and building professional data-driven applications. Detailed discussions and descriptions about how to build professional and practical database applications using this runtime object method are provided combined with four (4) real projects.

- Chapter 6 provides detailed discussions and analyses about three popular data insertion methods with Oracle XE 18c database:

  1) Using TableAdapter's DBDirect methods TableAdapter.Insert() method.
  2) Using the TableAdapter's Update() method to insert new records that have already been added into the DataTable in the DataSet.
  3) Using the Command object's ExecuteNonQuery() method.

  This chapter is also divided into two parts: Methods 1 and 2 are related to Visual Studio.NET design tools and wizards and therefore are covered in Part I. The third method is related to runtime object and therefore it is covered in Part II. Four (4) real projects are used to illustrate how to perform the data insertion into the Oracle XE 18c database. Some professional and practical data validation methods are also discussed in this chapter to confirm the data insertion.

- Chapter 7 provides discussions and analyses on three popular data updating and deleting methods with four real project examples:

  1) Using TableAdapter DBDirect methods such as TableAdapter.Update() and TableAdapter.Delete() to update and delete data directly again in the databases.
  2) Using TableAdapter.Update() method to update and execute the associated TableAdapter's properties such as UpdateCommand or DeleteCommand to save changes made for the table in the DataSet to the table in the database.

3) Using the runtime object method to develop and execute the Command's method ExecuteNonQuery() to update or delete data again in the database directly.

This chapter is also divided into two parts: Methods 1 and 2 are related to Visual Studio.NET design tools and wizards and therefore are covered in Part I. The third method is related to runtime object and it is covered in Part II. Four (4) real projects are used to illustrate how to perform the data updating and deleting against the database Oracle XE 18c. Some professional and practical data validation methods are also discussed in this chapter to confirm the data updating and deleting actions. The key points in performing the data updating and deleting actions against a relational database, such as the order to execute data updating and deleting between the parent and child tables, are also discussed and analyzed.

- Chapter 8 provides introductions and discussions about the developments and implementations of ASP.NET Web applications in Visual Basic.NET 2019 environment. At the beginning of Chapter 8, a detailed and complete description about the ASP.NET and the .NET Framework is provided, and this part is especially useful and important to students or programmers who do not have any knowledge or background in the Web application developments and implementations. Following the introduction section, a detailed discussion on how to install and configure the environment to develop the ASP.NET Web applications is provided. Some essential tools such as the Web server, IIS, and FrontPage Server Extension 2000 as well as the installation process of these tools are introduced and discussed in detail. Starting from Section 8.3, the detailed development and building process of ASP.NET Web applications to access the Oracle databases are discussed with four (4) real Web application projects. One popular database Oracle XE 18c is utilized as the target databases for those development and building processes.
- Chapter 9 provides introductions and discussions about the developments and implementations of ASP.NET Web services in Visual Basic.NET 2019 environment. A detailed discussion and analysis about the structure and components of the Web services is provided at the beginning of this chapter. One of the most popular databases, Oracle XE 18c, is discussed and used for three kinds of example Web service projects, which include:

1) WebServiceOracleSelect
2) WebServiceOracleInsert
3) WebServiceOracleUpdateDelete

Each Web service contains different Web methods that can be used to access different databases and perform the desired data actions such as Select, Insert, Update, and Delete via the Internet. To consume those Web services, different Web service client projects are also developed in this chapter. Both Windows-based and Web-based Web service client projects are discussed and built for each kind of Web services listed earlier. Totally, nine (9) projects, including the Web service and the associated Web service client projects, are developed in this chapter. All projects have been debugged and tested and can be run in most popular Windows compatible operating systems, such as Windows XP, Windows 7/8, and Windows 10.

1.4 How This Book Is Organized and How to Use This Book

This book is designed for both college students who are new to database programming with Visual Basic.NET and professional database programmers who has professional experience on this topic.

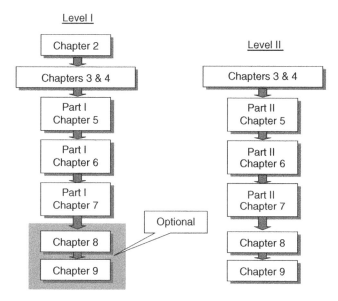

Figure 1.1 Two study levels in the book.

Chapters 2~4 provide the fundamentals on database structures and components, ADO.NET and LINQ components. Chapters 5~7 each is divided into two parts: fundamental part and advanced part. The data-driven applications developed with design tools and wizards provided by Visual Studio.NET, which can be considered as the fundamental part, have less coding loads and therefore they are more suitable to students or programmers who are new to the database programming with Visual Basic.NET. Part II contains the runtime object method and it covers a lot of coding developments to perform the different data actions against the database, and this method is more flexible and convenient to experienced programmers even a lot of coding jobs is concerned.

Chapters 8 and 9 give a full discussion and analysis about the developments and implementations of ASP.NET Web applications and Web services. These technologies are necessary to students and programmers who want to develop and build Web applications and Web services to access and manipulate data via Internet.

Based on the organization of this book we described earlier, this book can be used as two categories such as Level I and Level II, which is shown in Figure 1.1.

For undergraduate college students or beginning software programmers, it is highly recommended to learn and understand the contents of Chapters 2~4 and Part I of Chapters 5~7, since those are fundamental knowledge and techniques in database programming with Visual Basic. NET. Regarding Chapters 8 and 9, it is optional to instructors and it depends on the time and schedule available to instructors.

For experienced college students or software programmers who have already had some knowledge and techniques in database programming, it is recommended to learn and understand the contents of Part II of Chapters 5~7 as well as Chapters 8 and 9 since the runtime objects method and some sophisticated database programming techniques, such as joined-table query and nested stored procedures, are discussed and illustrated in those chapters with real examples. Also the ASP. NET Web applications and ASP.NET Web services are discussed and analyzed with many real database program examples for Oracle XE 18c database.

1.5   How to Use Appendices and Related Materials

Totally, nine (9) Appendices, Appendices A~I, are provided with the book to assist and help readers to easily and correctly download and install all required and necessary software and tools to build desired practical database projects. These Appendices provide crystal clear directions for readers to enable them to smoothly go through the entire installing and setup processes for each kind of software and development tool and make them ready to be used to build professional and practical database applications. The main functions and directions provided by these Appendices include:

- **Appendix A: Download and Install Oracle Database 18c XE.** Provides a complete and accurate direction to help users to complete downloading and installing this Oracle XE 18c Database with its engine.
- **Appendix B: Download and Install Oracle SQL Developer.** Provides an accurate direction to help users to complete downloading and installing this Oracle SQL Developer. This tool is a key component to build and develop any customer Oracle database, including our sample database **CSE_DEPT** with five data tables and keys.
- **Appendix C: Download and Install DevExpress WinForms.** Provides a complete direction to help users to complete downloading and installing this third-party tool. By using this tool, users can directly and conveniently insert any image into any table in Oracle database without any coding process. This product is a 30-day free trial version without any charge to the user.
- **Appendix D: How to Use the Sample Database.** To assist readers to quickly and easily build professional database application projects, a sample database, **CSE_DEPT,** is provided and used for entire book. This sample database is used to simulate a computer science and engineering department with five tables, **LogIn, Faculty, Course, Student,** and **StudentCourse.** This Appendix provides a clear picture to show readers how to download and duplicate this sample database in just some button clicks. Indeed, by using this Appendix and following up the directions, one can easily and quickly build this sample database without spending much time and efforts! It greatly simplifies the generation and building process of this sample database and therefore provides a quick shortcut for readers.
- **Appendix E: How to Export the Sample Database.** Opposite to Appendix D, this Appendix provides a way to show readers how to export our sample database **CSE_DEPT** to enable other users to import it to their blank database to simplify this database-building process. By following up the directions provided by this Appendix, readers can easily and quickly export their database to enable other users to import and make that database as their database. How easy it is!
- **Appendix F: Download and Install dotConnect Express.** This is a free-version third-party product that provides a data drive for Oracle data provider. To access an Oracle database from any programming environment, including Visual Basic.NET, a data drive is necessary to work as a translator or a bridge to setup up a connection between Visual Basic. NET and Oracle database engine. This Appendix provides a clear and complete direction to enable readers to quickly setup this connection.
- **Appendix G: How to Use User-Defined Windows/Web Forms.** To assist readers to speed up their database project developments, all Windows Forms and Web Pages used for all projects built in this book have been developed. Readers can use any of them by just simply adding them into their projects by using **Add|Existing Item** menu item. All built Windows Forms, including the **LogIn Form, Selection Form, Faculty Form,**

Course Form, and **Student Form,** and all built Web Pages, including the LogIn Page, Selection Page, Faculty Page, Course Page, and Student Page, can be found from a folder **VB Forms\Windows** and **VB Forms\Web,** which is located under the Students folder at the Wiley ftp site (refer to Figure 1.2).
- **Appendix H: Download and Install FrontPage Server Extension for Windows 10.** To run any project developed in Chapters 8 and 9, one needs to use Internet Information Services (IIS) provider. The FrontPage Server Extension can be considered as an administrator for IIS. To utilize the IIS more effectively and efficiently, it is recommend installing this extension if possible.

For instructors:

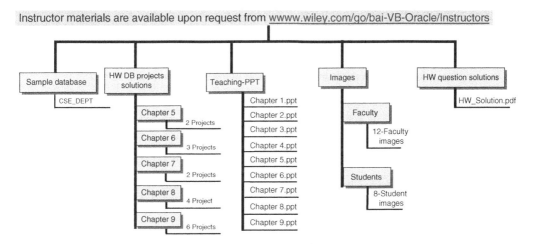

For students:

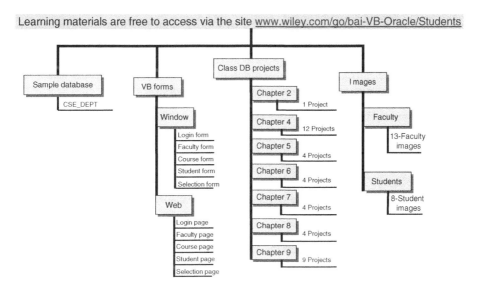

Figure 1.2 Book-related materials on Web site.

   – **Appendix I: Download and Install LinqConnect Express.** This is a free-version third-party product that provides a drive for LINQ to Oracle. To access and manipulate data records in an Oracle database via LINQ to Oracle, one needs to use some third-party tool or drive to setup a connection between any programming environment, including Visual Basic.NET, and the Oracle database engine. This Appendix provides a clear and complete direction to enable readers to quickly setup this connection and use this LINQ to Oracle technique to develop and build professional database applications.

1.6 How to Use Source Codes and Sample Database

All source codes in each project developed in this book are available and open to publics, and all projects are categorized and stored into the associated chapters, which are located at a folder **Class DB Projects** that is under the **Students** folder at the Wiley ftp site www.wiley.com/go/bai-VB-Oracle. You can copy or download those codes into your computer and run each project as you like. To successfully run those projects, the following conditions must be met:

- Visual Studio.NET 2019 or higher must be installed in your computer.
- The database management system, **Oracle Database Configuration Assistant,** must be installed in your computer.
- The sample database, **CSE_DEPT,** must be installed in your computer in the appropriate folders.
- To run projects developed in Chapters 8 and 9, in addition to conditions listed above, an Internet Information Services (IIS) such as FrontPage Server Extension 2000 or 2002 must be installed in your computer and it works as a pseudo server for those projects.
- Some third-party drives and tools, such as DevExpress WinForms, dotConnect for Oracle, LinqConnect Express, and Oracle SQL Developer, should have been installed in your computer.

All related teaching and learning materials, including the sample database, example projects, homework solutions, faculty and student images, as well as sample Windows forms and Web pages, can be found from the associated folders, **Instructors** or **Students,** located at the Wiley ftp site www.wiley.com/go/bai-VB-Oracle, as shown in Figure 1.2.

These materials are categorized and stored at different folders in two different sites based on the teaching purpose (for instructors) and learning purpose (for students):

1) **Sample Database** Folder: Contains our sample database, **CSE_DEPT** (Oracle XE 18c) with five (5) tables. Refer to Appendix D to get details in how to use this database for your applications or sample projects.
2) **Class DB Projects** Folder: Contains all sample projects developed in the book. Projects are categorized and stored at different Chapter subfolder based on the book chapter sequence. Readers can directly use the codes and GUIs of those projects by downloading them from this folder that is located under the **Students** folder at the Wiley ftp site.
3) **Images** Folder: Contains all sample faculty image files (under the **Images\Faculty** subfolder) and all student image files (under the **Images\Students** subfolder) used in all sample projects in the book. Readers can copy and paste those image files to their projects to use them.
4) **VB Forms** Folder: Contains all sampled Windows-based Forms (under the **VB Forms\ Window** subfolder) and Web-based Pages (under the **VB Forms\Web** subfolder) developed and implemented in all sample projects in the book. Readers can use those Forms or Pages by

adding them into their real projects with the **Add|Existing** Item menu item in the Visual Studio.NET environment.

5) **Teaching-PPT** Folder: Contains all MS-PPT teaching slides for each chapter.

6) **HW Question Solutions Folder:** Contains selected solutions for the homework Questions developed and used in the book. The solutions are categorized and stored at the different Chapter subfolder based on the book chapter sequence.

7) **HW DB Project Solutions Folder:** Contains all solutions for the homework Exercises developed and used in the book. The project solutions are categorized and stored at the different Chapter subfolder based on the book chapter sequence.

Folders 1~4 belong to learning materials for students; therefore, they are located at the sub-folder **Students** at the site: www.wiley.com/go/bai-VB-Oracle. Folders 1~3 and 5~7 belong to teaching materials for instructors, they are located at the sub-folder **Instructors** at the same site (password protected) and available upon requests by instructors.

1.7 Instructors and Customer Supports

The teaching materials for all chapters have been extracted and represented by a sequence of Microsoft Power Point files, each file for one chapter. The interested instructors can find them from the folder **Teaching-PPT** that is located at a sub-folder **Instructors** at the site www.wiley.com/go/bai-VB-Oracle and those instructor materials are available upon request from the book's listing on that site (password protected).

A selected homework Questions solution and all homework Exercise solutions are also available upon request from the site. E-mail support is available to readers of this book. When you send e-mail to us, please provide the following information:

- The detailed description about your problems, including the error message and debug message, as well as the error or debug number if it is provided.
- Your name, job title, and company name.
- Please send all questions to the e-mail address: ybai@jcsu.edu.

Detailed structure and distribution of all book-related materials in the Wiley site, including the teaching and learning materials, are shown in Figure 1.2.

All projects in the folder **Instructors|HW DB Project Solutions** are different from those in the **Students** folder since the former contained solutions to projects in the Exercises part, but the latter have no solutions.

2

Introduction to Databases

Ying Bai and Satish Bhalla

Databases have become an integral part of our modern day life. Today, we are an information-driven society. Large amounts of data are generated, analyzed, and converted into different information at each moment. A recent example of biological data generation is the Human Genome project that was jointly sponsored by the Department of Energy (DOE) and the National Institute of Health (NIH). Many countries participated in this venture for more than 10 years. The project was a tremendous success. It was completed in 2003 and resulted in the generation of huge amount of genome data, currently stored in databases around the world. The scientists will be analyzing this data in years to come.

Database technology has a direct impact on our daily lives. Decisions are routinely made by organizations based on the information collected and stored in the databases. A record company may decide to market certain albums in selected regions based on the music preference of teenagers. Grocery stores display more popular items at the eye level, and reorders are based on the inventories taken at regular intervals. Other examples include book orders by the libraries, club memberships, auto part orders, winter cloth stock by department stores, and many others.

Database management programs have been in existence since the sixties. However, it was not until the seventies when E. F. Codd proposed the then revolutionary Relational Data Model that database technology really took off. In the early eighties, it received a further boost with the arrival of personal computers and microcomputer-based data management programs like dBase II (later followed by dBase III and IV). Today, we have a plethora of vastly improved programs for PCs and mainframe computers, including Microsoft Access, SQL Server, IBM DB2, Oracle, Sequel Server, MySQL, and others.

This chapter covers the basic concepts of database design followed by implementation of a specific relational database to illustrate the concepts discussed here. The sample database, CSE_DEPT, is used as a running example. The database structure is shown by using Microsoft Access, Microsoft SQL Server, and Oracle databases with a real Oracle 18c XE database sample in details. The topics discussed in this chapter include:

- What are databases and database programs?
  - File Processing System
  - Integrated Databases
- Various approaches to developing a Database
- Relational Data Model and Entity-Relationship (ER) Model

Oracle Database Programming with Visual Basic.NET: Concepts, Designs, and Implementations, First Edition. Ying Bai.
© 2021 The Institute of Electrical and Electronics Engineers, Inc. Published 2021 by John Wiley & Sons, Inc.
Companion website: www.wiley.com/go/bai-VB-Oracle

- Identifying Keys
  - Primary Keys, Foreign Keys, and Referential Integrity
- Defining Relationships
- Normalizing the Data
- Implementing the Relational Sample Database
  - Create Microsoft SQL Server 2017 Express Sample Database

2.1 What Are Databases and Database Programs?

A modern day database is a structured collection of data stored in a computer. The term structured implies that each record in the database is stored in a certain format. For example, all entries in a phone book are arranged in a similar fashion. Each entry contains a name, an address, and a telephone number of a subscriber. This information can be queried and manipulated by database programs. The data retrieved in answer to queries becomes information that can be used to make decisions. The databases may consist of a single table or related multiple tables. The computer programs used to create, manage, and query databases are known as a DataBase Management Systems (DBMSs). Similar to the databases, the DBMSs vary in complexity. Depending on the need of a user, one can use either a simple application or a robust program. Some examples of these programs were given earlier.

2.1.1 File Processing System

File processing system (FPS) is a precursor of the integrated database approach. The records for a particular application are stored in a file. An application program is needed to retrieve or manipulate data in this file. Thus, various departments in an organization will have their own file processing systems with their individual programs to store and retrieve data. The data in various files may be duplicated and not available to other applications. This causes redundancy and may lead to inconsistency, meaning that various files that supposedly contain the same information may actually contain different data values. Thus, duplication of data creates problems with data integrity. Moreover, it is difficult to provide access to multiple users with the file processing systems without granting them access to the respective application programs, which manipulate the data in those files.

The FPS may be advantageous under certain circumstances. For example, if data is static and a simple application will solve the problem, a more expensive DBMS is not needed. For example, in a small business environment, you want to keep track of the inventory of the office equipment purchased only once or twice a year. The data can be kept in an Excel spreadsheet and manipulated with ease from time to time. This avoids the need to purchase an expensive database program and hiring a knowledgeable database administrator. Before the DBMS's became popular, the data was kept in files and application programs were developed to delete, insert, or modify records in the files. Since specific application programs were developed for specific data

These programs lasted for months or years before modifications were necessitated by business needs.

2.1.2 Integrated Databases

A better alternative to a file processing system is an integrated database approach. In this environment, all data belonging to an organization is stored in a single database. The database is not a mere collection of files; there is a relation between the files. Integration implies a logical relationship, usually provided through a common column in the tables. The relationships are also stored within the database. A set of sophisticated programs known as DBMS is used to store, access, and manipulate the data in the database. Details of data storage and maintenance are hidden from the user. The user interacts with the database through the DBMS. A user may interact either directly with the DBMS or via a program written in a programming language such as Visual C++, Java, Visual Basic, or Visual C#. Only the DBMS can access the database. Large organizations employ Database Administrators (DBA's) to design and maintain large databases.

There are many advantages of using an integrated database approach over that of a file processing approach:

1) **Data sharing:** The data in the database is available to a large numbers of users who can access the data simultaneously and create reports and manipulate the data given proper authorization and rights.
2) **Minimizing data redundancy:** Since all the related data exists in a single database, there is a minimal need of data duplication. The duplication is needed to maintain relationship between various data items.
3) **Data consistency and data integrity:** Reducing data redundancy will lead to data consistency. Since data is stored in a single database, enforcing data integrity becomes much easier. Furthermore, the inherent functions of the DBMS can be used to enforce the integrity with minimum programming.
4) **Enforcing standards**: DBAs are charged with enforcing standards in an organization. DBA takes into account the needs of various departments and balances it against the overall need of the organization. DBA defines various rules such as documentation standards, naming conventions, update and recovery procedures etc. It is relatively easy to enforce these rules in a Database System, since it is a single set of programs which is always interacting with the data files.
5) **Improving security:** Security is achieved through various means such as controlling access to the database through passwords, providing various levels of authorizations, data encryption, providing access to restricted views of the database etc.
6) **Data independence:** Providing data independence is a major objective for any database system. Data independence implies that even if the physical structure of a database changes, the applications are allowed to access the database as before the changes were implemented. In other words, the applications are immune to the changes in the physical representation and access techniques.

The downside of using an integrated database approach has mainly to do with exorbitant costs associated with it. The hardware, the software, and maintenance are expensive. Providing security, concurrency, integrity, and recovery may add further to this cost. Furthermore, since DBMS consists of a complex set of programs, trained personnel are needed to maintain it.

2.2   Develop a Database

Database development process may follow a classical Systems Development Life Cycle.

1) **Problem Identification** – Interview the user, identify user requirements, and perform preliminary analysis of user needs.
2) **Project Planning** – Identify alternative approaches to solving the problem. Does the project need a database? If so define the problem. Establish scope of the project.
3) **Problem Analysis** – Identify specifications for the problem. Confirm the feasibility of the project. Specify detailed requirements

4) **Logical Design** – Delineate detailed functional specifications. Determine screen designs, report layout designs, data models etc.
5) **Physical Design** – Develop physical data structures.
6) **Implementation** – Select DBMS. Convert data to conform to DBMS requirements. Code programs; perform testing.
7) **Maintenance** – Continue program modification until desired results are achieved.

An alternative approach to developing a database is through a phased process which will include designing a conceptual model of the system that will imitate the real-world operation. It should be flexible and change when the information in the database changes. Furthermore, it should not be dependent upon the physical implementation. This process follows following phases:

1) **Planning and Analysis** – This phase is roughly equivalent to the first three steps mentioned above in the Systems Development Life Cycle. This includes requirement specifications, evaluating alternatives, and determining input, output, and reports to be generated.
2) **Conceptual Design** – Choose a data model and develop a conceptual schema based on the requirement specification that was laid out in the planning and analysis phase. This conceptual design focuses on how the data will be organized without having to worry about the specifics of the tables, keys, and attributes. Identify the entities that will represent tables in the database, identify attributes that will represent fields in a table, and identify each entity attribute relationship. ER diagrams provide a good representation of the conceptual design.
3) **Logical Design** – Conceptual design is transformed into a logical design by creating a roadmap of how the database will look before actually creating the database. Data model is identified; usually, it is the relational model. Define the tables (entities) and fields (attributes). Identify primary and foreign key for each table. Define relationships between the tables.
4) **Physical Design** – Develop physical data structures; specify file organization and data storage etc. Take into consideration the availability of various resources including hardware and software. This phase overlaps with the implementation phase. It involves the programming of the database taking into account the limitations of the DBMS used.
5) **Implementation** – Choose the DBMS that will fulfill the user needs. Implement the physical design. Perform testing. Modify if necessary or until the database functions satisfactorily.

2.3 Sample Database

We will use a sample database CSE_DEPT to illustrate some essential database concepts. Tables 2.1~2.5 show sample data tables stored in this database.

The data in CSE_DEPT database is stored in five tables – LogIn, Faculty, Course, Student, and StudentCourse. A table consists of row and columns (Figure 2.1). A row represents a record, and the column represents a field. Row is called a tuple, and a column is called an attribute. For example, Student table has seven columns or fields – student_id, name, gpa, major, schoolYear, and email. It has five records or rows.

2.3.1 Relational Data Model

Data model is like a blue print for developing a database. It describes the structure of the database and various data relationships and constraints on the data. This information is used in building tables, keys, and defining relationships. Relational model implies that a user perceives

Table 2.1 LogIn table.

user_name	pass_word	faculty_id	student_id
abrown	america	B66750	
ajade	tryagain		A97850
awoods	smart		A78835
banderson	birthday	A52990	
bvalley	see		B92996
dangles	tomorrow	A77587	
hsmith	try		H10210
terica	excellent		T77896
jhenry	test	H99118	
jking	goodman	K69880	
sbhalla	india	B86590	
sjohnson	jermany	J33486	
ybai	come	B78880	

Table 2.2 Faculty table.

faculty_id	faculty_name	office	phone	college	title	email	fimage
A52990	Black Anderson	MTC-218	750-378-9987	Virginia Tech	Professor	banderson@college.edu	NULL
A77587	Debby Angles	MTC-320	750-330-2276	University of Chicago	Associate Professor	dangles@college.edu	NULL
B66750	Alice Brown	MTC-257	750-330-6650	University of Florida	Assistant Professor	abrown@college.edu	NULL
B78880	Ying Bai	MTC-211	750-378-1148	Florida Atlantic University	Associate Professor	ybai@college.edu	NULL
B86590	Davis Bhalla	MTC-214	750-378-1061	University of Notre Dame	Associate Professor	dbhalla@college.edu	NULL
H99118	Jeff Henry	MTC-336	750-330-8650	Ohio State University	Associate Professor	jhenry@college.edu	NULL
J33486	Steve Johnson	MTC-118	750-330-1116	Harvard University	Distinguished Professor	sjohnson@college.edu	NULL
K69880	Jenney King	MTC-324	750-378-1230	East Florida University	Professor	jking@college.edu	NULL

Table 2.3 Course table.

course_id	course	credit	classroom	schedule	enrollment	faculty_id
CSC-131A	Computers in Society	3	TC-109	M-W-F: 9:00-9:55 AM	28	A52990
CSC-131B	Computers in Society	3	TC-114	M-W-F: 9:00-9:55 AM	20	B66750
CSC-131C	Computers in Society	3	TC-109	T-H: 11:00-12:25 PM	25	A52990
CSC-131D	Computers in Society	3	TC-109	M-W-F: 9:00-9:55 AM	30	B86590
CSC-131E	Computers in Society	3	TC-301	M-W-F: 1:00-1:55 PM	25	B66750

Table 2.3 (Continued)

course_id	course	credit	classroom	schedule	enrollment	faculty_id
CSC-131I	Computers in Society	3	TC-109	T-H: 1:00-2:25 PM	32	A52990
CSC-132A	Introduction to Programming	3	TC-303	M-W-F: 9:00-9:55 AM	21	J33486
CSC-132B	Introduction to Programming	3	TC-302	T-H: 1:00-2:25 PM	21	B78880
CSC-230	Algorithms & Structures	3	TC-301	M-W-F: 1:00-1:55 PM	20	A77587
CSC-232A	Programming I	3	TC-305	T-H: 11:00-12:25 PM	28	B66750
CSC-232B	Programming I	3	TC-303	T-H: 11:00-12:25 PM	17	A77587
CSC-233A	Introduction to Algorithms	3	TC-302	M-W-F: 9:00-9:55 AM	18	H99118
CSC-233B	Introduction to Algorithms	3	TC-302	M-W-F: 11:00-11:55 AM	19	K69880
CSC-234A	Data Structure & Algorithms	3	TC-302	M-W-F: 9:00-9:55 AM	25	B78880
CSC-234B	Data Structure & Algorithms	3	TC-114	T-H: 11:00-12:25 PM	15	J33486
CSC-242	Programming II	3	TC-303	T-H: 1:00-2:25 PM	18	A52990
CSC-320	Object Oriented Programming	3	TC-301	T-H: 1:00-2:25 PM	22	B66750
CSC-331	Applications Programming	3	TC-109	T-H: 11:00-12:25 PM	28	H99118
CSC-333A	Computer Arch & Algorithms	3	TC-301	M-W-F: 10:00-10:55 AM	22	A77587
CSC-333B	Computer Arch & Algorithms	3	TC-302	T-H: 11:00-12:25 PM	15	A77587
CSC-335	Internet Programming	3	TC-303	M-W-F: 1:00-1:55PM	25	B66750
CSC-432	Discrete Algorithms	3	TC-206	T-H: 11:00-12:25 PM	20	B86590
CSC-439	Database Systems	3	TC-206	M-W-F: 1:00-1:55 PM	18	B86590
CSE-138A	Introduction to CSE	3	TC-301	T-H: 1:00-2:25 PM	15	A52990
CSE-138B	Introduction to CSE	3	TC-109	T-H: 1:00-2:25 PM	35	J33486
CSE-330	Digital Logic Circuits	3	TC-305	M-W-F: 9:00-9:55 AM	26	K69880
CSE-332	Foundations of Semiconductors	3	TC-305	T-H: 1:00-2:25 PM	24	K69880
CSE-334	Elec. Measurement & Design	3	TC-212	T-H: 11:00-12:25 PM	25	H99118
CSE-430	Bioinformatics in Computer	3	TC-206	Thu: 9:30-11:00 AM	16	B86590
CSE-432	Analog Circuits Design	3	TC-309	M-W-F: 2:00-2:55 PM	18	K69880
CSE-433	Digital Signal Processing	3	TC-206	T-H: 2:00-3:25 PM	18	H99118
CSE-434	Advanced Electronics Systems	3	TC-213	M-W-F: 1:00-1:55 PM	26	B78880
CSE-436	Automatic Control and Design	3	TC-305	M-W-F: 10:00-10:55 AM	29	J33486
CSE-437	Operating Systems	3	TC-303	T-H: 1:00-2:25 PM	17	A77587
CSE-438	Advd Logic & Microprocessor	3	TC-213	M-W-F: 11:00-11:55 AM	35	B78880
CSE-439	Special Topics in CSE	3	TC-206	M-W-F: 10:00-10:55 AM	22	J33486

Table 2.4 Student table.

student_id	student_name	gpa	credits	major	schoolYear	email	simage
A78835	Andrew Woods	3.26	108	Computer Science	Senior	awoods@college.edu	NULL
A97850	Ashly Jade	3.57	116	Information System Engineering	Junior	ajade@college.edu	NULL
B92996	Blue Valley	3.52	102	Computer Science	Senior	bvalley@college.edu	NULL
H10210	Holes Smith	3.87	78	Computer Engineering	Sophomore	hsmith@college.edu	NULL
T77896	Tom Erica	3.95	127	Computer Science	Senior	terica@college.edu	NULL

Table 2.5 StudentCourse table.

s_course_id	student_id	course_id	credit	major
1000	H10210	CSC-131D	3	CE
1001	B92996	CSC-132A	3	CS/IS
1002	T77896	CSC-335	3	CS/IS
1003	A78835	CSC-331	3	CE
1004	H10210	CSC-234B	3	CE
1005	T77896	CSC-234A	3	CS/IS
1006	B92996	CSC-233A	3	CS/IS
1007	A78835	CSC-132A	3	CE
1008	A78835	CSE-432	3	CE
1009	A78835	CSE-434	3	CE
1010	T77896	CSC-439	3	CS/IS
1011	H10210	CSC-132A	3	CE
1012	H10210	CSC-331	2	CE
1013	A78835	CSC-335	3	CE
1014	A78835	CSE-438	3	CE
1015	T77896	CSC-432	3	CS/IS
1016	A97850	CSC-132B	3	ISE
1017	A97850	CSC-234A	3	ISE
1018	A97850	CSC-331	3	ISE
1019	A97850	CSC-335	3	ISE
1020	T77896	CSE-439	3	CS/IS
1021	B92996	CSC-230	3	CS/IS
1022	A78835	CSE-332	3	CE
1023	B92996	CSE-430	3	CE
1024	T77896	CSC-333A	3	CS/IS
1025	H10210	CSE-433	3	CE
1026	H10210	CSE-334	3	CE
1027	B92996	CSC-131C	3	CS/IS
1028	B92996	CSC-439	3	CS/IS

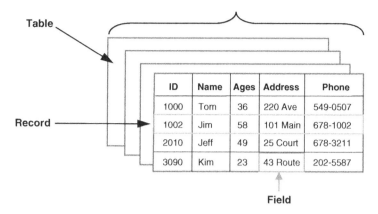

Figure 2.1 Records and fields in a table.

the database as made up of relations, a database jargon for tables. It is imperative that all data elements in the tables are represented correctly. In order to achieve these goals, designers use various tools. The most commonly used tool is ER Model. A well-planned model will give consistent results and will allow changes if needed later on. Following section further elaborates on the ER Model.

2.3.2 Entity-Relationship (ER) Model

ER model was first proposed and developed by Peter Chen in 1976. Since then Charles Bachman and James Martin have added some refinements, the model was designed to communicate the database design in the form of a conceptual schema. The ER model is based on the perception that the real world is made up of entities, their attributes, and relationships. The ER model is graphically depicted as ER diagrams (ERDs). ERDs are a major modeling tool; they graphically describe the logical structure of the database. ER diagrams can be used with ease to construct the relational tables and are a good vehicle for communicating the database design to the end user or a developer. The three major components of ERD are entities, relationships, and the attributes.

2.3.2.1 Entities
An entity is a data object, either real or abstract, about which we want to collect information. For example, we may want to collect information about a person, a place, or a thing. An entity in an ER diagram translates into a table. It should preferably be referred to as an entity set. Some common examples are departments, courses, and students. A single occurrence of an entity is an instance. There are four entities in the CSE_Dept database, LogIn, Faculty, Course, and Student. Each entity is translated into a table with the same name. An instance of the Faculty entity will be Alice Brown and her attributes.

2.3.2.2 Relationships
A database is made up of related entities. There is a natural association between the entities; it is referred to as relationship. For example,

- Students take courses
- Departments offer certain courses
- Employees are assigned to departments

The number of occurrences of one entity associated with single occurrence of a related entity is referred to as **cardinality**.

2.3.2.3 Attributes

Each entity has properties or values called attributes associated with it. The attributes of an entity map into fields in a table. *Database Processing* is one attribute of an entity called *Courses*. The domain of an attribute is a set of all possible values from which an attribute can derive its value.

2.4 Identifying Keys

2.4.1 Primary Key and Entity Integrity

An attribute that uniquely identifies one and only one instance of an entity is called a primary key. Sometimes a primary key consists of a combination of attributes. It is referred to as a *composite key*. *Entity integrity rule* states that no attribute that is a member of the primary (composite) key may accept a null value.

A **faculty_id** may serve as a primary key for the Faculty entity, assuming that all faculty members have been assigned a unique FaultyID. However, caution must be exercised when picking an attribute as a primary key. Last Name may not make a good primary key because a department is likely to have more than one person with the same last name. Primary keys for the CSE_DEPT database are shown in Table 2.6.

Primary keys provide a tuple level addressing mechanism in the relational databases. Once you define an attribute as a primary key for an entity, the DBMS will enforce the uniqueness of the primary key. Inserting a duplicate value for primary key field will fail.

Table 2.6 Faculty table.

faculty_id	faculty_name	title	office	phone	college	email	fimage
A52990	Black Anderson	Professor	MTC-218	750-378-9987	Virginia Tech	banderson@college.edu	NULL
A77587	Debby Angles	Associate Professor	MTC-320	750-330-2276	University of Chicago	dangles@college.edu	NULL
B66750	Alice Brown	Assistant Professor	MTC-257	750-330-6650	University of Florida	abrown@college.edu	NULL
B78880	Ying Bai	Associate Professor	MTC-211	750-378-1148	Florida Atlantic University	ybai@college.edu	NULL
B86590	Davis Bhalla	Associate Professor	MTC-214	750-378-1061	University of Notre Dame	dbhalla@college.edu	NULL
H99118	Jeff Henry	Associate Professor	MTC-336	750-330-8650	Ohio State University	jhenry@college.edu	NULL
J33486	Steve Johnson	Distinguished Professor	MTC-118	750-330-1116	Harvard University	sjohnson@college.edu	NULL
K69880	Jenney King	Professor	MTC-324	750-378-1230	East Florida University	jking@college.edu	NULL

2.4.2   Candidate Key

There can be more than one attribute which uniquely identifies an instance of an entity. These are referred to as *candidate keys*. Any one of them can serve as a primary key. For example, ID Number as well as Social Security Number may make a suitable primary key. Candidate keys that are not used as primary key are called *alternate keys*.

2.4.3   Foreign Keys and Referential Integrity

Foreign keys are used to create relationships between tables. It is an attribute in one table whose values are required to match those of primary key in another table. Foreign keys are created to enforce ***referential integrity*** which states that you may not add a record to a table containing a foreign key unless there is a corresponding record in the related table to which it is logically linked. Furthermore, the referential integrity rule also implies that every value of foreign key in a table must match the primary key of a related table or be null. MS Access also makes provision for cascade update and cascade delete which imply that changes made in one of the related tables will be reflected in the other of the two related tables.

   Consider two tables Course and Faculty in the sample database, CSE_DEPT. The Course table has a foreign key entitled faculty_id which is the primary key in the Faculty table. The two tables are logically related through the **faculty_id** link. Referential integrity rules imply that we may not add a record to the Course table with a faculty_id which is not listed in the Faculty table. In other words, there must be a logical link between the two related tables. Second, if we change or delete a faculty_id in the Faculty table, it must reflect in the Course table meaning that all records in the Course table must be modified using a cascade update or cascade delete (Tables 2.7).

2.5   Define Relationships

2.5.1   Connectivity

Connectivity refers to the types of relationships that entities can have. Basically, it can be *one-to-one, one-to-many, and many-to-many*. In ER diagrams, these are indicated by placing 1, M or N at one of the two ends of the relationship diagram. Figure illustrates the use of this notation.

Table 2.7   Course (Partial data shown);   Faculty (Partial data shown).

course_id	course	faculty_id		faculty_id	faculty_name	office
CSC-132A	Introduction to Programming	J33486		A52990	Black Anderson	MTC-218
CSC-132B	Introduction to Programming	B78880		A77587	Debby Angles	MTC-320
CSC-230	Algorithms & Structures	A77587		B66750	Alice Brown	MTC-257
CSC-232A	Programming I	B66750		B78880	Ying Bai	MTC-211
CSC-232B	Programming I	A77587		B86590	Davis Bhalla	MTC-214
CSC-233A	Introduction to Algorithms	H99118		H99118	Jeff Henry	MTC-336
CSC-233B	Introduction to Algorithms	K69880		J33486	Steve Johnson	MTC-118
CSC-234A	Data Structure & Algorithms	B78880		K69880	Jenney King	MTC-324

- A ***one-to-one*** **(1 : 1)** relationship occurs when one instance of entity A is related to only one instance of entity B. For example, **user_name** in the LogIn table and **user_name** in the Student table (Figure 2.2).
- A ***one-to-many*** **(1 : M)** relationship occurs when one instance of entity A is associated with zero, one, or many instances of entity B. However, entity B is associated with only one instance of entity A. For example, one department can have many faculty members; each faculty member is assigned to only one department. In CSE_DEPT database, One-to-many relationship is represented by **faculty_id** in the Faculty table and **faculty_id** in the Course table, **student_id** in the Student table and **student_id** in the StudentCourse table, **course_id** in the Course table and **course_id** in the StudentCourse table (Figure 2.3).
- A ***many-to-many*** **(M : N)** relationship occurs when one instance of entity A is associated with zero, one, or many instances of entity B. And one instance of entity B is associated with zero, one, or many instance of entity A. For example, a student may take many courses, and one course may be taken by more than one student (Figure 2.4).

In CSE_DEPT database, a many-to-many relationship can be realized by using the third table. For example, in this case, the StudentCourse that works as the third table set a many-to-many relationship between the Student and the Course tables.

This database design assumes that the course table only contains courses taught by all faculty members in this department for one semester. Therefore, each course can only be taught by a unique faculty. If one wants to develop a Course table that contains courses taught by all faculty in more than one semester, the third table, say FacultyCourse table, should be created to set up a many-to-many relationship between the Faculty and the Course table since one course may be taught by the different faculty for the different semester.

LogIn

user_name	pass_word
ajade	tryagain
awoods	smart
bvalley	see
hsmith	try
terica	excellent

Student

user_name	gpa	credits	student_id
ajade	3.26	108	A97850
awoods	3.57	116	A78835
bvalley	3.52	102	B92996
hsmith	3.87	78	H10210
terica	3.95	127	T77896

Figure 2.2 One-to-one relationship in the LogIn and the Student tables.

Faculty

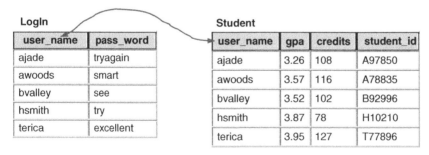

faculty_id	faculty_name	office
A52990	Black Anderson	MTC-218
A77587	Debby Angles	MTC-320
B66750	Alice Brown	MTC-257
B78880	Ying Bai	MTC-211
B86590	Davis Bhalla	MTC-214
H99118	Jeff Henry	MTC-336
J33486	Steve Johnson	MTC-118
K69880	Jenney King	MTC-324

Course

course_id	course	faculty_id
CSC-132A	Introduction to Programming	J33486
CSC-132B	Introduction to Programming	B78880
CSC-230	Algorithms & Structures	A77587
CSC-232A	Programming I	B66750
CSC-232B	Programming I	A77587
CSC-233A	Introduction to Algorithms	H99118
CSC-233B	Introduction to Algorithms	K69880
CSC-234A	Data Structure & Algorithms	B78880

Figure 2.3 One-to-many relationship between Faculty and Course tables.

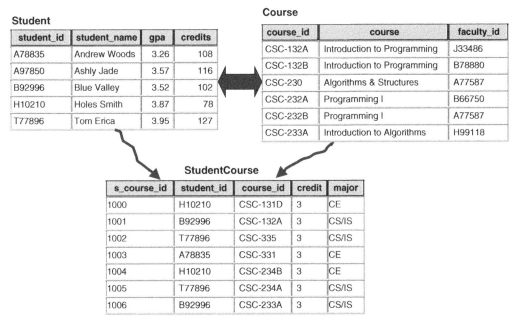

Figure 2.4 Many-to-many relationship between Student and Course tables.

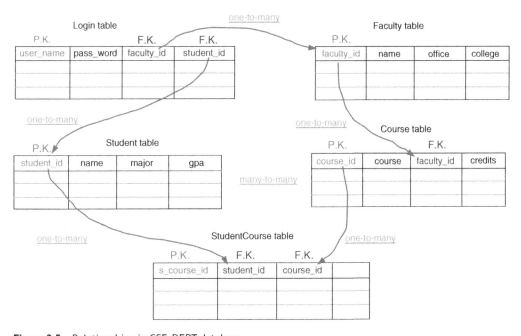

Figure 2.5 Relationships in CSE_DEPT database.

The relationships in CSE_DEPT database are summarized in Figure 2.5.

Database name: **CSE_DEPT**

Five entities are:

- LogIn
- Faculty

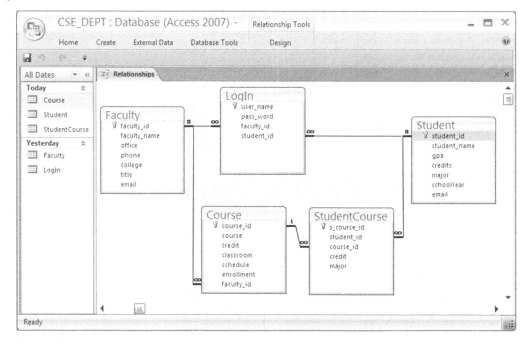

Figure 2.6 Relationships are illustrated using MS Access in the CSE_DEPT database. *Source*: Microsoft Corporation.

- Course
- Student
- StudentCourse

The relationships between these entities are shown below. **P.K.** and **F.K** represent the primary key and the foreign key, respectively.

Figure 2.6 displays the Microsoft Access relationships diagram among various tables in the CSE_ Dept database. One-to-many relationship is indicated by placing 1 at one end of the link and ∞ at the other. The many-to-many relationship between the Student and the Course table was broken down to two one-to-many relationships by creating a new StudentCourse table.

2.6 ER Notation

There are a number of ER notations available including Chen's, Bachman, Crow's foot, and a few others. There is no consensus on the symbols and the styles used to draw ERD's. A number of drawing tools are available to draw ERD's. These include ER Assistant, Microsoft Visio, and Smart Draw among others. Commonly used notations are shown in Figure 2.7.

2.7 Data Normalization

After identifying tables, attributes, and relationships, the next logical step in database design is to make sure that the database structure is optimum. Optimum structure is achieved by eliminating redundancies, various inefficiencies, and update and deletion anomalies that usually occur in the

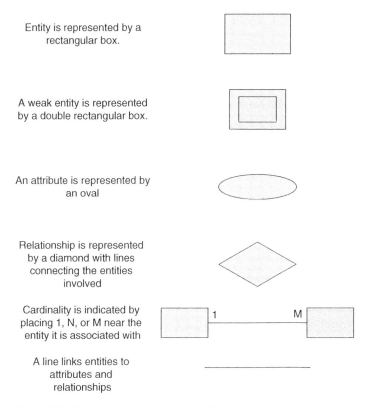

Entity is represented by a rectangular box.

A weak entity is represented by a double rectangular box.

An attribute is represented by an oval

Relationship is represented by a diamond with lines connecting the entities involved

Cardinality is indicated by placing 1, N, or M near the entity it is associated with

A line links entities to attributes and relationships

Figure 2.7 Commonly used symbols for ER notation.

unnormalized or partially normalized databases. Data normalization is a progressive process. The steps in the normalization process are called normal forms. Each normal form progressively improves the database and makes it more efficient. In other words, a database that is in second normal form (2NF) is better than the one in the first normal form (1NF), and the one in third normal form (3NF) is better than the one in 2NF. To be in the 3NF, a database has to be in the 1NF and 2NF. There are fourth and fifth normal forms but for most practical purposes, a database meeting the criteria of third normal form is considered to be of good design.

2.7.1   First Normal Form (1NF)

A table is in 1NF if values in each column are atomic, that is there are no repeating groups of data.

The following Faculty table (Table 2.8) is not normalized. Some faculty members have more than one telephone number listed in the phone column. These are called repeating groups.

In order to convert this table to the INF, the data must be atomic. In other words, the repeating rows must be broken into two or more atomic rows. Table 2.9 illustrates the Faculty table in 1NF where repeating groups have been removed. Now, it is in 1NF.

2.7.2   Second Normal Form (2NF)

A table is in 2NF if it is already in 1NF and every non-key column is fully dependent upon the primary key.

Table 2.8 Unnormalized Faculty table with repeating groups.

faculty_id	faculty_name	office	phone
A52990	Black Anderson	MTC-218, SHB-205	750-378-9987, 555-255-8897
A77587	Debby Angles	MTC-320	750-330-2276
B66750	Alice Brown	MTC-257	750-330-6650
B78880	Ying Bai	MTC-211, SHB-105	750-378-1148, 555-246-4582
B86590	Davis Bhalla	MTC-214	750-378-1061
H99118	Jeff Henry	MTC-336	750-330-8650
J33486	Steve Johnson	MTC-118	750-330-1116
K69880	Jenney King	MTC-324	750-378-1230

Table 2.9 Normalized Faculty table.

faculty_id	faculty_name	office	phone
A52990	Black Anderson	MTC-218	750-378-9987
A52990	Black Anderson	SHB-205	555-255-8897
A77587	Debby Angles	MTC-320	750-330-2276
B66750	Alice Brown	MTC-257	750-330-6650
B78880	Ying Bai	MTC-211	750-378-1148
B78880	Ying Bai	SHB-105	555-246-4582
B86590	Davis Bhalla	MTC-214	750-378-1061
H99118	Jeff Henry	MTC-336	750-330-8650
J33486	Steve Johnson	MTC-118	750-330-1116
K69880	Jenney King	MTC-324	750-378-1230

This implies that if the primary key consists of a single column, then the table in 1NF is automatically in 2NF. The second part of the definition implies that if the key is composite, then none of the non-key columns will depend upon just one of the columns that participates in the composite key.

The Faculty table in Table 2.9 is in 1NF. However, it has a composite primary key, made up of faculty_id and office. The phone number depends on a part of the primary key, the office and not on the whole primary key. This can lead to update and deletion anomalies mentioned above.

By splitting the old Faculty table (Figure 2.8) into two new tables, Faculty and Office, we can remove the dependencies mentioned earlier. Now, the faculty table has a primary key, faculty_id, and the Office table has a primary key, office. The non-key columns in both tables now depend only on the primary keys only.

2.7.3   Third Normal Form (3NF)

A table is in 3NF if it is already in 2NF and every non-key column is non-transitively dependent upon the primary key. In other words, all non-key columns are mutually independent, but at the same time, they are fully dependent upon the primary key only.

Old Faculty table in 1NF

faculty_id	faculty_name	office	phone
A52990	Black Anderson	MTC-218	750-378-9987
A52990	Black Anderson	SHB-205	555-255-8897
A77587	Debby Angles	MTC-320	750-330-2276
B66750	Alice Brown	MTC-257	750-330-6650
B78880	Ying Bai	MTC-211	750-378-1148
B78880	Ying Bai	SHB-105	555-246-4582
B86590	Davis Bhalla	MTC-214	750-378-1061
H99118	Jeff Henry	MTC-336	750-330-8650
J33486	Steve Johnson	MTC-118	750-330-1116
K69880	Jenney King	MTC-324	2750-378-1230

New Faculty table

faculty_id	faculty_name
A52990	Black Anderson
A52990	Black Anderson
A77587	Debby Angles
B66750	Alice Brown
B78880	Ying Bai
B78880	Ying Bai
B86590	Davis Bhalla
H99118	Jeff Henry
J33486	Steve Johnson
K69880	Jenney King

New Office table

office	phone	faculty_id
MTC-218	750-378-9987	A52990
SHB-205	555-255-8897	A52990
MTC-320	750-330-2276	A77587
MTC-257	750-330-6650	B66750
MTC-211	750-378-1148	B78880
SHB-105	555-246-4582	B78880
MTC-214	750-378-1061	B86590
MTC-336	750-330-8650	H99118
MTC-118	750-330-1116	J33486
MTC-324	750-378-1230	K69880

Figure 2.8 Converting Faculty table into 2NF by decomposing the old table in two, Faculty and Office.

Another way of stating this is that in order to achieve 3NF, no column should depend upon any non-key column. If column B depends on column A, then A is said to functionally determine column B, hence the term determinant. Another definition of 3NF says that the table should be in 2NF and only determinants it contains are candidate keys.

For the Course table in Table 2.10, all non-key columns depend on the primary key – course_id. In addition, name and phone columns also depend on faculty_id. This table is in 2NF but it suffers from update, addition, and deletion anomalies because of transitive dependencies. In order to conform to 3NF, we can split this table into two tables, Course and Instructor (Tables 2.11 and 2.12). Now, we have eliminated the transitive dependencies that are apparent in the Course table in Table 2.10.

2.8 Database Components in Some Popular Databases

All databases allow for storage, retrieval, and management of the data. Simple databases provide basic services to accomplish these tasks. Many database providers, like Microsoft SQL Server and Oracle, provide additional services which necessitates storing many components in the database other than data. These components such as views, stored procedures etc., are collectively called

Table 2.10 The old Course table.

course_id	course	classroom	faculty_id	faculty_name	phone
CSC-131A	Computers in Society	TC-109	A52990	Black Anderson	750-378-9987
CSC-131B	Computers in Society	TC-114	B66750	Alice Brown	750-330-6650
CSC-131C	Computers in Society	TC-109	A52990	Black Anderson	750-378-9987
CSC-131D	Computers in Society	TC-109	B86590	Davis Bhalla	750-378-1061
CSC-131E	Computers in Society	TC-301	B66750	Alice Brown	750-330-6650
CSC-131I	Computers in Society	TC-109	A52990	Black Anderson	750-378-9987
CSC-132A	Introduction to Programming	TC-303	J33486	Steve Johnson	750-330-1116
CSC-132B	Introduction to Programming	TC-302	B78880	Ying Bai	750-378-1148

Table 2.11 The new Course table.

course_id	course	classroom
CSC-131A	Computers in Society	TC-109
CSC-131B	Computers in Society	TC-114
CSC-131C	Computers in Society	TC-109
CSC-131D	Computers in Society	TC-109
CSC-131E	Computers in Society	TC-301
CSC-131I	Computers in Society	TC-109
CSC-132A	Introduction to Programming	TC-303
CSC-132B	Introduction to Programming	TC-302

Table 2.12 The new Instructor table.

faculty_id	faculty_name	phone
A52990	Black Anderson	750-378-9987
B66750	Alice Brown	750-330-6650
A52990	Black Anderson	750-378-9987
B86590	Davis Bhalla	750-378-1061
B66750	Alice Brown	750-330-6650
A52990	Black Anderson	750-378-9987
J33486	Steve Johnson	750-330-1116
B78880	Ying Bai	750-378-1148
A77587	Debby Angles	750-330-2276

database objects. In this section, we will discuss various objects that make up MS Access, SQL Server, and Oracle databases.

There are two major types of databases, *File Server* and *Client Server:*

In a File Server database, data is stored in a file and each user of the database retrieves the data, displays the data, or modifies the data directly from or to the file. In a Client Server database, the data is also stored in a file; however, all these operations are mediated through a master program called a server. MS Access is a File Server database, whereas Microsoft SQL Server and Oracle are Client Server databases. The Client Server databases have several advantages over the File Server databases. These include minimizing chances of crashes, provision of features for recovery, enforcement of security, better performance, and more efficient use of the network compared to the file server databases.

2.8.1 Microsoft Access Databases

Microsoft Access Database Engine is a collection of information stored in a systematic way that forms the underlying component of a database. Also called a Jet (Joint Engine Technology), it allows the manipulation of relational database. It offers a single interface that other software may use to access Microsoft databases. The supporting software is developed to provide security, integrity, indexing, record locking etc. By executing MS Access program, MSACCESS.EXE, you can see the database engine at work and the user interface it provides. Figure 2.9 shows how a Java application accesses the MS Access database via ACE OLE database provider.

2.8.1.1 Database File

Access database is made up of a number of components called objects which are stored in a single file referred to as *database file*. As new objects are created or more data is added to the database, this file gets bigger. This is a complex file that stores objects like tables, queries, forms, reports, macros, and modules. The Access files have an .mdb (Microsoft DataBase) extension. Some of these objects help user to work with the database; others are useful for displaying database information in a comprehensible and easy to read format.

2.8.1.2 Tables

Before you can create a table in Access, you must create a database container and give it a name with the extension .mdb. Database creation is a simple process and is explained in detail with an example, later in this chapter. Suffice it to say that a table is made up of columns and rows. Columns are referred to as fields, which are attributes of an entity. Rows are referred to as records also called tuples.

Figure 2.9 Microsoft Access database illustration.

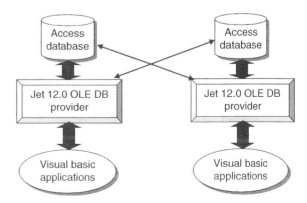

2.8.1.3 Queries

One of the main purposes of storing data in a database is that the data may be retrieved later as needed, without having to write complex programs. This purpose is accomplished in Access and other databases by writing SQL statements. A group of such statements is called a query. It enables you to retrieve, update, and display data in the tables. You may display data from more than one table by using a Join operation. In addition, you may insert or delete data in the tables.

Access also provides a visual graphic user interface to create queries. This bypasses writing SQL statements and makes it appealing to beginning and not so savvy users, who can use wizards or graphical user interface (GUI) to create queries. Queries can extract information in a variety of ways. You can make them as simple or as complex as you like. You may specify various criteria to get desired information, perform comparisons, or you may want to perform some calculations and obtain the results. In essence, operators, functions, and expressions are the building blocks for Access operation.

2.8.2 SQL Server Databases

The Microsoft SQL Server Database Engine is a service for storing and processing data in either a relational (tabular) format or as XML documents. Various tasks performed by the Database Engine include:

- Designing and creating a database to hold the relational tables or XML documents.
- Accessing and modifying the data stored in the database.
- Implementing Web sites and applications
- Building procedures
- Optimizing the performance of the database.

The SQL Server database is a complex entity, made up of multiple components. It is more complex than MS Access database which can be simply copied and distributed. Certain procedures have to be followed for copying and distributing an SQL server database.

SQL Server is used by a diverse group of professionals with diverse needs and requirements. To satisfy different needs, SQL Server comes in five editions, Enterprise edition, Standard edition, Workgroup edition, Developer edition, and Express edition. The most common editions are Enterprise, Standard, and Workgroup. It is noteworthy that the database engine is virtually the same in all of these editions.

SQL Server database can be stored on the disk using three types of files – primary data files, secondary data files, and transaction log files. Primary data files are created first and contain user-defined objects like tables and views, and system objects. These file have an extensions of .mdf. If the database grows too big for a disk, it can be stored as secondary files with an extension .ndf. The SQL Server still treats these files as if they are together. The data file is made up of many objects. The transaction log files carry .ldf extension. All transactions to the database are recorded in this file.

Figure 2.10 illustrates the structure of the SQL Server Database. Each Java application has to access the server, which in turn accesses the SQL database.

2.8.2.1 Data Files

A data file is a conglomeration of objects, which includes tables, keys, views, stored procedures, and others. All these objects are necessary for the efficient operation of the database.

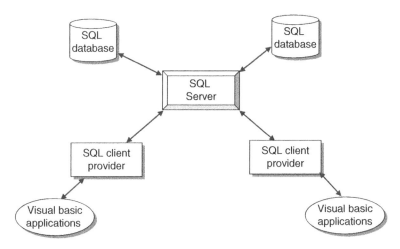

Figure 2.10   SQL Server database structure.

2.8.2.2   Tables

The data in a relational database resides in tables. These are the building blocks of the database. Each table consists of columns and rows. Columns represent various attributes or fields in a table. Each row represents one record. For example, one record in the Faculty table consists of name, office, phone, college, title, and email. Each field has a distinct data type, meaning that it can contain only one type of data such as numeric or character. Tables are the first objects created in a database.

2.8.2.3   Views

Views are virtual tables, meaning that they do not contain any data. They are stored as queries in the database, which are executed when needed. A view can contain data from one or more tables. The views can provide database security. Sensitive information in a database can be excluded by including non-sensitive information in a view and providing user access to the views instead of all tables in a database. The views can also hide the complexities of a database. A user can be using a view that is made up of multiple tables, whereas it appears as a single table to the user. The user can execute queries against a view just like a table.

2.8.2.4   Stored Procedures

Users write queries to retrieve, display, or manipulate data in the database. These queries can be stored on the client machine or on the server. There are advantages associated with storing SQL queries on the server rather than on the client machine. It has to do with the network performance. Usually, users use same queries over and over again; frequently different users are trying to access the same data. Instead of sending the same queries on the network repeatedly, it improves the network performance and executes queries faster if the queries are stored on the server where they are compiled and saved as stored procedures. The users can simply call the stored procedure with a simple command like *execute stored_procedure* A.

2.8.2.5   Keys and Relationships

A *primary key* is created for each table in the database to efficiently access records and to ensure *entity integrity*. This implies that each record in a table is unique in some way. Therefore, no two records can have the same primary key. It is defined as a globally unique identifier. Moreover, a primary key may not have null value, i.e. missing data. SQL server creates a unique index for each primary key. This ensures fast and efficient access to data. One or columns can be combined to designate a primary key.

In a relational database, relationships between tables can be logically defined with the help of *foreign keys*. A foreign key of one record in a table points specifically to a primary key of a record in another table. This allows a user to join multiple tables and retrieve information from more than one table at a time. Foreign keys also enforce *referential integrity*, a defined relationship between the tables which does not allow insertion or deletion of records in a table unless the foreign key of a record in one table matches a primary key of a record in another table. In other words, a record in one table cannot have a foreign key that does not point to a primary key in another table. Additionally, a primary key may not be deleted if there are foreign keys in another table pointing to it. The foreign key values associated with a primary key must be deleted first. Referential integrity protects related data, from corruption, stored in different tables.

2.8.2.6 Indexes

The indexes are used to find records, quickly and efficiently, in a table just like one would use an index in a book. SQL server uses two types of indexes to retrieve and update data – clustered and non-clustered.

Clustered index sorts the data in a table so that the data can be accessed efficiently. It is akin to a dictionary or a phone book where records are arranged alphabetically. So one can go directly to a specific alphabet and from there search sequentially for the specific record. The clustered indexes are like an inverted tree. The index of a structure is called a B-tree for binary-tree. You start with the root page at the top and find the location of other pages further down at secondary level, following to tertiary level and so on until you find the desired record. The very bottom pages are the leaf pages and contain the actual data. There can be only one clustered index per table because clustered indexes physically rearrange the data.

Non-clustered indexes do not physically rearrange the data as do the clustered indexes. They also consist of a binary tree with various levels of pages. The major difference, however, is that the leaves do not contain the actual data as in the clustered indexes; instead, they contain pointers that point to the corresponding records in the table. These pointers are called row locators.

The indexes can be unique where the duplicate keys are not allowed, or not unique which permit duplicate keys. Any column that can be used to access data can be used to generate an index. Usually, the primary and the foreign key columns are used to create indexes.

2.8.2.7 Transaction Log Files

A transaction is a logical group of SQL statements which carry out a unit of work. Client–server database uses a log file to keep track of transactions that are applied to the database. For example, before an update is applied to a database, the database server creates an entry in the transaction log to generate a before picture of the data in a table and then applies a transaction and creates another entry to generate an after picture of the data in that table. This keeps track of all the operations performed on a database. Transaction logs can be used to recover data in case of crashes or disasters. Transaction logs are automatically maintained by the SQL Server.

2.8.3 Oracle Databases

Oracle was designed to be platform independent making it architecturally more complex than the SQL Server database. Oracle database contains more files than SQL Server database.

The Oracle DBMS comes in three levels: Enterprise, Standard, and Personal. Enterprise edition is the most powerful and is suitable for large installations using large number of transactions in multi-user environment. Standard edition is also used by high-level multi-user installations. It lacks some of the utilities available in Enterprise edition. Personal edition is used in a single user environment for developing database applications. The database engine components are virtually the same for all three editions.

Oracle architecture is made up of several components including an Oracle server, Oracle instance, and an Oracle database. The Oracle server contains several files, processes, and memory structures. Some of these are used to improve the performance of the database and ensure database recovery in case of a crash. The Oracle server consists of an Oracle instance and an Oracle database. An Oracle instance consists of background processes and memory structures. Background processes perform input/output and monitor other Oracle processes for better performance and reliability. Oracle database consists of data files that provide the actual physical storage for the data.

2.8.3.1 Data Files

The main purpose of a database is to store and retrieve data. It consists of a collection of data that is treated as a unit. An Oracle database has a logical and physical structure. The logical layer consists of tablespaces, necessary for the smooth operation of an Oracle installation. Data files make up the physical layer of the database. These consist of three types of files: *data files* which contain actual data in the database, *redo logfiles* which contain records of modifications made to the database for future recovery in case of failure, and *control files* which are used to maintain and verify database integrity. Oracle server uses other files that are not part of the database. These include *parameter file* that defines the characteristics of an Oracle instance, *password file* used for authentication, and *archived redo log* files which are copies of the redo log files necessary for recovery from failure. A partial list of some of the components follows.

2.8.3.2 Tables

Users can store data in a regular table, partitioned table, index-organized table, or clustered table. A *regular table* is the default table as in other databases. Rows can be stored in any order. A *partitioned table* has one or more partitions where rows are stored. Partitions are useful for large tables which can be queried by several processes concurrently. *Index organized tables* provide fast key-based access for queries involving exact matches. The table may have index on one or more of its columns. Instead of using two storage spaces for the table and a B-tree index, a single storage space is used to store both the B-tree and other columns. A *clustered table* or group of tables share the same block called a cluster. They are grouped together because they share common columns and are frequently used together. Clusters have a cluster key for identifying the rows that need to be stored together. Cluster keys are independent of the primary key and may be made up of one or more columns. Clusters are created to improve performance.

2.8.3.3 Views

Views are like virtual tables and are used in a similar fashion as in the SQL Server databases discussed above.

2.8.3.4 Stored Procedures

In Oracle, functions and procedures may be saved as stored program units. Multiple input arguments (parameters) may be passed as input to functions and procedures; however, functions return only one value as output, whereas procedures may return multiple values as output. The advantages to creating and using stored procedures are the same as mentioned above for SQL server. By storing procedures on the server, individual SQL statements do not have to be transmitted over the network, thus reducing the network traffic. In addition, commonly used SQL statements are saved as functions or procedures and may be used again and again by various users thus saving rewriting the same code over and over again. The stored procedures should be made flexible so that different users are able to pass input information to the procedure in the form of arguments or parameters and get the desired output.

Figure 2.11 shows the syntax to create a stored procedure in Oracle. It has three sections – a header, a body, and an exception section. The procedure is defined in the header section. Input and output parameters, along with their data types, are declared here and transmit information to or from the procedure. The body section of the procedure starts with a key word BEGIN and consists of SQL statements. The exceptions section of the procedure begins with the keyword EXCEPTION and contains exception handlers which are designed to handle the occurrence of some conditions that changes the normal flow of execution.

Indexes are created to provide direct access to rows. An index is a tree structure. Indexes can be classified on their logic design or their physical implementation. Logical classification is based on application perspective, whereas physical classification is based on how the indexes are stored. Indexes can be partitioned or nonpartitioned. Large tables use partitioned indexes, which spreads an index to multiple table spaces thus decreasing contention for index look up and increasing manageability. An index may consist of a single column or multiple columns; it may be unique or non-unique. Some of these indexes are outlined below.

Function-based indexes precompute the value of a function or expression of one or more columns and stores it in an index. It can be created as a B-tree or as a bit map. It can improve the performance of queries performed on tables that rarely change.

Domain Indexes are application-specific and are created and managed by the user or applications. Single column indexes can be built on text, spatial, scalar, object, or LOB data types.

B-tree indexes store a list of row IDs for each key. Structure of a *B-tree* index is similar to the ones in the SQL Server described above. The leaf nodes contain indexes that point to rows in a table. The leaf blocks allow scanning of the index in either ascending or descending order. Oracle server maintains all indexes when insert, update, or delete operations are performed on a table.

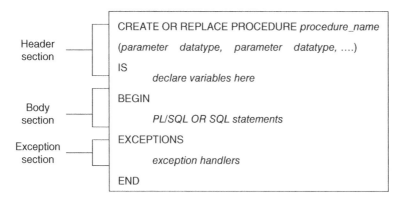

Figure 2.11 Syntax for creating a stored procedure in Oracle.

Bitmap indexes are useful when columns have low cardinality and a large number of rows. For example, a column may contain few distinct values like Y/N for marital status, or M/F for gender. A bitmap is organized like a B-tree where the leaf nodes store a bitmap instead of row IDs. When changes are made to the key columns, bit maps must be modified.

2.8.3.5 Initialization Parameter Files

Oracle server must read the initialization parameter file before starting an oracle database instance. There are two types of initialization parameter files: static parameter file and a persistent parameter file. An initialization parameter file contains a list of instance parameters, and the name of the database the instance is associated with name and location of control files and information about the undo segments. Multiple initialization parameter files can exist to optimize performance.

2.8.3.6 Control Files

A control file is a small binary file that defines the current state of the database. Before a database can be opened, control file is read to determine if the database is in a valid state or not. It maintains the integrity of the database. Oracle uses a single control file per database. It is maintained continuously by the server and can be maintained only by the Oracle server. It cannot be edited by a user or database administrator. A control file contains: database name and identifier, time stamp of database creation, tablespace name, names and location of data files and redo logfiles, current log files sequence number, archive and backup information.

2.8.3.7 Redo Log Files

Oracle's redo log files provide a way to recover data in the event of a database failure. All transactions are written to a redo log buffer and passed on to the redo log files.

Redo log files record all changes to the data, provide a recovery mechanism, and can be organized into groups. A set of identical copies of online redo log files is called a redo log file group. The Oracle server needs a minimum of two online redo logfile groups for normal operations. The initial set of redo log file groups and members are created during the database creation. Redo log files are used in a cyclic fashion. Each redo log file group is identified by a log sequence number and is overwritten each time the log is reused. In other words, when a redo log file is full then the log writer moves to the second redo log file. After the second one is full, first one is reused.

2.8.3.8 Password Files

Depending upon whether the database is administered locally or remotely, one can choose either operating system or password file authentication to authenticate database administrators. Oracle provides a password utility to create password file. Administrators use the GRANT command to provide access to the database using the password file.

2.9 Create Oracle 18c XE Sample Database

After you finished the installation of Oracle 18c Express Edition database (refer to Appendix A), you can begin to use it to connect to the server and build our database. To start, go to `Start\All Programs\Database Configuration Assistant`. The opened assistant is shown in Figure 2.12.

Figure 2.12 The home page of the Oracle Database 18c XE. *Source*: Oracle Database.

Starting from Oracle Database 18c Express Edition (XE), it comes with a container database as the default database. Additionally, you can add up to three (3) pluggable databases with free with the container database, so XE is a good start for getting familiar with the Multitenant architecture.

Since a default database **XE** has been created when installing Oracle 18c XE, and only a single instance can be created and used in the Oracle 18c XE, thus we need first to delete that default database and then create our sample database CSE_DEPT.

2.9.1 Delete the Default Database XE

Perform the following operations to delete the default database XE:

On the opened home page of the Database Configuration Assistant shown in Figure 2.12, select **Delete database** radio button and then click on the **Next** button to go to the next wizard, the **Select Database** wizard.

1) Click and select the default database **XE** and enter a desired password, as shown in Figure 2.13, and click on the **Next** button to continue.
2) Click on the **Next** button for the next wizard, **Management Option**, and **Finish** button on the Summary wizard to complete this deletion.
3) Click **Yes** button on the pop up message box to confirm this deleting action.
4) Finally click on the **Close** button when this deletion is completed to exit the Configuration Assistant.

2.9.2 Create a New Oracle 18c XE Sample Database

Now let's start to create a new Oracle 18c XE sample database CSE_DEPT.

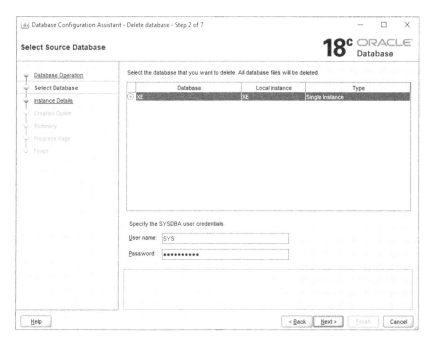

Figure 2.13 The Select Database wizard. *Source*: Oracle Database.

Open the **Database Configuration Assistant** again and perform the following operations to create our sample database CSE_DEPT:

1) On the first opened wizard, **Database Operation**, keep the default selection, **Create a database**, and click on the **Next** button.

2) The next wizard is for **Creation Mode** selection. Regularly, the default mode, **Typical configuration**, should be used. However, you may encounter a memory automatic management problem if your computer has a larger memory size, such as >4 GB. The reason for that is because when the memory is ≤4 GB, this memory automatic management function is enabled by Oracle 18c XE. Otherwise if your memory is >4 GB, that function is disabled. Thus, we prefer to select the **Advanced configuration** mode to avoid that problem.

   Check the **Advanced configuration** radio button and click on the **Next** button to continue (Figure 2.14).

3) The next page, **Deployment Type**, is displayed, and it is shown in Figure 2.15. Select the **XE Database** and click on the **Next** button to go to next wizard.

4) In the **Database Identification** page, enter our database name, **CSE_DEPT**, into the **Global database name** box, **XE** to the **SID** box and **csedb** into the **PDB name** box, as shown in Figure 2.16. The reason for **XE** as SID is because the Oracle 18c XE only allows single instance; thus, we need to keep SID with no change. Click on the **Next** button to go to the **Storage Option** page.

5) In the opened Storage Option wizard, check the **Use following for the database storage attributes** radio button as shown in Figure 2.17, and click on the **Next** button to go to the Configuration Options wizard.

6) For the next page, **Fast Recovery Option**, just click on the **Next** button without changing anything on that page since we do not care any recovery mode.

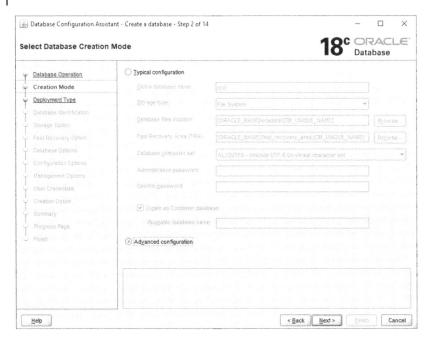

Figure 2.14 The opened Creation Mode wizard. *Source*: Oracle Database.

Figure 2.15 The Deployment wizard. *Source*: Oracle Database.

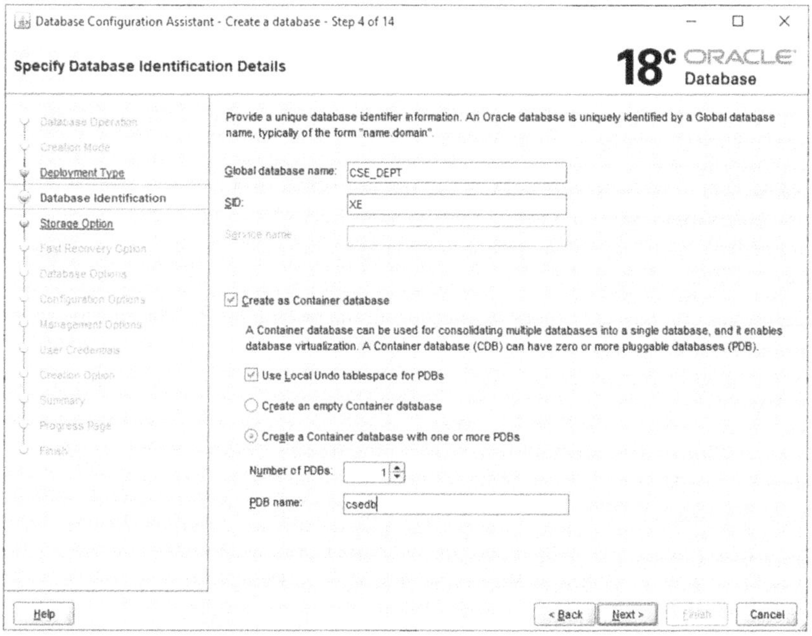

Figure 2.16   The Database Identification wizard. *Source*: Oracle Database.

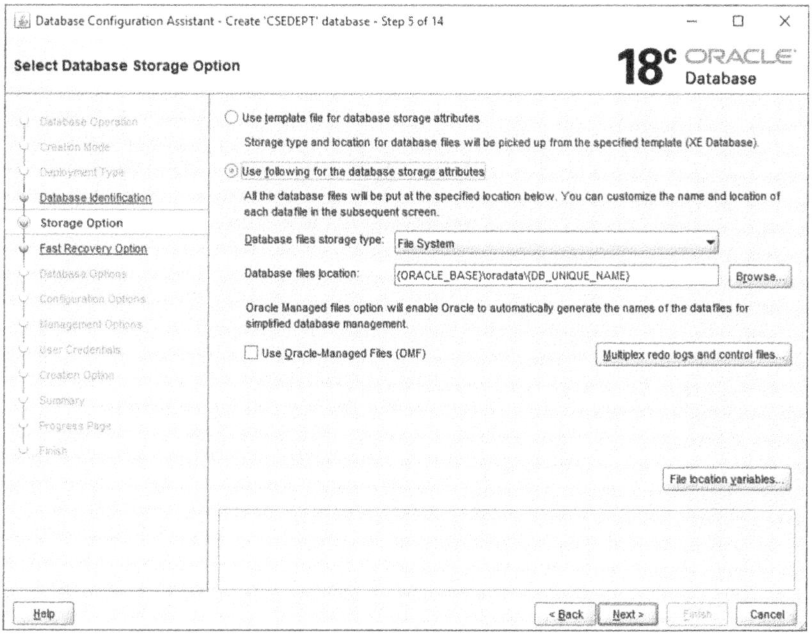

Figure 2.17   The Storage Option wizard. *Source*: Oracle Database.

7) On the opened **Network Configuration** wizard, check the **Create a new listener** checkbox and enter **1518** into the **Listener** box as a new listener. Click on the **Next** button to continue.

8) For the next page, **Data Vault Option**, just click on the **Next** button without changing anything on data vault.

9) On the **Configuration Options** page, keep the default selection for **Use Automatic Shared Memory Management**, and enter **1536** for SGA and **512** to PGA sizes, as shown in Figure 2.18. Then, click on the **Sample schemas** tab on the top, and check the **Add sample schemas to the database** checkbox, and click on the **Next** button. The reason for us to make these memory changes is to meet the requirements of Oracle 18c XE, and the total size for both SGA and PGA should be about 2 GB.

10) The next page is the **Management Options**, uncheck the default selection **Configure Enterprise Manager (EM) database express** since we do not need to use any EM for our database. Then click on the **Next** button to go to the **User Credential** page.

11) On the opened **User Credential** page, change the default selection to **Use the same administrative password for all accounts** by checking that radio button. Then enter the same administrative password as we did in the **Creation Mode** page (Figure 2.13), as shown in Figure 2.19. Click on the **Next** button on this page and **Yes** button on the pup up message box to confirm this password to open the **Creation Option** page.

12) In the opened **Creation Option** page, keep the default selection **Create database** and check the **Generate database creation scripts** checkbox, as shown in Figure 2.20, and then click on the **Next** button to open the **Summary** page.

13) On the opened **Summary** wizard, click on the **Finish** button to try to complete this database creation process. The **Progress** page is displayed to show the processing progress, as shown in Figure 2.21.

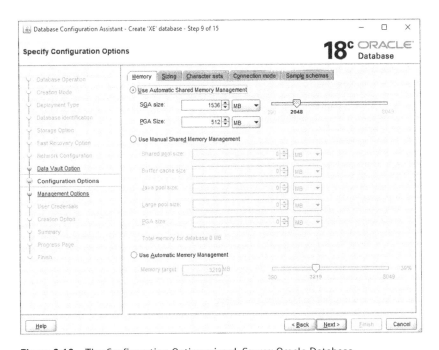

Figure 2.18 The Configuration Option wizard. *Source*: Oracle Database.

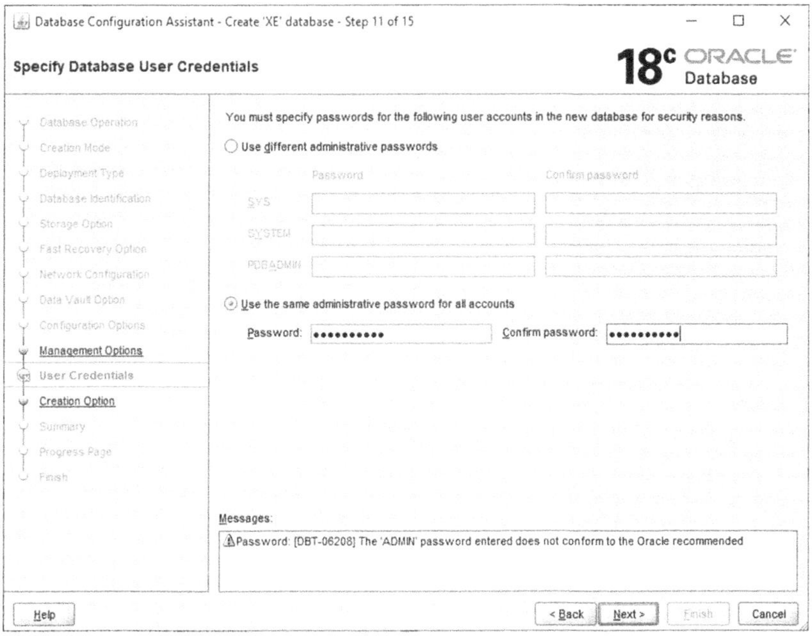

Figure 2.19 The User Credential wizard. *Source*: Oracle Database.

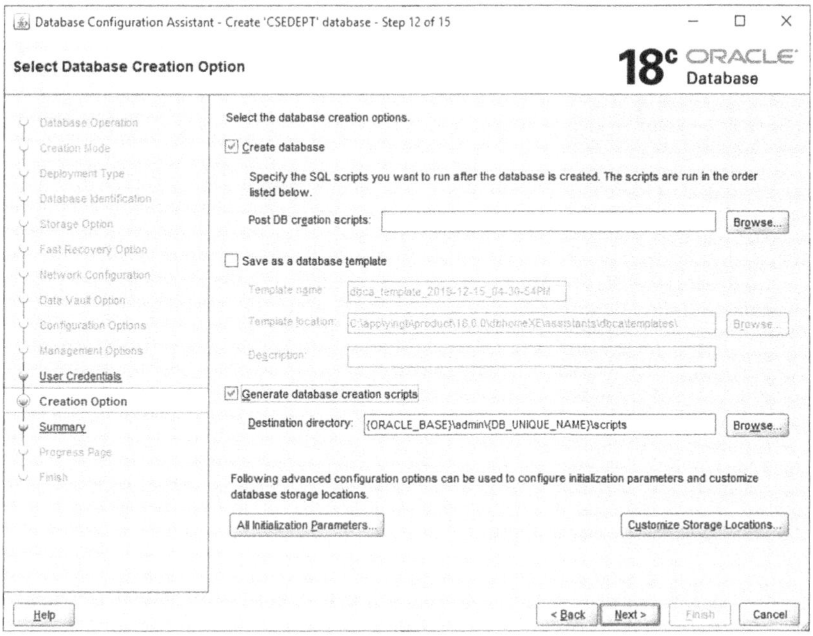

Figure 2.20 The Creation Option wizard. *Source*: Oracle Database.

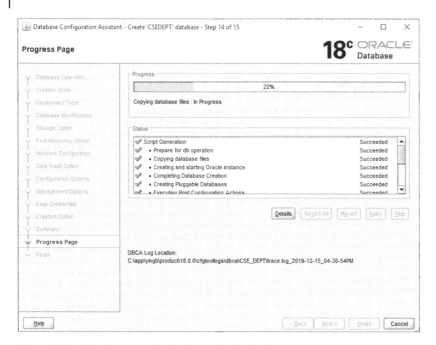

Figure 2.21 The Progress wizard. *Source*: Oracle Database.

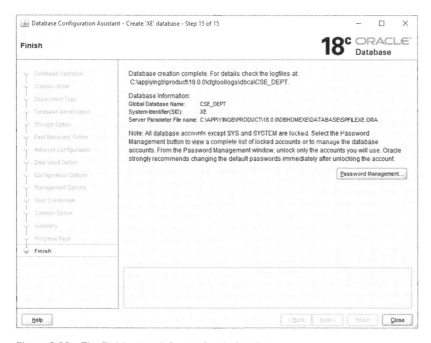

Figure 2.22 The Finish wizard. *Source*: Oracle Database.

14) Finally when the database creation process is done, a summary wizard is displayed, as shown in Figure 2.22. Click on the `Close` button to complete this creation and exit the Configuration Assistant.

After a new sample Oracle 18c XE database, CSE_DEPT, is created, we need to use some GUI to access it to manipulate data components, such as data items, data tables, and stored procedures. Among various GUIs, the Oracle SQL Developer is a good choice to perform those jobs. Refer to Appendix B to download and install the updated Oracle SQL Developer 19.2.1 since we need to use this tool to create and implement all data components, such as tables and procedures, in our sample database in the following chapters.

First, one needs to connect our sample database CSE_DEPT in the Oracle SQL Developer, and then you need to create data tables. For this sample database, you need to create five data tables: LogIn, Faculty, Course, Student, and StudentCourse. After five tables are created, you also need to set up relationships among them since Oracle I a relational database.

Now let us first connect to our sample database from the Oracle SQL Developer.

2.9.3 Connect to Our Sample Database from the Oracle SQL Developer

Open the Oracle SQL Developer by clicking on the icon stored in the taskbar. The opened Developer is shown in Figure 2.23. Perform the following operations to connect to our sample database CSE_DEPT:

1) Click on the green plus (+) icon on the upper-left corner under the `Connections` tab. A `New/Select Database Connection` wizard pops up, as shown in Figure 2.24.

2) Enter all pieces of required connection information into the related box, as shown in Figure 2.24. One critical point to be noted is the `Port`, which is `1518`, not default `1521`. Recalled that we modified this port number when we created a new listener during the creation of our sample database in last section. For the username, the `SYSTEM` is selected here and you need to enter your desired password that should be identical, this one you used during our sample database creation process in last part. Now click on the `Connect` button to start this connection process.

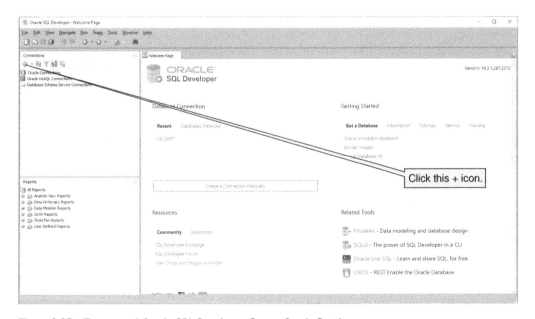

Figure 2.23 The opened Oracle SQL Developer. *Source*: Oracle Database.

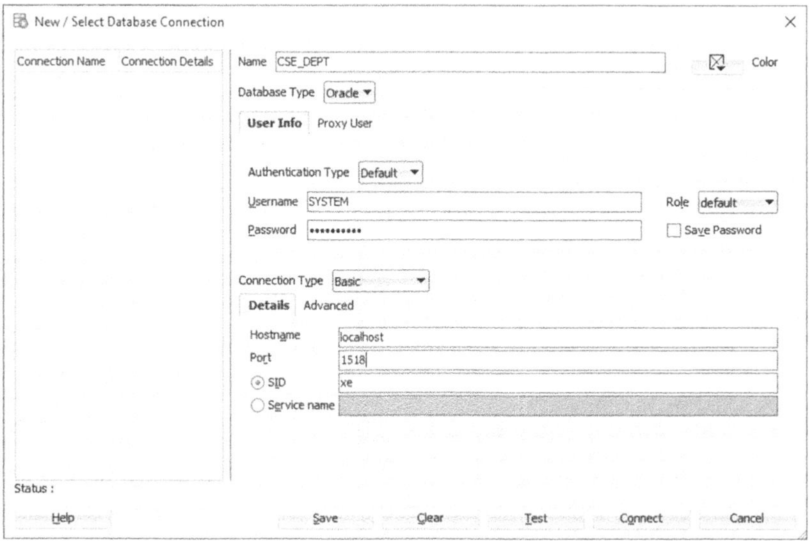

Figure 2.24 The opened New/Select Database Connection wizard. *Source*: Oracle Database.

3) For the pop upped input box, enter your password again to confirm this connection. Then click on the **OK** button to continue.
4) Immediately you can find that our sample database, **CSE_DEPT**, has been connected and displayed in the **Connections** panel under the **Oracle Connections** tab.
   Next, we need to create and add our five tables one by one into this sample database.

2.9.4 Create an Oracle User Account for the User Schema

After you created an Oracle 18c XE database, you need to create a customer Oracle database. To create the customer's database in Oracle18c XE, it is different to create a customer database in Microsoft SQL Server database management system (MDBS). In Oracle 18c XE, you need to create a new user or user account if you want to create a new customer database. Each user or user account is related to a schema or a database, and the name of each user is equal to the name of the associated schema or the database.

Therefore, you need to perform two steps to create a customer Oracle database:

1) Create a new customer user or user account.
2) Create Oracle database objects, such as tables, schemas, and relations under that user account.

First let us create a user account with Oracle SQL Developer now.

Perform the following operations to create a new user account CSE_DEPT:

1) In the opened database CSE_DEPT in the Oracle SQL Developer as shown in Figure 2.25, scroll down to the last folder named **Other Users**. Right click on this folder and select **Create User** item from the pop-up menu to open the Create User wizard, as shown in Figure 2.26.
2) Enter our user's name, **CSE_DEPT**, into the user Name box with your desired password. In our case, it is **oracle_18c**. Enter this password to both **New Password** and **Confirm Password** boxes, as shown in Figure 2.26. Please do not be confused for this user name and our database, **CSE_DEPT**. One is for our database, and another is for our user account. Of course, you can select different name for both of them. Here, we want to create all our components, including

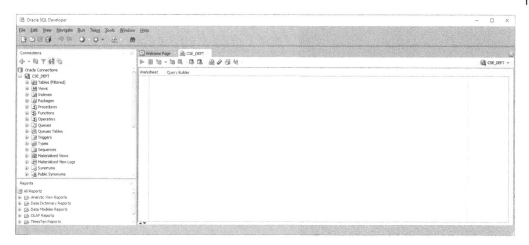

Figure 2.25 All data components related to our sample database CSE_DEPT. *Source*: Oracle Database.

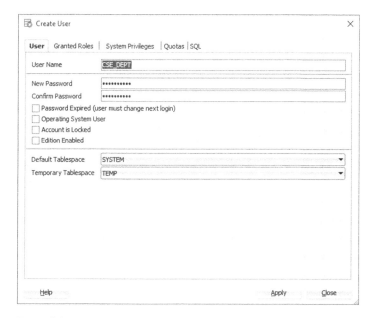

Figure 2.26 The opened Create User wizard. *Source*: Oracle Database.

tables, relations, and keys and embed them in our single user account, which can be considered as a sub-database.

3) For all options, such as **Password Expired, Operating System User, Account is Locked,** and **Edition Enabled**, just keep them unchecked with default status since we do not want to apply any limitations for our account.

4) Select **SYSTEM** and **TEMP** for the **Default Tablespace** and **Temporary Tablespace** since we need to assign this account with Administration privilege. The first completed wizard should match one that is shown in Figure 2.26.

5) For the **Granted Roles** set ups, we do not want to make any change to give any granted access to this user, thus click on the **System Privileges** tab to open its wizard, as shown in Figure 2.27.

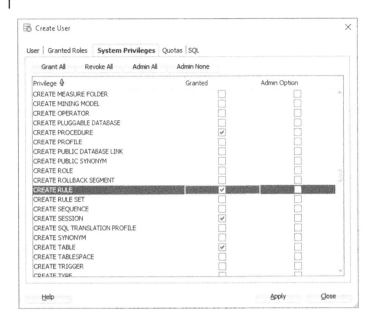

Figure 2.27 The opened System Privileges wizard. *Source*: Oracle Database.

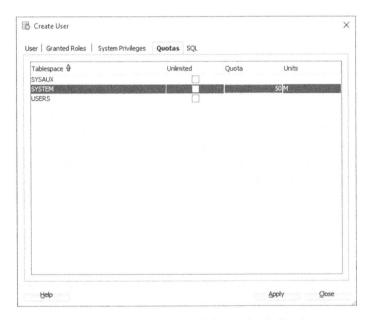

Figure 2.28 The opened Quotas wizard. *Source*: Oracle Database.

6) Select **CREATE PROCEDURE, CREATE RULE, CREATE SESSION,** and **CREATE TABLE** items by checking them from the list since we want to provide these privileges to enable the user to create new sessions, new procedures, and tables. Then, click on the **Quotas** tab to open its wizard, as shown in Figure 2.28.

7) Click on the **SYSTEM** line and enter **50** and **M** to the **Quota** and **Units** columns to provide 50 MB space to the **SYSTEM** user, as shown in Figure 2.28.

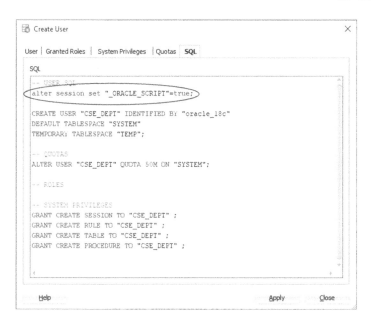

Figure 2.29 The opened and completed SQL wizard. *Source*: Oracle Database.

8) Finally open the **SQL** wizard by clicking on the **SQL** tab, as shown in Figure 2.29.

In Oracle database, two kinds of users, Container Database (CBD) user and Plugged Database (PDB) user, are existed. The former is called a common user but the latter is local user. To create a common user for CBD, one needs to use C## or c## as prefixes the user name. It is same to create a local user for PDB.

In order to create a local user for PDB, one needs to set a hidden parameter "_ORACLE_SCRIPT"=true, then one can create a user without a C## in front of the user name.

9) To use this hidden parameter, enter **alter session set "_ORACLE_SCRIPT"=true;** in the first line on this opened SQL wizard, as shown in Figure 2.29. This is critical important to create this local user account; otherwise, you will encounter an error when you apply this creation process.

10) Click on the **Apply** button to execute this creation. A successful execution message will be displayed to indicate the successful creation of this user account.

Now if you expand the **Other User** folder, you can find that our new created user, **CSE_DEPT**, has been created under this folder.

2.9.5 Create LogIn Table

Now expand our user account or sample database icon, **CSE_DEPT**, and we need to create and add all five tables into this database.

The first table we need to add is the LogIn table. Perform the following operations to create and add this table into our sample database:

1) Right click on the **Tables** icon and select **New Table** item from the popup menu.
2) On the opened **Create Table** wizard, keep the default **Schema** with no changed and enter **LOGIN** into the **Name:** box.
3) Refer to Table 2.1 to create each column as below.
4) Enter **USER_NAME** into **Name** column, select **NVERCHAR2** as **Data Type**, 50 as **Size**, and click on the space under the **PK** to make this column as a primary key.
5) Click on the + sign on the upper-right corner to add this column into our sample database.
6) In a similar way, complete all other columns including **PASS_WORD**, **FACULTY_ID**, and **STUDENT_ID** based on the data components in Table 2.1.
7) You can check on the **Advanced** checkbox to a detailed view for this table when you complete this table, as shown in Figure 2.30.
8) Click on the **OK** button to create and add this table into our sample database.

Now expand the **Tables** icon on the left and you can find our new created table **LOGIN**. Let us enter all data for each column one by one based on Table 2.1.

1) Click on our new created table **LOGIN** icon to open the detailed view for this table.
2) Click on the **Data** tab from the opened **LOGIN** table.
3) Click on the green color + icon (**Insert Row**) on the top to add a new row.
4) Enter the first record into this row based on Table 2.1.
5) In a similar way, add all rows to complete this table.

Finally go to **File|Save All** menu item to save these new added records. A **Commit Successful** message should be displayed in the **Message - Log** window under this table view if these records are successfully added into this table.

Your finished data records for this table should look like one shown in Figure 2.31.

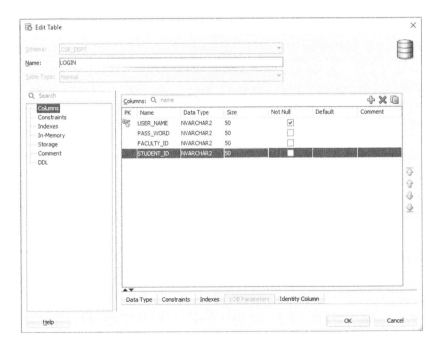

Figure 2.30 The completed design view of the LogIn table. *Source*: Oracle Database.

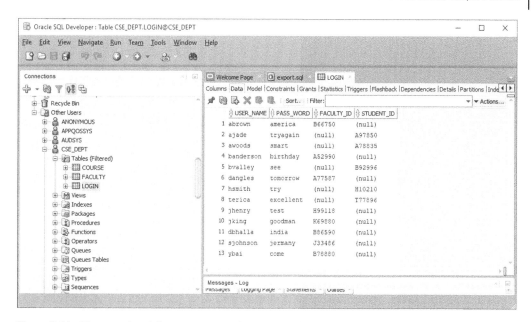

Figure 2.31 The completed data components for LogIn table. *Source*: Oracle Database.

2.9.6 Create Faculty Table

Right click on the **Tables** folder on the left and select the **New Table** item to open the design view of a new table, which is shown in Figure 2.32.

For this table, we have eight columns: **faculty_id, faculty_name, title, office, phone, college, email,** and **fimage**. The data types for the columns **faculty_id** and **faculty_name** are **nvarchar(50)**, and all other data types, except the **fimage** column, can be either **text** or **nvarchar(50)** since all of them are string variables. The data type for the **fimage** column is **BLOB** since all faculty images are stored in this column. The reason we selected the **nvarchar(50)** as the data type for the **faculty_id** is that a primary key can work for this data type but it does not work for the **text**.

Do not forget to enter **FACULTY** into the **Name:** box on the top as the name for this table. The finished design-view of the Faculty table should match one that is shown in Figure 2.32. Click on the **OK** button to create this Faculty table and add it into our sample database.

Now expand the **Tables** icon on the left and you can find our new created data table **FACULTY**. Let us enter all data for each column one by one based on Table 2.13.

1) Click on our new created table **FACULTY** icon to open the detailed view for this table.
2) Click on the **Data** tab from the opened **FACULTY** table.
3) Click on the green color **+** icon (**Insert Row**) on the top to add a new row.
4) Enter the first record into this row based on Table 2.13.
5) In a similar way, add all rows to complete this table.

Your finished **FACULTY** table should match one that is shown in Figure 2.33.

Finally go to **File | Save All** menu item to save these new added records. A Commit Successful message should be displayed in the **Message – Log** window under this table view if these records are successfully added into this table.

At this moment, just keep NULL for the **fimage** column and we will add actual faculty images later by using Visual Studio.NET and Devexpress controls.

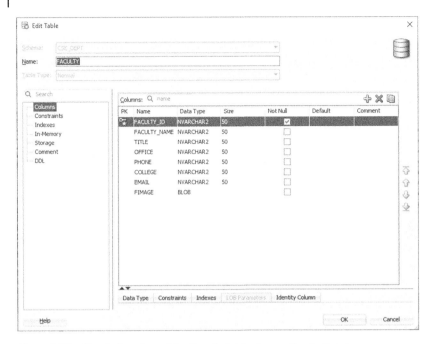

Figure 2.32   The design view of the Faculty table. *Source*: Oracle Database.

Table 2.13   The data in the Faculty table

faculty_id	faculty_name	office	phone	college	title	email	fimage
A52990	Black Anderson	MTC-218	750-378-9987	Virginia Tech	Professor	banderson@college.edu	NULL
A77587	Debby Angles	MTC-320	750-330-2276	University of Chicago	Associate Professor	dangles@college.edu	NULL
B66750	Alice Brown	MTC-257	750-330-6650	University of Florida	Assistant Professor	abrown@college.edu	NULL
B78880	Ying Bai	MTC-211	750-378-1148	Florida Atlantic University	Associate Professor	ybai@college.edu	NULL
B86590	Davis Bhalla	MTC-214	750-378-1061	University of Notre Dame	Associate Professor	dbhalla@college.edu	NULL
H99118	Jeff Henry	MTC-336	750-330-8650	Ohio State University	Associate Professor	jhenry@college.edu	NULL
J33486	Steve Johnson	MTC-118	750-330-1116	Harvard University	Distinguished Professor	sjohnson@college.edu	NULL
K69880	Jenney King	MTC-324	750-378-1230	East Florida University	Professor	jking@college.edu	NULL

2.9.7   Create Other Tables

In a similar way, create the rest of the three tables: **Course, Student,** and **StudentCourse.** Select **course_id, student_id,** and **s_course_id** as the primary keys for these tables (refer to Tables 2.14~2.16). For the data type selections, follow the directions below.

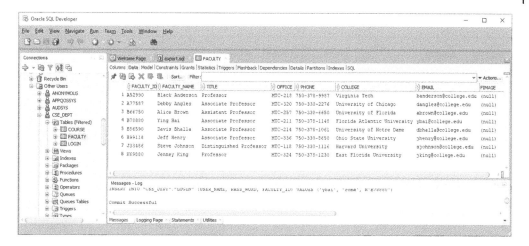

Figure 2.33 The completed Faculty table. *Source*: Oracle Database.

Table 2.14 The data in the Course table.

course_id	course	credit	classroom	schedule	enrollment	faculty_id
CSC-131A	Computers in Society	3	TC-109	M-W-F: 9:00-9:55 AM	28	A52990
CSC-131B	Computers in Society	3	TC-114	M-W-F: 9:00-9:55 AM	20	B66750
CSC-131C	Computers in Society	3	TC-109	T-H: 11:00-12:25 PM	25	A52990
CSC-131D	Computers in Society	3	TC-109	M-W-F: 9:00-9:55 AM	30	B86590
CSC-131E	Computers in Society	3	TC-301	M-W-F: 1:00-1:55 PM	25	B66750
CSC-131I	Computers in Society	3	TC-109	T-H: 1:00-2:25 PM	32	A52990
CSC-132A	Introduction to Programming	3	TC-303	M-W-F: 9:00-9:55 AM	21	J33486
CSC-132B	Introduction to Programming	3	TC-302	T-H: 1:00-2:25 PM	21	B78880
CSC-230	Algorithms & Structures	3	TC-301	M-W-F: 1:00-1:55 PM	20	A77587
CSC-232A	Programming I	3	TC-305	T-H: 11:00-12:25 PM	28	B66750
CSC-232B	Programming I	3	TC-303	T-H: 11:00-12:25 PM	17	A77587
CSC-233A	Introduction to Algorithms	3	TC-302	M-W-F: 9:00-9:55 AM	18	H99118
CSC-233B	Introduction to Algorithms	3	TC-302	M-W-F: 11:00-11:55 AM	19	K69880
CSC-234A	Data Structure & Algorithms	3	TC-302	M-W-F: 9:00-9:55 AM	25	B78880
CSC-234B	Data Structure & Algorithms	3	TC-114	T-H: 11:00-12:25 PM	15	J33486
CSC-242	Programming II	3	TC-303	T-H: 1:00-2:25 PM	18	A52990
CSC-320	Object Oriented Programming	3	TC-301	T-H: 1:00-2:25 PM	22	B66750

(Continued)

Table 2.14 (Continued)

course_id	course	credit	classroom	schedule	enrollment	faculty_id
CSC-331	Applications Programming	3	TC-109	T-H: 11:00-12:25 PM	28	H99118
CSC-333A	Computer Arch & Algorithms	3	TC-301	M-W-F: 10:00-10:55 AM	22	A77587
CSC-333B	Computer Arch & Algorithms	3	TC-302	T-H: 11:00-12:25 PM	15	A77587
CSC-335	Internet Programming	3	TC-303	M-W-F: 1:00-1:55 PM	25	B66750
CSC-432	Discrete Algorithms	3	TC-206	T-H: 11:00-12:25 PM	20	B86590
CSC-439	Database Systems	3	TC-206	M-W-F: 1:00-1:55 PM	18	B86590
CSE-138A	Introduction to CSE	3	TC-301	T-H: 1:00-2:25 PM	15	A52990
CSE-138B	Introduction to CSE	3	TC-109	T-H: 1:00-2:25 PM	35	J33486
CSE-330	Digital Logic Circuits	3	TC-305	M-W-F: 9:00-9:55 AM	26	K69880
CSE-332	Foundations of Semiconductors	3	TC-305	T-H: 1:00-2:25 PM	24	K69880
CSE-334	Elec Measurement & Design	3	TC-212	T-H: 11:00-12:25 PM	25	H99118
CSE-430	Bioinformatics in Computer	3	TC-206	Thu: 9:30-11:00 AM	16	B86590
CSE-432	Analog Circuits Design	3	TC-309	M-W-F: 2:00-2:55 PM	18	K69880
CSE-433	Digital Signal Processing	3	TC-206	T-H: 2:00-3:25 PM	18	H99118
CSE-434	Advanced Electronics Systems	3	TC-213	M-W-F: 1:00-1:55 PM	26	B78880
CSE-436	Automatic Control and Design	3	TC-305	M-W-F: 10:00-10:55 AM	29	J33486
CSE-437	Operating Systems	3	TC-303	T-H: 1:00-2:25 PM	17	A77587
CSE-438	Advd Logic & Microprocessor	3	TC-213	M-W-F: 11:00-11:55 AM	35	B78880
CSE-439	Special Topics in CSE	3	TC-206	M-W-F: 10:00-10:55 AM	22	J33486

Table 2.15 The data in the Student table

student_id	student_name	gpa	credits	major	schoolYear	email	simage
A78835	Andrew Woods	3.26	108	Computer Science	Senior	awoods@college.edu	NULL
A97850	Ashly Jade	3.57	116	Information System Engineering	Junior	ajade@college.edu	NULL
B92996	Blue Valley	3.52	102	Computer Science	Senior	bvalley@college.edu	NULL
H10210	Holes Smith	3.87	78	Computer Engineering	Sophomore	hsmith@college.edu	NULL
J77896	Tom Erica	3.95	127	Computer Science	Senior	terica@college.edu	NULL

Table 2.16 The data in the StudentCourse table.

s_course_id	student_id	course_id	credit	major
1000	H10210	CSC-131D	3	CE
1001	B92996	CSC-132A	3	CS/IS
1002	T77896	CSC-335	3	CS/IS
1003	A78835	CSC-331	3	CE
1004	H10210	CSC-234B	3	CE
1005	T77896	CSC-234A	3	CS/IS
1006	B92996	CSC-233A	3	CS/IS
1007	A78835	CSC-132A	3	CE
1008	A78835	CSE-432	3	CE
1009	A78835	CSE-434	3	CE
1010	T77896	CSC-439	3	CS/IS
1011	H10210	CSC-132A	3	CE
1012	H10210	CSC-331	2	CE
1013	A78835	CSC-335	3	CE
1014	A78835	CSE-438	3	CE
1015	T77896	CSC-432	3	CS/IS
1016	A97850	CSC-132B	3	ISE
1017	A97850	CSC-234A	3	ISE
1018	A97850	CSC-331	3	ISE
1019	A97850	CSC-335	3	ISE
1020	T77896	CSE-439	3	CS/IS
1021	B92996	CSC-230	3	CS/IS
1022	A78835	CSE-332	3	CE
1023	B92996	CSE-430	3	CE
1024	T77896	CSC-333A	3	CS/IS
1025	H10210	CSE-433	3	CE
1026	H10210	CSE-334	3	CE
1027	B92996	CSC-131C	3	CS/IS
1028	B92996	CSC-439	3	CS/IS

The data type selections for the **Course** table:

- course_id – nvarchar(50) (Primary key)
- credit – smallint
- enrollment – int
- faculty_id – nvarchar(50)
- All other columns – either nvarchar(50) or text

The data type selections for the **Student** table:

- student_id – nvarchar(50) (Primary key)
- student_name - nvarchar(50)

- gpa – float
- credits – int
- simage - BLOB
- All other columns – either nvarchar(50) or text

The data type selections for the **StudentCourse** table:

- s_course_id – int (Primary key)
- student_id – nvarchar(50)
- course_id – nvarchar(50)
- credit – int
- major – either nvarchar(50) or text

Enter the data that are shown in Tables 2.14~2.16 into each associated table, and save each table as Course, Student, and StudentCourse, respectively.

Similar to Faculty table, at this moment, just keep NULL for the **SIMAGE** column in the Student table and we will add actual student images later by using Visual Studio.NET and DevExpress Drive controls.

The finished Course table should match one that is shown in Figure 2.34. The finished Student table should match one that is shown in Figure 2.35. The finished StudentCourse table should match one that is shown in Figure 2.36.

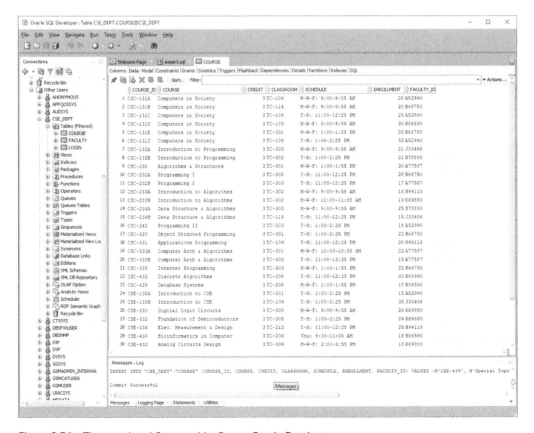

Figure 2.34 The completed Course table. *Source*: Oracle Database.

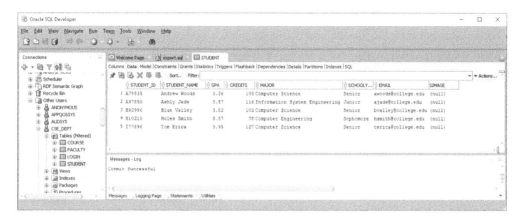

Figure 2.35 The completed Student table. *Source*: Oracle Database.

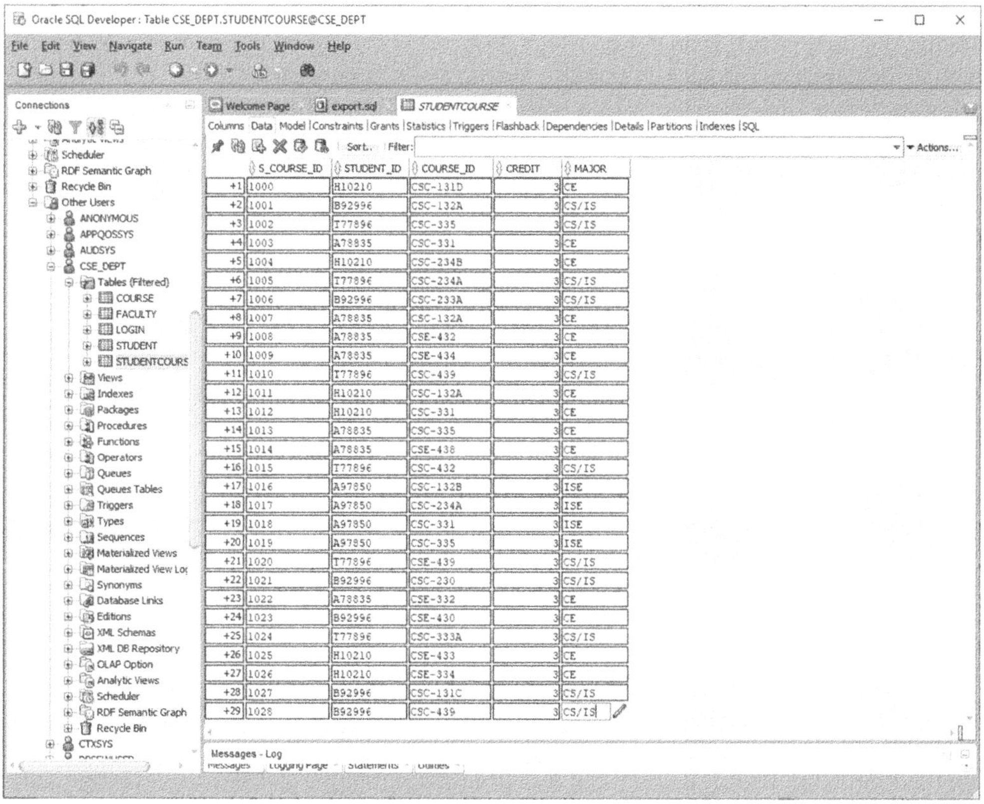

Figure 2.36 The completed StudentCourse table. *Source*: Oracle Database.

2.9.8 Create Relationships Among Tables

Next, we need to set up relationships among these five tables using the Primary and Foreign Keys. In Oracle 18c Express Edition database environment, the relationship between tables can be set by using the Property wizard under each table. Now let us begin to set up the relationship between the LogIn and the Faculty tables by using the Oracle SQL Developer.

2.9.8.1 Create Relationship Between LogIn and Faculty Tables

The relationship between the Faculty and the LogIn table is one-to-many, which means that the faculty_id is a primary key in the Faculty table, and it can be mapped into many faculty_id that are foreign keys in the LogIn table.

To set up this relationship, we can either do that by using this Oracle SQL Developer or use an Oracle SQL Developer extension, **Developer Modeler** that is involved in the Developer when it was installed. To make things simple and easy, we prefer to set up these relationships directly by using this Oracle SQL Developer.

Perform the following operations to set up this foreign key for the **LOGIN** table.

1) Click on the **LOGIN** table under our customer database account **CSE_DEPT** to open this table.
2) On the open **LOGIN** table, select the **Constraints** tab on the top and click on the **Edit** icon, as shown in Figure 2.37, to open the **Edit Table** wizard.
3) On the opened **Edit Table** wizard, as shown in Figure 2.38, click on the **Constraints** item on the left pane and click on the green color + icon, as shown in Figure 2.38, and select the **New Foreign Key Constraint** item from the popup menu.
4) Change the name of this Foreign Key, which is located at the second line under the **Name** column in the **Constraints** list, to **LOGIN_FACULTY_FK** (Figure 2.39).
5) Select **FACULTY** table from the **Table** box, **FACULTY_PK** from the **Constraints** box and **Cascade** from the **On Delete** box. Your completed wizard is shown in Figure 2.39.
6) Click on the **OK** button to add this foreign key to the **LOGIN** table.

Now you can find this new added foreign key, **LOGIN_FACULTY_FK**, from the top line in the **Constraints** wizard, as shown in Figure 2.40.

The reason to set up a cascaded relationship between the Primary key (**FACULTY_ID**) in the parent table **FACULTY** and the Foreign keys (**FACULTY_ID**) in the child table **LOGIN** is because we want to simplify the data updating and deleting operations between these tables in our relational database CSE_DEPT. You will have a better understanding about this cascading later when you learn how to update and delete data against a relational database in Chapter 7.

2.9.8.2 Create Relationship Between LogIn and Student Tables

In a similar way, you can create a foreign key for the **LOGIN** table and set up a one-to-many relationship between the **STUDENT** and the **LOGIN** tables.

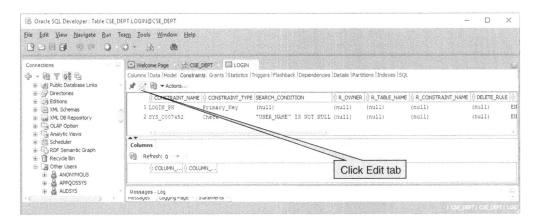

Figure 2.37 The opened Model view for the LOGIN table. *Source*: Oracle Database.

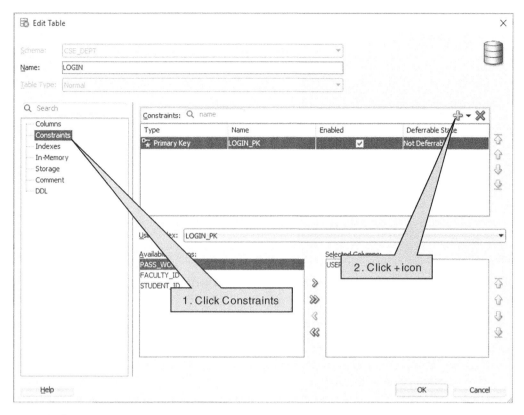

Figure 2.38 The opened Edit Table wizard. *Source*: Oracle Database.

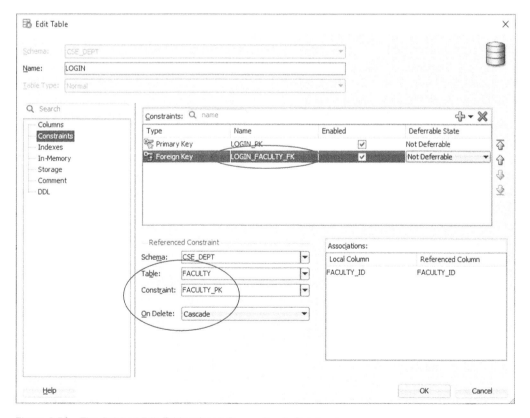

Figure 2.39 The finished Edit Table wizard. *Source*: Oracle Database.

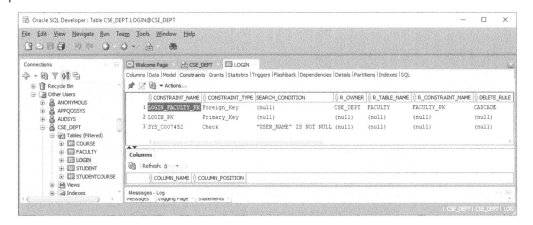

Figure 2.40 The added foreign key LOGIN_FACULTY_FK. *Source*: Oracle Database.

Perform the following operations to set up this relationship between **LOGIN** and **STUDENT** tables:

1) Click on the **LOGIN** table under our customer database **CSE_DEPT** to open it.
2) On the open **LOGIN** table, select the **Constraints** tab on the top and click on the **Edit** icon to open the **Edit Table** wizard.
3) On the opened **Edit Table** wizard, click on the **Constraints** item on the left pane and click on the green color+icon, and then select the **New Foreign Key Constraint** item from the popup menu.
4) Change the name of this Foreign Key, which is located at the second line under the **Name** column in the **Constraints** list, to LOGIN_STUDENT_FK (Figure 2.41).
5) Select **STUDENT** table from the **Table** box, **STUDENT_PK** from the **Constraints** box and **Cascade** from the **On Delete** box. Your completed wizard is shown in Figure 2.41.
6) Click on the **OK** button to add this foreign key to the **LOGIN** table.

Now you can find this new added foreign key, **LOGIN_STUDENT_FK**, from the third line in the Constraints wizard, as shown in Figure 2.42.

2.9.8.3 Create Relationship Between Faculty and Course Tables

The relationship between the **FACULTY** and the **COURSE** tables is one-to-many, and the **FACULTY_ID** in the **FACULTY** table is a Primary key and the **FACULTY_ID** in the **COURSE** table is a Foreign key.

Perform the following operations to set up this relationship between the **FACULTY** and the **COURSE** tables:

1) Click on the **COURSE** table under our customer account CSE_DEPT to open it.
2) On the open table, select the **Constraints** tab on the top and click on the **Edit** icon to open the **Edit Table** wizard.
3) On the opened **Edit Table** wizard, click on the **Constraints** item on the left pane and click on the green color+icon, and then select the **New Foreign Key Constraint** item from the popup menu.
4) Change the name of this Foreign Key, which is located at the second line under the **Name** column in the **Constraints** list, to **COURSE_FACULTY_FK** (Figure 2.43).

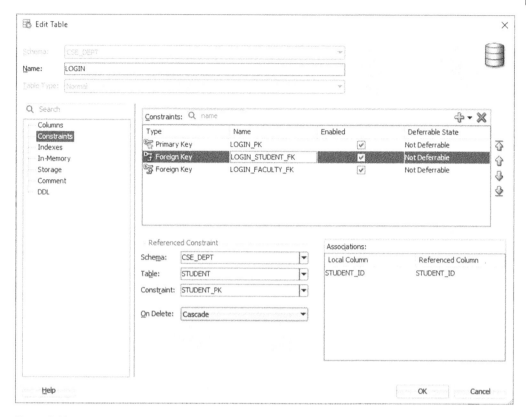

Figure 2.41 The created foreign key in the LOGIN and STUDENT tables. *Source*: Oracle Database.

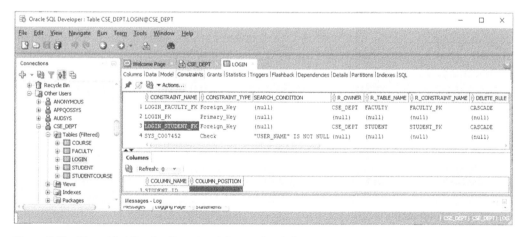

Figure 2.42 The added Foreign Key wizard. *Source*: Oracle Database.

5) Select **FACULTY** table from the **Table** box, **FACULTY_PK** from the **Constraints** box and **Cascade** from the **On Delete** box. Your completed wizard is shown in Figure 2.43.
6) Click on the **OK** button to add this foreign key to the **COURSE** table.

Now you can find this new added foreign key, **COURSE_FACULTY_FK**, from the top line in the **Constraints** wizard.

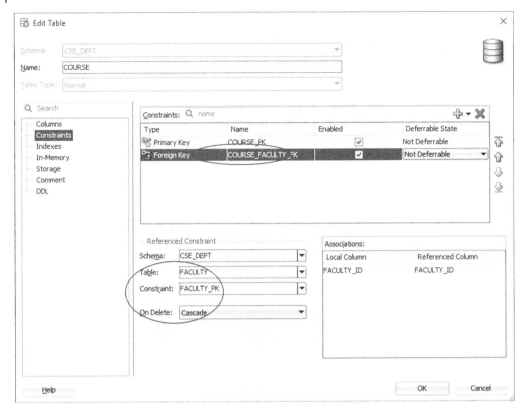

Figure 2.43 The finished foreign key for the COURSE table. *Source*: Oracle Database.

2.9.8.4 Create Relationship Between Student and StudentCourse Tables

The relationship between the **STUDENT** and the **STUDENTCOURSE** tables is one-to-many, and the **STUDENT_ID** in the **STUDENT** table is a Primary key and the **STUDENT_ID** in the **STUDENTCOURSE** table is a Foreign key.

Perform the following operations to set up this relationship between the **STUDENT** and the **STUDENTCOURSE** tables:

1) Click on the **STUDENTCOURSE** table under our customer account CSE_DEPT to open it.
2) On the open table, select the **Constraints** tab on the top and click on the **Edit** icon to open the **Edit Table** wizard.
3) On the opened **Edit Table** wizard, click on the **Constraints** item on the left pane and click on the green color + icon, and then select the **New Foreign Key Constraint** item from the pop-up menu.
4) Change the name of this Foreign Key, which is located at the second line under the **Name** column in the **Constraints** list, to **STUDENTCOURSE_STUDENT_FK**.
5) Select the **STUDENT** table from the **Table** box, **STUDENT_PK** from the **Constraints** box and **Cascade** from the **On Delete** box. In this way, these two tables have a cascaded deletion relationship for this column when a deleting action is performed later. Your completed wizard is shown in Figure 2.44.
6) Click on the **OK** button to set up this foreign key relationship.

Finally, let us handle the relationship between the **COURSE** and **STUDENTCOURSE** tables.

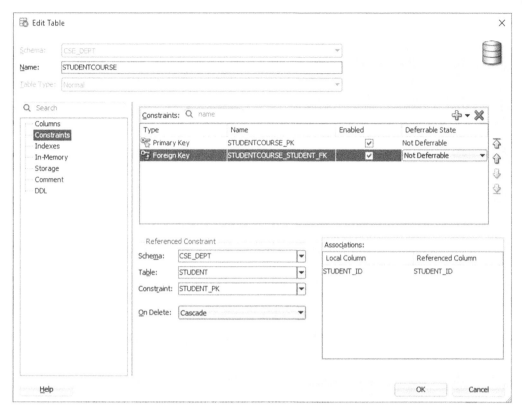

Figure 2.44 The finished foreign key for STUDENTCOURSE table. *Source*: Oracle Database.

2.9.8.5 Create Relationship Between Course and StudentCourse Tables

The relationship between the **COURSE** and the **STUDENTCOURSE** tables is one-to-many, and the **COURSE_ID** in the **COURSE** table is a Primary key and the **COURSE_ID** in the **STUDENTCOURSE** table is a Foreign key.

Perform the following operations to set up this relationship between the **COURSE** and the **STUDENTCOURSE** tables:

1) Click on the **STUDENTCOURSE** table under our customer database account **CSE_DEPT** to open it.
2) On the open table, select the **Constraints** tab on the top and click on the Edit icon to open the **Edit Table** wizard.
3) On the opened Edit Table wizard, click on the **Constraints** item on the left pane and click on the green color + icon, and then select the **New Foreign Key Constraint** item from the pop-up menu.
4) Change the name of this Foreign Key, which is located at the second line under the **Name** column in the **Constraints** list, to **STUDENTCOURSE_COURSE_FK**.
5) Select the **COURSE** table from the **Table** box, **COURSE_PK** from the **Constraints** box and **Cascade** from the **On Delete** box. In this way, these two tables have a cascaded deletion relationship for this column when a deleting action is performed later. Your completed wizard is shown in Figure 2.45.
6) Click on the **OK** button to set up this foreign key relationship.

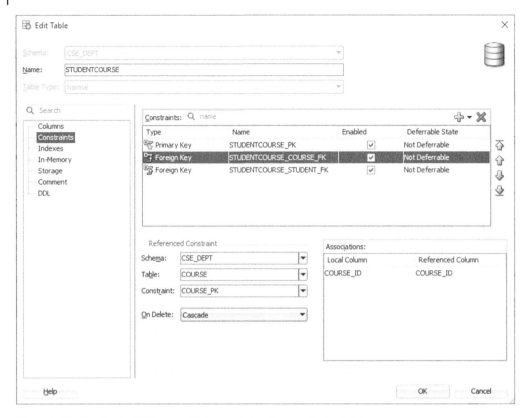

Figure 2.45 The finished Tables and Columns dialog. *Source*: Oracle Database.

At this point, we complete settings of the relationships among our five data tables. Go to `File|Save All` item to save these foreign keys setup. Now if you open the `Model` tab from the `LOGIN` table, you can find that two foreign keys, `LOGIN_FACULTY_FK` and `LOGIN_STUDENT_FK`, have been set up as shown in Figure 2.46.

Next, let us discuss how to store an image into the related column in Oracle database.

2.9.9 Store Images to the Oracle 18c Express Edition Database

When building Faculty and Student tables in Sections 2.9.6 and 2.9.7, we need to store faculty and student images into the Oracle 18c XE database directly. Due to the image property of Oracle 18c XE database, an image can be directly stored into the database column as a `Binary Large OBject` (BLOB) object in an Oracle database.

With the help of a product built by Developer Express Incorporated, or a user interface, DevExpress WinForms, we can directly insert an image into an Oracle database's column via Microsoft Visual Studio.NET platform with no coding process.

Refer to Appendix C to download and install this DevExpress WinForms from the site DevExpress.com. As it is done, this component has been added into Visual Basic.NET environment.

Now we will use Visual Studio.NET 2019 as an IDE and DevExpress WinForms as a tool to insert or store images into the related columns in the Oracle 18c XE database.

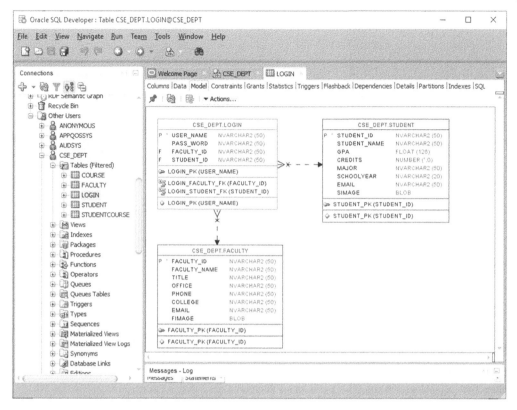

Figure 2.46 Relationships among LOGIN, FACULTY, and STUDENT tables. *Source*: Oracle Database.

First open Visual Studio.NET 2019 and create a new Visual Basic.NET Windows Form App project named `Oracle Image Project` and save it in any folder in your computer. Perform the following operations to complete this project creation process.

1) Select `Create a new project` item at the right-lower corner, which is under the Get started tab, to open the `Create a project` wizard, as shown in Figure 2.47.
2) Select the `Blank Solution` from the left by clicking on it, as shown in Figure 2.47, then click on the `Next` button to open the `Configure your new project` wizard, as shown in Figure 2.48.
3) Enter Oracle Image Solution into the `Project name` box as the name for this solution, and `C:\Temp` into the `Location` box for the location of this solution (Figure 2.48). Then, click on the **Create** button to create a blank solution. You can select any other folder if you like as the location for this project.
4) Right click on the new created blank solution `Oracle Image Solution` in the Solution Explorer window and select `Add|New Project` item from the pop-up menu to open the **Add New Project** wizard, as shown in Figure 2.49.
5) Make sure to select the **Windows Form App (.NET Framework)** for Visual Basic template on the left pane, and click on the `Next` button to continue.
6) On the opened `Configure your new project` wizard, as shown in Figure 2.50, enter `Oracle Image Project` into the **Project name** box as the name for this project, as shown in Figure 2.50. Keep the selected location with no change and click on the **Create** button to continue. The added project wizard is shown in Figure 2.51.

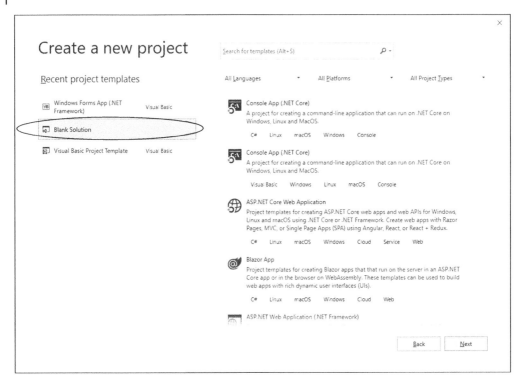

Figure 2.47 Create a blank solution Oracle Image Solution. *Source*: Oracle Database.

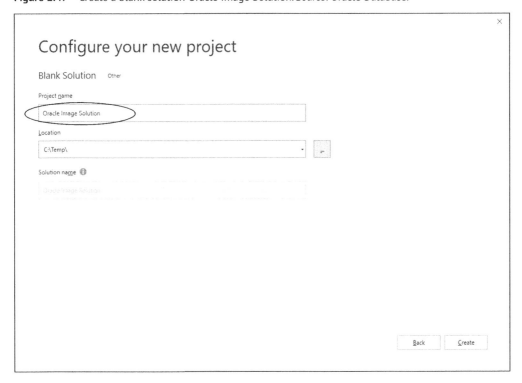

Figure 2.48 Enter the solution name and location. *Source*: Oracle Database.

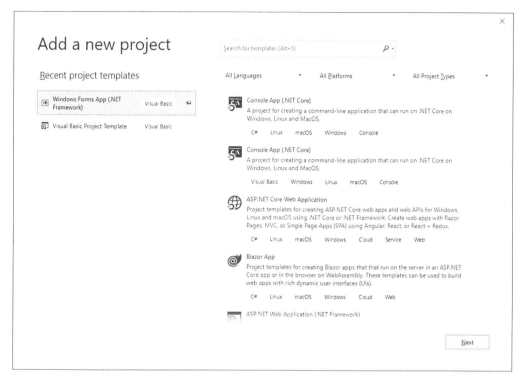

Figure 2.49 The opened Add new project wizard. *Source*: Oracle Database.

Configure your new project

Windows Forms App (.NET Framework)   Visual Basic   Windows   Desktop

Project name

Oracle Image Project

Location

C:\Temp\Oracle Image Solution

Framework

.NET Framework 4.7.2

Back   Create

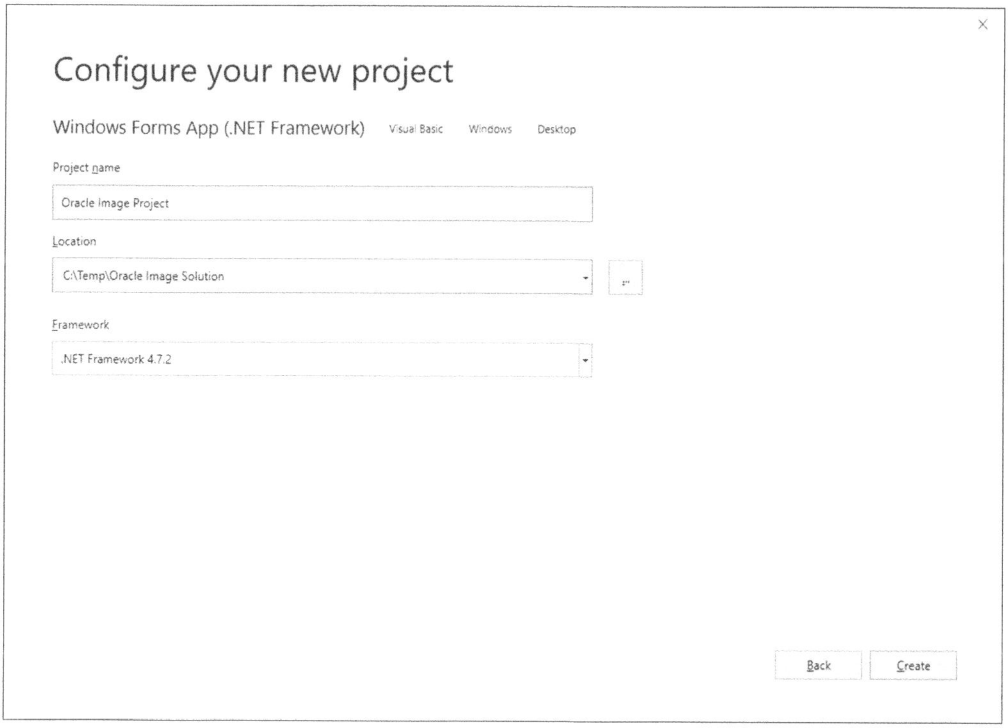

Figure 2.50 The opened Configure your new project wizard. *Source*: Oracle Database.

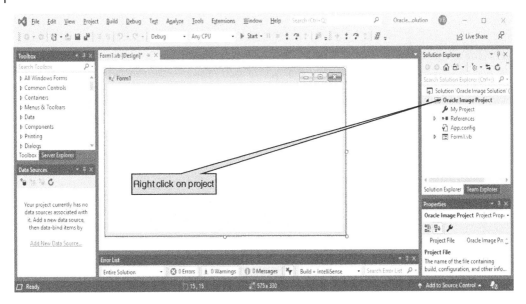

Figure 2.51 The new created project – Oracle Image Project. *Source*: Oracle Database.

Prior to using the Data Source tool in Visual Studio.NET to access our Oracle 18c XE database, we need to add some database drivers into the project to enable us to use it as an adaptor to connect and implement our sample database, and add images into our **FACULTY** and **STUDENT** tables. Let us start with **FACULTY** table.

2.9.9.1 Store Images into the FACULTY Table

Perform the following operations to complete these addition processes

1) Right click on our project `Oracle Image Project` from the Solution Explorer window (Figure 2.51), and select **Add | Reference** items from the pop-up menu to open the Reference Manager wizard, which is shown in Figure 2.52.

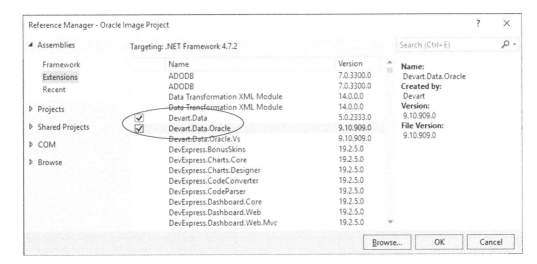

Figure 2.52 Two added data components. *Source*: Oracle Database.

2) Select the **Extensions** item from the left pane under **Assemblies** tab to open the component list contained all third-party-added components.
3) Select both **Devart.Data** and **Devart.Data.Oracle** items, as shown in Figure 2.52. If you cannot find these two items, you need to download and install **dotConnect Express** driver for Oracle database first. Refer to Appendix F to complete this job.
4) Click on the **OK** button to add both database driver components into our project.

Now if you go to Solution Explorer window and expand the **References** folder, you can find that both drivers have been added into our project.

Next, let us use one of Visual Studio.NET tools, **Data Source**, to connect and access our sample Oracle 18c XE database via the added database drivers.

1) Click on the **Add New Data Source** link, as shown in Figure 2.53, in the **Data Sources** window located at the lower-left corner (if this window is not shown up, go to **View|Other Windows|Data Sources** to open it), to open the **Data Source Configuration Wizard** to connect to our designed Oracle 18c XE database CSE_DEPT.
2) On the opened **Choose a Data Source Type** and **Choose a Database Model** wizards, keep the default **Database** and **DataSet** selection on these two wizards and click on the **Next** buttons to come to our database connection wizard, **Choose Your Data Connection** wizard. Click on the **New Connection. . .** button to open the **Add Connection** wizard, which is shown in Figure 2.54a.
3) Click on the **Change** button to open the **Change Data Source** wizard, as shown in Figure 2.54b.
4) Select **Oracle Database** from the **Data source** list on the left, and make sure that **dotConnect for Oracle** component is selected in the **Data provider** box, as shown in Figure 2.54b. Click on the **OK** button to return to Add Connection wizard.
5) On the returned Add Connection wizard, as shown in Figure 2.55, enter following parameters into the related box as the connection parameters:
   a) Server: **localhost:1518/CSE_DEPT**
   b) User Id: **CSE_DEPT**
   c) Password: **oracle_18c**

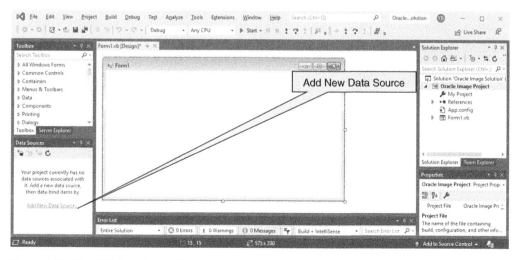

Figure 2.53 The Add Data Source link. *Source*: Oracle Database.

(a)

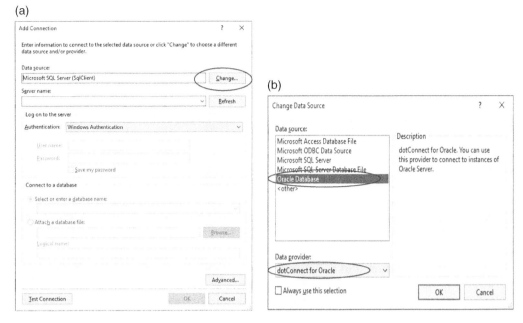

Figure 2.54 The opened Add Connection wizard. *Source*: Oracle Database.

Figure 2.55 The parameters used to connect to our sample database. *Source*: Oracle Database.

The Server contained the data source, it is formatted as `Host:Listener/Database`. The User Id is our user account, CSE_DEPT, and the password is oracle_18c.

6) Check the `Allow saving password` checkbox since we want to keep it.

7) You can click on the `Test Connection` button to test this connection. A successful connection message should be displayed if this connection is complete.

8) Click on the `OK` button to start this connection process.

9) On the opened `Data Source Configuration Wizard`, which is shown in Figure 2.56, check the `Yes, include sensitive data in the connection string` radio button since we want to keep all of above connection parameters to be used in the future in our project. For the same reason, also check the `Show the connection string that you will save in the application` checkbox. Click on the `Next` button to continue.

10) On the next wizard, check `Yes, save the connection as` checkbox to save our connection string as default one, which may be used in the future. Click on the `Next` button to go to the next wizard to select our database objects.

11) The `Choose Database Objects` wizard is opened, as shown in Figure 2.57. Expand the `Tables` and then `FACULTY` icons, then select `FACULTY_ID`, `FACULTY_NAME` and `FIMAGE` columns by checking each of them (of course you can select all columns as we will do this later, but right now we only need these columns for our demo purpose). Also change the DataSet name to `OracleImageDataSet` in the `DataSet name` box, as shown in Figure 2.57.

12) Click on the `Finish` button to complete this connection process.

Next let's use this created connection and DataSet object to connect and access to our sample database to perform faculty image insertion operations to the FACULTY table.

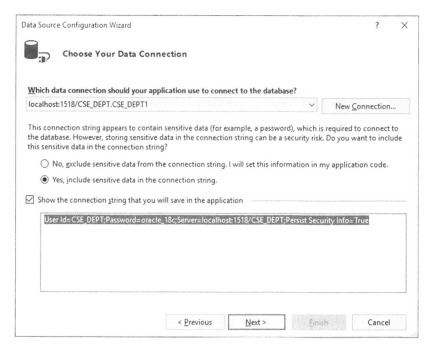

Figure 2.56 The opened Data Source Configuration wizard. *Source*: Oracle Database.

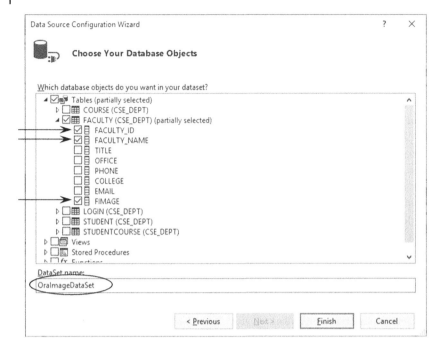

Figure 2.57 The connected database and data set OracleImageDataSet. *Source*: Oracle Database.

1) Return to our Visual Basic.NET project window, expand our DataSet and related Faculty table, `OracleImageDataSet` and `FACULTY`, in the Data Sources window. Click on the drop-down arrow on the right of the `FACULTY` table combo box and select the `Details` item, and then drag this `Details` item and place it into the Form window, as shown in Figure 2.58.

2) Now go to the Image object added on the Form window, `FIMAGE`, and click on an arrow box ▣ located at the upper-right corner to open the **PictureEdit Tasks** dialog box, and select **Stretch** from the **Size Mode** combo box. Then click on any place on the Form window to close that `PictureEdit Tasks` dialog box.

3) Click on the drop-down arrow on the right of the Faculty table combo box again and select the **GridView** item, and then drag this GridView item and place it into the Form window, as shown in Figure 2.59.

4) Now go to **File|Save All** item to save all of these additions and modifications to this Form window.

5) Then click on the **Start** button (green arrow on the tool bar) to run this Visual Basic project. As the project runs, the contents of three columns for all faculty members in this FACULTY table are displayed in both the Details and GridView except the faculty image `FIMAGE`, as shown in Figure 2.60.

6) To add an image to the `FIMAGE` box for the selected faculty member, click on an arrow for that faculty and first click (left-click) on the `FIMAGE` column in the GridView, and then right click on the `FIMAGE` column again. On the pop-up menu, select the **Load** item to load and add an image for the selected faculty member.

7) Browse to the related faculty image, in our case, all faculty images are in the folder: **C:/Students/Images/Faculty**, and select the associated faculty image, such as `Anderson.jpg` for the faculty member Black Anderson, by clicking on it, and click on the **Open** button to add it to the OracleImageDataSet.

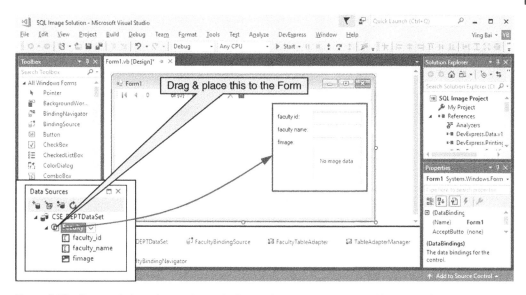

Figure 2.58 Drag and place three columns in Details format from Faculty table. *Source*: Oracle Database.

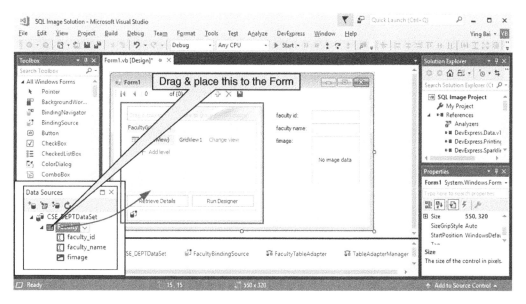

Figure 2.59 Drag and place three columns in GridView format on Faculty table. *Source*: Oracle Database.

 All faculty images are located at the Wiley site at the folder **Students/ Images/Faculty,** and you can copy those image files with folders and save them into your computer (refer to Figure 1.2 in Chapter 1 to get more details about these image files).

Figure 2.60 The opened Form for adding faculty images. *Source*: Oracle Database.

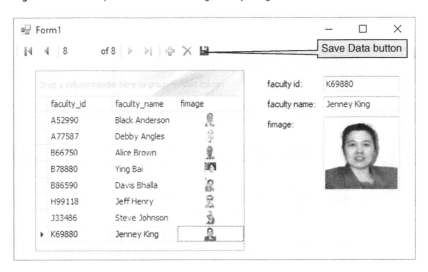

Figure 2.61 The opened Form for adding faculty images. *Source*: Oracle Database.

8) Then click on the **Save Data** button located at the upper-right corner on the tool bar to save this image into the database. Perform similar operations to add all faculty images into our sample database CSE_DEPT.

Your finished Form window is shown in Figure 2.61. The relationships between each faculty member and related image file are shown in Table 2.17.

Now you can test these image insertion operations by clicking each **FACULTY_ID** from the GridView box. Immediately, the selected faculty, including the **FACULTY_ID**, **FACULTY_NAME**, and **FIMAGE**, will be displayed in the Details View in this Form window, as shown in Figure 2.61.

Table 2.17 The image files in the Faculty table.

faculty_id	faculty_name	fimage
A52990	Black Anderson	Anderson.jpg
A77587	Debby Angles	Angles.jpg
B66750	Alice Brown	Brown.jpg
B78880	Ying Bai	Bai.jpg
B86590	Davis Bhalla	Davis.jpg
H99118	Jeff Henry	Nenry.jpg
J33486	Steve Johnson	Johnson.jpg
K69880	Jenney King	King.jpg

Figure 2.62 The modified FIMAGE column. *Source*: Oracle Database.

Now if you open the Oracle SQL Developer and our **FACULTY** table located under our user account database CSE_DEPT, click on the **Data** tab, you can find that all **NULL** values in the FIMAGE column (the last column) have been changed to **BLOB**, as shown in Figure 2.62.

2.9.9.2 Store Images into the STUDENT Table

In a similar way, you can add all students' images into the **STUDENT** table in our database CSE_DEPT. All students' images can be found from the Wiley site at a folder: **Students/Images/Students**. Refer to Figure 1.2 in Chapter 1 for more details about this folder. You can copy those image files and save them to your local folder if you like.

The relationships between each student and related image file are shown in Table 2.18.

You do not need to create a new project and redo everything as we did above. The only things you need to do include:

1) Add another new Windows Form object, **Form2.vb**, by right clicking on our project **Oracle Image Project** in the Solution Explorer window and select **Add|New Item**, then select **Form (Windows Forms)** from the mid-pane and click on the **Add** button to add it into our project.
2) Define the new added form, **Form2**, as the start-up form to direct the project to run that form first as the project starts. Go to **Projct|Oracle Image Project Properties** item to open the project properties wizard. Under the default tab, **Application**, select **Form2** from the **Startup form** combobox.

Table 2.18 The image files in the Student table.

student_id	student_name	simage
A78835	Andrew Woods	Woods.jpg
A97850	Ashly Jade	Jade.jpg
B92996	Blue Valley	Valley.jpg
H10210	Holes Smith	Smith.jpg
T77896	Tom Erica	Erica.jpg

3) Go to **File|Save All** to save this change.

Reconfigure the **OracleImageDataSet** to select the STUDENT table with three columns, **STUDENT_ID**, **STUDENT_NAME** and **SIMAGE**.

Following the steps below to complete this reconfiguration:

a) In the Visual Basic Form window, right click on the **OracleImageDataSet** in the Data Sources window, and select **Configure Data Source with Wizard...** item from the pop-up menu to open that configuration wizard.

b) Expand the **Tables** folder and expand the **STUDENT** table.

c) Check three columns: **STUDENT_ID**, **STUDENT_NAME**, and **SIMAGE**.

d) Your finished **STUDENT** table in the Configuration Wizard is shown in Figure 2.63. Click on the **Finish** button to complete this reconfiguration process.

In the Visual Basic.NET project window, exactly in the Oracle Image Project Form window, drag the **Details** and **GridView** of the **STUDENT** table and place them on the windows form object, **Form2**.

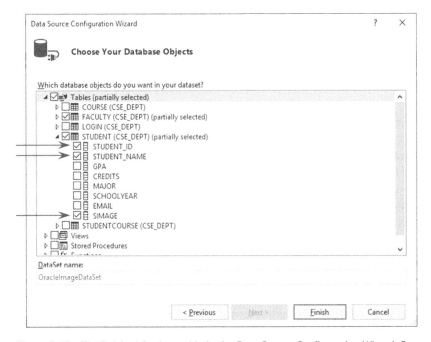

Figure 2.63 The finished Student table in the Data Source Configuration Wizard. *Source*: Oracle Database.

Figure 2.64 The completed Form for adding student images. *Source*: Oracle Database.

Also do not forget to set up the **Size Mode** property of the **SIMAGE** image box to **Stretch** as we did for the **Form1** for the faculty image **FIMAGE** object.

Now you can run the project to start adding all images for all students. Insert each student's image into the **SIMAGE** column in the **STUDENT** table by right clicking on each **SIMAGE** column, and select the **Load** item to locate and select related student's image file. Then click on the **Open** button to add each image into that column.

Do not forget to click on the **Save Data** button on the top to save these image additions. Your finished Form window should match one that is shown in Figure 2.64.

Now if you open the **STUDENT** table in our sample database **CSE_DEPT** by using either Oracle SQL Developer or Server Explorer in Visual Studio.NET environment, you can find that all data values in the **SIMAGE** columns have been changed to BLOB.

2.10   Chapter Summary

A detailed discussion and analysis of the structure and components about popular database systems are provided in this chapter. Some key technologies used to develop and design database are also given and discussed in this part. The procedure and components used to develop a relational database are analyzed in detailed with some real data tables in our sample database CSE_DEPT. The process in developing and building a sample database is discussed in detailed with the following points:

- Defining Relationships
- Normalizing the Data
- Implementing the Relational Database

In the second part of this chapter, a sample Oracle database built with Oracle 18c Express Edition, CSE_DEPT, is developed with an updated and popular database management system, Oracle 18c XE.

The detailed or step-by-step illustrations and explanations are provided for those development stages to provide readers a crystal clear picture in how to create a new Oracle 18c XE database and how to add a customer-made database and tables with the help of Oracle 18c XE and Oracle SQL

Developer, which are difficult or rarely to be found from most other books related to Oracle 18c XE developments.

The covered technologies include, but not limited to:

- Create a new Oracle database with the Oracle 18c XE environment.
- Create a new customer account with a new sample database or schema with the Oracle SQL Developer.
- Set up relationships between data tables with Oracle SQL Developer Modeler.
- Connect to created sample database from Visual Studio.NET 2019 with the help of a third party product, **dotConnect** data component.

The developed sample database will be used in the following chapters throughout the whole book.

At the end of this chapter, an easy and simple technique used to store or insert images into the Oracle 18c XE database is discussed with a real project. Step-by-step illustrations are provided to show readers how to use a third-party component, **DevExpress WindowUI**, to conveniently and quickly add either faculty or student images into the related columns in **FACULTY** or **STUDENT** tables in our sample database.

A possible reason why some powerful tools, such as Oracle Data Provider for .NET (ODP.NET) and Oracle Developer Tools for Visual Studio (ODT), are not used and discussed in this book is because some or all of those tools are out-of-date and they cannot catch up or meet the needs of quick developments of Microsoft Visual Studio.NET. For example, both ODP.NET and ODT can still support Visual Studio.NET 2015 or 2017, but today the updated version of Visual Studio.NET is 2019. By the releasing of this book proposal, there are no any new leases for both products to support Visual Studio.NET 2019.

Homework

I. True/False Selections

_____ 1   Database development process involves project planning, problem analysis, logical design, physical design, implementation, and maintenance

_____ 2   Duplication of data creates problems with data integrity.

_____ 3   If the primary key consists of a single column, then the table in 1NF is automatically in 2NF.

_____ 4   A table is in first normal form if there are no repeating groups of data in any column.

_____ 5   When a user perceives the database as made up of tables, it is called a Network Model.

_____ 6   *Entity integrity rule* states that no attribute that is a member of the primary (composite) key may accept a null value.

_____ 7   When creating data tables for the Oracle database, a blank field can be kept as a blank without any value in it.

_____ 8   To create data tables in an Oracle Server database, the data type for an image field can be a binary large object (BLOB).

_____ **9**   The name of each data table in Oracle Server database must be prefixed by the keyword ora.

_____ **10**   In each relational database table, it can contain multiple primary keys, but only one unique foreign key.

II.   **Multiple Choices**

1   There are many advantages to use an integrated database approach over that of a file processing approach. These include _____
   A   Minimizing data redundancy
   B   Improving security
   C   Data independence
   D   All of the above

2   Entity integrity rule implies that no attribute that is a member of the primary key may accept _____
   A   Null value
   B   Integer data type
   C   Character data type
   D   Real data type

3   Reducing data redundancy will lead to _____
   A   Deletion anamolies
   B   Data consistency
   C   Loss of efficiency
   D   None of the above

4   _____ keys are used to create relationships among various tables in a database
   A   Primary keys
   B   Candidate keys
   C   Foreign keys
   D   Composite keys

5   In a small university, the department of Computer Science has six faculty members. However, each faculty member belongs to only the computer science department. This type of relationship is called _____
   A   One-to-one
   B   One-to-many
   C   Many-to-many
   D   None of the above

6   The Client–Server databases have several advantages over the File Server databases. These include _____
   A   Minimizing chances of crashes
   B   Provision of features for recovery
   C   Enforcement of security
   D   Efficient use of the network
   E   All of the above

7 One can create the foreign keys between tables _____
   A Before any table can be created
   B When some tables are created
   C After all tables are created
   D With no limitations

8 To create foreign keys between tables, first one must select the table that contains a _____ key and then select another table that has a _____ key.
   A Primary, foreign
   B Primary, primary
   C Foreign, primary
   D Foreign, foreign

9 The data type nvarchar(50) in an Oracle Server database is a string with _____
   A Limited length up to 50 letters
   B Fixed length of 50 bytes
   C Certain number of letters
   D Varying length

10 For data tables in an Oracle Server Database, a blank field must be _____
   A Indicated by NULL Avoided
   B Kept as a blank
   C Either by NULL or a blank
   D Indicated by NULL

III. Exercises

1 What are the advantages to using an integrated database approach over that of a file processing approach

2 Define entity integrity and referential integrity. Describe the reasons for enforcing these rules.

3 Entities can have three types of relationships. It can be *one-to-one, one-to-many, and many-to-many*. Define each type of relationship. Draw ER diagrams to illustrate each type of relationship.

4 List all steps to create Foreign keys between data tables for the Oracle 18c Express Edition database in the Oracle SQL Developer Modeler. Illustrate those steps by using a real example. For instance, how to create foreign keys between the LogIn and the Faculty table.

5 List all steps to create Foreign keys between data tables for the Oracle 18c Express Edition database in the Oracle SQL Developer Modeler. Illustrate those steps by using a real example. For instance, how to create foreign keys between the StudentCourse and the Course table.

3

Introduction to ADO.NET

It has been a long story for software developers to generate and implement sophisticated data processing techniques to improve and enhance the data operations. The evolution of data access API is also a long process focusing predominantly on how to deal with relational data in a more flexible method. The methodology development has been focused on Microsoft-based APIs such as ODBC, OLEDB, Microsoft® Jet, Data Access Objects (DAO), and Remote Data Objects (RDO), in addition to many non-Microsoft-based APIs. These APIs did not bridge the gap between object-based and semi-structured (XML) data programming needs. Combine this problem with the task of dealing with many different data stores, nonrelational data like XML and applications applying across multiple languages are challenging topics and you should have a tremendous opportunity for complete rearchitecture. The ADO.NET is a good solution for these challenges.

3.1 The ADO and ADO.NET

ActiveX Data Object (ADO) is developed based on Object Linking and Embedding (OLE) and Component Object Model (COM) technologies. COM is used by developers to create reusable software components, link components together to build applications, and take advantage of Windows services. For recent decade, ADO has been the preferred interface for Visual Basic programmers to access various data sources, with ADO 2.7 being the latest version of this technology. The development history of data accessing methods can be traced back to the mid-1990s with Data Access Object (DAO), and then followed by Remote Data Object (RDO), which was based on the Open Database Connectivity (ODBC). In the late 1990s, the ADO that is based on OLEDB is developed. This technology is widely applied in most Object Oriented Programming and Database applications during the last decade.

Starting from ADO.NET 2.0, Microsoft released some new versions for this product, such as ADO.NET 3.5 with Visual Studio.NET 2008 and ADO.NET 4.0, which is released with Visual Studio.NET 2010. ADO.NET 4.3 is an update version of ADO.NET that is released with SQL Server 2017 and based mainly on the Microsoft .NET Framework 4.7.

The underlying technology applied in ADO.NET 3.5 is very different from the COM-based ADO. The ADO.NET Common Language Runtime provides bi-directional, transparent integration with COM. This means that COM and ADO.NET applications as well as components can use functionality from each system. But the ADO.NET 3.5 Framework provides developers with a significant number of benefits including a more robust, evidence-based security model, automatic memory

Oracle Database Programming with Visual Basic.NET: Concepts, Designs, and Implementations, First Edition. Ying Bai.
© 2021 The Institute of Electrical and Electronics Engineers, Inc. Published 2021 by John Wiley & Sons, Inc.
Companion website: www.wiley.com/go/bai-VB-Oracle

management native Web services support and Language Integrated Query (LINQ). For new development, the ADO.NET 3.5 is highly recommended as a preferred technology because of its powerful managed runtime environment and services.

Some important components included in the recent ADO.NET contain:

- LINQ to DataSet
- LINQ to SQL
- LINQ to Entities (ADO.NET Entity Framework)
- WCF Data Services (ADO.NET Data Services)
- XML and ADO.NET

ADO.NET 4.3 provides the following new features and components compared with the earlier versions:

- The ConnectRetryCount and ConnectRetryInterval connection string keywords (Connection String) let you control the idle connection resiliency feature.
- Streaming support from SQL Server to an application supports scenarios where data on the server is unstructured. See SqlClient Streaming Support for more information.
- Support has been added for asynchronous programming. See Asynchronous Programming for more information.

Figure 3.1 shows an overview of how the ADO.NET LINQ technologies relate to high-level programming languages and LINQ-enabled data sources.

This chapter will provide a detailed introduction to ADO.NET and its components, and these components will be utilized for the rest of the book.

In this chapter, you will:

- Learn the basic classes in ADO.NET and its architecture
- Learn the different ADO.NET Data Providers
- Learn about the Connection and Command components

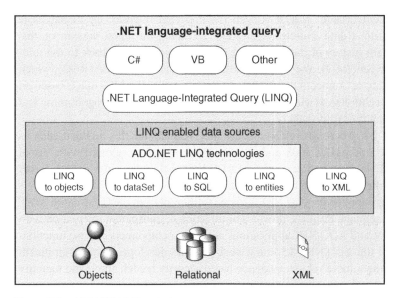

Figure 3.1 ADO.NET LINQ techniques.

- Learn about the Parameters collection component
- Learn about the DataAdapter and DataReader components
- Learn about the DataSet and DataTable components
- Learn about the Entity Framework (EF)
- Learn about the Entity Framework Tools (EFT)
- Learn about the Entity Data Model (EDM)

3.2   Overview of the ADO.NET

ADO.NET is a set of classes that expose data access services to the Microsoft .NET programmer. ADO.NET provides a rich set of components for creating distributed, data-sharing applications. It is an integral part of the Microsoft .NET Framework, providing access to relational, XML, and application data. ADO.NET supports a variety of development needs, including the creation of front-end database clients and middle-tier business objects used by applications, tools, languages, or Internet browsers.

All ADO.NET classes are located at the System.Data namespace with two files named System. Data.dll and System.Xml.dll. When compiling code that uses the System.Data namespace, reference both System.Data.dll and System.Xml.dll.

Basically speaking, ADO.NET provides a set of classes to support you to develop database applications and enable you to connect to a data source to retrieve, manipulate, and update data with your database. The classes provided by ADO.NET are core to develop a professional data-driven application and they can be divided into the following three major components:

- .NET Framework Data Provider
- DataSet
- DataTable

These three components are located at the different namespaces. The DataSet and the DataTable classes are located at the System.Data namespace. The classes of the Data Provider are located at the different namespaces based on the types of the Data Providers.

Data Provider contains four classes: Connection, Command, DataAdapter, and DataReader. These four classes can be used to perform the different functionalities to help you to:

1) Set a connection between a project and the data source using the Connection object
2) Execute data queries to retrieve, manipulate, and update data using the Command object
3) Move the data between a DataSet and a database using the DataAdapter object
4) Perform data queries from the database (read only) using the DataReader object

The DataSet class can be considered as a table container, and it can contain multiple data tables. These data tables are only a mapping to those real data tables in your database. But these data tables can also be used separately without connecting to the DataSet. In this case, each data table can be considered as a DataTable object.

The DataSet and DataTable classes have no direct relationship with the Data Provider class; therefore, they are often called Data Provider-independent components. Four classes such as Connection, Command, DataAdapter, and DataReader that belong to Data Provider are often called Data Provider-dependent components.

To get a clearer picture of the ADO.NET, let' us first take a look at the architecture of the ADO.NET.

3.3 The Architecture of the ADO.NET

The ADO.NET architecture can be divided into two logical pieces: command execution and caching.

Command execution requires features like connectivity, execution, and reading of results. These features are enabled with ADO.NET Data Providers. Caching of results is handled by the DataSet.

The Data Provider enables connectivity and command execution to underlying data sources. Note that these data sources do not have to be relational databases. Once a command has been executed, the results can be read using a DataReader. A DataReader provides efficient forward-only stream level access to the results. In addition, results can be used to render a DataSet a DataAdapter. This is typically called "filling the DataSet."

Figure 3.2 shows a typical architecture of the ADO.NET 2.0.

In this architecture, the data tables are embedded into the DataSet as a DataTable-Collection and the data transactions between the DataSet and the Data Provider such as SELECT, INSERT, UPDATE, and DELETE are made by using the DataAdapter via its own four different methods: SelectCommand, InsertCommand, UpdateCommand, and DeleteCommand, respectively. The Connection object is only used to set a connection between data sources and applications. The DataReader object is not used for this architecture. As you will see from a sample project in the following chapters, to execute the different methods under the DataAdapter to perform the data query is exactly to call the Command object with different parameters.

An alternative architecture of ADO.NET 2.0 is shown in Figure 3.3.

In this architecture, the data tables are not embedded into the DataSet but treated as independent data tables and each table can be considered as an individual DataTable object. The data transactions between the Data Provider and the DataTable are realized by executing the different methods of the Command object with the associated parameters. The ExecuteReader() method of the Command object is called when a data query is made from the data source, which is equivalent to execute an SQL SELECT statement, and the returned data should be stored to the DataReader object. When performing other data accessing operations such as INSERT, UPDATE, or DELETE, the ExecuteNonQuery() method of the Command object should be called with the suitable parameters attached to the Command object.

Keep these two ADO.NET architectures in minds, we will have a more detailed discussion for each component of the ADO.NET below. The sample projects developed in the following sections utilized these two architectures to perform the data query from and the data accessing to the data source.

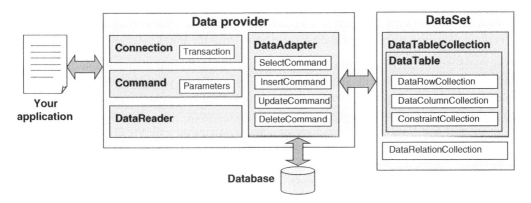

Figure 3.2 A typical architecture of the ADO.NET.

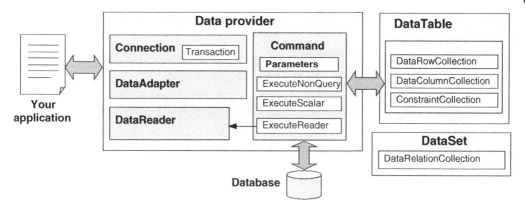

Figure 3.3 Another architecture of the ADO.NET.

3.4 The Components of ADO.NET

As we discussed in Section 3.2, ADO.NET is composed of three major components: Data Provider, DataSet, and DataTable. First let us take a look at the Data Provider.

3.4.1 The Data Provider

The Data Provider can also be called a data driver, and it can be used as a major component for your data-driven applications. The functionalities of the Data Provider, as its name means, are to:

- Connect your data source with your applications
- Execute different methods to perform the associated data query and data accessing operations between your data source and your applications
- Disconnect the data source when the data operations are done

The Data Provider is physically composed of a binary library file, and this library is in the DLL file format. Sometimes this DLL file depends on other DLL files, so in fact a Data Provider can be made up of several DLL files. Based on the different kinds of databases, Data Provider can have several versions, and each version is matched to each kind of database. The popular versions of the Data Provider are as follows:

- **O**pen **DataB**ase **C**onnectivity (**Odbc**) Data Provider (ODBC.NET)
- **O**bject **L**inking and **E**mbeding **DataB**ase (**OleDb**) Data Provider (OLEDB.NET)
- **SQL** Server (**Sql**) Data Provider (SQL Server.NET)
- **Oracle** (**Oracle**) Data Provider (Oracle.NET)

Each Data Provider can be simplified by using an associated keyword, which is the letters enclosed by the parentheses above. For instance, the keyword for the ODBC Data Provider is Odbc; the keyword for an SQL Server Data Provider is Sql, and so on.

In order to distinguish with the older Data Providers such as Microsoft ODBC, Microsoft OLE DB, Microsoft SQL Server, and Oracle, in some books all different Data Providers included in the ADO.NET are extended by a suffix NET, such as OLE DB.NET, ODBC.NET, SQL Server.NET, and Oracle.NET. Since most Data Providers discussed in this book belong to ADO.NET, generally we do not need to add that .NET suffix but we will add this suffix if the old Data Providers are used.

Table 3.1 Namespaces for different Data Providers, DataSet, and DataTable.

Namespaces	Descriptions
System.Data	Holds the DataSet and DataTable classes
System.Data.OleDb	Holds the class collection used to access an OLEDB data source
System.Data.SqlClient	Holds the classes used to access an SQL Server 7.0 data source or later
System.Data.Odbc	Holds the class collection used to access an ODBC data source
System.Data.OracleClient	Holds the classes used to access an Oracle data source

The different data providers are located at the different namespaces, and these namespaces hold the various data classes that you must import into your code in order to use those classes in your project.

Table 3.1 lists the most popular namespaces used by the different data providers and used by the DataSet and the DataTable.

Since the different Data Provider is located at the different namespace as shown in Table 3.1, you must first import the appropriate namespace into your Visual Basic.NET 2005 project, exactly into the each form's code window, whenever you want to use that Data Provider. Also all classes provided by that Data Provider must be prefixed by the associated keyword. For example, you must use "imports System.Data.OleDb" to import the namespace of the OLEDB.NET Data Provider if you want to use this Data Provider in your project, and also all classes belong to that Data Provider must be prefixed by the associated keyword OleDb, such as OleDbConnection, OleDbCommand, OleDbData-Adapter, and OleDbDataReader. The same thing holds true for all other Data Providers.

Although different Data Providers are located at the different namespaces and have the different prefixes, the classes of these Data Providers have the similar methods or properties with the same name. For example, no matter what kind of Data Provider you are using such as an OleDb, an Sql, or an Oracle, they have the methods or properties with the same name, such as Connection String property, Open() and Close() method, as well as the ExecuteReader() method. This provides the flexibility for the programmers and allows them to use different Data Providers to access the different data source by only modifying the prefix applied before each class.

The following sections provide a more detailed discussion for each specific Data Provider. These discussions will give you a direction or guideline to help you to select the appropriate Data Provider when you want to use them to develop the different data-driven applications.

3.4.1.1 The ODBC Data Provider

The .NET Framework Data Provider for ODBC uses native ODBC Driver Manager (DM) through COM interop to enable data access. The ODBC Data Provider supports both local and distributed transactions. For distributed transactions, the ODBC data provider, by default, automatically enlists in a transaction and obtains transaction details from Windows 2000 Component Services.

The ODBC .NET Data Provider provides access to ODBC data sources with the help of native ODBC drivers in the same way that the OleDb .NET Data Provider accesses native OLE DB providers.

The ODBC.NET supports the following Data Providers:

- SQL Server
- Microsoft ODBC for Oracle
- Microsoft Access Driver (*.mdb)

Some older database systems only support ODBC as the data access technique, which include older versions of SQL Server and Oracle as well as some third-party database such as Sybase.

3.4.1.2 The OLEDB Data Provider

The System.Data.OleDb namespace holds all classes used by the .NET Framework Data Provider for OLE DB. The .NET Framework Data Provider for OLE DB describes a collection of classes used to access an OLE DB data source in the managed space. Using the OleDbDataAdapter, you can fill a memory-resident DataSet that you can use to query and update the data source. The OLE DB.NET data access technique supports the following Data Providers:

- Microsoft Access
- SQL Server (7.0 or later)
- Oracle (9i or later)

One advantage of using the OLEDB.NET Data Provider is to allow users to develop a generic data-driven application. The so-called generic application means that you can use the OLEDB. NET Data Provider to access any data source such as Microsoft Access, SQL Server, Oracle, and other data source that support the OLEDB.

Table 3.2 shows the compatibility between the OLEDB Data Provider and the OLE DB.NET Data Provider.

3.4.1.3 The SQL Server Data Provider

This Data Provider provides access to a SQL Server version 7.0 or later database using its own internal protocol. The functionality of the Data Provider is designed to be similar to that of the .NET Framework data providers for OLE DB, ODBC, and Oracle. All classes related to this Data Provider are defined in a DLL file and are located at the System.Data.SqlClient namespace. Although Microsoft provides different Data Providers to access the data in SQL Server database, such as the ODBC and OLE DB, for the sake of optimal data operations, it is highly recommended to use this Data Provider to access the data in an SQL Server data source.

As shown in Table 3.2, this Data Provider is a new version and it can only work for the SQL Server version 7.0 and later. If an old version of SQL Server is used, you need to use either an OLE DB.NET or a SQLOLEDB Data Provider.

3.4.1.4 The Oracle Data Provider

This Data Provider is an add-on component to the .NET Framework that provides access to the Oracle database. All classes related to this Data Provider are located in the System.Data. OracleClient namespace. This provider relies upon Oracle Client Interfaces provided by the Oracle Client Software. You need to install the Oracle Client software on your computer to use this Data Provider.

Table 3.2 The compatibility between the OLEDB and OLEDB.NET.

Provider Name	Descriptions
SQLOLEDB	Used for Microsoft SQL Server 6.5 or earlier
Microsoft.Jet.OLEDB.4.0	Use for Microsoft JET database (Microsoft Access)
MSDAORA	Use for Oracle version 7 and later

Microsoft provides multiple ways to access the data stored in an Oracle database, such as Microsoft ODBC for Oracle and OLE DB, you should use this Data Provider to access the data in an Oracle data source since this one provides the most efficient way to access the Oracle database.

This Data Provider can only work for the recent versions of the Oracle database, such as 8.1.7 and later. For old versions of the Oracle database, you need to use either MSDAORA or an OLE DB.NET.

As we mentioned in the previous parts, all different Data Providers use the similar objects, properties, and methods to perform the data operations for the different databases. In the following sections, we will make a detailed discussion for these similar objects, properties, and methods used for the different Data Providers.

3.4.2 The Connection Class

As shown in Figures 3.2 and 3.3, the Data Provider contains four sub-classes and the Connection component is one of them. This class provides a connection between your applications and the database you selected to connect to your project. To use this class to setup a connection between your application and the desired database, you need first to create an instance or an object based on this class. Depends on your applications, you can create a global connection instance for your entire project or you can create some local connection objects for each of your form windows. Generally, a global instance is a good choice since you do not need to perform multiple open and close operations for connection objects. A global connection instance is used in all sample projects in this book.

The Connection object you want to use depends on the type of the data source you selected. Data Provider provides four different Connection classes and each one is matched to one different database. Table 3.3 lists these popular Connection classes used for the different data sources:

The New keyword is used to create a new instance or object of the Connection class. Although different Connection classes provide different overloaded constructors, two popular constructors are utilized widely for Visual Basic.NET. One of them does not accept any argument, but another one accepts a connection string as the argument and this constructor is the most commonly used for data connections.

The connection string is a property of the Connection class, and it provides all necessary information to connect to your data source. Regularly this connection string contains a quite few parameters to define a connection, but only five of them are popularly utilized for most data-driven applications:

1) Provider
2) Data Source
3) Database
4) User ID
5) Password

Table 3.3 The Connection classes and databases.

Connection Class	Associated Database
OdbcConnection	ODBC Data Source
OleDbConnection	OLE DB Database
SqlConnection	SQL Server Database
OracleConnection	Oracle Database

For different databases, the parameters contained in the connection string may have a little difference. For example, both OLE DB and ODBC databases need all of these five parameters to be included in a connection string to connect to OleDb or Odbc data source. But for the SQL Server database connection, you may need to use the Server to replace the Provider parameter, and for the Oracle database connection, you do not need the Provider and Database parameters at all for your connection string. You can find these differences in Section 5.18.1 in Chapter 5.

The parameter names in a connection string are case insensitive, but some of parameters such as the Password or PWD may be case sensitive. Many of the connection string properties can be read out separately. For example, one of properties, state, is one of the most useful property for your data-driven applications. By checking this property, you can get to know what is the current connection status between your database and your project, and this checking is necessary for you to make the decision which way your program suppose to go. Also you can avoid the unnecessary errors related to the data source connection by checking this property. For example, you cannot perform any data operation if your database has not been connected to your application. By checking this property, you can get a clear picture whether your application is connected to your database or not.

A typical data connection instance with a general connection string can be expressed by the following codes:

```
Connection = New xxxConnection("Provider=MyProvider;" & _
                "Data Source=MyServer;" & _
                "Database=MyDatabase;" & _
                "User ID=MyUserID;" & _
                "Password=MyPassWord;")
```

where *xxx* should be replaced by the selected Data Provider in your real application, such as OleDb, Sql, or Oracle. You need to use the real parameter values implemented in your applications to replace those nominal values such as MyServer, MyDatabase, MyUserID, and MyPassWord in your application.

The Provider parameter indicates the database driver you selected. If you installed a local SQL server and client such as the SQL Server 2017 Express on your computer, the Provider should be local host. If you are using a remote SQL Server instance, you need to use that remote server's network name. If you are using the default named instance of SQLX on your computer, you need to use *.\SQLEXPRESS* as the value for your Provider parameter. For the Oracle server database, you do not need to use this parameter.

The Data Source parameter indicates the name of the network computer on which your SQL server or Oracle server is installed and running.

The Database parameter indicates your database name.

The User ID and Password parameters are used for the security issue for your database. In most cases, the default Windows NT Security Authentication is utilized.

Some typical Connection instances used for the different databases are listed below:

OLE DB Data Provider for Microsoft Access Database

```
Connection = New OleDbConnection("Provider=Microsoft.ACE.
                OLEDB.12.0;" & _
                "Data Source=C:\\database\\CSE_DEPT.accdb;" & _
                "User ID-MyUserID;" & _
                "Password=MyPassWord;")
```

SQL Server Data Provider for SQL Server Database

```
Connection = New SqlConnection("Server=localhost;" + _
                "Data Source=Computer_name\SQLEXPRESS;" + _
                "Database=CSE_DEPT;" + _
                "Integrated Security=SSPI")
```

Oracle Data Provider for Oracle Database

```
Connection = New OracleConnection("Data Source=XE;" + _
                    "User ID=system;" + _
                    "Password=come")
```

Besides these important properties such as the connection string and state, the Connection class contains some important methods, such as the Open() and Close() methods. To make a real connection between your data source and your application, the Open() method is needed, and the Close() method is also needed when you finished the data operations and you want to exit your application.

3.4.2.1 The Open() Method of the Connection Class

To create a real connection between your database and your applications, the Open() method of the Connection class is called and it is used to open a connection to a data source with the property settings specified by the connection string. An important issue for this connection is that you must make sure that this connection is a bug-free connection, in other words, the connection is successful and you can use this connection to access data from your application to your desired data source without any problem. One of the efficient ways to do this is to use the Try. . ..Catch block to embed this Open() operation to try to find and catch the typical possible errors caused by this connection. An example coding of opening an OLEDB connection is shown in Figure 3.4.

The Microsoft.ACE.OLEDB.12.0 driver, which is a driver for the Microsoft Access 2007, is used as the Data Provider and the Microsoft Access 2007 database file **CSE_DEPT.accdb** is located at the **database\Access** folder at our local computer. The Open() method, which is embedded inside the Try. . ..Catch block, is called after a new OleDbConnection object is created to open this connection. Two possible typical errors, either an OleDbException or an InvalidOperationException,

```
Dim strConnectionString As String = " Provider=Microsoft.ACE.OLEDB.12.0;" & _
                            "Data Source=C:\\database\\Access\\CSE_DEPT.accdb;"

accConnection = New OleDbConnection(strConnectionString)

Try
    accConnection.Open()
Catch OleDbExceptionErr As OleDbException
    MessageBox.Show(OleDbExceptionErr.Message, "Access Error")
Catch InvalidOperationExceptionErr As InvalidOperationException
    MessageBox.Show(InvalidOperationExceptionErr.Message, "Access Error")
End Try

If accConnection.State <> ConnectionState.Open Then
    MessageBox.Show("Database Connection is Failed")
    Exit Sub
End If
```

Figure 3.4 An example code of the opening a connection.

could be happened after this Open() method is executed. A related message would be displayed if any one of those errors occurred and caught.

To make sure that the connection is bug-free, one of the properties of the Connection class, State, is used. This property has two possible values: Open or Closed. By checking this property, you can confirm that the connection is successful or not.

3.4.2.2   The Close() Method of the Connection Class

The Close() method is a partner of the Open() method, and it is used to close a connection between your database and your applications when you finished your data operations to the data source. You should close any connection object you connected to your data source after you finished the data access to that data source, otherwise a possible error may be encountered when you try reopen that connection in the next time as you run your project.

Unlike the Open() method, which is a key to your data access and operation to your data source, the Close() method does not throw any exceptions when you try to close a connection that has already been closed. So you do not need to use a Try. . ..Catch block to catch any error for this method.

3.4.2.3   The Dispose() Method of the Connection Class

The Dispose() method of the Connection class is an overloaded method, and it is used to releases the resources used by the Connection object. You need to call this method after the Close() method is executed to perform a cleanup job to release all resources used by the Connection object during your data access and operations to your data source. Although it is unnecessary for you to have to call this Dispose() method to do the cleanup job since one of system tools, Garbage Collection can periodically check and clean all resources used by unused objects in your computer, it is highly recommended for you to make this kind of coding to make your program more professional and efficient.

After the Close() and Dispose() methods executed, you can release your reference to the Connection instance by setting it to Nothing. A piece of example code is shown in Figure 3.5.

Now we finished the discussion for the first component defined in a Data Provider, the Connection object, let us take a look at the next object, the Command object. Since a close relationship is existed between the Command and the Parameter object, we discuss these two objects in one section.

3.4.3   The Command and the Parameter Classes

Command objects are used to execute commands against your database such as a data query, an action query, and even a stored procedure. In fact, all data accesses and data operations between your data source and your applications are achieved by executing the Command object with a set of parameters.

Command class can be divided into the different categories, and these categories are based on the different Data Providers. For the popular Data Providers, such as OLE DB, ODBC, SQL Server,

Figure 3.5   An example code for the cleanup of resources.

```
' clean up the objects used
accConnection.Close()
accConnection.Dispose()
accConnection = Nothing
```

and Oracle, each one has its own Command class. Each Command class is identified by the different prefix such as OleDbCommand, OdbcCommand, SqlCommand, and OracleCommand. Although these different Command objects belong to the different Data Providers, they have the similar properties and methods, and they are equivalent in functionalities.

Depends on the architecture of the ADO.NET, the Command object can have two different roles when you are using it to perform a data query or a data action. Refer to Figures 3.2 and 3.3 in this chapter. In Figure 3.2, if a TableAdapter is utilized to perform a data query and all data tables are embedded into the DataSet as a data catching unit, the Command object is embedded into the different data query method of the TableAdapter, such as SelectCommand, InsertCommand, UpdateCommand, and DeleteCommand and is executed based on the associated query type. In this case, the Command object can be executed indirectly, which means that you do not need to use any Executing method to run the Command object directly, instead you can run it by executing the associated method of the TableAdapter.

In Figure 3.3, each data table can be considered as an individual table. The Command object can be executed directly based on the attached parameter collection that is created and initialized by the user.

No matter which role you want to use for the Command object in your application, you should first create, initialize, and attach the Parameters collection to the Command object before you can use it. Also you must initialize the Command object by assigning the suitable properties to it in order to use the Command object to access the data source to perform any data query or data action. Some most popular properties of the Command class are discussed below.

3.4.3.1 The Properties of the Command Class

The Command class contains more than 10 properties, but only four of them are used popularly in most applications:

- Connection property
- CommandType property
- CommandText property
- Parameters property

The Connection property is used to hold a valid Connection object, and the Command object can be executed to access the connected database based on this Connection object.

The CommandType property is used to indicate what kind of command that is stored in the CommandText property should be executed. In other words, the CommandType property specifies how the CommandText property can be interpreted. Totally, three CommandType properties are available: Text, TableDirect, and StoredProcedure. The default value of this property is Text.

The content of the CommandText property is determined by the value of the CommandType property. It contains a complete SQL statement if the value of the CommandType property is Text. It may contain a group of SQL statements if the value of the CommandType property is StoredProcedure.

The Parameters property is used to hold a collection of the Parameter objects. You need to note that the Parameters is a collection but the Parameter is an object, which means that the former contains a group of objects and you can add the latter to the former.

You must first create and initialize a Parameter object before you can add that object to the Parameters collection for a Command object.

3.4.3.2 The Constructors and Properties of the Parameter Class

The Parameter class has four popular constructors, which are shown in Figure 3.6 (an SQL Server Data Provider is used as an example).

```
Dim oraParameter As New OracleParameter()
Dim oraParameter As New OracleParameter(ParamName, objValue)
Dim oraParameter As New OracleParameter(ParamName, OracleDbType)
Dim oraParameter As New OracleParameter(ParamName, OracleDbType, intSize)
```

Figure 3.6   Four constructors of the Parameter class in Oracle Provider.

Table 3.4   The data types and the associated Data Provider.

Data Type	Associated Data Provider
OdbcType	ODBC Data Provider
OleDbType	OLE DB Provider
SqlDbType	SQL Server Data Provider
OracleDBType	Oracle Data Provider

The first constructor is a blank one, and you need to initialize each property of the Parameter object one by one if you want to use this constructor to instantiate a new Parameter object. Three popular properties of a Parameter object are as follows:

- ParameterName
- Value
- DbType

The first property ParameterName contains the name of the selected parameter. The second property Value is the value of the selected parameter and it is an object. The third property DbType is used to define the data type of the selected parameter.

All parameters in the Parameter object must have a data type, and you can indicate a data type for a selected parameter by specifying the DbType property. ADO.NET and ADO.NET Data Provider have different definitions for the data types they provided. The DbType is the data type used by ADO.NET, but ADO.NET Data Provider has another four different popular data types and each one is associated with a Data Provider. Table 3.4 lists these data types as well the associated Data Providers.

Even the data types provided by ADO.NET and ADO.NET Data Provider are different, but they have a direct connection between them. As a user, you can use any data type you like, and the other one will be automatically changed to the corresponding value if you set one of them. For example, if you set the DbType property of a SqlParameter object to String, the SqlDbType parameter will be automatically set to Char. In this book, we always use the data types defined in the ADO.NET Data Provider since all parameters discussed in this section are related to the different Data Provider.

The default data type for the DbType property is String.

3.4.3.3   Parameter Mapping

When you add a Parameter object to the Parameters collection of a Command object by attaching that Parameter object to the Parameters property of the Command class, the Command object needs to know the relationship between that added parameter and the parameters you used in your SQL query string such as an SELECT statement. In other words, the Command object needs to

Table 3.5 The different parameter mappings.

Parameter Mapping	Associated Data Provider
Positional Parameter Mapping	ODBC Data Provider
Positional Parameter Mapping	OLE DB Provider
Named Parameter Mapping	SQL Server Data Provider
Named Parameter Mapping	Oracle Data Provider

identify which parameter used in your SQL statement should be mapped to this added parameter. Different parameter mappings are used for different Data Providers. Table 3.5 lists these mappings.

Both OLE DB and ODBC Data Providers used a so-called Positional Parameter Mapping, which means that the relationship between the parameters defined in an SQL statement and the added parameters into a Parameters collection is one-to-one in the order. In other words, the order in which the parameters appear in an SQL statement and the order in which the parameters are added into the Parameters collection should be exactly identical. The Positional Parameter Mapping is indicated with a question mark **?**.

For example, the following SQL statement is used for an OLE DB Data Provider as a query string:

```
SELECT id, user_name, pass_word FROM LogIn WHERE (user_name=?) AND
(pass_word=?)
```

The user_name and pass_word are mapped to two columns in the LogIn data table. Two dynamic parameters are represented by two question marks ? in this SQL statement. To add a Parameter object to the Parameters collection of a Command object accCommand, you need to use the **Add()** method as below:

```
accCommand.Parameters.Add("user_name", OleDbType.Char).Value =
txtUserName.Text
accCommand.Parameters.Add("pass_word", OleDbType.Char, 8).Value =
txtPassWord.Text
```

You must be careful with the order in which you add these two parameters, user_name and pass_word, and make sure that this order is identical with the order in which those two dynamic parameters (**?**) appear in the above SQL statement.

Both SQL Server and Oracle Data Provider used the Named Parameter Mapping, which means that each parameter, either defined in an SQL statement or added into a Parameters collection, is identified by the name. In other words, the name of the parameter appeared in an SQL statement or a stored procedure must be identical with the name of the parameter you added into a Parameters collection.

For example, the following Oracle statement is used for an Oracle Data Provider as a query string:

```
SELECT id, user_name, pass_word FROM LogIn WHERE (user_name = :Param1)
                                AND (pass_word = :Param2)
```

The **user_name** and **pass_word** are mapped to two columns in the LogIn data table. Compared with the above Oracle statement, two dynamic parameters are represented by two

```
Dim paramUserName As New OracleParameter
Dim paramPassWord As New OracleParameter

paramUserName.ParameterName = ":Param1"
paramUserName.Value = txtUserName.Text
paramPassWord.ParameterName = ":Param2"
paramPassWord.Value = txtPassWord.Text
```

Figure 3.7   An example of initializing the property of a Parameter object.

nominal parameters `:Param1` and `:Param2` in this Oracle statement. The equal operator is used as an assignment operator for two parameters. This format or syntax is required by the Oracle Data Provider.

Then you need two Parameter objects associated with your Command object, an example of initializing these two Parameter objects is shown in Figure 3.7.

Where two **ParameterName** properties are assigned with two dynamic parameters, `:Param1` and `:Param2`, respectively. Both **Param1** and **Param2** are nominal names of the dynamic parameters and a colon (:) symbol is prefixed before each parameter since this is the requirement of the Oracle database when a dynamic parameter is utilized in an Oracle statement.

You can see from this piece of codes, the name of each parameter you used for each Parameter object must be identical with the name you defined in your Oracle statement. Since the Oracle Data Provider use **Named Parameter Mapping**, you do not need to worry about the order in which you added Parameter objects into the Parameters collection of the Command object.

To add Parameter objects into a Parameters collection of a Command object, you need to use some methods defined in the **ParameterCollection** class.

3.4.3.4   The Methods of the ParameterCollection Class

Each ParameterCollection class has more than 10 methods, but only two of them are most often utilized in the data-driven applications, which are **Add()** and **AddWithValue()** methods. Each Parameter object must be added into the Parameters collection of a Command object before you can execute that Command object to perform any data query or data action.

As we mentioned in the last section, you do not need to worry about the order in which you added the parameter into the Parameter object if you are using a Named Parameter Mapping Data Providers such as an SQL Server or an Oracle. But you must pay attention to the order in which you added the parameter into the Parameter object if you are using a Positional Parameter Mapping Data Providers such as an OLE DB or an ODBC.

The Parameters property in the Command class is a collection of a set of Parameter objects. You need first to create and initialize a Parameter object, and then you can add that Parameter object to the Parameters collection. In this way, you can assign that Parameter object to a Command object.

To add Parameter objects to an Parameters collection of a Command object, two popular ways are generally adopted, **Add()** method and **AddWithValue()** method.

The **Add()** method is an overloaded method, and it has five different protocols, but only two of them are widely used. The protocols of these two methods are shown below.

```
ParameterCollection.Add( value As OracleParameter )
As OracleParameter
ParameterCollection.Add( parameterName As String, Value As Object )
```

The first method needs a Parameter object as the argument, and that Parameter object should have been created and initialized before you call this **Add()** method to add it into the collection if you want to use this method.

The second method contains two arguments. The first one is a String that contains the ParameterName and the second is an object that includes the value of that parameter.

The **AddWithValue()** method is similar to the second **Add()** method with the following protocol:

```
ParameterCollection.AddWithValue( parameterName As String, Value
As Object )
```

An example of using these two methods to add Parameter objects into a Parameters collection is shown in Figure 3.8.

The top section is used to create and initialize the Parameter objects, which we have discussed in the previous sections.

First the **Add()** method is executed to add two Parameter objects, **paramUserName** and **paramPassWord** to the Parameters collection of the Command object **oraCommand**. To use this method, two Parameter objects should have been initialized.

The second way to do this job is to use the **AddWithValue()** method to add these two Parameter objects, which is similar to the second protocol of the **Add()** method.

3.4.3.5 The Constructor of the Command Class

The constructor of the Command class is an overloaded method and it has multiple protocols. Four popular protocols are listed in Figure 3.9 (an Oracle Data Provider is used as an example).

The first constructor is a blank one without any argument. You have to create and assign each property to the associated property of the Command object separately if you want to use this constructor to instantiate a new Command object.

The second constructor contains two arguments: the first one is the parameter name that is a string variable and the second is the value that is an object. The following two constructors are similar to the second one, and the difference is that a data type and a data size argument are included.

```
Dim paramUserName As New OracleParameter
Dim paramPassWord As New OracleParameter

paramUserName.ParameterName = ":Param1"
paramUserName.Value = txtUserName.Text
paramPassWord.ParameterName = ":Param2"
paramPassWord.Value = txtPassWord.Text

oraCommand.Parameters.Add(paramUserName)
oraCommand.Parameters.Add(paramPassWord)

oraCommand.Parameters.AddWithValue(":Param1", txtUserName.Text)
oraCommand.Parameters.AddWithValue(":Param2", txtPassWord.Text)
```

Figure 3.8   Two methods to add Parameter objects in Oracle Provider.

```
Dim oraCommand As New OracleCommand()
Dim oraCommand As New OracleCommand(connString)
Dim oraCommand As New OracleCommand(connString, OracleConnection)
Dim oraCommand As New OracleCommand(connString, OracleConnection, OracleTransaction)
```

Figure 3.9   Three popular protocols of the constructor of the Command class.

```
Dim cmdString1 As String = "SELECT id, user_name, pass_word FROM Login "
Dim cmdString2 As String = "WHERE (user_name = :Param1 ) AND (pass_word = :Param2)"
Dim cmdString As String = cmdString1 & cmdString2
Dim paramUserName As New OracleParameter
Dim paramPassWord As New OracleParameter
Dim oraCommand As New OracleCommand

    paramUserName.ParameterName = ":Param1"
    paramUserName.Value = txtUserName.Text
    paramPassWord.ParameterName = ":Param2"
    paramPassWord.Value = txtPassWord.Text
    oraCommand.Connection = oraConnection
    oraCommand.CommandType = CommandType.Text
    oraCommand.CommandText = cmdString
    oraCommand.Parameters.Add(paramUserName)
    oraCommand.Parameters.Add(paramPassWord)
```

Figure 3.10   An example of creating a OracleCommand object.

A sample example of creating an **OracleCommand** object is shown in Figure 3.10. This example contains the following functionalities:

1) Create a OracleCommand object
2) Create two OracleParameter objects
3) Initialize two OracleParameter objects
4) Initialize the OracleCommand object
5) Add two Parameter objects into the Parameters collection of the Command object oraCommand

The top two lines of the coding create an Oracle statement with two dynamic parameters, user name and pass word. Then two strings are concatenated to form a complete string. Two OracleParameter and an OracleCommand objects are created in the following lines.

Then two OracleParameter objects are initialized with nominal parameters and the associated text box's contents. After this, the OracleCommand object is initialized with four properties of the Command class.

Now let's take care of the popular methods used in the Command class.

3.4.3.6   The Methods of the Command Class

In the last section, we discussed how to create an instance of the Command class and how to initialize the Parameters collection of a Command object by attaching Parameter objects to that Command object. Those steps are prerequisite to execute a Command object. The actual execution of a Command object is to run one of methods of the Command class to perform the associated data queries or data actions. Four popular methods are widely utilized for most data-driven applications and Table 3.6 lists these methods.

Table 3.6 Methods of the Command class.

Method Name	Functionality
ExecuteReader	Executes commands that return rows, such as a SQL SELECT statement. The returned rows are located in an OdbcDataReader, an OleDbDataReader, a SqlDataReader, or an OracleDataReader, depending on which Data Provider you are using.
ExecuteScalar	Retrieves a single value from the database.
ExecuteNonQuery	Executes a non-query command such as SQL INSERT, DELETE, UPDATE, and SET statements.
ExecuteXmlReader (SqlCommand only)	Similar to the ExecuteReader() method, but the returned rows must be expressed using XML. This method is only available for the SQL Server Data Provider.

As we mentioned in the last section, the Command object is a Data Provider-dependent object, so four different versions of the Command object are developed and each version is determined by the Data Provider the user selected and used in the application, such as the OleDbCommand, OdbcCommand, SqlCommand, and an OracleCommand. Although each Command object is dependent on the Data Provider, all methods of the Command object are similar in functionality and have the same roles in a data-driven application.

3.4.3.6.1 The ExecuteReader Method   The ExecuteReader() method is a data query method, and it can only be used to execute a read-out operation from a database. The most popular matched operation is to execute an SQL SELECT statement to return rows to a DataReader by using this method. Depending on which Data Provider you are using, the different DataReader object should be utilized as the data receiver to hold the returned rows. Remember, the DataReader class is a read-only class, and it can only be used as a data holder. You cannot perform any data updating by using the DataReader.

The following example coding can be used to execute an SQL SELECT statement, which is shown in Figure 3.11.

As shown in Figure 3.11, as the ExecuteReader() method is called, an SQL SELECT statement is executed to retrieve the `id, user_name` and `pass_word` from the **LOGIN** table.

The returned rows are assigned to the oraDataReader object. Please note that the OracleCommand object should already be created and initialized before the ExecuteReader() method can be called.

3.4.3.6.2 The ExecuteScalar Method   The ExecuteScalar() method is used to retrieve a single value from a database. This method is faster and has substantially less overhead than the ExecuteReader() method. You should use this method whenever a single value needs to be retrieved from a data source.

```
Dim cmdString As String = "SELECT id, user_name, pass_word FROM Login "
Dim oraCommand As New OracleCommand

    oraCommand.Connection = oraConnection
    oraCommand.CommandType = CommandType.Text
    oraCommand.CommandText = cmdString
    oraDataReader = oraCommand.ExecuteReader
```

Figure 3.11   An example code of running of ExecuteReader() method.

```
Dim cmdString As String = "SELECT pass_word FROM LogIn WHERE (user_name = ybai)"
Dim oraCommand As New OracleCommand
Dim passWord As String

    oraCommand.Connection = oraConnection
    oraCommand.CommandType = CommandType.Text
    oraCommand.CommandText = cmdString
    passWord = oraCommand.ExecuteScalar()
```

Figure 3.12   A sample code of using the ExecuteScalar() method.

```
Dim cmdString1 As String = "INSERT INTO LogIn (pass_word) VALUES ('come')"
Dim cmdString2 As String = "DELETE FROM LogIn WHERE (user_name = ybai)"
Dim oraCommand As New OracleCommand

    oraCommand.Connection = oraConnection
    oraCommand.CommandType = CommandType.Text
    oraCommand.CommandText = cmdString1
    oraCommand.ExecuteNonQuery()
    oraCommand.CommandText = cmdString2
    oraCommand.ExecuteNonQuery()
```

Figure 3.13   An example code of using the ExecuteNonQuery() method.

A sample coding of using this method is shown in Figure 3.12.

In this sample, the SQL SELECT statement is try to pick up a password based on the username **ybai**, from the **LOGIN** data table. This password can be considered as a single value. The ExecuteScalar() method is called after an OracleCommand object is created and initialized. The returned single value is a String, and it is assigned to a String variable **passWord**.

Section 5.4.5 in Chapter 5 provides an example of using this method to pick up a single value, which is a password, from the **LOGIN** data table from the **CSE_DEPT** database.

3.4.3.6.3   The ExecuteNonQuery Method   As we mentioned, the ExecuteReader() method is a read-out method, and it can only be used to perform a data query job. To execute the different SQL Statements such as INSERT, UPDATE, or DELETE commands, the ExecuteNonQuery() method is needed.

Figure 3.13 shows an example coding of using this method to insert to and delete a record from the **LOGIN** data table.

As shown in Figure 3.13, the first SQL statement is try to insert a new password into the **LOGIN** data table with a value **come**. After an OracleCommand object is created and initialized, the ExecuteNonQuery() method is called to execute this INSERT statement. Similar procedure is performed for the DELETE statement.

Now let's look at the last class in the Data Provider, DataReader.

3.4.4   The DataAdapter Class

The DataAdapter serves as a bridge between a DataSet and a data source for retrieving and saving data. The DataAdapter provides this bridge by mapping Fill, which changes the data in the DataSet to match the data in the data source, and Update, which changes the data in the data source to match the data in the DataSet.

The DataAdapter connects to your database using a Connection object and it uses Command objects to retrieve data from the database and populate those data to the DataSet and related classes such as DataTables also the DataAdapter uses Command objects to send data from your DataSet to your database.

To perform data query from your database to the DataSet, the DataAdapter uses the suitable Command objects and assign them to the appropriate DataAdapter properties such as SelectCommand, and execute that Command. To perform other data manipulations, the DataAdapter uses the same Command objects but assign them with different properties such as InsertCommand, UpdateCommand, and DeleteCommand to complete the associated data operations.

As we mentioned in the previous section, the DataAdapter is a sub-component of the Data Provider, so it is a Data Provider-dependent component. This means that the DataAdapter has different versions based on the used Data Provider. Four popular DataAdapters are OleDbDataAdapter, OdbcDataAdapter, SqlDataAdapter, and OracleDataAdapter. Different DataAdapters are located at the different namespaces.

If you are connecting to a SQL Server database, you can increase overall performance by using the SqlDataAdapter along with its associated SqlCommand and SqlConnection objects. For OLE DB-supported data sources, use the OleDbDataAdapter with its associated OleDbCommand and OleDbConnection objects. For ODBC-supported data sources, use the OdbcDataAdapter with its associated OdbcCommand and OdbcConnection objects. For Oracle databases, use the OracleDataAdapter with its associated OracleCommand and OracleConnection objects.

3.4.4.1 The Constructor of the DataAdapter Class

The constructor of the DataAdapter class is an overloaded method, and it has multiple protocols. Two popular protocols are listed in Table 3.7 (An Oracle Data Provider is used as an example).

The first constructor is most often used in the most data-driven applications.

3.4.4.2 The Properties of the DataAdapter Class

Some popular properties of the DataAdapter class are listed in Table 3.8.

3.4.4.3 The Methods of the DataAdapter Class

The DataAdapter has more than 10 methods available to help users to develop professional data-driven applications. Table 3.9 lists some most often used methods.

Among these methods, the Dispose, Fill, FillSchema, and Update are most often used methods. The Dispose method should be used to release the used DataAdapter after the DataAdapter completes its job. The Fill method should be used to populate a DataSet after the Command object is initialized and ready to be used. The FillSchema method should be called if you want to add a new DataTable into the DataSet, and the Update method should be used if you want to perform some data manipulations such as Insert, Update, and Delete with the database and the DataSet.

Table 3.7 The constructors of the DataAdapter class.

Constructor	Descriptions
SqlDataAdapter()	Initializes a new instance of a DataAdapter class
SqlDataAdapter(from)	Initializes a new instance of a DataAdapter class from an existing object of the same type

Table 3.8 The public properties of the DataAdapter class.

Properties	Descriptions
AcceptChangesDuringFill	Gets or sets a value indicating whether AcceptChanges is called on a DataRow after it is added to the DataTable during any of the Fill operations.
MissingMappingAction	Determines the action to take when incoming data does not have a matching table or column.
MissingSchemaAction	Determines the action to take when existing DataSet schema does not match incoming data.
TableMappings	Gets a collection that provides the master mapping between a source table and a DataTable.

Table 3.9 The public methods of the DataAdapter class.

Methods	Descriptions
Dispose()	Releases the resources used by the DataAdapter.
Fill()	Add or refreshe rows in the DataSet to match those in the data source using the **DataSet** name, and creates a DataTable.
FillSchema()	Adds a DataTable to the specified DataSet.
GetFillParameters()	Gets the parameters set by the user when executing an SQL SELECT statement.
ToString()	Returns a String containing the name of the component, if any. This method should not be overridden.
Update()	Calls the respective INSERT, UPDATE, or DELETE statements for each inserted, updated, or deleted row in the specified DataSet from a named DataTable.

Table 3.10 The events of the DataAdapter class.

Events	Descriptions
Disposed	Occurs when the component is disposed by a call to the Dispose() method.
FillError	Returned when an error occurs during a fill operation.

3.4.4.4 The Events of the DataAdapter Class

Two events available to the DataAdapter class, which are listed in Table 3.10.

Before we can complete this section, an example coding is provided to show readers how to use the DataAdapter to perform some data access and data actions between your DataSet and your database. Figure 3.14 shows an example of using an Oracle DataAdapter (assuming that a Connection object sqlConnection has been created).

Starting from step **A**, an SQL SELECT statement string is created with some other new object declarations, such as a new instance of OracleCommand class, a new object of OracleDataAdapter class and a new instance of the DataSet class. The DataSet class will be discussed in the following section, and it is used as a table container to hold a collection of data tables. The Fill method of the DataAdapter class can be used to populate the data tables embedded in the DataSet later.

In step **B**, the OracleCommand object is initialized with the Connection object, CommandType, and the command string.

```
A   Dim cmdString As String = "SELECT name, office, title, college FROM Faculty"
    Dim oraCommand As New OracleCommand
    Dim oraDataAdapter As OracleDataAdapter
    Dim oraDataSet As DataSet

B       oraCommand.Connection = oraConnection
        oraCommand.CommandType = CommandType.Text
        oraCommand.CommandText = cmdString

C       oraDataAdapter = New OracleDataAdapter(cmdString, oraConnection)
D       oraDataAdapter.SelectCommand = oraCommand
        oraDataSet = New DataSet()
        oraDataSet.Clear()
E       Dim intValue As Integer = oraDataAdapter.Fill(oraDataSet)
            If intValue = 0 Then
                MessageBox.Show("No valid faculty found!")
            End If

F       oraDataSet.Dispose()
        oraDataAdapter.Dispose()
        oraCommand.Dispose()
        oraCommand = Nothing
```

Figure 3.14   An example of using the OracleDataAdapter to fill the DataSet.

The instance of the OracleDataAdapter, oraDataAdapter, is initialized with the command string and the OracleConnection object in step **C**.

In step **D**, the initialized OracleCommand object, oraCommand, is assigned to the SelectCommand property of the oraDataAdapter. Also the DataSet is initialized and cleared to make it ready to be filled by executing the Fill() method of the oraDataAdapter to populate the data table in the DataSet later.

The Fill() method is called to execute a population of data from the **FACULTY** data table into the mapping of that table in the DataSet in step **E**.

An integer variable **IntValue** is used to hold the returned value of calling this Fill() method. This value is equal to the number of rows filled into the Faculty table in the DataSet. If this value is 0, which means that no matched row has been found from the **FACULTY** table in the database and 0 row has been filled into the Faculty table in the DataSet, an error message is displayed. Otherwise, this fill is successful.

In step **F**, all components used for this piece of codes are released by using the Dispose() method.

3.4.5   The DataReader Class

The DataReader class is a read-only class, and it can only be used to retrieve and hold the data rows returned from a database executing an ExecuteReader method. This class provides a way of reading a forward-only stream of rows from a database. Depends on the Data Provider you are using, four popular DataReaders are provided by four Data Providers. They are OdbcDataReader, OleDbDataReader, SqlDataReader, and OracleDataReader.

To create a DataReader instance, you must call the ExecuteReader() method of the Command object, instead of directly using a constructor since the DataReader class does not have any public constructor. The following code that is used to create an instance of the OracleDataReader is incorrect:

```
Dim oraDataReader As New OracleDataReader()
```

While the DataReader object is being used, the associated Connection is busy serving the DataReader, and no other operations can be performed on the Connection other than closing it. This is the case until the Close method of the DataReader is called. For instance, you cannot retrieve output parameters until after you call Close method to close the connected DataReader.

The **IsClosed** property of the DataReader class can be used to check if the DataReader has been closed or not, and this property returns a Boolean value. A True means that the DataReader has been closed. It is a good habit to call the Close method to close the DataReader each time when you finished data query using that DataReader to avoid the troubles caused by the multiple connections to the database.

Table 3.11 lists most public properties of the OracleDataReader class. All other DataReader classes have the similar properties.

The DataReader class has more than 50 public methods. Table 3.12 lists the most useful methods of the OracleDataReader class. All other DataReader classes have the similar methods.

Table 3.11 Popular properties of the SqlDataReader class.

Property Name	Value Type	Functionality
FieldCount	Integer	Gets the number of columns in the current row.
HasRows	Boolean	Gets a value that indicates whether the **SqlDataReader** contains one or more rows.
IsClosed	Boolean	Retrieves a Boolean value that indicates whether the specified **SqlDataReader** instance has been closed.
Item(Int32)	Native	Gets the value of the specified column in its native format given the column ordinal.
Item(String)	Native	Gets the value of the specified column in its native format given the column name.
RecordsAffected	Integer	Gets the number of rows changed, inserted, or deleted by execution of the Transact-SQL statement.
VisibleFieldCount	Integer	Gets the number of fields in the **SqlDataReader** that are not hidden.

Table 3.12 Popular methods of the OracleDataReader class.

Method Name	Functionality
Close()	Closes the opened SqlDataReader object.
Dispose()	Releases the resources used by the DbDataReader.
GetByte()	Gets the value of the specified column as a byte.
GetName()	Gets the name of the specified column.
GetString()	Gets the value of the specified column as a string.
GetValue()	Gets the value of the specified column in its native format.
IsDBNull()	Gets a value that indicates whether the column contains nonexistent or missing values.
NextResult()	Advances the data reader to the next result, when reading the results of batch Transact-SQL statements.
Read()	Advances the **OracleDataReader** to the next record.
ToString()	Returns a String that represents the current **Object**.

```
A    Dim cmdString As String = "SELECT name, office, title, college FROM Faculty"
     Dim oraCommand As New OracleCommand
     Dim oraDataReader As OracleDataReader

B        oraCommand.Connection = oraConnection
         oraCommand.CommandType = CommandType.Text
         oraCommand.CommandText = cmdString

C        oraDataReader = oraCommand.ExecuteReader
         If oraDataReader.HasRows = True Then
            While FacultyReader.Read()
               For intIndex As Integer = 0 To FacultyReader.FieldCount - 1
D                 FacultyLabel(intIndex).Text = FacultyReader.Item(intIndex).ToString
               Next intIndex
            End While
         Else
E               MessageBox.Show("No matched faculty found!")
         End If

         oraDataReader.Close()
         oraDataReader = Nothing
         oraCommand.Dispose()
         oraCommand = Nothing
```

Figure 3.15   An example code of using the OracleDataReader object.

When you run the ExecuteReader() method to retrieve data rows from a database and assign them to a DataReader object, each time the DataReader can only retrieve and hold one row. So if you want to read out all rows from a data table, a loop should be used to sequentially retrieve each row from the database.

The DataReader object provides the most efficient ways to read data from the database, and you should use this object whenever you just want to read the data from the database from the start to finish to populate a list on a form or to populate an array or collection. It can also be used to populate a DataSet or a DataTable.

Figure 3.15 shows an example coding of using the OracleDataReader object to continuously retrieve all records (rows) from the **FACULTY** data table suppose a Connection object **oraConnection** has been created.

Starting from section **A**, a new OracleCommand and an OracleDataReader object is created with a SQL SELECT statement string object. The Command object is initialized in Section **B**. In Section **C**, the ExecuteReader() method is called to retrieve data row from the **FACULTY** data table and assign the resulted row to the OracleDataReader object. By checking the **HasRows** property (refer to Table 3.11), one can determine whether a valid row has been collected or not. If a valid row has been retrieved, a **While** and **For...Next** loop is utilized to sequentially read out all rows one by one using the Read() method (refer to Table 3.12). The Item(Int32) property (refer to Table 3.11) and the ToString() method (refer to Table 3.12) are used to populate the retrieved row to a Label control collection object. The **FieldCount** property (refer to Table 3.11) is used as the termination condition for the **For...Next** loop, and its termination value is **FieldCount - 1** since the loop starts from 0, not 1. If the **HasRows** property returns a False, which means that no any row has been retrieved from the **FACULTY** table, an error message will be displayed in Section **D**. Finally, before we can finish this data query job, we need to clean up all sources we used. In Section **E**, the Close() and Dispose() (refer to Table 3.12) methods are utilized to finish this cleaning job.

Table 3.13 Popular Exceptions of the DataReader class.

Exception Name	Functionality
IndexOutOfRangeException	If an index does not exist within the range, array, or collection, this exception occurs.
InvalidCastException	If you try to convert a database value using one of Get methods to convert a column value to a specific data type, this exception occurs.
InvalidOperationException	If you perform an invalid operation, either a property or a method, this exception occurs.
NotSupportedException	If you try to use any property or method on a DataReader object that has not been opened or connected, this exception occurs.

Before we can finish this section and move to the next one, we need to discuss one more staff, which is the DataReader Exceptions. Table 3.13 lists often used Exceptions.

You can use the `Try...Catch` block to handle those Exceptions in your applications to avoid unnecessary debug process as your project runs.

3.4.6 The DataSet Component

The DataSet, which is an in-memory cache of data retrieved from a database, is a major component of the ADO.NET architecture. The DataSet consists of a collection of DataTable objects that you can relate to each other with DataRelation objects. In other words, a DataSet object can be considered as a table container that contains a set of data tables with the DataRelation as a bridge to relate all tables together. The relationship between a DataSet and a set of DataTable objects can be defined:

- A DataSet class holds a data table collection, which contains a set of data tables or DataTable objects, and the Relations collection, which contains a set of DataRelation objects. This Relations collection sets up all relationships among those DataTable objects.
- A DataTable class holds the Rows collection, which contains a set of data rows or DataRow objects, and the Columns collection, which contains a set of data columns or DataColumn objects. The Rows collection contains all data rows in the data table and the Columns collection contains the actual schema of the data table.

The definition of the DataSet class is a generic idea, which means that it is not tied to any specific type of database. Data can be loaded into a DataSet by using a TableAdapter from many different databases such as Microsoft Access, Microsoft SQL Server, Oracle, Microsoft Exchange, or any OLE DB or ODBC-compliant database.

Although not tied to any specific database, the DataSet class is designed to contain relational tabular data as one would find in a relational database.

Each table included in the DataSet is represented in the DataSet as a DataTable. The DataTable can be considered as a direct mapping to the real table in the database. For example, the LogIn data table, LogInDataTable, is a data table component or DataTable that can be mapped to the real table LogIn in the Department database. The relationship between any tables is realized in the DataSet as a DataRelation object. The DataRelation object provides the information that relates a child table to a parent table via a foreign key. A DataSet can hold any number of tables with any number of relationships defined between tables. From this point of view, a DataSet can be considered as a

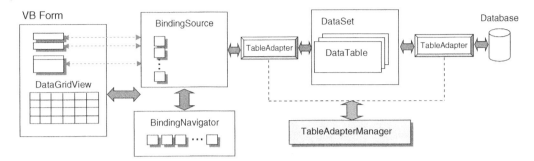

Figure 3.16 A global representation of the DataSet and other data objects.

mini database engine, so it can contain all information of tables it holds such as the column name and data type, all relationships between tables, and more important, it contains most management functionalities of the tables such as browse, select, insert, update, and delete data from tables.

A DataSet is a container and it keeps its data or tables in memory as XML files. In Visual Studio. NET 2008, when one wants to edit the structure of a DataSet, one must do that by editing an XML Schema or XSD file. Although there is a visual designer, the terminology and user interface are not consistent with a DataSet and its constituent objects.

With the Visual Basic.NET 2019, one can easily edit the structure of a DataSet and make any changes to the structure of that DataSet by using the DataSet Designer in the Data Source window. More importantly, one can graphically manipulate the tables and queries in a manner more directly tied to the DataSet rather than having to deal with an XML Schema (XSD).

As we mentioned before, when your build a data-driven project and set up a connection between your project and a database by using ADO.NET, the data tables in the DataSet can be populated with data coming from your database by using the data query methods or the Fill method. From this point of view, you can consider the DataSet as a *data source,* and it contains all mapped data tables from the database you connected to your project. In some books, the terminology *data source* means a DataSet.

Figure 3.16 shows a global relationship between the DataSet object, other data objects, and the Visual Basic.NET 2019 application.

Starting Visual Studio.NET 2008, a new class named **TableAdapterManager** is added into this structure to manage all TableAdapters. The TableAdapterManager class is not part of the .NET Framework. By default, a TableAdapterManager class is generated when you create a DataSet that contains related tables.

A DataSet can be typed or untyped, and the difference between them is that the typed DataSet object has a schema and the untyped DataSet does not. In your data-driven applications, you can select to use either kind of DataSet as you like. But the typed DataSet has more support in Visual Studio.NET 2019.

A typed DataSet object provides an easier way to access the content of the data table fields through strongly typed programming. The so-called strongly typed programming uses information from the underlying data scheme, which means that you can directly access and manipulate those data objects related to data tables. Another point is that a typed DataSet has a reference to an XML schema file and it has an extension of the .xsd.

3.4.6.1 The DataSet Constructor
The DataSet class has four public overloaded constructors, and Table 3.14 lists two most often used constructors. The first constructor is used to create a new instance of the DataSet class with a blank

Table 3.14 Popular constructors of the DataSet class.

Constructor	Functionality
DataSet()	Initializes a new instance of the **DataSet** class.
DataSet(String)	Initializes a new instance of a **DataSet** class with the given name.

Table 3.15 Public properties of the DataSet class.

Property Name	Type	Functionality
DataSetName	String	Gets or sets the name of the current DataSet.
DefaultViewManager	DataViewManager	Gets a custom view of the data contained in the **DataSet** to allow filtering, searching, and navigating using a custom DataViewManager
HasErrors	Boolean	Gets a value indicating whether there are errors in any of the **DataTable** objects within this **DataSet**.
IsInitialized	Boolean	Gets a value that indicates whether the **DataSet** is initialized.
Namespace	String	Gets or sets the namespace of the **DataSet**.
Tables	DataTableCollection	Gets the collection of tables contained in the **DataSet**.

parameter. The second constructor is used to create a new instance of the DataSet with the specific name of the new instance.

3.4.6.2 The DataSet Properties
The DataSet class has more than 15 public properties. Table 3.15 lists the most often used properties.

3.4.6.3 The DataSet Methods
The DataSet class has more than 30 public methods. Table 3.16 lists most often used methods.

Among those methods, the Clear, Dispose, and Merge methods are often used. Before you can fill a DataSet, it had better execute the Clear method to clean up the DataSet to avoid any possible old data. Often in your applications, you need to merge other DataSets or data arrays into the current DataSet object by using the Merge method. After you finished your data query or data action using the DataSet, you need to release it by executing the Dispose method.

3.4.6.4 The DataSet Events
DataSet class has three public events and Table 3.17 lists these events.

The Disposed event is used to trigger the Dispose event procedure as this event occurs. The Initialized event is used to make a mark to indicate that the DataSet has been initialized to your applications. The Mergefailed event is triggered when a conflict occurs and the EnforceConstraints property is set to True as you want to merge a DataSet with an array of DataRow objects, another DataSet, or a DataTable.

Before we can finish this section, we need to show your guys how to create, initialize, and implement a real DataSet object in a data-driven application. A piece of codes shown in Figure 3.17 is used

Table 3.16 Public methods of the DataSet class.

Method Name	Functionality
BeginInit()	Begins the initialization of a **DataSet** that is used on a form or used by another component. The initialization occurs at run time.
Clear()	Clears the **DataSet** of any data by removing all rows in all tables.
Copy()	Copies both the structure and data for this **DataSet**.
Dispose()	Releases the resources used by the MarshalByValueComponent.
GetChanges()	Gets a copy of the **DataSet** containing all changes made to it since it was last loaded, or since **AcceptChanges** was called.
HasChanges()	Gets a value indicating whether the **DataSet** has changes, including new, deleted, or modified rows.
Load()	Fills a **DataSet** with values from a data source using the supplied IDataReader.
Merge()	Merges a specified **DataSet**, **DataTable**, or array of DataRow objects into the current **DataSet** or **DataTable**.
Reset()	Resets the **DataSet** to its original state. Subclasses should override Reset to restore a **DataSet** to its original state.
ToString()	Returns a String containing the name of the Component, if any. This method should not be overridden.
WriteXml()	Writes XML data, and optionally the schema, from the **DataSet**.
WriteXmlSchema()	Writes the **DataSet** structure as an XML schema.

Table 3.17 Public events of the DataSet class.

Event Name	Descriptions
Disposed	Adds an event handler to listen to the Disposed event on the component.
Initialized	Occurs after the DataSet is initialized.
Mergefailed	Occurs when a target and source DataRow have the same primary key value, and EnforceConstraints is set to true.

to illustrate these issues, and an Oracle Data Provider is utilized for this example. Assuming that an **OracleConnection** object, **oraConnection**, has been created and initialized for this example.

Starting from step **A**, some initialization jobs are performed. An SQL SELECT statement is created, an OracleCommand object, an OracleDataAdapter object, and a DataSet object are also created. The integer variable **intValue** is used to hold the returned value from calling the Fill() method.

In **B**, the OracleCommand object is initialized by assigning the OracleConnection object to the Connection property, the CommandType.Text to the CommandType property and cmdString to the CommandText property of the OracleCommand object.

The initialized OracleCommand object is assigned to the SelectCommand property of the OracleDataAdapter object in step **C**. Then a new DataSet object **oraDataSet** is initialized and the **Clear()** method is called to clean up the DataSet object before it can be filled.

Then in step **D**, the Fill() method of the **OracleDataAdapter** object is executed to fill the **oraDataSet**. If this fill is successful, which means that the **oraDataSet** (exactly the DataTable

```
A    Dim cmdString As String = "SELECT name, office, title, college FROM Faculty"
     Dim oraCommand As New OracleCommand
     Dim oraDataAdapter As OracleDataAdapter
     Dim oraDataSet As DataSet
     Dim intValue As Integer

B         oraCommand.Connection = oraConnection
          oraCommand.CommandType = CommandType.Text
          oraCommand.CommandText = cmdString

C         oraDataAdapter.SelectCommand = oraCommand
          oraDataSet = New DataSet()
          oraDataSet.Clear()

D         intValue = oraDataAdapter.Fill(oraDataSet)
              If intValue = 0 Then
                 MessageBox.Show("No valid faculty found!")
              End If

E          oraDataSet.Dispose()
          oraDataAdapter.Dispose()
          oraCommand.Dispose()
          oraCommand = Nothing
```

Figure 3.17 An example of using the DataSet.

in the `oraDataSet`) has been filled by some data rows, the returned value should be greater than 0. Otherwise it means that some errors occurred for this fill and an error message will be displayed to warn the user.

Before the project can be completed, all resources used in this piece of codes should be released and clean up. These cleaning jobs are performed in step **E** by executing some related method such as Dispose().

You need to note that when the Fill() method is executed to fill a DataSet, The Fill() method retrieves rows from the data source using the SELECT statement specified by an associated the CommandText property. The Connection object associated with the SELECT statement must be valid, but it does not need to be open. If the connection is closed before a Fill() is called, it is opened to retrieve data, then closed. If the connection is open before Fill() is called, it still remains open.

The Fill operation then adds the rows to destination DataTable objects in the DataSet, creating the DataTable objects if they do not already exist. When creating DataTable objects, the Fill operation normally creates only column name metadata. However, if the `MissingSchemaAction` property is set to `AddWithKey`, appropriate primary keys and constraints are also created.

If the Fill() returns the results of an OUTER JOIN, the DataAdapter does not set a PrimaryKey value for the resulting DataTable. You must explicitly define the primary key to ensure that duplicate rows are resolved correctly.

You can use the Fill() method multiple times on the same DataTable. If a primary key exists, incoming rows are merged with matching rows that already exist. If no primary key exists, incoming rows are appended to the DataTable.

3.4.7 The DataTable Component

`DataTable` class can be considered as a container that holds the Rows and Columns collections, and the Rows and Columns collections contain a set of rows (or `DataRow` objects) and a set of columns (or `DataColumn` objects) from a data table in a database. The `DataTable` is a directly mapping to a real data table in a database or a data source and it store its data in a mapping area, or a block of memory space that is associated to a data table in a database as your project runs. The `DataTable` object can be used in two ways as we mentioned in the previous sections. One way is that a group of `DataTable` objects, each `DataTable` object is mapped to a data table in the real database, can be integrated into a `DataSet` object. All of these `DataTable` objects can be populated by executing the Fill method of the DataAdapter object (refer to the example in Section 3.3). The argument of the Fill method is not a `DataTable`, but a `DataSet` object since all `DataTable` objects are embedded into that `DataSet` object already. The second way to use the DataTable is that each `DataTable` can be considered as a single stand-alone data table object, and each table can be populated or manipulated by executing either the **ExecuteReader** or **ExecuteNonQuery** method of the Command object.

The `DataTable` class is located in the **System.Data** namespace and it is a Data Provider independent component, which means that only one set of `DataTable` objects are existed no matter what kind of Data Provider you are using in your applications.

The `DataTable` is a central object in the ADO.NET library. Other objects that use the DataTable include the `DataSet` and the `DataView`.

When accessing DataTable objects, note that they are conditionally case sensitive. For example, if one DataTable is named "faculty" and another is named "Faculty", a string used to search for one of the tables is regarded as case sensitive. However, if **faculty** exists and **Faculty** does not, the search string is regarded as case insensitive. A `DataSet` can contain two `DataTable` objects that have the same **TableName** property value but different Namespace property values.

If you are creating a `DataTable` programmatically, you must first define its schema by adding **DataColumn** objects to the **DataColumnCollection** (accessed through the Columns property). To add rows to a DataTable, you must first use the **NewRow** method to return a new **DataRow** object. The NewRow method returns a row with the schema of the DataTable, as it is defined by the table's DataColumnCollection. The maximum number of rows that a DataTable can store is 16,777,216.

The `DataTable` also contains a collection of Constraint objects that can be used to ensure the integrity of the data. The `DataTable` class is a member of the **System.Data** namespace within the .NET Framework class library. You can create and use a DataTable independently or as a member of a `DataSet`, and `DataTable` objects can also be used in conjunction with other .NET Framework objects, including the `DataView`. As we mentioned in the last section, you access the collection of tables in a `DataSet` through the Tables property of the `DataSet` object.

In addition to a schema, a `DataTable` must also have rows to contain and order data. The `DataRow` class represents the actual data contained in a table. You use the `DataRow` and its properties and methods to retrieve, evaluate, and manipulate the data in a table. As you access and change the data within a row, the `DataRow` object maintains both its current and original state.

3.4.7.1 The DataTable Constructor

The DataTable has four overloaded constructors, and Table 3.18 lists three most often used constructors.

You can create a `DataTable` object by using the appropriate `DataTable` constructor. You can add it to the `DataSet` by using the Add method to add it to the `DataTable` object's Tables collection.

You can also create `DataTable` objects within a `DataSet` by using the Fill or **FillSchema** methods of the `DataAdapter` object, or from a predefined or inferred XML schema using the **ReadXml**, **ReadXmlSchema**, or **InferXmlSchema** methods of the `DataSet`. Note that after you have added a `DataTable` as a member of the Tables collection of one DataSet, you cannot add it to the collection of tables of any other DataSet.

Table 3.18   Three popular constructors of the DataTable class.

Constructors	Descriptions
DataTable()	Initializes a new instance of the DataTable class with no arguments.
DataTable(String)	Initializes a new instance of the DataTable class with the specified table name.
DataTable(String, String)	Initializes a new instance of the DataTable class using the specified table name and namespace.

```
Dim FacultyDataSet As DataSet
Dim FacultyTable As DataTable

FacultyDataSet = New DataSet()
FacultyTable = New DataTable("Faculty")
FacultyDataSet.Tables.Add(FacultyTable)
```

Figure 3.18   An example of adding a DataTable into a DataSet.

When you first create a DataTable, it does not have a schema (that is, a structure). To define the schema of the table, you must create and add **DataColumn** objects to the Columns collection of the table. You can also define a primary key column for the table, and create and add Constraint objects to the Constraints collection of the table. After you have defined the schema for a **DataTable**, you can add rows of data to the table by adding **DataRow** objects to the Rows collection of the table.

You are not required to supply a value for the **TableName** property when you create a **DataTable**; you can specify the property at another time, or you can leave it empty. However, when you add a table without a **TableName** value to a **DataSet**, the table will be given an incremental default name of **Table*N***, starting with "Table" for Table0.

Figure 3.18 shows an example of creating a new DataTable and a DataSet, and then adding the DataTable into the DataSet object.

First you need to create two instances of the DataSet and the DataTable, respectively. Then you can add this new DataTable instance into the new DataSet object by using the Add method.

3.4.7.2   The DataTable Properties
The **DataTable** class has more than 20 properties. Table 3.19 lists some most often used properties.

Among these properties, the Columns and Rows properties are very important to us, and both properties are collections of DataColumn and DataRow in the current DataTable object. The Columns property contains a collection of DataColumn objects in the current DataTable, and each column in the table can be considered as a DataColumn object and can be added into this Columns collection. Similar situation happened to the Rows property. The Rows property contains a collection of DataRow objects that are composed of all rows in the current DataTable object. You can get the total number of columns and rows from the current DataTable by calling these two properties.

3.4.7.3   The DataTable Methods
The DataTable class has about 50 different methods with 33 public methods, and Table 3.20 lists some most often used methods.

Table 3.19 The popular properties of the DataTable class.

Properties	Descriptions
Columns	The data type of the Columns property is DataColumn-Collection, which means that it contains a collection of DataColumn objects. Each column in the DataTable can be considered as a DataColumn object. By calling this property, a collection of DataColumn objects existed in the DataTable can be retrieved.
DataSet	Gets the DataSet to which this table belongs.
IsInitialized	Gets a value that indicates whether the DataTable is initialized.
Namespace	Gets or sets the namespace for the XML representation of the data stored in the DataTable.
PrimaryKey	Gets or sets an array of columns that function as primary keys for the data table.
Rows	The data type of the Rows property is DataRowCollection, which means that it contains a collection of DataRow objects. Each row in the DataTable can be considered as a DataRow object. By calling this property, a collection of DataRow objects existed in the DataTable can be retrieved.
TableName	Gets or sets the name of the DataTable.

Table 3.20 The popular methods of the DataTable class.

Methods	Descriptions
Clear()	Clears the DataTable of all data.
Copy()	Copies both the structure and data for this DataTable.
Dispose()	Release the resources used by the MarshalByValue-Component.
GetChanges()	Gets a copy of the DataTable containing all changes made to it since it was last loaded, or since AcceptChanges was called.
GetType()	Gets the Type of the current instance.
ImportRow()	Copies a DataRow into a DataTable, preserving any property settings, as well as original and current values.
Load()	Fills a DataTable with values from a data source using the supplied IDataReader. If the DataTable already contains rows, the incoming data from the data source is merged with the existing rows.
LoadDataRow()	Finds and updates a specific row. If no matching row is found, a new row is created using the given values.
Merge()	Merge the specified DataTable with the current DataTable.
NewRow()	Creates a new DataRow with the same schema as the table.
ReadXml()	Reads XML schema and data into the DataTable.
RejectChanges()	Rolls back all changes that have been made to the table since it was loaded, or the last time AcceptChanges was called.
Reset()	Resets the DataTable to its original state.
Select()	Gets an array of DataRow objects.
ToString()	Gets the TableName and DisplayExpression, if there is one as a concatenated string.
WriteXml()	Writes the current contents of the DataTable as XML.

Among these methods, three of them are important to us: NewRow, ImportRow, and LoadDataRow. Calling NewRow adds a row to the data table using the existing table schema, but with default values for the row, and sets the DataRowState to Added. Calling ImportRow preserves the existing DataRowState along with other values in the row. Calling LoadDataRow is to find and update a data row from the current data table. This method has two arguments, the Value (As Object) and the Accept Condition (As Boolean). The Value is used to update the data row if that row were found and the Condition is used to indicate whether the table allows this update to be made or not. If no matching row found, a new row is created with the given Value.

3.4.7.4 The DataTable Events

The DataTable class contains 11 public events and Table 3.21 lists these events.

The most often used events are **ColumnChanged**, Initialized, **RowChanged** and **RowDeleted**. By using these events, one can track and monitor the real situations occurred in the **DataTable**.

Before we can finish this section, we need to show users how to create a data table and how to add data columns and rows into this new table. Figure 3.19 shows a complete example of creating a new data table object and adding columns and rows into this table. The data table is named FacultyTable.

Refer to Figure 3.19, starting from step **A**, a new instance of the data table **FacultyTable** is created and initialized to a blank table.

In order to add data into this new table, you need to use the Columns and Rows collections, and these two collections contain the DataColumn and DataRow objects. So next you need to create **DataColumn** and **DataRow** objects, respectively. Step **B** finished these objects declarations.

In step **C**, a new instance of the **DataColumn**, column, is created by using the New keyword. Two **DataColumn** properties, **DataType** and **ColumnName**, are used to initialize the first **DataColumn** object with the data type as integer (System.Int32) and with the column name as **FacultyId**, respectively. Finally, the completed object of the **DataColumn** is added into the **FacultyTable** using the Add method of the Columns collection class.

The second data column, with the column data type as string (**System.String**) and the column name as the **FacultyOffice**, is added into the **FacultyTable** in a similar way as we did for the first data column **FacultyId** in step **D**.

Table 3.21 The public events of the DataTable class.

Events	Descriptions
ColumnChanged	Occurs after a value has been changed for the specified DataColumn in a DataRow.
ColumnChanging	Occurs when a value is being changed for the specified DataColumn in a DataRow.
Disposed	Adds an event handler to listen to the Disposed event on the component.
Initialized	Occurs after the DataTable is initialized.
RowChanged	Occurs after a DataRow has been changed successfully.
RowChanging	Occurs when a DataRow is changing.
RowDeleted	Occurs after a row in the table has been deleted.
RowDeleting	Occurs before a row in the table is about to be deleted.
TableCleared	Occurs after a DataTable is cleared.
TableClearing	Occurs when a DataTable is being cleared.
TableNewRow	Occurs when a new DataRow is inserted.

```
A    'Create a new DataTable
     Dim FacultyTable As DataTable = New DataTable("FacultyTable")

B    'Declare DataColumn and DataRow variables
     Dim column As DataColumn
     Dim row As DataRow

C    'Create new DataColumn, set DataType, ColumnName and add to DataTable
     column = New DataColumn
     column.DataType = System.Type.GetType("System.Int32")
     column.ColumnName = "FacultyId"
     FacultyTable.Columns.Add(column)

D    'Create another column.
     column = New DataColumn
     column.DataType = Type.GetType("System.String")
     column.ColumnName = "FacultyOffice"
     FacultyTable.Columns.Add(column)

     'Create new DataRow objects and add to DataTable.
     Dim Index As Integer
     For Index = 1 To 10
E        row = FacultyTable.NewRow
         row("FacultyId") = Index
         row("FacultyOffice") = "TC- " & Index
         FacultyTable.Rows.Add(row)
F    Next Index
```

Figure 3.19 An example of creating a new table and adding data into the table.

Table 3.22 The completed FacultyTable.

FacultyId	FacultyOffice
1	TC-1
2	TC-2
3	TC-3
4	TC-4
5	TC-5
6	TC-6
7	TC-7
8	TC-8
9	TC-9
10	TC-10

In step **E**, a `For...Next` loop is utilized to simplify the procedure of adding new data rows into this `FacultyTable`. First, a loop counter Index is created, and a new instance of the `DataRow` is created with the method of the `DataTable – NewRow` (refer to Table 3.20). Totally, we create and add 10 rows into this FacultyTable object. For the first column `FacultyId`, the loop counter Index is assigned to this column for each row. But for the second column FacultyOffice, the building name combined with the loop counter Index, is assigned to this column for each row. Finally in step **F**, the `DataRow` object, row, is added into this `FacultyTable` using the Add method that belongs to the Rows collection class.

The completed `FacultyTable` should match one that is shown in Table 3.22.

3.4.8   ADO.NET Entity Framework

Most traditional databases use the relational model of data, such as Microsoft Access, SQL Server, and Oracle. But today almost all programming languages are object-oriented languages, and the object-oriented model of data structures are widely implemented in modern programs developed with those languages. Therefore, a potential contradiction is existed between the relational model of data in databases and the object-oriented model of programming applied in our real world today. Although some new components were added into the ADO.NET 2.0 to try to solve this contradiction, still it does not give a full solution for this issue.

A revolutionary solution of this problem came with the release of ADO.NET 4.1 based on the .NET Framework 4.1 and the addition of Language Integrated Query (LINQ) to Visual Studio.NET 2010. The main contributions of the ADO.NET 4.1 include that some new components, ADO.NET 4.1 Entity Framework (EF4.1) and ADO.NET 4.1 Entity Data Model Tools, are added into ADO.NET 4.1. With these new components, the contradiction existed between the relational model of data used in databases and the object-oriented programming projects can be fully resolved.

The first version of Entity Framework (EF1) was released in 2008, as part of .NET Framework 3.5 SP1 and Visual Studio 2008 SP1. The second version of Entity Framework, named Entity Framework 4.0, was released as part of .NET 4.0 on April 2010. The third version of Entity Framework, version 4.1, was released on April 12, 2011.

Starting with the EF4.1 release, it has shipped as the EntityFramework NuGet package. EF6 runs on the .NET Framework 4.x, which means that it runs only on Windows. Between versions 4.1 and 5.0, the EntityFramework NuGet package extended the EF libraries that shipped as part of .NET Framework.

Starting with EF6, it became an open source project and also moved completely out of the .NET Framework. This means that when you add the EntityFramework version 6 NuGet package to an application, you are getting a complete copy of the EF library that does not depend on the EF bits that ship as part of .NET Framework. This helped somewhat accelerate the pace of development and delivery of new features.

Entity Framework Core (EF Core) is a complete rewrite of EF6 that was first released in 2016. It ships in Nuget packages, the main one being Microsoft.EntityFrameworkCore. EF Core is a cross-platform product that can run on .NET Core or .NET Framework. EF Core was designed to provide a developer experience similar to EF6. Most of the top-level APIs remain the same, so EF Core will feel familiar to developers who have used EF6. Because of the similarity, we concentrate on the EF6 only in this chapter.

The architecture of EF6 is similar to EF4.1, which provides an abstract database structure that converts the traditional logic database structure to an abstract or object structure with three layers:

- Conceptual layer
- Mapping layer
- Logical layer

EF4.1 defines these three layers using a group of XML files, and these XML files provide a level of abstraction to enable users to program against the object-oriented Conceptual model instead of the traditional relational data model.

The Conceptual layer provides a way to allow developers to build object-oriented codes to access database, and each component in databases can be considered as an object or entity in this layer. The Conceptual Schema Definition Language (CSDL) is used in those XML files to define entities and relationships that will be recognized and used by the Mapping layer to setup mapping between

(a)   (b)

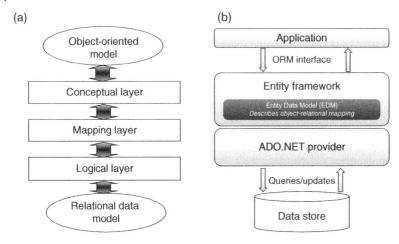

Figure 3.20   (a, b) The mapping relationship between three layers.

entities and relational data tables. The Mapping layer uses Mapping Schema Language (MSL) to establish mappings between entities in the Conceptual layer and the relational data structure in the Logical layer. The relational database schema is defined in an XML file using Store Schema Definition Language (SSDL) in the Logical layer. The Mapping layer works as a bridge or a converter to connect the Conceptual layer to the Logical layer and interpret between the object-oriented data model in the Conceptual layer and the relational data model in the Logical layer. This mapping that is shown in Figure 3.20a allows users to code against the Conceptual layer and map those codes into the Logical layer.

The architecture of implementing EF4.1 is shown in Figure 3.20b.

The EF4.1 is built on the existing ADO.NET provider model, with existing providers being updated additively to support the new Entity Framework functionality. Because of this, existing applications built on ADO.NET can be carried forward to the Entity Framework 4.1 easily with a programming model that is familiar to ADO.NET developers.

A useful data component is provided by the Conceptual layer to enable users to develop object-oriented codes, and it is called EntityClient. Exactly the EntityClient is a Data Provider with the associated components such as Connection (EntityConnection), Command (EntityCommand), and DataReader (EntityDataReader). The EntityClient is similar to other Data Providers we discussed in the previous sections in this chapter, but it includes new components and functionalities. Figure 3.21 shows the Entity Framework architecture for accessing data.

It can be found from Figure 3.21, the Entity Framework includes the EntityClient data provider. This provider manages connections, translates entity queries into data source-specific queries, and returns a data reader that the Entity Framework uses to materialize entity data into objects. When object materialization is not required, the EntityClient provider can also be used like a standard ADO.NET data provider by enabling applications to execute Entity SQL queries and consume the returned read-only data reader.

3.4.8.1 Advantages of Using the Entity Framework 6

In summary, using the Entity Framework 6 to write data-oriented applications provides the following benefits:

1) Reduced development time. The framework provides the core data access capabilities so developers can concentrate on application logic.

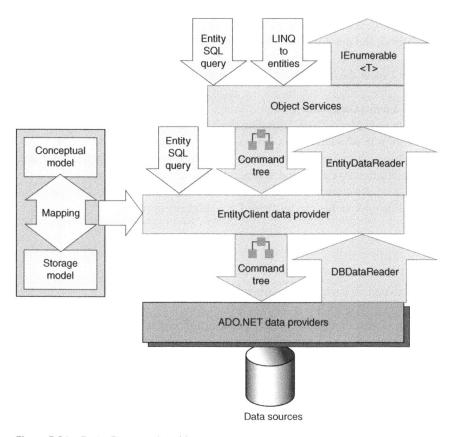

Figure 3.21 Entity Framework architecture.

2) Developers can work in terms of a more application-centric object model, including types with inheritance, complex members, and relationships. In .NET Framework 4, the Entity Framework also supports Persistence Ignorance through Plain Old CLR Objects (POCO) entities.

3) Applications are freed from hard-coded dependencies on a particular data engine or storage schema by supporting a conceptual model that is independent of the physical/storage model.

4) Mappings between the object model and the storage-specific schema can change without changing the application code.

5) Language-Integrated Query support (called LINQ to Entities) provides IntelliSense and compile-time syntax validation for writing queries against a conceptual model.

The Entity Framework uses the Entity Data Model (EDM) to describe the application-specific object or "conceptual" model against which the developer programs. The EDM builds on the widely known Entity Relationship model to raise the abstraction level above logical database schemas. The EDM was developed with the primary goal of becoming the common data model across a suite of developer and server technologies from Microsoft. Thus, an EDM created for use with the Entity Framework can also be leveraged with WCF Data Services (formerly ADO.NET Data Services), Windows Azure Table Storage, SharePoint 2010, SQL Server Reporting Services, and SQL Server PowerPivot for Excel, with more coming in the future.

The core of EF4.1 is its EDM, and the user can access and use this model using the ADO.NET 4.3 Entity Data Model Tools that includes the Entity Data Model item template, the Entity Data Model wizard, Entity Data Model Designer, entity mapping details, and the entity model browser.

In the following sections, we will discuss the Entity Data Model and how to use these Entity Data Model Tools to create, build, and develop Entity Data Model and implement it in your actual data-driven applications.

First let's take a closer look at the ADO.NET 4.3 Entity Data Model.

3.4.8.2 The ADO.NET 4.3 Entity Data Model

The ADO.NET 4.3 Entity Data Model (EDM) is a data model for defining application data as sets of entities and relationships to which common language runtime (CLR) types and storage structures can be mapped. This enables developers to create data access applications by programming against a conceptual application model instead of programming directly against a relational storage schema.

Entity Data Model design approaches can be divided into three categories:

1) Database First
2) Model First
3) Code First

Let's have a brief discussion for each of these components one by one.

3.4.8.2.1 *Database First* Entity Framework supports several approaches for creating Entity Data Models. Database First approach was historically the first one. It appeared in Entity Framework v1, and its support was implemented in Visual Studio 2008. This approach considers that an existing database is used, or the new database is created first, and then Entity Data Model is generated from this database with Entity Data Model Wizard.

All needed model changes in its conceptual (CSDL) and mapping (MSL) part are performed with Entity Data Model Designer. If the storage part needs changing, the database must be modified first, and then Entity Data Model is updated with Update Model Wizard.

Database First approach is supported in Visual Studio 2008/2010 for MS SQL Server only. However, there are third-party solutions that provide Database First support in Visual Studio for other database servers: DB2, EffiProz, Firebird, Informix, MySQL, Oracle, PostgreSQL, SQLite, Sybase, and VistaDB. Besides, there are third-party tools that extend or completely replace standard Entity Data Model Wizard, Entity Data Model Designer, and Update Model Wizard.

3.4.8.2.2 *Model First* A Model First approach was supported in Visual Studio 2010, which was released together with the second Entity Framework version (Entity Framework 4.0). In Model First approach, the development starts from scratch. At first, the conceptual model is created with Entity Data Model Designer, entities and relations are added to the model, but mapping is not created. After this Generate Database Wizard is used to generate storage (SSDL) and mapping (MSL) parts from the conceptual part of the model and save them to the **edmx** file. Then the wizard generates DDL script for creating database, which including tables and foreign keys.

If the model was modified, the Generate Database Wizard should be used again to keep the model and the database consistent. In such case, the generated DDL script contains DROP statements for tables, corresponding to old SSDL from the .**edmx** file and CREATE statements for tables, corresponding to new SSDL, generated by the wizard from the conceptual part. In Model First approach, developer should not edit storage part or customize mapping because they will be regenerated each time when Generate Database Wizard is launched.

Model First in Visual Studio 2010 is supported only for MS SQL Server. However, there are third-party solutions that provide support for other databases, such as Oracle, MySQL, and PostgreSQL.

Besides, there are third-party tools for complete replacement of Entity Data Model Designer and Generate Database Wizard in the context of Model First approach.

3.4.8.2.3 Code First   Entity Framework 4.1 Release to Web (RTW) is a new technique that is the first fullysupported go-live release of the DbContext API and Code First development workflow.

Code First allows you to define your model using Visual C# or Visual Basic.NET classes, optionally additional configuration can be performed using attributes on your classes and properties or by using a Fluent API. Your model can be used to generate a database schema or to map to an existing database.

The following tools are designed to help you work with the EDM:

- The ADO.NET 4.3 Entity Data Model item template is available for Visual Basic.NET project type, ASP.NET Web Site and Web Application projects, and launches the Entity Data Model Wizard.
- The Entity Data Model Wizard generates an EDM, which is encapsulated in an .edmx file. The wizard can generate the EDM from an existing database. The wizard also adds a connection string to the App.Config or Web.Config file and configures a single file generator to run on the conceptual model contained in the .edmx file. This single file generator will generate Visual C# or Visual Basic.NET code from the conceptual model defined in the .edmx file.
- The ADO.NET Entity Data Model Designer provides visual tools to view and edit the EDM graphically. You can open an .edmx file in the designer and create entities and map entities to database tables and columns.
- EdmGen.exe is a command-line tool that can be used to also generate models, validate existing models, and perform other functions on your EDM metadata files.

We will provide a detailed discussion for each of these tools in the following sections.

3.4.8.2.4 Entity Data Model Item Template   The ADO.NET 4.3 Entity Data Model item template is the starting point to the Entity Data Model tools. The ADO.NET 4.3 Entity Data Model item template is available for Visual C# and Visual Basic.NET project types. It can be added to Console Application, Windows Application, Class Library, ASP.NET Web Service Application, ASP.NET Web Application, or ASP.NET Web Site projects. You can add multiple ADO.NET 4.3 Entity Data Model items to the same project, with each item containing files that were generated from a different database and/or tables within the same database.

When you add the ADO.NET 4.3 Entity Data Model item template to your project, Visual Studio:

- Adds references to the System.Data, System.Data.Entity, System.Core, System.Security, and System.Runtime.Serialization assemblies if the project does not already have them.
- Starts the Entity Data Model Wizard. The wizard is used to generate an Entity Data Model (EDM) from an existing database. The wizard creates an .edmx file, which contains the model information. You can use the .edmx file in the ADO.NET Entity Data Model Designer to view or modify the model.
- Creates a source code file that contains the classes generated from the conceptual model. The source code file is auto-generated and is updated when the .edmx file changes, and is compiled as part of the project.

Next let's have a closer look at the Entity Data Model Wizard.

3.4.8.2.5 Entity Data Model Wizard   The Entity Data Model Wizard is used to generate an .edmx file. It also allows you to create a model from an existing database, or to generate an empty model.

The Entity Data Model Wizard starts after you add an ADO.NET 4.3 Entity Data Model to your project. The wizard is used to generate an Entity Data Model (EDM). The wizard creates an **.edmx** file that contains the model information. The **.edmx** file is used by the ADO.NET 4.3 Entity Data Model Designer, which enables you to view and edit the mappings graphically.

You can select to create an empty model or to generate the model from an existing database. Generating the model from an existing database is the recommended practice for this release of the EDM tools.

The Wizard also creates a source code file that contains the classes generated from the CSDL information encapsulated in the **.edmx** file. The source code file is auto-generated and is updated when the .edmx file changes.

Depending on your selections, the Wizard will help you with the following steps.

- **Choose the Model Contents**: By selecting **Generate from database**, you can generate an .edmx file from an existing database. Then the Entity Data Model Wizard will guide you through selecting a data source, database, and database objects to include in the conceptual model. By selecting **Empty model**, you can add an .edmx file that contains empty conceptual model, storage model, and mapping sections to your project. Select this option if you plan to use the Entity Designer to build your conceptual model and later generate a database that supports the model.
- **Choose the Database Connection**: You can choose an existing connection from the drop-down list of connections or click **New Database Connection** to open the **Connection Properties** dialog box and create a new connection to the database.
- **Choose your Database Objects**: You can select the tables, views, and stored procedures to include in the EDM.

Beginning with Visual Studio 2017, the **Choose Your Database Objects** dialog box also allows you to perform the following customizations:

1) Apply English-language rules for singulars and plurals to entity, entity set, and navigation property names when the .edmx file is generated.
2) Include foreign key columns as properties on entity types.

Upon closing, the Entity Data Model Wizard creates an .edmx file that contains the model information. The .edmx file is used by the Entity Designer, which enables you to view and edit the conceptual model and mappings graphically.

Now let's have a closer look at the real part – ADO.NET 4.3 Entity Data Model Designer.

3.4.8.2.6 Entity Data Model Designer   The ADO.NET 4.3 Entity Data Model Designer provides visual tools for creating and editing an Entity Data Model (EDM). You can use the Entity Model Designer to visually create and modify entities, associations, mappings, and inheritance relationships. You can also validate an .edmx file using the Entity Model Designer.

The ADO.NET Entity Data Model Designer includes the following components:

- A visual design surface for creating and editing the conceptual model. You can create, modify, or delete entities and associations.
- An Entity Mapping Details window to view and edit mappings. You can map entity types or associations to database tables and columns.
- An Entity Model Browser to give you a tree view of the EDM.
- Toolbox controls to create entities, associations and inheritance relationships.

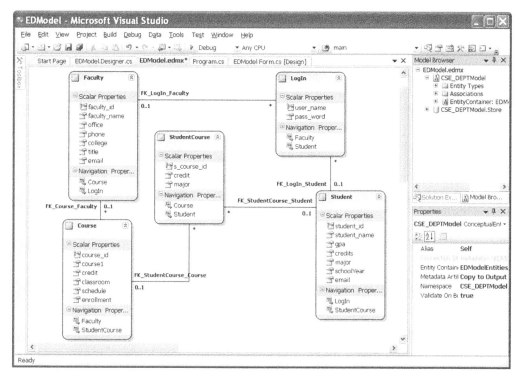

Figure 3.22 An example of the ADO.NET 4.3 Entity Data Model Designer. *Source:* AADO.NET 4.3 Entity Data Model Designer.

The ADO.NET 4.3 Entity Data Model Designer is integrated with the Visual Studio.NET 2017 components. You can view and edit information using the Properties window and errors are reported in the Error List.

Figure 3.22 shows an example of the ADO.NET 4.3 Entity Data Model Designer.

Two important functionalities of using the Entity Data Model Designer are:

Opening the ADO.NET Entity Data Model Designer
The ADO.NET 4.3 Entity Data Model Designer is designed to work with an .edmx file. The .edmx file is an encapsulation of three EDM metadata artifact files, the CSDL, the SSDL, and the MSL files. When you run the EDM Wizard an .edmx file is created and added to your solution. You open the ADO.NET Entity Data Model Designer by double-clicking on the .edmx file in the Solution Explorer.

Validating the EDM
As you make changes to the EDM, the ADO.NET Entity Data Model Designer validates the modifications and reports errors in the Error List. You can also validate the EDM at any time by right-clicking on the design surface and selecting **Validate Model**.

3.4.8.2.7 Entity Model Browser   The Entity Model Browser is a Visual Studio tool window that is integrated with the ADO.NET 4.3 Entity Data Model Designer. It provides a tree view of the Entity Data Model (EDM). The Entity Model Browser groups the information into two nodes.

The first node shows you the conceptual model. By expanding the underlying nodes, you can view all entity types and associations in the model.

The second node shows you the target database model. By expanding the underlying nodes, you can see what parts of the database tables, views, and stored procedures have been imported into the model.

The Entity Data Model Browser enables you to do the following:

- Clicking an item in the Model Browser makes it active in the **Properties** window and the **Mapping Details** window. You can use these windows to modify the properties and entity mappings.
- Create a function import from a stored procedure.
- Update the storage model when changes are made to the underlying database.
- Delete tables, views, and stored procedures from the storage model.
- Locate an entity type on the design surface. In the **Model Browser**, right-click the entity name in the tree view of the conceptual model and select **Show in Designer**. The visual representation of the model will be adjusted so that the entity type is visible on the design surface.
- Search the tree view of the conceptual and storage models. The search bar at the top of the Model Browser window allows you to search object names for a specified string.

The Entity Model Browser opens when the ADO.NET 4.3 Entity Data Model Designer is opened. If the Entity Model Browser is not visible, right-click on the main design surface and select **Model Browser**.

3.5 Chapter Summary

The main topic of this chapter is an introduction to the ADO.NET, which includes the architectures, organizations, and components of the ADO.NET.

Detailed discussions and descriptions are provided in this chapter to give readers both fundamental and practical ideas and pictures in how to use components in ADO.NET to develop professional data-driven applications. Two ADO.NET architectures are discussed to enable users to follow the directions to design and build their preferred projects based on the different organizations of the ADO.NET.

A history of the development of ADO.NET is first introduced in this chapter, which includes ADO.NET 2.0, ADO.NET 3.5 ADO.NET 4.1, and ADO.NET 4.3. Different data-related objects are discussed such as Data Access Object (DAO), Remote Data Object (RDO), Open Database Connectivity (ODBC), OLE DB, and the ADO. The difference between the ADO and the ADO.NET is provided in details.

Fundamentally, the ADO.NET is a class container, and it contains three basic components: Data Provider, DataSet, and DataTable. Furthermore, the Data Provider contains four sub-components: Connection, Command, TableAdapter, and DataReader. You should keep in mind that the Data Provider comes in multiple versions based on the type of the database you are using in your applications. So from this point of view, all four sub-components of the Data Provider are called Data Provider-dependent components. The popular versions of the Data Provider are:

- OLE DB Data Provider
- ODBC Data Provider
- Microsoft SQL Server Data Provider
- Oracle Data Provider

Each version of Data Provider is used for one specific database. But one exception is that both OLE DB and ODBC data Providers can work for some other databases, such as Microsoft Access,

Microsoft SQL Server, and Oracle databases. In most cases, you should use the matched version of the Data Provider for a specific database even the OLE DB and ODBC can work for that kind of database since the former can provide more efficient processing technique and faster accessing and manipulating speed compared with the latter.

To access and manipulate data in databases, you can use one of two ADO.NET architectures: you can use the DataAdapter to access and manipulate data in the DataSet that is considered as a DataTables collector by executing some properties of the DataAdapter, such as SelectCommand, InsertCommand, UpdateCommand, and DeleteCommand. Alternatively, you can treat each DataTable as a single table object and access and manipulate data in each table by executing the different methods of the Command object, such as ExecuteReader and ExecuteNonQuery.

A key point in using the Connection object of the Data Provider to setup connection between your applications and your data source is the connection string, which has the different format and style depending on the database you are using. The popular components of the connection string include Provider, Data Source, Database, Use ID, and Password. But some connection strings only use a limited number of components, such as the Data Provider for the Oracle database.

An important point in using the Command object to access and manipulate data in your data source is the Parameter component. The Parameter class contains all properties and methods that can be used to setup specific parameters for the Command object. Each Parameter object contains a set of parameters, and each Parameter object can be assigned to the Parameters collection that is one of property of the Command object.

By finishing this chapter, you should be able to:

- Understand the architecture and organization of the ADO.NET
- Understand three components of the ADO.NET, such as the Data Provider, DataSet, and the DataTable
- Use the Connection object to connect to an Microsoft Access, Microsoft SQL Server, and Oracle database
- Use the Command and Parameter objects to select, insert, and delete data using a string variable containing an SQL or an Oracle statement
- Use the DataAdapter object to fill a DataSet using the Fill method
- Read data from the data source using the DataReader object
- Read data from the DataTable using the SelectCommand property of the DataAdapter object
- Create DataSet and DataTable objects and add data into the DataTable object

In Chapter 4, we will discuss the data query technique with two methods: using Tools and Wizards provided by Visual Studio.NET 2019, and using the runtime object method to develop simple, but efficient data query applications with the Oracle Server database. Both methods are introduced in two parts: Part I: Using the tools and wizards provided by Visual Studio.NET 2019 to develop data query project, and Part II: Using the Runtime objects to perform the data query job for Oracle Server databases.

Homework

I. True/False Selections

_____ **1** ADO.NET is composed of four major components: Data Provider, DataSet, DataReader, and DataTable.

_____ **2** ADO is developed based on Object Linking and Embedding (OLE) and Component Object Model (COM) technologies.

_____ **3** ADO.NET is a new version of ADO, and it is based mainly on the Microsoft .NET Framework.

_____ **4** The Connection object is used to setup a connection between your data-driven application and your data source.

_____ **5** Both OLE DB and ODBC Data Providers can work for the SQL Server and Oracle databases.

_____ **6** Different ADO.NET components are located at the different namespaces. The DataSet and DataTable are located at the System.Data namespace.

_____ **7** The DataSet can be considered as a container that contains multiple data tables, but those tables are only a mapping of the real data tables in the database.

_____ **8** The ExecuteReader() method is a data query method, and it can only be used to execute a read-out operation from a database.

_____ **9** The SQL Server Data Provider used a so-called Named Parameter Mapping technique.

_____ **10** The DataTable object is a Data Provider-independent object.

II. Multiple Choices

1 To populate data from a database to a DataSet object, one needs to use the _____
   A Data Source
   B DataAdapter (TableAdapter)
   C Runtime object
   D Wizards

2 The Parameters property of the Command class _____
   A Is a Parameter object
   B Contains a collection of Parameter objects
   C Contains a Parameter object
   D Contains the parameters of the Command object

3 To add a Parameter object to the Parameters property of the Command object, one needs to use the _____ method that belongs to the _____
   A Insert, Command
   B Add, Command
   C Insert, Parameters collection
   D Add, Parameters collection

4 DataTable class is a container that holds the _____ and _____ objects
   A DataTable, DataRelation
   B DataRow, DataColumn
   C DataRowCollection, DataColumnCollection
   D Row, Column

5 The _____ is a property of the DataTable class, and it is also a collection of DataRow objects. Each DataRow can be mapped to a _____ in the DataTable
   A Rows, column
   B Columns, column
   C Row, row
   D Rows, row

6 The _____ Data Provider can be used to execute the data query for _____ data providers
   A SQL Server, OleDb, and Oracle
   B OleDb, SQL Server, and Oracle
   C Oracle, SQL Server ,and OleDb
   D SQL Server, Odbc, and Oracle

7 To perform a Fill() method to fill a data table, exactly it executes _____ object with suitable parameters
   A DataAdapter
   B Connection
   C DataReader
   D Command

8 The DataReader is a read-only class, and it can only be used to retrieve and hold the data rows returned from a database when executing a(n) _____ method.
   A Fill
   B ExecuteNonQuery
   C ExecuteReader
   D ExecuteQuery

9 One needs to use _____ method to release all objects used for a data-driven application before one can exit the project
   A Release
   B Nothing
   C Clear
   D Dispose

10 To ____ data between the DataSet and the database, the ___ object should be used
   A Bind, BindingSource
   B Add, TableAdapter
   C Move, TableAdapter
   D Remove, DataReader

III. Exercises

1 Explain two architectures of the ADO.NET and illustrate the functionality of these two architectures using block diagrams.

2 List three basic components of the ADO.NET and the different versions of the Data Provider as well as their sub-components.

3 Explain the relationship between the Command and Parameter objects. Illustrate how to add Parameter objects to the Parameters collection that is a property of the Command object using an example. Assuming that an Oracle Server Data Provider is used with two parameters: parameter_name: username, password, parameter_value: "NoName", "ComeBack".

4 Explain the relationship between the DataSet and DataTable. Illustrate how to use the Fill method to populate a DataTable in the DataSet. Assuming that the data query string is an Oracle SELECT statement: `SELECT faculty_id, faculty_name FROM Faculty`, and an Oracle Server Data Provider is utilized.

5 List three new features used for ADO.NET Entity Framework 4.3 to facility the database developments.

4

Introduction to Language-Integrated Query (LINQ)

Language-Integrated Query (LINQ) is a groundbreaking innovation in Visual Studio 2010 and the .NET Framework version 4.0 that bridges the gap between the world of objects and the world of data.

Traditionally, queries against data are expressed as simple strings without type-checking at compile time or IntelliSense support. Furthermore, you have to learn a different query language for each type of data source: Microsoft Access, SQL databases, XML documents, various Web services, and Oracle databases. LINQ makes a query as a first-class language construct in C# and Visual Basic. You write queries against strongly typed collections of objects using language keywords and familiar operators.

In Visual Studio.NET, you can write LINQ in Visual Basic.NET with SQL Server databases, XML documents, ADO.NET DataSets, and any collection of objects that supports IEnumerable or the generic IEnumerable(Of T) interface. As we mentioned in Chapter 3, LINQ support for the ADO.NET 4.1 Entity Framework is also planned, and LINQ providers are being written by third parties for many Web services and other database implementations.

You can use LINQ in new projects, or alongside non-LINQ in existing projects. The only requirement is that the project should be developed under the .NET Framework 3.5 environment or later.

Before we can dig deeper on LINQ, we had better have a general and global picture about the LINQ. Let's start from the basic introduction about the LINQ.

4.1   Overview of Language-Integrated Query

The LINQ pattern is established on the basis of a group of methods called standard query operators (SQOs). Most of these methods operate on sequences, where a sequence is an object whose type implements the IEnumerable(Of T) interface or the IQueryable(Of T) interface. The SQOs provide query capabilities including filtering, projection, aggregation, sorting, and more.

All SQO methods are located at the namespace System.Linq. To use these methods, one must declare this namespace with the directive like: **Imports System.Linq** in the namespace declaration section of the code windows.

There are some confused signs and terminologies, such as IEnumerable, IEnumerable(Of T), IQueryable, and IQueryable(Of T) interfaces. Let's have a closer look at these terminologies first.

Oracle Database Programming with Visual Basic.NET: Concepts, Designs, and Implementations, First Edition. Ying Bai.
© 2021 The Institute of Electrical and Electronics Engineers, Inc. Published 2021 by John Wiley & Sons, Inc.
Companion website: www.wiley.com/go/bai-VB-Oracle

4.1.1 Some Special Interfaces Used in LINQ

Four interfaces, IEnumerable, IEnumerable(Of T), IQueryable, and IQueryable(Of T), are widely used in LINQ via SQO. In fact, two interfaces, IEnumerable and IQueryable, are mainly used for the nongeneric collections supported by the earlier versions of C# and Visual Basic and the other two interfaces. IEnumerable(Of T) and IQueryable(Of T) are used to convert the data type of collections compatible with those in the System.Collection.Generic in Visual Basic.NET to either IEnumerable(Of T) (LINQ to Objects) or IQueryable(Of T) (LINQ to SQL), since LINQ uses a stronger typed collection or sequence as the data sources, and any data in those data sources must be converted to this stronger typed collection before the LINQ can be implemented. Most LINQ are performed on arrays or collections that implement the IEnumerable(Of T) or IEnumerable interfaces. But a LINQ to SQL query is performed on classes that implement the IQueryable(Of T) interface. The relationship between the IEnumerable(Of T) and the IQueryable(Of T) interfaces is IQueryable(Of T) implements IEnumerable(Of T), therefore, besides the SQO, the LINQ to SQL queries have additional query operators since it uses the IQueryable(Of T) interface.

4.1.1.1 The IEnumerable and IEnumerable(Of T) Interfaces

The IEnumerable(Of T) interface is a key part of LINQ to Objects and it allows all of early generic collection classes to implement it. This interface permits the enumeration of a collection's elements. All of the collections in the System.Collections.Generic namespace support the IEnumerable(Of T) interface. Here, T means the converted data type of the sequence or collection. For example, if you have an IEnumerable of *int*, expressed by IEnumerable(Of *int*), exactly you have a sequence or a collection of *ints*.

For nongeneric collections existed in the old version of Visual Basic, they support the IEnumerable interface, but they do not support the IEnumerable(Of T) interface because of the stronger typed property of the latter. Therefore, you cannot directly call those SQO methods whose first argument is an IEnumerable(Of T) using nongeneric collections. However, you can still perform LINQ using those collections by calling the Cast or OfType SQO to generate a sequence that implements IEnumerable(Of T).

Here, a coding example of using LINQ to Object is shown in Figure 4.1.

The type IEnumerable(Of int) plays two important roles in this piece of codes:

1) The query expression has a data source called **intArray** which implements IEnumerable(Of int).
2) The query expression returns an instance of IEnumerable(Of int).

```vbnet
// create an integer array
Dim myArray() As Integer = {1, 2, 3, 4, 5}

Dim intArray As IEnumerable(Of Integer) = myArray.Select(Function(i)  i)
Dim query = From num In intArray
            Where num >= 3
            Select num
For Each intResult In query
    Console.WriteLine(intResult)
Next
Console.WriteLine("Press any key to exit")
Console.ReadKey()
```

Figure 4.1 A coding example of using LINQ to Object query.

```
// create an integer array
Dim myArray() As Integer = {1, 2, 3, 4, 5}

Dim query As IEnumerable(Of Integer) = From num In myArray
                                       Where num >= 3
                                       Select num

    For Each intResult In query
        Console.WriteLine(intResult)
    Next
    Console.WriteLine("Press any key to exit")
    Console.ReadKey()
```

Figure 4.2   A modification of the coding example of using LINQ to Object query.

Every LINQ to Objects query expression, including the one shown above, will begin with a line of this type:

```
From x In y
```

In each case, the data source represented by the variable **y** must support the IEnumerable(Of T) interface. As you have already seen, the array of integers shown in this example supports that interface.

The query shown in Figure 4.1 can also be rewritten in a way that is shown in Figure 4.2.

This code makes explicit the type of the variable returned by this query, IEnumerable(Of int). In practice, you will find that most LINQ to Objects queries return IEnumerable(Of T), for different data type T.

By finishing these two examples, it should be clear to you that interface IEnumerable and IEnumerable(Of T) play a key role in LINQ to Objects queries. The former is used for the nongeneric collections and the latter is for the generic collections. The point is that a typical LINQ to Objects query expression not only takes a class that implements IEnumerable(Of T) as its data source, but it also returns an instance with the same type.

4.1.1.2   The IQueryable and IQueryable(OfT) Interfaces

As we discussed in the previous section, IQueryable and IQueryable(Of T) are two interfaces used for LINQ to SQL queries. Similar to IEnumerable and IEnumerable(Of T) interfaces, in which the SQO methods are defined as the static members in the Enumerable class, the SQO methods applied for the IQueryable(Of T) interface are defined as static members of the Queryable class. The IQueryable interface is mainly used for the nongeneric collections and the IQueryable(Of T) is used for generic collections. Another point is that the IQueryable(Of T) interface is inherited from the IEnumerable(Of T) interface from the Queryable class and the definition of this interface is

```
interface IQueryable(Of T): IEnumerable(Of T), Queryable
```

From this inheritance, one can treat an IQueryable(Of T) sequence as an IEnumerable(Of T) sequence.

Figure 4.3 shows an example of using the IQueryable interface to perform query to a sample database CSE_DEPT. A database connection has been made using the DataContext object before this piece of codes can be executed. The LogIn is the name of a table in this sample database and it has been converted to an entity before the LINQ can be performed. An IQueryable(Of T) interface, exactly a SQO, is utilized to perform this query. The LogIn works as a type in the IQueryable(Of T)

```
'create a database connection using the DataContext object
Dim cse_dept As CSE_DEPTDataContext

'create local string variables
Dim username As String = String.Empty
Dim password As String = String.Empty

'LINQ query expression
Dim loginfo As IQueryable(Of LogIn) = From lg In cse_dept.LogIns
                                      Where lg.user_name = txtUserName.Text &
                                      lg.pass_word = txtPassWord.Text
                                      Select lg
For Each log In loginfo
        username = log.user_name
        password = log.pass_word
Next
```

Figure 4.3 A coding example of using LINQ to SQL query.

interface to make sure that both input sequence and returned sequence are strongly typed sequence with the type of LogIn. The SQO fetches and returns the matched sequence and assigns them to the associated string variables using afor-each loop. Now let's have a closer look at the SQO.

4.1.2 Standard Query Operators

There are two sets of LINQ SQOs: one that operates on objects of type IEnumerable(Of T) and the other that operates on objects of type IQueryable(Of T). The methods that make up each set are static members of the Enumerable and Queryable classes, respectively. They are defined as extension methods of the type that they operate on. This means that they can be called using either static method syntax or instance method syntax.

In addition, several SQO methods operate on types other than those based on IEnumerable(Of T) or IQueryable(Of T). The Enumerable type defines two such methods that both operate on objects of type IEnumerable. These methods, Cast(Of TResult)(IEnumerable) and OfType(Of TResult)(IEnumerable), let you enable a non-parameterized or nongeneric, collection to be queried in the LINQ pattern. They do this by creating a strongly typed collection of objects. The Queryable class defines two similar methods, Cast(Of TResult)(IQueryable) and OfType(Of TResult)(IQueryable), which operate on objects of type Queryable.

The SQOs differ in the timing of their execution, depending on whether they return a singleton value or a sequence of values. Those methods that return a singleton value (for example, Average and Sum) execute immediately. Methods that return a sequence defer the query execution and return an enumerable object.

In the case of the methods that operate on in-memory collections, that is, those methods that extend IEnumerable(Of T), the returned enumerable object captures the arguments that were passed to the method. When that object is enumerated, the logic of the query operator is employed and the query results are returned. In contrast, methods that extend IQueryable(Of T) do not implement any querying behavior but build an expression tree that represents the query to be performed. The query processing is handled by the source IQueryable(Of T) object.

Calls to query methods can be chained together in one query, which enables queries to become arbitrarily complex. According to their functionality, the SQO can be divided into two categories: Deferred SQOs and non-deferred SQOs. Table 4.1 lists some most often used SQOs.

Because of the limitation of the space, we will select some most often used SQO methods and give a detailed discussion for them one by one.

Table 4.1 Most Often Used Standard Query Operators.

Standard Query Operator	Purpose	Deferred
All	Quantifiers	No
Any	Quantifiers	No
AsEnumerable	Conversion	Yes
Average	Aggregate	No
Cast	Conversion	Yes
Distinct	Set	Yes
ElementAt	Element	No
First	Element	No
Join	Join	Yes
Last	Element	No
OfType	Conversion	Yes
OrderBy	Ordering	Yes
Select	Projection	Yes
Single	Element	No
Sum	Aggregate	No
ToArray	Conversion	No
ToList	Conversion	No
Where	Restriction	Yes

4.1.3 Deferred Standard Query Operators

Both deferred SQOs and non-deferred SQOs are organized based on their purpose and we start this discussion based on the alphabet order.

AsEnumerable (Conversion Purpose)

The AsEnumerable operator method has no effect other than to change the compile-time type of *source* from a type that implements IEnumerable(Of T) to IEnumerable(Of T) itself. This means that if an input sequence has a type of IEnumerable(Of T), the output sequence will also be converted to one that has the same type, IEnumerable.

An example coding of using this operator is shown in Figure 4.4.

```
FacultyDataAdapter.SelectCommand = accCommand
FacultyDataAdapter.Fill(ds, "Faculty")
Dim facultyinfo = From fi In ds.Tables("Faculty").AsEnumerable()
                Where fi.Field(Of String)("faculty_name").Equals(ComboName.Text)
                Select fi

For Each fRow in facultyinfo
    'Display selected fRow elements...
Next
```

Figure 4.4 An example code for the operator AsEnumerable.

```
Dim fruits As New System.Collections.            ()
fruits.Add("apple")
fruits.Add("mango")
Dim query As              (Of String) =       .Cast(Of String).Select(Function(fruit) fruit)
For Each fruit In query
        .WriteLine(fruit)
Next
'the running result of this piece of codes is:

   apple
   mango
```

Figure 4.5 An example code for the operator Cast.

The key point for this query structure is the operator AsEnumerable(). Since different database systems use different collections and query operators, therefore those collections must be converted to the type of IEnumerable(Of T) in order to use the LINQ technique because all data operations in LINQ use a SQO methods that can perform complex data queries on an IEnumerable(Of T) sequence. A compiling error would be encountered without this operator.

Cast (Conversion Purpose)

A Cast operator provides a method for explicit conversion of the type of an object in an input sequence to an output sequence with specific type. The compiler treats *cast-expression* as type *type-name* after a type cast has been made. A point to be noticed is that the Cast operator method works on the IEnumerable interface, not IEnumerable(Of T) interface, and it can convert any object with an IEnumerable type to IEnumerable(Of T) type.

An example coding of using this operator is shown in Figure 4.5.

Join (Join Purpose)

A join of two data sources is the association of objects in one data source with objects that share a common attribute in another data source.

Joining is an important operation in queries that target data sources whose relationships to each other cannot be followed directly. In object-oriented programming, this could mean a correlation between objects that is not modeled, such as the backward direction of a one-way relationship. An example of a one-way relationship is a Customer class that has a property of type City, but the City class does not have a property that is a collection of Customer objects. If you have a list of City objects and you want to find all the customers in each city, you could use a join operation to find them.

The join methods provided in the LINQ framework are Join and GroupJoin. These methods perform equi-joins or joins that match two data sources based on equality of their keys. In relational database terms, Join implements an inner join, a type of join in which only those objects that have a match in the other data set are returned. The GroupJoin method has no direct equivalent in relational database terms, but it implements a superset of inner joins and left outer joins. A left outer join is a join that returns each element of the first (left) data source, even if it has no correlated elements in the other data source.

An example coding of using this operator is shown in Figure 4.6.

The issue is that we want to query all courses (course_id) taught by the selected faculty from the Course table based on the faculty_name. But the problem is that there is no faculty_name column

```
Dim courseinfo = Course.Join(Faculty, Function(ci) ci.faculty_id, _
                Function(fi) fi.faculty_id, _
                Function(ci, fi) New With {.faculty_name = ComboName.Text And course_id = ci.course_id})

For Each cid In courseinfo
    CourseList.Items.Add(cid.course_id)
Next
```

Figure 4.6   An example code for the operator Join.

```
Dim fruits As New System.Collections.          (2)
fruits.Add("Mango")
fruits.Add("Orange")
Dim query As          (Of String) = fruits.OfType(Of String)()
     .WriteLine("Elements of type 'string' are:" & vbCrLf)
For Each fruit As String In query
     .WriteLine(fruit)
Next
'the running result of this piece of codes is:

  Elements of type 'string' are:
  Mango
  Orange
```

Figure 4.7   An example code for the operator OfType.

in the Course table, and only faculty_id is associated with related course_id. Therefore, we have to get the faculty_id from the Faculty table first based on the faculty_name and then query the course_id from the Course table based on the queried faculty_id. This problem can be effectively solved using a join operator method shown in Figure 4.6.

OfType (Conversion Purpose)

This operator method is implemented using deferred execution. The immediate return value is an object that stores all the information that is required to perform the action. The query represented by this method is not executed until the object is enumerated either by calling its GetEnumerator method directly or using **For Each** in Visual Basic.NET.

An example coding of using this operator is shown in Figure 4.7.

The OfType(Of TResult)(IEnumerable) method returns only those elements in *source* that can be cast to type *TResult*. To instead receive an exception if an element cannot be cast to type *TResult*, use Cast(Of TResult)(IEnumerable).

This method is one of the few SQO methods that can be applied to a collection that has a non-parameterized type, such as an ArrayList. This is because OfType(Of TResult) extends the type IEnumerable. OfType(Of TResult) cannot only be applied to collections that are based on the parameterized IEnumerable(Of T) type but collections that are based on the non-parameterized IEnumerable type also.

By applying OfType(Of TResult) to a collection that implements IEnumerable, you gain the ability to query the collection using the SQOs. For example, specifying a type argument of Object to OfType(Of TResult) would return an object of type IEnumerable(Of Object) in Visual Basic, to which the SQOs can be applied.

```
Sub OrderByEx()
    'Create an array of Pet objects.
    Dim pets() As Pet = {New Pet With {.Name = "Barley", .Age = 8}, _
                          New Pet With {.Name = "Boots", .Age = 4}, _
                          New Pet With {.Name = "Whiskers", .Age = 1}}
    Dim query As IEnumerable(Of Pet) = pets.OrderBy(Function(pet)  pet.Age)
    For Each pt As Pet In query
        Console.WriteLine(pt.Name & " - " & pt.Age)
    Next
End Sub

'the running result of this piece of codes is:

    Whiskers - 1
    Boots - 4
    Barley - 8
```

Figure 4.8   An example code for the operator OrderBy.

OrderBy (Ordering Purpose)

This operator method is used to sort the elements of an input sequence in ascending order based on the keySelector method. The output sequence will be an ordered one in a type of IOrderedEnumerable(Of TElement). Both IEnumerable and IQueryable classes contain this operator method. An example coding of using this operator is shown in Figure 4.8.

Select (Projection Purpose)

Both IEnumerable and IQueryable classes contain this operator method.

This operator method is implemented using deferred execution. The immediate return value is an object that stores all the information that is required to perform the action. The query represented by this method is not executed until the object is enumerated either by calling its GetEnumerator method directly or using **For Each** in Visual Basic.NET.

This projection method requires the transform function, *selector*, to produce one value for each value in the source sequence, *source*. If *selector* returns a value that is itself a collection, it is up to the consumer to traverse the subsequences manually. In such a situation, it might be better for your query to return a single coalesced sequence of values. To achieve this, use the SelectMany method instead of Select. Although SelectMany works similarly to Select, it differs in that the transform function returns a collection that is then expanded by SelectMany before it is returned.

In query expression syntax, a **Select** in Visual Basic.NET clause translates to an invocation of Select. An example coding of using this operator is shown in Figure 4.9.

Where (Restriction Purpose)

Both IEnumerable and IQueryable classes contain this operator method.

This method is implemented using deferred execution. The immediate return value is an object that stores all the information that is required to perform the action. The query represented by this method is not executed until the object is enumerated either by calling its GetEnumerator method directly or using **For Each** in Visual Basic.NET.

An example coding of using this operator is shown in Figure 4.10.

In query expression syntax, a **Where** in Visual Basic.NET clause translates to an invocation of Where(Of TSource)IEnumerable(Of TSource), Func(Of TSource, Boolean).

```
Dim squares As IEnumerable(Of Integer) = Enumerable.Range(1, 5).Select(Function(x) x * x)
For Each num As Integer In squares
        .WriteLine(num)
Next
'the running result of this piece of codes is:

    1
    4
    9
    16
    25
```

Figure 4.9   An example code for the operator Select.

```
Dim fruits As New List(Of String)(New String() {"apple", "passionfruit", "banana", "mango", _
                                "orange", "blueberry", "grape", "strawberry"})
Dim query As IEnumerable(Of String) = fruits.Where(Function(fruit) fruit.Length < 6)

For Each  fruit in query
    Console.WriteLine(fruit)
Next
'the running result of this piece of codes is:

    apple
    mango
    grape
```

Figure 4.10   An example code for the operator Where.

4.1.4   Non-Deferred Standard Query Operators

Some most often used non-deferred SQOs methods are discussed in this section.

ElementAt (Element Purpose)

This operator method returns the element at a specified index in a sequence. If the type of *source* implements IList(Of T), that implementation is used to obtain the element at the specified index. Otherwise, this method obtains the specified element.

This method throws an exception if *index* is out of range. To instead return a default value when the specified index is out of range, use the ElementAtOrDefault(Of TSource) method.

An example coding of using this operator is shown in Figure 4.11.

First (Element Purpose)

This operator method returns the first element of an input sequence. The method First(Of TSource)(IEnumerable(Of TSource) throws an exception if the source contains no elements. To instead return a default value when the source sequence is empty, use the FirstOrDefault method.

An example coding of using this operator is shown in Figure 4.12.

Last (Element Purpose)

This operator method returns the last element of a sequence. The method Last(Of TSource) (IEnumerable(Of TSource)) throws an exception if *source* contains no elements. To instead return a default value when the source sequence is empty, use the LastOrDefault method.

```vb
'Create a string array
Dim names() As String = _
        {"Hartono, Tommy", "Adams, Terry", "Andersen, Henriette Thaulow" , "Hedlund, Magnus", "Ito, Shu"}
Dim name As String = names.ElementAt(2)

Console.WriteLine("The name chosen at position 2 is " & name)

'the running result of this piece of codes is:

    Andersen, Henriette Thaulow
```

Figure 4.11   An example code for the operator ElementAt.

```vb
'Create a string array
Dim numbers() As Integer = {9, 34, 65, 92, 87, 435, 3, 54, 83, 23, 87, 435, 67, 12, 19}

'Select the first element in the array
Dim first As Integer = numbers.First()

Console.WriteLine(first)

'the running result of this piece of codes is:

    9
```

Figure 4.12   An example code for the operator First.

```vb
Dim numbers() As Integer = {9, 34, 65, 92, 87, 435, 3, 54, 83, 23, 87, 67, 12, 19}

Dim last As Integer = numbers.Last()

Console.WriteLine(last)

'the running result of this piece of codes is 19
```

Figure 4.13   An example code for the operator Last.

An example coding of using this operator is shown in Figure 4.13.

Single (Element Purpose)

This operator method returns a single, specific element of an input sequence of values. The Single(Of TSource)(IEnumerable(Of TSource)) method throws an exception if the input sequence is empty. To instead return **Nothing** when the input sequence is empty, use SingleOrDefault.

An example coding of using this operator is shown in Figure 4.14.

ToArray (Conversion Purpose)

This operator method converts a collection to an array. This method forces query execution. The ToArray(Of TSource)(IEnumerable(Of TSource)) method forces immediate query evaluation and returns an array that contains the query results. You can append this method to your query in order to obtain a cached copy of the query results.

An example coding of using this operator is shown in Figure 4.15.

ToList (Conversion Purpose)

```
Dim fruits() As String = {"orange"}
Dim fruit As String = fruits.Single()
Console.WriteLine(fruit)
'the running result of this piece of codes is:  orange
```

Figure 4.14 An example code for the operator Single.

```
Module ToArrayTest
   Sub Main()
      Dim sArray As String() = {"G", "H", "a", "H", "over", "Jack"}
      Dim names As String() = sArray.OfType(Of String).ToArray()
      For Each name In names
         Console.WriteLine(name)
      Next
   End Sub
End Module
'the running result of this piece of codes is:
   GHaHoverJack
```

Figure 4.15 An example code for the operator ToArray.

```
Dim fruits() As String = {"apple", "banana", "mango",  "orange", "blueberry", "grape", "strawberry"}
Dim lengths As List(Of Integer) = fruits.Select(Function(fruit) fruit.Length).ToList()
For Each length As Integer In lengths
    Console.WriteLine(length)
Next
'the running result of this piece of codes is:
 5
 6
 5
 6
 9
 5
 10
```

Figure 4.16 An example code for the operator ToList.

This operator method converts a collection to a List(Of T). This method forces query execution. The ToList(Of TSource)(IEnumerable(Of TSource)) method forces immediate query evaluation and returns a List(Of T) that contains the query results. You can append this method to your query in order to obtain a cached copy of the query results.

An example coding of using this operator is shown in Figure 4.16.

Now we have a finished a detailed discussion about the SQO methods and they are actual methods to be executed to perform a LINQ. Next, we will go ahead to discuss the LINQ. We organize this part in the following sequence. First, we will provide an introduction about the LINQ. Then, we divide this discussion into seven sections:

1) Architecture and Components of LINQ
2) LINQ to Objects
3) LINQ to DataSet
4) LINQ to Entities
5) LINQ to XML
6) Visual Basic.NET Language Enhancement for LINQ
7) LINQ to Oracle

Two components, LINQ to DataSet and LINQ to Entities, belong to LINQ to ADO.NET. Now let's start with the first part: introduction to LINQ.

4.2   Introduction to LINQ

A query is basically an expression that retrieves data from a data source. Queries are usually expressed in a specialized query language such as Microsoft Access, SQL Server, Oracle, or XML document. Different languages have been developed over time for the various types of data sources, for example, Oracle for relational databases and XQuery for XML. Therefore, developers have had to learn a new query language for each type of data source or data format that they must support. LINQ simplifies this situation by offering a consistent model for working with data across various kinds of data sources and formats. In a LINQ, you are always working with objects. You use the same basic coding patterns to query and transform data in XML documents, Oracle databases, ADO. NET DataSets, .NET collections, and any other format for which a LINQ provider is available.

LINQ can be considered as a pattern or model that is supported by a collection of so-called SQO methods we discussed in the last section, and all those SQO methods are static methods defined in either IEnumerable or IQueryable classes in the namespace *System.Linq*. The data operated in LINQ are object sequences with the data type of either IEnumerable(Of T) or IQueryable(Of T), where T is the actual data type of the objects stored in the sequence.

From another point of view, LINQ can also be considered as a converter or bridge that sets up a mapping relationship between the abstract objects implemented in SQOs and the physical relational databases implemented in the real world. It is the LINQ that allows developers directly access and manipulate data in different databases using objects with the same basic coding patterns. With the help of LINQ, the headache caused by learning and using different syntaxes, formats, and query structures for different data sources in order to access and query them can be removed. The efficiency of database queries can be significantly improved and the query process can also be greatly simplified.

Structurally, all LINQ operations consist of three distinct actions:

1) Obtain the data source.
2) Create the query.
3) Execute the query.

In order to help you to have a better understanding about the LINQ and its running process, let's have an example to illustrate how the three parts of a query operation are expressed in source code. The example uses an integer array as a data source for convenience; however, the same concepts apply to other data sources, too.

The example codes are shown in Figure 4.17.

The exact running process of this piece of codes is shown in Figure 4.18.

```
Module

    Sub Main()
        '1. Data Source
        Dim numbers As Integer() = {0, 1, 2, 3, 4, 5, 6}

        '2. Query creation. The numQuery is an IEnumerable(Of Int)
        Dim numQuery = From num In numbers
                        Where (num Mod 2) = 0
                        Select num
        '3. Query execution.
        For Each num In numQuery
            .Write("{0,1} ", num)
        Next
            .WriteLine(vbNewLine & "Press any key to continue...")
            .ReadKey()
    End Sub

End Module

'the running result of this piece of codes is:  0  2  4  6
```

Figure 4.17   An example code for the LINQ.

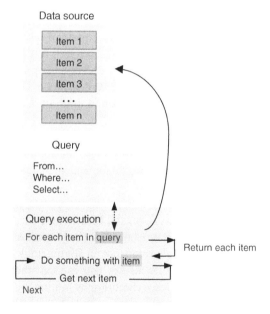

Figure 4.18   The running process of a LINQ.

The key point is in LINQ, the execution of the query is distinct from the query itself; in other words when you create a query in step 2, you have not retrieved any data and the real data query occurs in step 3, query execution using the For Each loop.

Let's have a closer look at this piece of codes and the mapped process to have a clear picture about the LINQ and its process.

The **Data Source** used in this example is an integer array *numbers*, it implicitly supports the generic IEnumerable(Of T) interface. This fact means it can be queried with LINQ. A query is executed in a For Each loop, and For Each requires IEnumerable or IEnumerable(Of T). Types that support IEnumerable(Of T) or a derived interface such as the generic IQueryable(Of T) are called queryable types.

> **From** [identifier] **In** [data source]
> **Let** [expression]
> **Where** [boolean expression]
> **Order By** [[expression](ascending/descending)], [optionally repeat]
> **Select** [expression]
> **Group** [expression] **By** [expression] **Into** [expression]

Figure 4.19 A typical query expression of LINQ.

The **Query** specifies what information to retrieve from the data source or sources. Optionally, a query also specifies how that information should be sorted, grouped, and shaped before it is returned. A query is stored in a query variable and initialized with a query expression.

A typical basic form of the query expression is shown in Figure 4.19.

Three clauses, **From**, **Where,** and **Select**, are mostly used for most LINQ.

The query used in this example returns all the even numbers from the integer array. The query expression contains three clauses: **From**, **Where,** and **Select**. If you are familiar with SQL, you will have noticed that the ordering of the clauses is reversed from the order in SQL. The **From** clause specifies the data source, the **Where** clause applies the filter, and the **Select** clause specifies the type of the returned elements. For now, the important point is that in LINQ, the query variable itself takes no action and returns no data. It just stores the information that is required to produce the results when the query is executed at some later point.

The **Query Execution** in this example is a deferred execution since all operator methods used in this query are deferred operators (refer to Table 4.1).

The **For Each** statement with an iteration variable *num* is used for this query execution to pick up each item from the data source and assign it to the variable *num*. A Console.Write() method is executed to display each received data item, and this query process will continue until all data items have been retrieved from the data source.

Because the query variable itself never holds the query results, you can execute it as often as you like. For example, you may have a database that is being updated continually by a separate application. In your application, you could create one query that retrieves the latest data, and you could execute it repeatedly at some interval to retrieve different results every time.

Queries that perform aggregation functions over a range of source elements must first iterate over those elements. Examples of such queries are **Count**, **Max**, **Average**, and **First**. These execute without an explicit **For Each** statement because the query itself must use **For Each** in order to return a result. Note also that these types of queries return a single value, not an IEnumerable collection. To force immediate execution of any query and cache its results, you can call the ToList(Of TSource) or ToArray(Of TSource) methods. You can also force execution by putting the **For Each** loop immediately after the query expression. However, by calling ToList or ToArray, you also cache all the data in a single collection object.

4.3 The Architecture and Components of LINQ

LINQ is composed of three major components: LINQ to Objects, LINQ to ADO.NET, and LINQ to XML. A detailed organization or the LINQ can be written as:

1) LINQ to Objects
2) LINQ to ADO.NET (LINQ to DataSet, LINQ to SQL, andLINQ to Entities)
3) LINQ to XML

Table 4.2   LINQ Related Namespaces.

Namespace	Purpose
System.Linq	Classes and interfaces that support LINQ are located at this namespace
System.Collections. Generic	All components related to IEnumerable and IEnumerable(Of T) are located at this namespace (LINQ to Objects)
System.Data.Linq	All classes and interfaces related to LINQ to SQL are defined in this namespace
System.XML.Linq	All classes and interfaces related to LINQ to XML are defined in this namespace
System.Data.Linq. Mapping	Map a class as an entity class associated with a physical database

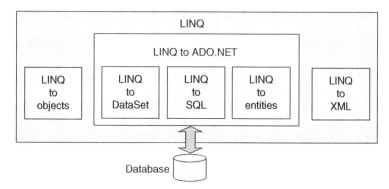

Figure 4.20   A typical LINQ architecture.

All of three components are located at the different namespaces provided by .NET Framework 4.0, which is shown in Table 4.2.

A typical LINQ architecture is shown in Figure 4.20.

Now let's give a brief introduction for each component in LINQ.

4.3.1   Overview of LINQ to Objects

The LINQ to Objects refers to the use of LINQ with any IEnumerable or IEnumerable(Of T) collection directly, without the use of an intermediate LINQ provider or API such as LINQ to SQL or LINQ to XML. The actual LINQ are performed using the SQO methods that are static methods of the static System.Linq.Enumerable class that you use to create LINQ to Objects queries. You can use LINQ to query any enumerable collections such as List(Of T), Array, or Dictionary(Of TKey, TValue). The collection may be user-defined or may be returned by a .NET Framework API.

In a basic sense, LINQ to Objects represents a new approach to collections, which includes arrays and in-memory data collections. In the old way, you had to write complex for each loops that specified how to retrieve data from a collection. In the LINQ approach, you write declarative code that describes what you want to retrieve.

In addition, LINQ offer three main advantages over traditional For Each loops:

1) They are more concise and readable, especially when filtering multiple conditions.
2) They provide powerful filtering, ordering, and grouping capabilities with a minimum of application code.
3) They can be ported to other data sources with little or no modification.

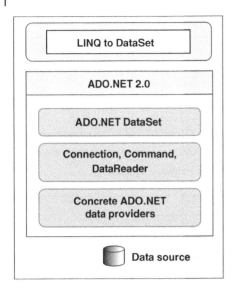

Figure 4.21 The relationship between LINQ to DataSet and ADO.NET 2.0.

In general, the more complex the operation you want to perform on the data, the more benefit you will realize using LINQ instead of traditional iteration techniques.

4.3.2 Overview of LINQ to DataSet

LINQ to DataSet belongs to LINQ to ADO.NET and it is a subcomponent of LINQ to ADO.NET.

LINQ to DataSet makes it easier and faster to query over data cached in a DataSet object. Specifically, LINQ to DataSet simplifies querying by enabling developers to write queries from the programming language itself, instead of using a separate query language. This is especially useful for Visual Studio developers, who can now take advantage of the compile-time syntax checking, static typing, and IntelliSense support provided by the Visual Studio in their queries.

LINQ to DataSet can also be used to query over data that has been consolidated from one or more data sources. This enables many scenarios that require flexibility in how data is represented and handled, such as querying locally aggregated data and middle-tier caching in Web applications. In particular, generic reporting, analysis, and business intelligence applications require this method of manipulation.

The LINQ to DataSet functionality is exposed primarily through the extension methods in the DataRowExtensions and DataTableExtensions classes. LINQ to DataSet builds on and uses the existing ADO.NET 2.0 architecture and is not meant to replace ADO.NET 2.0 in application code. Existing ADO.NET 2.0 code will continue to function in a LINQ to DataSet application. The relationship of LINQ to DataSet to ADO.NET 2.0 and the data store can be illustrated in Figure 4.21.

It can be found from Figure 4.21 that LINQ to DataSet is built based on ADO.NET 2.0 and uses its all components include Connection, Command, DataAdapter, and DataReader. The advantage of this structure is that all developers using ADO.NET 2.0 can continue their database implementations and developments without problem.

4.3.3 Overview of LINQ to SQL

LINQ to SQL belongs to LINQ to ADO.NET and it is a subcomponent of LINQ to ADO.NET.

LINQ to SQL is a component of .NET Framework version 4.0 that provides a run-time infrastructure for managing relational data as objects. In LINQ to SQL, the data model of a relational database is mapped to an object model expressed in the programming language of the developer with three layers. When the application runs, LINQ to SQL translates into SQL the LINQ in the object model and sends them to the database for execution. When the database returns the results, LINQ to SQL translates them back to objects that you can work with in your own programming language.

Two popular LINQ to SQL Tools, SQLMetal and Object Relational Designer, are widely used in developing applications of using LINQ to SQL. The SQLMetal provides a DOS-like template with a command window. Developers using Visual Studio typically use the Object Relational Designer, which provides a GUI for implementing many of the features of LINQ to SQL.

4.3.4 Overview of LINQ to Entities

LINQ to Entities belongs to LINQ to ADO.NET and it is a subcomponent of LINQ to ADO.NET.

Through the Entity Data Model (EDM) we discussed in Section 3.4.8.2 in Chapter 3, ADO.NET 4.3 exposes entities as objects in the .NET environment. This makes the object layer an ideal target for LINQ support. Therefore, LINQ to ADO.NET includes LINQ to Entities. LINQ to Entities enables developers to write queries against the database from the same language used to build the business logic. Figure 4.22 shows the relationship between LINQ to Entities and the Entity Framework, ADO.NET, and the data store.

It can be found that the Entities and EDM released by ADO.NET 4.3 locates at the top of this LINQ to Entities, and they are converted to the logical model by the Mapping Provider and interfaced to the data components such as Data Providers defined in ADO.NET 2.0. The bottom components used for this model are still "old" components that work for the ADO.NET 2.0.

Most applications are currently written on the relational databases and they are compatible with ADO.NET 2.0. At some point, these applications will have to interact with the data represented in a relational form. Database schemas are not always ideal for building applications, and the conceptual models of applications differ from the logical models of databases. The EDM released with

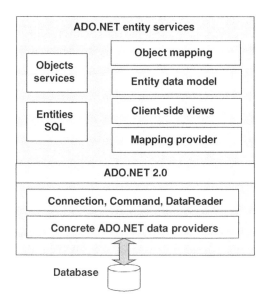

Figure 4.22 Relationship between LINQ to Entities, the Entity Framework, and ADO.NET.

ADO.NET 4.3 is a conceptual data model that can be used to model the data of a particular domain so that applications can interact with data as entities or objects.

4.3.5   Overview of LINQ to XML

LINQ to XML is a LINQ-enabled, in-memory XML programming interface that enables you to work with XML from within the .NET Framework programming languages.

LINQ to XML provides an in-memory XML programming interface that leverages the .NET LINQ Framework. LINQ to XML uses the latest .NET Framework language capabilities and is comparable to an updated, redesigned Document Object Model (DOM) XML programming interface. This interface was previously known as XLing in older prereleases of LINQ.

The LINQ family of technologies provides a consistent query experience for objects (LINQ), relational databases (LINQ to SQL), and XML (LINQ to XML).

At this point, we have finished an overview for LINQ family. Now let's go a little deep for those topics to get a more detailed discussion for each of them.

4.4   LINQ to Objects

As we mentioned in the previous section, LINQ to Objects is used to query any sequences or collections that are either explicitly or implicitly compatible with IEnumerable sequences or IENumerable(Of T) collections. Since any IEnumerable collection contains a sequence of objects with a data type that is compatible with IENumerable(Of T), therefore there is no need to use any LINQ API such as LINQ to SQL to convert or map this collection from an object model to a relational model, and the LINQ to Objects can be directly implemented to those collections or sequences to perform the queries.

Regularly LINQ to Objects is mainly used to query arrays and in-memory data collections. In fact, it can be used to query for any enumerable collections such as List(Of T), Array, or Dictionary(Of TKey, TValue). All of these queries are performed by executing SQO methods defined in the IEnumerable class. The difference between the IEnumerable and IENumerable(Of T) interfaces is that the former is used for nongeneric collections and the latter is used for generic collections. In Sections 4.1.3 and 4.1.4, we have provided a very detailed discussion about the SQOs. Now let's give a little more detailed discussion about the LINQ to Objects using those SQOs. We divide this discussion into the following four parts:

1) LINQ and ArrayList
2) LINQ and Strings
3) LINQ and File Directories
4) LINQ and Reflection

Let's starts with the first part: LINQ and ArrayList.

4.4.1   LINQ and ArrayList

When using LINQ to query nongeneric IEnumerable collections such as ArrayList, you must explicitly declare the type of the range variable to reflect the specific type of the objects in the collection. For example, if you have an ArrayList of **Student** objects, your From clause in a query should look like this:

```
Dim query = From s As Student In arrList
```

By specifying the type of the range variable *s* with **Student**, you are casting each item in the ArrayList *arrList* to a Student.

The use of an explicitly typed range variable in a query expression is equivalent to calling the Cast(Of TResult) method. Cast(Of TResult) throws an exception if the specified cast cannot be performed. Cast(Of TResult) and OfType(Of TResult) are the two SQO methods we discussed in Section 4.1.3 and these two methods operate on nongeneric IEnumerable types.

Let's illustrate this kind of LINQ with a Visual Basic.NET example project named **NonGenericLINQ.vb**. Create a new Visual Basic.NET Console App (.NET Framework) project and name it as **NonGenericLINQ** and enter the following codes that are shown in Figure 4.23 into the code window of this new project.

Let's have a closer look at this piece of codes to see how it works.

A) The **System.Collections** namespace is first added into this project since all nongeneric collections are defined in this namespace. In order to use any nongeneric collection such as ArrayList, you must import this namespace in this project before it can be used.
B) Modify the default module name from **Module1** to **NonGenericLINQ**. Also do this modification for the module project name **Module1.vb** to **NonGenericLINQ.vb** in the Solution Explorer window.
C) A new **Student** class with two properties is created and this class is used as a protocol for those objects to be created and added into the ArrayList nongeneric collection late.
D) A new instance of the ArrayList class **arrList** is created and initialized by adding four new Student objects.

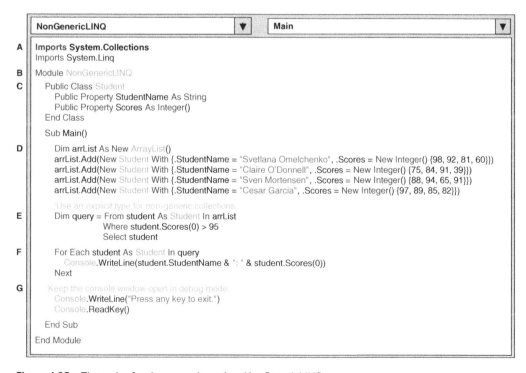

```vb
NonGenericLINQ                    ▼    Main                              ▼

A   Imports System.Collections
    Imports System.Linq

B   Module NonGenericLINQ
C       Public Class Student
            Public Property StudentName As String
            Public Property Scores As Integer()
        End Class

        Sub Main()
D           Dim arrList As New ArrayList()
            arrList.Add(New Student With {.StudentName = "Svetlana Omelchenko", .Scores = New Integer() {98, 92, 81, 60}})
            arrList.Add(New Student With {.StudentName = "Claire O'Donnell", .Scores = New Integer() {75, 84, 91, 39}})
            arrList.Add(New Student With {.StudentName = "Sven Mortensen", .Scores = New Integer() {88, 94, 65, 91}})
            arrList.Add(New Student With {.StudentName = "Cesar Garcia", .Scores = New Integer() {97, 89, 85, 82}})

            'Use an explicit type for non-generic collections
E           Dim query = From student As Student In arrList
                        Where student.Scores(0) > 95
                        Select student

F           For Each student As Student In query
                Console.WriteLine(student.StudentName & ": " & student.Scores(0))
            Next

G           'Keep the console window open in debug mode
            Console.WriteLine("Press any key to exit.")
            Console.ReadKey()

        End Sub
    End Module
```

Figure 4.23   The codes for the example project NonGenericLINQ.

E) A LINQ is created with the *student* as the range variable whose type is defined as Student by a Cast operator method. The filtering condition is that all student objects should be selected as long as their first Scores's value is greater than 95.

F) The *For Each* loop is used to pick up all query results one by one and assign it to the iteration variable *student*. A Console.WriteLine() method is executed to display each received data item, including the student's name and scores. This query process will continue until all data items have been retrieved from the ArrayList.

G) Two code lines here allow users to run this project in the Debugging mode. As you know, the Console window cannot be kept in the opening status if you run the project in the Debugging mode without these two lines of codes.

Before building the project, go to **Project** menu item and select **NonGenericLINQProject Properties** item to open the **Properties** wizard. Select the name of the **Startup object** as **NonGenericLINQ**. Now you can Build and Run the project, the running result should be

```
Svetlana Omelchenko: 98
Cesar Garcia: 97
Press any key to exit.
```

A complete Visual Basic.NET Console project NonGenericLINQProject can be found from the folder **Class DB Projects\Chapter 4\NonGenericLINQSolution** that is located under the Students folder at the Wiley ftp site (refer to Figure 1.2 in Chapter 1).

4.4.2 LINQ and Strings

LINQ can be used to query and transform strings and collections of strings. It can be especially useful with semi-structured data in text files. LINQ can be combined with traditional string functions and regular expressions. For example, you can use the Split or Split() method to create an array of strings that you can then query or modify using LINQ. You can use the IsMatch() method in the **where** clause of a LINQ. And you can use LINQ to query or modify the MatchCollection results returned by a regular expression.

You can query, analyze, and modify text blocks by splitting them into a queryable array of smaller strings using the Split() method. You can split the source text into words, sentences, paragraphs, pages, or any other criteria and then perform additional splits if they are required in your query. Many different types of text files consist of a series of lines, often with similar formatting, such as tab- or comma-delimited files or fixed-length lines. After you read such a text file into memory, you can use LINQ to query and/or modify the lines. LINQ also simplify the task of combining data from multiple sources.

Two example projects are provided in this part to illustrate (i) how to query a string to determine the number of numeric digits it contains and (ii) how to sort lines of structured text, such as comma-separated values, by any field in the line.

4.4.2.1 Query a String to Determine the Number of Numeric Digits

Because the String class implements the generic IEnumerable(Of T) interface, any string can be queried as a sequence of characters. However, this is not a common use of LINQ. For complex pattern matching operations, use the Regex class.

The following example queries a string to determine the number of numeric digits it contains. Note that the query is "reused" after it is executed the first time. This is possible because the query itself does not store any actual results.

Create a new Visual Basic.NET Console App (.NET Framework) project and name it as **QueryStringLINQ**. Change the Module name from Module1.vb to QueryStringLINQ.vb in the Solution Explorer window. Enter the codes shown in Figure 4.24 into the Sub Main() event.

Let's have a closer look at this piece of codes to see how it works.

A) A string object or a generic collection aString is created and this will work as a data source to be queried by LINQ to Objects.

B) The LINQ to Objects query is created and initialized with three clauses. The method IsDigit() is used as the filtering condition for the where clause and *ch* is the range variable. All digital element in this string collection will be filtered, selected, and returned. A Cast() operator is used for the returned query collection with an IEnumerable(Of T) interface, and T is replaced by the real data type *Char* here.

C) The query is executed using a For Each loop and c is an iteration variable. The queried digits are displayed using the Console.WriteLine() method.

D) The Count() method is executed to query the number of digits existing in the queried string. This query is "reused" because the query itself does not store any actual results.

E) Another query or the second query is created and initialized. The purpose of this query is to retrieve all letters before the first dash line in the string collection.

F) The second query is executed and the result is displayed using the **Console.Write()** method.

G) The purpose of these two coding lines is to allow users to exit the project.

Now you can run the project in Debugging mode by clicking **Debug|Start Debugging** menu item, and the running result of this project is

```
9 9 7 4 1 2 8 9
Count = 8
ABCDE99F
Press any key to exit
```

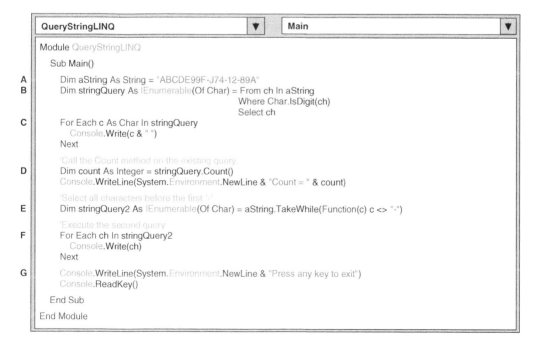

```
QueryStringLINQ                          ▼     Main                                    ▼

Module QueryStringLINQ

    Sub Main()

A       Dim aString As String = "ABCDE99F-J74-12-89A"
B       Dim stringQuery As IEnumerable(Of Char) = From ch In aString
                                           Where Char.IsDigit(ch)
                                           Select ch

C       For Each c As Char In stringQuery
            Console.Write(c & " ")
        Next

        'Call the Count method on the existing query
D       Dim count As Integer = stringQuery.Count()
        Console.WriteLine(System.Environment.NewLine & "Count = " & count)

        'Select all characters before the first '-'
E       Dim stringQuery2 As IEnumerable(Of Char) = aString.TakeWhile(Function(c) c <> "-")

        'Execute the second query
F       For Each ch In stringQuery2
            Console.Write(ch)
        Next

G       Console.WriteLine(System.Environment.NewLine & "Press any key to exit")
        Console.ReadKey()

    End Sub

End Module
```

Figure 4.24 The codes for the example project QueryStringLINQ.

A complete Visual Basic.NET Console project named **QueryStringLINQ Project** can be found from the folder **ClassDB Projects\Chapter 4\QueryStringLINQ Solution** that is under the **Students** folder located at the Wiley ftp site (refer to Figure 1.2 in Chapter 1).

Our first LINQ and Strings example is successful, and let's have a look at the second example.

4.4.2.2   Sort Lines of Structured Text by Any Field in the Line

This example project shows readers how to sort lines of structured text, such as comma-separated values, by any field in the line. The field may be dynamically specified at runtime. Assume that the fields in a sample text file scores.csv represent a student's ID number, followed by a series of four test scores.

Let's create a blank Solution named **SortLinesLINQ Solution** and add a new Visual Basic.NET Console App (.NET Framework) project named **SortLinesLINQ Project** into the Solution. Then save this Solution into an appropriate location in your computer. Then we need to create a sample text file **scores.csv** that will be used for our new project created above.

Open the NotePad editor and enter the following codes that are shown in Figure 4.25 into this opened text editor.

This file represents spreadsheet data. Column 1 is the student's ID, and columns 2 through 5 are test scores.

Click on the **File|Save As** menu item from the NotePad editor to open the Save As dialog box. Browse to the folder in which our new Visual Basic.NET Solution **SortLinesLINQ Solution** is located.Enter "**scores.csv**" into the File name box and click on the **Save** button to save this sample file. The point to be noticed is that the file name **scores.csv** must be enclosed by a pair of double quotation marks when you save this file in the extension **.csv**. Otherwise, the file will be saved with a text extension.

Close the NotePad editor and now let's develop the codes for our new Visual Basic.NET Console project **SortLinesLINQ**. In the Solution Explorer window, change the Module name from **Module1.vb** to **SortLinesLINQ.vb**.

Open the code window of our Visual Basic.NET Console App project **SortLinesLINQProject** and enter the codes shown in Figure 4.26 into the Code Window.

Let's have a closer look at this piece of codes to see how it works.

A) A local integer variable *sortField* is initialized to 1, which means that we want to use the first column in this string collection, student ID, as the filtering criteria. You can change this criterion by selecting any other column if you like.

```
111,   97,   92,   81,   60
112,   75,   84,   91,   39
113,   88,   94,   65,   91
114,   97,   89,   85,   82
115,   35,   72,   91,   70
116,   99,   86,   90,   94
117,   93,   92,   80,   87
118,   92,   90,   83,   78
119,   68,   79,   88,   92
120,   99,   82,   81,   79
121,   96,   85,   91,   60
122,   94,   92,   91,   91
```

Figure 4.25   The content of the sample text file scores.csv.

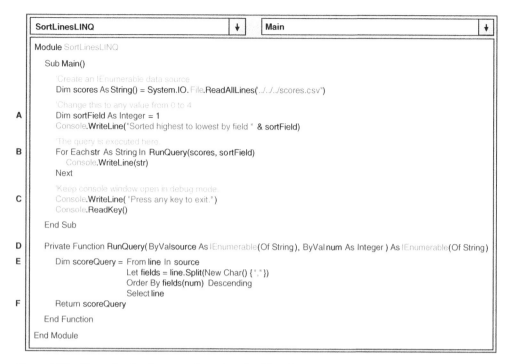

| SortLinesLINQ | ↓ | Main | ↓ |

```
Module SortLinesLINQ

    Sub Main()

        'Create an IEnumerable data source
        Dim scores As String() = System.IO.File.ReadAllLines("../../scores.csv")

A       'Change this to any value from 0 to 4
        Dim sortField As Integer = 1
        Console.WriteLine("Sorted highest to lowest by field " & sortField)

B       'The query is executed here.
        For Each str As String In RunQuery(scores, sortField)
            Console.WriteLine(str)
        Next

C       'Keep console window open in debug mode.
        Console.WriteLine("Press any key to exit.")
        Console.ReadKey()

        End Sub

D   Private Function RunQuery(ByVal source As IEnumerable(Of String), ByVal num As Integer) As IEnumerable(Of String)

E       Dim scoreQuery = From line In source
                         Let fields = line.Split(New Char() {","})
                         Order By fields(num) Descending
                         Select line
F       Return scoreQuery

    End Function

End Module
```

Figure 4.26   The codes for the example project SortLinesLINQ.

B) The query is built and executed by calling a function RunQuery() with two arguments: the data source *scores* and the filtering criteria *sortField*. The queried results are displayed by executing the method Console.WriteLine().

C) The purpose of these two coding lines is to allow users to run this project in a Debugging mode.

D) The body of the function RunQuery() starts from here. One point to be noticed is that the accessing mode for this function is Private, which means that all other event procedures defined in this console application can call and use this function.

E) The query is built with four clauses. The Split() method is used in the *Let* clause to allow the string to be split into different pieces at each comma. The queried result is distributed in a descending order using the Order By operator.

F) The queried result is returned to the calling method.

Now build and run the project by clicking the **Debug|Start Debugging** menu item, and the running result of this project is shown in Figure 4.27.

A complete Visual Basic.NET Console App project named **SortLinesLINQProject** can be found from the folder **Class DB Projects\Chapter 4\SortLinesLINQSolution** that is under the Students folder located at the Wiley ftp site (refer to Figure 1.2 in Chapter 1).

4.4.3   LINQ and File Directories

Many file system operations are essentially queries and are therefore well suited to the LINQ approach. Note that the queries for those file system are read-only. They are not used to change the contents of the original files or folders. This follows the rule that queries should not cause any side

```
Sorted highest to lowest by field 1:
116, 99, 86, 90, 94
120, 99, 82, 81, 79
111, 97, 92, 81, 60
114, 97, 89, 85, 82
121, 96, 85, 91, 60
122, 94, 92, 91, 91
117, 93, 92, 80, 87
118, 92, 90, 83, 78
113, 88, 94, 65, 91
112, 75, 84, 91, 39
119, 68, 79, 88, 92
115, 35, 72, 91, 70

Press any key to exit.
```

Figure 4.27 The running result of the project SortLinesLINQ.

effects. In general, any code (including queries that perform create/update/delete operators) that modifies source data should be kept separate from the code that just queries the data.

Different file operations or queries are existed for the file systems. The most typical operations include

1) Query for Files with a Specified Attribute or Name
2) Group Files by Extension (LINQ)
3) Query for the Total Number of Bytes in a Set of Folders (LINQ)
4) Query for the Largest File or Files in a Directory Tree (LINQ)
5) Query for Duplicate Files in a Directory Tree (LINQ)
6) Query the Contents of Files in a Folder (LINQ)

There is some complexity involved in creating a data source that accurately represents the contents of the file system and handles exceptions gracefully. The examples in this section create a snapshot collection of FileInfo objects that represents all the files under a specified root folder and all its subfolders. The actual state of each FileInfo may change in the time between when you begin and end executing a query. For example, you can create a list of FileInfo objects to use as a data source. If you try to access the Length property in a query, the FileInfo object will try to access the file system to update the value of Length. If the file no longer exists, you will get a FileNotFoundException in your query, even though you are not querying the file system directly. Some queries in this section use a separate method that consumes these particular exceptions in certain cases. Another option is to keep your data source updated dynamically using the FileSystemWatcher.

Because of the limitation of the space, here we only discuss one file operation or query, which is to open, inspect, and query the contents of files in a selected folder (the sixth operation).

4.4.3.1 Query the Contents of Files in a Folder

This example shows how to query over all the files in a specified directory tree, open each file, and inspect its contents. This type of technique could be used to create indexes or reverse indexes of the contents of a directory tree. A simple string search is performed in this example. However, more complex types of pattern matching can be performed with a regular expression.

Create a new Visual Basic.NET Console App (.NET Framework) project **QueryContentsLINQ Project** and add it into a Solution named **QueryContentsLINQ Solution**. Then enter the codes shown in Figure 4.28 into the code window. Let's have a look at this piece of codes to see how it works.

A) A string object startFolder is created and the value of this object is the default path of the Visual Studio.NET 2019, in which all files of the Visual Studio.NET 2019 are installed. You can modify this path if you installed your Visual Studio.NET 2019 at a different folder in your computer.

B) An IEnumerable(Of T) interface is used to define the data type of the queried files fileList. The real data type applied here is System.IO.FileInfo that is used to replace the nominaltype T. The method GetFiles() is executed to open and access the queried files with the file path as the argument of this method.

C) The query criterion *VisualStudio* that is a keyword to be searched by this query is assigned to a string object searchTerm that will be used in the following query process.

D) The LINQ is created and initialized with four clauses: From, Let, Where, and Select. The range variable file is selected from the opened files fileList. The method GetFileText() will be executed to read back the contents of the matched files using the Letclause. Two *Where* clauses are

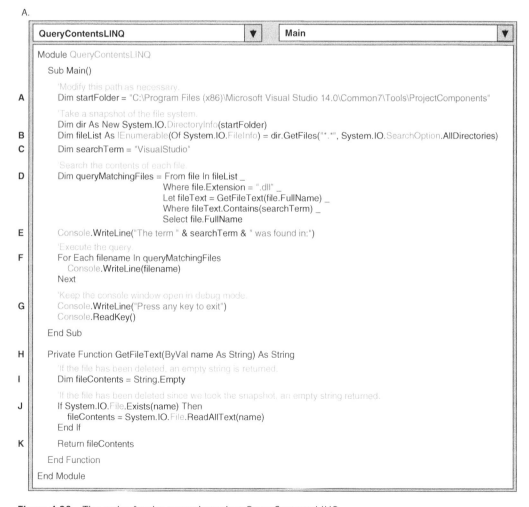

Figure 4.28 The codes for the example project QueryContentsLINQ.

used here to filter the matched files with both an extension .dll and a keyword *VisualStudio* in the file name.

E) The Console.WriteLine() method is executed to indicate that the following matched files contain the searched keyword *VisualStudio* in their file names.

F) The LINQ is executed to pick up all files that have a file name that contains the keyword *VisualStudio*, and all searched files are displayed using the method Console.WriteLine().

G) The purpose of these two coding lines is to allow users to run this project in a Debugging mode.

H) The body of the function GetFileText() starts from here. The point is that this method must be defined as a private function to indicate that this function can be called by all other procedures defined in this console application.

I) The string object fileContents is initialized with an empty string object.

J) The system method Exists() is executed to find all files whose names contain the keyword *VisualStudio*. All of matched files will be opened and the contents will be read back by the method ReadAllText() and assigned to the string object fileContents.

K) The read out fileContents object is returned to the calling method.

Before you can build this project, in the Solution Explorer window, change the Module name from **Module1.vb** to **QueryContentsLINQ.vb**. Now build and run the project by clicking the **Debug|Start Debugging** menu item. All files that have an extension .dll and under the path **C:\ Program Files (x86)\Microsoft Visual Studio\2019\Enterprise\Common7\Tools** and whose name contains the keyword *VisualStudio* are found and displayed as this project runs.

Press any key from the keyboard to exit this project.

A complete Visual Basic.NET Console App project **QueryContentsLINQ Project** can be found from the folder **Class DB Projects\Chapter 4\QueryContentsLINQ Solution** that is located under the Students folder at the Wiley ftp site (refer to Figure 1.2 in Chapter 1).

Next let's have a discussion about another query related to LINQ to Objects, the LINQ, and Reflection.

4.4.4 LINQ and Reflection

The .NET Framework 4.7 class library reflection APIs can be used to examine the metadata in a .NET assembly and create collections of types, type members, parameters, and so on that are in that assembly. Because these collections support the generic IEnumerable interface, they can be queried using LINQ to Objects query.

To make it simple and easy, in this section, we use one example project to illustrate how LINQ can be used with reflection to retrieve specific metadata about methods that match a specified search criterion. In this case, the query will find the names of all the methods in the assembly that return enumerable types such as arrays.

Create a new Visual Basic.NET Console App (.NET Framework) project and name it as **QueryReflectionLINQ Project** and add it into a Solution named **QueryReflectionLINQ Solution**. In the Solution Explorer window, change the module name from **Module1.vb** to **QueryReflectionLINQ.vb**. Open the code window and enter the codes shown in Figure 4.29 into this window.

Let's have a closer look at this piece of codes to see how it works.

A) The namespace System.Reflection is added into the namespace declaration part of this project since we need to use some components defined in this namespace in this coding.

B) An Assembly object that is created with the Load() method is executed to load and assign this new Assembly to the instance assembly.

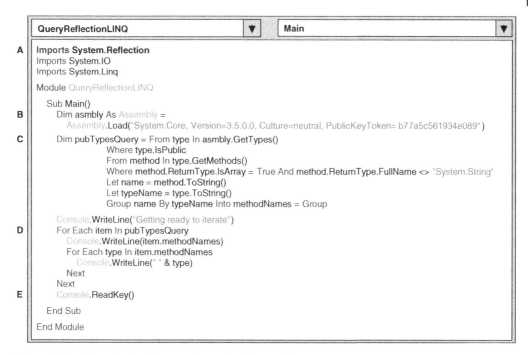

```
QueryReflectionLINQ        ▼    Main                        ▼

A   Imports System.Reflection
    Imports System.IO
    Imports System.Linq

    Module QueryReflectionLINQ

        Sub Main()
B           Dim asmbly As Assembly =
                Assembly.Load("System.Core, Version=3.5.0.0, Culture=neutral, PublicKeyToken= b77a5c561934e089" )

C           Dim pubTypesQuery = From type In asmbly.GetTypes()
                        Where type.IsPublic
                        From method In type.GetMethods()
                        Where method.ReturnType.IsArray = True And method.ReturnType.FullName <> "System.String"
                        Let name = method.ToString()
                        Let typeName = type.ToString()
                        Group name By typeName Into methodNames = Group

            Console.WriteLine("Getting ready to iterate")
D           For Each item In pubTypesQuery
                Console.WriteLine(item.methodNames)
                For Each type In item.methodNames
                    Console.WriteLine(" " & type)
                Next
            Next
E           Console.ReadKey()

        End Sub

    End Module
```

Figure 4.29 The codes for the example project QueryReflectionLINQ.

C) The LINQ is created and initialized with three clauses. The GetTypes() method is used to obtain the data type of all queried methods. The first Where clause is used to filter methods in the Public type. The second From clause is used to get the desired methods based on the data type Public. The second Where clause is used to filter all methods with two criteria: (i) the returning type of the method is array and (ii) the returning type of those methods should not be System. String. Also the queried methods' names are converted to string.

D) Two For Each loops are utilized here. The first one is used to retrieve and display the data type of the queried methods, and the second one is used to retrieve and display the names of the queried methods.

E) The purpose of this coding line is to allow users to run this project in a Debugging mode.

Now you can build and run the project by clicking the **Debug|Start Debugging** menu item. The running results are displayed in the console window.

A complete Visual Basic.NET Console project named **QueryReflectionLINQ Project** can be found from a folder **Class DB Projects\Chapter 4\QueryReflectionLINQ Solution**, which is located under the Students folder at the Wiley ftp site (refer to Figure 1.2 in Chapter 1).

4.5 LINQ to DataSet

As we discussed in the previous section, LINQ to DataSet is a subcomponent of LINQ to ADO.NET.

The DataSet, for which we provided a very detailed discussion in Chapter 3, is one of the most widely used components in ADO.NET, and it is a key element of the disconnected programming model that ADO.NET is built on. Despite this prominence, however, the DataSet has limited query capabilities.

LINQ to DataSet enables you to build richer query capabilities into DataSet using the same query functionality that is available for many other data sources. Because the LINQ to DataSet is built on the existing ADO.NET 2.0 architecture, the codes developed using ADO.NET 2.0 will continue to function in a LINQ to DataSet application without modifications. This is a very valuable advantage since any new components has its own architecture and tools with definite learning process to get it known.

Among all LINQ to DataSet query operations, the following three are most often implemented in most popular applications:

1) Perform operations to DataSet objects.
2) Perform operations to DataRow objects using the extension methods.
3) Perform operations to DataTable objects.

First, let's have a little deeper understanding about the LINQ to DataSet, or the operations to the DataSet objects.

4.5.1   Operations to DataSet Objects

Data sources that implement the IEnumerable(Of T) generic interface can be queried through-LINQ using the SQO methods. Using AsEnumerable SQO to query a DataTable returns an object which implements the generic IEnumerable(Of T) interface, which serves as the data source for LINQ to DataSet queries.

In the query, you specify exactly the information that you want to retrieve from the data source. A query can also specify how that information should be sorted, grouped, and shaped before it is returned. In LINQ, a query is stored in a variable. If the query is designed to return a sequence of values, the query variable itself must be an enumerable type. This query variable takes no action and returns no data; it only stores the query information. After you create a query, you must execute that query to retrieve any data.

In a query that returns a sequence of values, the query variable itself never holds the query results and only stores the query commands. Execution of the query is deferred until the query variable is iterated over in a **For Each** loop. This is called deferred execution, that is, query execution occurs sometime after the query is constructed. This means that you can execute a query as often as you want to. This is useful when, for example, you have a database that is being updated by other applications. In your application, you can create a query to retrieve the latest information and repeatedly execute the query, returning the updated information every time.

In contrast to deferred queries, which return a sequence of values, queries that return a singleton value are executed immediately. Some examples of singleton queries are Count, Max, Average, and First. These execute immediately because the query results are required to calculate the singleton result. For example, in order to find the average of the query results, the query must be executed so that the averaging function has input data to work with. You can also use the ToList(Of TSource) or ToArray(Of TSource) methods on a query to force immediate execution of a query that does not produce a singleton value. These techniques to force immediate execution can be useful when you want to cache the results of a query.

Basically, to perform a LINQ to DataSet query, three steps are needed:

1) Create a new DataSet instance
2) Populate the DataSet instance using the Fill() method
3) Query the DataSet instance using LINQ to DataSet

After a DataSet object has been populated with data, you can begin querying it. Formulating queries with LINQ to DataSet is similar to using LINQ against other LINQ-enabled data sources. Remember, however, that when you use LINQ over a DataSet object you are querying an enumeration of DataRow objects, instead of an enumeration of a custom type. This means that you can use any of the members of the DataRow class in your LINQ. This lets you to create rich and complex queries.

As with other implementations of LINQ, you can create LINQ to DataSet queries in two different forms: query expression syntax and method-based query syntax. Basically, the query expression syntax will be finally converted to the method-based query syntax as the compiling time if the query is written as the query expression, and the query will be executed by calling the SQO methods as the project runs.

4.5.1.1 Query Expression Syntax

A query expression is a query expressed in query syntax. A query expression is the first-class language construct. It is just like any other expression and can be used in any context in which a query expression is valid. A query expression consists of a set of clauses written in a declarative syntax similar to SQL or XQuery. Each clause in turn contains one or more expressions, and these expressions may themselves be either a query expression or contain a query expression.

A query expression must begin with a From clause and must end with a Select or Group clause. Between the first From clause and the last Select or Group clause, it can contain one or more of these optional clauses: Where, Order By, Join, Let, and even additional From clauses. You can also use the Into keyword to enable the result of a Join or Group clause to serve as the source for additional query clauses in the same query expression.

In all LINQ (including LINQ to DataSet), all of clauses will be converted to the associated SQO methods, such as From, Where, Order By, Join, Let, and Select, as the queries are compiled. Refer to Table 4.1 in this chapter to get the most often used SQOs and their definitions.

In LINQ, a query variable is always strongly typed and it can be any variable that stores a query instead of the results of a query. More specifically, a query variable is always an enumerable type that will produce a sequence of elements when it is iterated over in a For Each loop or a direct call to its method IEnumerator.MoveNext.

The following code example shows a simple query expression with one data source, one filtering clause, one ordering clause, and no transformation of the source elements. The Select clause ends the query.

An integer array is created here and this array works as a data source. The variable scoreQuery is a query variable and it contains only the query command and does not contain any query result. This query is composed of four clauses: From, Where, Order By, and Select. Both the first and the last clause are required and the others are optional. The query is casted to a type of IEnumerable(Of Int32) using an IEnumerable(Of T) interface. The testScore is an iteration variable that is scanned through the For Each loop to get and display each queried data when this query is executed. Exactly, when the For Each statement executes, the query results are not returned through the query variable scoreQuery. Rather, they are returned through the iteration variable testScore.

An alternative way to write this query expression is to use the so-called implicit typing of query variables. The difference between the explicit and implicit typing of query variables is that in the former situation, the relationship between the query variable scoreQuery and the Select clause is clearly indicated by the IEnumerable(Of T) interface, and this makes sure that the type of returned collection is IEnumerable(Of T) that can be queried by LINQ. In the latter situation, we do not exactly know the data type of the query variable and therefore an implicit type **scoreQuery** is used

```
Module QueryExpression
    Dim scores As Integer() = {90, 71, 82, 93, 75, 82}

    Sub main()
        'Query Expression.
        Dim scoreQuery As IEnumerable (Of Int32) = From score In scores
                                                   Where score > 80
                                                   Order By score Descending
                                                   Select score
        'Execute the query to produce the results
        For Each testScore In scoreQuery
            Console.Write("{0, 1} ", testScore)
        Next
        Console.WriteLine(vbNewLine & "Press any key to continue...")
        Console.ReadKey()
    End Sub

End Module
'Outputs: 93  90  82  82
```

Figure 4.30   The example codes for the query expression syntax.

```
Module QueryExpression
    Dim scores As Integer() = {90, 71, 82, 93, 75, 82}

    Sub main()
        'Query Expression.
        Dim scoreQuery = From score In scores
                         Where score > 80
                         Order By score Descending
                         Select score
        'Execute the query to produce the results
        For Each testScore In scoreQuery
            Console.Write("{0, 1} ", testScore)
        Next
        Console.WriteLine(vbNewLine & "Press any key to continue...")
        Console.ReadKey()
    End Sub

End Module
'Outputs: 93  90  82  82
```

Figure 4.31   The example codes for the query expression in implicit typing of query variable.

to instruct the compiler to infer the type of a query variable (or any other local variable) at the compiling time. The example codes written in Figure 4.30 can be expressed in another format that is shown in Figure 4.31 using the implicit typing of query variable.

Here, the implicit type is used to replace the explicit type IEnumerable(Of T) for the query variable and it can be converted to the IEnumerable(Of Int32) automatically as this piece of codes is compiled.

4.5.1.2   Method-Based Query Syntax

Most queries used in the general LINQ are written as query expressions using the declarative query syntax. However, the .NET common language runtime (CLR) has no notion of query syntax in itself. Therefore, at compile time, query expressions are converted to something that the CLR can understand – method calls. These methods are SQO methods, and they have names equivalent to query clauses such as **Where, Select, GroupBy, Join, Max, Average**, and so on. You can call them directly using method syntax instead of query syntax. In Sections 4.1.3 and 4.1.4, we have provided a very detailed discussion about the SQO methods. Refer to that section to get more details for those methods and their implementations.

In general, we recommend query syntax because it is usually simpler and more readable; however, there is no semantic difference between method syntax and query syntax. In addition, some queries, such as those that retrieve the number of elements that match a specified condition, or that retrieve the element that has the maximum value in a source sequence, can only be expressed as method calls. The reference documentation for the SQOs in the System.Linq namespace generally uses method syntax. Therefore, even when getting started writing LINQ, it is useful to be familiar with how to use method syntax in queries and in query expressions themselves.

We discussed the SQO with a quite few of examples using the method syntax in Sections 4.1.3 and 4.1.4. Refer to those sections to get more details in creating and using method syntax to directly call SQO methods to perform LINQ. In this section, we just give an example to illustrate the different format using the query syntax and the method syntax for a given data source.

Create a new Visual Basic Console App (.NET Framework) project **QueryMethodSyntax Project** and add it into a Solution **QueryMethodSyntax Solution**. Change the module name from **Module1.vb** to **QueryMethodSyntax.vb** in the Solution Explorer window. Enter the codes shown in Figure 4.32 into this Code Window. Let's have a look at this piece of codes to see how it works.

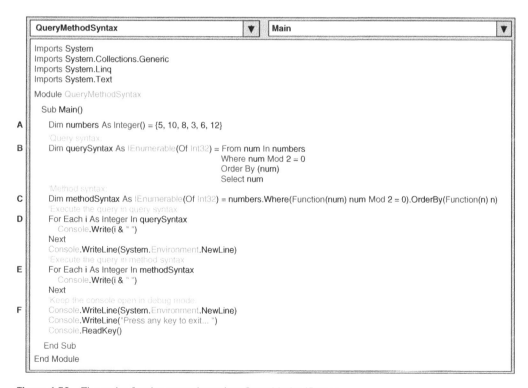

```vb
QueryMethodSyntax                          ▼   Main                                              ▼

Imports System
Imports System.Collections.Generic
Imports System.Linq
Imports System.Text

Module QueryMethodSyntax

    Sub Main()

A       Dim numbers As Integer() = {5, 10, 8, 3, 6, 12}
        'Query syntax:
B       Dim querySyntax As IEnumerable(Of Int32) = From num In numbers
                                                   Where num Mod 2 = 0
                                                   Order By (num)
                                                   Select num
        'Method syntax:
C       Dim methodSyntax As IEnumerable(Of Int32) = numbers.Where(Function(num) num Mod 2 = 0).OrderBy(Function(n) n)
        'Execute the query in query syntax:
D       For Each i As Integer In querySyntax
            Console.Write(i & " ")
        Next
        Console.WriteLine(System.Environment.NewLine)
        'Execute the query in method syntax:
E       For Each i As Integer In methodSyntax
            Console.Write(i & " ")
        Next
        'Keep the console open in debug mode:
F       Console.WriteLine(System.Environment.NewLine)
        Console.WriteLine("Press any key to exit... ")
        Console.ReadKey()

    End Sub
End Module
```

Figure 4.32 The codes for the example project QueryMethodSyntax.

A) An integer array is created and it works as a data source for this project.
B) The first query that uses a query syntax is created and initialized with four clauses. The query variable is named querySyntax with a type of IEnumerable(Of Int32).
C) The second query that uses a method syntax is created and initialized with the StandardQuery Operator methods Where() and Order By().
D) The first query is executed using a For Each loop and the query result is displayed by using the Console.Write() method.
E) The second query is executed and the result is displayed, too.
F) The purpose of these two coding lines is to allow users to run this project in a Debugging mode.

It can be found that the method syntax looks simpler in structure and easy to coding compared with the query syntax from this piece of codes. In facts, the first query with the query syntax will be converted to the second query with the method syntax as the project is compiled.

Now you can build and run the project. You can find that the running result is identical for both syntaxes.

A complete Visual Basic.NET Console project **QueryMethodSyntax Project** can be found from the folder **ClassDB Projects\Chapter 4\QueryMethodSyntax Solution** that is under the **Students** folder located at the Wiley ftp site (refer to Figure 1.2 in Chapter 1).

Besides the general and special properties of query expression discussed above, the following points are also important to understand query expressions:

1) Query expressions can be used to query and to transform data from any LINQ-enabled data source. For example, a single query can retrieve data from a DataSet, and produce an XML stream as output.
2) Query expressions are easy to master because they use many familiar C language constructs.
3) The variables in a query expression are all strongly typed, although in many cases you do not have to provide the type explicitly because the compiler can infer it if an implicit type var is used.
4) A query is not executed until you iterate over the query variable in a **For Each** loop.
5) At compile time, query expressions are converted to SQO method calls according to the rules set forth in the Visual Basic specification. Any query that can be expressed using query syntax can also be expressed using method syntax. However, in most cases, query syntax is more readable and concise.
6) As a rule when you write LINQ, we recommend that you use query syntax whenever possible and method syntax whenever necessary. There is no semantic or performance difference between the two different forms. Query expressions are often more readable than equivalent expressions written in method syntax.
7) Some query operations, such as Count or Max, have no equivalent query expression clause and must therefore be expressed as a method call. Method syntax can be combined with query syntax in various ways.
8) Query expressions can be compiled to expression trees or to delegates, depending on the type that the query is applied to. IEnumerable(Of T) queries are compiled to delegates. IQueryable and IQueryable(Of T) queries are compiled to expression trees.

Now let's start the LINQ to DataSet with the single table query.

4.5.1.3 Query the Single Table

LINQ work on data sources that implement the IEnumerable(Of T) interface or the IQueryable interface. The DataTable class does not implement either interface, so you must call the

AsEnumerable method if you want to use the DataTable as a source in the **From** clause of a LINQ.

As we discussed in Section 4.5.1, to perform LINQ to DataSet query, the first step is to create an instance of the DataSet and fill it with the data from the database. To fill a DataSet, a DataAdapter can be used with the Fill() method that is attached to that DataAdapter. Each DataAdapter can only fill a single DataTable in a DataSet.

In this section, we use an example to query a single DataTable using the LINQ to DataSet. Create a blank Solution **DataSetSingleTableLINQ Solution** and add a new Visual Basic.NET Console App (.NET Framework) project **DataSetSingleTableLINQ Project**. On the opened project, change the File Name property to **DataSetSingleTableLINQ.vb** in the Solution Explorer window.

First let's add some references into the project to access our sample Oracle database to perform data actions. Right-click on our project and select **Add|Reference** item to open the Reference Manager wizard. Select **Extensions** under the **Assemblies** tab on the left pane, and check both items, **Devart.Data** and **Devart.Data.Oracle,** from mid-pane to select them. Click on the **OK** button to add them into our project since we need them to connect to our sample Oracle database.

Open the code window and enter the codes shown in Figure 4.33 into this window.

A) The namespace, **Devart.Data.Oracle,** must be added into the namespace declaration section of this project since we need to use some Oracle data components, such as DataAdapter, Command, and Connection, to access our sample database to perform data actions.

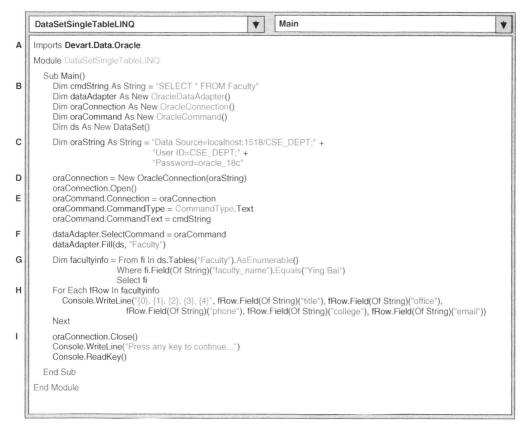

```vb
DataSetSingleTableLINQ                                    Main

A    Imports Devart.Data.Oracle

     Module DataSetSingleTableLINQ

         Sub Main()
B            Dim cmdString As String = "SELECT * FROM Faculty"
             Dim dataAdapter As New OracleDataAdapter()
             Dim oraConnection As New OracleConnection()
             Dim oraCommand As New OracleCommand()
             Dim ds As New DataSet()

C            Dim oraString As String = "Data Source=localhost:1518/CSE_DEPT;" +
                                        "User ID=CSE_DEPT;" +
                                        "Password=oracle_18c"

D            oraConnection = New OracleConnection(oraString)
             oraConnection.Open()
E            oraCommand.Connection = oraConnection
             oraCommand.CommandType = CommandType.Text
             oraCommand.CommandText = cmdString

F            dataAdapter.SelectCommand = oraCommand
             dataAdapter.Fill(ds, "Faculty")

G            Dim facultyinfo = From fi In ds.Tables("Faculty").AsEnumerable()
                               Where fi.Field(Of String)("faculty_name").Equals("Ying Bai")
                               Select fi
H            For Each fRow In facultyinfo
                 Console.WriteLine("{0}, {1}, {2}, {3}, {4}", fRow.Field(Of String)("title"), fRow.Field(Of String)("office"),
                                   fRow.Field(Of String)("phone"), fRow.Field(Of String)("college"), fRow.Field(Of String)("email"))
             Next
I            oraConnection.Close()
             Console.WriteLine("Press any key to continue...")
             Console.ReadKey()

         End Sub
     End Module
```

Figure 4.33 The codes for the example project DataSetSingleTableLINQ.

B) An Oracle query string is created to query all columns from the Faculty data table in the DataSet. Also all Oracle data components are created in this part including a non-OleDb data component, DataSet.

C) The connection string is declared since we need to use it to connect to our sample database CSE_DEPT that is developed in Oracle 18c XE. You need to modify this string based on the real parameters with which you built your database.

D) The Connection object oraConnection is initialized with the connection string and a connection is executed by calling the Open() method. Regularly a Try . . .Catch block should be used for this connection operation to catch up any possible exception. Here, we skip it since we try to make this connection coding simple.

E) The Command object is initialized with Connection, CommandType, and CommandText properties.

F) The initialized Command object is assigned to the SelectCommand property of the DataAdapter and the DataSet is filled with the Fill() method. The point is that only a single table, Faculty, is filled in this operation.

G) A LINQ to DataSet query is created with three clauses, From, Where, and Select. The data type of the query variable facultyinfo is an implicit and it can be inferred by the compiler as the project is compiled. The Faculty data table works as a data source for this LINQ to DataSet query; therefore, the AsEnumerable() method must be used to convert it to an IEnumerable(Of T) type. The Where clause is used to filter the desired information for the selected faculty member (faculty_name). All of these clauses will be converted to the associated SQO methods that will be executed to perform and complete this query.

H) The For Each loop then enumerates the enumerable object returned by selecting and yielding the query results. Because query is an Enumerable type, which implements IEnumerable(Of T), the evaluation of the query is deferred until the query variable is iterated over using the For Each loop. Deferred query evaluation allows queries to be kept as values that can be evaluated multiple times, each time yielding potentially different results.

I) Finally, the connection to our sample database is closed by calling the Close() method.

Now you can build and run this project by clicking **Debug|Start Debugging**. Related information for the selected faculty will be retrieved and displayed in the console window.

A completed and tested Visual Basic.NET Console App (.NET Framework) project named **DataSetSingleTableLINQ Project** can be found from a folder **ClassDB Projects\Chapter 4\ DataSetSingleTableLINQ Solution** that is under the **Students** folder located at the Wiley ftp site (refer to Figure 1.2 in Chapter 1).

4.5.1.4 Query the Cross Tables

A DataSet object must first be populated before you can query over it with LINQ to DataSet.

There are several different ways to populate a DataSet. From the example we discussed in the last section, we used the DataAdapter class with the Fill() method to do this population.

In addition to querying a single table, you can also perform cross-table queries in LINQ to DataSet. This is done by a join clause. A join is the association of objects in one data source with objects that share a common attribute in another data source, such as a faculty_id in the LogIn table and in the Faculty table. In object-oriented programming, relationships between objects are relatively easy to navigate because each object has a member that references another object. In external database tables, however, navigating relationships is not as straightforward. Database tables do not contain built-in relationships. In these cases, the Join operation can be used to match elements from each source. For example, given two tables that contain faculty information and course information, you could use a join operation to match course information and faculty for the same faculty_id.

The LINQ framework provides two join operators, Join and GroupJoin. These operators perform equi-joins, that is, joins that match two data sources only when their keys are equal. (By contrast, Transact-SQL supports join operators other than **Equals**, such as the **Less Than** operator.)

In relational database terms, Join implements an inner join. An inner join is a type of join in which only those objects that have a match in the opposite data set are returned.

In this section, we use an example project to illustrate how to use Join operator to perform a multi-table query using LINQ to DataSet. The functionality of this project is

1) To populate a DataSet instance, exactly populate two data tables, Faculty and Course, with two DataAdapters.
2) To Use LINQ to DataSet join query to perform the cross-table query

Now create a blank Solution **DataSetCrossTableLINQ Solution** and add a new Visual Basic. NET Console App (.NET Framework) project **DataSetCrossTableLINQ Project**. On the opened project, in the Solution Explorer window, change the **File Name** property to **DataSetCrossTableLINQ.vb**. Also add two references, **Devart.Data** and **Devart.Data.Oracle**, into our project by right-clicking on our project and select **Add|Reference** item.

Then open the code window and enter the codes shown in Figure 4.34 into this window.

A) The namespace, **Devart.Data,** must be added into the namespace declaration section since we need to use some Oracle data components, such as DataAdapter, Command, and Connection, to access our sample database to do data actions.

B) Two Oracle query strings are created to query some columns from the Faculty and the Course data tables in the DataSet. Also all Oracle data components, including two sets of Command and DataAdapter objects, are created in this part with a non-OleDb data component, DataSet. Each set of components is used to fill an associated data table in the DataSet.

C) The connection string is declared since we need to use it to connect to our sample database CSE_DEPT that is developed with Oracle 18c XE.

D) The Connection object oraConnection is initialized with the connection string and a connection is executed by calling the Open() method. Regularly, a Try . . .Catch block should be used for this connection operation to catch up any possible exception. Here, we skip it since we try to make this connection coding simple.

E) The facultyCommand object is initialized with Connection, CommandType, and CommandText properties.

F) The initialized facultyCommand object is assigned to the SelectCommand property of the facultyAdapter and the DataSet is filled with the Fill() method. The point is that only a single table, Faculty, is filled in this operation.

G) The courseCommand object is initialized with Connection, CommandType, and CommandText properties. The initialized courseCommand object is assigned to the SelectCommand property of the courseAdapter and the DataSet is filled with the Fill() method. The point is that only a single table, Course, is filled in this operation.

H) A LINQ to DataSet query is created with a Join clause. The data type of the query variable courseinfo is an implicit and it can be inferred by the compiler as the project is compiled. Two data tables, Faculty and Course, work as a joined data source for this LINQ to DataSet query; therefore, the AsEnumerable() method must be used to convert them to an IEnumerable(Of T)

```
DataSetCrossTableLINQ                              ▼   │  Main                              ▼

A   Imports Devart.Data.Oracle

    Module DataSetCrossTableLINQ

        Sub Main()
B           Dim strFaculty As String = "SELECT faculty_id, faculty_name FROM Faculty"
            Dim strCourse As String = "SELECT course_id, faculty_id FROM Course"
            Dim facultyAdapter As New OracleDataAdapter()
            Dim courseAdapter As New OracleDataAdapter()
            Dim oraConnection As New OracleConnection()
            Dim facultyCommand As New OracleCommand()
            Dim courseCommand As New OracleCommand()
            Dim ds As New DataSet()

C           Dim oraString As String = "Data Source=localhost:1518/CSE_DEPT;" +
                                       "User ID=CSE_DEPT;" +
                                       "Password=oracle_18c"

D           oraConnection = New OracleConnection(oraString)
            oraConnection.Open()

E           facultyCommand.Connection = oraConnection
            facultyCommand.CommandType = CommandType.Text
            facultyCommand.CommandText = strFaculty
F           facultyAdapter.SelectCommand = facultyCommand
            facultyAdapter.Fill(ds, "Faculty")

G           courseCommand.Connection = oraConnection
            courseCommand.CommandType = CommandType.Text
            courseCommand.CommandText = strCourse
            courseAdapter.SelectCommand = courseCommand
            courseAdapter.Fill(ds, "Course")

H           Dim courseinfo = From ci In ds.Tables("Course").AsEnumerable()
                             Join fi In ds.Tables("faculty").AsEnumerable()
                             On ci.Field(Of String)("faculty_id") Equals fi.Field(Of String)("faculty_id")
                             Where fi.Field(Of String)("faculty_name").Equals("Ying Bai")
                             Select New With {.course_id = ci.Field(Of String)("course_id")}

I           For Each cid In courseinfo
                Console.WriteLine(cid.course_id)
            Next

J           oraConnection.Close()
            facultyCommand.Dispose()
            courseCommand.Dispose()
            facultyAdapter.Dispose()
            courseAdapter.Dispose()

K           Console.WriteLine("Press any key to continue...")
            Console.ReadKey()

        End Sub

    End Module
```

Figure 4.34 The codes for the example project DataSetCrossTableLINQ.

type. Two identical fields, faculty_id that is a primary key in the Faculty table and a foreign key in the Course tables, works as a joined criterion to link two tables together. The Where clause is used to filter the desired course information for the selected faculty member (faculty_name). All of these clauses will be converted to the associated SQO methods that will be executed to perform and complete this query.

I) The For Each loop then enumerates the enumerable object returned by selecting and yielding the query results. Because query is an Enumerable type, which implements IEnumerable(Of T), the evaluation of the query is deferred until the query variable is iterated over using the For Each loop. Deferred query evaluation allows queries to be kept as values that can be evaluated multiple times, each time yielding potentially different results. All courses taught by the selected faculty are retrieved and displayed when this For Each loop is done.

J) Finally, the connection to our sample database is closed by calling the Close() method, and all data components used in this project are released.

K) These two coding lines are used to enable this console project to be run in the Debugging mode.

Now you can build and run this project. Click the **Debug|Start Debugging** menu item to run the project, and you can find that all courses (course_id) taught by the selected faculty member are retrieved and displayed in this console window.

A complete Visual Basic.NET Console App project **DataSetCrossTableLINQ Project** can be found from the folder **Class DB Projects\Chapter 4\DataSetCrossTableLINQ Solution** that is under the **Students** folder located at the Wiley ftp site (refer to Figure 1.2 in Chapter 1).

Next, let's take a look at querying typed DataSet with LINQ to DataSet.

4.5.1.5   Query Typed DataSet

If the schema of the DataSet is known at application design time, it is highly recommended that you use a typed DataSet when using LINQ to DataSet. A typed DataSet is a class that derives from a DataSet. As such, it inherits all the methods, events, and properties of a DataSet. Additionally, a typed DataSet provides strongly typed methods, events, and properties. This means that you can access tables and columns by name, instead of using collection-based methods. This makes queries simpler and more readable.

LINQ to DataSet also supports querying over a typed DataSet. With a typed DataSet, you do not have to use the generic Field() method or SetField() method to access column data. Property names are available at compile time because the type information is included in the DataSet. LINQ to DataSet provides access to column values as the correct type, so that the type mismatch errors are caught when the code is compiled instead of at run time.

Before you can begin querying a typed DataSet, you must generate the class using the DataSet Designer in Visual Studio 2019.

In this section, we show readers how to use LINQ to DataSet to query a typed DataSet. In fact, it is very easy to perform this kind of query as long as a typed DataSet has been created. There are two ways to create a typed DataSet: using the Data Source Configuration Wizard or using the DataSet Designer. Both belong to the Design Tools and Wizards provided by Visual Studio.NET 2019.

We will use the second method, DataSet Designer, to create a typed DataSet. The database we will use is our sample database CSE_DEPT developed with Oracle 18c XE.

Create a blank Solution **TypedDataSetLINQ Solution**, add a new Visual Basic.NET Console App (.NET Framework) project **TypedDataSetLINQ Project**, and change the File Name property from **Module1.vb** to **TypedDataSetLINQ.vb** in the Solution Explorer window.

Let's first create our typed DataSet. On the opened new project, right-click our new project **TypedDataSetLINQ Project** from the Solution Explorer window. Select the **Add|New Item** from the popup menu to open the **Add New Item** wizard, which is shown in Figure 4.35.

Click on the DataSet from the Template list and enter **CSE_DEPT_DataSet.xsd** into the Name box as the name for this DataSet. Click on the **Add** button to add this DataSet into our project. Your finished **Add New Item** wizard should match one that is shown in Figure 4.35.

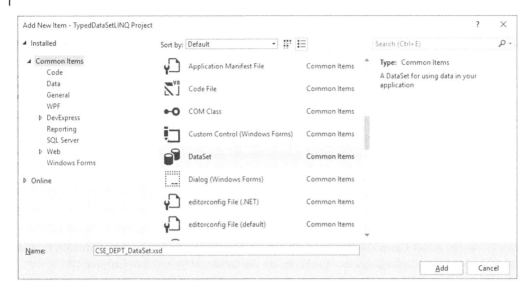

Figure 4.35 The opened Add New Item dialog box. *Source*: LINQ to DataSet.

Next we need to select our data source for our new DataSet. Go to **View|Server Explorer** menu to open the Server Explorer window and right-click the first folder **Data Connections** if you have not connected any data source. Then click on the **Add Connection** item from the popup menu to open the Add Connection wizard.

Click on the **Change** button on the right of Data source: box to open the Change Data Source wizard. Select **Oracle Database** from the **Data source** list and make sure that the **dotConnect for Oracle** is selected from the Data provider box. Then click on the OK button to return to the Add Connection wizard, as shown in Figure 4.36a.

Enter connection parameters shown in Figure 4.36a into the related box. The Password is **oracle_18c** that is created during we created our customer database CSE_DEPT in Chapter 2. Your finished Add Connection wizard should match one that is shown in Figure 4.36a.

You can click on the **Test Connection** button to test this connection. Click on the OK button to finish this process if the connection test is successful.

Now you can find that a new data connection folder has been added into the Server Explorer window with our sample database CSE_DEPT. Expand the Tables folder under this data source, you can find all five tables, which is shown in Figure 4.36b, in our sample database.

Open the DataSet Designer by double-clicking on the item **CSE_DEPT_DataSet.xsd** from the Solution Explorer window if it is not opened, drag the Faculty and the Course tables from the Server Explorer window and place them to the DataSet Designer. You can drag/place all five tables, but here we only need two of them. Exactly we only need the Faculty table in this project.

Now we have finished creating our typed DataSet and the connection to our data source. Next, we need to perform the coding to use LINQ to DataSet to perform the query to this typed DataSet. But first we need to add two references, **Devart.Data** and **Devart.Data.Oracle**, into our project since we need to use some Oracle database components to access and implement records from our sample database. Right-click on our project from the Solution Explorer window and select **Add|Reference** to open the Reference Manager wizard. Select the **Extensions** item from left and select these two data components from the mid pane, and click **OK** button to add them.

(a)

(b)

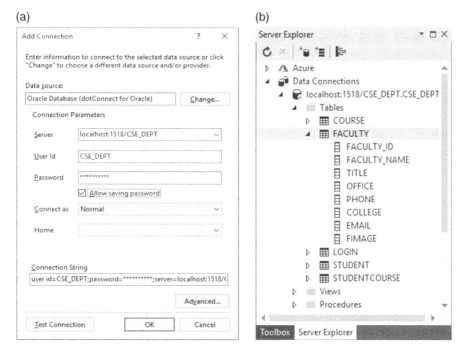

Figure 4.36 (a, b) The Add Connection dialog and the Server Explorer window. *Source*: Server Explorer window.

Double-click on our new project **TypedDataSetLINQ.vb** from the Solution Explorer window to open the code window. Enter the codes shown in Figure 4.37 into this window.

Let's have a closer look at this piece of codes to see how it works.

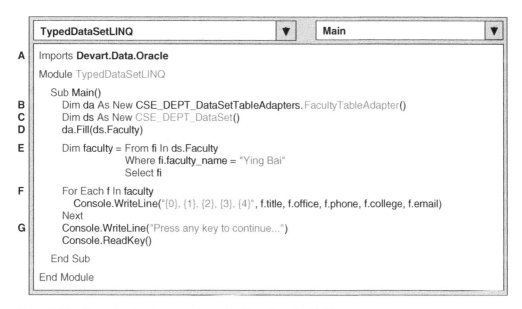

Figure 4.37 The codes for the example project TypedDataSetLINQ.

A) The namespace, Devart.Data.Oracle, must be added into the namespace declaration section since we need to use some Oracle data components, such as DataAdapter, Command, and Connection, to access our sample database to do data actions.

B) A new instance of the FacultyTableAdapter da is created since we need it to fill the DataSet later. All TableAdapters are defined in the CSE_DEPTDataSetTableAdapters namespace; therefore, we must prefix it in front of the FacultyTableAdapter class.

C) A new DataSet instance ds is also created.

D) The new instance of DataSet is populated with data using the Fill() method. Exactly only the Faculty table is filled with data obtained from the Faculty table in our sample database CSE_DEPT.

E) The LINQ to DataSet query is created with three clauses. The data type of the query variable is an implicit data type, and it can be inferred to the suitable type as the compiling time. Since we are using a typed DataSet, we can directly use the table name, Faculty, after the DataSet without worry about the Field(Of T) setup with the real table name.

F) The For Each loop is executed to perform this query and each queried column from the Faculty table is displayed using the Console.WriteLine() method. Compared with the same displaying operation in Figure 4.33 in Section 4.5.1.3, you can find that each column in the queried result can be accessed using its name in this operation since a typed DataSet is used in this project.

G) These two coding lines enable this console project to be run in the Debugging mode.

Now you can build the project. Click on the **Debug|Start Debugging** item to run the project, and you can find all pieces of information related to the selected faculty are retrieved and displayed in this console window. Our project is successful!

A completed Visual Basic.NET Console App project **TypedDataSetLINQ Project** can be found from the folder **ClassDB Projects\Chapter 4\TypedDataSetLINQ Solution** that is under the **Students** folder located at the Wiley ftp site (refer to Figure 1.2 in Chapter 1).

4.5.2 Operations to DataRow Objects Using the Extension Methods

The LINQ to DataSet functionality is exposed primarily through the extension methods in the DataRowExtensions and DataTableExtensions classes. In Visual Basic.NET, you can call either of these methods as an instance method on any object of type. When you use instance method syntax to call this method, omit the first parameter. The DataSet API has been extended with two new methods of the DataRow class, Field() and SetField(). You can use these to form LINQ expressions and method queries against DataTable objects. They are the recommended methods to use for accessing column values within LINQ expressions and method queries.

In this section, we show readers how to access and manipulate column values using the extension methods provided by the DataRow class, the Field() and SetField() methods. These methods provide easier access to column values for developers, especially regarding null values. The DataSet uses Value to represent null values, whereas LINQ uses the nullable type support introduced in the .NET Framework 2.0. Using the preexisting column accessor in DataRow requires you to cast the return object to the appropriate type. If a particular field in a DataRow can be null, you must explicitly check for a null value because returning Value and implicitly casting it to another type throws an InvalidCastException.

The Field() method allows users to obtain the value of a column from the DataRow object and handles the casting of DBNull.Value. Totally, the Field() method has six different prototypes. The

SetField() method, which has three prototypes, allows users to set a new value for a column from the DataRow object including handle a nullable data type whose value is null.

Now let's create a blank Solution **DataRowFieldLINQ Solution** and add a new Visual Basic. NET Console App (.NET Framework) project **DataRowFieldLINQ Project** to illustrate how to use the Field() method to retrieve some columns' values from the DataRow object. The database we will use is still our sample database CSE_DEPT. In the Solution Explorer window, change the File Name from **Module1.vb** to **DataRowFieldLINQ.vb**.

First let's add some references into the project to access our sample Oracle database to perform data actions. Right-click on our project and select **Add|Reference** item to open the Reference Manager wizard. Select **Extensions** under the **Assemblies** tab on the left pane and check both items, **Devart.Data** and **Devart.Data.Oracle**, from mid-pane to select them. Click on the **OK** button to add them into our project since we need them to connect to our sample Oracle database.

Open the code window and enter the codes shown in Figure 4.38 into this window. Let's have a closer look at this piece of codes to see how it works.

A) The namespace, Devart.Data.Oracle, must be added into the namespace declaration section of this project since we need to use some Oracle data components such as DataAdapter, Command, and Connection to access our sample Oracle database.

```
DataRowFieldLINQ ▼                              Main ▼

A   Imports Devart.Data.Oracle
    Module DataRowFieldLINQ

    Sub Main()
B       Dim cmdString As String = "SELECT * FROM Faculty"
        Dim dataAdapter As New OracleDataAdapter
        Dim oraConnection = New OracleConnection
        Dim oraCommand As New OracleCommand
        Dim ds = New DataSet

C       Dim oraString As String = "Data Source=localhost:1518/CSE_DEPT;" +
                                  "User ID=CSE_DEPT;" +
                                  "Password=oracle_18c"

D       oraConnection = New OracleConnection(oraString)
        oraConnection.Open()
E       oraCommand.Connection = oraConnection
        oraCommand.CommandType = CommandType.Text
        oraCommand.CommandText = cmdString
F       dataAdapter.SelectCommand = oraCommand
        dataAdapter.Fill(ds, "Faculty")
G       Dim dt As DataTable = ds.Tables("Faculty")
        Dim fRow As IEnumerable(Of DataRow) = dt.AsEnumerable

H       Dim FacultyID As String = (From fi In fRow
                                   Where fi.Field(Of String)("faculty_name").Equals("Ying Bai")
                                   Select fi.Field(Of String)(dt.Columns(0))).Single()

I       Console.WriteLine("The Selected FacultyID is: " & FacultyID)
J       oraConnection.Close()

K       Console.WriteLine("Press any key to continue...")
        Console.ReadKey()
    End Sub

    End Module
```

Figure 4.38 The codes for the example project DataRowFieldLINQ.

B) An Oracle query string is created to query all columns from the Faculty data table in the DataSet. Also all Oracle data components are created in this part including a non-OleDb data component, DataSet.

C) The connection string is declared since we need to use it to connect to our sample database CSE_DEPT that is developed with Oracle 18c XE.

D) The Connection object oraConnection is initialized with the connection string and a connection is executed by calling the Open() method. Regularly, a Try . . .Catch block should be used for this connection operation to catch up any possible exception. Here, we skip it since we try to make this connection coding simple.

E) The Command object is initialized with Connection, CommandType, and CommandText properties.

F) The initialized Command object is assigned to the SelectCommand property of the DataAdapter and the DataSet is filled with the Fill() method. The point is that only a single table, Faculty, is filled in this operation.

G) A single DataTable object, Faculty, is created and a DataRow object fRow is built based on the Faculty table with a casting (Of DataRow).

H) The query is created and executed with the Field() method to pick up a single column, faculty_id that is the first column in the Faculty table. The first prototype of the Field() method is used for this query. You can use any one of six prototypes if you like to replace this one. The SQO method Single() is also used in this query to indicate that we only need to retrieve a single column's value from this row.

I) The obtained faculty_id is displayed using the Console.WriteLine() method.

J) The database connection is closed after this query is done.

K) These two coding lines enable this console project to be run in the Debugging mode.

Now you can build and run this project to test the functionality of querying a single column from a DataRow object. Click the **Debug|Start Debugging** menu item to run the project. The desired faculty_id will be obtained and displayed in this console window.

A completed Visual Basic.NET Console App project **DataRowFieldLINQ Project** can be found from the folder **Class DB Projects\Chapter 4\DataRowFieldLINQ Solution** that is located under the **Students** folder at the Wiley ftp site (refer to Figure 1.2 in Chapter 1).

Before we can finished this section, we want to show users another example to illustrate how to modify a column's value using the SetField() method via the DataRow object.

Open Visual Studio.NET 2019 and create a blank Solution **DataRowSetFieldLINQ Solution** and add a new Visual Basic.NET Console App (.NET Framework) project **DataRowSetFieldLINQ Project**. Change the File Name property from **Module1.vb** to **DataRowSetFieldLINQ.vb** in the Solution Explorer window.

Add two references, Devart.Data and Devart.Data.Oracle, into the project. Open the code window and enter the codes shown in Figure 4.39 into this window.

The codes between steps **A** and **B** are identical with those we developed for our last project DataRwoFieldLINQ Project. Refer to that project to get more details for these codes and their functionalities. Let's take a closer look at this piece of codes to see how it works.

A) The namespace, **Devart.Data.Oracle**, must be added into the namespace declaration section since we need to use some Oracle data components, such as DataAdapter, Command, and Connection, to access to our sample database to perform some data actions.

B) A LINQ to DataSet query is created with the Field() method via DataRow object. This query should return a complete data row from the Faculty table.

C) The AcceptChanges() method is executed to allow the DataRow object to accept the current value of each DataColumn object in the Faculty table as the original version of the value for that column. This method is very important and there would be no original version of the DataColumn object's values without this method.

D) Now we call SetField() method to set up a new value to the column faculty_name in the Faculty table. This new name will work as the current version of this DataColumn object's value. The second prototype of this method is used here and you can try to use any one of other two prototypes if you like.

E) The Console.WriteLine() method is executed to display both original and the current values of the DataColumn object faculty_name in the Faculty table.

F) The database connection is closed after this query is done.

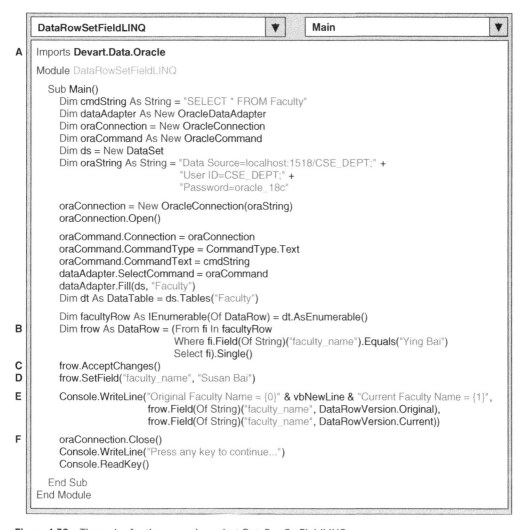

```vb
DataRowSetFieldLINQ                          Main

A   Imports Devart.Data.Oracle

    Module DataRowSetFieldLINQ

        Sub Main()
            Dim cmdString As String = "SELECT * FROM Faculty"
            Dim dataAdapter As New OracleDataAdapter
            Dim oraConnection = New OracleConnection
            Dim oraCommand As New OracleCommand
            Dim ds = New DataSet
            Dim oraString As String = "Data Source=localhost:1518/CSE_DEPT;" +
                             "User ID=CSE_DEPT;" +
                             "Password=oracle_18c"

            oraConnection = New OracleConnection(oraString)
            oraConnection.Open()

            oraCommand.Connection = oraConnection
            oraCommand.CommandType = CommandType.Text
            oraCommand.CommandText = cmdString
            dataAdapter.SelectCommand = oraCommand
            dataAdapter.Fill(ds, "Faculty")
            Dim dt As DataTable = ds.Tables("Faculty")

            Dim facultyRow As IEnumerable(Of DataRow) = dt.AsEnumerable()
B           Dim frow As DataRow = (From fi In facultyRow
                             Where fi.Field(Of String)("faculty_name").Equals("Ying Bai")
                             Select fi).Single()
C           frow.AcceptChanges()
D           frow.SetField("faculty_name", "Susan Bai")

E           Console.WriteLine("Original Faculty Name = {0}" & vbNewLine & "Current Faculty Name = {1}",
                             frow.Field(Of String)("faculty_name", DataRowVersion.Original),
                             frow.Field(Of String)("faculty_name", DataRowVersion.Current))

F           oraConnection.Close()
            Console.WriteLine("Press any key to continue...")
            Console.ReadKey()
        End Sub
    End Module
```

Figure 4.39 The codes for the example project DataRowSetFieldLINQ.

Now you can build and run the project to test the functionality of the method SetField(). Click on the **Debug|Start Debugging** menu item to run the project. You can find that both the original and the current version of the DataColumn object faculty_name are retrieved and displayed in the console window.

A completed Visual Basic.NET Console App project **DataRowSetFieldLINQ Project** can be found from the folder **Class DB Projects\Chapter 4\DataRowSetFieldLINQ Solution** that is located under the **Students** folder at the Wiley ftp site (refer to Figure 1.2 in Chapter 1).

4.5.3   Operations to DataTable Objects

Besides the DataRow operators defined in the DataRowExtensions class, there are some other extension methods that can be used to work for the DataTable class defined in the DataTableExtensions class.

Extension methods enable you to "add" methods to existing types without creating a new derived type, recompiling, or otherwise modifying the original type. Extension methods are a special kind of static method, but they are called as if they were instance methods on the extended type. For client code written in Visual Basic, there is no apparent difference between calling an extension method and the methods that are actually defined in a type.

The most common extension methods are the LINQ SQOs that add query functionality to the existing IEnumerable and IEnumerable(Of T) types. To use the SQOs, first bring them into scope with an Imports System.Linq directive. Then any type that implements IEnumerable(Of T) appears to have instance methods. You can see these additional methods in IntelliSense statement completion when you type a dot operator after an instance of an IEnumerable(Of T) type such as List(Of T) or Array.

Two extension methods defined in the DataTableExtensions class, AsEnumerable(), and CopyToDataTable(), are widely implemented in most data-driven applications. Because of the space limitation, we only give a brief discussion about the first method in this section.

The functionality of the extension method AsEnumerable() is to convert and return a sequence of type IEnumerable(Of DataRow) from a DataTable object. Some readers may have already noticed that we have used this method in quite a few example projects in the previous sections. For example, in the example projects DataRowFieldLINQ and DataRowSetFieldLINQ we discussed in the last section, you can find this method and its functionality. Refer to Figures 4.38 and 4.39 to get a clear picture about how to use this method to return a DataRow object.

4.6   LINQ to Entities

As we mentioned in the introduction to LINQ section, LINQ to Entities belongs to LINQ to ADO. NET and it is a subcomponent of LINQ to ADO.NET.

LINQ to Entities queries are performed under the control of the ADO.NET 4.3 Entity Framework (ADO.NET 4.3 EF6) and ADO.NET 4.0 Entity Framework Tools (ADO.NET 4.3 EFT). ADO.NET 4.3 EF6 enables developers to work with data in the form of domain-specific objects and properties, such as customers and customer addresses, without having to think about the underlying database tables and columns where this data is stored. To access and implement ADO.NET 4.3 EF6 and ADO. NET 4.3 EFT, developers need to understand the Entity Data Model (EDM) that is a core of ADO. NET 4.3 EF6.LINQ allows developers to formulate set-based queries in their application code, without having to use a separate query language. Through the Object Services infrastructure of Entity Framework, ADO.NET exposes a common conceptual view of data, including relational data, as objects in the .NET environment. This makes the object layer an ideal target for LINQ support.

This LINQ technology, LINQ to Entities, allows developers to create flexible, strongly typed queries against the Entity Framework object context using LINQ expressions and the LINQ SQOs directly from the development environment. The queries are expressed in the programming language itself and not as string literals embedded in the application code, as is usually the case in applications written on the Microsoft .NET Framework 4.0. Syntax errors as well as errors in member names and data types will be caught by the compiler and reported at compile time, reducing the potential for type problems between the EDM and the application.

LINQ to Entities queries use the Object Services infrastructure. The ObjectContext class is the primary class for interacting with an EDM as CLR objects. The developer constructs a generic ObjectQuery instance through the ObjectContext. The ObjectQuery generic class represents a query that returns an instance or collection of typed entities. The returned entity objects are updatable and are located in the object context. This is also true for entity objects that are returned as members of anonymous types.

4.6.1   The Object Services Component

Object Services is a component of the Entity Framework that enables you to query, insert, update, and delete data, expressed as strongly typed CLR objects that are instances of entity types. Object Services supports both LINQ and Entity SQL queries against types defined in an EDM. Object Services materializes returned data as objects and propagates object changes back to the persisted data store. It also provides facilities for tracking changes, binding objects to controls, and handling concurrency. Object Services is implemented by classes in the System.Data.Objects and System. Data.Objects. DataClasses namespaces.

4.6.2   The ObjectContext Component

The ObjectContext class encapsulates a connection between the .NET Framework and the database. This class serves as a gateway for Create, Read, Update, and Delete operations, and it is the primary class for interacting with data in the form of objects that are instances of entity types defined in an EDM. An instance of the ObjectContext class encapsulates the following:

- A connection to the database, in the form of an EntityConnection object.
- Metadata that describes the model, in the form of a MetadataWorkspace object.
- An ObjectStateManager object that manages objects persisted in the cache.

The Entity Framework tools consume a Conceptual Schema Definition Language (CSDL) file from a relational database and generate the object-layer code. This code is used to work with entity data as objects and to take advantage of Object Services functionality. This generated code includes the following data classes:

- A class that represents the EntityContainer for the model and is derived from the ObjectContext;
- Classes that represent entities and inherit from the EntityObject.

4.6.3   The ObjectQuery Component

The ObjectQuery generic class represents a query that returns a collection of zero or more typed entities. An object query always belongs to an existing object context. This context provides the connection and metadata information that is required to compose and execute the query.

4.6.4 LINQ to Entities Flow of Execution

Queries against the Entity Framework are represented by command tree queries, which execute against the object context. LINQ to Entities converts LINQ to command tree queries, executes the queries against the Entity Framework, and returns objects that can be used by both the Entity Framework and LINQ. The following is the process for creating and executing a LINQ to Entities query:

1) Construct an ObjectQuery instance from ObjectContext.
2) Compose a LINQ to Entities query in Visual Basic using the ObjectQuery instance.
3) LINQ SQOs and expressions in query are converted to command trees.
4) The query, in command tree representation, is executed against the data store. Any exceptions thrown on the data store during execution are passed directly up to the client.
5) Query results are materialized back to the client.

4.6.4.1 Construct an ObjectQuery Instance

The ObjectQuery generic class represents a query that returns a collection of zero or more typed entities. An object query is typically constructed from an existing object context, instead of being manually constructed, and always belongs to that object context. This context provides the connection and metadata information that is required to compose and execute the query. The ObjectQuery generic class implements the IQueryable generic interface whose builder methods enable LINQ to be incrementally built.

4.6.4.2 Compose a LINQ to Entities Query

Instances of the ObjectQuery generic class, which implements the generic IQueryable interface, serve as the data source for LINQ to Entities queries. In a query, you specify exactly the information that you want to retrieve from the data source. A query can also specify how that information should be sorted, grouped, and shaped before it is returned. In LINQ, a query is stored in a variable. This query variable takes no action and returns no data; it only stores the query information. After you create a query you, must execute that query to retrieve any data.

LINQ to Entities queries can be composed in two different syntaxes: query expression syntax and method-based query syntax. We have provided a very detailed discussion about the query expression syntax and method-based query syntax with real example codes in Sections 4.5.1.1 and 4.5.1.2 in this chapter. Refer to those sections to get a clear picture for these two syntaxes.

4.6.4.3 Convert the Query to Command Trees

To execute a LINQ to Entities query against the Entity Framework, the LINQ must be converted to a command tree representation that can be executed against the Entity Framework.

LINQ to Entities queries are comprised of LINQ SQOs (such as Select, Where, and Order By) and expressions. LINQ SQOs are not defined by a class but rather are static methods on a class. In LINQ, expressions can contain anything allowed by types within the System.Expressions namespace and, by extension, anything that can be represented in a lambda function. This is a superset of the expressions that are allowed by the Entity Framework, which are by definition restricted to operations allowed on the database, and supported by ObjectQuery.

In the Entity Framework, both operators and expressions are represented by a single type hierarchy, which are then placed in a command tree. The command tree is used by the Entity Framework to execute the query. If the LINQ cannot be expressed as a command tree, an exception

```
Dim FacultyInfo As              (Of String) = From fi In Faculties
                                Where fi.faculty_id = "B78880"
                                Select fi.faculty_name
```

Figure 4.40   An example of expression used in LINQ to Entities.

will be thrown when the query is being converted. The conversion of LINQ to Entities queries involves two subconversions: the conversion of the SQOs and the conversion of the expressions. In general, expressions in LINQ to Entities are evaluated on the server, so the behavior of the expression should not be expected to follow CLR semantics.

An example of an expression used in LINQ to Entities is shown in Figure 4.40.

4.6.4.4   Execute the Query

After the LINQ is created by the user, it is converted to a representation that is compatible with the Entity Framework (in the form of command trees), which is then executed against the store. At query execution time, all query expressions (or components of the query) are evaluated on the client or on the server. This includes expressions that are used in result materialization or entity projections.

A query expression can be executed in two ways. LINQ are executed each time the query variable is iterated over, not when the query variable is created; this is referred to as deferred execution. The query can also be forced to execute immediately, which is useful for caching query results. The following example shown in Figure 4.41 uses **Select** to return all the rows from Faculty and display the faculty names. Iterating over the query variable in the For Each loop causes the query to execute.

When a LINQ to Entities query is executed, some expressions in the query might be executed on the server and some parts might be executed locally on the client. Client-side evaluation of an expression takes place before the query is executed on the server. If an expression is evaluated on the client, the result of that evaluation is substituted for the expression in the query, and the query is then executed on the server. Because queries are executed on the data store, the data store configuration overrides the behavior specified in the client. Null value handling and numerical precision are examples of this. Any exceptions thrown during query execution on the server are passed directly up to the client.

4.6.4.5   Materialize the Query

Materialization is the process of returning query results back to the client as CLR types. InLINQ to Entities, query results data records are never returned; there is always a backing CLR type, defined

```
Dim faculties As ObjectQuery(Of Faculty) = cse_dept.Faculty

Dim FacultyNames As              (Of String) = From f In faculties
                                               Select f.faculty_name
            .WriteLine("Faculty Names:")
For Each fName In FacultyNames
            .WriteLine(fName)
Next
```

Figure 4.41   An example of executing the query.

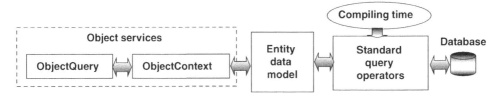

Figure 4.42 A simplified structure of LINQ to Entities.

by the user or by the Entity Framework, or generated by the compiler (anonymous types). All object materialization is performed by the Entity Framework. Any errors that result from an inability to map between the Entity Framework and the CLR will cause exceptions to be thrown during object materialization.

Query results are usually returned as one of the following:

- A collection of zero or more typed entity objects or a projection of complex types in the EDM.
- CLR types supported by the EDM.
- Inline collections.
- Anonymous types.
- IGrouping instances.
- IQueryable instances.

A simplified structure of LINQ to Entities is shown in Figure 4.42.

We have provided a very detailed discussion about the structure and components used in LINQ to Entities query; next, we need to illustrate these using some examples.

4.6.5 Implementation of LINQ to Entities

In order to use LINQ to Entities query to perform data actions against databases, one needs to have a clear picture about the infrastructure and fully understanding about components used in LINQ to Entities. The ADO.NET Entity Framework 6.0 and ADO.NET 4.3 Entity Data Model (EDM) include the Entity Data Model Wizard, Entity Data Model Designer, and Entity Model Browser. The EDM is used to provide a template or container to cover all entities and components used to connect, access, and implement data to the selected data source. The Model Designer provides a graphical user interface to enable users to design, set up, or review relationships among data tables with a model view. The Model Browser can be used to as a tool to enable users to create a new or open an existed entity model and browse or design schemas for the selected data source.

4.7 LINQ to XML

LINQ to XML was developed with LINQ over XML in mind and takes advantage of SQOs and adds query extensions specific to XML. LINQ to XML is a modernized in-memory XML programming API designed to take advantage of the latest .NET Framework language innovations. It provides both DOM and XQuery/XPath like functionality in a consistent programming experience across the different LINQ-enabled data access technologies.

There are two major perspectives for thinking about and understanding LINQ to XML. From one perspective, you can think of LINQ to XML as a member of the LINQ Project family of technologies with LINQ to XML providing an XML LINQ capability along with a consistent query experience for objects, relational database (LINQ to SQL, LINQ to DataSet, and LINQ to Entities), and other data access technologies as they become LINQ-enabled.

From another perspective, you can think of LINQ to XML as a full feature in-memory XML programming API comparable to a modernized, redesigned Document Object Model (DOM) XML Programming API plus a few key features from XPath and XSLT.

LINQ to XML is designed to be a lightweight XML programming API. This is true from both a conceptual perspective, emphasizing a straightforward, easy to use programming model, and from a memory and performance perspective. Its public data model is aligned as much as possible with the W3C XML Information Set.

4.7.1 LINQ to XML Class Hierarchy

First, let's have a global picture about the LINQ to XML Class Hierarchy that is shown in Figure 4.43. The following important points should be noticed when study this class hierarchy:

1) Although XElement is low in the class hierarchy, it is the fundamental class in LINQ to XML. XML trees are generally made up of a tree of XElements. XAttributes are name/value pairs associated with an XElement. XDocuments are created only if necessary, such as to hold a DTD or top-level XML processing instruction (XProcessingInstruction). All other XNodes can only be leaf nodes under an XElement, or possibly an XDocument (if they exist at the root level).
2) XAttribute and XNode are peers derived from a common base class XObject. XAttributes are not XNodes because XML attributes are really name value pairs associated with an XML element not nodes in the XML tree. Contrast this with W3C DOM.
3) XText and XCData are exposed in this version of LINQ to XML, but as discussed above, it is best to think of them as a semi-hidden implementation detail except when exposing text nodes is necessary. As a user, you can get back the value of the text within an element or attribute as a string or other simple value.
4) The only XNode that can have children is an XContainer, meaning either an XDocument or XElement. An XDocument can contain an XElement (the root element), an XDeclaration, an XDocumentType, or an XProcessingInstruction. An XElement can contain another XElement, an XComment, an XProcessingInstruction, and text (which can be passed in a variety of formats but will be represented in the XML tree as text).

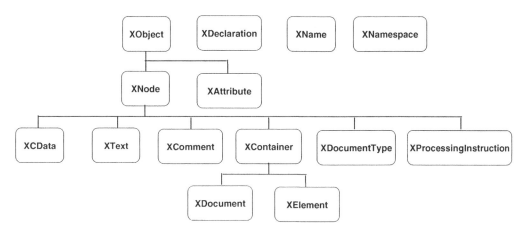

Figure 4.43 The LINQ to XML class hierarchy.

In addition to this class hierarchy, some other important components applied in XML also play key roles in LINQ to XML. One of them is the XML names.

XML names, often a complex subject in XML programming APIs, are represented simply in LINQ to XML. An XML name is represented by an XNamespace object (which encapsulates the XML namespace URI) and a local name. An XML namespace serves the same purpose that a namespace does in your .NET Framework-based programs, allowing you to uniquely qualify the names of your classes. This helps ensure that you do not run into a name conflict with other users or built-in names. When you have identified an XML namespace, you can choose a local name that needs to be unique only within your identified namespace.

4.7.2   Manipulate XML Elements

LINQ to XML provides a full set of methods for manipulating XML. You can insert, delete, copy, and update XML content. Before we can continue to discuss these data actions, first we need to illustrate how to create a sample XML element file using LINQ to XML.

4.7.2.1   Creating XML from Scratch

LINQ to XML provides a powerful approach to creating XML elements. This is referred to as functional construction. Functional construction lets you create all or part of your XML tree in a single statement. For example, to create a facultiesXElement, you could use the following code that is shown in Figure 4.44.

By indenting, the XElement constructor resembles the structure of the underlying XML. Functional construction is enabled by an XElement constructor that takes a params object. An example of the Functional construction is shown below:

```
public XElement(XName faculty_name, params object[] contents)
```

The contents parameter is extremely flexible, supporting any type of object that is a legitimate child of an XElement. Parameters can be any of the following:

- A *string,* which is added as text content. This is the recommended pattern to add a string as the value of an element; the LINQ to XML implementation will create the internal XText node.
- An XText, which can have either a string or CData value, added as child content. This is mainly useful for CData values; using a *string* is simpler for ordinary string values.
- An XElement, which is added as a child element.
- An XAttribute, which is added as an attribute.
- An XProcessingInstruction or XComment, which is added as child content.
- An IEnumerable, which is enumerated, and these rules are applied recursively.

```
Dim faculties As XElement = New XElement("faculties",
                    New XElement("faculty",
                    New XElement("faculty_name", "Patrick Tones"),
                    New XElement("phone", "750-378-0144"),
                    New XElement("title", "Associate Professor"),
                    New XElement("office", "MTC-387"),
                    New XElement("college", "Main University"),
                    New XElement("email", "ptones@college.edu"),
                    New XElement("faculty_id", "P68042")))
```

Figure 4.44   A sample XML file created using LINQ to XML.

```
......
    Dim qty As                = New            ("quantity", GetQuantity())
......
Public Function GetQuantity() As Integer
        Return 55
End Function
```

Figure 4.45 A sample functional construction.

- Anything else, ToString() is called and the result is added as text content.
- *null*, which is ignored.

The term CDATA, meaning *character data*, is used for distinct, but related purposes in the markup languages SGML and XML. The term indicates that a certain portion of the document is general *character data*, rather than noncharacter data or character data with a more specific, limited structure.

In the above example showing functional construction, a string ("Patrick Tones") is passed into the faculty_name XElement constructor. This could have been a variable (for example, new XElement ("faculty_name," facultyName)), it could have been a different type besides string (for example, new XElement ("quantity," 55)), and it could have been the result of a function call like one that is shown in Figure 4.45.

It could also have even been an IEnumerable**(Of** XElement**)**. For example, a common scenario is to use a query within a constructor to create the inner XML. The code shown in Figure 4.46 reads faculties from an array of Person objects into a new XML element faculties. Notice how the inner body of the XML, the repeating faculty element, and, for each faculty, the repeating phone were generated by queries that return an IEnumerable.

When an objective of your program is to create an XML output, functional construction lets you begin with the end in mind. You can use functional construction to shape your goal output document and either create the subtree of XML items inline or call out to functions to do the work.

Functional construction is instrumental in *transforms*, which belongs to XML Transformation. Transformation is a key usage scenario in XML, and functional construction is well suited for this task.

Now let's use this sample XML file to discuss the data manipulations using LINQ to XML.

```
Class
    Public faculty_name As String
    Public PhoneNumbers As String()
End Class
Sub Main()

Dim persons As          () = {New          With {.faculty_name = "Patrick Tones", .PhoneNumbers = {"750-555-0144",
                             "750-555-0145"}}, New        With {.faculty_name = "Gretchen Rivas", .PhoneNumbers =
                             {"750-555-0163"}}}
Dim faculties As          = New            ("faculties", From f In persons
                                                Select New        ("faculty",
                                                New        ("fname", f.faculty_name),
                                                From p In f.PhoneNumbers
                                                Select New        ("phone", p)))
         .WriteLine(faculties)
End Sub
```

Figure 4.46 A sample query using LINQ to XML.

```
A    Dim mobilePhone As XElement = New XElement("phone", "750-555-0168")
         faculty.Add(mobilePhone)

B        Dim mobilePhone As XElement = New XElement("phone", "750-555-0168")
         Dim firstPhone As XElement = faculty.Element("phone")
         firstPhone.AddAfterSelf(mobilePhone)

C        Dim mobilePhone As XElement = New XElement("phone", "750-555-0168")
         Console.WriteLine(mobilePhone.Parent)      'will print out null

D    faculty.Add(mobilePhone)
         Console.WriteLine(mobilePhone.Parent)      'will print out faculty

E    faculty2.Add(mobilePhone)

F    faculty2.Add(New XElement(mobilePhone))
```

Figure 4.47   Some sample codes of using LINQ to XML to insert XML.

4.7.2.2   Insert XML

You can easily add content to an existing XML tree. To add another phoneXElement, one can use the **Add()** method that is shown in section **A** in Figure 4.47.

This code fragment will add the mobilePhone XElement as the *last* child of faculty. If you want to add to the beginning of the children, you can use AddFirst(). If you want to add the child in a specific location, you can navigate to a child before or after your target location by using AddBeforeSelf() or AddAfterSelf(). For example, if you wanted mobilePhone to be the second phone, you could do the coding that is shown in section **B** in Figure 4.47.

Let's take a look a little deeper at what is happening behind the scenes when adding an element child to a parent element. When you first create an XElement, it is *unparented*. If you check its Parent property you will get back null, which is shown in section **C** in Figure 4.47.

When you use the Add() method to add this child element to the parent, LINQ to XML checks to see if the child element is unparented, if so, LINQ to XML *parents* the child element by setting the child's Parent property to the XElement that Add() was called on. Section **D** in Figure 4.47 shows this situation.

This is a very efficient technique which is extremely important since this is the most common scenario for constructing XML trees.

To add mobile Phone to another faculty, such as faculty2, refer to the codes shown in section **E** in Figure 4.47.

Again, LINQ to XML checks to see if the child element is parented. In this case, the child is already parented. If the child is already parented, LINQ to XML clones the child element under subsequent parents. This situation can be illustrated by the codes that are shown in section **F** in Figure 4.47.

4.7.2.3   Update XML

To update XML, you can navigate to the XElement whose contents you want to replace and then use the ReplaceNodes() method. For example, if you wanted to change the phone number of the first phone XElement of a faculty, you could do the codes that are shown in section **A** in Figure 4.48.

The method SetElement() is designed to work on simple content. With the SetElement(), you can operate on the parent. For example, we could have performed the same update we

A	faculty.Element("phone").ReplaceNodes("750-555-0155")
B	faculty.SetElement("phone", "750-555-0155")
C	faculty.SetElement("office", "MTC-119")
D	faculty.SetElement("office", **null**)

Figure 4.48   Some sample codes of using LINQ to XML to update XML.

demonstrated above on the first phone number using the code that is shown in section **B** in Figure 4.48.

The results would be identical. If there had been no phone numbers, an XElement named **"phone"** would have been added under faculty. For example, you might want to add an office to the faculty. If an office is already there, you can update it. If it does not exist, you can insert it. This situation is shown in section **C** in Figure 4.48.

Also, if you use SetElement() with a value of **null**, the selected XElement will be deleted. You can remove the office element completely using the code that is shown in section **D** in Figure 4.48. Attributes have a symmetric method called SetAttribute(), which has the similar functionality as SetElement().

4.7.2.4   Delete XML

To delete XML elements, navigate to the content you want to delete and call the Remove() method. For example, if you want to delete the first phone number for a faculty, enter the following code that is shown in section **A** in Figure 4.49.

The Remove() method also works over an IEnumerable, so you could delete all of the phone numbers for a faculty in one call that is shown in section **B** in Figure 4.49.

You can also remove all of the content from an XElement using the RemoveNodes() method. For example, you could remove the content of the first faculty's first office with the statement that is shown in section **C** in Figure 4.49. Another way to remove an element is to *set* it to **null** using the SetElement() method, which we talked about in the last section, Update XML. An example code is shown in section **D** in Figure 4.49.

4.7.3   Manipulate XML Attributes

There is substantial symmetry between working with XElement and XAttribute classes. However, in the LINQ to XML class hierarchy, XElement and XAttribute are quite distinct and do not derive from a common base class. This is because XML attributes are not nodes in the XML tree; they are unordered name/value pairs associated with an XML element. LINQ to XML makes this distinction, but in practice, working with XAttribute is quite similar to working with XElement. Considering the nature of an XML attribute, where they diverge is understandable.

A	faculty.Element("phone").Remove()
B	faculty.Elements("phone").Remove()
C	faculties.Element("faculty").Element("office").RemoveNodes()
D	faculty.SetElement("phone", **null**)

Figure 4.49   Some sample codes of using LINQ to XML to delete XML.

```
Dim Faculty = <faculties>
    <faculty>
      <faculty_name>Patrick Tones</faculty_name>
      <phone type="home">750-555-0144</phone>
      <phone type="work">750-555-0145</phone>
    </faculty>
```

Figure 4.50 A sample XML attributes.

```
Dim faculty As XElement = New XElement("faculty",
                    New XElement("faculty_name", "Patrick Tones"),
                    New XElement("phone",
                    New XAttribute("type", "home"), "750-555-0144"),
                    New XElement("phone", New XAttribute("type", "work"), "750-555-0145"))
```

Figure 4.51 A sample code to create an XAttribut.

4.7.3.1 Add XML Attributes

Adding an XAttribute is very similar to adding a simple XElement. In the sample XML that is shown in Figure 4.50, notice that each phone number has a *type* attribute that states whether this is a home, work, or mobile phone number.

You create an XAttribute using functional construction the same way you would create an XElement with a simple type. To create a faculty using functional construction, enter the codes that are shown in Figure 4.51.

Just as you use the SetElement() method to update, add, or delete elements with simple types, you can do the same using the SetAttribute(XName, object) method on XElement. If the attribute exists, it will be updated. If the attribute does not exist, it will be added. If the value of the objectis **null**, the attribute will be deleted.

4.7.3.2 Get XML Attributes

The primary method for accessing an XAttribute is by using the Attribute(XName) method on XElement. For example, to use the *type* attribute to obtain the contact's home phone number, one can use the piece of codes that are shown in section **A** in Figure 4.52.

Notice that how the Attribute(XName) works similarly to the Element(XName) method. Also, notice that there are some differences between the Attribute() and the SetAttributeValue() methods.

```
A   For Each p In faculty.Elements("phone")
        If p.Attribute("type") = "home" Then
            Console.Write("Home phone is: " & p.ToString)
        End If
    Next

B   faculty.Elements("phone").First().Attribute("type").Remove()

C   faculty.Elements("phone").First().SetAttributeValue("type", txtBox.Value)
```

Figure 4.52 A sample code to get and delete an XAttribut.

4.7.3.3 Delete XML Attributes

If you want to delete an attribute, you can use Remove() or SetAttributeValue(XName, Object. Value) method passing null as the value of object. For example, to delete the type attribute from the first phone using the Remove() method, use the code that is shown in section **B** in Figure 4.52.

Alternatively you can use the SetAttributeValue() method with a DBNull.Value argument to perform this deleting operation. An example code is shown in section **C** in Figure 4.52.

We have provided a very detailed discussion about the basic components on manipulating XML elements and attributes; now, let's go a little deep on the query XML with LINQ to XML.

4.7.4 Query XML with LINQ to XML

The major differentiator for LINQ to XML and other in-memory XML programming APIs is LINQ. LINQ provides a consistent query experience across different data models as well as the ability to mix and match data models within a single query. This section describes how to use LINQ with XML. The following section contains a few examples of using LINQ across data models.

SQOs form a complete query language for IEnumerable(Of T). SQOs show up as extension methods on any object that implements IEnumerable(Of T) and can be invoked like any other method. This approach, calling query methods directly, can be referred to as explicit dot notation. In addition to SQOs are query expressions for five common query operators:

- Where
- Select
- SelectMany
- OrderBy
- GroupBy

Query expressions provide an ease-of-use layer on top of the underlying explicit dot notation similar to the way that for each is an ease-of-use mechanism that consists of a call to GetEnumerator() and a While loop. When working with XML, you will probably find both approaches useful. An orientation of the explicit dot notation will give you the underlying principles behind XML LINQ and help you to understand how query expressions simplify things.

The LINQ to XML integration with LINQ is apparent in three ways:

1) Leveraging SQOs
2) Using XML query extensions
3) Using XML transformation

The first is common with any other LINQ enabled data access technology and contributes to a consistent query experience. The last two provide XML-specific query and transform features.

4.7.4.1 Standard Query Operators and XML

LINQ to XML fully leverages SQOs in a consistent manner exposing collections that implement the IEnumerable interface. We have provided a very detailed discussion about the SQOs in Sections 4.1.2~4.1.4 in this chapter. Review those sections for details on how to use SQOs. In this section, we will cover two scenarios that occasionally arise when using SQOs.

First, let's create a XElement with multiple elements that can be queried using a single Select SQO. Enter the codes that are shown in Figure 4.53 to create this sample XElement.

```
Dim faculties = <Faculties>
                <!-- contact -->
                <faculty_name>Patrick Tones</faculty_name>
                <phone type="home">750-555-0144</phone>
                <phone type="work">750-555-0145</phone>
                <office>MTC-319</office>
                <title>Associate Professor</title>
                <email>ptones@college.edu</email>
                <!-- contact -->
                <faculty_name>Greg River</faculty_name>
                <office>MTC-330</office>
                <title>Assistant Professor</title>
                <email>griver@college.edu</email>
                <!-- contact -->
                <faculty_name>Scott Money</faculty_name>
                <phone type="home">750-555-0134</phone>
                <phone type="mobile">750-555-0177</phone>
                <office>MTC-335</office>
                <title>Professor</title>
                <email>smoney@college.edu</email>
            </Faculties>
```

Figure 4.53 A sample code to create an XElement.

```
Dim f As New XElement("Faculties",
                From c In faculties.Elements("faculty")
                Select New Object() _
                {
                  New XComment("faculty"),
                  New XElement("faculty_name", c.Element("faculty_name")), c.Elements("phone"),
                  New XElement("office", c.Element("office"))
                })
```

Figure 4.54 A sample code to perform the query to an XElement.

In this XElement, the faculty information is directly created under the root <faculties> element rather than under each separate <faculty> elements. In this way, we flatten out our faculty list and make it simple to be queried.

To use the SQO Select to perform the LINQ to XML query, you can use a piece of sample codes that are shown in Figure 4.54. Notice that we used an array initializer to create the sequence of children that will be placed directly under the faculty element.

4.7.4.2 XML Query Extensions

XML-specific query extensions provide you with the query operations you would expect when working in an XML tree data structure. These XML-specific query extensions are analogous to the XPath axes. For example, the Elements() method is equivalent to the XPath* (star) operator. The following sections describe each of the XML-specific query extensions.

The Elements query operator returns the child elements for each XElement in a sequence of XElements (IEnumerable(Of XElement)). For example, to get the child elements for every faculty in the faculty list, you could do the following:

```
ForEach fiAsXElementIn faculties.Elements("Faculties").Elements()
Console.WriteLine(fi)
Next
```

Note that the two Elements() methods used in this example are different, although they do identical things. The first Elements is calling the XElement method Elements(), which returns an IEnumerable(Of XObject) containing the child elements in the single XElement faculties. The second Elements() method is defined as an extension method on IEnumerable(Of XObject). It returns a sequence containing the child elements of every XElement in the list.

If you want all of the children with a particular name, you can use the Elements(XName) overload. A piece of sample codes is shown below:

```
ForEach piAsXElementIn faculties.Elements("Faculties").Elements("phone")
Console.WriteLine(pi)
Next
```

This would return all phone numbers related to all children.

4.7.4.3 Using Query Expressions with XML

There is nothing unique in the way that LINQ to XML works with query expressions so we will not repeat information in here. The following shows a few simple examples of using query expressions with LINQ to XML.

The query shown in section **A** in Figure 4.55 retrieves all of the offices from the faculties, orders them by faculty_name, and then returns them as **String** (the result of this query is IEnumerable(Of string)).

The query shown in section **B** in Figure 4.55 retrieves all faculty members from faculty that have the faculty_id that starts from B and have an area code of 750 ordered by the faculty_name. The result of this query is IEnumerable(Of XElement). Another example shown in section **C** in Figure 4.55 retrieving the students that have a GPA that is greater than the average GPA.

4.7.4.4 Using XPath and XSLT with LINQ to XML

LINQ to XML supports a set of "bridge classes" that allow it to work with existing capabilities in the System.Xml namespace, including XPath and XSLT. A point to be noticed is that System.Xml supports only the 1.0 version of these specifications in "Orcas."

Extension methods supporting XPath are enabled by referencing the System.Xml.XPath namespace by adding this namespace typing: Imports System.Xml.XPath in the namespace declaration section on the code window of each project.

```
A    Dim query = From fi In faculties.Elements("faculty")
                 Where fi.Element("office") = "MTC-3.*"
                 Order By f.Element("faculty_name")
                 Select fi.Element("faculty_name")

B    Dim query = From fi In faculties.Elements("faculty"), p In fi.Elements("phone")
                 Where fi.Element("faculty_id") = "B.*" & p.Value.StartsWith("750")
                 Order By fi.Element("faculty_name")
                 Select fi

C    Dim query = From s In students.Elements("student"), average In students.Elements("student").
                 Average(Function(x As Integer) x.Element("gpa"))
                 Where (s.Element("gpa") > average)
                 Select s
```

Figure 4.55 A sample code to perform the query using query expressions with XML.

```
Dim faculties = New XElement("Faculties",
                             From f In db.Faculties
                             Where f.faculty_id = "B*"
                             Select New XElement("Faculty",
                             New XAttribute("facultyName", f.faculty_name),
                             New XElement("Office", f.office),
                             New XElement("Title", f.title),
                             New XElement("Phone", f.phone),
                             New XElement("Email", f.email)))
Console.WriteLine(faculties)
```

Figure 4.56 A sample code to perform the query using mixing XML.

This brings into scope CreateNavigator overloads to create XpathNavigator objects, XPathEvaluate overloads to evaluate an XPath expression, and XPathSelectElement[s] overloads that work much like SelectSingleNode and XPatheXelectNodes methods in the System.Xml DOM API. To use namespace-qualified XPath expressions, it is necessary to pass in a NamespaceResolver object, just as with DOM.

For example, to display all elements with the name "phone," the following codes are used:

```
ForEach phone In faculties.XPathSelectElements("//phone")
Console.WriteLine(phone)
Next
```

Likewise, XSLT is enabled by referencing the System.Xml.Xsl namespace by typing: Imports System.Xml.Xsl in the namespace declaration section on the code window of each project. That allows you to create an XPathNavigator using the XDocumentCreateNavigator() method and pass it to the Transform() method.

4.7.4.5 Mixing XML and Other Data Models

LINQ provides a consistent query experience across different data models via SQOs and the use of lambda expressions that will be discussed in the next section. It also provides the ability to mix and match LINQ enabled data models/APIs within a single query. This section provides a simple example of two common scenarios that mix relational data with XML, using our CSE_DEPT sample database.

4.7.4.5.1 Reading from a Database to XML   Figure 4.56 shows a simple example of reading from the CSE_DEPT database (using LINQ to SQL) to retrieve the faculties from the Faculty table and then transforming them into XML.

4.7.4.5.2 Reading XML and Updating a Database   You can also read XML and put that information into a database. For this example, assume that you are getting a set of faculty members updates in XML format. For simplicity, the update records contain only the phone number changes.

First let's create a sample XML, which is shown in Figure 4.57.

To accomplish this update, you query for each facultyUpdate element and call the database to get the corresponding Faculty record. Then, you update the Faculty column with the new phone number. A piece of sample cods to fulfill this functionality is shown in Figure 4.58.

At this point, we have finished the discussion about the LINQ to XML. Next, we will have a closer look at the Visual Basic.NET language enhancement for LINQ.

```
<facultyUpdates>
  <facultyUpdate>
    <faculty_id>D55990</faculty_id>
    <phone>750-555-0103</phone>
  </facultyUpdate>
  <facultyUpdate>
    <faculty_id>E23456</faculty_id>
    <phone>750-555-0143</phone>
  </facultyUpdate>
</facultyUpdates>
```

Figure 4.57   A sample XML.

```
For Each fi In facultyUpdates.Elements("facultyUpdate")
      Dim faculty As Faculty = db.Faculties.
      First(Function(f) f.faculty_id = fi.Element("faculty_id"))
      faculty.Phone = fi.Element("phone")
Next

db.SubmitChanges()
```

Figure 4.58   A piece of sample codes to read and update database.

4.8   Visual Basic.NET Language Enhancement for LINQ

Visual Basic.NET introduces several language extensions to support the creation and use of higher-order, functional style class libraries. The extensions enable construction of compositional APIs that have equal expressive power of query languages in domains such as relational databases and XML.

Starting from Visual Basic.NET 2008, significant enhancements have been added into Visual Basic.NET, and these enhancements are mainly developed to support the LINQ. LINQ is a series of language extensions that supports data querying in a type-safe way; it was released with the Visual Studio.NET 2008.The data to be queried, which we have discussed in the previous sections in this chapter, can take the form of objects (LINQ to Objects), databases (LINQ-enabled ADO.NET, which includes LINQ to SQL, LINQ to DataSet, and LINQ to Entities), XML (LINQ to XML), and so on.

In addition to those general LINQ topics, special improvements on LINQ are made for Visual Basic.NET. The main components of these improvements include

- Lambda expressions
- Extension methods
- Implicitly typed local variables
- Query expressions

Let's have a detailed discussion for these topics one by one.

4.8.1   Lambda Expressions

Lambda expressions are a language feature that is similar in many ways to anonymous methods. If lambda expressions had been developed and implemented into the language first, there would have been no need for anonymous methods. The basic idea of using lambda expressions is that you can treat code as data. In fact, a lambda expression is a function or subroutine without a name that can be used wherever a delegate is valid. Lambda expressions can be functions or subroutines and can be single-line or multi-line. You create lambda expressions using the Function or Sub keyword, just as you create a standard function or subroutine. However, lambda expressions are included in a statement.

You can pass values from the current scope to a lambda expression. Unlike named functions, a lambda expression can be defined and executed at the same time. Anonymous methods and lambda expressions extend the range of the values to include code blocks. This concept is common in functional programming.

The syntax of lambda expressions in Visual Basic.NET can be expressed as a function or a subroutine declaration followed by an expression that can be considered as the function or subroutine body. For more complicated lambda expressions, a statement block can be followed and embedded. A simple example of lambda expression used in Visual Basic.NET looks like:

```
Dim var = Fucntion(Argument list...) function body or expression
```

where var on the left side of the function is the returned running result of the function. The Argument list contains all inputs to the function. The function body is a simple expression in most situations. This lambda expression can be read as *input Argument and output var*.

For more complicated lambda expressions, a statement block should be adopted.

The syntax of a lambda expression resembles that of a standard function or subroutine. The differences are

- A lambda expression does not have a name.
- Lambda expressions cannot have modifiers, such as Overloads or Overrides.
- Single-line lambda functions do not use an As clause to designate the return type. Instead, the type is inferred from the value that the body of the lambda expression evaluates to. For example, if the body of the lambda expression is f.office = "MTC-332", its return type is Boolean.
- In multi-line lambda functions, you can either specify a return type using an As clause or omit the As clause so that the return type is inferred. When the As clause is omitted for a multi-line lambda function, the return type is inferred to be the dominant type from all the Return statements in the multi-line lambda function. The *dominant type* is a unique type that all other types supplied to the Return statement can widen to. If this unique type cannot be determined, the dominant type is the unique type that all other types supplied to the Return statement can narrow to. If neither of these unique types can be determined, the dominant type is Object. For example, if the expressions supplied to the Return statement contain values of type Integer, Long, and Double, the resulting type is Double. Both Integer and Long widen to Double and only Double. Therefore, Double is the dominant type.
- The body of a single-line function must be an expression that returns a value, not a statement. There is no Return statement for single-line functions. The value returned by the single-line function is the value of the expression in the body of the function.
- The body of a single-line subroutine must be single-line statement.
- Single-line functions and subroutines do not include an End Function or End Sub statement.
- You can specify the data type of a lambda expression parameter using the As keyword, or the data type of the parameter can be inferred. Either all parameters must have specified data types or all must be inferred.
- Optional and Paramarray parameters are not permitted.
- Generic parameters are not permitted.

```
Dim increment1 = Function(x)  x + 1
Dim increment2 = Function(x)
                    Return x + 2
                End Function
Dim writeline1 = Sub(x) Console.WriteLine(x)
Dim writeline2 = Sub(x)
                    Console.WriteLine(x)
                End Sub
```

Figure 4.59 A piece of sample codes for lambda expressions.

Another example of using lambda expressions is shown in Figure 4.59.

For the first two lambda expressions, both are expressed using Function followed by the function body. The difference is that the first is a single-line expression but the second is a multi-line expression with the Return and End Function statements involved.

The second two lambda expressions are expressed using two subroutines, with one in a single-line and another one is multi-line expressions.

In some situations, the lambda expressions are combined with the LINQ to simplify the query operations. One example is

```
Dim faculty AsEnumerable = IEnumerable(Of Faculty).Where(faculties,
Function(f)  f.faculty_name = "Ying Bai")
```

Here, the SQO method Where() is used as a filter in this query. The input is an object with a type of faculties, and the output is a string variable. The compiler is able to infer that "f" refers to a faculty because the first parameter of the Where() method is IEnumerable(Of Faculty), such that T must, in fact, be Faculty. Using this knowledge, the compiler also verifies that Faculty has a faculty_name member. Finally, there is no returnkeyword specified. In the syntactic form, the return member is omitted but this is merely syntactic convenience. The result of the expression is still considered to be the return value.

Lambda expressions also support a more verbose syntax that allows you to specify the types explicitly as well as execute multiple statements. An example of this kind of syntax is

```
Return IEnumerable(Of Faculty).Where(faculties, (Function(Faculty f)
{id = faculty_id Return f.faculty_id = id})
```

Here, the IEnumerable(Of Faculty) class is used to allow us to access and use the static method Where() since all SQO methods are static methods defined in either Enumerable or Queryable classes.

As you know, a static method is defined as a class method and can be accessed and used by each class in which that method is defined. Is that possible for us to access a static method from an instance of that class? Generally, this will be considered as a stupid question since that is impossible. Is there any way to make it possible? The answer is maybe. To get that question answered correctly, let's go to the next topic.

4.8.2 Extension Methods

Extension methods enable developers to add custom functionality to data types that are already defined without creating a new derived type. Extension methods make it possible to write a method that can be called as if it were an instance method of the existing type.

Regularly, static methods can only be accessed and used by classes in which those static methods are defined. For example, all SQO methods, as we discussed in Sections 4.1.3 and 4.1.4, are static methods defined in either Enumerable or Queryable classes and can be accessed by those classes directly. But those static methods cannot be accessed by any instance of those classes.

When building and using extension methods, the following points should be noted:

1) An extension method can be only a Sub procedure or a Function procedure. You cannot define an extension property, field, or event. All extension methods must be marked with the extension attribute <Extension()> from the System.Runtime.CompilerServices namespace.
2) The first parameter in an extension method definition specifies which data type the method extends. When the method is run, the first parameter is bound to the instance of the data type that invokes the method.
3) Extension methods can be declared only within modules. Typically, the module in which an extension method is defined is not the same module as the one in which it is called. Instead, the module that contains the extension method is imported, if it needs to be, to bring it into scope. After the module that contains the extension method is in scope, the method can be called as if it were an ordinary instance method.
4) When an in-scope instance method has a signature that is compatible with the arguments of a calling statement, the instance method is chosen in preference to any extension method. The instance method has precedence even if the extension method is a better match.

Let's use an example to illustrate these important points and properties. Figure 4.60 shows a piece of codes that defines an instance and an extension method in the module Conversion.

In this example, both methods have the same name but different signatures. Let's have a closer look at this piece of codes to see how it works.

A) The namespace System.Runtime.CompilerServices is imported first since we need to use some extension attributes defined in that namespace.
B) First, a class ExampleClass is created with an instance method ConvertToUpper(). The first argument of this instance method is an integer. To call and execute this instance method, one must first create a new instance based on the class ExampleClass and then call that method. The second argument is a string to be returned with the uppercase when this instance method is done.
C) The extension method is declared with the different signature. The type of the first argument of this class method is Long, and the second argument is also a string to be returned as the

```
A   Imports System.Runtime.CompilerServices
    Module Conversion

B     Class ExampleClass
        'Define an instance method named ConvertToUpper.
        Public Function ConvertToUpper(ByVal m As Integer, ByVal aString As String) As String
          Console.WriteLine(vbNewLine & "Instance Method is called ")
          Return aString.ToUpper
        End Function
      End Class

C     <Extension()>
      Function ConvertToUpper(ByVal ec As ExampleClass, ByVal n As Long, ByVal aString As String) As String
        Console.WriteLine(vbNewLine & "Extension Method is called ")
        Return aString.ToUpper
      End Function

    End Module
```

Figure 4.60 An example of defining class and instance method.

```
Module VBExtensions

    Sub Main()

A       Dim exClass As New ExampleClass
        Dim input As String = "Hello"
        Dim index_ext As Long = 5
        Dim index_ins As Integer = 1

        'The following statement calls the extension method.
B       Console.WriteLine(exClass.ConvertToUpper(index_ext, input))

        'The following statement calls the instance method.
C       Console.WriteLine(exClass.ConvertToUpper(index_ins, input))

        Console.WriteLine(vbNewLine & "Press any key to exit ")
        Console.ReadKey()
    End Sub

End Module
```

Figure 4.61 An example of calling class and instance method.

uppercase when this class method is executed. To call and execute this class method, one can directly call it with the class name prefixed in front of this method.

Figure 4.61 shows a piece of codes to illustrate how to distinguish these two methods when calling them with different signatures.

As we mentioned, to call the extension methods defined in a module, a different module should be created, here the module VBExtensions is used for this purpose. Now let's use an example project to illustrate this extension calling.

Open Visual Studio.NET 2019 and create a blank Solution **VBExtensions Solution**, and add a new Console App (.NET Framework) project **VBExtensions Project**. Enter the codes shown in Figure 4.61 into the code window of this project.

Let's have a closer look at this piece of codes to see how it works.

A) An instance of the class ExampleClass, exClass, is created since we need to call the instance method ConvertToUpper() defined in that class in another module named VB_Extensions. Conversion. Also some local variables are declared here.
B) First, we try to call the extension method with the type of the first argument as a Long.
C) Then we try to call the instance method with the first argument as an integer.

Now right-click on our project **VBExtensions Project** from the Solution Explorer window and select **Add|Module** item from the popup menu to open the Add New Item wizard. Click on the **Module** item from the list and change the name in the Name: box from **Module1.vb** to **Conversion.vb**. Then click on the **Add** button to add this module into the project. Enter the codes shown in Figure 4.60 into this module code window.

Now build and run the project. The running result is shown in Figure 4.62.

In some situations, the query would become very complicated if one wants to call those static methods from any instance of those classes. To solve this complex issue, extension methods are developed to simplify the query structures and syntax.

To declare an extension method from an existing static method, just redefine that existing static method with the <Extension()> keyword. For example, to make the class method ToUpper() an

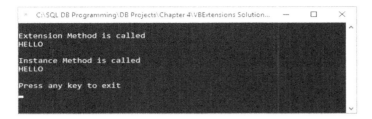

Figure 4.62 The running result of the execution of the extension method.

```
Imports System.Runtime.CompilerServices
Module Conversion

    Class ExampleClass
        'Define an instance method named ConvertToUpper.
        Public Function ConvertToUpper(ByVal m As Integer, ByVal aString As String) As String
            Console.WriteLine(vbNewLine & "Instance Method is called ")
            Return aString.ToUpper
        End Function
    End Class

    <Extension()>
    Function ConvertToUpper(ByVal ec As ExampleClass, ByVal n As Long, ByVal aString As String) As String
        Console.WriteLine(vbNewLine & "Extension Method is called ")
        Return aString.ToUpper
    End Function

    <Extension()>
    Function ToUpper(ByVal ec As ExampleClass, ByVal aString As String) As String
        Console.WriteLine(vbNewLine & "Extension ToUpper() Method is called ")
        Return aString.ToUpper
    End Function

End Module
```

A
B

Figure 4.63 Declare the class method ToUpper() to extension method.

extension method, redefine that method with the <Extension()> keyword in a module, as shown the codes that have been highlighted in bold in Figure 4.63.

Now the class method ToUpper() has been converted to an extension method and can be accessed by any instance of the class ExampleClass.

A completed project **VB Extensions Project** can be found in the folder **Class DB Projects\Chapter 4\VB Extensions Solution** that is located under the **Students** folder at the Wiley ftp site (refer to Figure 1.2 in Chapter 1).

4.8.3 Implicitly Typed Local Variables

In LINQ, there is another language feature known as implicitly typed local variables that instructs the compiler to infer the type of a local variable. Instead of explicitly specifying a type when you declare and initialize a variable, you can now enable the compiler to infer and assign the type. This is referred to as *local type inference*. Local type inference works only when you are defining a local variable inside a method body, with Option Infer set to On. On is the default for new projects in LINQ.

As you know, with the addition of anonymous types to Visual Basic.NET, a new problem becomes a main concern, which is that if a variable is being instantiated that is an unnamed type, as in an

```
Module ImpLocal

  Class faculty
     Public faculty_id As String
     Public faculty_name As String
  End Class

  Sub Main()

     faculty = New With {.faculty_id = "B78880", .faculty_name = "Ying Bai"}
     Console.WriteLine("faculty information {0}, {1}", faculty.faculty_id & ". " & faculty.faculty_name)

  End Sub
End Module
```

Figure 4.64   Declare an anonymous type variable.

```
Module ImpLocal

  Class faculty
     Public faculty_id As String
     Public faculty_name As String
  End Class

  Sub Main()

     Dim faculty = New With {.faculty_id = "B78880", .faculty_name = "Ying Bai"}
     Console.WriteLine("faculty information {0}, {1}", faculty.faculty_id & ". " & faculty.faculty_name)

  End Sub
End Module
```

Figure 4.65   Declare an anonymous type variable using implicitly typed local variable.

anonymous type, of what type variable would you assign it to? LINQ belong to strongly typed queries with two popular types: IEnumerable(Of T) and IQueryable(Of T), as we discussed at the beginning of this chapter. Figure 4.64 shows an example of this kind of variable with an anonymous type.

A compiling error will be encountered when this piece of codes to be compiled since the data type of the variable faculty is not indicated. In Visual Basic.NET language enhancement for LINQ, a new terminology, implicitly typed local variable, is developed to solve this kind of anonymous type problem. Refer to Figure 4.65, the codes written in Figure 4.64 can be rewritten as codes shown in Figure 4.65.

This time there would be no error if you compile this piece of codes since the keyword *Dim* informs the compiler to implicitly infer the variable type from the variable's initializer. In this example, the initializer for this implicitly typed variable faculty is a string collection. This means that all implicitly typed local variables are statically type checked at the compile time; therefore, an initializer is required to allow compiler to implicitly infer the type from it.

The implicitly typed local variables mean that those variables are just local within a method, for example, the faculty is valid only inside the Main() method in the previous example. It is impossible for them to escape the boundaries of a method, property, indexer, or other block because the type cannot be explicitly stated, and *Dim* is not legal for fields or parameter types.

Another important terminology applied in Visual Basic.NET language enhancement for LINQ is the object initializers. Object initializers are used in query expressions when you have to create an anonymous type to hold the results of a query. They also can be used to initialize objects of named

```
Imports VB_Extensions.ImpLocal
Module ObjInitializer

    Sub Main()

        Dim fi = New faculty With {.faculty_id = "B78880",
                                    .faculty_name = "Ying Bai"}
    End Sub

End Module
```

Figure 4.66 An example of using the object initializer.

types outside of queries. Using an object initializer, you can initialize an object in a single line without explicitly calling a constructor.

Object initializers basically allow the assignment of multiple properties or fields in a single expression. For example, a common pattern for object creation is shown in Figure 4.66.

In this example, there is no constructor of faculty that takes a faculty id and name; however, there are two properties, faculty_id and faculty_name, which can be set once an instance fi is created. Object initializers allow creating a new instance with all necessary initializations being performed at the same time as the instantiation process.

4.8.4 Query Expressions

To perform any kind of LINQ, such as LINQ to Objects, LINQ to ADO.NET, LINQ to XML, a valid query expression is needed. The query expressions implemented in Visual Basic.NET have a syntax that is closer to SQL statements and are composed of some clauses. Regularly, a query expression can be expressed in a declarative syntax similar to that of SQL or XQuery. At compile time, query syntax is converted into method calls to a LINQ provider's implementation of the SQO extension methods. Applications control which SQOs are in scope by specifying the appropriate namespace with an Imports statement.

One of the most popular query expressions is the For Each statement. As this For Each is executed, the compiler converts it into a loop with calls to methods such as GetEnumerator() and MoveNext(). The main advantage of using the For Each loop to perform the query is that it provides a significant simplicity in enumerating through arrays, sequences, and collections and return the terminal results in an easy way. A syntax of query expression is shown in Figure 4.67.

Generally, a query expression is composed of two blocks. The top block in Figure 4.67 is the *from-clause* block and the bottom block is the *query-body* block. The *from-clause* block only takes

```
Dim query_variable = From [identifier] In [data source]
                     Let [expression]
                     Where [boolean expression]
                     Order By [[expression](ascending/descending)], [optionally repeat]
                     Select [expression]
                     Group [expression] By [expression] Into [expression]

For Each  range_variable  In query_variable

    'pick up or retrieve back each element from the range_variable....

Next
```

Figure 4.67 A typical syntax of query expression.

```
Sub Main()

    Dim faculty As IEnumerable(Of Faculty) = From f In Faculty
                                             Let f.college <> "U.*"
                                             Where f.title = "Professor"
                                             Order By f.faculty_name Ascending
                                             Select f.phone, f.email
        'Execute the query to produce the results
        For Each fi In faculty
            Console.WriteLine("{0}, {1}, {2}, {3}", fi.faculty_name, fi.title, fi.phone, fi.email)
        Next

End Sub
```

Figure 4.68 A real example of query expression.

charge of the data query information (no query results), but the *query-body* block performs the real query and contains the real query results.

Refer to syntax represented in Figure 4.67, the following components should be included in a query expression:

- A query variable must be defined first in either explicitly (IEnumerable(Of T)) or implicitly (Dim) type
- A query expression can be represented in either query syntax or method syntax
- A query expression must start with a **From** clause and must end with a **Select** or **Group** clause. Between the first **From** clause and the last **Select** or **Group** clause, it can contain one or more of these optional clauses: **Where**, **Order By**, **Join**, **Let**, and even additional **From** clauses

In all LINQ (including LINQ to DataSet), all of clauses will be converted to the associated SQO methods, such as From(), Where(), OrderBy(), Join(), Let(), and Select(), as the queries are compiled. Refer to Table 4.1 in this chapter to get the most often used SQOs and their definitions.

In LINQ, a query variable is always strongly typed and it can be any variable that stores a query instead of the results of a query. More specifically, a query variable is always an enumerable type that will produce a sequence of elements when it is iterated over in a **For Each** loop or a direct call to its method IEnumerator.MoveNext().

A very detailed discussion about the query expression has been provided in Sections 4.5.1.1 and 4.5.1.2 in this chapter. Refer to those sections to get more details for this topic.

Before we can finish this chapter, a real query example implemented in our project is shown in Figure 4.68.

In fact, the Let clause is not necessary in this query block and it can be combined with the Where clause. Generally, the Let clause is used to perform some non-Boolean operations but the Where clause is used to perform Boolean operations.

So far, we have provided a detailed discussion about LINQ in Visual Basic.NET with most popular techniques and implementations. All sample projects involved in this chapter have been debugged and tested and can be used directly in real applications.

4.9 LINQ To Oracle

As we discussed in the previous sections in this chapter, LINQ provides some popular tools to help users to build and develop various projects to access and manipulate records in databases. Those popular tools include LINQ to Objects, LINQ to DataSet, LINQ to SQL, and LINQ to Entities.

Among them, only LINQ to SQL and LINQ to Entities allow users to access the real database to perform data actions. Also the LINQ to SQL and LINQ to Entities can only work for SQL databases. Thus in order to use LINQ to Oracle, we need to use some drives provided by third-party products, such as LINQ to Oracle (LinqConnect) provided by Devart and Oracle Data Access Components (ODAC) provided by Oracle, to build our LINQ to Oracle projects to access and manipulate our sample Oracle database.

In fact, we try to use the LINQ to Oracle and EDM provided by the Devart as a tool to build a fundamental end-to-end LINQ to Oracle scenario for selecting, adding, modifying, and deleting data against our sample database. As you know, LINQ to Oracle queries can perform not only the data selection but also the data insertion, updating, and deletion actions. The standard LINQ to Oracle queries include

- Select
- Insert
- Update
- Delete

To perform any of these operations or queries, we need to use entity classes and DataContext object we discussed in Section 4.6.1 in Chapter 4 to do LINQ to Oracle actions against our sample database.

Due to the space limitations, we will concentrate our discussion for this LINQ to Oracle in Section 8.6 in Chapter 8, where a detailed introduction and discussion about the LINQ to Oracle are provided, and a completed Web Application project LINQWebOracle Project is also given with detailed coding developments and step-by-step illustrations.

4.10   Chapter Summary

LINQ, which is built on .NET Frameworks 3.5, is a new technology released with Visual Studio. NET 2008 by Microsoft in 2008. LINQ is designed to query general data sources represented in different formats, such as Objects, DataSet, SQL Server database, Entities, and XML. The innovation of LINQ bridges the gap between the world of objects and the world of data.

An introduction to LINQ general programming guide is provided at the first part in this chapter. Some popular interfaces widely used in LINQ, such as IEnumerable, IEnumerable(Of T), IQueryable, and IQueryable(Of T), and SQOs including the deferred and non-deferred SQO, are discussed in that part.

An introduction to LINQ is given in the second section in this chapter. Following this introduction, a detailed discussion and analysis about the LINQ that is implemented for different data sources is provided based on a sequence listed below:

1) Architecture and Components of LINQ
2) LINQ to Objects
3) LINQ to DataSet
4) LINQ to Entities
5) LINQ to XML
6) Visual Basic.NET Language Enhancement for LINQ

Both literal introductions and actual examples are provided for each part listed above to give readers not only a general and global picture about LINQ technique applied for different data, but also practical and real feeling about the program codes developed to realize the desired functionalities.

Fifteen real projects are provided in this chapter to help readers to understand and follow up all techniques discussed in this chapter.

After finishing this chapter, readers should be able to

- Understand the basic architecture and components implemented in LINQ;
- Understand the functionalities of SQOs;
- Understand general interfaces implemented in LINQ, such as LINQ to Objects, LINQ to DataSet, LINQ to Entities, and LINQ to XML;
- Understand the Visual Basic.NET language enhancement for LINQ;
- Design and build real applications to apply LINQ to perform data actions to all different data sources;
- Develop and build applications to apply Visual Basic.NET language enhancement for LINQ to perform all different queries to data sources.

Starting from the next chapter, we will concentrate on the database programming with Visual Basic.NET using the real projects.

Homework

I. True/False Selections

_____ **1** LINQ are built based on .NET Frameworks 3.5.

_____ **2** Most popular interfaces used for LINQ are IEnumerable, IEnumerable(Of T), IQueryable, and IQueryable(Of T).

_____ **3** IEnumerable interface is used to convert data type of data source to IEnumerable(Of T) that can be implemented by LINQ.

_____ **4** IEnumerable interface is inherited from the class IQueryable.

_____ **5** All Standard Query Operator methods are static methods defined in the IEnumerable class.

_____ **6** IEnumerable and IQueryable interfaces are mainly used for the nongeneric collections supported by the earlier versions of Visual Basic.NET.

_____ **7** All LINQ expressions can only be represented as query syntax.

_____ **8** All LINQ expressions will be converted to the Standard Query Operator methods during the compile time by CLR.

_____ **9** The query variable used in LINQ contains both the query information and the returned query results.

_____ **10** LINQ to DataSet and LINQ to Entities belong to LINQ to ADO.NET.

II. Multiple Choices

1 The difference between the interfaces IEnumerable and IEnumerable(Of T) is that the former is mainly used for _____, but the latter is used for _____

  A Nongeneric collections, generic collections

  B Generic collections, nongeneric collections

  C All collections, partial collections

  D .NET Frameworks 2.0, .NET Frameworks 3.5

2 The query variable used in LINQ contains_____

  A Query information and query results

  B Query information

  C Query results

  D Standard Query Operator

3 All Standard Query Operator (SQO) methods are defined as_____, this means that these methods can be called either as class methods or as instance methods

  A Class methods

  B Instance method

  C Variable methods

  D Extension methods

4 One of SQO methods, AsEnumerable() operator method, is used to convert the data type of the input object from_____ to _____

  A IQuerable(Of T), IEnumrable(Of T)

  B IEnumerable(Of T), IEnumerable(Of T)

  C Any, IEnumerable(Of T)

  D All of them

5 LINQ to Objects is used to query any sequences or collections that are either explicitly or implicitly compatible with _____ sequences or _____ collections

  A IQuerable, IQuerable(Of T)

  B IEnumerable, IEnumerable(Of T)

  C Deferred SQO, non-deferred SQO

  D Generic, nongeneric

6 LINQ to DataSet is built on the _____ architecture, the codes developed by using that version of ADO.NET will continue to function in a LINQ to DataSet application without modifications

  A ADO.NET 2.0

  B ADO.NET 3.0

  C ADO.NET 3.5

  D ADO.NET 4.0

7   The relationship between XAttribute and XNode is _____.
   A XAttirbute is equivalent to XNode
   B XAttribute and Anode are derived based on different bass class
   C XAttribute and Anode are derived based on same bass class
   D None of above

8   LINQ to Entities_____.
   A Belongs to LINQ to ADO.NET
   B Is a subcomponent of LINQ to ADO.NET
   C Query data by using the Object Services infrastructure
   D All of above

9   LINQ to Entities queries are performed under the control of the _____ and the _____
   A .NET Frameworks 3.5, ADO.NET 3.5
   B ADO.NET 4.0 Entity Framework, ADO.NET 4.0 Entity Framework Tools
   C IEnumerable(Of T), IQueryable(Of T)
   D Entity Data Model, Entity Data Model Designer

10 To access and implement ADO.NET 4.0 EF and ADO.NET 4.0 EFT, developers need to understand the _____ that is a core of ADO.NET 4.0 EF
   A SQLMetal
   B Object Relational Designer
   C Generic collections
   D Entity Data Model

11 Lambda expressions are a language feature that is similar in many ways to _____ methods
   A Standard Query Operator
   B anonymous
   C Generic collection
   D IQuerable

12 Extension methods are defined as those methods that can be called as either _____ methods or _____ methods
   A Class, instance
   B IEnumerable(Of T), IQueryable(Of T)
   C Generic, nongeneric
   D Static, dynamic

13 In LINQ, the data type *var* is used to define a(n) _____, and the real data type of that variable can be inferred by the _____ during the compiling time.
   A Generic variable, debugger
   B implicitly typed local variable, compiler
   C Nongeneric variable, builder
   D IEnumerable(Of T) variable, loader

14 In LINQ, the query expression must start with a _____ clause and must end with a _____ or _____ clause

    A Begin, Select, End

    B Select, Where, Order By

    C From, Select, Group

    D query variable, range variable, For Each loop

15 The DataContext is a class that is used to establish a _____ between your project and your database. In addition to this role, the DataContext also provide the function to _____ operations of the Standard Query Operators to the SQL statements that can be run in real databases

    A Relationship, perform

    B Reference, translate

    C Generic collections, transform

    D Connection, convert

III. Exercises

1 Explain the architecture and components of the LINQ and illustrate the functionality of these using a block diagram.

2 Explain the execution process of a LINQ using the For Each statement.

3 Explain the definitions and functionalities of the Standard Query Operator methods.

4 Explain the relationship between the LINQ expressions and Standard Query Operator methods

5 Explain the definitions and functionalities of IEnumerable, IEnumerable(Of T), IQueryable, and IQueryable(Of T) interfaces.

```
Module Example4_78
   Sub Main()
      Dim fruits As New List(Of String)(New String() {"apple", "passionfruit", "banana", "mango", _
                                          "orange", "blueberry", "grape", "strawberry"})

      Dim query = From fruit In fruits
                  Where fruit.Length < 6
                  Select fruit

      For Each f In query
         Console.WriteLine(f)
      Next

   End Sub
End Module
```

Figure 4.69 A LINQ to Object query.

6 A query used for LINQ to Objects, which is represented by a query syntax, is shown in Figure 4.69. Try to convert this query expression to a method's syntax.

7 Explain the difference between the class method and the instance method and try to illustrate the functionality of an extension method and how to build an extension method by using an example.

8 List three steps of performing the LINQ to DataSet queries.

5

Query Data from Oracle Database with Visual Basic.NET

Starting from Visual Studio 2005, Visual Basic.NET added some new components and wizards to simplify the data access, and inserting and updating functionalities for database development and applications. Compared to Visual Studio 2005, Visual Studio 2017 added more new components to simplify the data accessing, and inserting and updating functionalities. Quite a number of new features such as Windows Communication Foundation (WCF), Windows Presentation Foundation (WPF), and Language Integrated Query (LINQ) had been added into Visual Studio.NET 2017.

The transition from the Visual Studio.NET 2008 to the Visual Studio.NET 2019 is more about extending the language to cope with new Windows 10 features than a radical of the language itself. Visual Basic.NET 2019 describes new features in the Visual Basic language and Code Editor. The features include developing apps for Android, iOS, Windows, Linux, Web, and Cloud and also code fast, debug and diagnose with ease, test often, and release with confidence. You can also extend and customize Visual Studio by building your own extensions. One of the significant differences between the Visual Studio.NET 2008 and Visual Studio.NET 2019 is that the former is built based on the .NET Framework 3.5, and the latter is built based on .NET Framework 4.7.

Starting from Visual Studio.NET 2019, Microsoft provides a quite few new development tools and wizards to help users to build and develop database programming easily and efficiently. One of the most popular tools is the cross-platform development, which contains Redgate Data Tools and .NET Core.

The Redgate Data Tools provide the following features:

- Redgate ReadyRoll Core helps you develop migration scripts, manage database changes using source control, and safely automate deployments of SQL Server database changes alongside applications changes.
- Redgate SQL Prompt Core helps you write SQL more quickly and accurately with the help of intelligent code completion. SQL Prompt auto-completes database and system objects and keywords and offers column suggestions as you type. This results in cleaner code and fewer errors because you don't have to remember every column name or alias.

NET Core is a general purpose, modular, cross-platform, and open source implementation of the .NET Standard and contains many of the same APIs as the .NET Frame-work.

The Toolbox window in Visual Studio.NET 2019 also contains data components that enable you to quickly and easily build simple database applications without needing to touch very complicated coding process. Combined these data components with wizards, which are located in the Data Source wizard and related to ADO.NET, one can easily develop binding relationships between

Oracle Database Programming with Visual Basic.NET: Concepts, Designs, and Implementations, First Edition. Ying Bai.
© 2021 The Institute of Electrical and Electronics Engineers, Inc. Published 2021 by John Wiley & Sons, Inc.
Companion website: www.wiley.com/go/bai-VB-Oracle

the data source and controls on the Visual Basic windows form object; furthermore, one can build simple Visual Basic project to navigate, scan, retrieve, and manipulate data stored in the data source with a few of lines of codes.

This chapter is divided to two parts: Part I provides a detailed description and discussion in how to use Visual Studio.NET 2019 tools and wizards to build simple but efficient database applications without touching complicated coding. In Part II, a deeper digging in how to develop advanced database applications using runtime objects is presented. More complicated coding technology is provided in this part. Some real examples are presented in detail with these two parts to enable readers to have a clear picture about the development of professional database applications in simple and efficient ways. This chapter concentrates only on the data query applications.

In this chapter, you will

- Learn and understand the most useful tools and wizards used in developing data query applications.
- Learn and understand how to connect a database with different components provided in data providers and configure this connection with wizards.
- Learn and understand how to use BindingSource object to display database tables' contents using `DataGridView`.
- Learn and understand how to bind a DataSet (data source) to various controls in the windows form object.
- Learn and understand how to configure and edit TableAdapter to build special queries
- Learn and understand how to retrieve data using the LINQ technology from the data source to simplify and improve the efficiency of the data query.
- Build and execute simple dynamic data query commands to retrieve desired data.

To successfully complete this chapter, you need to understand topics such as Fundamentals of Databases, which is introduced in Chapter 2, ADO.NET that is discussed in Chapter 3, and LINQ to DataSet discussed in Chapter 4. Also a sample database developed in Chapter 2 will be used through this Chapter.

Part I: Data Query with Visual Studio.NET Design Tools and Wizards

Before we can start, a preview of a completed sample database application is necessary, and this preview can give readers a feeling about how a database application works and what it can do. The database used for this project is our sample database **CSE_DEPT** that we built in Chapter 2.

5.1   A Completed Sample Database Application Example

This sample application is composed of five Visual Basic.NET forms, named **LogIn, Selection, Faculty, Student,** and **Course** forms. It is designed to map a Computer Science and Engineering Department in a university and allow users to scan and browse all pieces of information about a typical Computer Science and Engineering department, which including faculty members, courses taught by selected faculty, students, and courses taken by the associated student.

Each form, except the **Selection**, is associated with one or two data tables in our sample database **CSE_DEPT**, which was developed in Chapter 2. The relationship between the form and related data tables is shown in Table 5.1.

Table 5.1 Relationship between the Form and Data Table.

VB Form	Tables in Sample Database
LogIn	LOGIN
Faculty	FACULTY
Course	COURSE
Student	STUDENT, STUDENTCOURSE

Controls on each form are bound to the associated fields in certain data table located in the `CSE_DEPT` database. As the project runs, a data query will be executed via a dynamic Oracle statement that is built during the configuration of each TableAdapter in the Data Source wizard. The retrieved data will be reflected on the associated controls that have been bound to those data fields.

Go to the folder `Class DB Projects\Chapter 5` located at the Wiley ftp site under the `Students` folder (refer to Figure 1.2 in Chapter 1) to find an executable file `SampleWizards Project.exe` that is located under the project folder `SampleWizards Solution\ SampleWizards Project\bin\Debug`. Double-click on that `.exe` file to run it.

As the project runs, a LogIn form is displayed to ask users to enter username and password, as shown in Figure 5.1. Enter `jhenry` and `test` as username and password. Then click on the `LogIn` button to call the LogIn TableAdapter to execute a query to pick up a record that matches the username and password entered by the user from the LogIn table located in the CSE_DEPT database. If a matched record is found based on the username and password, the next window form, `Selection,` will be displayed to allow user to continue to select and check the desired information related to faculty, course, or student, which is shown in Figure 5.2.

Select the default information – `Faculty Information` by clicking the OK button, and the `Faculty` form appears as shown in Figure 5.3.

All faculty names in the CSE department are listed in a ComboBox control on the form. Select the desired faculty name from the ComboBox control by clicking on the drop-down arrow and click on the desired faculty name. To query all information for this faculty, click on the `Select` button to execute a pre-built dynamic Oracle statement. All information related to the selected faculty will be fetched from the faculty table in our sample database and reflected on five label controls in the Faculty form, as shown in Figure 5.3. A faculty photo will also be displayed in a PictureBox control in the form.

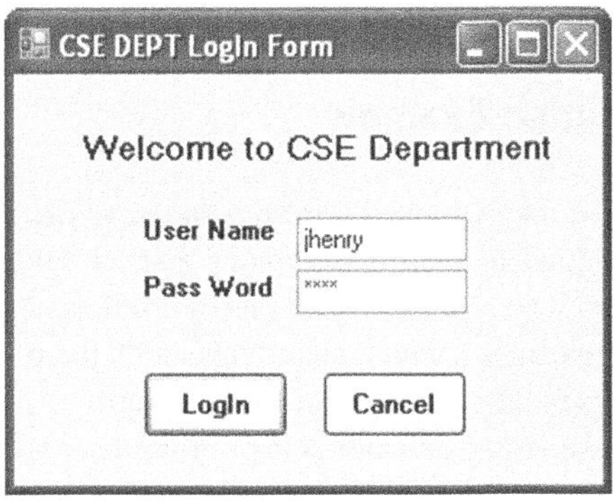

Figure 5.1 The LogIn Form. *Source:* Microsoft Corporation.

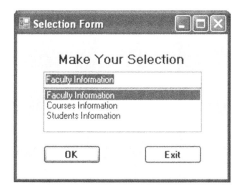

Figure 5.2 The Selection Form. *Source:* Microsoft Corporation.

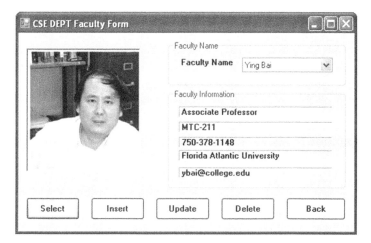

Figure 5.3 The Faculty Form. *Source:* Microsoft Corporation.

The **Back** button is used to return to the Selection Form to enable users to make other selections to obtain the associated information.

Click on the **Back** button to return to the Selection Form and then select the **Course Information** item to open the **Course** form. Select the desired faculty name from the ComboBox control and click the **Select** button to retrieve courses taught by this faculty, which will be displayed in the Course ListBox, as shown in Figure 5.4.

An interesting thing is that when you select the specified course by clicking on it from the Course list, all information related to that course such as the course title, course schedule, classroom, credits, and course enrollment will be reflected on each associated textbox control under the Course Information frame control.

Click on the **Back** button to return to the Selection Form and select the **Student Information** to open the **Student** form. You can continue to work on this form to see what will happen to this form.

In the following sections, we will discuss how to design and build a similar project **SelectWizard** step by step.

Open Windows Explorer and create a new folder **Class DB Projects\Chapter 5** under your root drive. Then open Visual Studio 2019 and create a blank solution **SelectWizard**

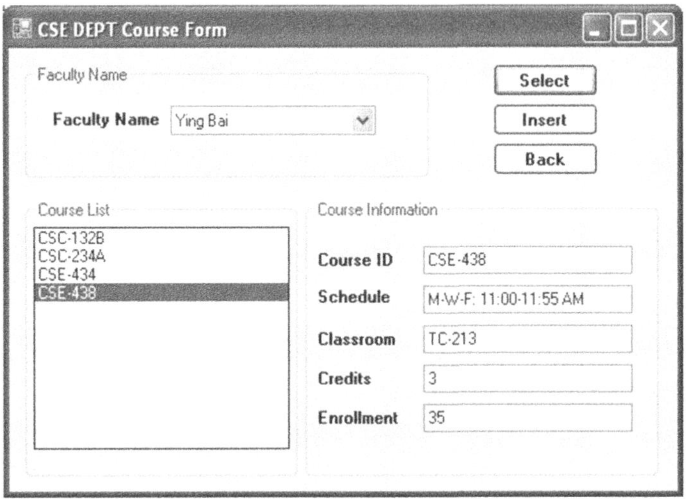

Figure 5.4 The Course Form. *Source:* Microsoft Corporation.

`Solution` and add a new `Windows Forms App (.NET Framework)` project `SelectWizard Project`. Save the solution to the folder `Class DB Projects\Chapter 5`.

Let's first concentrate on the .NET design tools and wizards related to data source.

5.2   Visual Studio.NET Design Tools and Wizards

When building a Windows Forms App (.NET Framework) application that needs to interface to database, a powerful and simple way is to use the design tools and wizards provided by Visual Studio.NET. With this technique, the length of coding process can be significantly reduced, and the developing procedures can also be greatly simplified. Now let's first take a look at those components resided in the Toolbox window.

5.2.1   Data Components in the Toolbox Window

Each database related to a Windows Forms App application contains three components that can be used to develop a database application using the data controls in the Toolbox: `DataSet,` `BindingSource,` and `TableAdapter`. Two other useful components are the `DataGridView` and the `BindingNavigator`. Some of these components are located in the Toolbox window as shown in Figure 5.5.

5.2.1.1   The DataSet
A DataSet object can be considered as a container and it is used to hold data from one or more data tables. It maintains the data as a group of data tables with optional relationships defined between those tables. The definition of the DataSet class is a generic idea, which means that it is not tied to any specific type of database. Data can be loaded into a DataSet using a TableAdapter from many different databases such as Microsoft Access, Microsoft SQL Server, Oracle, Microsoft Exchange, Microsoft Active Directory, or any OLE DB or ODBC compliant database when your application begins to run or the `Form_Load()` event procedure is called if one used an `DataGridView` object.

Although not tied to any specific database, the DataSet class is designed to contain relational tabular data as one would find in a relational database. Each table included in the DataSet is represented in the DataSet as a DataTable. The DataTable can be considered as a direct mapping to the real table in the database. For example, the LogIn data table, LogInDataTable, is a data table com-

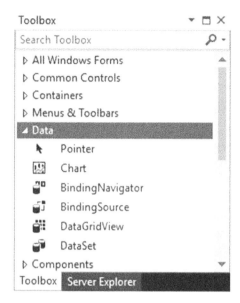

Figure 5.5 The Data components in Toolbox window. *Source:* Microsoft Corporation.

ponent or DataTable that can be mapped to the real table LogIn in the CSE_DEPT database. The relationship between any tables is realized in the DataSet as a DataRelation object. The DataRelation object provides the information that relates a child table to a parent table via a foreign key. A DataSet can hold any number of tables with any number of relationships defined between tables. From this point of view, a DataSet can be considered as a mini database engine, so it can contain all information of tables it holds such as the column name and data type, all relationships between tables, and more important, it contains most management functionalities of the tables such as browse, select, insert, update, and delete data from tables.

With the Visual Basic.NET 2019, one can easily edit the structure of a DataSet and make any changes to the structure of that DataSet using the Dataset Designer in the Data Source window. Most importantly, one can graphically manipulate the tables and queries in a manner more directly tied to the DataSet rather than having to deal with an XML Schema (XSD).

In summary, the DataSet object is a very powerful component that can contain multiple data tables with all information related to those tables. Using this object, one can easily browse, access, and manipulate data stored in it. We will explore this component in more detail in the following sections when a real project is built.

When you build a data-driven project and set up a connection between your project and a database using the ADO.NET, the DataTables in the DataSet can be populated with data of your database using data query methods or the `Fill()` method. From this point of view, you can consider the DataSet as a *data source* and it contains all mapped data from the database you connected to your project.

Refer to Figure 5.6 for a global picture of the DataSet and other components in the Toolbox window to obtain more detailed ideas for this issue.

5.2.1.2 DataGridView

The next useful data component defined in the Toolbox window is the **DataGridView**.

Like its name, you can consider the DataGridView as a view container, and it can be used to bind data from your database and display the data in a tabular or a grid format. You can use the

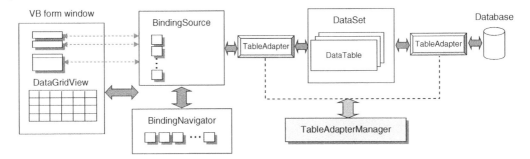

Figure 5.6 The relationship between data components.

DataGridView control to show read-only views of a small amount of data or you can scale it to show editable views of very large sets of data. The DataGridView control provides many properties that enable you to customize the appearance of the view and properties that allow you to modify the column headers and the data displayed in the grid format. You can also easily customize the appearance of the DataGridView control by choosing among different properties. Many types of data stores can be used as a database, or the DataGridView control can operate with no data source bound to it.

By default, a DataGridView control has the following properties:

- Automatically displays column headers and row headers that remain visible as users scroll the table vertically.
- Has a row header that contains a selection indicator for the current row.
- Has a selection rectangle in the first cell.
- Has columns that can be automatically resized when the user double-clicks the column dividers.
- Automatically supports visual styles on Windows XP and the Windows Server 2003 family when the EnableVisualStyles method is called from the application's Main method.

Refer to Figure 5.6 to get a relationship between the DataGridView and other data components. A more detailed description in how to use the DataGridView control to bind and display data in Visual Basic.NET 2019 will be provided in Section 5.5 in this chapter.

5.2.1.3 BindingSource

The `BindingSource` component has two functionalities. First, it provides a layer of indirection when binding the controls on a form to data in the data source. This is accomplished by binding the BindingSource component to your data source and then binding the controls on your form to the BindingSource component. All further interactions with the data, including navigating, sorting, filtering, and updating, are accomplished with calls to the BindingSource component.

Second, the BindingSource component can act as a strongly typed data source. Adding a type to the BindingSource component with the Add method creates a list of that type.

Exactly, the BindingSource control works as a bridge to connect the data-bound controls on your Visual Basic forms with your data source (DataSet). The BindingSource control can also be considered as a container object and it hold all mapped data from the data source. As a data-driven project runs, the DataSet will be filled with data from the database using a TableAdapter. Also the BindingSource control will create a set of data that are mapped to those filled data in the DataSet. The BindingSource control can hold this set of mapped data and create a one-to-one connection between the DataSet and the BindingSource. This connection is very useful when you perform data binding between controls on the Visual Basic form and data in the DataSet, exactly you set up a connection between your controls on the Visual Basic form and those mapped data in the BindingSource object. As your project runs and the data are needed to be reflected on the associated controls, a request to BindingSource is issued and the BindingSource control will control the data accessing to the data source (DataSet) and data updating in those controls. For instance, the DataGridView control will send a request to the BindingSource control when a column sorting action is performed, and the latter will communicate with the data source to complete this sorting.

When perform a data binding in Visual Basic.NET 2019, you need to bind the data referenced by the BindingSource control to the DataSource property of your controls on the forms.

5.2.1.4 BindingNavigator

The **BindingNavigator** control allows user to scan and browse all records stored in the data source (DataSet) one by one in a sequence. The BindingNavigator component provides a standard UI with buttons and arrows to enable users to navigate to the first and the previous records as well as the next and the last records in the data source. It also provides textbox controls to display how many records existed in the current data table and the current displayed record's index.

As shown in Figure 5.6, the BindingNavigator is also bound to the BindingSource component as other component did. When the user clicks either the Previous or the Next button on the BindingNavigator UI, a request is sent to the BindingSource for the previous or the next record, and in turn, this request is sent to the data source for picking up the desired data.

5.2.1.5 TableAdapter

From Figure 5.6, one can find that a **TableAdapter** is equivalent to an adapter and it just works as a connection media between the database and DataSet, and between the BindingSource and the DataSet. This means that the TableAdapter has double functionalities when it works as different roles for the different purposes. For example, as you develop your data-driven applications using the design tools, the data in the database will be populated to the mapped tables in the DataSet using the TableAdapter's Fill() method. The TableAdapter also works as an adapter to coordinate the data operations between the BindingSource and the DataSet when the data-bound controls in Visual Basic form need to be filled or updated.

The TableAdapter belongs to designer-generated component and you cannot find this component from the Toolbox window. The function of a TableAdapter is to connect your DataSet objects with their underlying databases, and it will be created automatically when you add and configure new data sources via design tools such as Data Source Configuration Wizard when you build your applications.

The TableAdapter is similar to DataAdapter in that both components can handle the data operations between DataSet and the database, but the TableAdapter can contain multiple queries to support multiple tables from the database, allowing one TableAdapter to perform multiple queries to your DataSet. Another important difference between the TableAdapter and the Data Adapter is that each TableAdapter is a unique class that is automatically generated by Visual Studio.NET 2019 to work with only the fields you have selected for a specific database object.

The TableAdapter class contains queries used to select data from your database. Also it contains different methods to allow users to fill the DataSet with some dynamic parameters in your project with data from the database. You can also use the TableAdapter to build different query statements such as Insert, Update, and Delete based on the different data operations. A more detailed exploration and implementation of TableAdapter with a real example will be provided in the following sections.

5.2.1.6 TableAdapter Manager

Starting Visual Studio.NET 2008, a new class named **TableAdapterManager** is added into this structure to manage all TableAdapters. The TableAdapterManager class is not part of the .NET Framework. By default, a TableAdapterManager class is generated when you create a DataSet that contains related tables.

5.2.2 Data Source Window

Two Integrated Development Environment (IDE) features included in the Visual Studio.NET, the `Data Sources` Window and the `Data Source Configuration Wizard`, are used to assist you to set up data access using the new classes, such as DataConnector and TableAdapter.

The Data Sources window is used to display the data sources or available databases in your project. You can use the Data Sources window to directly create a user interface (consisting of data-bound controls) by dragging items from the Data Sources window onto Visual Basic.NET forms in your project. Each item inside the Data Sources window has a drop-down control list where you can select the type of control to create prior to dragging it onto a form. You can also customize the control list with additional controls, such as controls that you have created.

A more detailed description on how to use the Data Sources window to develop a data-driven project is provided in Section 5.4.

5.2.2.1 Add New Data Sources and Oracle Database References

When the first time you create a new data-driven project in Visual Basic.NET 2019 environment, there is no any data source that has been connected to your project and therefore, the Data Source window is blank with no data source in there. For example, in our new created project `SelectWizard Project`, after it is created and opened, you can find and open the Data Sources window by clicking on the `View|Other Windows|Data Sources` menu item, which is shown in Figure 5.7.

The opened Data Sources window is blank since you have no any database connected to this new project. To add a new data source or database to this new project, you can click on the `Add New Data Source` link at the bottom of this window. Now the `Data Source Configuration Wizard` will be displayed. You need to use this wizard to select your desired database to be connected with your new project.

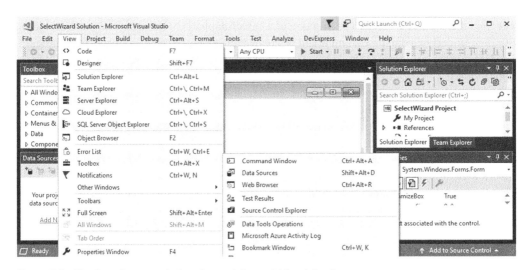

Figure 5.7 The Data Sources window. *Source:* Microsoft Visual Studio.

To access different databases, various data providers that work as an adaptor or a data driver are needed. These adaptors provide various functions, such as connect to target data source, access, retrieve, insert, update, and delete data from the data source. For Oracle database, regularly the following four popular tools are provided to work as this kind of adaptor or driver:

1) Oracle Data Provider for .NET (ODP.NET)
2) Oracle Data Access Components for .NET (ODAC.NET)
3) Oracle Developer Tools for Visual Studio.NET (ODT.NET)
4) A Third-Party Product, dotConnect, provided by Devart Inc.

For all four data drivers listed above, the top three are provided by Oracle Corporation and they are free to use. Moreover, the Devart also provided a free of charge version software, dotConnect Express, to provide basic driver functions for Oracle database. An issue in selecting these drivers is the versions. All drivers provided by Oracle are relatively out-of-date and cannot meet the needs of quickly developments of Visual Studio.NET even they are free in charge. An example is that until today, January 2020, all Oracle drivers still support Visual Studio.NET 2017 even through the version of Visual Studio.NET had been updated to 2019 since 2018.

Based on this reason, we adopted the third-party product, **dotConnect**, as our driver in this book to use it as an adaptor to access and implement our Oracle 18c XE sample database CSE_DEPT built in Chapter 2.

Refer to Appendix F to download and install this free driver for Oracle to your computer. Then we need to add some references related to this driver into our project to enable the compiler to know this driver as the project building time. Perform the following operations to add these references:

1) Right-click on our new created project **SelectWizard Project** from the Solution Explorer window and select **Add | Reference** item from the popup menu.
2) Click on the **Extensions** item on the left pane on the opened Reference Manager wizard, as shown in Figure 5.8, and select **Devart.Data** and **Devart.Data.Oracle** from the mid-pane by checking both of them, as shown in Figure 5.8.
3) Click on the **OK** button to add them into our project.

Now let's return to our opened Data Source Configuration wizard to continue our job.

5.2.2.2 Data Source Configuration Wizard

The opened **Data Source Configuration Wizard** is shown in Figure 5.9.

Using the **Data Source Configuration Wizard**, you can select your desired data source or database that will be connected to your new project. The **Data Source Configuration Wizard** supports three (3) types of data sources:

1) The first option, **Database**, allows you to select a data source for a database server on your local computer or on a remote server. The examples for this kind of data sources are Oracle 18c Express Edition, Microsoft Data Engine (MSDE) 2000, or SQL Server 2018. This option also allows you to choose either an Oracle database or a SQL Server database. The difference between a SQL Server database and a SQL Server database file is that the former is a complete database that integrates the database management system with data tables to form a body or a package, but the latter is only a database file.
2) The second option, Service, enable you to select a data source that is located at a Web service.
3) The third option, Object, allows you to bind your user interface to one of your own database classes.

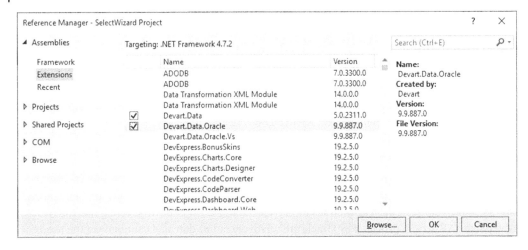

Figure 5.8 The finished reference selection wizard. *Source:* Microsoft Visual Studio.

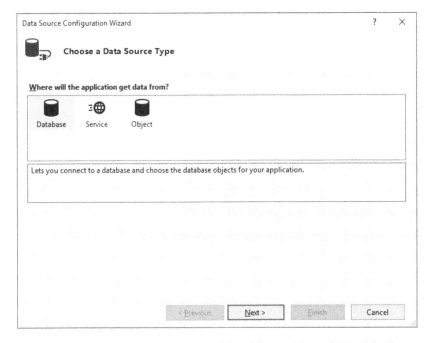

Figure 5.9 The Data Source Configuration Wizard. *Source:* Microsoft Visual Studio.

Click on the **Next** button to continue.

Only one default model, **DataSet**, is allowed to be selected on the next wizard shown in Figure 5.10. Click on the **Next** button to continue to the next step.

The first time when you run this wizard there is no preexisting connections available, but on subsequent uses of the wizard you can reuse previously created connections. To make a new connection, click on the **New Connection** and **Change** buttons, the Change Data Source wizard is displayed, as shown in Figure 5.11.

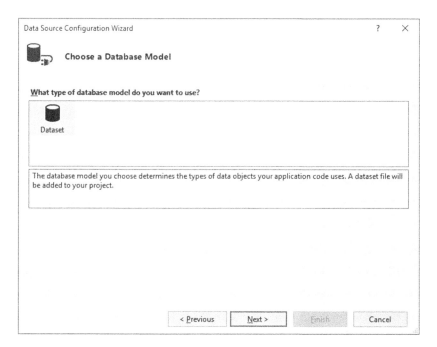

Figure 5.10 Choose a database model in the Data Source Configuration Wizard. *Source:* Microsoft Visual Studio.

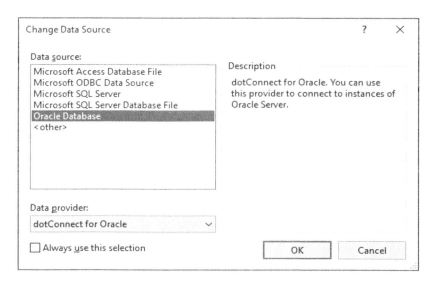

Figure 5.11 The Change Data Source wizard. *Source:* Microsoft Visual Studio.

Select `Oracle Database` from the `Data source:` box and make sure that the data provider is `dotConnect for Oracle` in the `Data provider:` box and click on the `OK` button.

On the opened Add Connection wizard, which is shown in Figure 5.12a, in the Server box, enter `localhost:1518/CSE-DEPT` as the Server name, and `CSE_DEPT` as the User ID and `oracle_18c` as the Password. You can also click on the `Test Connection` button to test this database connection. Remember to check the `Allow saving password` checkbox to save our password. Click on the `OK` button to go to the next wizard.

(a)

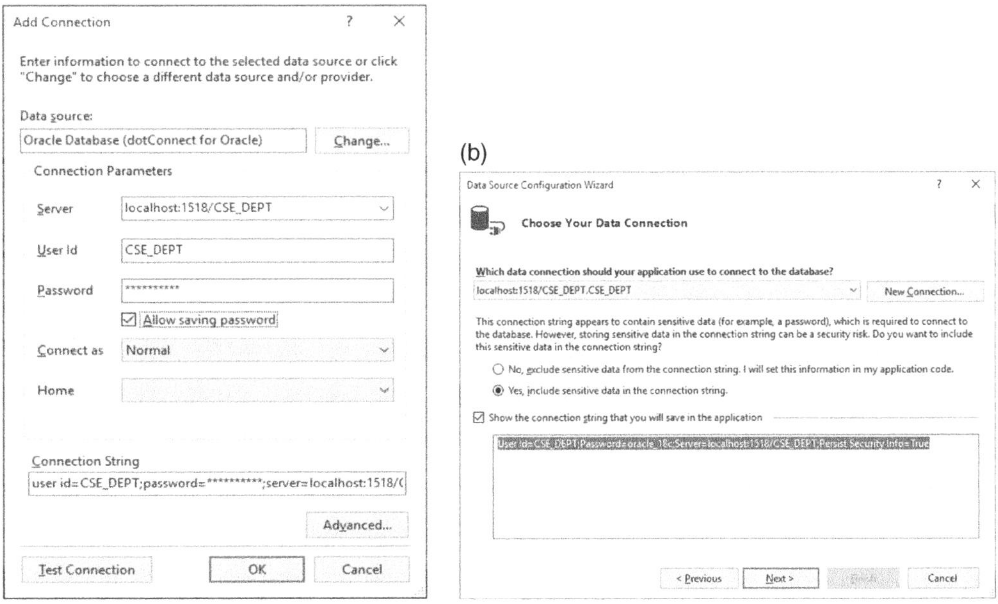

(b)

Figure 5.12 (a, b) The Add Connection and Change Data Source wizards. *Source:* Microsoft Visual Studio.

On the next wizard, check the **Show the connection string...** checkbox to display your data source connection string, which is shown in Figure 5.12b. Also click on the **Yes, include sensitive data in the connection string** radio button to keep our password to be used later. Click on the **Next** button to continue. Click on the **Next** button for the next wizard to the connection string.

In the opened **Choose Your Database Objects** wizard shown in Figure 5.13, expand the **Tables** icon to select all tables in our database. Change the DataSet to **CSE_DEPTDataSet**, in the **DataSet name:** box, as shown in Figure 5.13. Then click on the **Finish** button to complete this Data Source Configuration process.

When you finish selecting your database objects, all selected objects should have been added into your new instance of your DataSet class, in this example, it is **CSE_DEPTDataSet** that is located at the **DataSet name** box shown in Figure 5.13. Exactly, the data in all tables in your database (**CSE_DEPT**) should have been copied to those mapped tables in your DataSet object (**CSE_DEPTDataSet**), and you can use Preview Data to view data in each table in the DataSet. The wizard will build your SELECT statements for you automatically.

An important issue is that as you finished this Data Source Configuration and closed this Wizard, the connection you set between your application and your database is closed. You need to use data query, data manipulation methods, or the Fill() method to reopen this connection if you want to perform any data action between your application and your database later.

After the Data Source Configuration is finished, a new data source is added into your project, exactly it is added into the Data Source window, which is shown in Figure 5.14.

The data source added into your project is exactly a DataSet object that contains all data tables that are mappings to those tables in your real database. As shown in Figure 5.13, the data source window displays the data source or tables as a tree view, and each table is connected to this tree via a node. If you click on the arrow node that is prefixed in each table, all columns of the selected table will be displayed.

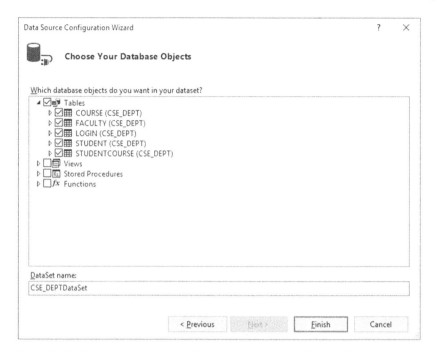

Figure 5.13 Choose Your Database Objects wizard. *Source:* Microsoft Visual Studio.

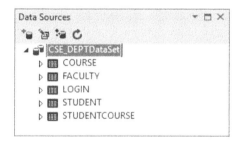

Figure 5.14 The added data source. *Source:* Microsoft Visual Studio.

Even after the data source is added into your project, you still have controllability over this data source. This means that you can still make some modifications to the data source, exactly make modifications to the tables and data source-elated methods. To do this job, you need to know something about another component, DataSet Designer, which is also located in the Data Source window.

5.2.2.3 DataSet Designer

The DataSet Designer is a group of visual tools used to create and edit a typed DataSet and the individual items that make up that DataSet. The DataSet Designer provides visual representations of the objects contained in the DataSet. Using the DataSet Designer, you can create and modify TableAdapters, TableAdapter Queries, DataTables, DataColumns, and DataRelations.

To open the DataSet Designer, right-click on any place inside the Data Source window and select **Edit DataSet with Designer**. Our DataSet Designer is shown in Figure 5.15.

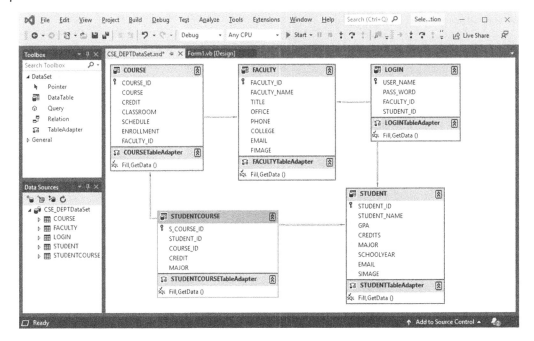

Figure 5.15 A sample DataSet Designer. *Source:* Microsoft Visual Studio.

In our sample database, we have five tables: `LogIn, Faculty, Course, Student,` and `StudentCourse`. To edit an item, just right-click on the associated component for which you want to modify. For example, if you want to edit the `LogIn` table, right-click on that table and choose your selections from the popup menu. You can add new queries, new relationships, new keys, and even new columns to the `LogIn` table. Also you can modify any built-in method of the TableAdapter, exactly the `LogInTableAdapter` in this example.

In addition to multiple editing abilities mentioned above, you can perform the following popular data operations using the DataSet Designer:

- Configure: configure and build data operations such as building a data query by modifying the default methods of the TableAdapter such as `Fill()` and `GetData().`
- Delete: delete the whole table.
- Rename: rename the table.
- Preview Data: view the contents of the table in a grid format.

To open a preview data for our Faculty table, right-click on the `CSE_DEPTDataSet` in the Data Sources window and select `Preview Data` item from the popup menu. Then expand the Faculty table and click and select `Fill, GetData()` sub-item, and click on the `Preview` button under the `Selected object` box, as shown in Figure 5.16.

The preview data for our Faculty table is shown in Figure 5.17. The Preview Data is a very powerful tool and it allows users to preview the contents of a data table.

Based on above discussions, it can be seen that the DataSet Designer is a powerful tool to help users to design and manipulate data source or DataSet even the data source has been added into your project. But it has one more important function, which is to allow users to add any missing table to your project. In some cases, if you have forgotten to add a data table or you add a wrong table (according to my experience, this has happened a lot for students who selected the wrong

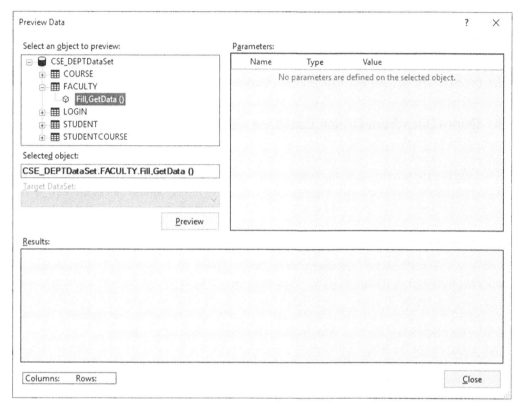

Figure 5.16 The opened Preview Data wizard. *Source:* Microsoft Visual Studio.

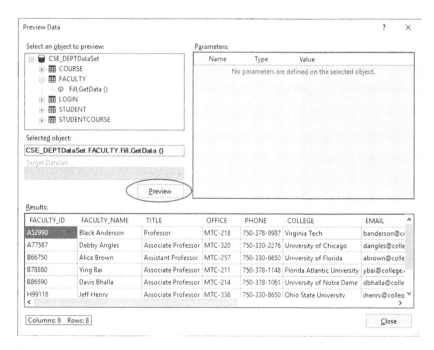

Figure 5.17 An example of the Preview Data for Faculty table. *Source:* Microsoft Visual Studio.

data source), you need to use this function to add that missed table or first delete the wrong table and add the correct one.

To perform adding a missed table, just right-click a blank area of the designer surface and choose **Add|DataTable**. You can also use this functionality to add a TableAdapter, Query, or a Relation to this DataSet. A more detailed exploration of DataSet Designer will be provided in Section 5.4.3.

5.3 Query Data from Oracle Database Using Design Tools and Wizards

So far we have introduced and discussed most design tools located at both Visual Studio.NET 2019 Toolbox and Data Source window. In the following sections, we will illustrate how to utilize those tools and wizards to build a data-driven application using our project **SelectWizard Project**. First, let's take care of all graphic user interfaces (GUIs) in this project.

5.3.1 Application User Interface

We made a similar demo for this sample data-driven application in Section 5.1. This project is composed of five forms, named **LogIn, Selection, Faculty, Student,** and **Course**. The project is designed to map a Computer Science and Engineering Department in a university and allow users to scan and browse all information about the department including faculty, courses taught by selected faculty, student, and courses taken by the associated students.

Each form, except the Selection Form, is associated with one or two data tables in our sample database CSE_DEPT, which was developed in Chapter 2. The relationships between each form and tables are shown in Table 5.2.

Controls on each form are bound to the associated fields in certain data table located in the CSE_DEPT database. As the project runs, a data query will be executed via a dynamic query statement that is built during the configuration of each TableAdapter in the Data Source wizard. The retrieved data will be reflected on the associated controls that have been bound to those data fields.

The database used in this sample project, which was built in Chapter 2, is an Oracle 18c XE database since it is compatible with Oracle database, and more important, it is free and can be easily downloaded from the Oracle Database Development site. Refer to Appendix A to get details in how to download and install Oracle 18c XE database. You can use other database such as Microsoft Access or Oracle for this project. The only thing you need to do is to select the desired data source when you add and connect that data source to your project.

All of these five forms are available from the folder **Students\VB Forms\Window** located at the Wiley ftp site (refer to Figure 1.2 in Chapter 1). You can copy and paste those forms to your project if you want to save time. However, here we want to provide a detailed discussion about how to build those forms.

Let's begin to develop this sample project with five forms.

Table 5.2 Relationship between each form and data table.

VB Form	Tables in Sample Database
LogIn	LOGIN
Faculty	FACULTY
Course	COURSE
Student	STUDENT, STUDENTCOURSE

5.3.1.1 The LogIn Form

On our new created project **SelectWizard Project** perform the following modifications to this project:

1) Remove the default form window **Form1.vb** in the Solution Explorer window by right-clicking on **Form1.vb** and select the **Delete** item from the popup menu. Click on the **OK** button to confirm this deleting action.

2) Add the **LogIn Form.vb** into this project. First right-click on our project **SelectWizard Project** in the Solution Explorer window and select the **Add|Existing Item** from the popup menu. Browse to the folder **Students\VB Forms\Window** that is located at the Wiley Web site (refer to Figure 1.2 in Chapter 1), select the **LogIn Form.vb** by checking it, and click on the **Add** button.

3) Open the GUI of the new added LogIn Form by right-clicking on it and select the **View Designer** item. Change the name of this form from **Form1** to **LogInForm** by doing that in the **Name** property in the Property window.

4) Also in the Property window, change the title of this form to **CSE_DEPT LogIn Form** by doing that in the **Text** property.

5) In the Solution Explorer window, click on the **LogInForm** to select it and go to the Property window to change the **StartPosition** property to **CenterScreen**.

6) This form contains seven controls shown in Table 5.3. The finished LogIn form is shown in Figure 5.18.

In a similar way, add all other four forms, **Faculty Form.vb**, **Course Form.vb**, **Student Form.vb,** and **Selection Form.vb**, into the project.

Now click on our project **SelectWizard Project** in the Solution Explorer window to select it and then go to **View|Property Pages** to open the project property wizard. Click on the drop-down arrow on the **Startup form:** combo box and select the **LogInForm** as our startup form.

You should set the **LogIn** button, **cmdLogIn**, as the default button by choosing this button from the **AcceptButton** property of the LogIn Form window.

5.3.1.2 The Selection Form

This form allows users to select the different windows form to connect to the different data tables and furthermore to browse data from the associated table. No data table is connected to this form.

Five controls shown in Table 5.4 should have been added into this form. The complete Selection Form is shown in Figure 5.19.

Table 5.3 Controls on the LogIn form.

Type	Name	Text	TabIndex
Label	Label1	Welcome to CSE Department	0
Label	Label2	User Name	1
Textbox	txtUserName		2
Label	Label3	Pass Word	3
Textbox	txtPassWord		4
Button	TabLogIn	TabLogIn	5
Button	ReadLogIn	ReadLogIn	6
Button	btnCancel	Cancel	7

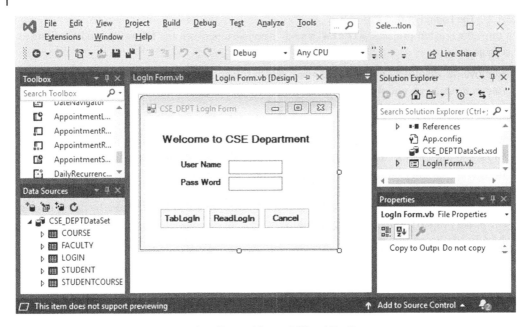

Figure 5.18 The finished project window. *Source:* Microsoft Visual Studio.

Table 5.4 Objects for the Selection form.

Type	Name	Text	TabIndex	DropDownStyle
Label	Label1	Make Your Selection	0	
ComboBox	ComboSelection	Faculty Information	1	Simple
Button	btnOK	OK	2	
Button	btnExit	Exit	3	
Form	SelectionForm	Selection Form		

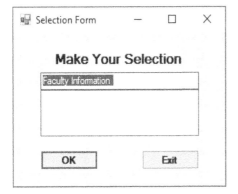

Figure 5.19 The completed Selection form. *Source:* Microsoft Visual Studio.

One needs to select the **OK** button, **btnOK**, as the default button by choosing this button from the **AcceptButton** property of the Selection Form window. Also you need to select the **CenterScreen** from the **StartPosition** property of the Selection Form window.

5.3.1.3 The Faculty Form

The Faculty Form contains controls that are related to faculty information stored in the Faculty table in our sample database CSE_DEPT, which was built in Chapter 2.

Totally, 28 controls shown in Table 5.5 are included in this Faculty Form window. The finished Faculty form should match one that is shown in Figure 5.20.

Table 5.5 Controls on the Faculty form.

Type	Name	Text	TabIndex	DropDownStyle
Label	Label1	Faculty Image	0	
TextBox	txtImage		1	
PictureBox	PhotoBox			
GroupBox	FacultyBox	Faculty Name & Query Method	2	
Label	Label2	Faculty Name	2.0	
ComboBox	ComboName		2.1	DropDownList
Label	Label3	Query Method	2.2	
ComboBox	ComboMethod		2.3	DropDownList
GroupBox	FacultyInfoBox	Faculty Information	3	
Label	Label4	Faculty ID	3.0	
TextBox	txtID		3.1	
Label	Label5	Name	3.2	
TextBox	txtName		3.3	
Label	Label6	Title	3.4	
TextBox	txtTitle		3.5	
Label	Label7	Office	3.6	
TextBox	txtOffice		3.7	
Label	Label8	Phone	3.8	
TextBox	txtPhone		3.9	
Label	Label9	College	3.10	
TextBox	txtCollege		3.11	
Label	Label10	Email	3.12	
TextBox	txtEmail		3.13	
Button	btnSelect	Select	4	
Button	btnInsert	Insert	5	
Button	btnUpdate	Update	6	
Button	btnDelete	Delete	7	
Button	btnBack	Back	8	
Form	FacultyForm	CSE DEPT Faculty Form		

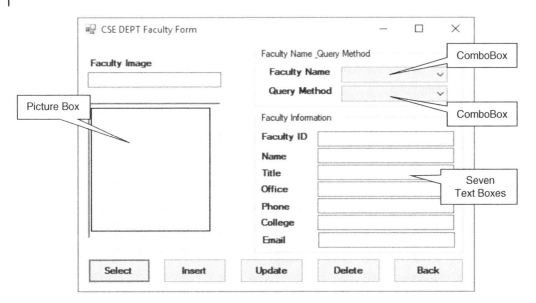

Figure 5.20 The finished Faculty form. *Source:* Microsoft Visual Studio.

One needs to choose the `Select` button, `btnSelect`, as the default button by choosing this button from the `AcceptButton` property of the Faculty form. Also you need to select the `CenterScreen` from the `StartPosition` property of the Faculty form.

In this Chapter, we only use the `Select` button to make data query to the data source. Other buttons will be used for the following chapters.

5.3.1.4 The Course Form

This form is used to connect to the Course table in your data source to retrieve course information associated with a specified faculty member selected by the user. Recall in Chapter 2, we developed a sample database CSE_DEPT and the Course table is one of five tables built in that database. A one-to-many relationship is existed between the Faculty and the Course table, which is connected using a primary key `FACULTY_ID` in the Faculty table and a foreign key `FACULTY_ID` in the Course table. We will use this relationship to retrieve data from the Course table based on the `FACULTY_ID` in both tables.

Totally, 25 controls shown in Table 5.6 are used in this form. Add these controls into this Course form window. The finished Course Form window is shown in Figure 5.21.

In this Chapter, we only use the `Select` button to make data query to the data source. The Insert and other buttons will be used in Chapters 6 and 7 for other data actions, such as data insertion, and data updating and deleting operations against our sample database.

5.3.1.5 The Student Form

The Student Form is used to collect and display student information including the courses taken by the student. As we mentioned in Section 5.1, the Student form needs two data tables in the database; the Student table and the StudentCourse table. This is a typical example of using two data tables for one graphical user interface (form).

Add 29 controls shown in Table 5.7 into the Student Form window. Your finished Student Form window is shown in Figure 5.22.

Table 5.6 Controls on the Course form.

Type	Name	Text	TabIndex	DropDownStyle
GroupBox	NameBox	Faculty Name & Query Method	0	
Label	Label1	Faculty Name	0.0	
ComboBox	ComboName		0.1	DropDownList
Label	Label2	Query Method	0.2	
ComboBox	ComboMethod		0.3	DropDownList
GroupBox	CourseBox	Course List	1	
ListBox	CourseList		1.0	
GroupBox	CourseInfoBox	Course information	2	
Label	CourseIDLabel	Course ID	2.0	
TextBox	txtID		2.1	
Label	CourseLabel	Course	2.2	
TextBox	txtCourse		2.3	
Label	ScheduleLabel	Schedule	2.4	
TextBox	txtSchedule		2.5	
Label	ClassRoomLabel	Classroom	2.6	
TextBox	txtClassRoom		2.7	
Label	CreditsLabel	Credits	2.8	
TextBox	txtCredits		2.9	
Label	EnrollLabel	Enrollment	2.10	
TextBox	txtEnroll		2.11	
Button	btnSelect	Select	3	
Button	btnInsert	Insert	4	
Button	btnUpdate	Update	5	
Button	btnDelete	Delete	6	
Button	btnBack	Back	7	
Form	CourseForm	CSE DEPT Course Form		

Make sure that you set up the following properties for controls and objects:

- Make the `Select` button as the default button by selecting this button from the `AcceptButton` property of the Student form window.
- Select the `CenterScreen` from the `StartPosition` property of the Student Form.
- Set the `BorderStyle` property of the `ListBox` control, CourseList, to `FixedSingle`.

Also in this Student Form, we use TextBoxes to binding and display the student's information. All courses, which are represented by the `course_id`, taken by the student are reflected and displayed in a `ListBox` control, CourseList.

5.4 Use Visual Studio Wizards and Design Tools to Query and Display Data

After all GUIs are completed, we need to use the data source added into this new project to access our sample database CSE_DEPT. In Section 5.2.2.2, we have provided a detailed discussion about how to add a new data source and how to configure a new added data source in a data-driven appli-

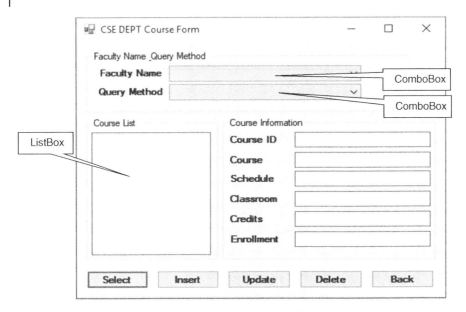

Figure 5.21 The completed Course form. *Source:* Microsoft Visual Studio.

cation. Now we will illustrate how to use those tools and wizards to connect and access our sample database to retrieve and display required information for the selected window forms and associated data tables.

5.4.1 Query and Display Data Using the DataGridView and Detail Controls

Now we have added a data source into your Visual Basic.NET 2019 project. Before we can develop this data-driven project, we want to show a popular but important functionality provided by the Toolbox window, `DataGridView`. As we discussed this issue in Section 5.2.1.2, the DataGridView is a view container and it can be used to bind data from your database and display the data in a tabular or a grid format in your Visual Basic form windows.

To use this tool, you can add a new blank form to the project SelectWizard and name this new form as `Grid Form`. Go to `Project|Add Windows Form` to open the Add New Item wizard. Select `Windows Form` from the Template list and enter `Grid Form.vb` into the `Name` box and click on the `Add` button.

Make the new added form `Grid_Form` be selected and open the Data Source window. You can view data of any table in your data source window. The two popular views are `Full Table` view and `Detail` view for specified columns.

Here we use the Faculty table as an example to illustrate how to use these two views.

5.4.1.1 View the Entire Table

To view a full Faculty table, expand the **FACULTY** table from the Data Source window, click on the drop-down arrow, and select the `DataGridView` item. Then drag the **FACULTY** table to the `Grid_Form`, as shown in Figure 5.23 (refer to Figure 2.59 in Chapter 2).

As soon as you drag the Faculty table to the Grid Form, a set of graphical components is created and added into your form automatically, which include the browsing arrows, Addition, Delete, and Save buttons. This set of components is to help you to view data from the selected table.

Now you can run your project by clicking on the Start button. But wait a moment! One more thing before running the project is to check whether you have selected your Grid Form as the startup

Table 5.7 Controls on the Student form.

Type	Name	Text	TabIndex	DropDownStyle
PictureBox	PhotoBox			
GroupBox	StudentNameBox	Student Name & Method	0	
Label	Label1	Student Name	0.0	
ComboBox	ComboName		0.1	DropDownList
Label	Label2	Query method	0.2	
ComboBox	ComboMethod		0.3	DropDownList
GroupBox	CourseSelectedBox	Course Selected	1	
ListBox	CourseList		1.0	
GroupBox	StudentInfoBox	Student Information	2	
Label	Label3	Student ID	2.0	
TextBox	txtID		2.1	
Label	Label4	Student Name	2.2	
TextBox	txtName		2.3	
Label	Label5	School Year	2.4	
TextBox	txtSchoolYear		2.5	
Label	Label6	GPA	2.6	
TextBox	txtGPA		2.7	
Label	Label7	Major	2.8	
TextBox	txtStatus		2.9	
Label	Label8	Credits	2.10	
TextBox	txtCredits		2.11	
Label	Label9	Email	2.12	
TextBox	txtEmail		2.13	
Button	btnSelect	Select	3	
Button	btnInsert	Insert	4	
Button	btnUpdate	Update	5	
Button	btnDelete	Delete	6	
Button	btnBack	Back	7	
Form	StudentForm	CSE DEPT student form		

object from the project property menu. To do that, go to `Project|SelectWizard Properties`, on the opened window, select the `Grid_Form` from the `Startup form` box. Now run the project and you can find that the entire Faculty table is shown in this grid view tool, as shown in Figure 5.24.

Using this grid view tool, you can not only view data from the Faculty table but also you can add new data into and delete data from the table by clicking the **Add** (**+**) or **Delete** (**x**) button to do that. Just type the new data in the new line after you click the **Add** button if you want to add new data or move to the data you want to delete by clicking browsing arrow on the top of the form window and then click the **Delete** button. One thing you need to know is that these modifications only take effect to data in your data tables in the DataSet, and it has nothing to do with data in your database yet.

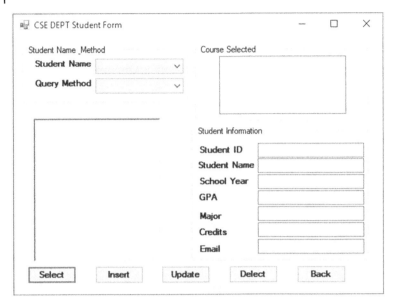

Figure 5.22 The completed Student form. *Source:* Microsoft Visual Studio.

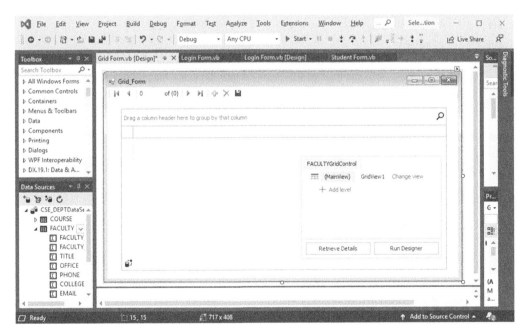

Figure 5.23 The DataGridView tool. *Source:* Microsoft Visual Studio.

When you drag the Faculty table from the data source window to the Grid Form, what was happened behind this dragging? Let's take a little more look at this issue.

First, you may already find that four components, FacultyBindingSource, FacultyTableAdapter, FacultyBindingNavigator, and TableAdapterManager, have been added into this form as you perform this dragging. As we mentioned in Sections 5.2.1.1–5.2.1.5, those components are objects or

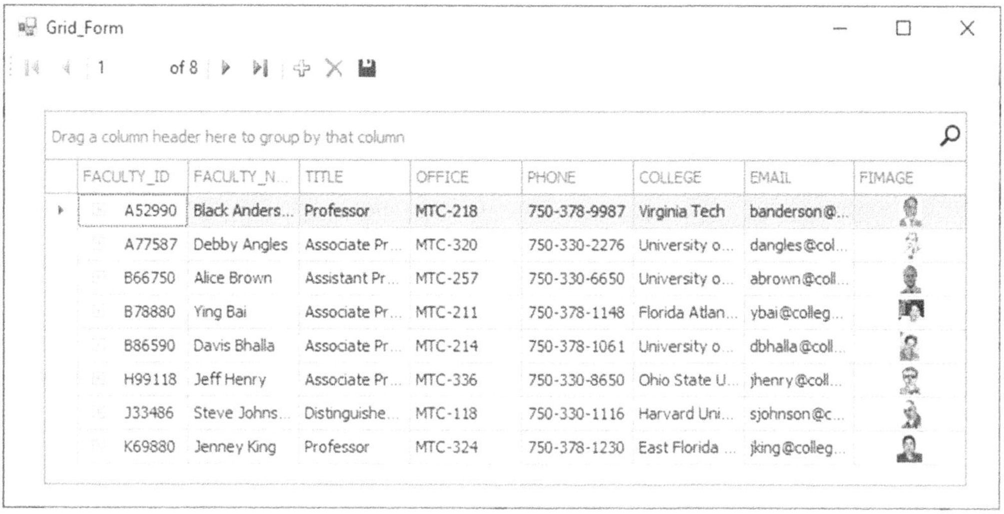

FACULTY_ID	FACULTY_N...	TITLE	OFFICE	PHONE	COLLEGE	EMAIL	FIMAGE
A52990	Black Anders...	Professor	MTC-218	750-378-9987	Virginia Tech	banderson@...	
A77587	Debby Angles	Associate Pr...	MTC-320	750-330-2276	University o...	dangles@col...	
B66750	Alice Brown	Assistant Pr...	MTC-257	750-330-6650	University o...	abrown@coll...	
B78880	Ying Bai	Associate Pr...	MTC-211	750-378-1148	Florida Atlan...	ybai@colleg...	
B86590	Davis Bhalla	Associate Pr...	MTC-214	750-378-1061	University o...	dbhalla@coll...	
H99118	Jeff Henry	Associate Pr...	MTC-336	750-330-8650	Ohio State U...	jhenry@coll...	
J33486	Steve Johns...	Distinguishe...	MTC-118	750-330-1116	Harvard Uni...	sjohnson@c...	
K69880	Jenney King	Professor	MTC-324	750-378-1230	East Florida ...	jking@colleg...	

Figure 5.24 The entire table view for the Faculty table. *Source:* Microsoft Visual Studio.

instances that are created based on their associated classes such as the BindingSource, BindingNavigator, and TableAdapter as you drag the Faculty table into your form window.

Second, let's look at the situation occurred to the program codes. Open the Solution Explorer window and select the **Grid Form.vb** and then click on the **View Code** button to open the Code window. Browse to the **Grid_Form_Load()** event procedure and you can find a line of code shown below has been already added into this procedure:

```
Me.FacultyTableAdapter.Fill(Me.CSE_DEPTDataSet.Faculty)
```

It looks like that the **Fill()** method, which belongs to the FacultyTableAdapter, is called to load data from the database into your DataGridView tool. The **Fill()** is a very powerful method and it performs an equivalent operation as an SELECT statement did. To make your guys more clear, open the data source window and right-click on any place inside that window. Select the **Edit the DataSet with Designer** item to open the DataSet Designer Wizard. Right-click on the bottom line on the Faculty table, in which the **Fill()** and the **GetData()** methods are shown, and then select the **Configure** item to open the **TableAdapter Configuration Wizard**. You will find that a complete SELECT statement is already in there:

```
SELECT faculty_id, faculty_name, title, office, college, phone,
email, fimage FROM Faculty
```

This statement will be executed when the **Fill()** method is called by the FacultyTable-Adapter as the **Grid_Form_Load()** event procedure runs when the project is started. The data returned from executing this statement will be filled to the grid view tool in the Faculty form.

5.4.1.2 View Each Record or the Specified Columns with Detail View

To view each record from the Faculty table, first delete the **DataGridView** item from the Grid_ Form window. Then go to the Data Source window and expand the **Faculty** table. Click the drop-down arrow and select the **Detail** item. Drag the Faculty table from the data source window to the **Grid_Form** window (refer to Figure 2.58 in Chapter 2).

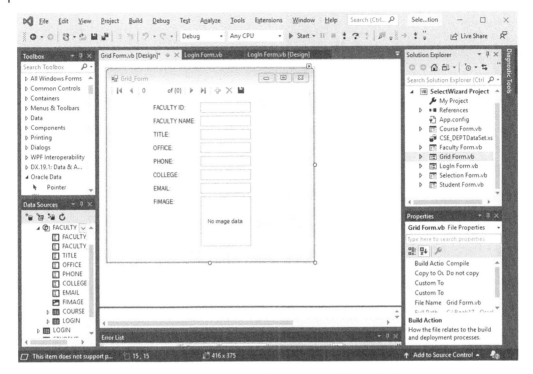

Figure 5.25 The Detail view for specified columns. *Source:* Microsoft Visual Studio.

Immediately, you can find that three new objects, `FacultyBindingSource`, `FacultyTableAdapter` and `FacultyBindingNavigator`, are added into the project. All column headers in the Faculty table are displayed, which is shown in Figure 5.25.

Now go to the `fimage` box and click on the arrow ▶ located at the upper-right corner of that box to open the `PictureEdit Tasks` wizard. Select the `Stretch` item from the `Size Mode` property box to set up the faculty image displaying mode.

Now click on the `Start` button to run your project, and the first record in the Faculty table is displayed in this Detail tool. To view each record, you can click on the forward arrow on the top of the form to scan all records from the top to the bottom of the Faculty table. An example record of a faculty named Ying Bai is shown in Figure 5.26.

If you only want to display some specified columns from the Faculty table, go to the Data Source window and select the Faculty table. Expand the table to display the individual columns and drag the desired column from the data source window onto the Grid Form window. For each column you drag, an individual data-bound control is created on the Grid Form, accompanied by an appropriately titled label control. When you run your project, the first record with the specified columns will be retrieved and displayed on the form, and you can scan all records by clicking the forward arrow.

Well, the `DataGridView` is a powerful tool and allow users to view all data from a table. But generally, we do not want to perform that data view like an inline query statement did. The so-called inline query statement means that the query statement must be already defined in full before your project runs. In other words, you cannot add any parameter into this statement after your project runs, which we called dynamic or runtime query statements, and all parameters

Figure 5.26 The running status of the Detail view for each record. *Source:* Microsoft Visual Studio.

must be predefined before your project runs. But running query statements dynamically is a very popular style for today's database operations, and in the following sections we will concentrate on this technique.

5.4.2 Use DataSet Designer to Edit the Structure of the DataSet

After a data source is added into your new project, you can edit the DataSet structure based on your applications if you want to develop a dynamic query statement. The following DataSet Structures can be edited using the DataSet Designer:

- Build user-defined query in an Oracle query statement format.
- Modify the method of the TableAdapter to match the users' preference.

Now let's begin to develop a dynamic query statement or a user-defined query with an example. We still use the sample project **SelectWizard** and start from the **LogIn** table.

Open the data source window and right-click any place inside the window, and select **Edit DataSet with Designer** to open the **DataSet Design Wizard**. Locate the **LogIn** table and right-click on the bottom line, in which two methods – **Fill()** and **GetData()** – are displayed, and select the **Add Query** item from the popup menu.

On the opened **TableAdapter Configuration** Wizard, perform the following operations to build this customer query:

1) On the opened Choose a Command Type wizard, keep the default radio button selection **Use SQL statements** checked, and click on the **Next** button.
2) On the opened Choose a Query Type wizard, keep the default radio button selection **SELECT which returns rows** checked, and click on the **Next** button.

3) In the next wizard, click on the **Query Builder** button to open the Query Builder window to build our desired dynamic query. The opened Query Build wizard is shown in Figure 5.27.
4) Move the cursor to the intersection cell of the **USER_NAME** row and the **Filter** column, type **=?** and press the *Enter* key from the keyboard. Perform the same operation to the intersection cell of the **PASS_WORD** row and the **Filter** column.
5) Your finished query is displayed in the bottom text pane, as shown in Figure 5.27.

Query Builder provides a graphical user interface (GUI) for creating data queries, and it is composed of graphical panes and text panes. The top two panes are graphical panes and the third pane is the text pane. You can select desired columns from the top graphical pane, and each column you selected will be added into the second graphical pane. Using the second graphical pane, you can install desired criteria to build user-defined queries. The query you built will be translated and presented by a real query statement in the text pane.

By default, all columns in the LogIn table are selected in the top graphical pane. You can decide which column you want to query by checking the associated checkbox in front of each column. In this application, we prefer to select all columns from the top graphical pane. The selected columns will be displayed in the second graphical pane, which is also shown in Figure 5.27.

Since we try to build a dynamic Oracle query for the **LOGIN** table, what we want to do is: when the project runs, the **username** and **password** are entered by the user, and those two items will be dynamically embedded into an SELECT statement that will be sent to the data source, exactly to the **LOGIN** table, to check if the username and password entered by the user can be found from the LogIn table. If a match is found, that matched record will be read back from the DataSet to the BindingSource via the TableAdapter and furthermore reflected on the bound controls on the Visual Basic.NET 2019 LogIn form.

The problem is that when we build this query, we do not know the values of username and password, which will be entered by the user as the project runs. In other words, these two parameters are dynamic parameters. In order to build a dynamic query with two dynamic parameters, we need

Figure 5.27 The Query Build window. *Source:* Microsoft Visual Studio.

to use two question marks "?" to temporarily replace those two parameters in the SELECT statement. We do this by typing an equal symbol followed by a question mark in the **Filter** column for **USER_NAME** and **PASS_WORD** rows in the second graphical pane, which is shown in Figure 5.27. The two question marks will become two dynamic parameters, represented by **:Param1** and **:Param2**, after you press the *Enter* key from the keyboard. The prefixed colon (:) means that this is a dynamic parameter and this is the typical representation method for the dynamic parameters used in an Oracle database query.

Now let's go to the text pane and you can find that a **WHERE** clause is attached at the end of the SELECT statement, which is shown in Figure 5.27. The clause

```
WHERE (USER_NAME = :PARAM1) AND (PASS_WORD = :PARAM2)
```

is used to set up a dynamic criterion for this SELECT statement. Two dynamic parameters **PARAM1** and **PARAM2** will be replaced later by the actual username and password entered by the user as the project runs. You can consider the colon symbol as a * in C++, which works as an address. So we leave two addresses that will be filled later by two real dynamic parameters, username and password, as the project runs.

Click on the **OK** button to return to the Configuration wizard. This wizard shows the complete query we built from the last step in the text format to ask your confirmation, and you can make any modification if you want. Click on the **Next** button to go to the next step since we do not need to do any modification to this query.

The next wizard shown in Figure 5.28 provides you with two options: (i) it allows you to modify the **Fill()** method to meet your specified query for your application and (ii) it allows you to modify the **GetData()** method that returns a new data table filled with the results of the query statement.

For this application, we need to modify the name of the **FillBy** method by attaching **UserNamePassWord** to the end of this Fill method, which is shown in Figure 5.28. We will use this method in our project to run this dynamic query statement. Click on the **Next** button to go to the next wizard.

The next wizard shows the result of your TableAdapter configuration. If everything is going smoothly, all statements and methods should be created and modified successfully, as shown in Figure 5.29. Click on the **Finish** button to complete this configuration.

Before we can begin to do our coding job, we need to bind data to controls on the LogIn form to set up the connection or binding relationship between each control on the LogIn form and each data item on the data source.

5.4.3 Bind Data to the Associated Controls in LogIn Form

Open the Solution Explorer window and right-click on the LogIn form, and then select the **View Designer** button from the popup menu to open its graphical user interface. Now we want to use the BindingSource to bind controls in the LogIn form, exactly the User Name and Pass Word TextBoxes, to the associated data fields in the LogIn table in the data source.

Click on the **User Name** TextBox and go to the **DataBindings** property that is located in the top section of the Property Window. Expand the property to display the individual items and then select the **Text** item. Click on the drop-down arrow to expand the following items:

- Other Data Sources
- Project Data Sources
- CSE_DEPTDataSet

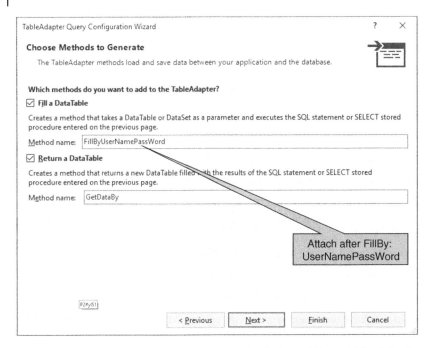

Figure 5.28 The Choose Methods to Generate wizard. *Source:* Microsoft Visual Studio.

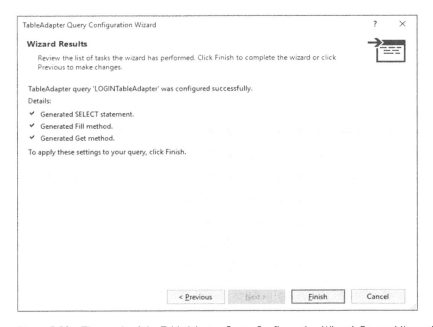

Figure 5.29 The result of the TableAdapter Query Configuration Wizard. *Source:* Microsoft Visual Studio.

The expansion result is shown in Figure 5.30.

Then expand the **LOGIN** table and select the **USER_NAME** column by clicking on it. In this way, we finished the data binding and set up a connection between the User Name TextBox control on the LogIn form and the **USER_NAME** column in the LogIn table in our sample database.

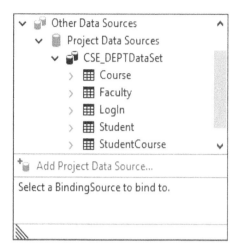

Figure 5.30 The DataBindings property. *Source:* Microsoft Visual Studio.

You can find that three objects, `CSE_DEPTDataSet`, `LogInBindingSource,` and `LogInTableAdapter,` have been added into the project and displayed at the bottom of the window after you finish this binding operation.

When you perform the first data binding, there is no any BindingSource available since you have not performed any binding before. You can browse to the desired data column and select it to finish this binding. Once you finish the first binding, a new BindingSource object is created, and all the following data bindings should use that new created BindingSource to perform all data bindings.

Well, is that easy? Yes. Perform the similar operations for the `Pass Word` TextBox to bind it with the `PASS_WORD` column in the LogIn table in the data source. But one point you need to note is: When we perform the data binding for the User Name TextBox, there is no BindingSource object available because you have not performed any data binding before, and the User Name is the first control you want to bind. You need to perform those steps as we did above. However, after you finish the first binding, a new BindingSource object, `LogInBindingSource`, is created. You need to use this BindingSource object to handle all other data binding jobs for all other controls on the LogIn form.

Let's perform the data binding for the `Pass Word` TextBox now.

Click that TextBox to select it, then go to the `DataBindings` property, select the `Text` item, and then click on the drop-down arrow. This time you will find that a new BindingSource object, `LogInBindingSource`, is shown up (Figure 5.31).

Expand this new binding source object and select the `PASS_WORD` column by clicking on it. The data binding for `PASS_WORD` is done.

Some readers may have noted that when we call the `Fill()` method, exactly the `FillByUserNamePassWord()`, from the LogInTableAdapter, we fill the LogIn form with

Figure 5.31 The created BindingSource object LogInBindingSource. *Source:* Microsoft Visual Studio.

four columns; **USER_NAME, PASS_WORD, FACULTY_ID,** and **STUDENT_ID** from the LogIn table. In fact, we only need to fill two textbox controls on the form: **txtUserName** and **txtPassWord** with two associated columns in the LogIn table; **USER_NAME** and **PASS_WORD.** We need to know if we can find matched username and password with those entered by the user in the LogIn table. If both matched items can be found in the LogIn table, which means that the login is successful and we can continue for the next step. Two bound-control on the form, **txtUserName** and **txtPassWord,** will be filled with the identical values stored in the LogIn table. It looks like that this does not make sense. In fact, we do not want to retrieve any column from the LogIn table, but instead, we only want to find the matched items of username and password to those entered by the user, for two columns in the LogIn table: **USER_NAME** and **PASS_WORD.** If we can find matched username and password, we do not care whether to fill the **FACULTY_ID** and **STUDENT_ID** or not. If no matched items can be found, this means that the login is failed and a warning message should be given.

Before we can go ahead for our coding, one thing we need to point out is the displaying style of the password in the textbox control **txtPassWord.** Generally, the password letters will be represented by a sequence of star * when users enter them as the project runs. To make this happened to our project, you need to set the **PasswordChar** property of the textbox control **txtPassWord** to *.

Now it is the time for us to develop codes that are related to those objects we created in the previous steps such as the BindingSource and TableAdapter to complete the dynamic query. The operation sequences of the LogIn form are shown below:

1) When the project runs, the user needs to enter the username and password to two textbox controls, **txtUserName** and **txtPassWord.**
2) Then the user will click on the **LogIn** button on the form to execute the LogIn event procedure.
3) The LogIn event procedure will first create some local variables or objects that will be used for the data query and displaying of the next form, **SelectionForm.**
4) Then the procedure will call the **FillByUserNamePassWord()** query method to fill the LogIn form.

5) If this Fill is successful, which means that a pair of matched data items for username and password has been found from the LogIn table, the next window form, **SelectionForm**, will be displayed for the next step.
6) Otherwise, a warning message is displayed.

The new objects created in step 3 include a new object of the LogInTableAdapter class, a new object of the next window form class, **SelectionForm**, since we need to use the LogInTableAdapter object to call the **FillByUserNamePassWord()** method and to use a new object to show the next window form **SelectionForm**.

Keep those points in mind and now let's begin to do the coding for the LogIn button's event procedure.

5.4.4   Develop Codes to Query Data Using the Fill() Method

Right-click on the LogIn form from the Solution Explorer window and click on the **View Designer** from the popup menu to open its graphical user interface. Double-click on the **TabLogIn** button to open its event procedure.

Based on step 3 in the above operation sequence, first we need to create two local objects: the **LogInTableApt** is an object of the LogInTableAdapter class and the **selForm** is an object of the **SelectionForm** class. The new created objects are shown in the top two lines (**A**) in Figure 5.32.

You need to note that all TableAdapters in this project are located in the namespace **CSE_ DEPTDataSetTableAdapters**. You need to use this namespace to access the desired TableAdapter.

Let's have a closer look at this piece of codes to see how it works:

B) Before to fill the LogIn table, clean up that table in the DataSet. As we mentioned in Section 5.2.1.1, the DataSet is a table holder and it contains multiple data tables. But these data tables are only mappings to those real data tables in the database. All data can be loaded into these tables in the DataSet using the TableAdapter when your project runs. Here a property **ClearBeforeFill**, which belongs to the TableAdapter, is set to **True** to perform this cleaning job for that mapped LogIn data table in the DataSet.
C) Now we need to call the Fill() method we modified in Section 5.4.2, exactly the **FillByUserNamePassWord()**, to fill the LogIn data table in the DataSet. Because we have already bound two textbox controls on the LogIn form, **txtUserName** and **txtPassWord**,

```
┌─────────────────────────────────────────┬──────────────────────────────────┐
│ TabLogIn                            ▼    │ Click                        ▼   │
├──────────────────────────────────────────────────────────────────────────────┤
│   Private Sub TabLogIn_Click(sender As Object, e As EventArgs) Handles TabLogIn.Click
│       Dim LogInTableApt As New CSE_DEPTDataSetTableAdapters.LogInTableAdapter
│ A     Dim selForm As New SelectionForm
│
│ B     LogInTableApt.ClearBeforeFill = True
│ C     LogInTableApt.FillByUserNamePassWord(CSE_DEPTDataSet.LogIn, txtUserName.Text, txtPassWord.Text)
│ D     If CSE_DEPTDataSet.LogIn.Count = 0 Then
│ E         MessageBox.Show("No matched username/password found!")
│ F       Exit Sub
│       End If
│ G     selForm.Show()
│ H     Me.Hide()
│   End Sub
│ ─────────────────────────────────────────────────────────────────────────────
│   Private Sub btnCancel_Click(sender As Object, e As EventArgs) Handles btnCancel.Click
│       Me.Close()
│   End Sub
└──────────────────────────────────────────────────────────────────────────────┘
```

Figure 5.32   The codes of the LogIn button's event procedure.

with two columns in the LogIn data table in the DataSet, `USER_NAME` and `PASS_WORD`, using the LogInBindingSource, so these two filled columns in the LogIn data table will also be reflected in those two bound textbox controls, `txtUserName` and `txtPassWord`, when this Fill() method is executed.

This Fill() method has three arguments; the first one is the data table, in this case it is the LogIn table that is held by the DataSet, CSE_DEPTDataSet. The following two parameters are dynamic parameters that were temporarily replaced by two question marks '?' when we modify this Fill() method in Section 5.4.2. Now we can use two real parameters, `txtUserName.Text` and `txtPassWord.Text,` to replace those two question marks to complete this dynamic query.

D) If a matched username and password is found from the LogIn table in the database, the Fill() method will fill the LogIn table in the DataSet, and at the same time, these two filled columns will be reflected on two bound textbox controls on the LogIn form, `txtUserName` and `txtPassWord`. The Count property of the LogIn table in the DataSet will be set. Otherwise, this property will be reset to 0. By checking this property, we will know if this Fill is successful or not, or if a matched username and password is found from the database.

If this property is 0, which means that no matched item is found from the database, and therefore no column is filled for the LogIn data table in the DataSet, the login is failed.

E) Then a warning message is displayed to ask users to handle it.

F) An `Exit Sub` is executed to exit the event procedure. You need to note that exit the event procedure does not mean to exit the project and your project still run and wait for the next login process.

G) If the login process is successful, the next window form, Selection form, will be shown to allow us to continue to the next step.

H) After displaying the next form, the current form, LogIn form, should be hidden by calling the `Hide()` method. The keyword `Me` represent the current window form.

The code for the `Cancel` button's event procedure is very simple. The `Close()` method should be called to terminate our project if this button is clicked by the user.

Before we can test this piece of cods by running the project, perform the following two operations:

1) Make sure that the LogIn form has been selected as the Start form from the project property window. To confirm this, go to `Project|SelectWizard Properties` to open the `Application` window and select the `LogInForm` from the `Start form` box.

2) Remove all codes inside the `LogInForm_Load()` event procedure since those codes are generated by the system automatically and we do not need those codes.

Now click on the Start button to run the project. Your running project should match one that is shown in Figure 5.33.

Enter a valid username such as `jhenry` to the User Name textbox and a valid password such as `test` to the Pass Word textbox and then click on the `TabLogIn` button. The `FillByUserNamePassWord()` method will be called to fill the LogIn table in the data source. Because we entered correct username and password, this fill will be successful and the next form, SelectionForm, will be shown up.

Now try to enter a wrong username or password and then click on the `TabLogIn` button, a Messagebox will be displayed, which is shown in Figure 5.34, to ask user to handle this situation.

In this section, we used the LogIn form and LogIn table to show readers how to perform a dynamic data query and fill a mapped data table in the DataSet from those columns in a data table in the database using the Visual Studio.NET tools and data wizards. The coding is relatively simple

Figure 5.33 The running status of the LogIn form. *Source:* Microsoft Visual Studio.

Figure 5.34 The warning message. *Source:* Microsoft Visual Studio.

and easy to follow. In the next section, we try to discuss how to use another method provided by the TableAdapter to pick up a single value from the database.

5.4.5 Use Return a Single Value to Query Data for LogIn Form

Many people may have experienced forgetting either the username or the password when they try to log on to a specified Web site to perform a purchasing, ordering, or try to obtain some information. In this section, we show users how to use a method to retrieve a single data value from the database. This method belongs to the TableAdapter.

We still use the LogIn form and LogIn table as an example. Suppose you forget your password, but you want to login to this project using the LogIn form with your username. Using this example, you can retrieve your password using your username.

The DataSet Designer allows us to edit the structure of the DataSet. As we discussed in Section 5.4.2, using this Designer, you can configure an existing query, add a new query, or add a new column and even a new key. The **Add Query** method allows us to add a new data query with a SELECT statement which returns a single value.

Open the LogIn form window from the Solution Explorer window and open the Data Source window. Right-click on any place inside the Data Source window and select the **Edit DataSet with Designer**, then locate the LogIn table, and right-click on the bottom line of that table, which contains our modified method **FillByUserNamePassWord()**. Then select **Add|Query** to open the **TableAdapter Query Configuration** Wizard. Perform the following operation to build this query:

1) On the opened wizard, keep the default selection **Use SQL statements**, which means that we want to build a query with SQL Statements, then click on the **Next** button, and choose the **SELECT which returns a single value** radio button. Click on the **Next** to go to the next wizard and click on the **Query Builder** button to build our query.

2) Delete the default query from the third pane by highlighting entire query and right-clicking on that query, and then selecting the **Delete** from the popup menu.

3) Then right-click on the top pane and select **Add Table** item from the popup menu to open the **Add Table** wizard, select the **LOGIN (CSE_DEPT)** table and click on the **Add** button, and then click on the **Close** button to close this **Add Table** wizard.

4) Select the **PASS_WORD** and **USER_NAME** columns from the LogIn table by checking those two related checkboxes.

5) Uncheck the **Output** checkbox from the **USER_NAME** column since we do not want to use it as the output, instead we need to use it as a criterion for this query.

6) Type **=?** on the **Filter** field from the **USER_NAME** column and press the **Enter** key from your keyboard. Your finished **Query Builder** is shown in Figure 5.35.
The query statement

SELECT PASS_WORD FROM CSE_DEPT.LOGIN WHERE (USER_NAME = :PARAM1)

indicates that we want to select a password from the LogIn table based on the **username** that is a dynamic parameter, and this parameter will be entered by the user when the project runs. Click on the **OK** button to go to the next wizard.

7) The next wizard is used to confirm your terminal query statement. Click on the **Next** button to go to the next wizard.

8) This wizard asks you to choose a function name for your query. Change the default name to a meaningful name such as **PassWordQuery** and then click on the **Next** button. A successful query result will be displayed if everything is fine. Click on the **Finish** button to complete this configuration.

Now let's do our coding for the LogIn form. For the testing purpose, first we need to add a temporary button to the LogIn form to perform this password checking function. Go to the ToolBox window and drag a button control to the LogIn form and set up the following properties to this button:

Figure 5.35 The finished Query Builder. *Source:* Microsoft Visual Studio.

`Name = `**`btnPW`**` and `` Text = ``**`PassWord`**

Then open the Solution Explorer window, select and open the LogIn form, double-click on the new added **PassWord** button to open its event procedure, and enter the codes shown in Figure 5.36 into this event procedure.

Let's have a closer look at this piece of codes to see how it works:

A) Create two local String variables. The **passWord** is used to hold the returning queried single value of the **PASS_WORD**. The **Result** is used to compose a resulting string that contains the returned password from the query.
B) Call the query, **PassWordQuery()**, with a dynamic parameter **username** that is entered by the user as the project runs. If this query found a valid password from the LogIn table based on the **username** entered by the user, that password will be returned and assigned to the local string variable **passWord**.
C) If this query cannot find any matched password, a blank string will be returned and assigned to the variable **passWord**. A Messagebox with a warning message will be displayed. The program will be directed to exit this subroutine.
D) If the query calling is successful, then a valid password is returned and assigned to the variable **passWord**. A composed string combined with the returned password is made and assigned to the String variable **Result**.
E) A Messagebox is used to display this found password.

Click on the Start button to run the project and your running project should match one that is shown in Figure 5.37a. Enter a username such as **jking** to the **User Name** box and click on the **PassWord** button. The returned password is displayed in a message box, which is shown in Figure 5.37b.

Now you can remove the temporary button **PassWord** and its event procedure from this LogIn form if you like since we need to continue to develop our project.

In the following sections, we will discuss how to develop more professional data-driven project using more controls and methods. We still use the **SelectWizard Project** as an example project and continue with the Selection Form.

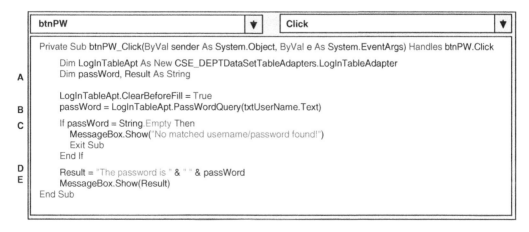

Figure 5.36 The codes for the btnPW button's event procedure.

(a)

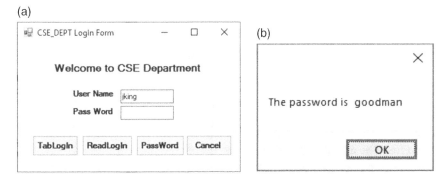

(b)

Figure 5.37   (a, b) The running status of the LogIn form. *Source:* Microsoft Visual Studio.

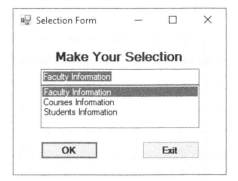

Figure 5.38   The Selection form. *Source:* Microsoft Visual Studio.

5.4.6   Develop the Codes for the Selection Form

As we discussed in Section 5.3.1.2, if the login process is successful, the **SelectionForm** window should be displayed to allow users to continue to the next step. Figure 5.38 shows an opened **SelectionForm** window.

Each piece of information in the ComboBox control is associated with a form window and is also associated with a group of data stored in a data table in the database.

The operation steps for this form are summarized as below:

1) When this form is opened, three pieces of information will be displayed in a ComboBox control to allow users to make a selection to browse the information related to that selection.
2) When the user clicks on the **OK** button, the selected form should be displayed to enable the user to browse the related information.

Based on the operation step 1, the coding to display three pieces of information should be located in the **Form_Load()** event procedure since this event procedure should be called first by the system as the project runs.

Open the Selection Form window and click on the View Code button to open its Code window. Select the **SelectionForm Events** item from the **Class Name** combo box and choose the **Load** item from the **Method Name** combo box to open its **SelectionForm_Load()** event procedure, and enter the codes shown in Figure 5.39 into this event procedure.

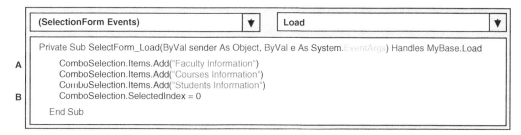

Figure 5.39   The codes for the Selection Form_Load event procedure.

Let's have a closer look at this piece of codes to see how it works:

A) The **Add** method of the ComboBox control is called to add all three pieces of information. The argument of this method must be String variable and have to be enclosed by the double quotation marks.

B) The **SelectedIndex** of this ComboBox control is reset to 0, which means that the first item, Faculty Information, is selected as the default information.

According to operation step 2 described above, when the **OK** button is clicked, the form related to the information selected by the user should be displayed to allow users to browse information from that form. On the opened Designer View of the SelectionForm object, double-click on the **OK** button to open its event procedure and enter the codes shown in Figure 5.40 into this procedure.

Let's have a closer look at this piece of codes to see how it works:

A) First create three new objects based on three classes. One needs to note that when you add any new Window Form into your project, the new item is a class, not an object. You need to create a new object or instance based on that class to use it.

B) Open the FacultyForm window if the user selected the **Faculty Information**.

C) Open the StudentForm window if the user selected the **Student Information**.

D) Open the CourseForm window if the user selected the **Course Information**.

The last coding for this form is the **Exit** button. Open the graphical user interface of the **SelectionForm** and double-click on the **Exit** button to open its event procedure. Enter the codes shown in Figure 5.41 into this procedure.

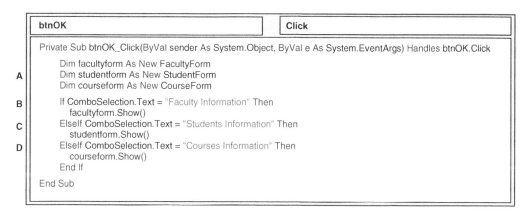

Figure 5.40   The codes for the OK button's event procedure.

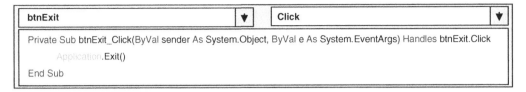

btnExit ▼	Click ▼

```
Private Sub btnExit_Click(ByVal sender As System.Object, ByVal e As System.EventArgs) Handles btnExit.Click
        Application.Exit()
End Sub
```

Figure 5.41 The codes for the Exit button's click event procedure.

This piece of codes is very simple. As the user clicks on the **Exit** button, the project is exited and terminated by calling the **Exit()** method.

Suppose the user selected the first item – Faculty Information. A Faculty form window will be displayed and it is supposed to be connected to a Faculty table in the database. If the user selected a faculty name from the ComboBox control and clicked on the **Select** button on that form (refer to Figure 5.3), all pieces of information related to that faculty should be displayed on seven text-boxes and a PictureBox on that form.

Now let's first see how to perform the data binding to bind controls on the Faculty form to the associated columns in the Faculty table in the database.

5.4.7 Query Data from the Faculty Table for the Faculty Form

First, let's open the Faculty form window from the Solution Explorer window and perform the following data bindings.

1) Select the Faculty ID textbox **txtID** by clicking on it, then go to the Properties Window and select the **DataBindings** property, select the **Text** item, and click on the drop-down arrow. Expand the following items (Figure 5.42a):

- Other Data Sources
- Project Data Sources
- CSE_DEPTDataSet
- Faculty

Then select the **FACULTY_ID** column from the Faculty table by clicking on it. In this way, you finish the binding between the textbox control **txtID** on the Faculty form and the **FACULTY_ID**

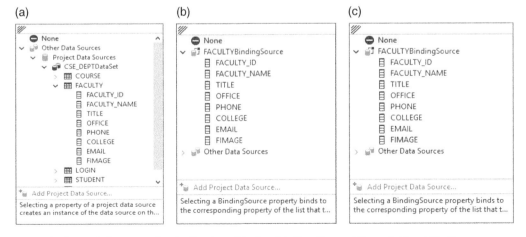

Figure 5.42 (a~c) The expansion for Faculty table data binding. *Source:* Microsoft Visual Studio.

column in the Faculty table. As soon as you finish this data binding, immediately you can find that three components are displayed under your form: CSE_DEPTDataSet, FacultyBindingSource, and FacultyTableAdapter.

2) Perform a similar operation for the next textbox **txtName** in the Faculty form to bind the **Name** and the **FACULTY_NAME** column in the Faculty table. Go to the **DataBindings** property and then select the **Text** item, and click on the drop-down arrow. This time you will find that a new object **FacuktyBindingSource** has been created. As we discussed in Section 5.4.3, as soon as you finished the first data binding, a new binding object related to the data-binding source will be created and served for the form in which the binding source is located. We need to use this binding source to bind our **Name** control. Expand this binding source until you find the Faculty table and then click on the **FACULTY_NAME** column to finish this binding. An example of this expansion is shown in Figure 5.42b.

3) In a similar way, you can finish the data binding for the rest of textbox controls; **txtTitle, txtOffice, txtPhone, txtCollege,** and **txtEmail**. The binding relationship is: txt-Title→**TITLE** column, txtOffice→**OFFICE** column, txtPhone→**PHONE** column, txtCol-lege→**COLLEGE,** and txtEmail→**EMAIL** column in the Faculty table.

4) For the data binding of the PictureBox control, **PhotoBox**, which should be connected to the **FIMAGE** column in the Faculty table, perform a similar operation. The difference is that when selected the **PhotoBox** and go to the **DataBindings** property, you need to select the **Image** (not **Text**) item to do this binding, which is shown in Figure 5.42c.

Next, we need to use the DataSet Designer to build our data query with a SELECT statement and modify the name of the **FillBy()** method for the FacultyTableAdapter. Perform the following operations to complete this query building process:

1) In the Data Source window, right-click on any place inside that window and select **Edit DataSet with Designer** item to open the DataSet Designer Wizard.

2) Locate the Faculty table and right-click on the bottom line of the Faculty table and select the **Add|Query** item to open the TableAdapter Configuration Wizard.

3) On the opened Wizard, click on the **Next** to keep the default command type – **Use SQL statements** and click on the **Next** button to keep the default query type – **SELECT which returns rows** for the next wizard. Then click on the **Query Builder** button to open the Query Builder wizard, as shown in Figure 5.43.

4) In the middle graphical pane, move your cursor to the **Filter** column along the **FACULTY_NAME** row, then type a question mark **?,** and press the **Enter** key from your keyboard. In this way, a **WHERE** clause with a dynamic parameter represented by = **:PARAM1** is added into the query.

5) Your finished Query Builder should match one that is shown in Figure 5.43.

6) Click on the **OK** and the **Next** buttons to modify the name of the **FillBy()** method to **FillByFacultyName**. Click on the **Next** and then the **Finish** buttons to complete this configuration.

Now let's develop the codes for querying the faculty information using this Faculty form with the Faculty data table in the database.

5.4.8 Develop Codes to Query Data from the Faculty Table

In this section, we divide the coding job into two parts. Querying data from the Faculty table using the query Select method is discussed in Part I and retrieving data using the LINQ method is provided in Part II. Furthermore, we only take care of the coding for the **Select** and the

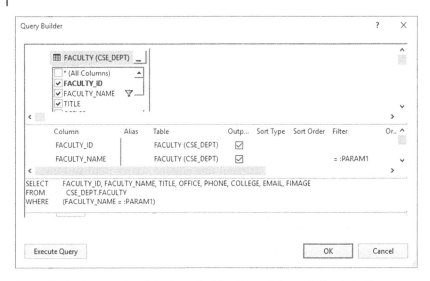

Figure 5.43 An example of the Query Builder. *Source:* Microsoft Visual Studio.

Back buttons' click event procedures in this section. The coding for all other buttons will be discussed and coded in later sections.

5.4.8.1 Develop Codes to Query Data Using the TableAdapter Method

As we mentioned above, the pseudo-code or the operation sequence of this data query can be described as:

- After the project runs, the user has completed the login process and selected the Faculty Information item from the Selection Form.
- The Faculty form will be displayed to allow users to select the desired faculty name from the Faculty Name ComboBox control.
- Then the user can click on the **Select** button to make a query to the Faculty data table to get all pieces of information related to that desired faculty.

The main coding job is performed inside the **Select** button's click event procedure. Prior to that coding, we need to do a query to get all default faculty names and add them into the Faculty Name ComboBox. Since these faculty names should be displayed first as the project runs, we need to do this coding in the **Form_Load** event procedure.

Open the **Faculty Form** Code Window and the **FacultyForm_Load** event procedure. Remove all original codes and enter the codes shown in Figure 5.44 into this procedure. A user-defined subroutine **CurrentFaculty()** is called to get all faculty members from the database and display them in the Faculty Name combo box, **ComboName**.

Now we need to do the coding for the **Select** button's click event procedure.

Right-click on the **Faculty Form.vb** from the Solution Explorer window and select the **View Designer** to open the Faculty form window. Then double-click on the **Select** button to open its event procedure. Enter the codes shown in Figure 5.45 into this event procedure.

Let's have a closer look at this piece of codes to see how it works:

A) First create a new FacultyTableAdapter object, **FacultyTableApt**. In Visual Basic.NET 2019, you have to create a new instance or object based on the data class if you want to use any method or property that belongs to that class.

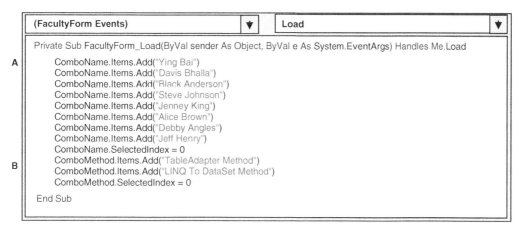

Figure 5.44 The codes for the FacultyForm_Load event procedure.

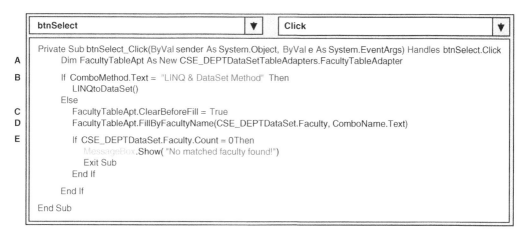

Figure 5.45 The codes for the Select button's event procedure.

B) If the user selected the LINQ & DataSet Method, a user-defined subroutine `LINQtoDataSet()` that will be built later is called to do a LINQ to DataSet query.

C) Otherwise, the SELECT query method has been selected. First, we need to clean up the Faculty table before it can be filled by setting the `ClearBeforeFill` property to `True`.

D) Call the method `FillByFacultyName()` to fill the Faculty table with a dynamic parameter, Faculty Name, which is selected by the user from the Faculty Name ComboBox control as the project runs.

E) By checking on the `Count` property of the Faculty table that is involved in our DataSet, we can confirm whether this fill is successful or not. If this property is equal to 0, which means that no matched record has been found from the Faculty table in the database, and therefore no any record or data has been filled into the Faculty table in our DataSet, a warning message is given for this situation to require users to handle this problem. The user can either continue to select correct faculty name or exit the project. If this property is nonzero, which indicates that this fill is successful and a matched faculty name is found and the Faculty table in our DataSet has been filled. All information related to the matched faculty will be displayed in seven textboxes and a PictureBox.

As we mentioned, in this section, we only perform the coding for the **Select** and the **Back** buttons. The coding for all other buttons will be provided in the later sections.

The coding for the **Back** button is very simple. The Faculty form will be removed from the screen and from the project or from the memory, when this button is clicked. A **Close()** method is used for this purpose, which is shown in Figure 5.46.

Next, we need to develop the codes to use LINQ to DataSet method to perform this faculty data query.

5.4.8.2 Develop Codes to Query Data Using the LINQ to DataSet Method

The faculty data query can be significantly integrated and improved using the LINQ to DataSet technology. We have already provided a complete discussion about this technology in Chapter 4. Refer to that chapter to get more details for this issue. In this part, we will concentrate on the coding for this kind of query.

Open the Code Window of the **FacultyForm** if it is not opened, create a user-defined subroutine and enter the codes, which are shown in Figure 5.47, into this window.

Let's have a closer look at this piece of codes to see how it works:

A) First the default **Fill()** method of the FacultyTableAdapter is executed to load data from the Faculty table in the database into the Faculty table in our DataSet. This step is necessary since the LINQ technique is applied with the DataSet and the DataSet must contain the valid data in all tables before this technique can be implemented.

B) A typical LINQ query structure is created and executed to retrieve all related information for the selected faculty member. The **facultyinfo** is an implicitly typed local variable. The Visual

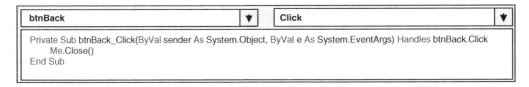

```
btnBack                                    ▼    Click                              ▼

Private Sub btnBack_Click(ByVal sender As System.Object, ByVal e As System.EventArgs) Handles btnBack.Click
    Me.Close()
End Sub
```

Figure 5.46   The codes for the Back button.

```
FacultyForm                                ▼    LINQtoDataSet                     ▼

     Private Sub LINQtoDataSet()
A        FACULTYTableAdapter.Fill(CSE_DEPTDataSet.FACULTY)
B        Dim facultyinfo = From fi In CSE_DEPTDataSet.FACULTY
                         Where fi.Field(Of String)("faculty_name").Equals(ComboName.Text)
                         Select fi
C        For Each fRow In facultyinfo
D           txtID.Text = fRow.FACULTY_ID
            txtName.Text = fRow.FACULTY_NAME
            txtTitle.Text = fRow.TITLE
            txtOffice.Text = fRow.OFFICE
            txtPhone.Text = fRow.PHONE
            txtCollege.Text = fRow.COLLEGE
            txtEmail.Text = fRow.EMAIL
E           Dim img As System.IO.MemoryStream = New System.IO.MemoryStream(fRow.FIMAGE)
F           PhotoBox.Image = System.Drawing.Image.FromStream(img)
         Next
     End Sub
```

Figure 5.47   The codes for the LINQ to DataSet subroutine.

Basic.NET 2019 will be able to automatically convert this variable to a suitable data type, in this case, it is a DataSet, when it sees it. An iteration variable **fi** is used to iterate over the result of this query from the Faculty table. Then, a SELECT statement is executed with the WHERE clause.

C) A **For Each** loop is utilized to pick up each column from the selected data row **fRow**, which is obtained from the **facultyinfo** we get from the LINQ query.

D) For all records represented by text, assign each column to the associated textbox to display it in the FacultyForm window.

E) Since all faculty images were stored as binary data in our sample database, thus a conversion from those binary data back to images is necessary before each of them can be assigned to the **PhotoBox.image** property. First, all binary data are converted to the stream with a system method **System.IO.MemoryStream()**.

F) Then another system method, **System.Drawing.Image.FromStream()**, is utilized to convert the related stream to the image and assign it to the **PhotoBox.image**.

Now we are ready to test our project. Click on the **Start** button to run the project. Enter **jhenry** as the username and **test** as the password on the LogIn form. Click on the **TabLogIn** button to open the Selection Form window, select the **Faculty Information** item, and then click on the **OK** button to open the Faculty form.

To perform this query using the TableAdapter Method, keep the default method in the Query Method ComboBox and select **Ying Bai** from the Faculty Name ComboBox, and click on the **Select** button. All information related to this faculty with a faculty picture will be displayed, as shown in Figure 5.48.

To test querying the faculty data using the LINQ to DataSet method, select the **LINQ to DataSet Method** from the Query Method combobox. Then select a desired faculty name from the Faculty Name ComboBox and click on the **Select** button. You can find that the same query result can be retrieved and displayed in this form. Click on the **Back** and then the **Exit** button in the Selection Form to exit our project.

Figure 5.48 The running status of the Faculty form window. *Source:* Microsoft Visual Studio.

At this point, we complete the designing and building our Faculty Form. Next, we will take care of our Course Form.

5.4.9 Query Data from the Course Table for the Course Form

The functions of this form are illustrated as the following steps:

1) This form allows users to find all courses taught by the selected faculty from the **Faculty Name** ComboBox when users click on the **Select** button. All courses, in fact all **course_id**, are displayed in the Course ListBox.
2) The detailed information for each course, such as the course title, course schedule, classroom, credits, and enrollment, can be obtained by clicking on the desired **course_id** from the Course ListBox and displayed in five TextBox controls.
3) The **Back** button allows users to return to the Selection Form to make some other selections to obtain desired information related to those selections.

In this section, we only take care of two buttons, the **Select** and the **Back**, and the coding for the other buttons will be discussed in the later chapters.

5.4.9.1 Build the Course Queries Using the Query Builder

For step 1 shown above, in order to find the courses taught by the selected faculty from the Course table, we need first to obtain the selected faculty ID that is associated with the selected faculty from the **Faculty Name** ComboBox when users click the **Select** button because no faculty name is available in the Course table. The only available information in the Course table is the **faculty_id**. So we need first to create a query that returns a single value (**faculty_id**) based on the selected faculty name from the Faculty table and then we can create another query in the Course table to find the courses (**course_id**) taught by the selected faculty based on the **faculty_id** obtained from the Faculty table.

Now let's do the first job, to create a query to obtain the associated **FACULTY_ID** from the Faculty table based on the selected faculty name in the **Faculty Name** ComboBox in the Course form:

1) Open the DataSet Designer Wizard, right-click on the bottom line of the Faculty table, and select **Add|Query** to open the TableAdapter Query Configuration Wizard.
2) Keep the default selection **Use SQL statements** and click on the **Next** button to go to the next wizard.
3) Check the radio button of **SELECT which returns a single value** to choose this query type and click on the **Next** button to go the next wizard.
4) Click on the **Query Builder** to build our query.
5) On the opened Query Builder wizard, remove the default query from the text pane or the third pane by highlighting it, right-clicking on it, and selecting the **Delete**. Then right-click on the top pane and select **Add Table** item to open the Add Table wizard. Select the Faculty table by clicking on it from the table list, click on the **Add,** and the **Close** buttons to add this table.
6) Select the **FACULTY_ID** and the **FACULTY_NAME** from the Faculty table by checking on them in the top pane and uncheck the **Output** checkbox for the **FACULTY_NAME** row in the mid-pane since we do not want to query the **FACULTY_NAME** but only use it as the criterion to find the **FACULTY_ID**.
7) Then type a question mark on the **Filter** column for the **FACULTY_NAME** row and press the **Enter** key in your keyboard. Your finished query is shown in Figure 5.49.

Figure 5.49 The finished query for the FACULTY_ID. *Source:* Microsoft Visual Studio.

8) The query statement shown in the text pane or the third pane is

```
SELECT FACULTY_ID FROM CSE_DEPT.FACULTY WHERE (FACULTY_NAME = :PARAM1)
```

9) Click on the OK and the **Next** buttons to go to the next wizard. Enter the FindFacultyIDByName into the box as our function name and then click on the **Next** and the **Finish** buttons to complete this query building.

Now let's continue to build our second query to find the courses (**COURSE_ID**) taught by the selected faculty from the Course table. Open the DataSet Designer to create our desired query and modify the **Fill()** method for the CourseTableAdapter:

1) Open the Data Source window if it not opened. Then right-click on any place inside this window and select the **Edit DataSet with Designer** item to open the DataSet Designer Wizard.
2) Right-click on the bottom line of the Course table and choose the **Add|Query** item to open the TableAdapter Configuration Wizard.
3) Keep the default selection **Use SQL statements** and click on the **Next** button to go to the next wizard. In the next wizard, keep the default selection **SELECT which returns rows** unchanged and click on the **Next** button.
4) Then click on the **Query Builder** to open the Query Builder window, which is shown in Figure 5.50.
5) Keep the default selections for the top graphical pane even we only need the **COURSE_ID** column and we will show your guys why we need to keep these default items later. Go to the **Filer** column along the **FACULTY_ID** row, and type a question mark (?) and press the **Enter** key from your keyboard. This is equivalent for us to set a dynamic parameter for this SELECT statement.
6) The completed query statement is displayed in the text pane and the content of this statement is

```
SELECT COURSE_ID, COURSE, CREDIT, CLASSROOM, SCHEDULE, ENROLLMENT,
FACULTY_ID
FROM COURSE
WHERE (FACULTY_ID = :PARAM1)
```

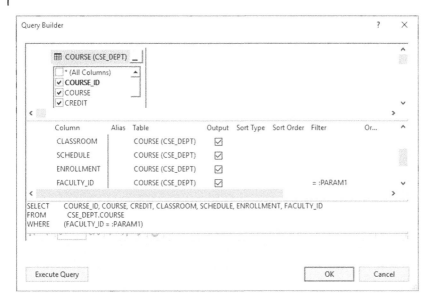

Figure 5.50 The Query Builder. *Source:* Microsoft Visual Studio.

7) The dynamic parameter `:PARAM1` is a temporary parameter and it will be replaced by the real parameter `FACULTY_ID` as the project runs.
8) Click on the `OK` and then the `Next` button to return to the TableAdapter Configuration Wizard to modify the `Fill()` method. Change the `FillBy` method to the `FillByFacultyID()`. Then click on the `Next` and the `Finish` button to complete this configuration.

The next step is to binding the controls from the Course form to the associated data column in the `Course` table in the DataSet. Right-click on the `Course Form.vb` from the Solution Explorer window and select the `View Designer` from the popup menu to open the Course form window.

5.4.9.2 Bind Data Columns to the Associated Controls in the Course Form
First, we need to bind the `CourseList` to the `COURSE_ID` column in the Course table in the DataSet. Recall that there are many course records with the same `FACULTY_ID` in this Course table when we built this sample database in Chapter 2. Those multiple records with the same `FACULTY_ID` are distinguished by the different `COURSE_ID` taught by that faculty. To binding a ListBox to those multiple course records with the same `FACULTY_ID`, we cannot continue to use the binding method we used before for textbox controls in the previous sections. This is a specialty of binding a ListBox control. The special point is that the relationship between the ListBox and the data items in a table is one-to-many, which means that a ListBox can contain multiple items, in this case, the CourseList can contain many `COURSE_ID`. So the binding of a ListBox control is exactly to bind a ListBox to a table in the DataSet, exactly to the `COURSE` table in this application.

Perform the following operation to complete this binding:

1) Click on the `CourseList` control from the Course form and go to the `DataSource` property. Then click on the drop-down arrow to expand the data source until the `COURSE` table is found. Select this table by clicking on it. Figure 5.51a shows this expansion situation.
2) Go to the `DisplayMember` property and expand the Course table to find the `COURSE_ID` column, and select it by clicking on this item (Figure 5.51b).

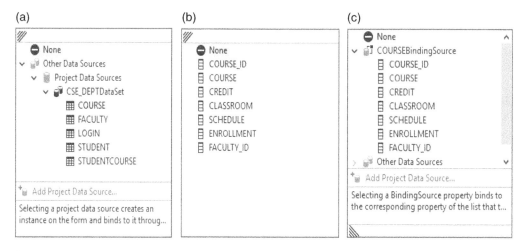

Figure 5.51 (a~c) The expansion of the data source. *Source:* Microsoft Visual Studio.

In this way, we set up a binding relationship between the **Course ListBox** in the Course form and the **COURSE** data table in the DataSet.

Now let's do the second binding and bind six textbox controls in the Course form to six columns in the Course data table in the DataSet. Perform the following operations to complete this binding:

1) Keep the Course form opened and then select the **Course ID** textbox from the Course form.
2) Go to the **DataBindings** property and expand to the **Text** item. Click on the drop-down arrow and you will find that a **CourseBindingSource** object is already in there for this project. Expand this **CourseBindingSource** until you find the **COURSE_ID** column, which is shown in Figure 5.51c, and then choose it by clicking on the **COURSE_ID** column.

In this way, a binding is set up between the **Course ID** textbox in the Course form and the **COURSE_ID** column in the Course table in the DataSet.

Set up all other four data bindings for the following five textbox controls: **Course**, **Schedule**, **Classroom**, **Credits,** and **Enrollment**, in a similar way.

One point you need to note is the order of performing these two bindings. You must first perform the binding for the CourseList control and then perform the binding for six Textboxes.

Now we can answer the question why we need to keep the default selections at the top graphical pane when we build our query in the Query Builder (refer to Figure 5.50). The reason for this is that we need those columns to perform data binding for our six textbox controls here. In this way, each textbox control in the Course form is bound with the associated data column in the Course table in the DataSet. After this kind of binding relationship is set up, all data columns in the data table Course in the DataSet will be updated by the data columns in the Course data table in our real database each time when a **FillByFacultyID()** method is executed. At the same time, all six textboxes' content will also be updated since those textbox controls have been bound to those data columns in the Course data table in the DataSet.

Ok, now it is the time for us to make coding for this form.

5.4.9.3 Develop Codes to Query Data for the Course Form

Based on the analysis of the functionality of the Course form we did above, when the user selected a faculty name and click on the **Select** button, all courses, exactly all **COURSE_ID**, taught by that faculty should be listed in the Course ListBox. To check the details for each course, click the

COURSE_ID from the CourseList control and all detailed information related to the selected **COURSE_ID** will be displayed in six textbox controls. The coding is divided into two parts. The first part is to query data using the TableAdapter method and the second part is to perform the data query using the LINQ to DataSet method.

5.4.9.3.1 Query Data From the Course Table Using the TableAdapter Method Open the Code Window of the Course Form window and click on the drop-down arrow from the Class Name ComboBox to select the (**CourseForm Events**) item. Then click on the drop-down arrow from the Method Name ComboBox to select the **Load** to open the **CourseForm_Load** event procedure. Replace all original codes with the codes shown in Figure 5.52 in this event procedure.

The **Add** method is used to add all faculty names into the ComboBox. Resetting the SelectedIndex property to 0 is to select the first faculty and the first method as the default one from the ComboBox as the project runs.

Open the Course form window by right-clicking on the **Course Form.vb** in the Solution Explorer window and selecting the **View Designer** from the popup menu. Then double-click on the **Select** button to open its event procedure. Enter the codes shown in Figure 5.53 into this event procedure.

Let's have a closer look at this piece of codes to see how it works:

A) A new course table adapter object is created based on the CourseTableAdapter class that is located at the namespace CSE_DEPTDataSetTableAdapters.
B) A new faculty table adapter object is also created based on the FacultyTable- Adapter class. A local string variable **strFacultyID** is declared and it is used to hold the returned **FACULTY_ID** when our built query **FindFacultyIDByName()** is executed later.
C) Before the query **FindFacultyIDByName()** is executed, the faculty table adapter is first cleaned up.
D) The query **FindFacultyIDByName()** is called with an argument that is the faculty name selected by the user when the project runs. The returned **FACULTY_ID** is assigned to the local string variable **strFacultyID**.
E) If the returned value is an empty string, which means that no matched **FACULTY_ID** can be found and this calling is failed, an error message is displayed and the procedure is exited.

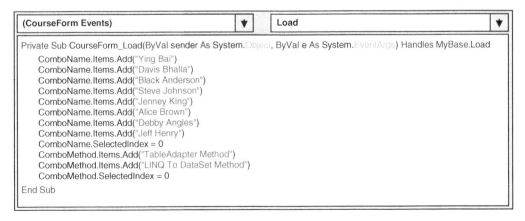

```
(CourseForm Events)  ▼        Load  ▼

Private Sub CourseForm_Load(ByVal sender As System.Object, ByVal e As System.EventArgs) Handles MyBase.Load
      ComboName.Items.Add("Ying Bai")
      ComboName.Items.Add("Davis Bhalla")
      ComboName.Items.Add("Black Anderson")
      ComboName.Items.Add("Steve Johnson")
      ComboName.Items.Add("Jenney King")
      ComboName.Items.Add("Alice Brown")
      ComboName.Items.Add("Debby Angles")
      ComboName.Items.Add("Jeff Henry")
      ComboName.SelectedIndex = 0
      ComboMethod.Items.Add("TableAdapter Method")
      ComboMethod.Items.Add("LINQ To DataSet Method")
      ComboMethod.SelectedIndex = 0
End Sub
```

Figure 5.52 The codes for the CourseForm_Load event procedure.

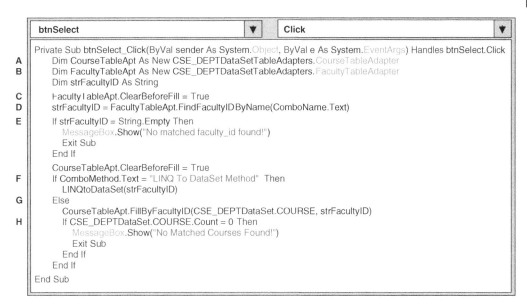

```
btnSelect ▼          Click ▼

    Private Sub btnSelect_Click(ByVal sender As System.Object, ByVal e As System.EventArgs) Handles btnSelect.Click
A       Dim CourseTableApt As New CSE_DEPTDataSetTableAdapters.CourseTableAdapter
B       Dim FacultyTableApt As New CSE_DEPTDataSetTableAdapters.FacultyTableAdapter
        Dim strFacultyID As String

C       FacultyTableApt.ClearBeforeFill = True
D       strFacultyID = FacultyTableApt.FindFacultyIDByName(ComboName.Text)

E       If strFacultyID = String.Empty Then
            MessageBox.Show("No matched faculty_id found!")
            Exit Sub
        End If

        CourseTableApt.ClearBeforeFill = True
F       If ComboMethod.Text = "LINQ To DataSet Method"  Then
            LINQtoDataSet(strFacultyID)
G       Else
            CourseTableApt.FillByFacultyID(CSE_DEPTDataSet.COURSE, strFacultyID)
H           If CSE_DEPTDataSet.COURSE.Count = 0 Then
                MessageBox.Show("No Matched Courses Found!")
                Exit Sub
            End If
        End If
    End Sub
```

Figure 5.53 The codes for the Select button's click event procedure.

F) If the user selected the **LINQ To DataSet Method**, a user-defined subroutine **LINQtoDataSet()** that will be built later is called to perform this data query using the LINQ to DataSet method.

G) Otherwise, the TableAdapter method is selected by the user and the query we built in the DataSet Designer, **FillByFacultyID()**, will be called to fill the Course table in our DataSet using a dynamic parameter **:PARAM1** that is replaced by our real parameter **strFacultyID** now (refer to Figure 5.50).

H) To check whether this fill is successful, the **Count** property of the Course table is detected. If this property is reset to 0, which means that no any data item is filled into our Course table in our DataSet, the fill is failed and a warning message will be displayed to require users to handle this situation. Otherwise, the fill is successful and all courses (**COURSE_ID**) taught by the selected faculty will be filled into the Course table and loaded into the Course ListBox control in our Course form, and furthermore, the detailed course information including the course ID, course schedule, classroom, credits, and enrollment for the selected **COURSE_ID** in the Course ListBox will be displayed in the six textbox controls since these textboxes have been bound to those related data columns in the Course table.

Return to the Course form window (View Designer) and double-click on the **Back** button to open its event procedure and enter the code, **Me.Close()** into this event procedure.

Next let's handle the coding for the querying data using the LINQ to DataSet method.

5.4.9.3.2 Query Data From the Course Table Using the LINQ to DataSet Method The project will be directed to calling the **LINQtoDataSet()** subroutine if the user selected the **LINQ to DataSet** method from the **Query Method** ComboBox. Refer to Chapter 4 to get more details about the data query between LINQ to DataSet. In this part, we will develop the codes to use this method to perform the data query from the Course table in our DataSet.

Open the Code Window of the **CourseForm** if it is not opened, create a new subroutine **LINQtoDataSet()**, and enter the codes, which are shown in Figure 5.54, into this subroutine.

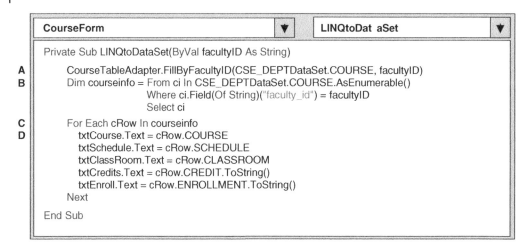

Figure 5.54 The codes for the LINQ to DataSet subroutine.

Let's have a closer look at this piece of codes to see how it works:

A) First, the default **Fill()** method of the CourseTableAdapter is executed to load data from the Course table in the database into the Course table in our DataSet. This step is necessary since the LINQ technique is applied with the DataSet and the DataSet must contain the valid data in all tables before this technique can be implemented.

B) A typical LINQ query structure is created and executed to retrieve all related information for the selected **FACULTY_ID**. The **courseinfo** is an implicitly typed local variable. The Visual Basic.NET 2019 will be able to automatically convert this variable to a suitable data type, in this case, it is a DataSet, when it sees it. An iteration variable **ci** is used to iterate over the result of this query from the Course table. Then a SELECT statement is executed with the **WHERE** clause.

C) A For Each loop is utilized to pick up each column from the selected data row **cRow**, which is obtained from the **courseinfo** we get from the LINQ query.

D) Assign each column to the associated textbox to display it in the CourseForm window.

That is! The all coding job is done.

Let's test our project by running it. Click on the **Start** button to run our project. Complete the login process and select the **Course Information** from the Selection Form. Then click on the **OK** button to open our Course form, which is shown in Figure 5.55.

On the opened Course form, select the default faculty name **Ying Bai** and keep the default query method **TableAdapter Method** from the Query Method ComboBox, and click on the **Select** button to test this data query using the TableAdapter method. The filled **COURSE_ID** is displayed in the Course ListBox, as shown in Figure 5.55.

Now let's go one more step forward by just clicking on a **COURSE_ID** from the Course ListBox, the detailed information about that selected **COURSE_ID** including the course, schedule, classroom, credits, and enrollment will be displayed in the six textbox controls. This makes sense since those textbox controls have been bound to those six associated columns in the Course table in our DataSet. As you click one **COURSE_ID** from the Course ListBox, effectively you selected and picked up one course record from the Course table. Recall that the Course ListBox is bound to the Course table in our DataSet using the CourseBindingSource when we perform this data binding in

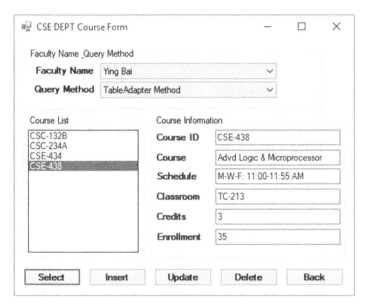

Figure 5.55 The running status of the Course form. *Source:* Microsoft Visual Studio.

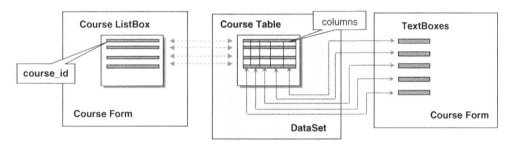

Figure 5.56 The relationships between Course ListBox, Course table and TextBox.

Section 5.4.9.2. For the selected course record, six columns of that record have been bound to the six textbox controls in the form, so the data related to those columns will also be reflected on these six textbox controls. These relationships can be represented and illustrated by a diagram shown in Figure 5.56.

It is very interesting, is not it?

Yes! This is the power provided by Visual Basic.NET. Using those Tools and Wizards in Visual Studio.NET, it is very easy to develop a professional database programming in the Visual Basic.NET environment, and it becomes a fun to develop a database programming in Visual Basic.NET 2019.

You can select the **LINQ to DataSet Method** from the Query Method ComboBox to test the course data query with that method. The same query results can be obtained and displayed in the CourseForm.

We have the last form, which is the Student form, and we want to leave this as the homework for students to allow them to finish the building and developing of the data connection and operation between the Student form and the Student table as well as the StudentCourse table.

For your reference, a completed project **SelectWizard Project**, including the source codes, graphical user interface designs, Data Source, and Query Builders, can be found from the folder

`Class DB Projects\Chapter 5\SelectWizard Solution` that is located under the `Students` folder at the Wiley ftp site (refer to Figure 1.2 in Chapter 1).

Part II: Data Query with Runtime Objects

Unlike the sample data-driven application programs we developed in Part I, where quite a few design tools and wizards provided by Visual Studio.NET are utilized to help users to do those developments such as the DataSet, BindingSource, BindingNavigator, and TableAdapter, the sample project developed in this part has nothing to do with those tools and wizards. This means that we create those ADO.NET 4.5 objects by directly writing Visual Basic.NET 2019 codes without the aid of Visual Studio.NET design-time wizards and tools as well as the auto-generated codes. All data-driven objects are created and implemented during the period of the project runs. In other words, all those objects are created dynamically.

The shortcoming of using those Visual Studio.NET tools and wizards in creating data connections is that the auto-generated connection codes related to tools and wizards are embedded into the programs, and those connection codes are machine-dependent. Once that piece of connection information in the programs is complied, it cannot be modified. In other words, those programs cannot be distributed to and run in other platforms.

Compared with tools and wizards, there are some advantages of using the runtime objects to make the data operations for your Visual Basic.NET 2019 project. One of the most important advantages is that it provides programmers more flexibility in creating and implementing connection objects and data operation objects related to ADO.NET and allows users to use different methods to access and manipulate data from the data source and the database. But anything has both good and bad side, and it is also true here. The flexibility also brings some complexicity. For example, you have to create and use different data providers and different commands to access the different databases by using the different codes. Unlike the sample project we developed in the last part, in which you can use tools and wizards to select any data source you want and produce the same coding for the different data sources, in this part you must specify the data provider and command type based on your real data source to access the data in your project. But before we can continue to do that, a detailed understanding of the connection and data operations classes is very important, and those classes are directly related to the ADO. NET. Although some discussions have been provided in Chapter 3, we will make a more detailed discussion for this topic in this section in order to make readers have a clear picture about this issue.

5.5 Introduction to Runtime Objects

The definition of runtime objects can be described as: objects or instances used for data connections and operations in a data-driven application are created and implemented during the period of a project runs, in other words, those objects are created and utilized dynamically. To understand what kind of objects are most popularly used in a data-driven application, let's first have a detailed discussion about the most useful classes provided by ADO.NET.

Based on Chapter 3, the ADO.NET architecture can be divided into three components: Data Provider, DataSet, and a DataTable. These three components are directly related to different associated classes, which are shown in Figure 5.57.

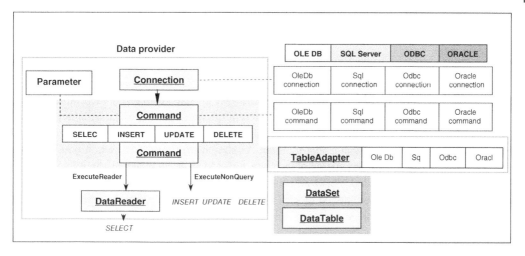

Figure 5.57 Classes provided by ADO.NET.

Data Provider contains four components:

1) Data **Connection**
2) Data **Command**
3) **DataReader**
4) **TableAdapter**

All components inside the Data Provider are Data Provider-dependent components, which means that all components including the Connection, Command, TableAdapter (DataAdapter), and DataReader are identified and named based on the real data provider, or database the user used. For example, the Data Provider used for Oracle Server database must be identified and named by a prefix such as the `Oracle`, such as:

- Data Connection component: `Oracle`Connection
- Data Command component: `Oracle`Command
- DataAdapter (TableAdapter):   `Oracle`DataAdapter (`Oracle`TableAdapter)
- DataReader components: `Oracle`DataReader

Same definition is needed to all other three Data Providers. All classes, methods, properties, and constants of these four types of Data Provider are located at four different namespaces: `System.Data.OleDb`, `System.Data.SqlClient`, `System.Data.Odbc`, and `System.Data.OracleClient`. However, Microsoft stopped supports for Oracle database in recent years, thus we need to use a third-party driver, `dotConnect` for Oracle, in this book.

As shown in Figure 5.57, four data providers are popularly used in database programming in Visual Basic.NET 2019. One must create the correct connection object based on your real database using the specific prefix.

However, two components in the ADO.NET, DataSet and DataTable, are Data Provider-independent. These two components are located at `System.Data` namespace. You do not need to use any prefix when you use these two components in your applications. Both DataSet and the DataTable can be filled using the DataAdapter or the TableAdapter components.

ADO.NET provides different classes to allow users to develop a professional data-driven application using the different methods. Among those methods, two popular methods will be discussed in this part in detail.

The first method is to use the so-called DataSet-DataAdapter method to build a data-driven application. DataSet and DataTable classes can have different roles when they are implemented in a real application. Multiple DataTables can be embedded into a DataSet and each table can be filled, inserted, updated, and deleted using the different query method of a DataAdapter such as the SelectCommand, InsertCommand, Update-Command, or DeleteCommand when one develops a data-driven application using this method. As shown in Figure 5.57, when you use this method, the Command and Parameter objects are embedded or attached to the TableAdapter object (represented by a shaded block) and the DataTable object is embedded into the DataSet object (represented by another shaded block). This method is relatively simple since you do not need to call some specific objects such as the DataReader with specific method such as the **ExecuteReader** or **ExecuteNonQuery** to complete this data query. You just call the associated command of the TableAdapter to finish this data operation. But this simplicity brings some limitations for your applications. For instance, you cannot access different data tables separately to perform multiple specific data operations.

The second method is to allow you to use each object individually, which means that you do not have to use the DataAdapter to access the Command object or use the DataTable with DataSet together. This provides more flexibility. In this method, no DataAdapter or DataSet is needed, and you can only create a new Command object with a new Connection object and then build a query statement and attach some useful parameter into that query for the new created Command object. You can fill any DataTable by calling the **ExecuteReader()** method to a DataReader object and also you can perform any data manipulation by calling the **ExecuteNonQuery()** method to the desired DataTable.

In this section, we provide another sample project **OracleSelectRTObject Project** to cover two methods, which are associated with an Oracle 18c XE database.

To understand better for these two methods, we need to have a clear picture in how to develop a data-driven application using the related classes and methods provided by ADO.NET.

5.5.1 Procedure of Building a Data-Driven Application Using Runtime Object

Recall that we discussed the architecture and important classes of the ADO.NET in Chapter 3. To connect and implement a database with your Visual Basic.NET project, you need follow the sequence listed below:

1) Create a new Connection String with correct parameters.
2) Create a new Connection Object using the suitable Connection String built in step 1.
3) Call the **Open()** method to open this database connection with the correct block such as **Try...Catch** block.
4) Create a new TableAdapter (DataAdapter) object.
5) Create a new DataTable object that is used to be filled with data.
6) Call the suitable command/object such as the SelectCommand (or the Fill()) or the DataReader to make data query.
7) Fill the data to the bound controls on the Visual Basic.NET 2019 form.
8) Release the TableAdapter, Command, DataTable, and the DataReader used.
9) Close the database Connection Object if no more database operation is needed.

Now let's first develop a sample project to access the data using the runtime object for Oracle 18c XE database.

5.6 Query Data From Oracle Server Database Using Runtime Object

As we discussed in Chapter 3, one needs to use the different data providers to access the different database. To meet this request, ADO.NET provides some popular different namespaces for different data providers, such as `System.Data.OleDb` for OLEDB database and `System.Data.SqlClient` for SQL Server. Because the Microsoft stopped supports to Oracle database, in this book, we will use a third-party driver, dotConnect for Oracle, as the data provider for our sample database CSE_DEPT, which is an Oracle 18c XE database.

5.6.1 Access to Oracle Server Database

Basically, similar runtime objects and structures can be utilized to develop a data-driven project that can access the different databases. For example, all three kinds of data provides need to use the Connection, Command, TableAdapter, and DataReader objects to perform data queries to either a DataSet or a DataTable. The DataSet and the DataTable components are data provider-independent, but the first four objects are data provider-dependent. This means that one must use the different prefix to specify what kind of data provider is utilized for certain databases. A prefix `Oracle` would be used if an Oracle data provider is utilized, such as `OracleConnection`, `OracleCommand`, `OracleTableAdapter,` and `OracleDataReader`.

The differences between the data-driven applications that can access the different databases are the data provider-dependent components. Among them, the Connection String is a big issue. Different data provider needs to use the different connection string to make the connection to the associated database.

Regularly a Connection String is composed of five parts:

- Provider
- Data Source
- Database
- User ID
- Password

A typical data connection instance with a general connection string can be expressed by the following codes:

```
Connection = New xxxConnection("Provider=MyProvider;" & _
                               "Data Source=MyServer;" & _
                               "Database=MyDatabase;" & _
                               "User ID=MyUserID;" & _
                               "Password=MyPassWord;")
```

where **xxx** should be replaced by the selected data provider in your real application, such as `OleDb`, `Sql`, or `Oracle`. You need to use the real parameter values implemented in your applications to replace those nominal values such as **MyProvider**, **MyServer**, **MyDatabase**, **MyUserID**, and **MyPassWord** in your application.

The **Provider** parameter indicates the database driver you selected. If you installed a local Oracle Server database and a client such as the Oracle 18c XE on your computer, the provider should be *localhost*. If you are using a remote Oracle Server instance, you need to use that *remote server's network name*. If you are using the default named instance of XE on your computer, you need to use *.\XE* as the value for your provider parameter. Similar values can be used for other server database.

The **Data Source** parameter indicates the name of the network computer on which your Oracle server is installed and running. The **Database** parameter indicates your database name.

The `User ID` and `Password` parameters are used for the security issue for your database. In most cases, the default Windows NT Security Authentication is utilized.

You can also use the OLEDB as the SQL Server database provider. A sample connection string to be connected to a SQL Server database using the OLEDB data provider can be expressed:

```
Connection = New OleDbConnection("Provider=SQLOLEDB;" +
                                 "Data Source=MyServer_Name;" +
                                 "Initial Catalog =CSE_DEPT;" +
                                 "Integrated Security = SSPI;"
```

You need to use the real parameter values implemented in your applications to replace those nominal values such as `MyServer_Name`, your database name (here we used our target database name `CSE_DEPT`) in your application.

When you want to connect to the Oracle Server database using `OracleClient`, the connection string is a little different with those strings shown above. The Provider parameter should be replaced by the `Server` parameter and the `User ID` and the `Password` parameters should be replaced by the actual security parameter. A sample connection string to be used to connect to an Oracle Server database with the `OracleClient` is

```
Connection = New OracleConnection("Server=XE;" +
                                  "Data Source=localhost:1518/CSE_
                                   DEPT;" +
                                  "User Id=CSE_DEPT;" +
                                  "Password=oracle_18c"
```

where the value for the `Data Source` parameter is *Computer Name:Database Listener/User Database* since we installed the Express Edition of Oracle 18c Server in our local computer. The User ID is exactly a user account or a schema, `CSE_DEPT` in our case. The Password is a password we used when we create our user account or user database.

When you build a connection string to be used by an Oracle database using the OLEDB provider, you can use the same parameters as those shown in the typical connection string with three exceptions: the `Provider`, `Database`, and `Data Source` parameters. First, to connect to an Oracle database, a third-party driver should be used for the `Provider` parameter. Second, regularly the `Database` parameter is not needed when connecting to a default Oracle database, such as XE, because the default `tnsnames.ora` file contains this piece of information, and this `tnsnames.ora` file is created as you installed and configured the Oracle client on your computer. Third, by default, the `Data Source` will not be used to indicate the computer name on which the Oracle is installed and running. This information is included in the `tnsnames.ora` file, too.

In the following sections, we will discuss how to develop the professional data-driven applications connecting to an Oracle Server database using our third-party data providers.

In this section, we use an Oracle 18c XE sample database and connect it with our example project using the dotConnect for Oracle data provider. The Oracle Server database used in this sample project is `CSE_DEPT`, which was developed in Chapter 2 and it is located at the folder `Students\ Sample Database` that can be found from the Wiley ftp site (refer to Figure 1.2 in Chapter 1). The advantages of using the Express Edition of Oracle 18c include, but not limited to:

- The Oracle 18c Express Edition is fully compatible with Oracle 18c database and has full functionalities of the latter.
- The Oracle 18c Express Edition can be easily download from the Oracle site with free of charge.

- The Oracle SQL Developer can also be downloaded and installed on your local computer with free of charge. You can use this tool to build and manage your database easily and conveniently.

Now we need to create a Visual Basic.NET 2019 project named `OracleSelectRTObject Project` with five form windows: `LogIn`, `Selection`, `Faculty`, `Course`, and `Student`.

Let's first create a new blank solution `OracleSelectRTObject Solution` and add a new `Windows Forms App (.NET Framework)` project `OracleSelectRTObject Project`. Save the solution to the folder `C:\Class DB Projects\Chapter 5`.

5.6.2 Declare Global Variables and Runtime Objects for the Oracle Provider

Open the default window `Form1` by double-clicking on the `Form1.vb` from the Solution Explorer window and then right-click on this form and click on the `Delete` item and `OK` button to a MessageBox to remove this form from our project. This deletion will cause a compiling error and we will fix this later.

Now we need to add all five Visual Basic form windows from the folder `Students\VB Forms\ Window` that is located at the Wiley ftp site (refer to Figure 1.2 in Chapter 1) to this project. Perform the following operations to complete this adding action:

1) Click on the `Project|Add Existing Item` and browse to the folder `Students\VB Forms\Window` that is located at the Wiley ftp site (refer to Figure 1.2 in Chapter 1).
2) Press and hold the `Ctrl` key on your keyboard and click on five forms one by one: `LogIn Form.vb`, `Selection Form.vb`, `Faculty Form.vb`, `Course Form.vb`, and `Student Form.vb`. Click on the `Add` button to add these forms into our current project.

All data components related to the Oracle Server Data Provider that is supplied by dotConnect for Oracle are located at the namespace `Devart.Data` and `Devart.Data.Oracle`. To access and use these components, one needs to add above two namespaces as references into our project and imports them into the Code Window of our project. Perform the following operations to add those references into our project:

1) Right-click on our new project `OracleSelectRTObject Project` from the Solution Explorer window and select `Add|Reference` item from the popup menu.

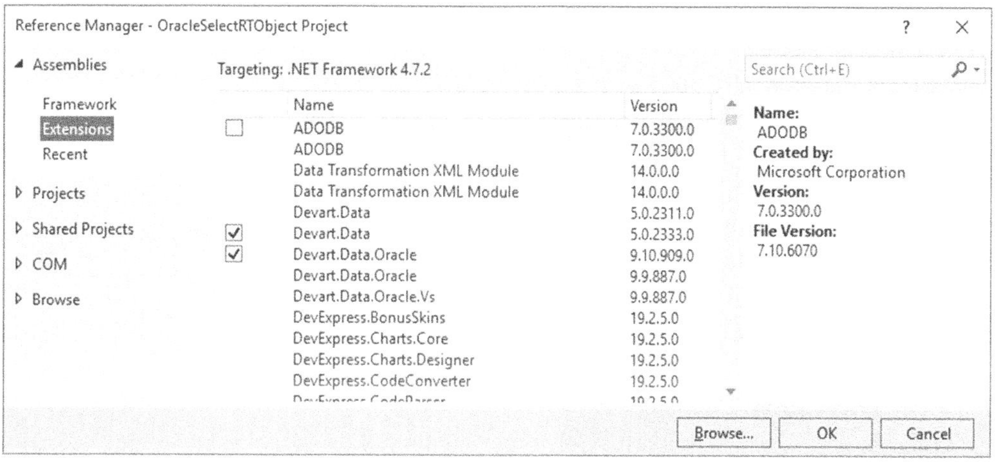

Figure 5.58 The opened Reference Manager wizard. *Source:* Microsoft Visual Studio.

2) Select the **Extensions** item from the left pane and check two checkboxes, **Devart.Data** and **Devart.Data.Oracle**, as shown in Figure 5.58, to select them.
3) Then click on the **OK** button to add them into our project.

Next let's declare these namespaces in a global method (**Module**) to allow Visual Basic.NET to know that you want to use this specified Data Provider.

Starting from Visual Basic.NET 2010, the **Module** class is resumed by Microsoft. By using this class, we can declare some global variables used by a whole Visual Basic.NET project. One candidate for this kind of global variables is the connection object since it will be used by all five forms in our project.

Now create a new module **connModule** by perform the following operations:

1) Go to the **Project|Add Module** menu item to open the Add New Item wizard.
2) Go to the **Name** box and change the module's name to **connModule.vb** and click on the **Add** button.
3) In the opened module Code Window, enter the codes shown in Figure 5.59.

The namespaces, **Devart.Data** and **Devart.Data.Oracle**, are declared at the top of this window since we need to use data components provided by the third party, dotConnect for Oracle, to connect to the Oracle Server Data Provider in this project. The connection instance **oraConnection** is created with the **OracleConnection** class since we need this connection object for our whole project.

Now let's fix the error caused by our deleting the default form window Form1.

1) Go to the **Project|OracleSelectRTObject Project Properties** menu to open the project property window.
2) Keep the **Application** tab selected and make sure that the **LogInForm** is located in the **Startup form** box. If not, select the **LogInForm** as the Startup form.

5.6.3 Query Data Using Runtime Objects for the LogIn Form

In this application, we want to use two methods to perform the data query from our LogIn table: the DataSet-TableAdapter method and the DataReader method. Recall when we built our LogIn Form in Section 5.3.1.1, two buttons, **TabLogIn** and the **ReadLogIn**, are created, as shown in Figure 5.60.

The **TabLogIn** button is used to trigger the TableAdapter method and the **ReadLogIn** button is for DataReader method.

Since the connection job is the first thing you need to do before you can make any data query, you need to do the connection job in the first event procedure, **Form_Load()** event procedure, to allow the connection to be made first as your project runs.

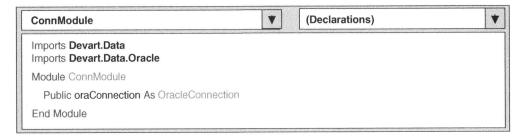

Figure 5.59 The declaration of the namespace for the Oracle Server Data Provider.

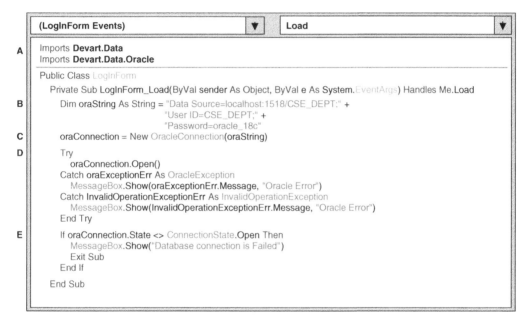

Figure 5.60 The LogIn form window. *Source:* Microsoft Visual Studio.

```
(LogInForm Events) ▼        Load ▼

A   Imports Devart.Data
    Imports Devart.Data.Oracle

    Public Class LogInForm
        Private Sub LogInForm_Load(ByVal sender As Object, ByVal e As System.EventArgs) Handles Me.Load
B           Dim oraString As String = "Data Source=localhost:1518/CSE_DEPT;" +
                                      "User ID=CSE_DEPT;" +
                                      "Password=oracle_18c"
C           oraConnection = New OracleConnection(oraString)
D           Try
               oraConnection.Open()
            Catch oraExceptionErr As OracleException
               MessageBox.Show(oraExceptionErr.Message, "Oracle Error")
            Catch InvalidOperationExceptionErr As InvalidOperationException
               MessageBox.Show(InvalidOperationExceptionErr.Message, "Oracle Error")
            End Try

E           If oraConnection.State <> ConnectionState.Open Then
               MessageBox.Show("Database connection is Failed")
               Exit Sub
            End If

        End Sub
```

Figure 5.61 The codes for the database connection.

5.6.3.1 Connect to the Data Source with the Runtime Object

Open the Code Window for the LogIn Form and click on the drop-down arrow in the **Class Name** ComboBox and select the **(LogInForm Events)**. The go to the **Method Name** ComboBox and click on the drop-down arrow to select the **Load** method to open the **LogInForm_Load()** event procedure and enter the codes shown in Figure 5.61 into this event procedure. Let's have a closer look at this piece of codes to see how it works.

A) The namespaces, **Devart.Data** and **Devart.Data.Oracle**, are imported first since we need to use data components related to Oracle Data Provider to query our sample Oracle database.

B) An **OracleConnection** String is created first and the connection string is used to connect our project with the sample database. Please note that this connection string is different with one we created in the last section. The Server parameter is combined with the Data Source by a value of **localhost**, which means that the Oracle Server is installed in our local computer. The Data Source parameter also contains the database listener and database itself, in our case, they are **1518/CSE_DEPT** as we created our sample database in Chapter 2. The username and password are those when we created and used during our database creation process. In our case, they are **CSE_DEPT** and **oracle_18c**, respectively.

C) A new instance of **OracleConnection** class, **oraConnection**, is created with the connection string as an argument.

D) A **Try...Catch** block is utilized to try to catch up any mistake caused by opening this connection. The advantage of using this kind of strategy is to avoid unnecessary system debug process and simplify this debug procedure.

E) This step is used to confirm that our database connection is successful. If not, an error message is displayed and the project is exited.

After a database connection is successfully made, next we need to use this connection to access the Oracle Server database to perform our data query jobs.

5.6.3.2 Coding for Method 1: Using the TableAdapter to Query Data

In this section, we will discuss how to create and use the runtime objects to query the data from the Oracle Server database using the TableAdapter method.

Open the **TabLogIn** button's Click event procedure and enter the codes shown in Figure 5.62 into this procedure.

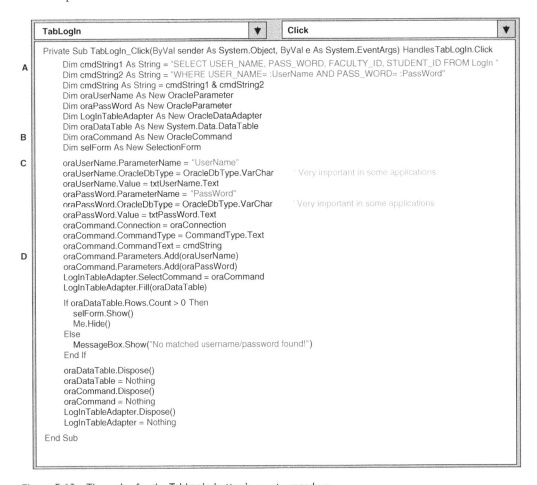

```
TabLogIn                                          ▼   │ Click                                              ▼

     Private Sub TabLogIn_Click(ByVal sender As System.Object, ByVal e As System.EventArgs) Handles TabLogIn.Click
A        Dim cmdString1 As String = "SELECT USER_NAME, PASS_WORD, FACULTY_ID, STUDENT_ID FROM LogIn "
         Dim cmdString2 As String = "WHERE USER_NAME= :UserName AND PASS_WORD= :PassWord"
         Dim cmdString As String = cmdString1 & cmdString2
         Dim oraUserName As New OracleParameter
         Dim oraPassWord As New OracleParameter
         Dim LogInTableAdapter As New OracleDataAdapter
         Dim oraDataTable As New System.Data.DataTable
B        Dim oraCommand As New OracleCommand
         Dim selForm As New SelectionForm

C        oraUserName.ParameterName = "UserName"
         oraUserName.OracleDbType = OracleDbType.VarChar     ' Very important in some applications
         oraUserName.Value = txtUserName.Text
         oraPassWord.ParameterName = "PassWord"
         oraPassWord.OracleDbType = OracleDbType.VarChar     ' Very important in some applications
         oraPassWord.Value = txtPassWord.Text
         oraCommand.Connection = oraConnection
         oraCommand.CommandType = CommandType.Text
         oraCommand.CommandText = cmdString
D        oraCommand.Parameters.Add(oraUserName)
         oraCommand.Parameters.Add(oraPassWord)
         LogInTableAdapter.SelectCommand = oraCommand
         LogInTableAdapter.Fill(oraDataTable)

         If oraDataTable.Rows.Count > 0 Then
           selForm.Show()
           Me.Hide()
         Else
           MessageBox.Show("No matched username/password found!")
         End If

         oraDataTable.Dispose()
         oraDataTable = Nothing
         oraCommand.Dispose()
         oraCommand = Nothing
         LogInTableAdapter.Dispose()
         LogInTableAdapter = Nothing
     End Sub
```

Figure 5.62 The codes for the TabLogIn button's event procedure.

Let's have a closer look at this piece of codes to see how it works:

A) Since the query string applied in this application is relatively long, we break it into two sub-string; **cmdString1** and **cmdString2**. Then we combine them to form a complete query string **cmdString**. One point you need to know is the relational operator applied in the Oracle Server database, which is different with that used in the Microsoft Access or SQL Server database. The criteria of the data query are represented using an equal operator that is located between the desired data column and a nominal parameter in the Microsoft Access. In the Oracle Server database, this equal operator is still be used. Another point is that a method is used to add the parameters into the Parameters collection. Unlike the method we utilized before, here we first create two **OracleParameter** objects and initialize these two objects with the parameter's name and dynamic data value separately.

B) The Command object **oraCommand** is created based on the **OracleCommand** class and initialized using a blank command constructor.

C) Two dynamic parameters are assigned to the **OracleParameter** objects, **oraUser-Name** and **oraPassWord**, separately. The parameter's name must be identical with the name of dynamic parameter in the Oracle statement string. The **Values** of two parameters should be equal to the contents of two associated textbox controls, which will be entered by the user as the project runs.

D) Two parameter objects are added into the Parameters collection that is the property of the Command object using the **Add()** method, and the command object is ready to be used. It is then assigned to the method **SelectCommand()** of the TableAdapter.

An important issue for this piece of codes is that a space is attached at the end of the **SELECT** statement at the top coding line to give an interval between this clause and the next clause **WHERE**. You must add this space on the end of the first query; otherwise, a possible query error would be encountered if you missed this space.

Now let's take a look at the codes for the second method.

5.6.3.3 Coding for Method 2: Using the DataReader to Query Data

Open the **ReadLogIn** button's Click event procedure and enter the codes shown in Figure 5.63 into this event procedure.

Most codes in the top section are identical with those codes in the **TabLogIn** button's event procedure with two exceptions. First, a DataReader object is created to replace the TableAdapter to perform the data query, and second the DataTable is removed from this event procedure since we do not need it for our data query in this method.

Let's have a closer look at this piece of codes to see how it works:

A) As we did in the coding for the method 1, the comparator = is used in the second query string, and this is the requirement of the Oracle Server database.

B) Two **OracleParameter** objects are created and they will be used to fill two dynamic parameters used in this application. The dynamic parameters will be entered by the user when the project runs.

C) Tow Parameter objects are filled by two dynamic parameters; note that the **ParameterName** property is used to hold the nominal value of the dynamic parameter **:UserName**. The nominal value must be identical with that defined in the Oracle query statement. Same situation is true for the value of the second nominal parameter **:PassWord**.

D) The **ExecuteReader()** method is called to perform the data query and the returned data should be filled in the DataReader.

Figure 5.63 The codes for the ReadLogIn button's event procedure.

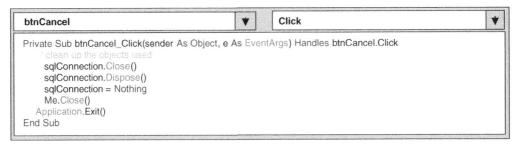

Figure 5.64 The codes for the Cancel button's event procedure.

E) If the returned DataReader contains some queried data, its **HasRows** property should be True, and then the project should go to the next step and the Selection Form should be displayed.

The codes for the **Cancel** command button's event procedure are shown in Figure 5.64.

To release the Connection object, a **Close()** method is called first. Then the **Dispose()** method and the **Nothing** property is used to finish this release. Finally, the system method **Me.Close()** is called to close the whole project. The keyword **Me** represents the current form window – the LogIn form. Please note that the Connection instance would not be released if this **Cancel** button were not clicked. In the normal case, we still need to use this Connection object for the following data queries if the login process is successful.

It is the time for us to test our project. Click on the Start button to begin our project. Enter **jhenry** and **test** as the username and the password into the two textboxes on the LogIn form window and then click on the **TabLogIn** button. The Selection form is displayed if this login is successful. Try to test the **ReadLogIn** button with a similar way.

Click on the **Cancel** button to terminate the project.

5.6.4 The Coding for the Selection Form

This coding process is very similar to those we did for the **SelectionForm** in the project **SelectWizard Project**. The coding process can be divided into three parts:

1) Coding for the **SelectionForm_Load()** event procedure
2) Coding for the **OK** button's Click event procedure
3) Coding for the **Exit** button's Click event procedure

Open the Code Window of the **SelectionForm** and the **SelectionForm_Load()** event procedure, enter the codes, which are shown in Figure 5.65, into this event procedure.

The codes for this event procedure are straightforward with no tricks. We add three pieces of information related to the CSE_DEPT using the **Add()** method to the Selection combo box in the **SelectionForm** window to allow users to select one of them to perform the related data query.

The coding process for the second step is for the **OK** button's Click event procedure. Open this event procedure by double-clicking the **OK** button from the **SelectionForm** window and enter the codes, which are shown in Figure 5.66, into this event procedure.

When the **OK** button is clicked by the user, first we create three instances for three form windows. Then we need to check which piece of information has been selected by the user from the Selection combo box. Based on that selection, we direct the program to the associated form window using the **Show()** method.

Finally, we come to the coding for the third step, coding for the **Exit** button's Click event procedure. Open the **Exit** button's Click event procedure and enter the codes shown in Figure 5.67 into this procedure. Before we can terminate our project, we need first to close our database connection. Then we call a system method **Application.Exit()** to terminate our project.

5.6.5 Query Data Using Runtime Objects for the Faculty Form

First let's take a look at the codes for the **Form_Load()** event procedure. Enter the codes shown in Figure 5.68 into this event procedure.

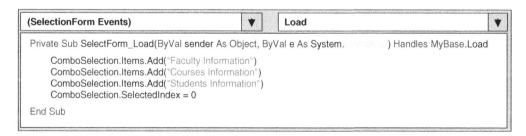

Figure 5.65 The codes for the SelectionForm_Load event procedure.

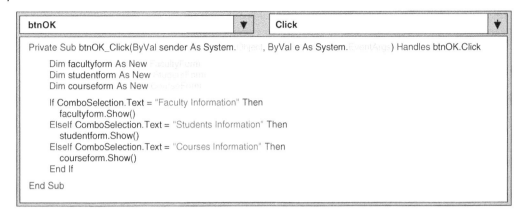

btnOK	▼	Click	▼

```
Private Sub btnOK_Click(ByVal sender As System.Object, ByVal e As System.EventArgs) Handles btnOK.Click

    Dim facultyform As New FacultyForm
    Dim studentform As New StudentForm
    Dim courseform As New CourseForm

    If ComboSelection.Text = "Faculty Information" Then
        facultyform.Show()
    ElseIf ComboSelection.Text = "Students Information" Then
        studentform.Show()
    ElseIf ComboSelection.Text = "Courses Information" Then
        courseform.Show()
    End If

End Sub
```

Figure 5.66 The codes for the OK Click button's event procedure.

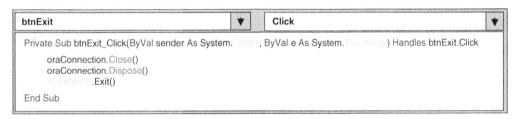

btnExit	▼	Click	▼

```
Private Sub btnExit_Click(ByVal sender As System.Object, ByVal e As System.EventArgs) Handles btnExit.Click

        oraConnection.Close()
        oraConnection.Dispose()
        Application.Exit()

End Sub
```

Figure 5.67 The codes for the Exit Click button's event procedure.

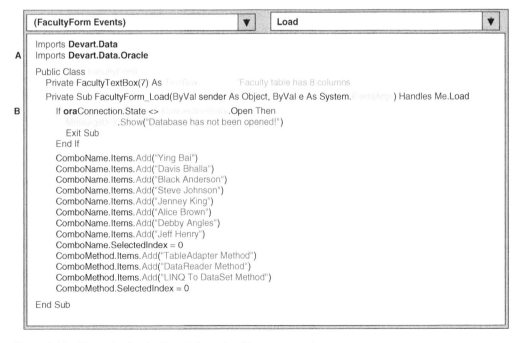

(FacultyForm Events)	▼	Load	▼

```
    Imports Devart.Data
A   Imports Devart.Data.Oracle

    Public Class FacultyForm
        Private FacultyTextBox(7) As TextBox       'Faculty table has 8 columns

        Private Sub FacultyForm_Load(ByVal sender As Object, ByVal e As System.EventArgs) Handles Me.Load

B           If oraConnection.State <> ConnectionState.Open Then
                MessageBox.Show("Database has not been opened!")
                Exit Sub
            End If

            ComboName.Items.Add("Ying Bai")
            ComboName.Items.Add("Davis Bhalla")
            ComboName.Items.Add("Black Anderson")
            ComboName.Items.Add("Steve Johnson")
            ComboName.Items.Add("Jenney King")
            ComboName.Items.Add("Alice Brown")
            ComboName.Items.Add("Debby Angles")
            ComboName.Items.Add("Jeff Henry")
            ComboName.SelectedIndex = 0
            ComboMethod.Items.Add("TableAdapter Method")
            ComboMethod.Items.Add("DataReader Method")
            ComboMethod.Items.Add("LINQ To DataSet Method")
            ComboMethod.SelectedIndex = 0
        End Sub
```

Figure 5.68 The codes for the FacultyForm_Load() event procedure.

Let's have a closer look at this piece of codes to see how it works:

A) The namespaces of the Oracle Data Provider, `Devart.Data` and `Devart.Data.Oracle`, are utilized for the Oracle Server database in this section.
B) The database connection status is first checked to make sure that our database has been connected to our project for all data queries to be executed later.

Next coding job is for the `Select` button's event procedure. Open the Faculty form window and the `Select` button's click event procedure. Enter the codes shown in Figure 5.69 into this procedure. Let's have a look at this piece of codes to see how it works.

A) The query string is created with the query parameter or the dynamic parameter, which is `:facultyName`. Also do not forget to leave a space at the end of the top query string after the table name `Faculty`.
B) An `OracleParameter` object, `paramFacultyName`, is created and it is used to hold the dynamic parameter's name and value later.
C) Two Data Provider-dependent objects are created, and they are: `oraCommand` and `oraDataReader`. The `oraDataTable` is a Data Provider-independent object.
D) The DataSet instance is used for data query using the `LINQ To DataSet` method.
E) The `OracleParameter` object, `paramFacultyName`, is initialized by assigning it with parameter's name and parameter's value.
F) The `OracleCommand` object, `oraCommand`, is initialized by assigning it with three related values.
G) The OracleParameter object, `paramFacultyName`, is added into the `OracleCommand` object to complete the initialization process of the OracleCommand object.
H) A user-defined subroutine `ShowFaculty()` is called to retrieve the faculty image in the column `FIMAGE` in the Faculty table and display it in the PictureBox control `PhotoBox` in the Faculty form. More detailed discussions about this subroutine will be given later.
I) If the `TableAdapter Method` is selected, a blank data table `oraDataTable` will be filled by the FacultyTableAdapter to get all columns in the Faculty table in our sample database and paste them into this table.
J) To inspect if this `Fill()` is successful, one can check the `Count` property of the data rows. If it is > 0, another user-defined subroutine `FillFacultyTable()` is called to assign each column to the associated textbox in the Faculty form. More detailed discussions about this subroutine will be given later. Otherwise, an error message would be displayed to indicate that this query is failed.
K) Then all used components, including the oraDataTable and FacultyTableAdapter, will be cleared and disposed.
L) If the `Data Reader Method` is used, the `ExecuteReader` command is assigned to the `oraDataReader` to make it ready to perform data query with this reader.
M) By checking the `HasRows` property, it can be known whether that ExecuteReader command is executed successfully. If it is True, another user-defined subroutine `FillFacultyReader()` is called to read each row and column, furthermore to assign each column to the associated textbox in the Faculty form. Otherwise, a piece of error information is displayed to indicate that this reading is failed.
N) The oraDataReader is released after this reading query.
O) If the `LINQ to DataSet Method` is chosen, the initialized `oraCommand` is assigned to the SelectCommand property of the TableAdapter and the `Fill()` method is executed to fill a blank DataSet with all data of the `Faculty` table in the database.

Figure 5.69 The modified codes for the Select button's event procedure.

P) A typical LINQ query structure is created and executed to retrieve all related information for the selected faculty member. The `facultyinfo` is an implicitly typed local variable. The Visual Basic.NET 2019 will be able to automatically convert this variable to a suitable data type, in this case, it is a DataSet, when it sees it. An iteration variable `fi` is used to iterate over the result of this query from the Faculty table. Then, a SELECT statement is executed with the WHERE clause.

Q) A **For Each** loop is utilized to pick up each column from the selected data row **fRow**, which is obtained from the **facultyinfo** we get from the LINQ query, and assign it to the related textbox in the Faculty form window. The only exception is the column **FIMAGE** that contains a faculty image and it will be retrieved by the user-defined subroutine **ShowFaculty()** to be discussed later.

R) Finally, after all query operations are done, the oraCommand object is released.

Now let's take a look at the codes for five user-defined subroutine procedures used in the above **Select** button's Click event procedure. The first one is the **FillFacultyTable()**, and its codes are shown in Figure 5.70.

Let's have a closer look at this piece of codes to see how it works:

A) To access the DataTable object, one must use some suitable properties of the DataTable class. The **DataRow** and the **DataColumn** are two important properties. Using them, we can scan the whole DataTable to get each column from each row. The integer variable **pos1** is used as a loop counter later to retrieve the data from the DataTable and assign them to the associated bound textbox control on the Faculty form.

B) Next, we need to initialize the module-level object array **FacultyTextBox** by creating instances of the **TextBox** control. Recall that although we have eight columns in our Faculty table, but only seven of them are Text and the last column is Image and it contains all faculty images, so the size of this textbox array is 7 (from 0 to 6) since we only need to pick up seven Text columns and assign them to the related seven TextBox in the Faculty form.

C) Then another user-defined subroutine procedure **MapFacultyTable()**, which will be built later, is called to set a correct mapping relationship between each textbox object in the TextBox array and the data column retrieved from the DataTable.

D) Two **For Each...Next** loops are utilized to assign each data column read out of the DataTable to the mapped textbox control on the Faculty form window. Exactly in this application, we have

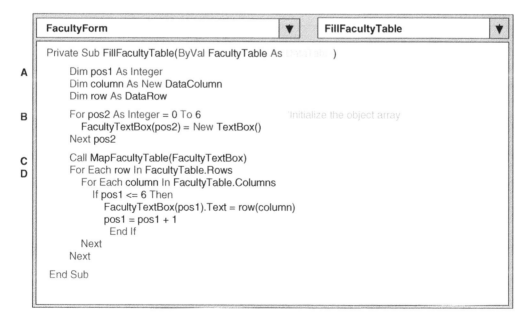

Figure 5.70 The codes for the user-defined subroutine procedure FillFacultyTable.

only one row (one record) selected from the Faculty table based on the faculty name, so the outer loop is only executed by one time and the inner loop is executed by seven times (0~6 columns) to get seven columns whose data type are Text. That is the reason why we used an `If-Then-EndIf` loop. Because the distribution order of the textbox controls in the Faculty form and the column order in the query string (`cmdString1`) is not identical, we need this `MapFacultyTable()` subroutine procedure to align them.

The detailed codes for this subroutine procedure `MapFacultyTable()` are shown in Figure 5.71.

The order of textboxes on the right-hand side of the equal symbol is the order of the queried columns in the query string, `cS1`, but the distribution order of seven textbox controls on the Faculty form window is different. By performing this assignment, the seven textbox controls on the Faculty form window can have a one-to-one mapping relation with the queried columns in the Faculty table.

Now let's take a look at another subroutine procedure `FillFacultyReader()`. This subroutine is used to retrieve the queried Text data from the `DataReader` and distribute them to the seven textbox controls on the Faculty form window. The detailed codes for this subroutine procedure are shown in Figure 5.72.

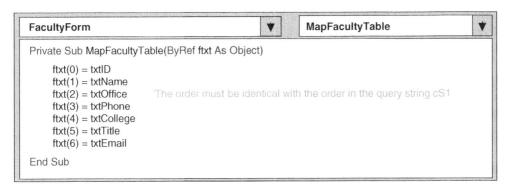

Figure 5.71 The codes for the user-defined subroutine procedure MapFacultyTable.

Figure 5.72 The codes for the subroutine procedure FillFacultyReader.

Let's have a closer look at this piece of codes to see how it works:

A) Seven instances of a TextBox array, **FacultyTextBox**, is created and initialized. These are mapped to seven Text columns in the Faculty table in the database.

B) The user-defined subroutine procedure **MapFacultyTable()** is called to set up the correct mapping between the seven textbox controls on the Faculty form window and seven columns in the Faculty table in our sample database.

C) A **While** loop is executed if the loop condition **Read()** method is True, which means that a valid data are read out from the **DataReader**. This method will return a False if no any valid data can be read out from the **DataReader**, which means that all data have been read out. Here, in fact, this **While** loop is only executed one time since we have only one row (one record) read out from the **DataReader**.

D) A **For...Next** loop is utilized to pick up each (Text) data column read out from the **DataReader** object and assign each of them to the associated textbox control on the Faculty form window. The **Item** property with the index is used here to identify each data from the **DataReader**. A point to be noted is the terminal number of the column to be read out, which is **FieldCount − 2** (=7), not **FieldCount − 1** (=8), since the last column is used to store all faculty images with the data type of Image (not Text).

The coding for the **Back** button's click event procedure is simple, just put **Me.Close()** into that event procedure. The purpose of this coding is to return to the Selection Form.

Finally, let's take care of the user-defined subroutine **ShowFaculty()**, which is used to get all faculty images from the Faculty table and display them on the **PhotoBox** in the Faculty form window. Figure 5.73 shows the codes for this subroutine.

Let's have a closer look at this piece of codes to see how it works:

A) Three arguments are passed into this subroutine, **fda** (OracleDataAdapter), **scmd** (OracleCommand), and **dt** (DataSet). First, the OracleCommand **scmd** that has been initialized is assigned to the SelectCommand property to make it ready to perform this data query operation. Then the **Fill()** method is executed to get all columns from the Faculty table in the database and fill them into the DataSet **dt**.

B) Since all images stored in the **FIMAGE** column in the Faculty table are binary bytes, thus they need to be clearly converted to the **Byte()** type before they can be displayed in the PictureBox in the Faculty form window. The converted results are assigned to an intermediate variable **bImage()**. Since only one row is collected or filled, so the property **Rows(0)** is used here.

C) This resulted **Byte()** must be further converted to an image in the memory stream format with a system method **System.IO.MemoryStream()** and assign this result to another variable **img**.

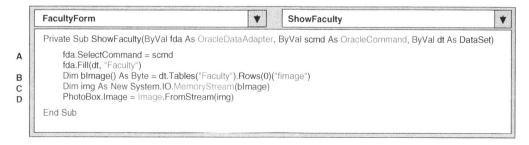

Figure 5.73 The codes for the subroutine procedure ShowFaculty().

D) Finally, the `img` is extracted to the real Image format using `Imag.FromStream()` method and assigned to the `Image` property of the PhotoBox.

Before we can finish this section, we want to show readers some alternative ways to retrieve images from a SQL Server database and display them on VB.NET Form.

5.6.5.1 Using Three Methods to Retrieve Images from Oracle Server Database

Three different methods, TableAdapter, DataReader, and LINQ to DataSet, are introduced in this section to retrieve images from Oracle Server database and display them in some Visual Basic.NET Window Forms.

Figure 5.74 shows a coding example with these methods. This piece of codes is very similar to those shown in Figure 5.69. The first two methods, `TableAdapter` and `DataReader`, use two user-defined subroutines, `FillFacultyTable()` and `FillFacultyReader()`, to perform this images retrieving and displaying, but the third method, `LINQ to DataSet`, use codes as shown in part **C** to do this image retrieving action. Now let's first take a look at two subroutines, `FillFacultyTable()` and `FillFacultyReader()`, to see how they works.

Figure 5.75 shows the modified codes for the subroutine `FillFacultyTable()`.

The `FIMAGE` column in the Faculty table is first converted to the `Byte()` type using the `CType()` method in part **A** and then it is converted to memory stream format in part **B**. Finally, it is mapped to the `Image` format using `FromStream()` method.

The modified codes for the subroutine `FillFacultyReader()` are shown in Figure 5.76.

A completed project `OracleSelectRTO_3Image Project` that contained these three query methods can be found from the folder `OracleSelectRTO_3Image Solution` located at the folder `Students\Class DB Projects\Chapter 5` in the Wiley ftp site (refer to Figure 1.2).

5.6.6 Query Data Using Runtime Objects for the Course Form

Now let's develop the codes for the Course Form. First let's do the coding for the `CourseForm_Load()` event procedure. Open that event procedure from the Course Form.

Basically, the codes of this event procedure are similar to those we did for the same event procedure in Section 5.4.9.3.1 (Figure 5.52). The only modifications are (refer to Figure 5.77):

A) A database connection status is checked to make sure that all following data query operations are valid.
B) Another query method, DataReader Method, is added into this form.

The next coding job is for the `Select` button's event procedure. One important issue is that there is no `FACULTY_NAME` column available in the Course table, and each course or `COURSE_ID` is only related to a `FACULTY_ID` in the Course table. In order to get the `FACULTY_ID` that is associated with the selected faculty name, one must first go to the Faculty table to perform a query to obtain it. In this situation, a join query is a desired method to complete this functionality.

5.6.6.1 Retrieve Data from Multiple Tables Using Tables JOINS

To have a clear picture why we need to use the Join query method for this data action, let's first take a look at the data structure in our sample database. A part of Faculty and Course data table in the CSE_DEPT database is shown in Table 5.8.

The `FACULTY_ID` in the Faculty table is a primary key, but it is a foreign key in the Course table. The relationship between the Faculty and the Course table is one-to-many. What we want to do is to pick up all `COURSE_ID` from the Course table based on the selected faculty name that is located in the Faculty table. The problem is that no faculty name is available in the Course table and we

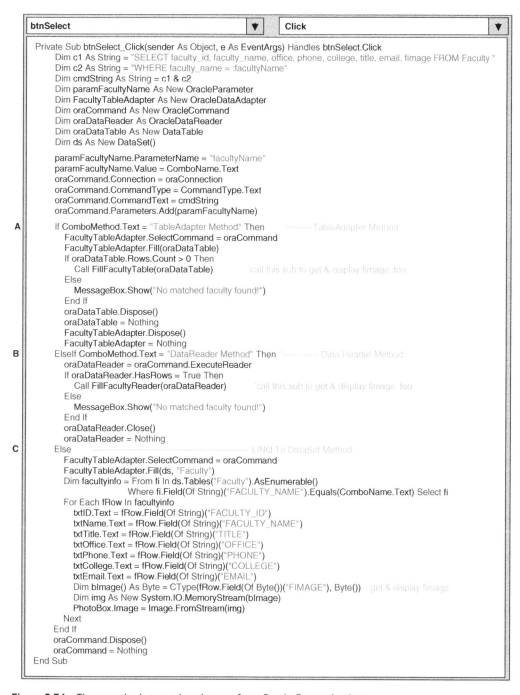

```
btnSelect  ▼        Click  ▼

  Private Sub btnSelect_Click(sender As Object, e As EventArgs) Handles btnSelect.Click
      Dim c1 As String = "SELECT faculty_id, faculty_name, office, phone, college, title, email, fimage FROM Faculty "
      Dim c2 As String = "WHERE faculty_name = :facultyName"
      Dim cmdString As String = c1 & c2
      Dim paramFacultyName As New OracleParameter
      Dim FacultyTableAdapter As New OracleDataAdapter
      Dim oraCommand As New OracleCommand
      Dim oraDataReader As OracleDataReader
      Dim oraDataTable As New DataTable
      Dim ds As New DataSet()

      paramFacultyName.ParameterName = "facultyName"
      paramFacultyName.Value = ComboName.Text
      oraCommand.Connection = oraConnection
      oraCommand.CommandType = CommandType.Text
      oraCommand.CommandText = cmdString
      oraCommand.Parameters.Add(paramFacultyName)

A     If ComboMethod.Text = "TableAdapter Method" Then           '-------TableAdapter Method
         FacultyTableAdapter.SelectCommand = oraCommand
         FacultyTableAdapter.Fill(oraDataTable)
         If oraDataTable.Rows.Count > 0 Then
            Call FillFacultyTable(oraDataTable)            'call this sub to get & display fimage, too
         Else
            MessageBox.Show("No matched faculty found!")
         End If
         oraDataTable.Dispose()
         oraDataTable = Nothing
         FacultyTableAdapter.Dispose()
         FacultyTableAdapter = Nothing
B     ElseIf ComboMethod.Text = "DataReader Method" Then    '------------ Data Reader Method
         oraDataReader = oraCommand.ExecuteReader
         If oraDataReader.HasRows = True Then
            Call FillFacultyReader(oraDataReader)        'call this sub to get & display fimage, too
         Else
            MessageBox.Show("No matched faculty found!")
         End If
         oraDataReader.Close()
         oraDataReader = Nothing
C     Else          ----------------------------------------------- LINQ To DataSet Method
         FacultyTableAdapter.SelectCommand = oraCommand
         FacultyTableAdapter.Fill(ds, "Faculty")
         Dim facultyinfo = From fi In ds.Tables("Faculty").AsEnumerable()
                           Where fi.Field(Of String)("FACULTY_NAME").Equals(ComboName.Text) Select fi
         For Each fRow In facultyinfo
            txtID.Text = fRow.Field(Of String)("FACULTY_ID")
            txtName.Text = fRow.Field(Of String)("FACULTY_NAME")
            txtTitle.Text = fRow.Field(Of String)("TITLE")
            txtOffice.Text = fRow.Field(Of String)("OFFICE")
            txtPhone.Text = fRow.Field(Of String)("PHONE")
            txtCollege.Text = fRow.Field(Of String)("COLLEGE")
            txtEmail.Text = fRow.Field(Of String)("EMAIL")
            Dim bImage() As Byte = CType(fRow.Field(Of Byte())("FIMAGE"), Byte())   get & display fimage
            Dim img As New System.IO.MemoryStream(bImage)
            PhotoBox.Image = Image.FromStream(img)
         Next
      End If
      oraCommand.Dispose()
      oraCommand = Nothing
  End Sub
```

Figure 5.74   Three methods to retrieve images from Oracle Server database.

cannot directly get all **COURSE_ID** based on the faculty name. An efficient way to do this is to use a query with two joined tables, which means that we can perform a query by joining two different tables – Faculty and Course to pick up those **COURSE_ID** records. To join these two tables, we need to use the primary key and the foreign key, **FACULTY_ID**, to set up this relationship. In other

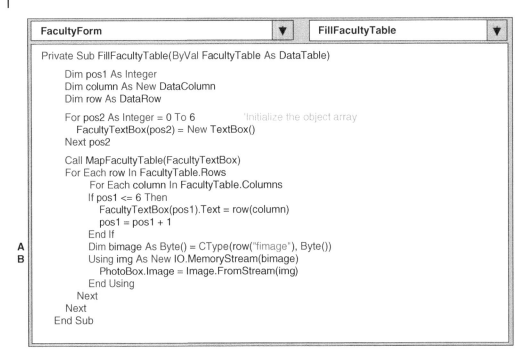

Figure 5.75 The modified codes for the subroutine FillFacultyTable().

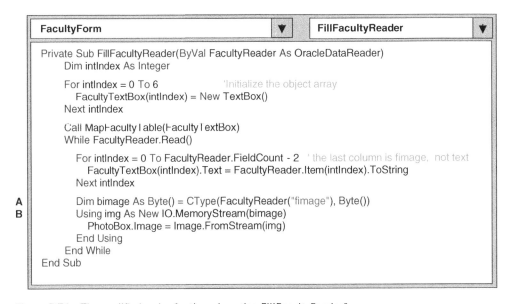

Figure 5.76 The modified codes for the subroutine FillFacultyReader().

words, we want to obtain all courses, exactly all **COURSE_ID**, from the Course table based on the faculty name in the Faculty table. But in the Course table, we only have course name and the associated **FACULTY_ID** information available. Similarly, in the Faculty table, we only have faculty name and the associated **FACULTY_ID** information available. The result is: we cannot set up a direct relationship between the faculty name in the Faculty table and the **COURSE_ID** in the

Figure 5.77 The codes for the CourseForm_Load() event procedure.

Table 5.8 A part of Faculty and Course data table.

Faculty Table			Course Table		
faculty_id	faculty_name	office	course	faculty_id	classroom
A52990	Black Anderson	MTC-218	Computers in Society	A52990	TC-109
A77587	Debby Angles	MTC-320	Computers in Society	A52990	TC-109
B66750	Alice Brown	MTC-257	Introduction to Programming	J33486	TC-303
B78880	Ying Bai	MTC-211	Introduction to Programming	B78880	TC-302
H99118	Jeff Henry	MTC-336	Algorithms & Structures	A77587	TC-301
J33486	Steve Johnson	MTC-118	Programming I	A77587	TC-303
K69880	Jenney King	MTC-324	Introduction to Algorithms	H99118	TC-302

Course table, but we can build an indirect relationship between them via **FACULTY_ID** since the **FACULTY_ID** works as a bridge to connect two tables together using the primary and foreign key.

A query statement with two joined tables, Faculty and Course, can be represented as:

```
SELECT Course.course_id, Course.course FROM Course, Faculty
WHERE (Course.faculty_id = Faculty.faculty_id) AND (Faculty.faculty_
name = :name)
```

The **:name** is a dynamic parameter and it will be replaced by the real faculty name as the project runs.

One point to be noted is that the syntax of this query statement is defined in the ANSI 89 standard and is relatively out of date. Microsoft will not support this out-of-date syntax in the future. So it is highly recommended to use a new syntax for this query statement, which is defined in the ANSI 92 standard and it looks like:

```
SELECT Course.course_id, Course.course FROM Course JOIN Faculty
ON (Course.faculty_id = Faculty.faculty_id) AND (Faculty.faculty_
name = :name)
```

Now let's use this inner join method to develop our query for this Course form. The modified codes are shown in Figure 5.78.

Let's have a closer look at this piece of codes to see how it works:

A) The joined table query string is declared at the beginning of this method. Here two columns are queried. The first one is the **COURSE_ID** and the second is the course name. The reason for this is that we need to use the **COURSE_ID**, not course name, as the identifier to pick up each course' detailed information from the Course table when the user clicks and selects the

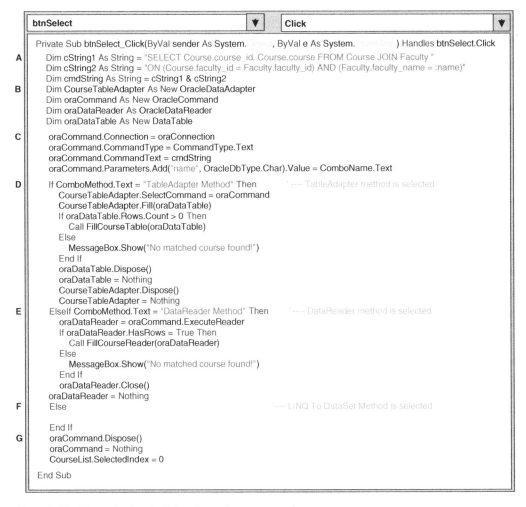

Figure 5.78 The codes for the Select button's event procedure.

COURSE_ID from the CourseList box. Exactly we only need the **COURSE_ID** column for this query, but it does not matter if other column such as the course is included in this query.

B) Some new Oracle objects are created such as the **CourseTableAdapter**, **oraCommand**, **oraDataReader**, and **oraDataTable**. All of these objects should be prefixed by the keyword **ora** to indicate that all those components are related to the Oracle Server Data Provider.

C) The **oraCommand** object is initialized with the connection string, command type, command text, and command parameter. The parameter's name must be identical with the dynamic nominal name **:name**, which is defined in the query string and it is exactly located after the equal symbol in the ON clause. The parameter's value is the content of the **Faculty Name** combo box, which should be entered by the user as the project runs later.

D) If the TableAdapter method is selected by the user, the **Fill()** method of the TableAdapter is executed to fill the Course table. The **FillCourseTable()** subroutine is called to fill the **COURSE_ID** into the CourseList box.

E) Otherwise if the DataReader method is selected by the user, the **ExecuteReader()** method is executed to read back all **COURSE_ID**, and the user-defined subroutine **FillCourseReader()** is called to fill the **COURSE_ID** into the CourseList box.

F) For the third query method, LINQ To DataSet, we leave the codes for this part as a home work project to enable students to handle that.

G) Finally, some cleaning jobs are preformed to release objects used for this query.

Now let's build codes for two user-defined subroutine procedures used in this part, **FillCourseTable()** and **FillCourseReader()**. These two subroutines are used to fill the CourseList box control on the Course form window using the queried data. Figure 5.79 shows the codes for these two user-defined subroutine procedures.

A) Before we can fill the CourseList box, a cleaning job is needed. This cleaning is very important and necessary. Otherwise multiple repeat courses (**COURSE_ID**) would be displayed in this ListBox if you forget to do this cleaning job.

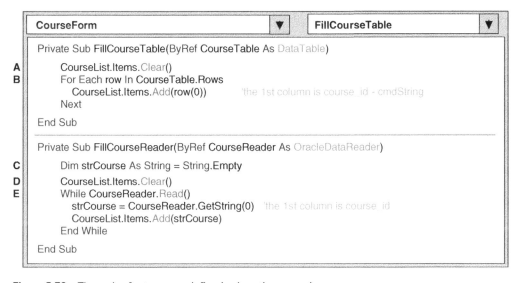

```
CourseForm               ▼    FillCourseTable          ▼

   Private Sub FillCourseTable(ByRef CourseTable As DataTable)
A      CourseList.Items.Clear()
B      For Each row In CourseTable.Rows
          CourseList.Items.Add(row(0))        'the 1st column is course_id - cmdString
       Next
   End Sub

   Private Sub FillCourseReader(ByRef CourseReader As OracleDataReader)
C      Dim strCourse As String = String.Empty
D      CourseList.Items.Clear()
E      While CourseReader.Read()
          strCourse = CourseReader.GetString(0)   'the 1st column is course_id
          CourseList.Items.Add(strCourse)
       End While
   End Sub
```

Figure 5.79   The codes for two user-defined subroutine procedures.

B) A **For Each** loop is used to scan all rows of the filled Course table. Recall that we filled 2 columns from the Course table in the database to this Course table in the DataTable object starting with the first column **COURSE_ID** (refer to query string **cString1** in Figure 5.78). Now we can pick up the first column, **COURSE_ID** (column index = 0) for each returned row of the Course table. Then the **Add()** method is used to add each retrieved **row(0)** that equals to **COURSE_ID** into the CourseList Box.

C) For the **FillCourseReader()** subroutine, a local string variable **strCourse** is created and this variable can be considered as an intermediate variable that is used to temporarily hold the queried data from the Course table.

D) Similarly, we need to clean up the CourseList box before it can be filled.

E) A **While** loop is utilized to retrieve each first column's data (**GetString(0)**) whose column index is 0 and the data value is the **COURSE_ID**. The queried data first is assigned to the intermediate variable **strCourse** and then it is added into the CourseList box using the **Add()** method.

Next, we need to take care of the coding for the **CourseList_SelectedIndexChanged()** event procedure. The detailed course information related to the selected **COURSE_ID** from the CourseList box should be displayed in six textbox controls when the user clicked and selected a **COURSE_ID** from the CourseList box. The codes for this event procedure are shown in Figure 5.80. Let's have a closer look at this piece of codes to see how it works:

A) The query string is created with six queried columns such as **COURSE_ID, COURSE, CREDIT, CLASSROOM, SCHEDULE,** and **ENROLLMENT**. The query criterion is **COURSE_ID**. The reason why we query the **COURSE_ID** using the **COURSE_ID** as a criterion is that we want to make this query complete and neat. In the WHERE clause, a dynamic parameter **courseid** is used in the query string, and this format is required by Oracle Server database operation. Also the nominal name of the dynamic parameter is changed to **:courseid**.

B) All data components related to Oracle Server Data Provider are created and these objects are used to perform the data operations between the database and our project. All of these classes should be prefixed by the keyword **Oracle** and all objects should be prefixed by the keyword **ora** since in this project we used an Oracle Server data provider.

C) The **oraCommand** object is initialized with the connection string, command type, command text, and command parameter.

D) The parameter's name must be identical with the dynamic nominal name **:courseid**, which is defined in the query string, exactly after the equal symbol in the WHERE clause. The parameter's value is the **COURSE_ID** in the CourseList ListBox control.

E) If the **DataAdapter Method** is selected by the user, the Fill() method is called to fill the Course table and the user-defined subroutine procedure **FillCourseTextBox()** is executed to fill six textboxes to display the detailed course information for the selected **COURSE_ID** from the CourseList box.

F) Otherwise, the **DataReader Method** is selected. The ExecuteReader() method is executed to read back the detailed information for the selected **COURSE_ID**, and the user-defined subroutine procedure **FillCourseReaderTextBox()** is called to fill those pieces of course information into six textboxes.

G) Finally, a cleaning job is performed to release objects used for this query.

The codes for two user-defined subroutine procedures, **FillCourseTextBox()** and **FillCourseReaderTextBox()**, are shown in Figure 5.81.

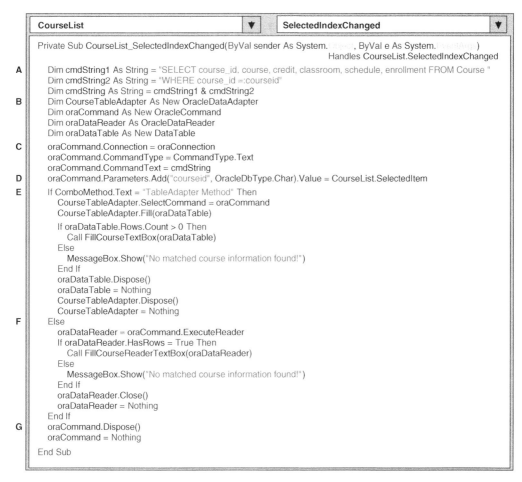

CourseList ▼	SelectedIndexChanged ▼

```
Private Sub CourseList_SelectedIndexChanged(ByVal sender As System.        , ByVal e As System.            )
                                                      Handles CourseList.SelectedIndexChanged
A      Dim cmdString1 As String = "SELECT course_id, course, credit, classroom, schedule, enrollment FROM Course "
       Dim cmdString2 As String = "WHERE course_id =:courseid"
       Dim cmdString As String = cmdString1 & cmdString2
B      Dim CourseTableAdapter As New OracleDataAdapter
       Dim oraCommand As New OracleCommand
       Dim oraDataReader As OracleDataReader
       Dim oraDataTable As New DataTable

C      oraCommand.Connection = oraConnection
       oraCommand.CommandType = CommandType.Text
       oraCommand.CommandText = cmdString
D      oraCommand.Parameters.Add("courseid", OracleDbType.Char).Value = CourseList.SelectedItem

E      If ComboMethod.Text = "TableAdapter Method" Then
           CourseTableAdapter.SelectCommand = oraCommand
           CourseTableAdapter.Fill(oraDataTable)

           If oraDataTable.Rows.Count > 0 Then
               Call FillCourseTextBox(oraDataTable)
           Else
               MessageBox.Show("No matched course information found!")
           End If
           oraDataTable.Dispose()
           oraDataTable = Nothing
           CourseTableAdapter.Dispose()
           CourseTableAdapter = Nothing
F      Else
           oraDataReader = oraCommand.ExecuteReader
           If oraDataReader.HasRows = True Then
               Call FillCourseReaderTextBox(oraDataReader)
           Else
               MessageBox.Show("No matched course information found!")
           End If
           oraDataReader.Close()
           oraDataReader = Nothing
       End If
G      oraCommand.Dispose()
       oraCommand = Nothing

   End Sub
```

Figure 5.80   The codes for the CourseList_SelectedIndexChanged procedure.

Let's have a closer look at this piece of codes to see how it works:

A) As we mentioned in the coding process for the Faculty form window, the DataTable can be scanned using two important objects: **DataRow** and **DataColumn**. You must use these two objects to access the DataTable to retrieve data stored in that DataTable.

B) The module-level object array, **CourseTextBox()**, are created and initialized here. For any object or object array, it should be created using the **New** operator. Six textbox objects are created and they can be mapped to six textbox controls in the Course form window. We use these six textbox objects to display the detailed course information for the selected **COURSE_ID** from the CourseList box later.

C) Another user-defined subroutine procedure **MapCourseTable()** is executed to setup a one-to-one mapping relation between each textbox control on the Course form window and each queried column in the queried row. This step is necessary since the distribution order of six textbox controls on the Course form is different with the column order in the query string.

D) A double **For Each** loop is utilized to retrieve all columns and all rows from the DataTable. Exactly the outer loop is only executed by one time since we only query one record (one row) course's information based on the selected **COURSE_ID** from the Course data table. The inner

```
CourseForm                     ▼        FillCourseTextBox                    ▼

   Private Sub FillCourseTextBox(ByVal CourseTable As DataTable)
A      Dim pos1 As Integer
       Dim row As DataRow
       Dim column As DataColumn
B      For pos2 As Integer = 0 To 5              'Initialize the object array
           CourseTextBox(pos2) = New TextBox
       Next pos2
C      Call MapCourseTable(CourseTextBox)
D      For Each row In CourseTable.Rows
           For Each column In CourseTable.Columns
               CourseTextBox(pos1).Text = row(column)
               pos1 = pos1 + 1
           Next
       Next
   End Sub

   Private Sub FillCourseReaderTextBox(ByVal CourseReader As OracleDataReader)
E      Dim intIndex As Integer
F      For intIndex = 0 To 5                     'Initialize the object array
           CourseTextBox(intIndex) = New TextBox
       Next intIndex
G      Call MapCourseTable(CourseTextBox)
H      While CourseReader.Read()
           For intIndex = 0 To CourseReader.FieldCount - 1
               CourseTextBox(intIndex).Text = CourseReader.Item(intIndex).ToString
           Next intIndex
       End While
   End Sub
```

Figure 5.81 The codes for two user-defined subroutine procedures.

loop is exactly executed by six times to pick up six pieces of course-related information that contains the course title, classroom, credit, schedule, and the enrollment. Then the retrieved information is assigned to each textbox control in the textbox array, which will be displayed in that textbox control in the Course form later.

E) For the subroutine **FillCourseReaderTextBox()**, a loop counter **intIndex** is first created and it is used to create six textbox objects array and retrieve data from the DataReader later.

F) This loop is used to create the textbox objects array and perform the initialization for those objects.

G) Same functionality as described in step **C**.

H) A **While** and a **For...Next** loop are used to pick up all six pieces of course-related information from the **DataReader** one by one. The **Read()** method is used as the **While** loop's condition. A returned True means that a valid data are read out from the **DataReader**, and a returned False means that no any valid data have been read out from the **DataReader**, in other words, no more data are available and all data have been read out. The **For...Next** loop uses the **FieldCount - 1** as the termination condition since the index of the first data field is 0, not 1, in the **DataReader** object. Each read-out data are converted to a string and assigned to the associated textbox control in the textbox objects array.

The detailed codes for the subroutine **MapCourseTable()** is shown in Figure 5.82.

This piece of codes is straightforward with no trick. The order of the textboxes on the right-hand side of the equal operator is the column order of the query string, **cmdString1**. By assigning each

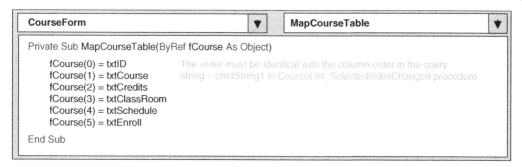

Figure 5.82   The codes for the subroutine MapCourseTable.

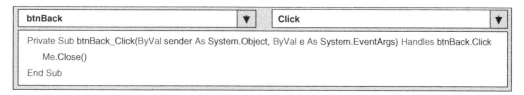

Figure 5.83   The codes for the Back button's click event procedure.

textbox control on the Course form window to each of its partner, the textbox in the textbox objects array in this order, a one-to-one mapping relationship is built and the data retrieved from the **DataReader** can be exactly mapped to and displayed in the associated textbox control.

The last coding process is for the Back button's Click event procedure. This coding is very simple and the codes are shown in Figure 5.83.

Now you can test the codes we just developed for the CourseForm class by running the project now. After the LogIn process, select the **Course Information** from the Selection form to start the course information query process.

5.6.7   Query Data Using Runtime Objects for the Student Form

Now let's finally come to the coding process for the **Student** Form window in our project. The Student form window is shown in Figure 5.84 for your convenience.

The function for this form is to pick up all pieces of information related to the selected student such as the **student id, student name, gpa, credits, major, school year, email**, and **image** and display them in seven textboxes and a PictureBox **PhotoBox** when the **Select** button is clicked by the user. Also all courses (**COURSE_ID**) taken by that student are displayed in the CourseList box. Apparently, this function needs to make two queries to the two different tables, the **STUDENT** and the **STUDENTCOURSE** tables, respectively.

The codes for this form are similar to those we did for the Faculty form with one important difference, which is the query type. In order to improve the querying efficiency and make the codes simple, two stored procedures are developed and implemented in this section. Using the stored procedures, the query can be significantly simplified and integrated, and the efficiency of the data query can also be improved.

Let's start from the **Form_Load**() event procedure. The codes for this event procedure are shown in Figure 5.85. Let's have a closer look at this piece of codes to see how it works:

A) The namespaces of the Oracle Server data class library are imported to provide the prototypes of all data components to be created and used in this procedure.

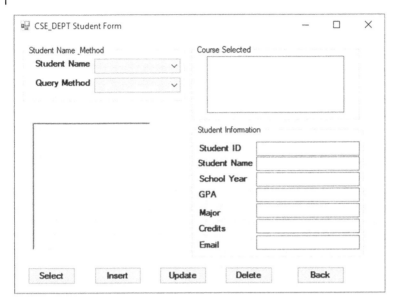

Figure 5.84 The Student form window. *Source:* Microsoft Visual Studio.

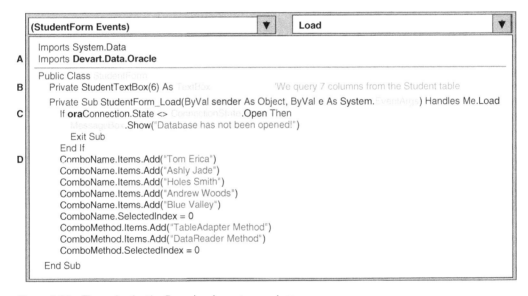

Figure 5.85 The codes for the Form_Load event procedure.

B) A form-level textbox array **StudentTextBox()** is declared and it is used to hold the detailed student's information as the project runs, and those pieces of information will be displayed in seven textboxes in the Student form later.

C) The database connection is checked first before we can perform any data operation between the project and the database related.

D) All sampled students' names and query methods are added into the related combo box, and the default item is the first one in both combo boxes.

Next let's take a look at the coding process for the `Select` button's click event procedure. When this `Select` button is clicked by the user, seven pieces of student information and the student's image are displayed in seven related textboxes and a PictureBox, and all courses (`COURSE_ID`) taken by that student are displayed in the CourseList box. Regularly two queries are needed for this operation. However, in order to save time and space, we want to use two stored procedures to replace two queries to improve the query integrity and efficiency. Let's go a little deep for the stored procedure.

5.6.7.1 Query Student Data Using Stored Procedures

Stored procedures are nothing more than functions or procedures applied in any project developed in any programming language. This means that stored procedures can be considered as functions or subroutines, and they can be called easily with any arguments and they can also return any data with certain type. One can integrate multiple query statements into a single stored procedure to perform multiple queries at a time, and those statements will be precompiled by the Oracle Server to form an integrated target body. In this way, the precompiled body is insulated with your codes developed in Visual Basic.NET environment. You can easily call the stored procedure from your Visual Basic.NET project as the project runs. The result of using the stored procedure is that the performance of your data-driven application can be greatly improved and the data query's speed can be significantly faster. Also when you develop a stored procedure, the database server automatically creates an execution plan for that procedure, and the developed plan can be updated automatically whenever a modification is made to that procedure by the database server.

Regularly, there are three types of stored procedures: system stored procedures, extended stored procedures, and custom stored procedures. The system stored procedures are developed and implemented for administrating, managing, configuring, and monitoring the server. The extended stored procedures are developed and applied in the dynamic linked library (dll) format. This kind of stored procedures can improve the running speed and save the running space since they can be dynamically linked to your project. The custom stored procedures are developed and implemented by users for their applications.

Unlike other databases, if a stored procedure developed in the Oracle database needs to return data such that a stored procedure needs to execute a SELECT statement, then that stored procedure must be embedded into a package. The package in Oracle is a class and it can contain variables, functions, and procedures. Therefore, the stored procedures in the Oracle can be divided into two parts: stored procedures and packages. The stored procedures that don't need to return any data (by executing the INSERT, UPDATE, and DELETE statements) can be considered as a pure stored procedures, but the stored procedures that need to return data (by executing the SELECT statement) must be embedded into a package and therefore a package should be used.

5.6.7.2 The Syntax of Creating a Stored Procedure in the Oracle

The syntax of creating a stored procedure in the Oracle is shown in Figure 5.86.

The keyword `REPLACE` is used for the modified stored procedures. Recall that in the SQL Server, the keyword `ALTER` is used for any stored procedure that has been modified since it was created. In Oracle, the keyword `CREATE OR REPLACE` is used to represent any procedure that is either a newly created or a modified.

Followed the procedure's name, all input or output parameters are declared inside the braces. After the keyword `AS`, the stored procedure's body is displayed. The body begins with the keyword `BEGIN` and ends with the keyword `END`. You need to note that a semi-colon must be followed after each query statement and after the keyword `END`.

```
CREATE OR REPLACE PROCEDURE  Procedure name
{
        Param1's name      Param1's data type,
        Param2's name      Param2's data type,
        ……..
}
AS
    BEGIN
    (Your query Statements, such as INSERT, UPDATE or DELETE);
    END;
```

Figure 5.86   The syntax of creating a stored procedure in Oracle.

```
CREATE OR REPLACE PROCEDURE  InsertProcedure
{
        studentId          VARCHAR2,
        name               VARCHAR2,
        credit             NUMBER
}
AS
    BEGIN
    INSERT INTO Student(student_id, s_name, s_credit)
    VALUES(studentId, name, credit);
    END;
```

Figure 5.87   The syntax of creating a stored procedure in Oracle.

```
CREATE OR REPLACE PACKAGE  Package name
AS
        Definition for the returned Cursor;
        Definition for the stored procedure
END;
CREATE OR REPLACE PACKAGE BODY  Package name
AS
    Stored procedure prototype
    AS
    BEGIN
      OPEN  Returned cursor FOR
      (Your SELECT Statements);
    END;
END;
```

Figure 5.88   The syntax of creating a package in Oracle.

An example of creating a stored procedure in Oracle is shown in Figure 5.87.

The length of data type for each parameter is not necessary since this allows those parameters to have a varying length value.

5.6.7.3   The Syntax of Creating a Package in the Oracle

To create stored procedure that returns data, one need to embed the stored procedure into a package. The syntax of creating a package is shown in Figure 5.88.

The syntax of creating a package contains two parts: The package definition part and the package body part. The returned data type, CURSOR, is first defined since the cursor can be used to return a group of data. Following the definition of the cursor, the stored procedure, exactly the protocol of the stored procedure, is declared with the input and the output parameters (cursor works as the output argument).

Following the package definition part is the body part. The protocol of the stored procedure is redeclared at the beginning, and then the body begins with the opening of the cursor and assigns the returning result of the following SELECT statement to the cursor. Similarly, each statement must be ended with a semi-colon, including the command **END**.

An example of creating a **FacultyPackage** in the Oracle is shown in Figure 5.89.

The stored procedure is named **SelectFacultyID** with two parameters; the input parameter **FacultyName** and the output parameter **FacultyID**. The keywords **IN** and **OUT** followed the associated parameter are used to indicate the input/output direction of the parameter. The length of the stored procedure name is limited to 30 letters in the Oracle. Unlike the stored procedure name created in the SQL Server, there is no any prefix applied for each procedure's name.

Unlike the SQL Server database, Visual Studio.NET 2019 does not provide a GUI to help users to directly create, edit, and manipulate the Oracle database components such as tables, views, and stored procedures inside the Visual Studio.NET environment. However, the Oracle SQL Developer did provide a GUI tool to allow users to create and manipulate database components such as tables, views, indexes, stored procedures, and packages directly in that Developer environment.

In this section, we will use the Oracle SQL Developer to create our packages with our desired stored procedures to query students' courses.

5.6.7.4 Create Two Oracle Packages for Student Form

There are two data parts in the Student Form, the detailed student's information part that contains student's information, such as student's name, student_id, gpa, school year, major, email and student's image, and the student's courses part that includes all courses taken by the selected student. Thus, we need to create two packages to perform these two queries for two sets of data.

First let's create our first package, **Student_Info**, with the Oracle SQL Developer.

Open the Oracle SQL Developer and connect to our database by entering the system password. Then expand the **Other Users** folder and our sample database folder **CSE_DEPT**. Perform the following operations to create this package:

```
CREATE OR REPLACE PACKAGE  FacultyPackage
AS
        TYPE  CURSOR_TYPE  IS  REF  CURSOR;
        PROCEDURE SelectFacultyID (FacultyName IN CHAR,
                        FacultyID  OUT  CURSOR_TYPE);
END;
CREATE OR REPLACE PACKAGE BODY  FacultyPackage
AS
    PROCEDURE SelectFacultyID (FacultyName IN CHAR,
                    FacultyID  OUT  CURSOR_TYPE)
    AS
    BEGIN
      OPEN  FacultyID  FOR
      SELECT faculty_id, title, office, email FROM Faculty
      WHERE faculty_name = FacultyName;
    END;
END;
```

Figure 5.89 An example of creating a Faculty Package in Oracle.

1) Right-click on the **Packages** folder and select the **New Package** item.
2) On the opened Create Package wizard, enter the package name **STUDENT_INFO**, as shown in Figure 5.90. Click on the **OK** button.
3) On the opened Package Definition wizard, enter the codes shown in Figure 5.91 into this wizard as the package definition.
4) Click on the drop-down arrow and select **Compile** item to compile this package. A **Compiled** message should be displayed in the Message-Log window if this compiling is successful.
5) Now right- click on our new created package, **STUDENT_INFO**, under the **Packages** folder and select the **Create Body** item to add package body into this package.
6) On the opened **Package Body** wizard, enter the codes that are highlighted and shown in Figure 5.92 into this body wizard.
7) Click on the drop-down arrow and select **Compile** item to compile this package body. A **Compiled** message should be displayed in the Message-Log window if this compiling is successful, as shown in Figure 5.93.
8) Your finished package, **Student_Info**, is shown in Figure 5.93.

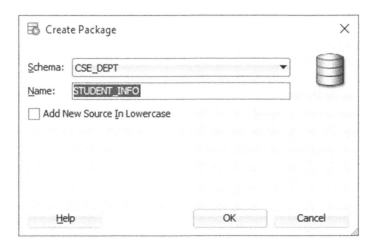

Figure 5.90 The opened New Package wizard. *Source:* Microsoft Visual Studio.

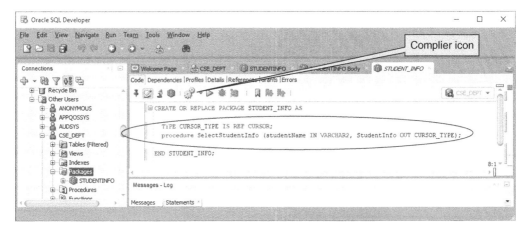

Figure 5.91 The opened Package Definition wizard. *Source:* Oracle Database.

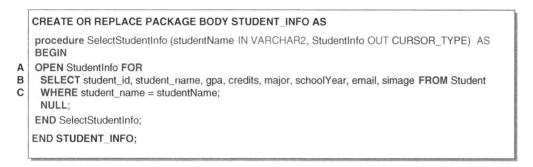

```
CREATE OR REPLACE PACKAGE BODY STUDENT_INFO AS

  procedure SelectStudentInfo (studentName IN VARCHAR2, StudentInfo OUT CURSOR_TYPE)  AS
  BEGIN
A   OPEN StudentInfo FOR
B    SELECT student_id, student_name, gpa, credits, major, schoolYear, email, simage FROM Student
C    WHERE student_name = studentName;
    NULL;
  END SelectStudentInfo;

  END STUDENT_INFO;
```

Figure 5.92 The finished Package Body wizard.

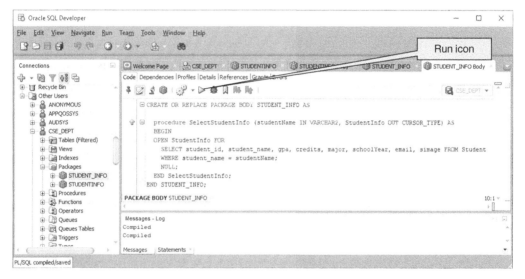

Figure 5.93 Finished package Student_Info. *Source:* Oracle Database.

Let's have a closer look at this piece of codes to see how it works:

A) The **OPEN StudentInfo FOR** command is used to assign the returned data columns from the following query to the cursor variable **StudentInfo**.

B) The **SELECT** query is executed to get all columns from the **STUDENT** table.

C) The input argument, **studentName**, is assigned to the **STUDENT_NAME** column as a query criterion for this package.

In fact, it is unnecessary to build this query as a package due to its simplicity, but here we prefer to use this query as an example to illustrate the building process for an Oracle package.

Now we can test this package in this Oracle SQL Developer environment to confirm its correctness. Click on the green arrow (**Run**) button on the task bar, as shown in Figure 5.93, to run this package. The opened Run PL/SQL wizard is shown in Figure 5.94.

Enter a student's name, such as **Tom Erica**, into the **Input Value** box (Figure 5.94), and click on the **OK** button to run this package. You may need to re-enter the system password to run this package.

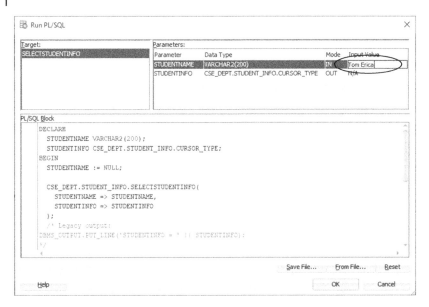

Figure 5.94 The opened Run PL/SQL wizard. *Source:* Microsoft Visual Studio.

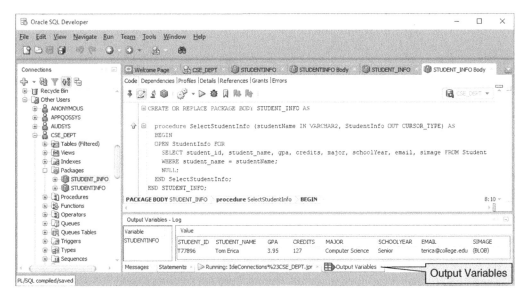

Figure 5.95 The running result of package STUDENT_INFO. *Source:* Oracle Database.

To check the running result, click on the `Output Variables` tab at the lower-right corner, and all eight selected columns related to the student named `Tom Erica` on the `STUDENT` table are displayed under the `Value` tab, as shown in Figure 5.95.

Next let's create another package, `STUDENT_COURSE`, for this Student form. This package contains two procedures: the first stored procedure is used to get the `student_id` from the `Student` table based on the selected student name and the second one is used to obtain the courses taken by the selected student based on the `student_id`. The reason why we need to use two queries is we want to query all courses (`course_id`s) taken by the selected student based on the student's name, not the **student_id**, from the **StudentCourse** table. But there is only **student_id** column available in the **StudentCourse** table and no student name available in that table. The student name can only be obtained from the **Student** table. So we need first to make a query to the **Student** table to get the **student_id** based on the student's name and then make the second query to the **StudentCourse** table to get all courses (exactly all **course_id**) based on the **student_id**.

Perform the following steps to build this package **STEDNET_COURSE**:

1) On the opened Oracle SQL Developer, expand our sample database **CSE_DEPT** under the **Other Users** folder and then right-click on the **Packages** folder and select the **New Package** item.
2) On the opened Create Package wizard, enter the package name **STUDENT_COURSE**, and click on the **OK** button.
3) On the opened Package Definition wizard, enter the codes shown in Figure 5.96 into this wizard as the package definition. The procedure is **SelectStudentCourse** with two arguments, **studentName** and **StudentCourse**, respectively.
4) Click on the drop-down arrow and select **Compile** item to compile this package. A **Compiled** message should be displayed in the Message-Log window if this compiling is successful, as shown in Figure 5.96.
5) Now right-click on our new created package, **STUDENT_COURSE**, under the **Packages** folder in the left pane and select the **Create Body** item to add package body into this package.
6) On the opened **Package Body** wizard, enter the codes that are highlighted and shown in Figure 5.97 into this body wizard.
7) Click on the drop-down arrow and select **Compile** item to compile this package body. A **Compiled** message should be displayed in the Message-Log window if this compiling is successful, as shown in Figure 5.98.
8) Your finished package, **STUDENT_COURSE**, is shown in Figure 5.98.

Let's have a closer look at this piece of codes to see how it works (Figure 5.97).

A) The procedure **SelectStudentCourse** is re-declared here. But an **IS** operator is attached at the end of this prototype to replace an **AS** operator to indicate that this procedure needs to use a local variable **studentID**, and this variable will work as an intermediate variable to hold the returned **student_id** from the first query in **C**.
B) A local variable **studentID** is declared here with a data type of **VARCHAR2(50)**.

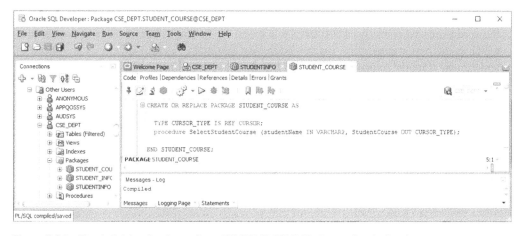

Figure 5.96 The definition for the package STUDENT_COURSE. *Source:* Oracle Database.

```
CREATE OR REPLACE PACKAGE BODY  STUDENT_COURSE  AS

A   procedure SelectStudentCourse (studentName IN VARCHAR2, StudentCourse OUT CURSOR_TYPE) IS
B   studentID VARCHAR2(50);
    BEGIN
C     SELECT student_id INTO studentID FROM Student
      WHERE student_name = studentName;
D     OPEN StudentCourse FOR SELECT course_id FROM StudentCourse
      WHERE student_id = studentID;
      NULL;
    END SelectStudentCourse;
    END STUDENT_COURSE;
```

Figure 5.97 The code body for the package STUDENT_COURSE.

Figure 5.98 The finished package STUDENT_COURSE. *Source:* Oracle Database.

C) Starting from the **BEGIN**, our two query statements are placed below. The first query is to get the **student_id** from the **STUDENT** table based on the input parameter **studentName**, which is the first argument of this procedure. An **SELECT...INTO** statement is utilized to temporarily store the returned **student_id** into the intermediate variable **studentID**.

D) The **OPEN StudentCourse FOR** command is used to assign the returned **course_id** to the output cursor variable **StudentCourse**.

Similarly as we did before, we can test this package in this Oracle SQL Developer environment to confirm its correctness. Click on the green arrow (**Run**) button on the task bar to run this package. The opened Run PL/SQL wizard is shown in Figure 5.99.

Enter one of sample students' names, **Tom Erica**, into the **Value** box, and then click on the **OK** button to run our stored procedure. The running result can be obtained by clicking on the **Output Variables** tab, as shown in Figure 5.100.

Now that our two packages have been tested successfully, it is time for us to develop our codes in Visual Basic.NET to call these two packages to perform related queries.

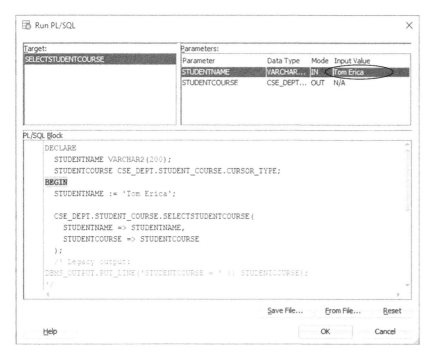

Figure 5.99 The opened Run PL/SQL wizard. *Source:* Microsoft Visual Studio.

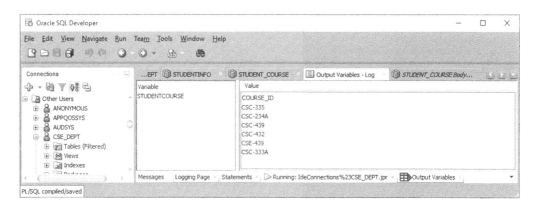

Figure 5.100 The running result of the package STUDENT_COURSE. *Source:* Oracle Database.

5.6.7.5 Query Data Using the Oracle Package for the Student Form

Open our project `OracleSelectRTObject Project` and the GUI of the `Student` form and double-click on the `Select` button to open its event procedure. Enter the codes shown in Figure 5.101 into this event procedure:

A) Two Oracle packages and stored procedures' names are assigned to two string variables `strStudentInfo` and `strStudentCourse`, respectively. These two names must be identical with those we created in two packages: `Student_Info.SelectStudentInfo` and `Student_Course.SelectStudentCourse`.

B) All data components are created in this section, which include two TableAdapters, two DataTables, two Command objects, and a DataReader.

btnSelect ▼	Click ▼

```
      Private Sub btnSelect_Click(sender As Object, e As EventArgs) Handles btnSelect.Click
A        Dim strStudentInfo As String = "Student_Info.SelectStudentInfo"
         Dim strStudentCourse As String = "Student_Course.SelectStudentCourse"
B        Dim StudentTableAdapter, StudentCourseTableAdapter As New OracleDataAdapter
         Dim oraCmdStudent, oraCmdStudentCourse As New OracleCommand
         Dim oraStudentTable, oraStudentCourseTable As New DataTable
         Dim oraDataReader As OracleDataReader

C        PhotoBox.SizeMode = PictureBoxSizeMode.StretchImage

D        Call BuildCommand(oraCmdStudent, strStudentInfo)
E        oraCmdStudent.Parameters.Add("studentName", OracleDbType.VarChar, ComboName.Text,
                                                               ParameterDirection.Input)

F        If ComboMethod.Text = "TableAdapter Method" Then          ' TableAdapter Method selected
            StudentTableAdapter.SelectCommand = oraCmdStudent
            StudentTableAdapter.Fill(oraStudentTable)
G           If oraStudentTable.Rows.Count > 0 Then
               Call FillStudent(oraStudentTable)
H           Else
               MessageBox.Show("No matched student found!")
            End If
I        Else                                       ' DataReader Method selected
            oraDataReader = oraCmdStudent.ExecuteReader
J           If oraDataReader.HasRows = True Then
               Call FillStudentReader(oraDataReader)
K           Else
               MessageBox.Show("No matched student found!")
            End If
L           oraDataReader.Close()
         End If

M        Call BuildCommand(oraCmdStudentCourse, strStudentCourse)
N        oraCmdStudentCourse.Parameters.Add("studentName", OracleDbType.VarChar, ComboName.Text,
                                                               ParameterDirection.Input)
O        oraCmdStudentCourse.Parameters.Add("StudentCourse", OracleDbType.Cursor, ParameterDirection.Output)
P        oraDataReader = oraCmdStudentCourse.ExecuteReader
Q        If oraDataReader.HasRows = True Then
            Call FillCourseReader(oraDataReader)
R        Else
            MessageBox.Show("No matched course found!")
         End If

S        oraStudentTable.Dispose()
         oraStudentCourseTable.Dispose()
         StudentTableAdapter.Dispose()
         StudentCourseTableAdapter.Dispose()
         oraCmdStudent.Dispose()
         oraCmdStudentCourse.Dispose()

      End Sub
```

Figure 5.101   The codes for the Select button's Click event procedure.

C) The student's image PictureBox, **PhotoBox**, is configured by setting its **SizeMode** to Stretch Image to make sure that the image is completely displayed in that box.

D) A user-defined subroutine **BuildCommand()** is called to initialize the first Command object with the correct Connection, CommandType, and CommandText properties. In order to execute our packages, those properties should be initialized as follows:
- CommandType = CommandType.**StoredProcedure**
- CommandText = **strStudent** = "**Student_Info.SelectStudentInfo**"

E) The unique input parameter to the first stored procedure **SelectStudentInfo** is the **studentName**, which will be selected by the user from the student name combo box (**ComboName.Text**) as the project runs. This dynamic parameter must be added into the **Parameters** collection that is the property of the Command class using the `Add()` method before the stored procedure can be executed. This `Add()` method has 14 overloaded versions and we used one of them. The key issue is that the added parameter's direction must be clearly indicated using the `ParameterDirection` data type when using this method to add any new dynamic parameter in Oracle database applications. Thus, the type of `ParameterDirection.Input` is used here to define that this `studentName` is an input parameter to this stored procedure. This direction must be clearly indicated for Oracle database implementations. The third argument of this method is the parameter's value, which is a student's name selected by the users from the student's name combo box as the project runs.

F) If the query method, `TableAdapter Method`, is selected, the initialized Command object `oraCmdStudent` is then assigned to the SelectCommand property of the TableAdapter to make it ready to be used. Then the `Fill()` method is called to fill the `oraStudentTable`, which is exactly to call our first stored procedure to fill the `oraStudentTable`.

G) If this filling is successful, the `Count` property should be greater than 0, which means that at least one row has been filled into the `oraStudentTable`, and another user-defined subroutine, `FillStudent()`, is called to fill seven textboxes and student's image PictureBox in the Student form with eight pieces of retrieved columns from the stored procedure.

H) Otherwise, an error message is displayed if this fill operation is failed.

I) If the `DataReader Method` is selected by the user, the `ExecuteReader()` method that is a member function of the Oracle Command class is called to perform a reading operation, exactly to call our stored procedure `SelectStudentInfo`, to retrieve all eight columns from the **STUDENT** table based on the input student's name and assign them to the OracleDataReader object, `oraDataReader`.

J) If the property of that reader, `HasRow`, is true, which means that DataReader did read back some rows, the subroutine `FillStudentReader()` is called to fill all seven textboxes and the PhotoBox in the Student form window with the read rows.

K) Otherwise, an error message is displayed.

L) A cleaning job is performed to close the used Data Reader object `oraDataReader`.

M) The subroutine `BuildCommand()` is called again to initialize our second Command object `oraCmdStudentCourse`. The values to be assigned to the properties of this Command object are
   - CommandType = CommandType.`StoredProcedure`
   - CommandText = `strStudentCourse` = "`Student_Course.SelectStudentCourse`"

The purpose of using this Command object again and the following codes is to use the Data Reader query method to call our second package/stored procedure `Student_Course.SelectStudentCourse` to get all courses (`course_id`) taken by the selected student.

N) The input parameter to that second stored procedure is the `studentName`, and it must be added into the Parameters collection using the `Add()` method as we did in step **E** above.

O) As we know, the second stored procedure has an output data sequence with a data type of `Cursor`, thus another overloading version of this `Add()` method is utilized to indicate the Data Type is an `OracleDbType.Cursor` type on the second argument, and the direction is a `ParameterDirection.Output` on the third argument for this method.

P) The `ExecuteReader()` method that is a member function of the Oracle Command class is called to perform a reading operation, exactly to call our second stored procedure `SelectStudentCourse()`, to retrieve all courses (`course_id`) from the **STUDENTCOURSE** table based on the input student's name and assign them to the OracleDataReader object, `oraDataReader`.

Q) If the property of that reader, `HasRow`, is true, which means that DataReader did read back some rows, the subroutine `FillCourseReader()` is called to get all courses (`course_id`) ad display them on the CourseList box.

R) Otherwise, an error message is displayed.

S) A sequence of cleaning jobs is performed to close all objects used in the event procedure.

The codes for the subroutine **BuildCommand()** are shown in Figure 5.102.

This piece of codes is straightforward with no trick. Different properties of the Command class, such as the Connection String, Command Type, and Command Text, are assigned to the Command object. The only point is the data type of the first argument, **cmdObj**, which is a reference (**ByRef**). A reference in Visual Basic.NET is equivalent to a memory address or a pointer in C++, and the argument **cmdObj** is called in Passing-By-Reference. When an argument is passing in this mode, the object **cmdObj** will work as both an input and an output, and they will be stored at the same memory address when this subroutine is completed. We can use this **cmdObj** as a returned object for this subroutine.

The codes of the subroutine **FillStudent()** are shown in Figure 5.103.

The function of this piece of codes is to fill seven textboxes and the student's image PictureBox in the Student form with eight columns data obtained from the Student table, **student_id**, **student_name**, **gpa**, **credits**, **major**, **schoolYear**, **email**, and **simage**, and it is the first query we discussed above.

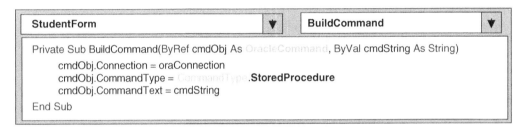

```
StudentForm ▼          BuildCommand ▼

Private Sub BuildCommand(ByRef cmdObj As OracleCommand, ByVal cmdString As String)
    cmdObj.Connection = oraConnection
    cmdObj.CommandType = CommandType.StoredProcedure
    cmdObj.CommandText = cmdString
End Sub
```

Figure 5.102   The codes for the subroutine BuildCommand().

```
StudentForm ▼          FillStudent ▼

Private Sub FillStudent(ByVal StudentTable As DataTable)
    Dim pos1 As Integer
    Dim row As DataRow
    Dim column As DataColumn

    For pos2 As Integer = 0 To 6          'Initialize the textbox array
        StudentTextBox(pos2) = New TextBox
    Next pos2

    Call MapStudentTextBox(StudentTextBox)
    For Each row In StudentTable.Rows
        For Each column In StudentTable.Columns
            If pos1 <= 6 Then
                StudentTextBox(pos1).Text = row(column)
                    pos1 = pos1 + 1
            End If
            Dim bimage As Byte() = CType(row("simage"), Byte())
            Using img As New IO.MemoryStream(bimage)
                PhotoBox.Image = Image.FromStream(img)
            End Using
        Next
    Next
End Sub
```

Figure 5.103   The codes for the subroutine FillStudent().

The **StudentTextBox** array is initialized, and then the subroutine **MapStudentTextBox()** is called to set up a one-to-one mapping relationship between the **StudentTextBox** array and seven textboxes in the Student form.

A nested **For Each** loop is executed to pick up each column's data from the queried row. Exactly only one row data that matches to the selected student name is obtained from the Student table; therefore, the outer-loop is only executed one time. The reason of using double loop is that both the **DataRow** and the **DataColumn** are classes, and in order to pick up data from any DataTable, one must use the objects **row** and **column**, which are instances of the **DataRow** and **DataColumn**, as the index to access each row or column of DataTable instead of using an integer. The local integer variable **pos1** works as an index for the **StudentTextBox** array.

Since the column **SIMAGE** stored all student's images with binary data type or **BLOB** format, thus a **CType()** method is used to retrieve this **SIMAGE** and convert it to a memory stream type, and finally a system method **FromStream()** is utilized to convert it to the Image type, and assigned to the student's PictureBox, **PhotoBox**'s Image property.

The codes for the subroutine **FillStudentReader()** are shown in Figure 5.104.

This subroutine is very similar to another subroutine **FillFacultyReader()** we discussed in Section 5.6.5.1, exactly in Figure 5.76. Please refer to that subroutine to get more details about it. The only change is to replace the keyword, Faculty, with Student in this subroutine.

For other user-defined subroutine procedures used in this form, **FillCourseReader()** and **MapStudentTextBox()**, their codes are similar to those we developed in the Course form window. For your convenience, we list them here again with some simple explanations.

The codes for the subroutine, **FillCourseReader()**, are shown in Figure 5.105. This subroutine is identical with one we discussed in Section 5.6.6.1, exactly in Figure 5.79.

The function of this subroutine is to fill the CourseList box with all courses (**COURSE_ID**) taken by the selected student, and all queried courses are stored in the StudentCourse table, which are obtained by executing the second query to the StudentCourse table based on the **STUDENT_ID**.

After the CourseList box is cleared, a **While** loop is executed to pick up each **COURSE_ID** from the StudentCourse table as long as the **Read()** method returns a True. The first column of the

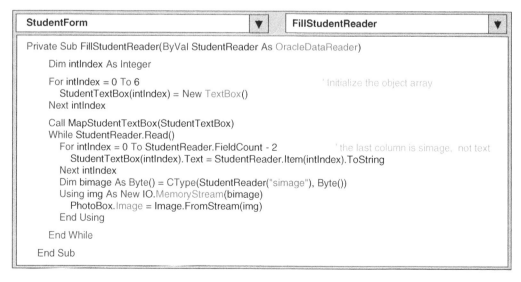

Figure 5.104 The codes for the subroutine FillStudentReader().

method `GetString(0)`, which is the `COURSE_ID`, is assigned to the local String variable `strCourse`, and then it is added into the CourseList box by executing the `Add()` method.

The codes for the subroutine `MapStudentTextBox()` are shown in Figure 5.106.

The purpose of this piece of codes is to set up a one-to-one mapping relationship between each textbox control in the `StudentTextBox` array and each column data in our first query string, `strStudent`. Each textbox control in the `StudentTextBox` array is related to an associated textbox control in the Student form such as `STUDENT_ID`, `STUDENT_NAME`, `GPA`, `CREDITS`, `MAJOR`, `SCHOOLYEAR`, and `EMAIL`. Since the distribution order of those textboxes in the `StudentTextBox` array may be different with the order of those column data in our first query, a correct order relationship is needed to be set up after calling this subroutine.

Another important point is the data type of the argument `sTextBox`, which is a nominal reference variable of the `StudentTextBox` array. A reference data type (`ByRef`) should be used for this argument in order to get the modified textbox controls in the `StudentTextBox` array when this subroutine returns to our main procedure.

The codes for the `Back` button's Click event procedure are simple, open that event procedure and just enter `Me.Close()` into that procedure.

Now we can begin to run this project to call those two stored procedures from our Visual Basic. NET project. Click on the Start Debugging button to run our project, enter username and password and select the `Student Information` item to open the Student form window, which is shown in Figure 5.107.

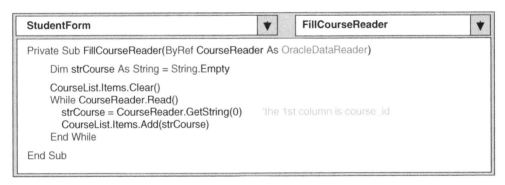

Figure 5.105   The codes for the subroutine FillCourseReader().

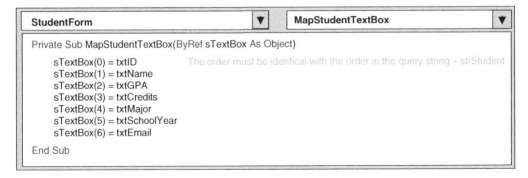

Figure 5.106   The codes for the subroutine MapStudentTextBox().

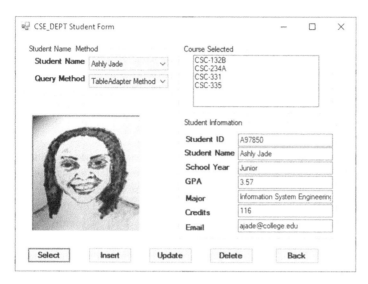

Figure 5.107 The running status of the Student form.

Select a student such as **Ashly Jade** from the Student Name combo box and click on the **Select** button. All pieces of information related to this student and all courses taken by this student are displayed in seven textboxes and the CourseList box, as shown in Figure 5.107. Our project to call two Oracle packages and stored procedures is very successful!

5.7 Chapter Summary

The main topic of this chapter is to develop professional data-driven applications in Visual Basic.NET 2019 environment with four different methods. The data query is the main task of this chapter.

The first method is to utilize Wizards and Tools provided by Visual Studio.NET 2019 and ADO. NET to build simple but powerful data query projects, and the second is to use the Runtime Object method to build the potable projects. The LINQ To DataSet is introduced as the third method to query data from the different data tables. Using the Oracle packages and stored procedures to access Oracle databases is also discussed in this chapter as the fourth query method.

Comparably, the first method is simple, and it is easy to be understood and learned by students who are beginner to Visual Basic.NET and databases. This method utilizes a lot of powerful tools and wizards provided by Visual Studio.NET and ADO.NET to simplify the coding process, and most codes are auto-generated by the .NET Framework and Visual Studio.NET 2019. The user can use those tools and wizards to easily perform data operations, such as adding new data source, making data binding, and connecting to the selected data source. The shortcoming of this method is that a lot of coding jobs are performed by the system behind the screen, so it is hard to enable users to have a clear and detailed picture about what is really happened behind those tools and wizards. The most codes are generated by the system automatically in the specific locations, so it is not easy to translate and execute those codes in other platforms.

The Runtime Object method is utilized as the second method. This method allows users to dynamically create all data-related objects and perform the associated data operations after the project runs. Because all objects are generated by the codes, it is very easy to translate and execute this kind of projects in other platforms. This method provides a clear view for the users and enables them to have a global and detailed picture in how to control the direction of the project with the codes based on the users' idea and feeling. The shortcoming of this method is that a lot of codes make the project complicated and hard to be accepted by the beginners.

The LINQ To DataSet method is an updated method provided by .NET Framework. With this method, a general query object can be produced and executed in higher efficiency disregard what kind of language the user is using. In other words, this method is a language- or query-independent method and this makes this method simple and more efficiency compared with another two methods discussed above.

Using the Oracle packages and stored procedures to access Oracle databases to retrieve required data is introduced and discussed as the last method in this chapter. The advantage of using this method is that multiple queries can be combined into a single stored procedure to greatly simplify the query procedures and therefore to improve the query efficiency for some complicated query actions.

Some example projects use two or three different data query methods, such as TableAdapter method, runtime object method, and LINQ To DataSet method, to perform query operations against the Oracle databases. A sequence of line-by-line illustrations is provided for each sample project. The readers can obtain the solid knowledge and practical experience in how to develop a professional data query application after they finish this chapter.

By finishing the Part I in this chapter, you should be able to:

- Use the tools and wizards provided by Visual Studio.NET 2019 and ADO.NET to develop the simple but powerful data-driven applications to perform data query to Oracle 18c Express databases.
- Use the OracleConnection class to connect to Oracle 18c Express database.
- Perform data binding to a DataGridView using two methods.
- Use the OracleCommand class to execute the data query with dynamic parameters to the sample database.
- Use the OracleDataAdapter to fill a DataSet and a DataTable object with Oracle server database.
- Use the OracleDataReader class to query and process data with Oracle server database.
- Set properties for the OracleCommand objects to construct a desired query string for Oracle server database.

By finishing the Part II in this chapter, you should be able to:

- Use the Runtime objects to develop the professional data-driven applications to perform data query to Oracle 18c Express database.
- Use the OracleConnection class to dynamically connect to Oracle 18c Express database.
- Use the OracleCommand class to dynamically execute the data query with dynamic parameters to Oracle server database.
- Use the OracleDataAdapter to dynamically fill a DataSet and a DataTable object with Oracle server database.
- Use the OracleDataReader class to dynamically query and process data with Oracle server database.
- Set properties for the OracleCommand objects dynamically to construct a desired query string for Oracle server database.
- Use LINQ To DataSet method to perform data query for Oracle server database.
- Use Oracle SQL Developer to create, debug, and test Oracle packages and stored procedures.
- Use Oracle packages and stored procedures to perform the data query from Visual Basic.NET.

In Chapter 6, we will discuss the data inserting technique with Oracle server database. Both methods are introduced in two parts: Part I: using the tools and wizards provided by Visual Studio. NET 2019 to develop data inserting query, and Part II: using the Runtime objects and LINQ To DataSet to perform the data inserting job for the Oracle server database.

Homework

I. True/False Selections

_____ 1   Data Provider-dependent objects are Connection, Command, TableAdapter, and DataReader.

_____ 2   The `Fill()` method belongs to the TableAdapter class.

_____ 3   To move data between the bound controls on a form window and the associated columns in the data source, a BindingSource is needed.

_____ 4   To set up the connection between the bound controls on a form window and the associated columns in the data source, a TableAdapter is needed.

_____ 5   All TableAdapter classes are located in the namespace DataSetTableAdapters.

_____ 6   Running the `Fill()` method is equivalent to execute the `ExecuteReader()` method.

_____ 7   The DataSet can be considered as a container that contains multiple data tables, but those tables are only a mapping of the real data tables in the database.

_____ 8   To run the `Fill()` method to fill a table is exactly to fill a data table that is located in the DataSet, not a real data table in the database.

_____ 9   By checking the Count property of a data table, one can determine whether a fill-table-operation is successful or not.

_____ 10   The DataTable object is a Data Provider-independent object.

_____ 11   If one needs to include the `SELECT` statements in an Oracle stored procedure, one can directly create a stored procedure and call it from Visual Basic.NET.

_____ 12   A Package should be used if one wants to return multiple columns from a query to an Oracle database.

_____ 13   You can create, edit, manipulate, and test stored procedures for an Oracle Server database inside the Oracle SQL Developer environment.

_____ 14   To call an Oracle Server stored procedure, one must set the CommandType property of the Command object to `Procedure.`

_____ **15** To set up a dynamic parameter in an SELECT statement in an Oracle Server database, a =: symbol must be prefixed before the nominal variable.

_____ **16** The name of the dynamic parameter in an SELECT statement in an Oracle Server database may be different with the name of the nominal parameter that is assigned to the **Parameters** collection of the Command object.

_____ **17** To assign a dynamic parameter in an SELECT statement in an Oracle Server database, the keyword = must be used as the assignment operator.

_____ **18** The Oracle SQL Developer provides a GUI to assist users to create Oracle packages and stored procedures.

_____ **19** Two popular ways to query data from any database are using **Fill**() method that belongs to the TableAdapter class and or calling **ExecuteReader** method that belongs to the Command class.

_____ **20** A DataTable can be considered as a collection of DataRowCollection and DataColumnCollection, and the latter contain DataRow and DataColumn objects.

II. Multiple Choices

1 To connect a database dynamically, one needs to use the _____
  A Data Source
  B TableAdapter
  C Runtime object
  D Tools and Wizards

2 Four popular data providers are _____
  A ODBC, DB2, JDBC, and SQL
  B SQL, ODBC, DB2, and Oracle
  C ODBC, OLEDB, SQL, and Oracle
  D Oracle, OLEDB, SQL, and DB2

3 To modify a DataSet, one needs to use the _____ Wizard.
  A DataSet configuration
  B DataSet edit
  C TableAdapter configuration
  D Query Builder

4 To bind a label with the associated column in a data table, one can use _____
  A BindingNavigator
  B TableAdapter
  C DataSet
  D BindingSource

5　The _____ keyword should be used as an assignment operator for the WHERE clause with a dynamic parameter for a data query in an Oracle Server database.
　A =
　A LIKE
　B =:
　C @=

6　The _____ data provider can be used to execute the data query for _____ data providers.
　A SQL Server, OleDb and Oracle
　B OleDb, SQL Server and Oracle
　C Oracle, SQL Server and OleDb
　D SQL Server, Odbc and Oracle

7　To perform a `Fill()` method to fill a data table, exactly it executes _____ object with suitable parameters.
　A DataAdapter
　B Connection
　C DataReader
　D Command

8　To fill a list box or combo box control, one must ____ by using the ____ method.
　A Remove all old items, Remove()
　B Remove all old items, ClearBeforeFill()
　C Clean up all old items, CleanAll()
　D Clear all old items, ClearAll()

9　A _____ accessing mode should be used to define a connection object if one wants to use that connection object _____ for the whole project.
　A Private, locally
　B Protected, globally
　C Public, locally
　D Public, globally

10　To ____ data between the DataSet and the database, the ___ object should be used
　A Bind, BindingSource
　B Add, TableAdapter
　C Move, TableAdapter
　D Remove, DataReader

11　The keyword _____ will be displayed before a stored procedure's name if one modified an Oracle Server stored procedure.
　A CREATE
　B CREATE OR REPLACE
　C REPLACE
　D ALTER

12　To perform a runtime data query to an Oracle Server database, one needs to use _____.
　A OleDb Data Provider
　B SQL Server Data Provider

C Both (a) and (b)

D Oracle Client Provider

13 To query data from any database using the run time object method, two popular methods are _____ and _____

A DataSet, TableAdapter

B TableAdapter, Fill

C DataReader, ExecuteReader

D TableAdapter, DataReader

14 To create a new Oracle stored procedure that needs to return columns, one needs to create a _____ and include that stored procedure in that _____.

A Stored procedure, package

B Procedure, package

C Package, package

D Package, stored procedure

15 If you want to develop a stored procedure that makes multiple queries with multiple data tables, you need to use the _____ method.

A DataReader

B Fill

C ExecuteQuery

D ExecuteNonQuery

III. Exercises

1 Using the tools and wizards provided by Visual Studio.NET and ADO.NET to complete the data query for the Student form in the **SelectWizard** project. The project is located at the folder **Class DB Projects\Chapter 5** at the Wiley ftp site under the **Students** folder (refer to Figure 1.2 in Chapter 1).

2 Using **LINQ To DataSet** method to build the data query for the **Select** button's click event procedure in the Course form in the **OracleSelectRTObject** project. The project is located at the folder **Class DB Projects\Chapter 5** at the Wiley ftp site under the **Students** folder (refer to Figure 1.2 in Chapter 1).

3 Develop a method by adding some codes into the **TabLogIn_Click()** event procedure of the project **OracleSelectRTObject** to allow users to try the login process only three times. A warning message should be displayed and the project should be exited after three times of trying to login if all of them are failed.

4 Build an Oracle package and a stored procedural named **FACULTY_COURSE** and **SELECT_COURSEID** for the Course form via the Oracle SQL Developer to get all **COURSE_ID** based on the faculty name. Two queries need to be created in that stored procedure: (i) Query **FACULTY_ID** from the **FACULTY** table based on the selected **FACULTY_NAME** and (ii) Query all **COURSE_ID** based on the **FACULTY_ID** obtained from the first query.

5 Modify the project `OracleSelectRTObject`, which is located at the folder Class DB Projects\Chapter 5 at the Wiley ftp site under the Students folder (refer to Figure 1.2 in Chapter 1), exactly the codes in the Course Form Select button's click event procedure to call the Oracle package and stored procedure built in last project to query all `course_id` based on the selected faculty name. These modifications include two parts:

a) Add one more query method, `Stored Procedure Method`, in the `CourseForm_Load` event procedure in the Course Form.

b) Add the related codes in the `Select` button's click event procedure in the Course Form to allow user to select the `Stored Procedure Method` to call the Oracle package and stored procedure built in the last project to get all `course_id` based on the selected faculty name on the combo box, `comboName`. One may need to add one more `ElseIf` block to cover and hold those codes.

6

Insert Data into Oracle Database with Visual Basic.NET

We spent a lot of time in discussion and explanation of data query in the last chapter by using two different methods. In this chapter, we will concentrate on inserting data into the DataSet and the database. Insert data into the DataSet or exactly insert data into the data tables in the DataSet is totally different with inserting data into the database or inserting data into the data tables in the database. The former is only to insert data into a mapping of the data table in the DataSet, and this insertion has nothing to do with the real data tables in the database. In other words, the data inserted into the mapping data tables in the DataSet are not to be inserted into the data tables in the real database. The latter is to insert the data into the data tables in the real database.

As you know, ADO.NET provided a disconnected working mode for the database access applications. The so-called disconnected mode means that your data-driven applications will not always keep the connection with your database, and this connection may be disconnected after you setup your DataSet and load all data from the data tables in your database into those data table mappings in your DataSet, and most time you are just working on the data between your applications and your data table mappings in your DataSet. The main reason of using this mode is to reduce the overhead of a large number of connections to the database and improve the efficiency of data transferring and implementations between the users' applications and the data sources.

In this chapter, we will provide two parts to show readers how to insert data into the database; inserting data into the database using the Visual Studio.NET design tools and wizards is discussed in the first part, and inserting data to the database using the run-time object method is shown in the second part.

When finished this chapter, you will

- Understand the working principle and structure on inserting data to the database using the Visual Studio.NET design tools and wizards.
- Understand the procedure of configuring the TableAdapter object by using the TableAdapter Query Configuration Wizard and build the query to insert data into the database.
- Design and develop special procedures to validate data before and after accessing the database to insert data.
- Understand the working principle and structure of inserting data to the database using the run time object method.
- Insert data into the DataSet using LINQ to DataSet method.
- Design and build Oracle stored procedures to perform the data inserting action.

Oracle Database Programming with Visual Basic.NET: Concepts, Designs, and Implementations, First Edition. Ying Bai.
© 2021 The Institute of Electrical and Electronics Engineers, Inc. Published 2021 by John Wiley & Sons, Inc.
Companion website: www.wiley.com/go/bai-VB-Oracle

To successfully complete this chapter, you need to understand topics such as Fundamentals of Databases, which was introduced in Chapter 2, ADO.NET that was discussed in Chapter 3. Also a sample database CSE_DEPT that was developed in Chapter 2 will be used through this chapter.

In order to save time and avoid the repeatability, we will use the project `SelectWizard` we developed in the last chapter. Recall that some command buttons on the different form windows in that project have not been coded, such as `Insert`, `Update`, and `Delete`, and some buttons or exactly the event procedures related to those buttons will be developed and built in this chapter. We only concentrate on the coding for the `Insert` button in this chapter.

Part I: Insert Data with Visual Basic.NET Design Tools and Wizards

In this part, we discuss inserting data into the database using the Visual Studio.NET design tools and wizards. We develop two methods to perform this data inserting: first, we use the TableAdapter DBDirect method, `TableAdapter.Insert()`, to directly insert data into the database. Second, we discuss how to insert data into the database by first adding new records into the DataSet and then updating those new records from the DataSet to the database using the `TableAdapter.Update()` method. Both methods utilize the TableAdapter's direct and indirect methods to complete the data insertion. The database we try to use is Oracle 18c Express Database, `CSE_DEPT`, which is developed in Chapter 2 and located at the folder `Students\Sample Database` at the Wiley ftp site (refer to Figure 1.2 in Chapter 1).

6.1   Insert Data into a Database

Generally, there are many different ways to insert data into any database in Visual Studio.NET. Regularly, three methods are widely utilized:

1) Using the TableAdapter's DBDirect methods, specifically such as the `TableAdapter.Insert()` method.
2) Using the TableAdapter's `Update()` method to insert new records that have already been added into the DataTable in the DataSet.
3) Using the Command object combined with the `ExecuteNonQuery()` method.

When using method 1, one can directly access the database and execute commands such as the `TableAdapter.Insert()` or `TableAdapter.Update()` to manipulate data in the database without requiring DataSet or DataTable objects to reconcile changes in order to send updates to a database. As we mentioned at the beginning of this chapter, inserting data into a table in the DataSet is different with inserting data into a table in the database. If you are using a DataSet to store data in your applications, you need to use the `TableAdapter.Update()` method since the `Update()` method can trigger and send all changes (updates, inserts, and deletes) to the database.

A good choice is to use the `TableAdapter.Insert()` method when your application uses objects to store data (for example, you are using textboxes to store your data), or when you want finer control over creating new records in the database.

In addition to inserting data into the database, method 2 can be used for other data operations such as update and delete data from the database. You can build associated command objects and assign them to the appropriate TableAdapter's properties such as the UpdateCommand and DeleteCommand. The point is that when these properties are executed, the data manipulations only occur to the data table in the DataSet, not in the database. In order to make those data modifications occur in the real database, the TableAdapter's `Update()` method is needed to update those modifications in the database.

Exactly, the terminal execution of inserting, updating, and deleting data of both methods 1 and 2 is performed by method 3. In other words, both methods 1 and 2 need method 3 to complete those data manipulations, which means that both methods need to execute the Command object, more precisely, the `ExecuteNonQuery()` method of the Command object, to finish those data operations again the database.

Because methods 1 and 2 are relatively simple, in this part, we will concentrate on inserting data into the database using the TableAdapter methods. First, we discuss how to insert new records directly into the database using the `TableAdapter.Insert()` method and then we discuss how to insert new records into the DataSet and then into a database using the `TableAdapter.Update()` method. Method 3 will be discussed in Part II since it contains more completed coding process related to the run-time objects.

6.1.1 Insert New Records into a Database Using the TableAdapter.Insert Method

When using this TableAdapter DBDirect method to perform data manipulations to a database, the main query must provide enough information in order for the DBDirect methods to be created correctly. The so-called main query is the default or original query methods such as `Fill()` and `GetData()` when you first time open any TableAdapter by using the TableAdapter Configuration Wizard. The enough information means that the data table must contain completed definitions. For example, if a TableAdapter is configured to query data from a table that does not have a primary key column defined, it does not generate DBDirect methods.

Table 6.1 lists three TableAdapter DBDirect methods.

It can be found from Table 6.1 that the `TableAdapter.Update()` method has two functionalities: first, it directly makes all changes in the database based on the parameters contained in the `Update()` method, and the second job is to update all changes made in the DataSet to the database based on the associated properties of the TableAdapter such as the InsertCommand, UpdateCommand, or DeleteCommand.

In this chapter, we only take care of the inserting data, so only top two methods are discussed in this chapter. The third method will be discussed in Chapter 7.

Table 6.1 TableAdapter DBDirect Methods.

TableAdapter DBDirect Method	Description
TableAdapter.Insert	Adds new records into a database allowing you to pass in individual column values as method parameters.
TableAdapter.Update	Updates existing records in a database. The Update method takes original and new column values as method parameters. The original values are used to locate the original record, and the new values are used to update that record. The TableAdapter.Update method is also used to reconcile changes in a dataset back to the database by taking a DataSet, DataTable, DataRow, or array of DataRows as method parameters.
TableAdapter.Delete	Deletes existing records from the database based on the original column values passed in as method parameters.

6.1.2 Insert New Records into a Database Using the TableAdapter.Update Method

To use this method to insert data into the database, one needs to perform the following two steps:

1) Add new records to the desired DataTable by creating a new DataRow and adding it to the Rows collection.
2) After the new rows are added to the DataTable, call the `TableAdapter.Update()` method. You can control the amount of data to be updated by passing an entire DataSet, a DataTable, an array of DataRows, or a single DataRow.

In order to provide a detailed discussion and explanation how to use these two methods to insert new records into the database, a real example will be very helpful. Let's first create a new Visual Basic.NET project to handle these issues.

6.2 Insert Data into Oracle Database Using a Sample Project InsertWizard

We have provided a very detailed introduction about the design tools and wizards in Visual Studio. NET in Section 5.2 in Chapter 5, such as DataSet, BindingSource, TableAdapter, Data Source window, Data Source Configuration window, and DataSet Designer. We need to use those staff to develop our data-inserting sample project based on the `SelectWizard Project` developed in the last chapter. First let us copy that project and do some modifications on that project to get our new project. The advantage of creating our new project in this way is that you do not need to redo the data source connection and configuration since those jobs have been performed in the last chapter.

6.2.1 Create a New InsertWizard Project

Open the Windows Explorer and create a new folder `Class DB Projects\Chapter 6` and perform the following operational steps to create this new project.

1) Open the Visual Studio.NET 2019 and go to `File|New Project` menu item, select the `Blank Solution,` and click on the `Next` button.
2) Enter `InsertWizard Solution` into the `Project name` box and then select the folder `Class DB Projects\Chapter 6` from the `Location` box and click on the `Create` button.
3) On the opened Studio window, go to the Solution Explorer window and right click on the new created solution and select the `Add|New Project` item from the popup menu to open the `Add a new project` wizard.
4) Select the `Windows Forms App (.NET Framework)` template under the `Recent project templates` and click on the `Next` button.
5) Enter `InsertWizard Project` into the `Project name` box and click on the `Create` button to add this new project into our solution.
6) In the Solution Explorer window, remove the `Form1.vb`, since we do not need it.
7) Now we need to add three Forms, Faculty Form, Course Form, and Student Form, into this new project. In the Solution Explorer window, right click on the new created project `InsertWizard Project` and select `Add|Existing Item` to open the Windows Explorer. Browse to the folder `VB Forms|Window` that is located at the Wiley ftp site under the `Students` folder and select the following items by checking each of them one by one:
   a) Faculty Form.vb[1]
   b) Faculty Form.designer.vb[2]

   c) Faculty Form.resx[3]

   d) Course Form.vb[1]

   e) Course Form.designer.vb[2]

   f) Course Form.resx[3]

   g) Student Form.vb[1]

   h) Student Form.designer.vb[2]

   i) Student Form.resx[3]

8) When add these items, a trick is: first, you have to add only the first item, say, **Faculty Form.vb** (indicated with a superscript 1), then in the Solution Explorer window you must expand, say, **Faculty Form.vb** and click on the **FacultyForm** under that **Faculty Form.vb** folder to select it, then right click on the Project and select the **Add|Existing Item** to add the second (2), and then the third item (3) one by one.

9) Click on the **Add** button to add them into this new project.

Now some error messages may be shown up in the Error List, do not worry and we can fix them. First, we need to configure our database connection to build our DataSet object. Refer to Section 5.2.2.2 in Chapter 5 to complete this database connection and build our DataSet object, **CSE_DEPTDataSet**.

Next we need to rebuild three TableAdapter query functions, **FillByFacultyName()**, **FindFacultyIDByName()**, and **FillByFacultyID()**, to erase the rest errors. Refer to Sections 5.4.7 and 5.4.9.1 in Chapter 5 to complete these query function rebuilding. The reason we need to rebuild these query functions is try to use the select button's event procedure to confirm our data updating and deleting actions later.

Now you may need to open the **Faculty Form.designer.vb** and **Course Form.designer.vb** to replace all **SelectWizard** with **InsertWizard** for all **CSE_DEPTDataSet** definitions. An easy way to do these corrections is just double click the related error message in the Error List to find those locations and make the corresponding replacements.

The final error is about the removing of the default Form, **Form1**, since we want to use our Faculty Form as the default and startup Form in this project. Go to the Solution Explorer window and open the App file **Application.Designer.vb**, which is under the folder **My Project|Application.myapp**. Change the last object for the **Me.MainForm** = line from **Form1** to **FacultyForm**, as shown below.

```
<Global.System.Diagnostics.DebuggerStepThroughAttribute()> _
Protected Overrides Sub OnCreateMainForm()
Me.MainForm = Global.UpdateDeleteWizard_Project.FacultyForm
End Sub
```

You also need to set this **FacultyForm** as the Startup form by going to **Project|Insert-Wizard Project Properties** window and replace the default **Form1** with our **FacultyForm** in the **Startup form** box.

Now you can go to **Build\Rebuild InsertWizard Project** to rebuild this project and then go to **File|Save All** to save these changes for the new project.

6.2.2 Application User Interfaces

As you know from the last chapter, five form windows work as the user interfaces for the **SelectWizard** project: **LogIn, Selection, Faculty, Course,** and **Student.** Of all these five form windows, three of them contain the **Insert** command button and they are:

Faculty, Course, and Student. Therefore, we only need to work on these three forms to perform the data insertion to our database. Now let us concentrate on the Faculty form to perform the data insertion into our **FACULTY** table in our Oracle database.

First let us concentrate on the data validation before the data insertion.

6.2.3 Validate Data Before the Data Insertion

The most popular validation way is to make sure that each data item stored in the related control is not NULL, but it contains a value. In other words, we want to make sure that all pieces of data have valid values, either a real value or a NULL value, before they can be inserted into the database.

In this application, we try to validate each piece of faculty information, which is stored in the associated textbox, to make sure that it is not an empty string. To make this validation simple, we develop a control collection and add all of those textboxes into this collection. In this way, we do not need to check each textbox, instead we can use the For Each . . . Next loop to scan the entire collection to find the empty textbox.

6.2.3.1   Visual Basic Collection and .NET Framework Collection Classes

There are two kinds of collection classes available for the Visual Basic.NET 2019 applications, one is Visual Basic collection class and the other is the .NET Framework collection class. One of the most important differences between them is the index of the starting value. The index of the Visual Basic collection class is 1-based, which means that the index starts from 1. The index value in the .NET Framework collection class is 0-based, which means that the index starts from 0. The namespace for the Visual Basic collection class is **Microsoft.VisualBasic**, and the namespace for the .NET Framework collection class is **System.Collections.Generic**. A generic collection is useful when every item in the collection has the same data type.

To create a Microsoft Visual Basic collection object **newVBCollection**, one can use:

```
Dim newVBCollection As New Microsoft.VisualBasic.Collection() or
Dim newVBCollection As New Collection()
```

The first declaration uses the full name of the collection class, which means that both the class name and the namespace are included. The second declaration uses only the collection class name with the default namespace.

To create a .NET Framework collection object **newNETCollection**, the following declaration can be used:

```
Dim newNETCollection As New System.Collections.Generic.
Dictionary(Of String, String)
```

or

```
Dim newNETCollection As New Dictionary(Of String, String)
```

The first declaration uses the full class name and the second one only uses the class name with the default namespace. Both declarations work well for the Visual Basic.NET applications. The new created .NET Framework collection object contains two arguments, the item key and the item content, and both are in the string format.

Now let us begin to develop the codes for this data validation using this collection component for our application.

6.2.3.2   Validate Data Using the Generic Collection

First, we need to create the generic collection object for our Faculty form. Since this collection will be used by the different procedures in this form, so a form-level or a class-level object should be

Figure 6.1 The form-level collection object.

created. Open the Code Window of the Faculty form and enter the codes that are shown in Figure 6.1 into the form's general declaration section.

The so-called form's general declaration section, which is located just under the class header, is used to create all form-level variables or objects. First, we create a form-level string variable **FacultyName,** and this variable will be used to temporarily store the faculty name entered by the user in the **txtName** textbox, and this faculty name will be used later by the **Select** button event procedure to validate the new inserted faculty data. Second, the generic collection object, **FacultyCollection**, is created with two arguments: item key and the item content. The code in bold, in which the default namespace is utilized, also works fine. Here we comment it out to illustrate that we prefer to use the full class name to create this collection object.

In order to use the collection object to check all textboxes, one needs to add all textboxes into the collection object after the collection object **FacultyCollection** is created by using the **Add()** method. The following two points should be noted:

1) First, we need to emphasize the order to perform this validation check. As the project starts, all textboxes are blank. The user needs to enter all pieces of faculty information into the appropriate textbox. Then the user clicks on the **Insert** button to perform this data insertion. The time to add all textboxes into the collection object should be after the user finished entering all pieces of information into all textboxes, not before. Also each time when you finish data validation by checking all textboxes, all textboxes should be removed from that collection since the collection only allows those textboxes to be added by one time.

2) Another point to be noted is that in order to simplify this data validation, in this application we need all textboxes to be filled with certain information or an NULL needs to be entered if no information will be entered. In other words, we do not allow any textbox to be empty. The data insertion will not be performed until all textboxes are nonempty in this application.

Based on these assumptions, we need to create two user-defined subroutines to perform this adding and removing textboxes from the collection object, respectively.

Open the Faculty Form and then double click on the **Insert** button to open its event procedure. Enter the codes that are shown in Figure 6.2 into this event procedure.

Let us take a closer look at this piece of codes to see how it works.

A) First, we need to create an instance of the **KeyValuePair** structure, and this structure instance contains two arguments, the **Key** and the **Value**, which are related to a collection component. In **B**, it can be found that both a key and the content of the associated textbox are added into the collection **FacultyCollection** when the user-defined subroutine **CreateFacultyCollection()** is called. We need both the key and the value of a textbox to validate the data for each textbox, which is to check whether a textbox is empty, the Value of that textbox is used, and to identify the emptied textbox, the Key of the textbox is used.

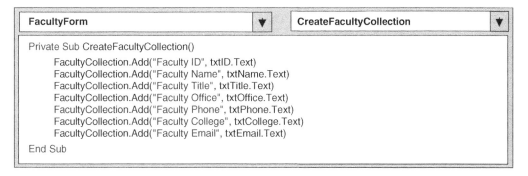

```
btnInsert            ▼      Click                          ▼

     Private Sub btnInsert_Click(sender As Object, e As EventArgs) Handles btnInsert.Click
A         Dim strCheck As KeyValuePair(Of String, String)
B         Call CreateFacultyCollection()
C         For Each strCheck In FacultyCollection
             If strCheck.Value = String.Empty Then
                 MessageBox.Show(strCheck.Key & " is empty, continue?")
                 RemoveFacultyCollection()
                 Exit Sub
             End If
          Next strCheck
     End Sub
```

Figure 6.2   The codes for the Insert button event procedure.

```
FacultyForm              ▼      CreateFacultyCollection             ▼

     Private Sub CreateFacultyCollection()
          FacultyCollection.Add("Faculty ID", txtID.Text)
          FacultyCollection.Add("Faculty Name", txtName.Text)
          FacultyCollection.Add("Faculty Title", txtTitle.Text)
          FacultyCollection.Add("Faculty Office", txtOffice.Text)
          FacultyCollection.Add("Faculty Phone", txtPhone.Text)
          FacultyCollection.Add("Faculty College", txtCollege.Text)
          FacultyCollection.Add("Faculty Email", txtEmail.Text)
     End Sub
```

Figure 6.3   The codes for the subroutine CreateFacultyCollection().

B) Next we need to call the subroutine **CreateFacultyCollection()** to add all textboxes into the collection **FacultyCollection**. Refer to Figure 6.3 for the detailed codes for this subroutine later.

C) A **For Each** loop is utilized to scan all textboxes to check and identify if any textbox is empty from the **FacultyCollection**. If any textbox is empty by checking its Value, that textbox will be identified by its Key and a messagebox is used to ask users to fill some information to it. Then the subroutine **RemoveFacultyCollection()** is called to remove all textboxes that have been added into the collection in the subroutine **CreateFacultyCollection()** since the collection only allows those textboxes to be added by one time. The project will be exited if this situation happened. The detailed codes for the user-defined subroutine **RemoveFacultyCollection()** are shown in Figure 6.4.

Now let us take care of the codes for the subroutine **CreateFacultyCollection()**, which are shown in Figure 6.3.

The codes are very simple and straightforward. Each textbox is added into the collection by using the **Add()** method with two parameters: the first one is the so-called **Key** parameter represented in a string format and the second is the content of each textbox, which is considered as the **Value** parameter. In this way, each textbox can be identified by its **Key**. Of course each textbox can also be identified by the index, but remember that the index starts from 0, not 1, since it is a .NET Framework collection instead of a Visual Basic collection.

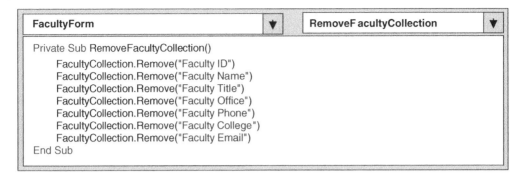

Figure 6.4 The codes for the subroutine RemoveFacultyCollection().

To remove all textboxes from the collection, another user-defined subroutine procedure **RemoveFacultyCollection()** is called. The codes for it are shown in Figure 6.4.

The key parameter of each textbox is used as the identifier for each textbox and the **Remove()** method is called to remove all textboxes from the collection object.

Next we need to handle some initialization coding jobs for the data insertion.

6.2.4 Initialization Coding Process for the Data Insertion

In this section, we need to handle the coding for the following event procedure:

- Coding for a user-defined subroutine procedure **CurrentFaculty()** to get and display all current faculty members in the Faculty Name combo box, **comboName**.
- Coding for the Form_Load event procedure to add two more insertion methods, **TableAdapter. Insert()** and **TableAdapter.Update()**, into the combo box **comboMethod** to display two data insertion methods.

The user-defined subroutine procedure **CurrentFaculty()** needs to retrieve all faculty members from the **FACULTY** table and then display them in the Faculty Name combo box.

Open the Faculty Form code window and type the codes shown in Figure 6.5 into this window to create this subroutine procedure.

The purpose of this procedure is to load all faculty members, exactly all faculty names, from the **FACULTY** table and place them into the **ComboName** combo box, from which each of them can be selected by users later.

Let us have a closer look at this piece of codes to see how it works.

A) First, a DataRow object **row** is declared since we need to use this object to get each related row from the **FACULTY** table.
B) The **Fill()** method is executed to load all faculty records from the **FACULTY** table in our sample database and fill them into the **FACULTY** table in the DataSet. By checking the **Count** property, we can confirm whether this fill is successful or not. It is failed, a 0 is returned and a massage is displayed and the program is exited.
C) Prior to add faculty names into the **ComboName** combo box, it is first cleared.
D) A **For Each** loop is used to retrieve each row record, **faculty_name** that is the second column with an index of 1, from the filled **FACULTY** table, and add it into the **ComboName** combo box.
E) The first faculty name is selected by setting the SelectedIndex value as 0.

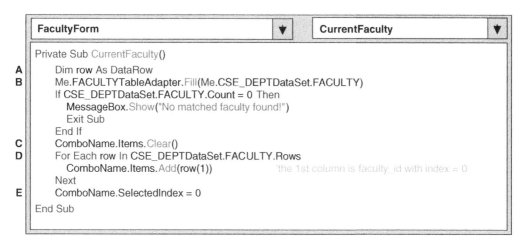

Figure 6.5 The codes for the subroutine procedure CurrentFaculty().

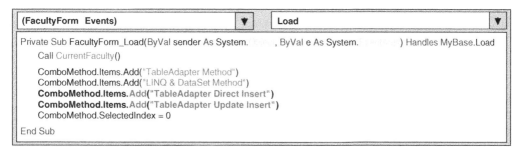

Figure 6.6 The codes for the Form_Load event procedure.

Next let us do our coding for the Form_Load event procedure to add two more insertion methods, **TableAdapter.Insert()** and **TableAdapter.Update()**, into the combo box **comboMethod** to display two data insertion methods. Open the Faculty Form_Load event procedure and add the codes shown in Figure 6.6 into this event procedure.

Now we need to take care of the coding process for the data insertion. Because we are using the design tools to perform this job, so first we need to configure the TableAdapter and build the insert query using the TableAdapter Query Configuration Wizard.

6.2.5 Build the Insert Query

As we mentioned, two methods will be discussed in this part: one is to insert new records using the TableAdapter DBDirect method **TableAdapter.Insert()** to insert data into the database and the other one is to use the **TableAdapter.Update()** method to insert new records into the database. Let us concentrate on the first method.

6.2.5.1 Configure the TableAdapter and Build the Data Inserting Query
In order to use the **TableAdapter.Insert()** DBDirect method to access the database, we need first to configure the TableAdapter and build the Insert query. Perform the following operations to build this data insertion query:

1) Open the Data Source window by going to **View|Other Windows|Data Sources**.
2) Right click on any place inside the Data Sources window and select the **Edit the DataSet with Designer** from the popup menu to open this Designer.

3) Then go to the **FACULTY** table and right click on the bottom item on the **FACULTY** table and select the **Add|Query** item from the popup menu to open the TableAdapter Query Configuration Wizard.
4) Keep the default selection **Use SQL statements** unchanged and click on the **Next** to go to the next wizard.
5) Select and check the **INSERT** item from this wizard since we need to perform inserting new records query, and then click on the **Next** again to continue.
6) Click on the **Query Builder** button since we want to build our insert query. The opened Query Builder wizard is shown in Figure 6.7.
7) The default Insert query statement is matched to our requirement since we want to add a new faculty record that contains all pieces of new information about that inserted faculty, which includes the **faculty_id**, **faculty_name**, **office**, **phone**, **college**, **title**, **email** and **fimage**. Click on the **OK** button to go to the next wizard.
8) Click on the **Next** button to confirm this query and continue to the next step.
9) Modify the query function name from the default one to the **InsertFaculty** and click on the **Next** button to go to the last wizard.
10) Click on the **Finish** button to complete this query building and close the wizard.

Immediately you can find that a new query function has been added into the Faculty TableAdapter as the last item.

Now that we have finished the configuration of the TableAdapter and building of the insert query, it is time for us to develop the codes to run the TableAdapter to complete this data insertion query. We need to develop the codes for the first method – using the TableAdapter DBDirect method, **TableAdapter.Insert()**.

6.2.6   Develop Codes to Insert Data Using the TableAdapter.Insert Method

Open the graphical user interface of the Faculty Form by clicking on the View Designer button from the Solution Explorer window and then double click the **Insert** button to open its Click event procedure. Then add the codes that are shown in Figure 6.8 into this event procedure.

Recall that we have created some codes for this event procedure in Section 6.2.3.2 to perform the data validation, so the old codes are highlighted with the gray color in the background. Let us have a closer look at this piece of codes to see how it works.

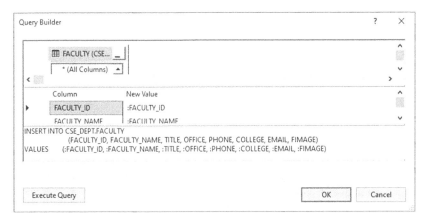

Figure 6.7   The opened Query Builder wizard. *Source:* Microsoft Visual Studio.

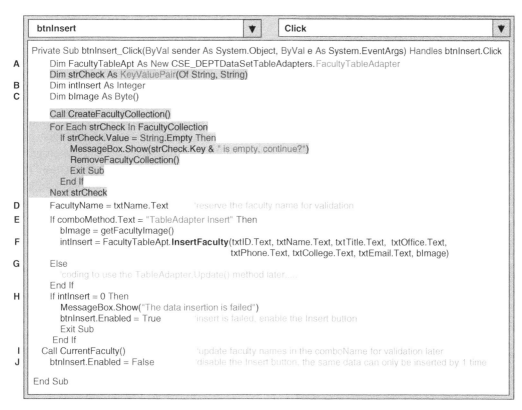

Figure 6.8 The codes for the Insert button event procedure.

A) First, we need to create a TableAdapter object for the FacultyTableAdapter class since we need this object to perform inserting data directly into the database. As we know, all TableAdapters in this application are located at the namespace **CSE_DEPTDataSetTableAdapters**, so this namespace must be prefixed before the desired TableAdapter class.

B) A local integer variable **intInsert** is declared here, and it is used to hold the returned value from execution of the **TableAdapter.Insert()** method. The value of this returned integer, which indicates how many records have been successfully inserted or affected to the database, can be used to determine whether this data insertion is successful or not. A returned value of zero means that no record has been added or affected to the database, in other words, this insertion is failed.

C) Some necessary components used to convert an image object from the memory stream to the binary byte array are declared here, which include a **Byte()** array object **bImage**.

D) The form-level variable **FacultyName** is used to temporarily hold the faculty name entered by the user from the textbox **txtName** since we need this name to validate this record insertion later.

E) If the user selected the **TableAdapter Insert** method to perform this data insertion, first we need to call a user-defined function **getFacultyImage()** to get a desired faculty image to be inserted into the database and convert it to the **Byte()** format. The detailed codes for this function will be discussed later.

F) The query function **InsertFaculty()**, which we built in the last section by using the TableAdapter Query Configuration Wizard, is called to complete this data insertion job. Eight pieces of new information, which is about the new inserted faculty and entered by the user into seven textboxes with a selected faculty image, will be inserted to the Faculty table in the database. A key issue is that the order of these eight pieces of information must be identical with those inputs located in the query `InsertFaculty()` we built in the last section.

G) If the user selected the `TableAdapter.Update()` method to perform this data insertion, the coding for that method will be discussed in the next section.

H) If this data insertion is successful, the returned integer will reflect the number of records that have been inserted into the database correctly. A returned value of zero indicates that this insertion is failed. A message box will be displayed with a warning message and the program will be exited. One point we need to emphasize is that when performing a data insertion, the same data can only be inserted into the database by one time, and the database does not allow multiple insertions of the same data item. To avoid multiple insertions, in this application (generally in most popular applications), we will disable the `Insert` button after one record is inserted successfully (refer to step **J** below). If the insertion is failed, we need to recover or re-enable the `Insert` button to allow users to try another insertion later.

I) As we mentioned before, when we perform the data validation to validate this data insertion, an SELECT statement will be executed to retrieve the new inserted record from the database. The new inserted faculty name should be added into the combo box `comboName` for the validation to be performed later. The user-defined subroutine `CurrentFaculty()` is executed for this purpose.

J) As we mentioned in **H**, the database does not allow the multiple insertions of the same data item into the database. So after the data insertion is successful, we need to disable the `Insert` button to protect it from being clicked again.

From the above explanations, we know that it is a good way to avoid the multiple insertions of the same data item into the database by disabling the `Insert` button after that insertion is successfully completed. A question arises: When and how this button can be enabled again to allow us to insert some other different new records if we want to do that later? The solution to this question is to develop another event procedure to handle this issue.

Try to think about it, the time when we want to insert new different data item into the database, first we must enter each piece of new information into each associated TextBox such as `txtID`, `txtName`, `txtOffice`, `txtPhone`, `txtTitle`, `txtCollege,` and `txtEmail`. In other words, anytime as long as the content of a textbox is changed, which means that a new different record will be inserted, we should enable the `Insert` button at that moment to allow users to perform this new insertion. Visual Basic.NET did provide an event called `TextChanged` and an associated event procedure for the textbox control. So we need to use this event procedure to enable the `Insert` button as long as a `TextChanged` event occurs.

Another question arises: with which textbox's `TextChanged` event occurring, we should trigger the associated event procedure to enable the `Insert` button to allow users to insert a new record? Is any textbox's `TextChanged` event? To answer this question, we need to review the data issue in the database. As you know, in our sampling database CSE_DEPT (exactly in our Faculty data table), it identifies a record based on its primary key. In other words, only those records with different primary keys can be considered as different records. So the solution to our question is: only the content of the TextBox that stores the primary key, in our case it is the `txtID` whose stores the `faculty_id`, is changed, it means that a new record will be inserted, and as this happened, that TextBox's `TextChanged` event procedure should be triggered to enable the `Insert` button.

Most databases, including the Oracle, do not allow multiple data insertions of the same data item into the databases. Each data item or record can only be added or inserted into the database by one time. The popular way to avoid this situation to be happened is to disable the Insert button after one insertion is done.

To open the **TextChanged** event procedure for the textbox **txtID**, open the Designer View of the Faculty form window and then double click on the **Faculty ID** textbox to open its **TextChanged** event procedure. Change the event procedure's name from the **txtID_TextChanged** to **FacultyInfoChanged** and enter the codes shown in Figure 6.9 into this event procedure.

The codes for this event procedure are simple: enable the **Insert** button by setting the **Enabled** property of that button to **True** as the **txtID** TextChanged event occurs.

Now let's take care of the user-defined function **getFacultyImage()**. The detailed codes for this function are shown in Figure 6.10. Let's have a closer look at this piece of codes.

A) Some necessary components used to convert an image object from the memory stream to the binary byte array and select desired faculty image to be inserted into the database are declared here, which include a **MemoryStream()** variable **ms**, an **OpenFileDialog** object **dlg** and a **Byte()** array object **bimage**.

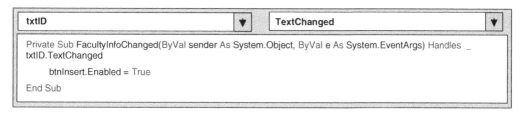

Figure 6.9   The codes for the txtID TextChanged event procedure.

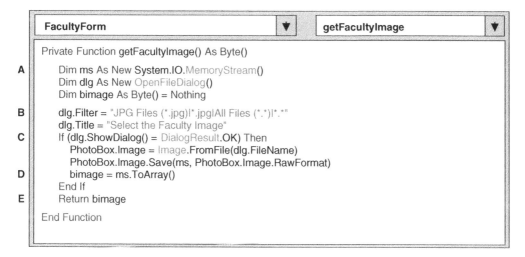

Figure 6.10   Detailed codes for the user-defined function getFcaultyImage().

B) Then we need to select the desired faculty image by using a FileDialog and a selecting criterion with certain image-related extensions as well as a title.

C) If this faculty image selection process is successful, the selected image will be assigned and displayed in the **PhotoBox** with **FromFile(dlg.FileName)** property. Then this image file is converted from the MemoryStream format to the binary **Byte()** array format, or called **RawFormat**.

D) The converted Byte array **ms.ToArray()** is assigned to the **bimage** array.

E) Finally the converted Byte(), **bimage**, is returned to the main event procedure. If this reading and conversion operation is failed, a null byte() or **Nothing**, is returned. Otherwise a successfully converted byte() is returned.

Now we finished the codes for the first data insertion method, let's continue to do our coding process for the second method.

6.2.7   Develop Codes to Insert Data Using the TableAdapter.Update Method

When a data-driven application uses DataSet to store data, as we did for this application by using the **CSE_DEPTDataSet**, one can use the **TableAdapter.Update()** method to insert or add a new record into the database.

To insert a new record into the database using this method, two steps are needed:

1) First adding new records to the desired data table in the DataSet. For example, in this application, the Faculty table in the DataSet **CSE_DEPTDataSet**.

2) Then call the **TableAdapter.Update()** method to update new added records from the data table in the DataSet to the data table in the database. The amount of data to be updated can be controlled by passing the different argument in the **Update()** method, either an entire DataSet, a DataTable, an array of DataRow, or a single DataRow.

Now let's develop our codes based on the above two steps to insert data using this method.

Open the Designer View of the Faculty form window and double click on the **Insert** button to open its event procedure. We have already developed most codes for this procedure in the last section, and now we need to add the codes to perform the second data insertion method. Browse to the **Else** block (step **G** in Figure 6.8), and enter the codes that are shown in Figure 6.11 into this block.

In order to distinguish between the new added codes and the old codes that have been developed before, all old codes are highlighted in the gray background color. Let us take a closer look at this piece of new inserted codes to see how it works.

A) First, we need to declare a new object of the DataRow class, **newFacultyRow**. Each DataRow object can be mapped to a real row in a data table. Since we are using the DataSet to manage all data tables in this project, the DataSet must be prefixed before the DataRow object. Also we need to create a row in the Faculty data table, the FacultyRow is selected as a DataRow class.

B) Next we need to create a new object of the **NewFacultyRow** class.

C) A user-defined function **InsertFacultyRow()** is called to add all pieces of information about the new inserting faculty, which is stored in seven textboxes, into this new created DataRow object. The detailed codes and the function of this user-defined function will be explained later. This function returns a completed DataRow in which all pieces of information about the new record have been added.

D) The completed DataRow is then added into the Faculty table in our DataSet object. One point to be noted is that adding a new record into the data table in the DataSet is nothing to do with adding a new record into the data table in the database. The data tables in the DataSet are only

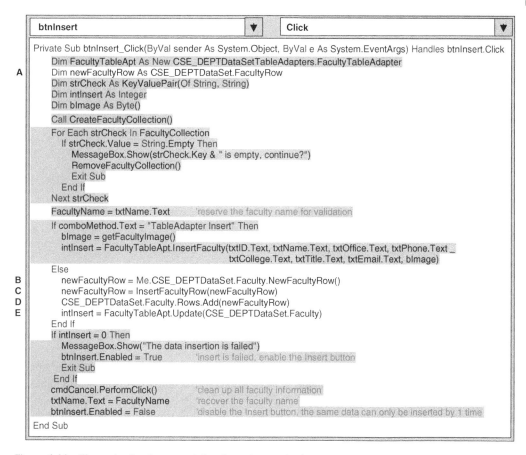

```
btnInsert                          ▼        Click                                    ▼

    Private Sub btnInsert_Click(ByVal sender As System.Object, ByVal e As System.EventArgs) Handles btnInsert.Click
        Dim FacultyTableApt As New CSE_DEPTDataSetTableAdapters.FacultyTableAdapter
A       Dim newFacultyRow As CSE_DEPTDataSet.FacultyRow
        Dim strCheck As KeyValuePair(Of String, String)
        Dim intInsert As Integer
        Dim bImage As Byte()
        Call CreateFacultyCollection()
        For Each strCheck In FacultyCollection
            If strCheck.Value = String.Empty Then
                MessageBox.Show(strCheck.Key & " is empty, continue?")
                RemoveFacultyCollection()
                Exit Sub
            End If
        Next strCheck
        FacultyName = txtName.Text            'reserve the faculty name for validation
        If comboMethod.Text = "TableAdapter Insert" Then
            bImage = getFacultyImage()
            intInsert = FacultyTableApt.InsertFaculty(txtID.Text, txtName.Text, txtOffice.Text, txtPhone.Text _
                                             txtCollege.Text, txtTitle.Text, txtEmail.Text, bImage)
        Else
B           newFacultyRow = Me.CSE_DEPTDataSet.Faculty.NewFacultyRow()
C           newFacultyRow = InsertFacultyRow(newFacultyRow)
D           CSE_DEPTDataSet.Faculty.Rows.Add(newFacultyRow)
E           intInsert = FacultyTableApt.Update(CSE_DEPTDataSet.Faculty)
        End If
        If intInsert = 0 Then
            MessageBox.Show("The data insertion is failed")
            btnInsert.Enabled = True          'insert is failed, enable the Insert button
            Exit Sub
        End If
        cmdCancel.PerformClick()              'clean up all faculty information
        txtName.Text = FacultyName            'recover the faculty name
        btnInsert.Enabled = False             'disable the Insert button, the same data can only be inserted by 1 time
    End Sub
```

Figure 6.11   The codes for the second data insertion method.

mappings of those real data tables in the database. To add this new record into the database, one needs to perform the next step.

E) The TableAdapter's method **Update()** is executed to make this new record be added into the real database. As we mentioned before, you can control the amount of data to be added into the database by passing the different arguments. Here we only want to add one new record into the Faculty table, so a data table is passed as the argument. This **Update()** method supposes to return an integer value to indicate whether this update is successful or not. The value of this returned integer is equal to the number of rows that have been successfully inserted into the database. A returned value of zero means that this updating is failed since no new row has been added into the database.

Now let us develop the codes for the user-defined function **InsertFacultyRow()**. Open the code window and enter the codes that are shown in Figure 6.12 into this function.

Let's have a closer look at this piece of codes to see how this function works.

A) In Visual Basic.NET, unlike C/C++ or Java, the subroutines and functions are different. A procedure that returns data is called a function, but a procedure that does not return any data is called a subroutine. The function **InsertFacultyRow()** needs to return a completed DataRow object, and the returned data type is indicated at the end of the function header after the keyword **As**. The argument is also a DataRow object, but it is a new created blank DataRow object. The data type of the argument is very important. Here we used passing by reference

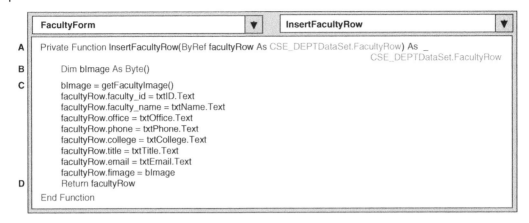

FacultyForm ▼	InsertFacultyRow ▼

```
A   Private Function InsertFacultyRow(ByRef facultyRow As CSE_DEPTDataSet.FacultyRow) As _
                                                        CSE_DEPTDataSet.FacultyRow
B       Dim bImage As Byte()

C       bImage = getFacultyImage()
        facultyRow.faculty_id = txtID.Text
        facultyRow.faculty_name = txtName.Text
        facultyRow.office = txtOffice.Text
        facultyRow.phone = txtPhone.Text
        facultyRow.college = txtCollege.Text
        facultyRow.title = txtTitle.Text
        facultyRow.email = txtEmail.Text
        facultyRow.fimage = bImage
D       Return facultyRow
    End Function
```

Figure 6.12   The codes for the user-defined function InsertFacultyRow().

mode for this argument. The advantage of using this mode is that the passed variable is an address of the DataRow object. Any modification to this object, such as adding new elements to this DataRow, is permanent and the modified object can be completely returned to the calling procedure.

B) In order to convert the selected faculty image from the stream format to Byte() format, a local variable **bImage** is declared first here.

C) Eight pieces of new faculty information stored in the associated textboxes and converted image are added into this new DataRow object, exactly added into a new row of the faculty table in the DataSet.

D) Finally this completed DataRow object is returned to the calling procedure. Another advantage of using this passing by reference mode is that we do not need to create another local variable as the returned variable, instead we can directly use this passed argument as the returned data.

At this point, we have completed the coding process for our data insertion by using two methods.

Now let us test our codes by running our project. You have two ways to test the project. One way is to run the project in a formal way, which means that you run the project starting from the LogIn form, Selection form and then the Faculty form. The second way, which is more flexible, is to directly starting from the Faculty form.

Now you can run the project in either way. We prefer to run it in the first way. Make sure that the Startup form is **LogInForm**, and then click on the Start Debugging button to run the project. Enter the correct username and password to the LogIn form and select the Faculty Information from the Selection form window to open the Faculty form.

Let's test the first method, **TableAdapter.Insert()** by selecting it from the combo box. Enter following seven pieces of new information for this new inserting faculty member into the associated textbox, as shown in Figure 6.13.

Faculty ID:	T56789
Name:	Williams Tom
Title:	Associate Professor
Office:	MTC-222
Phone:	750-330-1660
College:	University of Miami
Email:	wtom@college.edu

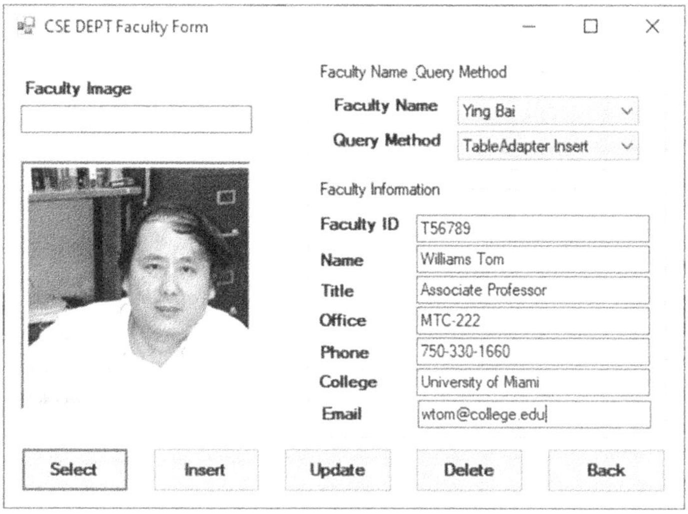

Figure 6.13 The running status of inserting a new faculty. *Source:* Microsoft Visual Studio.

After all pieces of new information have been entered into all associated textboxes, click on the **Insert** button to execute this data insertion using the first method. When the faculty image selection dialog appears, browse to the location where the desired image is located, and open that image in the **PhotoBox**. All available faculty image files are located at the folder **Instructors\ Images\Faculty** on the Wiley ftp site (refer to Figure 1.2 in Chapter 1). You may need to copy those files into a folder in your local drive and use them later. In this project, the image file **Tom.JPG** is located at **C:\Instructors\Images**). If this insertion is successful, no message box will be displayed, and the **Insert** button is disabled to avoid the same data to be added into the database more than one time.

Now let's confirm this data insertion by retrieving this inserted faculty from our database. Go to the **Faculty Name** combo box, and you can see that the new inserted faculty, **Williams Tom**, has been there. Click it and you can find that all eight pieces of information related to this new inserted faculty are displayed in seven textboxes and PhotoBox, as shown in Figure 6.14.

Click on the **Back** button to terminate the project.

You can also try to use the second method, **TableAdapter.Update()**, to insert a new faculty record into our sample database.

A point to be noted is that you had better to removing this new inserted faculty since we need to keep our database neat, and also we may need to perform this insertion in the following projects again. A good way to do this removing is to use the Sever Explorer inside this Visual Basic.NET environment. Click on the database icon to connect to our database **CSE_DEPT**, open the **FACULTY** table by right clicking on it and selecting the **Retrieve Data** item. Then you can edit or delete any row on that table.

Next we want to discuss how to insert a new record using the stored procedure.

6.2.8 Insert Data into the Database Using the Stored Procedures

In this section, we discuss how to insert new records into the database using the stored procedures. To make it simple, we will use the Course Form to discuss how to insert a new course record into the **COURSE** table in the database using a stored procedure.

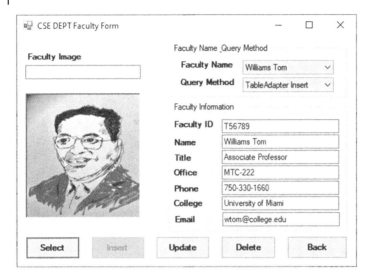

Figure 6.14 The confirmation result of the new inserted faculty member. *Source:* Microsoft Visual Studio.

As we discussed in Section 5.6.7.2 in Chapter 5, building an Oracle stored procedure is different with building a SQL stored procedure. In Oracle, a stored procedure that contains one or more **SELECT** queries and needs to return some data items should be embedded into an Oracle package, but a stored procedure that does not need to return any data item can be considered as a standard stored procedure. If a stored procedure contains some queries that do not need to return any data item, such as **INSERT**, **UPDATE** and **DELETE**, it does not need to be embedded into any package.

Now we need to build our stored procedure named **InsertCourseSP** under the Course table using the Oracle SQL Developer, and then we need to modify the codes for the **Form_Load** event procedure of the Course Form and develop the codes for the Insert button's Click event procedure. The code modifications and code developments include:

1) Add one more item **Stored Procedure Insert** into the combo box **ComboMethod** in the Form_Load event procedure in the Course Form to allow users to select this method to perform the data insertion using this method.
2) Add one **If** block in the **Insert** button Click event procedure to allow users to select the method, **Stored Procedure Insert**, and to call the built stored procedure to perform the data insertion.

Let us first create and build our stored procedure **InsertCourseSP** under the Course table using the Oracle SQL Developer.

6.2.8.1   Build the Stored Procedure InsertCourseSP Using the Oracle SQL Developer

Open the Oracle SQL Developer and connect to our database by entering the system password. Then expand the **Other Users** folder and our sample database folder **CSE_DEPT**. Perform the following operations to create this stored procedure.

1) Right click on the **Procedures** folder and select the **New Procedure** item.
2) On the opened Create Procedure wizard, enter **INSERTCOURSESP** into the **Name:** box as the procedure's name, as shown in Figure 6.15.
3) Click on the green color plus symbol (+) on the upper-right corner to add all seven input parameters one by one with the data type shown in Figure 6.15.
4) Click on the **OK** button to open the procedure code window.

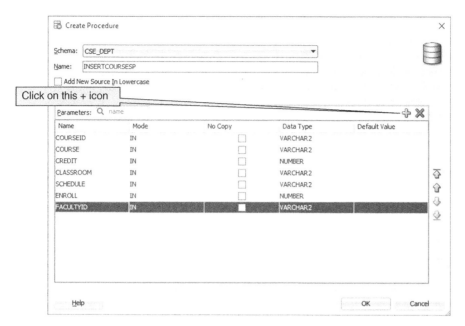

Figure 6.15 The Create Procedure wizard. *Source:* Microsoft Visual Studio.

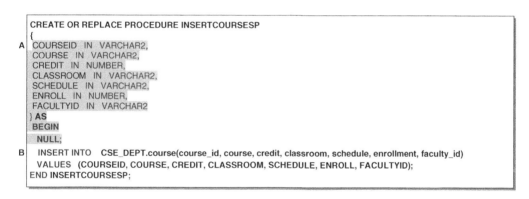

Figure 6.16 The code body for the procedure.

On the opened procedure code window, enter the codes shown in Figure 6.16 into the procedure body section, which is just under the **BEGIN** and **NULL;** command.

A) The top seven items are input parameters we added into this procedure.
B) The **INSERT INTO** query is created by us with seven nominal input data items followed with associated seven input parameters.

Your completed procedure is shown in Figure 6.17.

Now expand the **Compile** icon and click on the **Compile** item to compile our procedure, a **Compiled** statement should be displayed in the Message window if everything is fine. Also you can find our procedure **INSERTCOURSESP** just under the **Procedures** folder in the left pane (Figure 6.17). You may need to refresh that folder by right clicking on the folder and selecting the **Refresh** item on the popup menu if you cannot find our procedure.

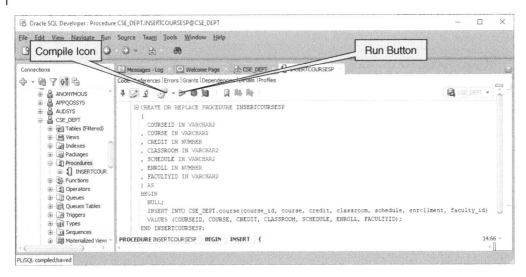

Figure 6.17 The completed procedure INSERTCOURSESP(). *Source:* Oracle Database.

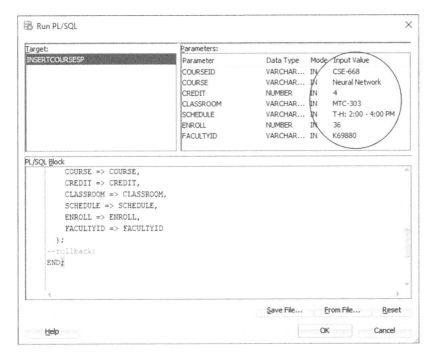

Figure 6.18 The running status of the procedure INSERTCOURSESP(). *Source:* Microsoft Visual Studio.

We can directly test this stored procedure in this Oracle SQL Developer environment to confirm its performance. To do this testing, just click on the green arrow button to run this procedure.

As the **Run PL/SQL** wizard appears, as shown in Figure 6.18, enter the following input parameters as a new course record for the faculty member Jenney King into the **Input Value** column, as shown in Figure 6.18:

Course_ID:	CSE-668
Course:	Neural Network
Credit:	4
Classroom:	MTC-303
Schedule:	T-H: 2:00-4:00 PM
Enroll:	36
Faculty_ID:	K69880

Then click on the **OK** button to run this procedure. You may need to confirm this running process by reentering your system password again. The running steps are displayed in the Running window.

To check this running result, two ways can be used. One way is to try to run this procedure again, but an error would be encountered and an error message is displayed to indicate that no duplicated record can be inserted into the same database.

Another way is to open the **COURSE** table in this Oracle SQL Developer environment to check this insertion. To do this check, expand the **Tables** folder just under our user database **CSE_ DEPT**, right click on our **COURSE** table, and select **Open** item. On the opened **COURSE** table, click on the **Data** tab on the top to open the data view for all courses. Scroll down to the bottom and you will find that our new inserted course, **CSE-668** with all related fields, has been inserted into this table, as shown in Figure 6.19.

6.2.8.2 Modify the Codes to Perform the Data Insertion Using the Stored Procedure

The first modification to the Course Form is to add one more item **Stored Procedure Insert** into the combo box **ComboMethod** in the Form_Load event procedure. Open the Form_Load event procedure in the code window of the Course Form window and add one more line of the code, which is highlighted in bold and shown in Figure 6.20 into this event procedure. The codes we developed before are highlighted in the gray color as the background.

Next let us perform the second code developments, and this development is performed inside the **Insert** button's Click event procedure. Open the **Insert** button's event procedure on the Course Form and enter the codes that are shown in Figure 6.21 into this event procedure.

To make this piece of codes simple, we did not develop any code to do this pre-data inspection. In fact, this checking and validation is necessary in most actual applications. We leave this coding

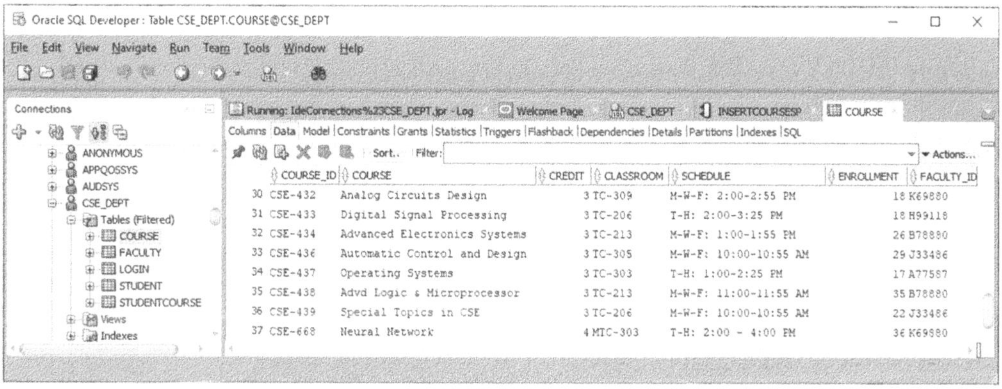

Figure 6.19 The running result of procedure INSERTCOURSESP(). *Source:* Oracle Database.

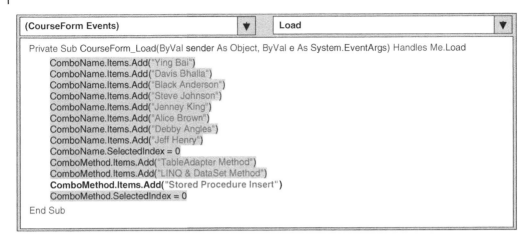

Figure 6.20 The modified codes in the Form_Load() event procedure.

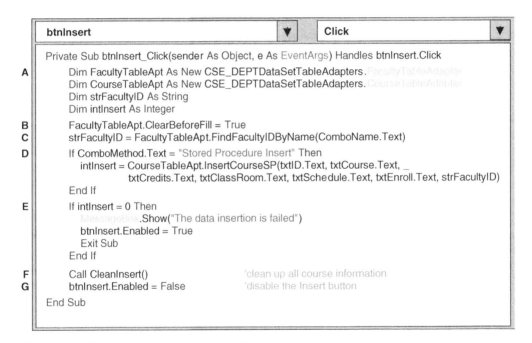

Figure 6.21 The codes in the Insert button's Click event procedure.

process as homework to the readers, and one can refer to Section 6.2.3 to build this data validation function.

Let's have a closer look at this piece of codes to see how it works.

A) Some data action components such as TableAdapters and local variables used for this procedure are declared and created first. The string variable **strFacultyID** is used to store the queried **FACULTY_ID** from the execution of the first query, and the integer variable **intInsert** is used to hold and check the running result of the data insertion operation.

B) Since no **FACULTY_NAME** column is available in the Course table and the only available column in that table is the **FACULTY_ID**. Therefore two queries are needed for inserting a new course record into the Course table; (i) query to the Faculty table to get the matched **FACULTY_ID** based on the faculty name selected by the user and (ii) query to the Course table to insert a new course based on the **FACULTY_ID** obtained from the first query. Prior to performing the first query, the Faculty TableAdapter is cleaned up first.

C) The first query is executed by calling the query function **FindFacultyIDByName()** we built in Section 5.4.9.1 in Chapter 5 to get the matched **FACULTY_ID** based on the faculty name selected by the user from the **ComboName** box.

D) If the user selected the **Stored Procedure Insert** method to perform this course data insertion, the stored procedure **InsertCourseSP()** we built in the last section is called to perform this new course record insertion operation. One point to be noted is that the order of the inserting columns in this calling stored procedure must be identical with that order in the stored procedure we built in the last section. Otherwise you may encounter a mismatching error during the project runs.

E) By checking the returned value that stored in the local integer variable **intInsert**, we can determine whether this data insertion is successful or not. If this stored procedure returns a zero, which means that no any record has been inserted into the Course table, a warning message is displayed to indicate this situation and the project is exited.

F) Otherwise the data insertion is successful. A user-defined subroutine procedure **CleanInsert()** is executed to clean up all six pieces of new course information from six textboxes in this Course Form window.

G) To avoid multiple insertions for the same record, the **Insert** button is disabled after this successful data insertion.

The detailed codes for the user-defined subroutine procedure **CleanInsert()** is shown in Figure 6.22. The codes are used to clean up all six textboxes in the Course Form window.

Finally let us build our stored procedure query function via the TableAdapter Query Configuration Wizard. This query function provides an interface between our Visual Basic.NET project and Oracle stored procedure to enable a TableAdapter to access the Stored Procedure we built in the Oracle SQL Developer to perform this data inserting function. Perform the following steps to build this interface query function:

1) Open the TableAdapter Query Configuration Wizard by right clicking on the Data Source window and select **Edit DataSet with Designer** item from the popup menu.

2) Then right click on the bottom line under the **COURSE** table and select the **Add Query** item.

3) On the opened Configuration Wizard, check the **Use existing stored procedure** radio button and click on the **Next** button to go to the next wizard.

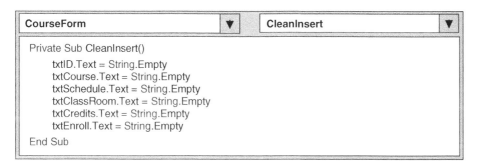

Figure 6.22   The codes for the subroutine CleanInsert().

4) Click on the drop down arrow on the `Select the stored procedure to call` box and select our built procedure `CSE_DEPT.INSERTCOURSESP` from the list to open its `Value Setup` wizard. Since we do not want to test this procedure again, thus click on the `Cancel` button to skip this step. Click on the `Next` button to continue.

5) On the next wizard, select the `No value` radio button since this insert procedure will not return any value when it is executed and click on the `Next` button again.

6) Click on the `Next` button for the next wizard since we want to keep the name for this procedure. In the final wizard, click on the `OK` button to ignore the warning message.

From the codes shown in Figure 6.21, it can be found that there is no difference between calling a query function and calling a stored procedure to perform this data insertion. Yes, that is true for this data action since a stored procedure is exactly a function or a collection of functions to perform some special functions or functionalities. One point we need to note is that by using the TableAdapter Query Configuration Wizard, we cannot create a stored procedure that can perform multiple data actions to the multiple different data tables since each TableAdapter can only access the associated data table. However, by using the run-time object method to insert data into the database, which we will discuss it in Part II, one stored procedure can access multiple different data tables and fulfill multiple different data manipulation operations.

At this point, we have finished developing our sample project to insert data into the Oracle Server database. Now we can run our project to test inserting new course record using the stored procedure method.

However, before you can do this running and testing, make sure that the Course Form should be a Startup Form as the project runs. To make this happen, perform the following operations:

- Go to `Project|InsertWizard Project Properties` menu item to open the Project Properties wizard.
- Locate the `Startup form` box, click on the drop down arrow from that box, and select the Course Form as the first Form as the project runs.

Now click on the `Start` button to run the project. On the opened Course Form window, select the faculty member `Jenney King` from the Faculty Name combo box, and select the `Stored Procedure Insert` method from the Query Method combo box. Then enter the following six pieces of new course information into the associated textbox:

Course ID:	`CSC-538`
Course:	`Special Topics in CS`
Schedule:	`M-W-F: 1:00 – 1:55 PM`
Classroom:	`TC-309`
Credits:	`3`
Enrollment:	`25`

Click on the `Insert` button to try to insert this new course into the **COURSE** table in our sample database. Immediately you can find that all six textboxes are cleaned up after this data insertion and the `Insert` button is disabled.

To confirm and validate this data insertion, just keep the selected faculty member `Jenney King` unchanged in the Faculty Name combo box, and click on the `Select` button to try to retrieve all courses taught by this faculty. You can find that the new inserted course `CSC-538` has been added into the CourseList box. To get the details of that course, just click on that **COURSE_ID** (`CSC-538`) from the CourseList box, and you can find the detailed information for that course is displayed in six textboxes, as shown in Figure 6.23.

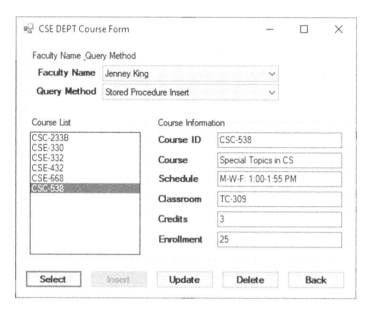

Figure 6.23 The running result of calling the stored procedure. *Source:* Microsoft Visual Studio.

Click on the **Back** button to terminate our project.

A completed project **InsertWizard Project** can be found from a folder **InsertWizard Solution** folder at **Class DB Projects\Chapter 6** that is located at the Wiley ftp site under the **Students** folder (refer to Figure 1.2 in Chapter 1).

Next we will discuss how to insert data into the Oracle Server database using the runtime object method.

Part II: Data Insertion with Runtime Objects

Inserting data into the database using the run-time objects method is a flexible and professional way to perform the data insertion job in Visual Basic.NET environment. Compared with the method we discussed in Part I, in which Visual Studio.NET design tools and wizards are utilized to insert data into the database, the run-time objects method provides more sophisticated techniques to do this job efficiently and conveniently even a more complicated coding job is performed.

Relatively speaking, the methods we discussed in the first part are easy to learn and coding, but some limitations are existed for those methods. First, each TableAdapter can only access the associated data table to perform data actions such as Inserting Data to that table only. Second, each query function built by using the TableAdapter Query Configuration Wizard can only perform a single query such as Data Insertion. Third, after the query function is built, no modifications can be made to that function dynamically, which means that the only times when you can modify that query function either before the project runs or after the project stops. In other words, you cannot modify that query function during the period when project is running.

To overcome those shortcomings, we will discuss how to insert data using the run-time object method in this part. Three sections are covered in this part: inserting data using the general runtime object method is discussed first. Inserting data into the database using the LINQ to DataSet query is introduced in the second section. Inserting data using the stored procedures is presented in the third section.

Generally, you need to use the TableAdapter to perform data actions against the database if you developed your applications using the Visual Studio.NET design tools and wizards in the design time. However, you should use the DataAdapter to make those data manipulations if you developed your projects using the run-time objects method.

6.3   The General Run-Time Objects Method

We have provided a very detailed introduction and discussion about the run time objects method in Section 5.5 in Chapter 5. Refer to that section to get more detailed information about this method. For your convenience, we highlight some important points and general methodology of this method as well as some keynotes in using this method to perform the data actions against the databases.

As you know, ADO.NET provides different classes to help users to develop professional data-driven applications by using the different methods to perform specific data actions such as inserting data, updating data, and deleting data. For the data insertion, two popular methods are widely applied:

1) Add new records into the desired data table in the DataSet and then call the **DataAdapter. Update**() method to update the new added records from the table in the DataSet to the table in the database.
2) Build the insert command using the Command object and then call the command's method **ExecuteNonQuery**() to insert new records into the database. Or you can assign the built command object to the **InsertCommand** property of the DataAdapter and call the **ExecuteNonQuery**() method from the **InsertCommand** property.

The first method is to use the so-called DataSet-DataAdapter method to build a data-driven application. DataSet and DataTable classes can have different roles when they are implemented in a real application. Multiple DataTables can be embedded into a DataSet, and each table can be filled, inserted, updated, and deleted by using the different properties of a DataAdapter, such as SelectCommand, InsertCommand, UpdateCommand, or DeleteCommand, when the DataAdapter's **Update**() method is executed. The DataAdapter will perform the associated operations based on the modifications you made for each table in the DataSet. For example, if you add new rows into a table in the DataSet, then you call this DataAdapter's **Update**() method. This method will perform an **InsertCommand** process based on your modifications. The DeleteCommand will be executed if you delete rows from the table in the DataSet and call this **Update**() method. This method is relative simple since you do not need to call some specific methods such as the **ExecuteNonQuery**() to complete these data queries. But this simplicity brings some limitations for your applications. For instance, you cannot access different data tables individually to perform multiple specific data operations. This method is very similar to the second method we discussed in Part I, so we will not continue to provide any discussion for this method in this part.

The second method is to allow you to use each object individually, which means that you do not have to use the DataAdapter to access the Command object, or use the DataTable with DataSet together. This provides more flexibility. In this method, no DataAdapter or DataSet is needed, and you only need to create a new Command object with a new Connection object, and then build a query statement and attach some useful parameter into that query for the new created Command object. You can insert data into any data table by calling the **ExecuteNonQuery**() method that belongs to the Command class. We will concentrate on this method in this part.

In this section, we provide a sample project named `OracleInsertRTObject` to illustrate how to insert new records into an Oracle database using the run-time object method.

Now let us first develop a sample project `OracleInsertRTObject` to insert data into the Oracle database using the run-time object method. Recall in Sections 5.6.5~5.6.7 in Chapter 5, we discussed how to select data for the Faculty, Course, and Student Form windows using the run-time object method. For the Faculty Form, a regular run time selecting query is performed, and for the Course Form, a run-time joined-table selecting query is developed. For the Student table, the stored procedures are used to perform the run-time data query.

We will concentrate on inserting data to the Faculty table from the Faculty Form window using the run-time object method in this part.

In order to avoid the duplication on the coding process, we will modify an existing project named `OracleSelectRTObject` we developed in Chapter 5 to create our new project `OracleInsertRTObject` used in this section.

6.4   Insert Data into the Oracle Database Using the Run-Time Object Method

Open the Windows Explorer and create a new folder `Class DB Projects\Chapter 6` if you have not, and then browse to the folder `Class DB Projects\Chapter 5` located at the Wiley ftp site under the Students folder (refer to Figure 1.2 in Chapter 1). Copy the project `OracleSelectRTObject Solution` and paste it to the new folder created above. Change the names of the Solution and Project to `OracleInsertRTObject`, change the name of the project `OracleSelectRTObject.vbproj` to `OracleInsertRTObject.vbproj`. Also change the name `OracleSelectRTObject.vbproj.user` to `OracleInsertRTObject.vbproj.user`. Then double click on the `OracleInsertRTObject.vbproj` to open this project. On the opened project, perform the following modifications to get our desired project:

- Go to `Project|OracleInsertRTObject Properties` menu item to open the project's property window. Change the **Assembly name** and the **Root namespace** from `OracleSelectRTObject Project` to `OracleInsertRTObject Project`, respectively.
- Click on the **Assembly Information** button to open the Assembly Information wizard. Change the **Title** and the **Product** to `OracleInsertRTObject Project`. Click on the **OK** button to close this wizard.

Go to the `File|Save All` and `Build|Rebuild OracleInsertRTObject Project` to save those modifications and rebuild the project. Now we are ready to develop our graphic user interfaces based on our new project `OracleInsertRTObject Project`.

6.4.1   Insert Data into the Faculty Table for the Oracle Database

Let's first discuss inserting data into the Faculty table in the Oracle database. To insert data into the Faculty data table, we can use the Faculty Form window we built in the last section.

The codes for this data insertion are divided into three steps; the data validation before the data insertion, data insertion using the run-time object method, and the data validation after the data insertion. The purpose of the first step is to confirm that all inserted data that stored in each associated textbox should be complete and valid. In other words, all textboxes should be nonempty. The third step is used to confirm that the data insertion is successful or in other words, the new inserted record should be in the desired table in the database, and it can be read back and displayed in the Faculty Form window. Let us begin with the coding process for the first step now.

6.4.1.1 Validate Data Before the Data Insertion

This data validation can be performed by calling one user-defined subroutine and one user-defined function. The subroutine is named **InitFacultyInfo()**, and it is used to setup a mapping relationship between each item in the string array **FacultyTextBox()** and each textbox. The user-defined function is named **CheckFacultyInfo()**, and it is used to scan and check all textboxes to make sure that no one of them is empty.

Open the code window of the Faculty Form window, and enter the codes shown in Figure 6.24 into this window to create a user-defined subroutine **InitFacultyInfo()**.

The **FacultyTextBox()** is a zero-based string array and it starts its index from 0. All seven textboxes related to faculty information are assigned to this array. In this way, it is easier for us to scan and check each of textbox to make sure that no one of them is empty.

In a similar way, enter the codes shown in Figure 6.25 into this code window to create a user-defined function **CheckFacultyInfo()**. The operational procedure is:

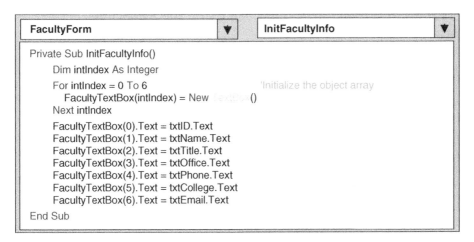

```
FacultyForm   ▼      InitFacultyInfo   ▼

Private Sub InitFacultyInfo()
    Dim intIndex As Integer
    For intIndex = 0 To 6                    'Initialize the object array
        FacultyTextBox(intIndex) = New TextBox()
    Next intIndex
    FacultyTextBox(0).Text = txtID.Text
    FacultyTextBox(1).Text = txtName.Text
    FacultyTextBox(2).Text = txtTitle.Text
    FacultyTextBox(3).Text = txtOffice.Text
    FacultyTextBox(4).Text = txtPhone.Text
    FacultyTextBox(5).Text = txtCollege.Text
    FacultyTextBox(6).Text = txtEmail.Text
End Sub
```

Figure 6.24 The codes for the user-defined subroutine InitFacultyInfo().

```
FacultyForm   ▼      CheckFacultyInfo   ▼

     Private Function CheckFacultyInfo() As Integer
         Dim pos As Integer
A        For pos = 0 To 6
             If FacultyTextBox(pos).Text = String.Empty Then
                 MessageBox.Show("Fill all Faculty Information box, enter a NULL for blank column")
                 Return 1
                 Exit Function
             End If
         Next
B        If txtImage.Text = "" Then
             MessageBox.Show("If no faculty image selected later, a default image will be used")
         End If
         Return 0
     End Function
```

Figure 6.25 The codes for the function CheckFacultyInfo().

A) A **For** loop is used to scan each textbox in the **FacultyTextBox()** string array to check whether any of them is empty. A message will be displayed if this situation happened and the function is existed to allow user to fill up all textboxes.

B) This step is a pre-check operation to make sure that a valid faculty image, either a default or a desired one, will be inserted into the database. If users do not select any faculty image in the following steps, a default faculty photo will be used, and we need to display a message to indicate this situation. The function returns a zero to indicate that this validation is successful. Otherwise a nonzero (1) will be returned to indicate that this validation is failed.

Now let us develop the code for the **Insert** button's Click event procedure to call the subroutine and the function we built above to perform the data validation before the data insertion. Open the **Insert** button's Click event procedure and enter the codes that are shown in Figure 6.26 into this event procedure.

The function of this piece of codes is straightforward and easy to be understood. First the user-defined subroutine **InitFacultyInfo()** is called to set up the mapping relationship between each item in the string array **FacultyTextBox()** and each textbox. Then the user-defined function **CheckFacultyInfo()** is executed to check and make sure that no one textbox is empty. If any of textboxes is empty, the function returns a nonero value and the procedure is exited to allow users to re-enter information to the associated textboxes until all of them are filled with the desired information.

At this point, we completed the coding process for the data validation before the data insertion. Before we can do our coding process for the data insertion, we need first to modify some codes in the Form_Load event procedure to make this data validation more professional.

6.4.1.2 Modify Codes in the Form_Load Event Procedure

In the previous procedure, all faculty members are added into the Faculty Name combo box, **ComboName**, with the predefined faculty members. This makes sense since we only need to query some faculty members without any changing to the **FACULTY** table in our sample database. However, if that table were changed by inserting, updating, or deleting actions, that table would be modified. Thus, we need to build a method to get all current faculty members in real time to reflect any changes made to the table.

A new user-defined subroutine, **CurrentFaculty()**, is built with the codes shown in Figure 6.27. Let us have a closer look at this piece of codes to see how it works.

A) The accessing mode of this subroutine is **Public**, it means that it can be used by any other Forms in this project. The argument is a **ComboBox** object. Two data components, Oracle Data Reader **oraReader** and Oracle Command **oraCommand**, are generated since we need to use them to perform faculty name query actions.

```
btnInsert                              ▼    Click                          ▼

    Private Sub btnInsert_Click(sender As Object,  e As EventArgs) Handles btnInsert.Click
        Dim pos As Integer
         InitFacultyInfo()
         pos = CheckFacultyInfo()
         If pos <> 0 Then
            Exit Sub
         End If
```

Figure 6.26 The first piece of codes for the Insert button's Click event procedure.

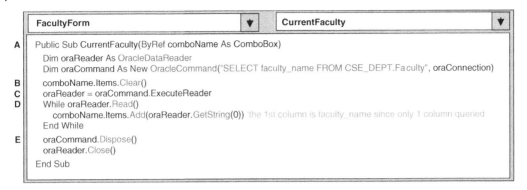

Figure 6.27 The codes for the new subroutine CurrentFaculty().

B) The **Faculty Name** combo box, **comboName**, is first cleared to make it ready to be filled with all faculty names queried from the **FACULTY** table later.

C) The **ExecuteReader()** method is executed to read and query the **FACULTY** table to get all faculty names and assign them to the Oracle Data Reader, **oraReader**.

D) A **While** loop is executed to pick up each faculty name and add it into the Faculty Name combo box, **comboName**, one by one. The condition for this loop is the **read()** method, which returns a Boolean value to indicate whether a valid faculty name is returned (True) or no faculty name is available (False). The **GetString(0)** method returns the first column from the reading results. The index 0 indicates the first column since we only queried one column, so it makes sense.

E) A cleaning job is performed to clean both used components.

Use this **CurrentFaculty()** subroutine to replace eight coding lines originally in this Form_Load event procedure to dynamically add current faculty names into the Faculty Name combo box, **ComboName**, as shown in Figure 6.28 (**A**).

Now we can continue to perform our coding jobs for the data insertion actions.

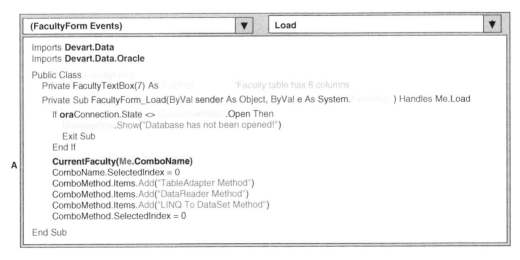

Figure 6.28 The modified codes for the Form_Load() event procedure.

6.4.1.3   Insert Data into the Faculty Table

The main coding job is performed inside the **Insert** button's Click event procedure. We have already developed some codes at the beginning of this procedure in the last section. Now let us continue to complete this coding process.

Open the **Insert** button Click event procedure and enter the codes that are shown in Figure 6.29 into this event procedure. The codes we developed before for this event procedure are highlighted with the gray color.

A) The **INSERT** statement is declared first and it contains eight parameters followed by the command **VALUES**. Each input parameter is prefixed by **:** symbol since this is the requirement for the Oracle database.

B) The data components used to perform the data insertion are declared here, which include the **OracleDataAdapter** and **OracleCommand**. One local integer variable, **intInsert**, is also declared at this part. The variable **intInsert** is used to hold the returned value of executing the **ExecuteNonQuery()** method of the Command class.

C) The Command instance is initialized with the Connection, CommandType and CommandText properties of the Command class.

D) Another user-defined subroutine **InsertParameters()** is called to fill parameters to the **Parameters** collection of the Command instance. Figure 6.30 shows the detailed codes for this subroutine later. Another way to execute this insert action, whose codes have been indicated as comments, is to call the FacultyDataAdapter with its property named **InsertCommand** and a related or an attached method ExecuteNonQuery().

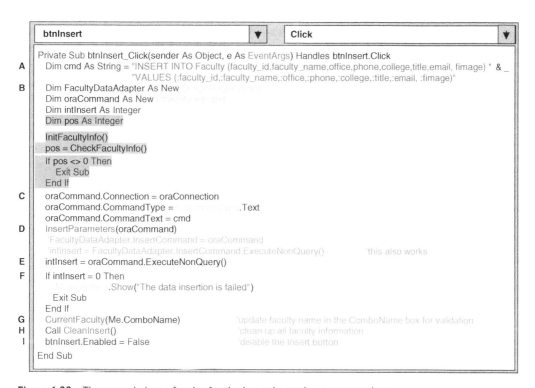

```
btnInsert                    ▼      Click                           ▼

      Private Sub btnInsert_Click(sender As Object, e As EventArgs) Handles btnInsert.Click
A        Dim cmd As String = "INSERT INTO Faculty (faculty_id,faculty_name,office,phone,college,title,email, fimage) " & _
                              "VALUES (:faculty_id,:faculty_name,:office,:phone,:college,:title,:email, :fimage)"
B        Dim FacultyDataAdapter As New
         Dim oraCommand As New
         Dim intInsert As Integer
         Dim pos As Integer

         InitFacultyInfo()
         pos = CheckFacultyInfo()
         If pos <> 0 Then
             Exit Sub
         End If
C        oraCommand.Connection = oraConnection
         oraCommand.CommandType =              .Text
         oraCommand.CommandText = cmd
D        InsertParameters(oraCommand)
          'FacultyDataAdapter.InsertCommand = oraCommand
          'intInsert = FacultyDataAdapter.InsertCommand.ExecuteNonQuery()          'this also works
E        intInsert = oraCommand.ExecuteNonQuery()
F        If intInsert = 0 Then
                          .Show("The data insertion is failed")
             Exit Sub
         End If
G        CurrentFaculty(Me.ComboName)                 'update faculty name in the ComboName box for validation
H        Call CleanInsert()                           'clean up all faculty information
I        btnInsert.Enabled = False                    'disable the Insert button
      End Sub
```

Figure 6.29 The second piece of codes for the Insert button's event procedure.

E) The **ExecuteNonQuery()** method returns an integer as the feedback to indicate whether this insertion is successful or not. The value of this returned integer equals to the number of new inserted records into the Faculty data table.

F) A zero means that no any new record has been inserted into the Faculty table and this insertion is failed. A warning message would be displayed and the procedure is exited if this situation happened.

G) The new inserted faculty name is added into the **Faculty Name** combo box by executing the **CurrentFaculty()** procedure for the validation purpose.

H) A cleaning job is performed to clean up the contents of all textboxes that contain the new-inserted faculty information, except the **Faculty ID**.

I) The **Insert** button is then disabled after this data insertion to avoid the multiple insertions of the same data. This button will be enabled again when the content of the Faculty ID textbox is changed, which means that a new different record is ready to be inserted into the Faculty table.

The detailed codes for the user-defined subroutine **InsertParameters()** are shown in Figure 6.30.

This piece of codes is easy, each piece of faculty-related information stored on the associated textbox is assigned to each matched parameter by using the **Add()** method. A user-defined function, **getFacultyImage()**, is called to get either a selected or a default faculty image. A local **Byte()** variable **bImage** is declared first to hold the selected faculty image.

One point to be noted is that the **:** symbol must be prefixed before each parameter since this is the requirement of the Oracle database operations. Another point to be noted is the type used for images in the Oracle database. Instead of using a Binary type for an image in the SQL Server database, a Blob (Binary Large Object) is used as the type for an image in the Oracle database.

The codes for the user-defined subroutine **CleanInsert()** are shown in Figure 6.31. The function of this piece of codes is simple, just clean up the contents of all textboxes that stored six pieces of new inserted faculty information, except the textbox FacultyID. The faculty PictureBox, **PhotoBox**, is also cleaned up by assigning **Nothing** to the **Image** property.

Another coding job is for the Faculty ID textbox, exactly for the **TextChanged** event procedure of the Faculty ID textbox. As we mentioned, in order to avoid multiple insertions of the same data, the **Insert** button should be disabled after one data is inserted into the database. This **Insert** button will be enabled again when the content of the Faculty ID textbox is changed, which means

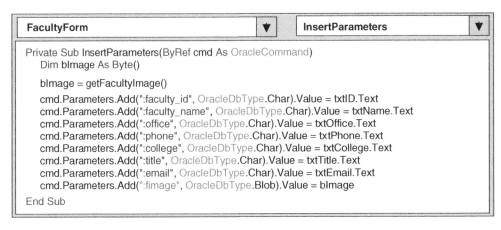

```
FacultyForm                           ▼    InsertParameters                    ▼

Private Sub InsertParameters(ByRef cmd As OracleCommand)
    Dim bImage As Byte()

    bImage = getFacultyImage()
    cmd.Parameters.Add(":faculty_id", OracleDbType.Char).Value = txtID.Text
    cmd.Parameters.Add(":faculty_name", OracleDbType.Char).Value = txtName.Text
    cmd.Parameters.Add(":office", OracleDbType.Char).Value = txtOffice.Text
    cmd.Parameters.Add(":phone", OracleDbType.Char).Value = txtPhone.Text
    cmd.Parameters.Add(":college", OracleDbType.Char).Value = txtCollege.Text
    cmd.Parameters.Add(":title", OracleDbType.Char).Value = txtTitle.Text
    cmd.Parameters.Add(":email", OracleDbType.Char).Value = txtEmail.Text
    cmd.Parameters.Add(":fimage", OracleDbType.Blob).Value = bImage
End Sub
```

Figure 6.30 The codes for the user-defined subroutine InsertParameters().

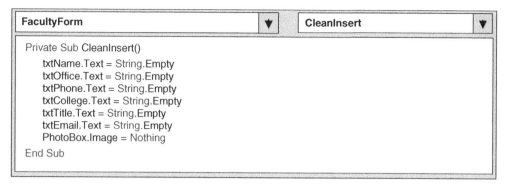

Figure 6.31 The codes for the user-defined subroutine CleanInsert().

that a different new record is ready to be inserted into the database. The codes for that event procedure are simple. Just open the Faculty ID textbox's **TextChanged** event procedure and enter one coding line: **btnInsert.Enabled = True** into that event procedure.

The codes for the user-defined function **getFacultyImage()** are basically similar to those codes for the same function we built in Figure 6.10 in Section 6.2.6. The only difference is that an **Else** clause is added with three-line codes to enable users to click the **Cancel** button for the **FileDialog** to not select any image for that insertion. In that case, a default faculty image, **Default.jpg** located at the folder **C:\Images**, will be used (Figure 6.32).

At this point, we have finished all coding development for this data insertion action for the Faculty Form window. Before we can run the project to test the function of this data insertion, we need to develop the codes to perform a post-validation for this data insertion.

6.4.1.4 Validate Data After the Data Insertion
To validate the new inserted faculty record, the same Faculty Form window can be used and the function of this validation is to read back the inserted data from the database and display them on the Faculty Form to confirm that the data insertion is successful. In fact, we can use the codes we

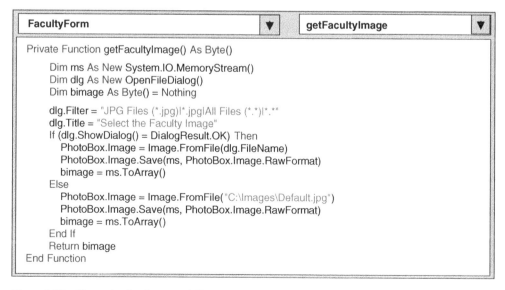

Figure 6.32 The codes for the user-defined function getFacultyImage().

developed for the `Select` button's Click event procedure in Chapter 5 to perform this data query and confirmation.

Now we have finished all coding process for data insertion and the pre-data validation as well as the post-data insertion. Let's run the project to test the functionalities of the codes we developed above. Since we want to add a default faculty photo for this data insertion, so make sure that your default faculty photo file has been already saved into the desired location. For this test, we want to display a default faculty photo `Default.jpg` and we have stored this image file in our default folder, which is `C:\Images`. You need to do the same setups if you want to run this project to test this insertion.

Now starts the project. After the project begins to run, enter the suitable username and password such as `jhenry` and `test` to the LogIn Form, and then select the `Faculty Information` item from the Selection Form to open the Faculty Form window. Then enter the following data into this form as a new faculty record:

- `M99875`   Faculty ID textbox
- `Mhamed Jones`   Faculty Name textbox
- `Professor`   Title textbox
- `MTC-225`   Office textbox
- `750-330-5587`   Phone textbox
- `University of Chicago`   College textbox
- `mjones@college.edu`   Email textbox

Then click on the `Insert` button to open the FileDialog to select default faculty image. Click on the `OK` button for the popup MessageBox. Click on the `Cancel` button on the opened FileDialog to select our default faculty image `Default.jpg`. All textboxes, except the Faculty ID, are immediately cleaned up and the `Insert` button is disabled after this data insertion operation.

To check and validate this faculty record insertion, click on the drop-down arrow of the Faculty Name combobox and you can find that the new inserted faculty name `Mhamed Jones` has been in there. Click that name to select it and then click on the `Select` button to try to read back that new inserted record from the database and display it in this Faculty Form window. All pieces of information about that new inserted faculty record, including the default faculty image, are displayed in the associated textboxes and PhotoBox, as shown in Figure 6.33. Our data insertion is successful.

One potential bug existed in this data validation is that each time when you enter a new piece of faculty information into the database; the faculty name must not be identical. Some readers may argue for this: the different faculty member is identified by the faculty ID, not by name, and the faculty ID is the primary key in the Faculty table. Yes, that is true. But the issue is that in this application, we use the faculty name, not faculty ID, as the criterion to perform this `SELECT` query. This means that the query criterion is based on the faculty name, not faculty ID.

Click on the `Back` and then `Exit` buttons to terminate our project.

Another way to confirm this faculty record insertion is to open our sample database using the Server Explorer. To do that, go to `View` menu and click on the `Server Explorer` item to open this window. Click on our sample database to connect it and expand the `Tables` folder. Right click on `FACULTY` table and select `Retrieve Data` item to open this table. You can find that the new inserted faculty member `Mhamed Jones` has been inserted into this table, as shown in Figure 6.34.

Figure 6.33 The new inserted faculty record in the Faculty Form window. *Source:* Microsoft Visual Studio.

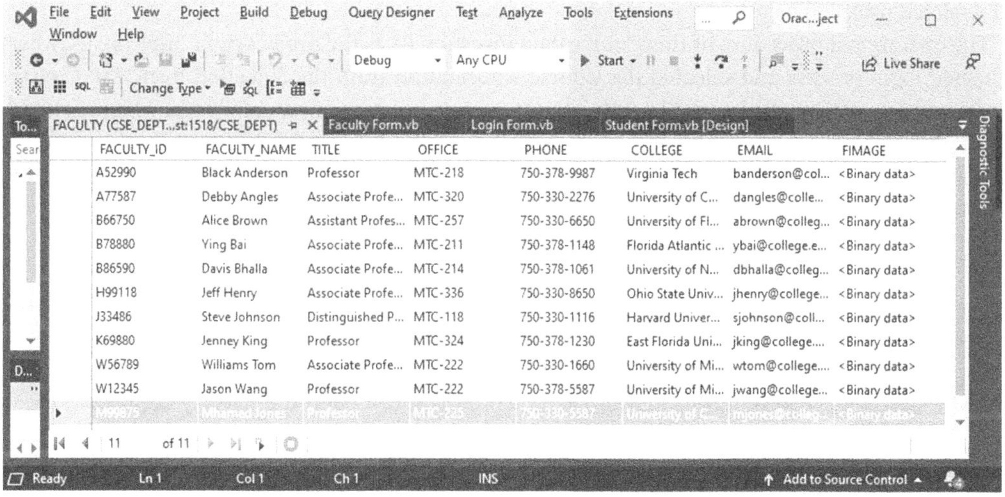

Figure 6.34 The new inserted faculty member Mhamed Jones. *Source:* Oracle Database.

A completed project `OracleInsertRTObject Project` can be found from the folder `Class DB Projects\Chapter 6\OracleInsertRTObject Solution` that is located at the Wiley ftp site under the `Students` folder (refer to Figure 1.2 in Chapter 1).

Basically there is no significant difference between inserting data into the Oracle, Microsoft Access or the SQL Server databases. The only differences are:

- The Connection string and the query strings.
- The `SELECT`, `INSERT` query strings and Parameter strings.

6.5 Insert Data into the Database Using Stored Procedures

In this section, we discuss how to insert data into the database using the stored procedures with run-time object method. We provided a very detailed introduction about the Oracle packages and the Oracle stored procedures and illustrated how to use these methods to perform the data query for the Student Form and **STUDENT** table in our sample database in Section 5.6.7.1 in Chapter 5. Refer to that part to get detailed information and descriptions about the stored procedures.

We try to use the Course Form and **COURSE** table to illustrate how to insert a new course record into the **COURSE** data table based on the selected faculty (**faculty_id**) in our sample database at this part.

6.5.1 Insert Data into the Oracle Database Using Stored Procedures

To save time and space, we can modify the project **OracleInsertRTObject Project** to create a new project named **OracleInsertRTObjectSP Project** and use the Student Form window to perform the data insertion using the stored procedures. Recall that when we developed that project, an **Insert** button is added into the Student Form window. We can use this button to trigger the data insertion function using the stored procedures.

Create a blank Solution **OracleInsertRTObjectSP Solution** in the folder **C:\Class DB Projects\Chapter 6**, copy and paste the existing project **OracleInsertRTObject Project** to that Solution folder, and rename it to our new project **OracleInsertRTObjectSP Project**. Refer to Section 6.4 to perform renaming and modifications to the project namespaces and related project files.

The operational procedure of this Course data insertion is: as the project runs, after the user has finished login process and selected the Course Information from the Selection form, the Course Form window will be displayed. The form allows users to enter one new course record represented by seven pieces of new course information into the appropriate textboxes based on the selected faculty member. By clicking on the **Insert** button, a new course record is inserted into the **COURSE** table in our database.

Let's first develop the codes for our Oracle stored procedures.

 One possible problem when you test your project by inserting more data into the Faculty table is that too many records are added into the database. To remove those unused records, you can open the Faculty table from the Server Explore or Oracle SQL Developer and then delete those records from the Faculty table

6.5.1.1 Develop Stored Procedures in Oracle Database

Recall that when we built our sample database CSE_DEPT in Chapter 2, there is no faculty name column in the **COURSE** table, and the only relationship existed between the **FACULTY** and the **COURSE** tables is the **FACULTY_ID**, which is a primary key in the **FACULTY** table but a foreign key in the **COURSE** table. As the project runs and the Course Form window is shown up, the user needs to insert new course data based on the faculty name, not the faculty ID. So for this new course data insertion, we need to perform two queries with two tables: first we need to make a query to the **FACULTY** table to get the **FACULTY_ID** based on the faculty name selected by the user, and second we can insert a new course record based on the **FACULTY_ID** we obtained from our first query. These two queries can be combined into a single stored procedure.

In addition to using stored procedures, another solution to avoid performing two queries is to use a joined table query to combine these two queries together to complete a course query, as we did for the Course Form in Section 5.6.6.1 in Chapter 5. However, it is more flexible and convenient to use stored procedures to perform multiple queries, especially when the queries are for multiple different data tables.

Now let us develop our stored procedures to combine these two queries to complete this data insertion. The stored procedure is named **INSERT_FACULTYCOURSE**.

Open the Oracle SQL Developer and connect to our database by entering the system password. Then expand the **Other Users** folder and our sample database folder **CSE_DEPT**. Perform the following operations to create this stored procedure.

1) Right click on the **Procedures** folder and select the **New Procedure** item.
2) On the opened Create Procedure wizard, enter **INSERT_FACULTYCOURSE** into the **Name:** box as the procedure's name.
3) Click on the green color plus symbol (**+**) on the upper-right corner to add all seven input parameters one by one with the data type shown in Figure 6.35.
4) Click on the **OK** button to open the procedure code window.

On the opened procedure code window, enter the codes shown in Figure 6.36 into the procedure body section, which is just under the **BEGIN** command.

The function of this stored procedure is:

A) All input parameters are listed in this part. The **FCAULTYNAME** is selected by the user from the Faculty Name combo box, and all other input parameters should be entered by the user to the associated textbox in the Course form window.
B) A local variable **FID** is declared and it is used to hold the returned query result, **faculty_id**, from the execution of the first query to the Faculty table in **D**.
C) The first query is executed to pick up the matched **faculty_id** from the Faculty table based on the first input parameter, **FACULTYNAME**.
D) The second query is to insert a new course record into the **COURSE** table. The last parameter in the **VALUES** list is the **FID**, which is obtained from the first query.

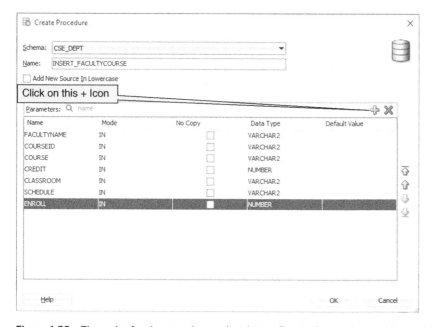

Figure 6.35 The codes for the stored procedure Insert_FacultyCourse. *Source:* Microsoft Visual Studio.

```
     CREATE OR REPLACE PROCEDURE INSERT_FACULTYCOURSE
     (
A     FACULTYNAME IN VARCHAR2
     , COURSEID IN VARCHAR2
     , COURSE IN VARCHAR2
     , CREDIT IN NUMBER
     , CLASSROOM IN VARCHAR2
     , SCHEDULE IN VARCHAR2
     , ENROLL IN NUMBER
     ) AS
     BEGIN
B     DECLARE FID VARCHAR2(20);
C     BEGIN SELECT faculty_id INTO FID FROM FACULTY
     WHERE faculty_name = FACULTYNAME;
D     INSERT INTO CSE_DEPT.course(course_id, course, credit, classroom, schedule, enrollment, faculty_id)
     VALUES (COURSEID, COURSE, CREDIT, CLASSROOM, SCHEDULE, ENROLL, FID);
     END;
     END INSERT_FACULTYCOURSE;
```

Figure 6.36 The code body for the procedure.

The codes for this stored procedure are simple and easy to be understood. One point you should know is the order of parameters in the **VALUES** parameter list. This order must be identical with the column order in the **COURSE** table at our sample database **CSE_DEPT**. Otherwise an error may be encountered when this stored procedure is executed.

Your completed procedure is shown in Figure 6.37.

Now expand the **Compile** icon and click on the **Compile** item to compile our procedure, a **Compiled** statement should be displayed in the Message window if everything is fine. Also you can find our procedure **INSERT_FACULTYCOURSE** just under the **Procedures** folder in the left pane (Figure 6.37). You may need to refresh that folder by right clicking on the folder and selecting the **Refresh** item on the popup menu if you cannot find our procedure.

We can directly test this stored procedure in this Oracle SQL Developer environment to confirm its performance. To do this testing, just click on the green arrow button to run this procedure.

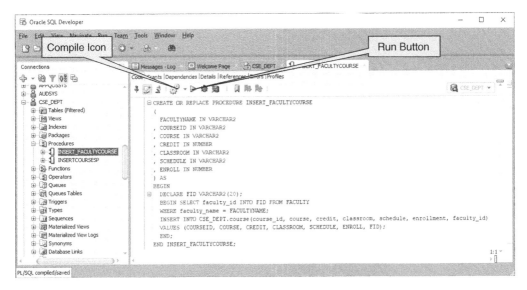

Figure 6.37 The completed code body for the procedure. *Source:* Oracle Database.

As the `Run PL/SQL` wizard appears, as shown in Figure 6.38, enter input parameters as a new course record for the faculty member `Ying Bai` into the `Input Value` column, as shown in Figure 6.38.

Then click on the `OK` button to run this procedure. You may need to confirm this running process by reentering your system password again. The running steps are displayed in the Running window.

To check this running result, one can open the `COURSE` table in this Oracle SQL Developer environment to check this insertion. Expand the `Tables` folder just under our user database `CSE_DEPT`, right click on our `COURSE` table and select `Open` item. On the opened `COURSE` table, click on the `Data` tab on the top to open the data view for all courses. Scroll down to the bottom and you will find that our new inserted course, `CSE-688` with all related fields, has been inserted into this table, as shown in Figure 6.39.

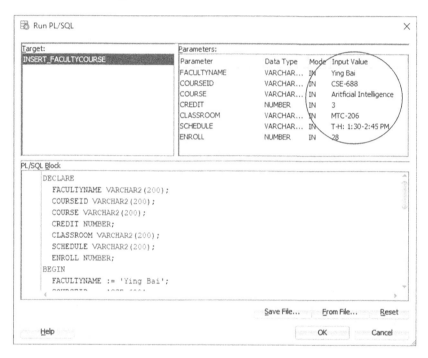

Figure 6.38 The input parameters for a new course record. *Source:* Microsoft Visual Studio.

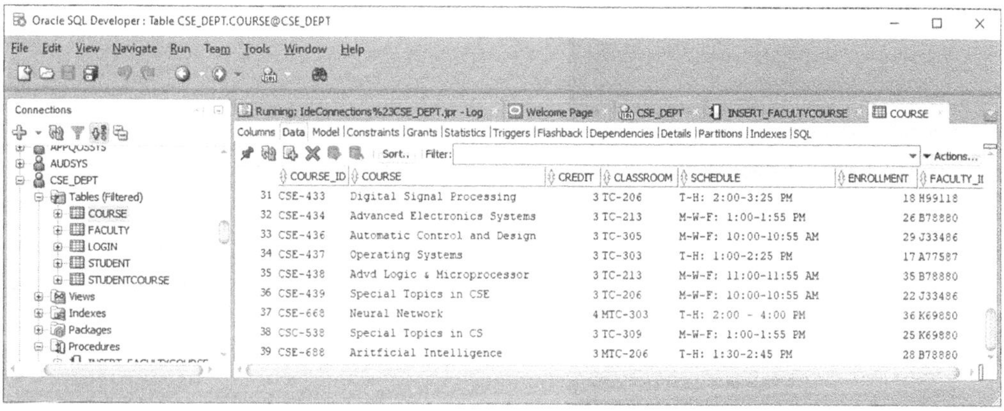

Figure 6.39 The running result of the stored procedure. *Source:* Oracle Database.

Another way to do this insertion checking or confirmation is to open the **COURSE** table in our sample database from the Server Explorer window in the Visual Studio.NET 2019 environment. Same result can be obtained for this new course insertion.

Next we need to develop the codes in Visual Basic.NET environment to call this stored procedure to insert a new course record into the database from our user interface.

6.5.1.2 Develop Codes to Call Stored Procedures to Insert Data into the Course Table

The coding process of the data insertion is divided into four steps; code modifications in the Form_ Load event procedure, the data validation before the data insertion, data insertion using the stored procedure, and the data validation after the data insertion. The purpose of the second step is to confirm that all inserted data that stored in each associated textbox should be complete and valid. In other words, all textboxes should be nonempty. The third step is used to confirm that the data insertion is successful, in other words, the new inserted data should be in the desired table in the database and can be read back and displayed in the form window. Let us begin with the coding process for the first step now.

6.5.1.2.1 Modify the Codes in the Form_Load Event Procedure The main purpose of this code modification is to retrieve all current actual faculty members from our **FACULTY** table in our sample database and display them in the **Faculty Name** Combo Box correctly. Recall that those codes in the original Form_Load event procedure, all faculty members are added into this combo box by a fixed sequence, not retrieved from our database.

Thus, we need to use a user-defined subroutine **CurrentFaculty()**, which was a Public subroutine built in Section 6.4.1.2, to replace those original codes.

Open the Form_Load event procedure under the Course Form window and enter the codes shown in Figure 6.40 into this procedure to replace original 8-line's codes. Let us have a closer look at these two coding lines to see how they work.

A) Since this user-defined subroutine is defined in the Faculty Form window, thus a new object of that Form, **faculty**, is declared first.

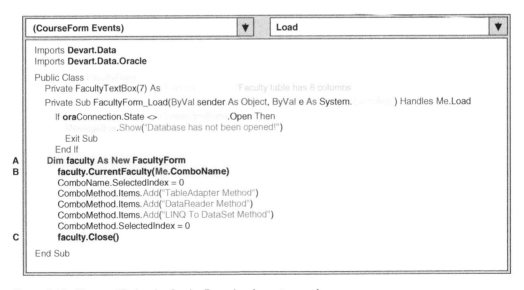

Figure 6.40 The modified codes for the Form_Load event procedure.

B) The user-defined subroutine, **CurrentFaculty()**, which is a **Public** subroutine and it is prefixed by a Faculty Form object **faculty**, is called with an argument **Me.ComboName**. The argument is the **Faculty Name** combo box defined in the Course Form, not in the Faculty Form, thus a keyword **Me** is prefixed. The keyword **Me** represents the current Form, the Course Form.

C) The object **faculty** is closed after its function.

Next let us take care of the codes for the pre-validation operations.

6.5.1.2.2 *Validate Data Before the Data Insertion* Two user-defined procedures, **InitCourseInfo()** and **CheckCourseInfo()**, are developed in this part to perform the data validation before the data insertion action. Open the code window of the Course Form and enter the codes shown in Figure 6.41 into this window to create a user-defined subroutine procedure **InitCourseInfo()** and a user-defined function **CheckCourseInfo()**. Let us take a look at these pieces of codes to see how they work.

A) A **For** loop is used to create a new textbox array.

B) The content of each textbox is assigned to the **Text** property of the associated textbox in that textbox array initialized in step **A**.

C) To check each textbox, a **For** loop is utilized to scan the **CourseTextBox** array. A warning message is displayed, and the function returns a nonzero value to the calling procedure to indicate that this checking is failed if any textbox is empty.

D) Otherwise a zero is returned to indicate that this checking is successful.

Now let us do our coding process for the data validation before the data insertion.

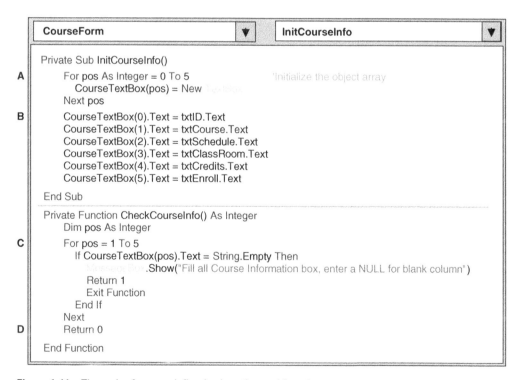

```
CourseForm ▼                              InitCourseInfo ▼

   Private Sub InitCourseInfo()
A      For pos As Integer = 0 To 5            'Initialize the object array
          CourseTextBox(pos) = New Textbox
       Next pos
B      CourseTextBox(0).Text = txtID.Text
       CourseTextBox(1).Text = txtCourse.Text
       CourseTextBox(2).Text = txtSchedule.Text
       CourseTextBox(3).Text = txtClassRoom.Text
       CourseTextBox(4).Text = txtCredits.Text
       CourseTextBox(5).Text = txtEnroll.Text

   End Sub

   Private Function CheckCourseInfo() As Integer
       Dim pos As Integer

C      For pos = 1 To 5
          If CourseTextBox(pos).Text = String.Empty Then
             MessageBox.Show("Fill all Course Information box, enter a NULL for blank column")
             Return 1
             Exit Function
          End If
       Next
D      Return 0

   End Function
```

Figure 6.41 The codes for user-defined subroutine and function.

This data validation can be performed by calling one subroutine `InitCourseInfo()` and one function `CheckCourseInfo()`, which we have discussed above, in the `Insert` button's Click event procedure. Open the `Insert` button's Click event procedure and enter the codes that are shown in Figure 6.42 into this event procedure.

The function of this piece of codes is straightforward and easy to be understood. First the subroutine `InitCourseInfo()` is called to set up one-to-one relationship between each item in the `CourseTextBox()` array and each associated textbox that stores a piece of course information. Next the function `CheckCourseInfo()` is executed to make sure that the new course information is completed and valid, in other words, no textbox is empty.

Now let's develop and complete the codes to call the stored procedure to perform the new course data insertion.

6.5.1.2.3 Develop Codes to Call Stored Procedures Open the `Insert` button's Click event procedure and add the codes that are shown in Figure 6.43 into this event procedure. The codes we

```
btnInsert ▼          Click ▼

Private Sub btnInsert_Click(sender As Object, e As EventArgs) Handles btnInsert.Click
    Dim pos As Integer

    InitCourseInfo()
    pos = CheckCourseInfo()
    If pos <> 0 Then
        Exit Sub
    End If
```

Figure 6.42 The first coding part for the Insert button's event procedure.

```
btnInsert ▼          Click ▼

    Private Sub btnInsert_Click(ByVal sender As System.Object, ByVal e As System.EventArgs) Handles btnInsert.Click
A       Dim cmdString As String = "CSE_DEPT.Insert_FacultyCourse"
B       Dim pos, intInsert As Integer
        Dim oraCommand As New OracleCommand

        InitCourseInfo()
        pos = CheckCourseInfo()
        If pos <> 0 Then
            Exit Sub
        End If
C       oraCommand.Connection = oraConnection
        oraCommand.CommandType = CommandType.StoredProcedure
        oraCommand.CommandText = cmdString
D       InsertParameters(oraCommand)
E       intInsert = oraCommand.ExecuteNonQuery()
F       oraCommand.Dispose()
        oraCommand = Nothing
G       If intInsert = 0 Then
            MessageBox.Show("The data insertion is failed")
            Exit Sub
        End If
H       'CleanInsert()                      'clean up all course information
I       btnInsert.Enabled = False           'disable the Insert button

    End Sub
```

Figure 6.43 The modifications to the Insert button's Click event procedure.

developed in the last section have been highlighted with the gray color as the background. Let us take a look at those new added codes to see how they work.

A) The query string is assigned with the name of the stored procedure we developed in Section 6.5.1.1 in this chapter. One of the most important points to call stored procedures is that the query string must be exactly identical with the name of the stored procedure to be called. When the Visual Basic.NET project could not find the stored procedures, a time up error would be encountered because the query string does not match the name of the stored procedure.

B) Some other components and variables used in this procedure are declared here. The local integer variable `intInsert` is used to hold the returned value of execution of the `ExecuteNonQuery()` method. The Oracle Command object `oraCommand` is created here, too.

C) The Command object is initialized with the suitable components. Two important points to be noted are CommandType and CommandText. The former must be assigned with the property of `StoredProcedure` to indicate that the command type of this Command object is stored procedure and a stored procedure will be called when this Command is executed. The name of the stored procedure must be assigned to the CommandText property of the Command object to provide the direction for the Visual Basic.NET project.

D) The user-defined subroutine `InsertParameters()`, whose detailed codes will be shown in Figure 6.44, is executed to fill all input parameters into the Parameters collection of the Command object to finish the initialization of the Command.

E) The `ExecuteNonQuery()` method of the Command class is executed to call the stored procedure to perform this new course data insertion.

F) The Command object is cleaned up and released after this data insertion.

G) The `ExecuteNonQuery()` method will return an integer to indicate whether this calling is successful or not. The returned value equals to the number of rows or records that have been successfully added into the database. A zero means that no row or record has been inserted into the database, and this data insertion is failed. In that case, a warning message is displayed and the procedure is exited.

H) After a record has been inserted into the Course table, all six pieces of information stored in all textboxes, except the Course ID, can be cleaned up. This line can be commented out since this operation is not necessary.

I) Also the `Insert` button is disabled to avoid multiple insertions of the same data into the database.

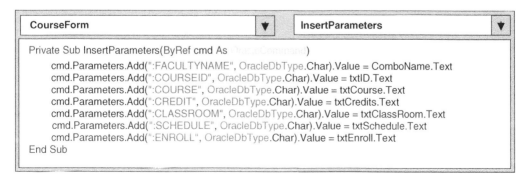

Figure 6.44 The codes for the user-defined subroutine InsertParameters().

The detailed codes for the user-defined subroutine `InsertParameters()` are shown in Figure 6.44.

The function of this subroutine is to assign each piece of information stored in each textbox to the associated input parameter we defined in the Oracle stored procedure `INSERT_FACULTYCOURSE`. One key point is that the name of each parameter, which is represented as a string and located at the first argument's position, must be identical with each input parameter's name we defined in the stored procedure. For example, the name of the parameter `:FACULTYNAME` used in here must be identical with the input parameter's name `FACULTYNAME` in the input parameter's list we defined at the beginning of the stored procedure `INSERT_FACULTYCOURSE`. Also the parameter's order used in here must be identical with the order used for those input parameters in our procedure. A runtime error would be encountered if the name or the order of parameter is not matched with the associated parameter's name or order in the stored procedure as the project runs. Refer to Figure 6.36 for all parameters' names and order defined in the stored procedure.

Now we have finished the coding process for this data insertion operation. Let us run the project to test the new data insertion using the stored procedures. Click on the Start Debugging button to start the project, enter the suitable username and password such as **jhenry** and **test** to the LogIn form, and select the `Course Information` item from the Selection form to open the Course form window.

Select the faculty member `Debby Angles` from the Faculty Name combobox and enter the following data into the associated textbox as the information for a new course:

- `CSC-623`   Course ID textbox
- `Adaptive Fuzzy Logics` Course Title textbox
- `M-W-F: 9:00 - 9:55 AM` Schedule textbox
- `MTC-309`   Classroom textbox
- `3`   Credits textbox
- `32`   Enrollment textbox

Your finished information window should match one that is shown in Figure 6.45.

A hiding issue is that the PL/SQL engine can do char-to-number conversions automatically since we did not convert `CREDIT` and `ENROLL` to number, but they works.

Click on the `Insert` button to call the stored procedure to insert this new course record into the database. Immediately, the `Insert` button is disabled after this data insertion to avoid multi-insertion for same record. Is our data insertion successful? To answer this question, we need to perform the data validation in the next section.

6.5.1.2.4 *Validate Data After the Data Insertion*   To confirm and validate this new course record insertion, we can use the `Select` button's Click event procedure to retrieve this new course record from the database and display it in this Course form.

Select the faculty member `Debby Angles` from the Faculty Name combobox and click on the `Select` button. All courses taught by this faculty are displayed in the CourseList box. The last item, `CSC-623`, is the course we just added into the Course table in the last section. Click on that `course_id` and all pieces of related course information are displayed in six textboxes, which is shown in Figure 6.46. This is the evidence that our data insertion using the stored procedure is successful!

A completed project `OracleInsertRTObjectSP Project` that includes the data insertion using the stored procedure can be found from the folder `Class DB Projects\Chapter 6\`

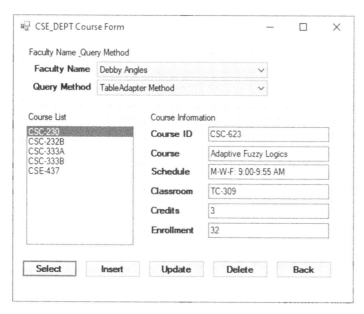

Figure 6.45 The running status of the Course Form window. *Source:* Microsoft Visual Studio.

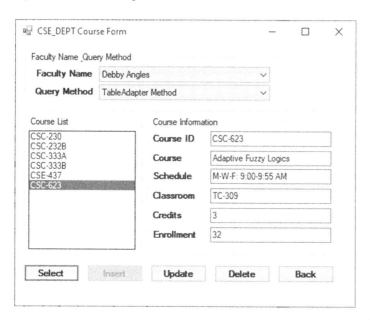

Figure 6.46 The data validation process. *Source:* Microsoft Visual Studio.

OracleInsertRTObjectSP Solution located at the Wiley ftp site under the **Students** folder (refer to Figure 1.2 in Chapter 1).

6.6 Insert Data into the Database Using the LINQ To DataSet Method

As we discussed in Chapter 4, Language-Integrated Query (LINQ) is a powerful method provided by Visual Studio.NET, and the .NET Framework bridges the gap between the world of objects and the world of the data. In Visual Studio.NET, you can write LINQ queries in Visual Basic.NET with

Oracle databases, XML documents, ADO.NET DataSets, and any collection of objects that supports IEnumerable or the generic IEnumerable(Of T) interface.

LINQ can be considered as a pattern or model that is supported by a collection of so-called Standard Query Operator methods we discussed in Section 4.1 in Chapter 4, and all those Standard Query Operator methods are static methods defined in either IEnumerable or IQueryable classes in the namespace `System.Linq`. The data operated in LINQ query are object sequences with the data type of either IEnumerable(Of T) or IQueryable(Of T), where T is the actual data type of the objects stored in the sequence.

LINQ is composed of three major components: LINQ to Objects, LINQ to ADO.NET, and LINQ to XML. The LINQ to ADO.NET contains LINQ to DataSet, LINQ to SQL and LINQ to Entities. In this section, we will concentrate our discussion on inserting data into the Oracle database using the LINQ to DataSet model.

Generally, the popular method to insert a new record into the database using the LINQ query follows three steps listed below:

1) Create a new object that includes the column data to be submitted.
2) Add the new Row object to the LINQ to SQL Table collection associated with the target table in the database.
3) Call the ExecuteNonQuery() method.

In this part, we will build a Console App project to illustrate how to insert a new course record into the **COURSE** table in our sample database.

6.6.1 Insert Data into the Oracle Database Using the LINQ to DataSet Queries

As we discussed in Sections 4.5.1.4 and 4.5.2 in Chapter 4, a cross table query and a single row query can be executed by using the LINQ To DataSet techniques. Here we need to use these models to perform this new course record insertion into the **COURSE** table with the selected faculty_id in the following sequences:

1) Perform the first single-row query to **FACULTY** table to get the desired faculty_id based on faculty name.
2) Perform the second LINQ To DataSet query to insert a new course record into the **COURSE** table.

Refer to Sections 4.5.1.4 and 4.5.2 in Chapter 4 to get more detailed descriptions about these methods and implementation examples.

Now let us build this Console project `OracleLinqDataSet` in Visual Studio.NET 2019. Perform the following operational steps to build this project:

1) Create a new folder, `OracleLinqDataSet Solution`, under the default folder `C:\Class DB Projects\Chapter 6` with the Windows Explorer.
2) Open Visual Studio.NET 2019 and go to `New Project` menu item.
3) Select the item `Console App (.NET Framework)` – Visual Basic, click on the `Next`.
4) Enter `OracleLinqDataSet` into the `Project Name` box.
5) Browse to our default folder, `C:\Class DB Projects\Chapter 6`, and use it as the location to save our new project.
6) Click on `Create` button and change Module name to `OracleLinqDataSet.vb`.
7) On the created project, add a Reference by right clicking on our new project from the Solution Explorer window, and select the `Add|Reference` item.
8) Click on the `Extensions` item on the left pane to find both namespaces, `Devart.Data` and `Devart.Data.Oracle`, and click on the `OK` button to add them.

9) On the opened Module code window, enter the namespace directive, **Imports Devart. Data.Oracle**, on the top of this window.

10) Then enter the codes shown in Figure 6.47 into this **Sub Main**() as the body for this Module.

Let's have a closer look at this piece of codes to see how it works

A) Two query strings are generated first, **fString** and **cString**, one is for **FACULTY** table and the other is for the **COURSE** table. The first query is used to get a matched faculty_id based on selected faculty name, and the second is an insertion query. To make it simple, only one dynamic parameter, faculty_id (**:fid**), is used for this query and all others are predefined parameters, and can be inserted into the **COURSE** table directly.

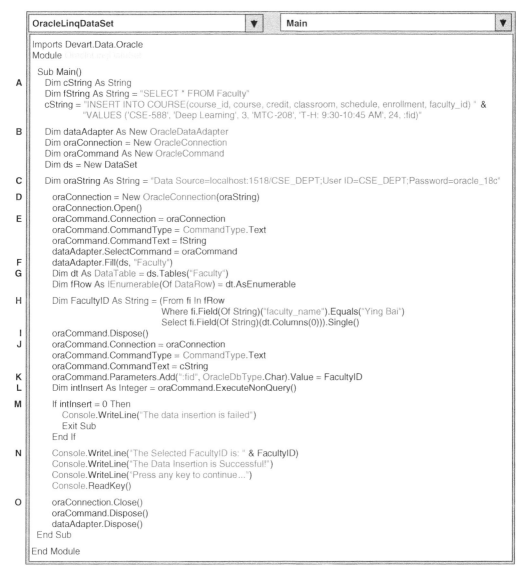

```
OracleLinqDataSet  ▼        Main                    ▼

     Imports Devart.Data.Oracle
     Module

         Sub Main()
A           Dim cString As String
            Dim fString As String = "SELECT * FROM Faculty"
            cString = "INSERT INTO COURSE(course_id, course, credit, classroom, schedule, enrollment, faculty_id) " &
                      "VALUES ('CSE-588', 'Deep Learning', 3, 'MTC-208', 'T-H: 9:30-10:45 AM', 24, :fid)"

B           Dim dataAdapter As New OracleDataAdapter
            Dim oraConnection = New OracleConnection
            Dim oraCommand As New OracleCommand
            Dim ds = New DataSet

C           Dim oraString As String = "Data Source=localhost:1518/CSE_DEPT;User ID=CSE_DEPT;Password=oracle_18c"

D           oraConnection = New OracleConnection(oraString)
            oraConnection.Open()
E           oraCommand.Connection = oraConnection
            oraCommand.CommandType = CommandType.Text
            oraCommand.CommandText = fString
            dataAdapter.SelectCommand = oraCommand
F           dataAdapter.Fill(ds, "Faculty")
G           Dim dt As DataTable = ds.Tables("Faculty")
            Dim fRow As IEnumerable(Of DataRow) = dt.AsEnumerable

H           Dim FacultyID As String = (From fi In fRow
                                       Where fi.Field(Of String)("faculty_name").Equals("Ying Bai")
                                       Select fi.Field(Of String)(dt.Columns(0))).Single()
I           oraCommand.Dispose()
J           oraCommand.Connection = oraConnection
            oraCommand.CommandType = CommandType.Text
            oraCommand.CommandText = cString
K           oraCommand.Parameters.Add(":fid", OracleDbType.Char).Value = FacultyID
L           Dim intInsert As Integer = oraCommand.ExecuteNonQuery()

M           If intInsert = 0 Then
               Console.WriteLine("The data insertion is failed")
               Exit Sub
            End If

N           Console.WriteLine("The Selected FacultyID is: " & FacultyID)
            Console.WriteLine("The Data Insertion is Successful!")
            Console.WriteLine("Press any key to continue...")
            Console.ReadKey()

O           oraConnection.Close()
            oraCommand.Dispose()
            dataAdapter.Dispose()
         End Sub

     End Module
```

Figure 6.47 The codes for the OracleLingDataSet module.

B) Some data components, including an Oracle DataAdapter, one Oracle Connection, one Oracle Command, and one DataSet, are declared here since we need to use them to perform data queries later.

C) The Oracle database connection string is defined and it is used to connect to our sample database first to perform the following data actions.

D) An Oracle Connection object is generated with the connection string, and then it is opened for the all following data transactions against our sample database.

E) The first Oracle Command object is initialized with connection object, command type, and command string `fString`, which is for the **FACULTY** table query to retrieve a matched faculty_id, and assigned to the `SelectCommand` property of the Oracle DataAdapter to perform a select query based on the given faculty name.

F) Then the `Fill()` method is executed to fill the DataSet with all queried faculty records from the **FACULTY** table in our sample database.

G) Two new objects are declared here, a Data Table `dt` and a Data Row `fRow`. The former is used to hold a **FACULTY** table and the latter is used to hold a Data Row.

H) A LINQ To DataSet query is executed to retrieve back the desired faculty_id that is located at `Columns(0)` in the **FACULTY** table based on the selected faculty name.

I) The job of the first Oracle Command is done, and it is released.

J) The second Oracle Command object is initialized with the course query string `cString`, and it is used to insert a new course record into the **COURSE** table.

K) The queried faculty_id from the first query is assigned to the unique dynamic parameter, `fid`, on the course query string `cString` to make it ready to be inserted into the **COURSE** table.

L) The ExecuteNonQuery() method is executed to insert a new course record into the **COURSE** table. This method will return an integer value to indicate whether this operation is successful or not.

M) If a zero is returned, which means that this insertion is failed and a warning message is displayed to indicate this situation and the program is exited.

N) Otherwise if a nonzero value is returned, this value indicates the number of records that have been successfully inserted into the database. The queried faculty_id and a successful insertion message are displayed on the screen.

O) Some cleaning jobs are performed to release all used objects.

Now you can run this Console project, and the related successful messages with the queried faculty_id will be displayed. Press any key to stop this project.

To confirm this insertion action, one can open the **COURSE** table in our sample database from the Server Explorer window. The new inserted course record, **CSE-588**, can be found at the last line on the **COURSE** table for the selected faculty member **Ying Bai**.

6.7 Chapter Summary

Five popular data insertion methods are discussed and analyzed with the Oracle 18c XE database in this chapter:

1) Using TableAdapter's DBDirect methods `TableAdapter.Insert()` method.
2) Using the `TableAdapter's Update()` method to insert new records that have already been added into the DataTable in the DataSet.
3) Using the Command object's `ExecuteNonQuery()` method.
4) Using stored procedures method.
5) Using LINQ to DataSet query method.

Method 1 is developed using the Visual Studio.NET Design Tools and Wizards, and it allows users to directly access the database and execute the TableAdapter's methods such as `TableAdapter.Insert()` and `TableAdapter.Update()` to manipulate data in the database without requiring DataSet or DataTable objects to reconcile changes in order to send updates to a database. As we mentioned at the beginning of this chapter, inserting data into a table in the DataSet is different with inserting data into a table in the database. If you are using the DataSet to store data in your applications, you need to use the `TableAdapter.Update()` method since the `Update()` method can trigger and send all changes (updates, inserts, and deletes) in the DataSet to the database.

A good habit is to try to use the `TableAdapter.Insert()` method when your application uses objects to store data (for example, you are using TextBoxes to store your data), or when you want finer control over creating new records in the database.

Method 2 allows users to insert new data into a database with two steps. First, the new record can be added into the data table that is located in the DataSet, and second the `TableAdapter.Update()` method can be executed to update the whole table in the DataSet to the associated table in the database.

Method 3 is a Run-Time Object method, and this method is more flexible and convenient, and it allows users to insert data into multiple data tables with the different functionalities.

Method 4 uses stored procedures to replace the general query functions, and this method promises users with more powerful controllability and flexibility on data insertions, especially for data insertions with multiple queries to multiple tables.

Method 5 is a powerful technique coming with .NET Framework, Visual Studio.NET, and LINQ that were released by Microsoft recently.

This chapter is divided into two parts. Part I provides a detailed discussion and analysis of inserting data into the Oracle 18c XE database using the Visual Studio.NET Design Tools and Wizards. It is simple and easy to develop data insertion projects with these tools and wizards. The disadvantage of using these tools and wizards is that the data can only be inserted to limited destinations, for example, to certain data table. Part II presents the Run-Time Object method to improve the efficiency of the data insertion and provides more flexibility in data insertion.

Four (4) real projects are provided in this chapter to give readers a clear and direct picture in developing professional data insertion applications in Visual Basic.NET environment.

Homework

I. True/False Selections

_____ 1   Three popular data insertion methods are the TableAdapter.Insert(), TableAdapter.Update(), and ExecuteNonQuery() method of the Command class.

_____ 2   Unlike the Fill() method, a valid database connection must be set before a new data can be inserted in the database.

_____ 3   One can directly insert new data or new records into the database using the TableAdapter.Update() method.

_____ **4** When executing an INSERT query, the order of the input parameters in the VALUES list can be different with the order of the data columns in the database.

_____ **5** To insert data into an Oracle database using stored procedures, a stored procedure can be built in the TableAdapter Query Configuration Wizard.

_____ **6** The difference between the Visual Basic collection class and the .NET Framework collection class is that two collections start with the different index, the former starts from 1, but the latter starts from 0.

_____ **7** When performing a data insertion action, the same data can be inserted into the database multiple times.

_____ **8** To insert data into the database using the TableAdapter.Update() method, the new data should be first inserted into the table in the DataSet and then the Update() method is executed to update that new data into the table in the database.

_____ **9** To insert data into an Oracle 18c XE database using the stored procedures, one can create and test the new stored procedure in the Oracle SQL Developer environment.

_____ **10** To call stored procedures to insert data into a database, the parameters' names must be identical with those names of the input parameters defined in the stored procedures.

II. Multiple Choices

1 To insert data into the database using the TableAdapter.Insert() method, one needs to use the _____ to build the _____.
  A Data Source, Qury Buildcr
  B TableAdapter Query Configuration Wizard, Insert query
  C Runtime object, Insert query
  D Server Explorer, Data Source

2 To insert data into a database using the TableAdapter.Update() method, one needs first to add new data into the _____, then update that data into the database.
  A Data table
  B Data table in the database
  C DataSet
  D Data table in the DataSet

3 To insert data into the database using the TableAdapter.Update() method, one can update _____
  A One data row only
  B Multiple data rows
  C The whole data table
  D Either of above

4 Because the ADO.NET provides a disconnected mode to the database, to insert a new record into the database, a valid _____ must be established.

A DataSet

B TableAdapter

C Connection

D Command

5 The _____ operator should be used as an assignment operator for the WHERE clause with a dynamic parameter for a data query in an Oracle database.

A =:

B LIKE

C :

D @

6 To confirm a stored procedure built in the Oracle SQL Developer for an Oracle database, one can _____ the stored procedure to make sure it works.

A Build

B Run

C Debug

D Create

7 To confirm a stored procedure built in the Oracle SQL Developer for an Oracle database, one should select the _____ item before run the stored procedure.

A Save

B Save As

C Compile

D Update

8 To insert data into an Oracle 18c XE database using the INSERT query, the parameters' data type must be _____.

A OleDbType

B SqlDbType

C OracleType

D OracleDbType

9 To insert data using stored procedures, the CommandType property of the Command object must be equal to _____.

A CommandType.InsertCommand

B CommandType.StoredProcedure

C CommandType.Text

D CommandType.Insert

10 To insert data using stored procedures, the CommandText property of the Command object must be equal to _____.

A The content of the CommandType.InsetCommand

B The content of the CommandType.Text

C The name of the Insert command

D The name of the stored procedure

III. Exercises

1 Using Oracle SQL Developer to build a stored procedure for Oracle database. The name for this procedure is **INSERT_STUDENTSP**.

Using following input parameters as a new record for this inserting student:

- SID   `student_id`   VARCHAR2
- SNAME   `student_name` VARCHAR2
- GPA   `gpa`   VARCHAR2
- MAJOR   `major`   VARCHAR2
- SYEAR   `schoolYear`   VARCHAR2
- CREDITS `credits`   NUMBER
- EMAIL   `email`   VARCHAR2
- SIMAGE   `simage`   BLOB

2 Create a Visual Basic.NET project **OracleInsertStudent Project** to call the stored procedure built above to insert a new student record into the **STUDENT** table in the sample database **CSE_DEPT**. Validate this new insertion by using the **Select** button on the Student Form. You can use/copy the **Student** Form with the **Insert** button event procedure in a completed project **OracleInsertRTObjectSP Project** that can be found from a folder: **Class DB Projects\Chapter 6** in the Wiley ftp site under the **Students** folder (refer to Figure 1.2 in Chapter 1). You may need to copy and modify that project to make it your new project **OracleInsertStudent Project**.

3 Figure 6.48 shows a piece of Visual Basic codes used to call a stored procedure **INSERT_NEWCOURSESP** in an Oracle database to insert a new course record into the **COURSE** table in our sample database **CSE_DEPT**. Please finish the coding process for the subroutine **InsertParameters()** and create an associated stored procedure using the Oracle SQL Developer.

```
Private Sub btnInsert_Click(ByVal sender As System.        , ByVal e As System.            ) Handles btnInsert.Click
    Dim cmdString As String = "INSERT_NEWCOURSESP"
    Dim intInsert As Integer
    Dim oraCommand As New OracleCommand

    oraCommand.Connection = oraConnection
    oraCommand.CommandType =            .StoredProcedure
    oraCommand.CommandText = cmdString
    InsertParameters(oraCommand)
    intInsert = oraCommand.ExecuteNonQuery()
    oraCommand.Dispose()
    oraCommand = Nothing

    If intInsert = 0 Then
                   .Show("The data insertion is failed")
        Exit Sub
    End If
    btnInsert.Enabled = False        'disable the Insert button
End Sub
```

Figure 6.48 The codes to call the Oracle stored procedure.

Compile and test this stored procedure inside the Oracle SQL Developer with the following elements for this new course:

A	Faculty Name	`Ying Bai`
B	Course ID	`CSE-590`
C	Course	`Machine Learning`
D	Credit	`3`
E	Classroom	`MTC-438`
F	Schedule	`M-W-F: 3:00 - 3:50 PM`
G	Enrollment	`28`

You need to use two queries for this stored procedure, (i) query a valid faculty_id from the Faculty table based on the faculty name, (ii) insert a new course record into the Course table for the selected `faculty_id`.

4 Using the tools and wizards provided by Visual Basic.NET and ADO.NET to perform the data insertion for the Student form in the `InsertWizard` project. The project file can be found from the folder `Class DB Projects\Chapter 6` that is located at the Wiley ftp site under the `Students` folder (refer to Figure 1.2 in Chapter 1). The new student record includes

A	student_id	`J36785`
B	student_name	`James Stevenson`
C	credits	`86`
D	gpa	`3.08`
E	major	`Computer Engineering`
F	schoolYear	`Junior`
G	email	`jstevenson@college.edu`
H	simage	`C:\Images\Default.jpg`

The image file `Default.jpg` can be found from the folder `Images\Students`, which is located at the Wiley ftp site under the `Students` folder (refer to Figure 1.2 in Chapter 1). You can validate this insertion by opening the `STUDENT` table in our sample database `CSE_DEPT` via Server Explorer window in Visual Studio.NET.

Hint: You do not need to generate any new query function to do this insertion, instead you can directly use a default `Insert()` query method provided by TableAdapter. A point to be noted is the argument style and dynamic parameters used for this insertion.

5 Using the Runtime Objects to complete the insert data query for the Student form by using the project `OracleInsertRTObject Project`. The project file can be found from the folder `Class DB Projects\Chapter 6` that is located at the Wiley ftp site under the `Students` folder (refer to Figure 1.2 in Chapter 1). The new student record is:

A	student_id	`W58766`
B	student_name	`Aversion Wang`
C	credits	`35`
D	gpa	`3.38`

E	major	Computer Science
F	schoolYear	Freshman
G	email	awang@college.edu
H	simage	C:\Images\Wang.jpg

The image file **Wang.jpg** can be found from the folder **Images\Students**, which is located at the Wiley ftp site under the **Students** folder (refer to Figure 1.2 in Chapter 1). You can validate this insertion by opening the **STUDENT** table in our sample database **CSE_DEPT** via Server Explorer window in Visual Studio.NET.

Perform this insertion by using the **Insert** button's Click event procedure on the Student Form window.

7

Data Updating and Deleting with Visual Basic.NET

In this Chapter, we will discuss how to update and delete data against the Oracle databases. Basically, many different methods can be provided and supported by Visual Basic.NET and .NET Framework to help users to perform the data updating and deleting against the database. Among them, three popular methods are widely implemented:

1) Using TableAdapter DBDirect methods, such as `TableAdapter.Update()` and `TableAdapter.Delete()`, to update and delete data directly against the databases.
2) Using `TableAdapter.Update()` method to update and execute the associated TableAdapter's properties, such as UpdateCommand or DeleteCommand, to save changes made from the table in the DataSet to the table in the database.
3) Using the run time object method to develop and execute the Command method `ExecuteNonQuery()` to update or delete data against the database directly.

Both methods 1 and 2 need to use Visual Studio.NET Design Tools and Wizards to create and configure suitable TableAdapters, build the associated queries using the Query Builder, and call those queries from Visual Basic.NET applications. The difference between methods 1 and 2 is that method 1 can be used to directly access the database to perform the data updating and deleting in a single step, but method 2 needs two steps to perform the data updating or deleting. First, the data updating or deleting are performed to the associated tables in the DataSet, and then those updated or deleted data are updated to the tables in the database by executing the `TableAdapter.Update()` method.

This Chapter is divided into two parts: Part I provides discussions on data updating and deleting using methods 1 and 2, or in other words, using the `TableAdapter.Update()` and `TableAdapter.Delete()` methods provided by the Visual Studio.NET Design Tools and Wizards. Part II presents the data updating and deleting using the run time object method to develop command objects to execute the `ExecuteNonQuery()` method dynamically. Updating and deleting data using the stored procedures and the LINQ to DataSet query method are also discussed in Part II.

When finished this chapter, you will be able to:

- Understand the working principle and structure on updating and deleting data against the database using the Visual Studio.NET Design Tools and Wizards.
- Understand the procedures in how to configure the TableAdapter object by using the TableAdapter Query Configuration Wizard and build the query to update and delete data against the database.

Oracle Database Programming with Visual Basic.NET: Concepts, Designs, and Implementations, First Edition. Ying Bai.
© 2021 The Institute of Electrical and Electronics Engineers, Inc. Published 2021 by John Wiley & Sons, Inc.
Companion website: www.wiley.com/go/bai-VB-Oracle

- Design and develop special procedures to validate data before and after the data updating and deleting.
- Understand the working principle and structure on updating and deleting data against the database using the runtime object method.
- Design and build LINQ to DataSet query to update and delete data.
- Design and build stored procedures to perform the data updating and deleting.

To successfully complete this chapter, you need to understand topics such as Fundamentals of Databases, which was introduced in Chapter 2, ADO.NET that was discussed in Chapter 3 and LINQ techniques discussed in Chapter 4. Also a sample database CSE_DEPT that was developed in Chapter 2 will be used through this Chapter.

In order to save time and avoid any duplication, we will use some sample projects, such as `InsertWizard` and `OracleInsertRTObject`, we developed in the previous chapters, and modify them to create new associated projects used in this Chapter. Recall that some command buttons on the different form windows in those projects have not been coded, such as `Update` and `Delete`, and those buttons or exactly the event procedures related to those buttons will be developed and built in this chapter. We only concentrate on the coding for the `Update` and `Delete` buttons in this Chapter.

Part I: Data Updating and Deleting with Visual Studio.NET Design Tools and Wizards

In this part, we discuss updating and deleting data against the database using the Visual Studio.NET Design Tools and Wizards. We will develop two methods to perform these data actions: first, we use the TableAdapter DBDirect methods, `TableAdapter.Update()`, and `TableAdapter.Delete()` to directly update or delete data in the database. Second, we discuss how to update or delete data in the database by first updating or deleting records in the DataSet and then updating those records' changes from the DataSet to the database using the `TableAdapter.Update()` method. Both methods utilize the so-called TableAdapter's direct and indirect methods to complete the data updating or deleting. The database we try to use is our sample database built with the Oracle 18c XE database, `CSE_DEPT`, which was developed in Chapter 2, and it can be found from the folder `Sample Database` located at the Wiley ftp site under the `Students` folder (refer to Figure 1.2 in Chapter 1).

7.1   Update or Delete Data Against Oracle Databases

We have already provided a very detailed discussion about the TableAdapter DBDirect methods in Section 6.1.1 in Chapter 6. To use these methods to directly access the database to make the desired manipulations to the data stored in the database, one needs to use Visual Studio.NET Design Tools and Wizards to create and configure the associated TableAdapters. However, there are some limitations existed when these DBDirect methods are utilized. For example, each TableAdapter is associated with a unique data table in the DataSet; therefore, the data updating or deleting can only be executed for that data table by using the associated TableAdapter. In other words, the specified TableAdapter cannot be used to update or delete data from any other data tables except the data table that is related to the created TableAdapter.

7.1.1 Updating and Deleting Data from Related Tables in a DataSet

When updating or deleting data against related tables in a DataSet, it is important to update or delete data in the proper sequence in order to reduce the chance of violating referential integrity constraints. The order of command execution will also follow the indices of the `DataRowCollection` in the DataSet. To prevent data integrity errors from being raised, the best practice is to update or delete data against the database in the following sequence:

1) Child table: delete records.
2) Parent table: insert, update, and delete records.
3) Child table: insert and update records.

For our sample database CSE_DEPT, all five tables are related to different primary keys and foreign keys. For example, among the LogIn, Faculty and Course tables, the `faculty_id` works as a key to relate these three tables together. It is a primary key in the Faculty table, but a foreign key in both LogIn and the Course tables. In order to update or delete data from any of those tables, one needs to follow the sequence above. As a case of updating or deleting a record against the database, the following data operations need to be performed:

1) First that record should be removed or deleted from the child tables, `LOGIN` and `COURSE` tables, respectively.
2) Then that record can be updated or deleted from the parent table, `FACULTY` table.
3) Finally that updated record can be reflected back into the child tables such as `LOGIN` and `COURSE` tables by the data updating operation. There are no any data actions for the data deleting operations for the child tables.

It would be terribly complicated if we try to update a completed record (includes updating the primary key) for an existing data in our sample database, and in practice, it is unnecessary to update a primary key for any record since the primary key has the same lifetime as a database. A better and popular way to do this kind of updating is to remove those undesired records and then insert new records with new primary keys. Therefore, in this Chapter, we will concentrate on updating existing data in our sample database without touching the primary key. For data deleting, we can delete a full record with the primary key involved, and all related records in the child tables will also be deleted since all keys in all tables have been set in a `Cascade On Delete` mode when we built these data tables for our sample database `CSE_DEPT` in Section 2.9.4 in Chapter 2.

7.1.2 Using TableAdapter.Update and TableAdapter.Delete Methods

Three typical TableAdapter's DBDirect methods are listed in Table 6.1 in Chapter 6. For your convenience, we redraw that table in this section again, which is shown in Table 7.1.

Both DBDirect methods, `TableAdapter.Update()` and `TableAdapter.Delete()`, need the original column values as the parameters when these methods are executed. The `TableAdapter.Update()` method needs both the original and the new column values to perform the data updating. Another point to be noted is that when the application uses the object to store the data, for instance, in our sample project we use textbox objects to store our data; thus, you should use this DBDirect method to perform the data manipulations against the database.

Table 7.1 TableAdapter DBDirect Methods.

TableAdapter DBDirect Method	Description
TableAdapter.Insert	Adds new records into a database allowing you to pass in individual column values as method parameters.
TableAdapter.Update	Updates existing records in a database. The Update method takes original and new column values as method parameters. The original values are used to locate the original record, and the new values are used to update that record. The TableAdapter.Update method is also used to reconcile changes in a dataset back to the database by taking a DataSet, DataTable, DataRow, or array of DataRows as method parameters.
TableAdapter.Delete	Deletes existing records from the database based on the original column values passed in as method parameters.

7.1.3 Update or Delete Data Against Database Using TableAdapter.Update Method

You can use the `TableAdapter.Update()` method to update or edit records in a database. This method provides several overloads that perform different operations depending on the parameters passed in. It is important to understand the results of calling these different method signatures.

To use this method to update or delete data against the database, one needs to perform the following two steps:

1) Change or delete records from the desired DataTable based on the selected data rows from the table in the DataSet
2) After the rows have been modified or deleted from the DataTable, call the `TableAdapter.Update()` method to reflect those modifications to the database. You can control the amount of data to be updated by passing an entire DataSet, a DataTable, an array of DataRows, or a single DataRow.

Table 7.2 describes the behavior of the various `TableAdapter.Update()` methods.

Table 7.2 Variations of Tableadapter.Update() method.

Update Method	Description
TableAdapter.Update(DataTable)	Attempt to save all changes in the DataTable to the database. (This includes removing any rows deleted from the table, adding rows inserted to the table, and updating any rows in the table that have changed)
TableAdapter.Update(DataSet)	Although the parameter takes a dataset, the TableAdapter attempts to save all changes in the TableAdapter's associated DataTable to the database. (This includes removing any rows deleted from the table, adding rows inserted in the table, and updating any rows in the table that have changed.)
TableAdapter.Update(DataRow)	Attempt to save changes in the indicated DataRow to the database.
TableAdapter.Update(DataRows())	Attempt to save changes in any row in the array of DataRows to the database.
TableAdapter.Update("new column values", "original column values")	Attempts to save changes in a single row that is identified by the original column values.

Different parameters or arguments can be passed into these five variations of this method. The parameter DataTable, which is located in a DataSet, is a data table mapping to a real data table in the database. When a whole DataTable is passed, any modification to that table will be updated and reflected in the associated table in the database. Similarly, if a DataSet is passed, all DataTables in that DataSet will be updated and reflected to those tables in the database.

The last variation of this method is to pass the original columns and the new columns of a data table to perform this updating. In fact, this method can be used as a DBDirect method to access the database to manipulate data.

In order to provide a detailed discussion and explanation in how to use these two methods to update or delete records against the database, a real example will be very helpful. Let us first create a new Visual Basic.NET project to handle these issues.

7.2 Update and Delete Data For Oracle 18c XE Database

We have provided a very detailed introduction about the Design Tools and Wizards in Visual Studio.NET in Section 5.2 in Chapter 5. The popular design tools and wizards include the DataSet, BindingSource, TableAdapter, Data Source window, Data Source Configuration window, and DataSet Designer. We need to use those tools to develop our data updating and deleting sample project based on the `InsertWizard` project developed in Chapter 6. First let us copy that project and do some modifications on that project to get our new project. The advantage of creating our new project in this way is that you do not need to redo the data source connection and configuration since those jobs have been performed in the previous project.

7.2.1 Create a New UpdataDeleteWizard Project

Open the Windows Explorer and create a new folder `Class DB Projects\Chapter 7` and perform the following operational steps to create this new project.

1) Open the Visual Studio.NET 2019 and go to `File|New Project` menu item, select the `Blank Solution` and click on the `Next` button.
2) Enter `UpdateDeleteWizard Solution` into the `Project name` box, then select the folder `Class DB Projects\Chapter 7` from the `Location` box and click on the `Create` button.
3) On the opened Studio window, go to the Solution Explorer window and right click on the new created solution and select the `Add|New Project` item from the popup menu to open the `Add a new project` wizard.
4) Select the `Windows Forms App (.NET Framework)` template under the `Recent project templates` and click on the `Next` button.
5) Enter `UpdateDeleteWizard Project` into the `Project name` box and click on the `Create` button to add this new project into our solution.
6) As the new project is opened, go to the Solution Explorer window and right click on the `Form1.vb`, and select `Delete` from the popup menu to remove this Form.
7) Now we need to add three Forms, Faculty Form, Course Form, and Student Form into this new project. In the Solution Explorer window, right click on the new created project `UpdateDeleteWizard Project` and select `Add|Existing Item` to open the Windows Explorer. Browse to the folder `VB Forms|Window` that is located at the Wiley ftp

site under the **Students** folder and select the following items by checking each of them one by one:

a) Course Form.vb,[1] Course Form.designer.vb,[2] Course Form.resx[3]
b) Faculty Form.vb,[1] Faculty Form.designer.vb,[2] Faculty Form.resx[3]
c) Student Form.vb,[1] Student Form.designer.vb,[2] Student Form.resx[3]

8) When adding these items, a trick is: first you have to add only the first item, say, **Faculty Form.vb**, then you must expand, say, **Faculty Form.vb** and click on the **FacultyForm** under that **Faculty Form.vb** folder to select it, then right click on the Project and select the **Add|Existing Item** to add the second, and then the third item.

9) Click on the **Add** button to add them into this new project.

Now some error messages may be shown up in the Error List, do not worry and we can fix them one by one.

First, we need to configure our database connection to build our DataSet object. Refer to Section 5.2.2.2 in Chapter 5 to complete this database connection and build our DataSet object, **CSE_DEPTDataSet**.

Next we need to rebuild three TableAdapter query functions, **FillByFacultyName()**, **FindFacultyIDByName()**, and **FillByFacultyID()** to erase the rest errors. Refer to Sections 5.4.7 and 5.4.9.1 in Chapter 5 to complete this query function rebuilding. The reason we need to rebuild these query functions is try to use the Select button's event procedure to confirm our data updating and deleting actions later.

Now you may need to open the **Faculty Form.designer.vb** and **Course Form. designer.vb** to replace all **SelectWizard** with **UpdateDeleteWizard** for all **CSE_DEPTDataSet** definitions. An easy way to do these corrections is just double click the related error message in the Error List to find those locations and make the corresponding replacements.

The final error is about the removing of the default Form, Form1, since we want to use our Faculty Form as the default and startup Form in this project. Go to the Solution Explorer window and open the App file **Application.Designer.vb**, which is under the folder **My Project|Application.myapp**. Change the last object for the **Me.MainForm =** line from **Form1** to **FacultyForm**, as shown below.

```
<Global.System.Diagnostics.DebuggerStepThroughAttribute()> _
Protected Overrides Sub OnCreateMainForm()
Me.MainForm = Global.UpdateDeleteWizard_Project.FacultyForm
\End Sub
```

Now you can go to **Build\Rebuild UpdateDeleteWizard Project** to rebuild this project and then go to **File|Save All** to save these changes for the new project.

7.2.2 Application User Interfaces

Recall that when we developed the project **SelectWizard**, there are five command buttons located in the Faculty form window: **Select**, **Insert**, **Update**, **Delete**, and **Back**. In this section, we need to use both **Update** and **Delete** buttons, exactly these two buttons' event procedures, to perform the data updating and deleting actions against the database. To check these updating and deleting actions, we can use the Faculty Form with some codes modifications to perform these confirmations for **FACULTY** table.

7.2.3 Validate Data Before the Data Updating and Deleting

This data validation can be neglected because when we performed a data query by clicking on the `Select` button, and the retrieved data should be a complete set of data and can be displayed in the Faculty Form window. This means that all textboxes have been filled by the related faculty information and no one is empty, no matter we do some modifications or not, all textboxes is full. So this prevalidation for the data updating and deleting can be ignored.

7.2.4 Build the Update and Delete Queries

As we mentioned, two methods will be discussed in this part: one is to update or delete records using the TableAdapter DBDirect method and the other one is to use the `TableAdapter. Update()` method to update modified records from the DataSet first and then in the database. First, let us concentrate on the first method.

Now let us build our data updating and deleting queries using the TableAdapter Query Configuration Wizard and Query Builder.

7.2.4.1 Configure the TableAdapter and Build the Data Updating Query

Open the Data Source window and connect to our sample database CSE_DEPT. Then perform the following operations to build the data updating query:

1) On the opened wizard, click on the `Edit the DataSet with Designer` icon that is located at the second left on the toolbar in the Data Source window to open this DataSet Designer.
2) Right click on the bottom item of the `FACULTY` table and select the **Add | Query** item from the popup menu to open the TableAdapter Query Configuration Wizard.
3) Keep the default selection `Use SQL statements` unchanged and click on the `Next` to go to the next wizard.
4) Select and check the `UPDATE` item from this wizard since we need to perform updating data query and then click on the `Next` button again to continue.
5) Click on the `Query Builder` button since we want to build our updating query. The opened Query Builder wizard is shown in Figure 7.1.
6) Remove all contents from the `faculty_id` and `faculty_name` rows under the `Filter` and `Or` columns. Uncheck the `Set` checkbox from the `faculty_id` row under the column `Set`, enter a question mark (`?`) to the `faculty_id` row under the column `Filter`, and press the `Enter` key from the keyboard. Change the name of the parameter `:Param1` to `:fid` for the `Filer` column in the `faculty_id` row.
7) Remove all rows under the last row, `fimage`, and your finished query builder wizard should match one that is shown in Figure 7.1.
8) Click on the `OK` button to go to the next wizard. Click on the `Next` to confirm this query and continue to the next step.
9) Modify the query function name from the default one to the `UpdateFaculty` and click on the `Next` to go to the last wizard.
10) Click on the `Finish` button to complete this query building and close this wizard.

7.2.4.2 Build the Data Deleting Query

Open the `Edit DataSet with Designer` wizard and right click on the last item from the `FACULTY` table and select the `Add Query` item to open TableAdapter Query

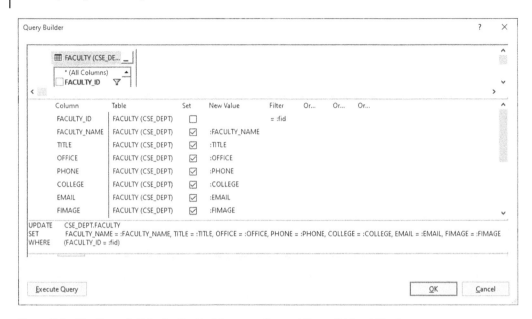

Figure 7.1 The Query Builder for the Update query. *Source:* Microsoft Visual Studio.

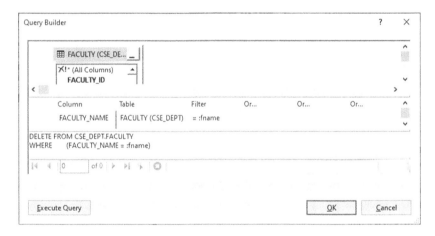

Figure 7.2 The Query Builder for the Delete query. *Source:* Microsoft Visual Studio.

Configuration Wizard. Perform the following operations to build the data deleting query:

1) On the opened wizard, keep the default selection **Use SQL statements** unchanged and click on the **Next** button to go to the next wizard.
2) Select and check the **DELETE** item from this wizard since we need to perform deleting data query. Then click on the **Next** button again to continue.
3) Click on the **Query Builder** button since we want to build our deleting query. The opened Query Builder wizard is shown in Figure 7.2.
4) Delete all rows from the mid-pane. Then click on the first cell just under the **Column** box, click on the drop-down arrow and select the **FACULTY_NAME** item.

5) Enter a question mark (**?**) into to the **Filter** column along the **faculty_name** row and press the **Enter** key on the keyboard.
6) Change the name of the dynamic parameter **:Param1** to **:fname**, and press the **Enter** key from the keyboard.
7) Your finished query builder should match one that is shown in Figure 7.2. Click on the **OK** button to go to the next wizard.
8) Click on the **Next** button to confirm this query and continue to the next step.
9) Modify the query function name to the **DeleteFaculty** and click on the **Next** button.
10) Click on the **Finish** button to complete this query building and close the wizard. Immediately you can find that a new query function **DeleteFaculty** has been added into the Faculty TableAdapter as the last item.

Next let us develop the codes to call these built query methods to perform the related data updating and deleting actions.

7.2.5 Develop Codes to Update Data Using the TableAdapter DBDirect Method

To perform the data updating using the built query method, some modifications to the original codes in the Faculty form are necessary. We divided these modifications into two subsections: codes modifications and codes creations.

7.2.5.1 Modifications of the Codes
The first modification is to modify the codes inside the **Form_Load()** event procedure in the Faculty Form class, exactly is to add two new updating methods and a user-defined subroutine **CurrentFaculty()**, into the Query Method combo box:

1) **TableAdapter DBDirect Method**
2) **TableAdapter.Update Method**

Open this event procedure and add those items into the **Form_Load()** event procedure using the **Add()** method. Your modified codes for this procedure have been highlighted with bold style and shown in Figure 7.3.

The second modification is to generate a new user-defined subroutine **CurrentFaculty()** as we did for the last project to get the most updated faculty members from the **FACULTY** table in our database and display them in the Faculty Name combo box **ComboName**.

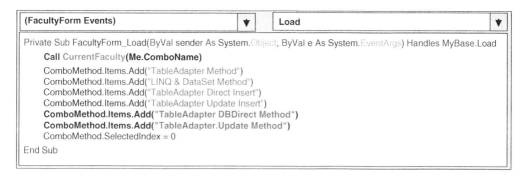

Figure 7.3 The modified codes for the Form_Load event procedure.

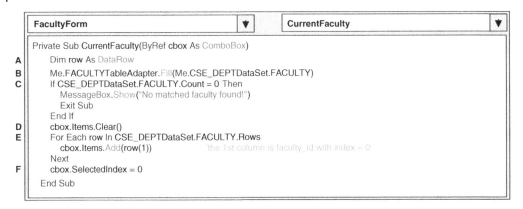

| FacultyForm | ▼ | CurrentFaculty | ▼ |

```
        Private Sub CurrentFaculty(ByRef cbox As ComboBox)
A           Dim row As DataRow
B           Me.FACULTYTableAdapter.Fill(Me.CSE_DEPTDataSet.FACULTY)
C           If CSE_DEPTDataSet.FACULTY.Count = 0 Then
               MessageBox.Show("No matched faculty found!")
               Exit Sub
            End If
D           cbox.Items.Clear()
E           For Each row In CSE_DEPTDataSet.FACULTY.Rows
               cbox.Items.Add(row(1))            'the 1st column is faculty_id with index = 0
            Next
F           cbox.SelectedIndex = 0
        End Sub
```

Figure 7.4   The codes for the user defined subroutine CurrentFaculty().

Open the code window of the Faculty Form and enter the codes shown in Figure 7.4 into this window to build our user-defined subroutine **CurrentFaculty()**.

Let us have a closer look at this piece of codes to see how it works.

A) First, a DataRow object **row** is created, and it will be used as a loop variable to get all faculty rows and add each of them into the Faculty Name combo box later.

B) The **Fill()** method on the **FACULTYTableAdapter** is executed to retrieve all faculty records from the database and fill them into the **FACULTY** table in our DataSet.

C) By checking the **Count** property of our filled **FACULTY** table, which should equal to the number of rows that have been filled successfully, we can confirm this fill function, either success (return's number > 0) or failed (return's number = 0). If the latter case occurred, a warning message is displayed to indicate this case and the subroutine is exited.

D) If this fill is success, the Faculty Name combo box is first cleared to make it ready to receive all faculty members.

E) A For Each loop is used to repeatedly retrieve each faculty name located at the first column of the filled **FACULTY** table and add each of them into the combo box by using the **Add()** method one by one.

F) Finally, the first faculty name is selected by setting the **SelectedIndex** as 0.

7.2.5.2   Creations of the Codes

The main coding process to perform this data updating is developed inside the **Update** button's Click event procedure in the Faculty Form window. Open this event procedure and enter the codes that are shown in Figure 7.5 into this event procedure.

Let us have a closer look at this piece of new added codes to see how it works.

A) All objects and variables used in this event procedure are declared here first. An instance of the FacultyTableAdapter class is created first since we need to use it to perform the data updating. A new row object of **FacultyRow** class is also created since we need this object to update the data in the DataSet to the table in the database later when we use another method, **TableAdapter.Update()**, to perform the data updating. The local integer variable **intUpdate** is used to hold the returned value of calling the TableAdapter DBDirect method to update the database. The local String variable **strFacultyID** is used to hold the returned **faculty_id** value when executing the second method, **TableAdapter.Update()**, to update the database in the next step.

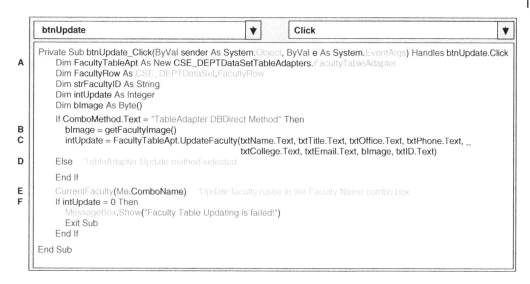

| btnUpdate ▼ | Click ▼ |

```
     Private Sub btnUpdate_Click(ByVal sender As System.Object, ByVal e As System.EventArgs) Handles btnUpdate.Click
A       Dim FacultyTableApt As New CSE_DEPTDataSetTableAdapters.FacultyTableAdapter
        Dim FacultyRow As CSE_DEPTDataSet.FacultyRow
        Dim strFacultyID As String
        Dim intUpdate As Integer
        Dim bImage As Byte()

        If ComboMethod.Text = "TableAdapter DBDirect Method" Then
B           bImage = getFacultyImage()
C           intUpdate = FacultyTableApt.UpdateFaculty(txtName.Text, txtTitle.Text, txtOffice.Text, txtPhone.Text, _
                                      txtCollege.Text, txtEmail.Text, bImage, txtID.Text)
D       Else    'TableAdapter Update method selected

        End If

E       CurrentFaculty(Me.ComboName)    'Update faculty name in the Faculty Name combo box
F       If intUpdate = 0 Then
            MessageBox.Show("Faculty Table Updating is failed!")
            Exit Sub
        End If

     End Sub
```

Figure 7.5 The codes for the Update command button's Click event procedure.

B) The user defined subroutine `getFacultyImage()` is called to get the image for the faculty member to be updated.

C) If the user selected the first method, `TableAdapter DBDirect` method, to perform this data updating, the updating function we built in Section 7.2.4.1 is called to update the selected faculty. This function will return an integer to indicate whether this function calling is successful or not. The value returned is equal to the number of rows that have been successfully updated in the database.

D) If the user selected the second method, `TableAdapter.Update()`, to update this record, the related codes that will be developed later are executed to first update that record in the DataSet and then update it to the database.

E) For the validation purpose, we need to update the Faculty Name combo box, `CmboName`, with the current faculty members by calling the user defined subroutine `CurrentFaculty()`.

F) If the returned value of executing the updating function is equal to zero, which means that no row or record has been updated after calling that query function, a warning message is displayed and the procedure is exited.

Now let's continue to develop the codes for the second data updating method.

7.2.6 Develop Codes to Update Data Using the TableAdapter.Update Method

Open the `Update` button's Click event procedure if it is not opened and add the codes that are shown in Figure 7.6 into this event procedure. Let us take a closer look at this piece of new added codes to see how it works. The codes we developed in the previous step are highlighted by the gray color as the background.

Let's have a closer look at this piece of codes to see how it works.

A) In order to update a selected row from the Faculty table in the DataSet, we need first to identify that row. Visual Studio.NET provides a default method, which is defined as `FindBy()`, to do that. However, that method needs a primary key as a criterion to perform a query to locate the desired row from the table. In our case, the primary key for our Faculty table is the

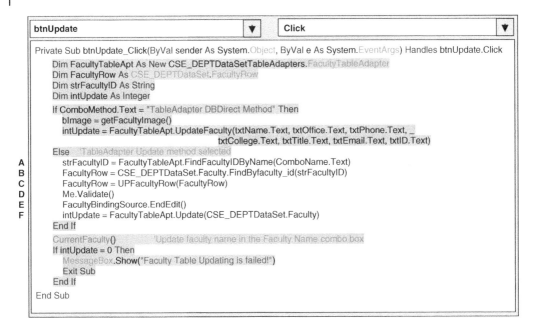

Figure 7.6 The codes for the second data updating method.

faculty_id. To find the **faculty_id**, we can use a query function **FindFacultyIDByName()** we built in Section 5.4.9.1 in Chapter 5 with the Faculty Name as a query criterion. One point to be noted to run this function is that the parameter Faculty Name must be old faculty name because in order to update a faculty row, we must first find the old faculty row based on the old name. So the content in the combo box Faculty Name, **ComboName.Text**, is used as the old faculty name.

B) After the **faculty_id** is found, the default method **FindByfaculty_id()** is executed to locate the desired row from the Faculty table, and the desired data row is returned and assigned to the local variable **FacultyRow**.

C) A user-defined function **UPFacultyRow()** is called to assign all pieces of updated faculty information to the desired rows. In this way, the faculty information, exactly a row in the Faculty table in the DataSet, is updated.

D) The **Validate()** command closes out the editing of a control, in our case, closes any editing for textbox control in the Faculty form.

E) The **EndEdit()** method of the binding source writes any edited data in the controls back to the record in the DataSet. In our case, any updated data entered into the textbox controls will be reflected to the associated column in the DataSet.

F) Finally the **Update()** method of the TableAdapter sends updated data back to the database. The argument of this method can be a whole DataSet, a DataTable in the DataSet, or a DataRow in a DataTable. In our case, we used the Faculty DataTable as the argument for this method.

The detailed codes for the user-defined function **UPFacultyRow()** are shown in Figure 7.7. The functionality of this function is straightforward and easy to be understood.

The argument of this function is a DataRow object, and it is passed by a reference to the function. The advantage of passing an argument in this way is that any modifications performed to DataRow object inside the function can be returned to the calling procedure without needing another

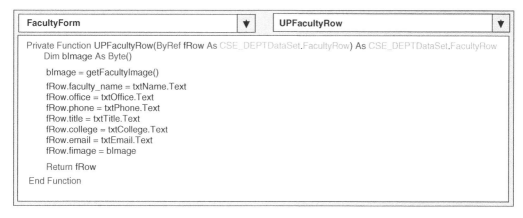

Figure 7.7   The codes for the user-defined function UPFacultyRow().

returned variable to be created. The updated faculty information stored in the associated textbox is assigned to associated column of the DataRow in the Faculty table in the DataSet. In this way, the selected DataRow in the Faculty table is updated.

At this point, we finished the coding development for two methods to update the data in a database. Next we discuss how to delete data from the database.

7.2.7   Develop Codes to Delete Data Using the TableAdapter DBDirect Method

To delete data from a database, you can use either the TableAdapter DBDirect method **TableAdapter.Delete()** or the **TableAdapter.Update()** method. Or, if your application does not use TableAdapters, you can use the run time object method such as ExecuteNonQuery to create command object to delete data from a database.

The **TableAdapter.Update()** method is typically used when your application uses DataSets to store data, whereas the **TableAdapter.Delete()** method is typically used when your application uses objects, for example in our case we used textboxes, to store data.

Open the Faculty form window and double click on the **Delete** button to open its event procedure. Enter the codes that are shown in Figure 7.8 into this event procedure.

A) All data components and objects as well as variables used in this event procedure are declared and created here. The object of the FacultyTableAdapter class is created first since we need to use its **Update()** and **Delete()** methods to delete data later. A button object of the **MessageboxButtons** class is created, and we need to use these two buttons to confirm the data deleting later. The **FacultyRow** is used to locate the DataRow in the Faculty DataTable, and it is also used for the second deleting method. The local variable **Answer** is an instance of DialogResult class, and it is used to hold the returned value of calling the MessageBox function. This variable can be replaced by an integer variable if you like.

B) First a MessageBox function is called to confirm that a data deleting will be performed from the Faculty data table.

C) If the returned value of calling this MessageBox function is **Yes,** which means that the user has confirmed that this data deleting is fine, the data deleting will be performed in the next step.

D) If the user selected the first method, the TableAdapter DBDirect method, the query function we built in Section 7.2.4.2 will be called to perform the data deleting from the Faculty table in the database.

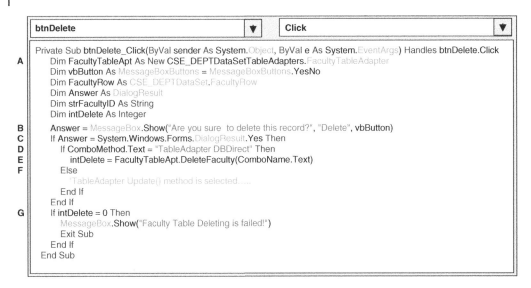

```
btnDelete                                      ▼      Click                                          ▼

    Private Sub btnDelete_Click(ByVal sender As System.Object, ByVal e As System.EventArgs) Handles btnDelete.Click
A       Dim FacultyTableApt As New CSE_DEPTDataSetTableAdapters.FacultyTableAdapter
        Dim vbButton As MessageBoxButtons = MessageBoxButtons.YesNo
        Dim FacultyRow As CSE_DEPTDataSet.FacultyRow
        Dim Answer As DialogResult
        Dim strFacultyID As String
        Dim intDelete As Integer
B       Answer = MessageBox.Show("Are you sure  to delete this record?", "Delete", vbButton)
C       If Answer = System.Windows.Forms.DialogResult.Yes Then
D          If ComboMethod.Text = "TableAdapter DBDirect" Then
E             intDelete = FacultyTableApt.DeleteFaculty(ComboName.Text)
F          Else
              'TableAdapter Update() method is selected.....
           End If
        End If
G       If intDelete = 0 Then
           MessageBox.Show("Faculty Table Deleting is failed!")
           Exit Sub
        End If
    End Sub
```

Figure 7.8   The codes for the Delete button's Click event procedure.

E) The execution result of the first method is stored in the local variable intDelete.

F) If the user selected the second method, **TableAdapter.Update()**, the associated codes that will be developed in the next step will be executed to delete data first from the DataTable in the DataSet and then from the data table in the database by executing the **Update()** method.

G) The returned value of calling either the **TableAdapter.Delete()** method or the **TableAdapter.Update()** method is an integer, and it is stored in the variable **intDelete**. The value of this returned data is equal to the number of deleted data rows in the database or deleted DataRows in the DataSet. A returned zero means that no data row has been deleted and this data deleting has failed. In that case, a warning message is displayed and the procedure is exited.

Now let's develop the codes for the data deleting using the second method.

7.2.8   Develop Codes to Delete Data Using the TableAdapter.Update Method

Add the codes that are shown in Figure 7.9 into the **Delete** button's Click event procedure, exactly into the **Else** block for the second deleting method. The codes we developed in the previous step have been highlighted with gray background color.

Let us have a close look at this piece of new added codes to see how it works.

A) To identify the DataRow to be deleted from the DataTable, the user built query method **FindFacultyIDByName()** is utilized. Since that method needs to use the **faculty_id** as the query qualification, therefore we need first retrieve it.

B) After the **faculty_id** is found, the default method **FindByfaculty_id()** is executed to locate the desired DataRow from the Faculty table, and the desired DataRow is returned and assigned to the local variable **FacultyRow**.

C) The **Delete()** method of the **FacultyRow** is executed to delete the selected DataRow from the Faculty DataTable in the DataSet.

D) The **TableAdapter.Update()** method is executed to update that deleted DataRow to the data row in the database.

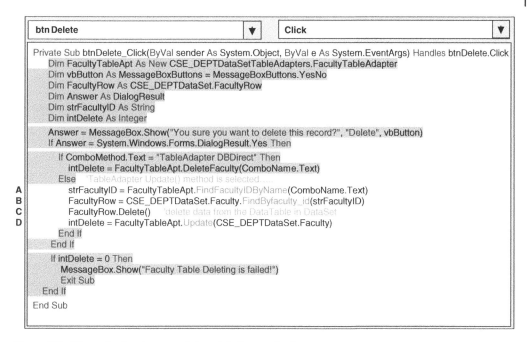

| btn Delete | ▼ | Click | ▼ |

```
Private Sub btnDelete_Click(ByVal sender As System.Object, ByVal e As System.EventArgs) Handles btnDelete.Click
    Dim FacultyTableApt As New CSE_DEPTDataSetTableAdapters.FacultyTableAdapter
    Dim vbButton As MessageBoxButtons = MessageBoxButtons.YesNo
    Dim FacultyRow As CSE_DEPTDataSet.FacultyRow
    Dim Answer As DialogResult
    Dim strFacultyID As String
    Dim intDelete As Integer

    Answer = MessageBox.Show("You sure you want to delete this record?", "Delete", vbButton)
    If Answer = System.Windows.Forms.DialogResult.Yes Then

        If ComboMethod.Text = "TableAdapter DBDirect" Then
            intDelete = FacultyTableApt.DeleteFaculty(ComboName.Text)
        Else        'TableAdapter Update() method is selected
            strFacultyID = FacultyTableApt.FindFacultyIDByName(ComboName.Text)
            FacultyRow = CSE_DEPTDataSet.Faculty.FindByfaculty_id(strFacultyID)
            FacultyRow.Delete()        'delete data from the DataTable in DataSet
            intDelete = FacultyTableApt.Update(CSE_DEPTDataSet.Faculty)
        End If
    End If

    If intDelete = 0 Then
        MessageBox.Show("Faculty Table Deleting is failed!")
        Exit Sub
    End If
End Sub
```

A
B
C
D

Figure 7.9 The codes for the second data deleting method.

Before we can run the project to test our codes for the data updating and deleting, let us first complete the codes for the data validations for those data actions. In fact, we can use the **Select** button's event procedure to do this validation.

Another issue is the Startup Form, which means that which Form should be displayed first as the project runs. Because in this project we only have three Forms such as Faculty Form, Course Form and Student Form; thus, we need to select which one should be run first as the project runs. To do this selection, go to **Project|UpdateDeleteWizard Project Properties** menu item to open the Project Properties wizard, then locate the Startup form box and select the **FacultyForm** from that box as our startup Form.

7.2.9 Validate the Data After the Data Updating and Deleting

As we mentioned in the previous section, we do not need to develop any code for these data validations since we can use the codes we developed for the **Select** button's Click event procedure to perform these validations.

Now let us run the project to test our codes for the data updating and data deleting. Make sure that the updating faculty photo file **Michael.jpg** has been stored at a folder in your C driver. This photo file can be found from the folder **Instructors\Images\Faculty** located in the Wiley ftp site under the **Instructors** folder (refer to Figure 1.2 in Chapter 1). Now run the project, finish the login process, and then open the Faculty form. Keep the default faculty member **Ying Bai** in the Faculty Name combobox selected and click the **Select** button to query detailed information for this faculty.

To update this faculty record, you can use either the **TableAdapter DBDirect** or the **TableAdapter.Update** method as you like by selecting it from the **Query Method** combo

Figure 7.10 The running status of the Updated Faculty Form window. *Source:* Microsoft Visual Studio.

box. Keep the Faculty ID unchanged and then enter the following information to the associated textboxes as an updated Faculty record:

- **Michael Bai**   Faculty Name textbox
- **Professor**   Title textbox
- **MTC-255**   Office textbox
- **750-378-1155**   Phone textbox
- **Duke University**   College textbox
- **mbai@college.edu**   Email textbox
- **Michael.jpg**   Faculty Image textbox

Your finished new faculty information window should match one that is shown in Figure 7.10.

Click on the **Update** button to select the desired faculty image and try to update this faculty record in the Faculty table. To confirm this data updating action, click on the drop-down arrow of the Faculty Name combo box and you will find that the updated faculty name **Michael Bai** has been in there. Select this name and select the **TableAdapter Method** from the **Query Method** combo box and click on the **Select** button to retrieve this updated faculty record and display it in the associated textboxes. You can find that the original faculty record is indeed updated, which is shown in Figure 7.11.

To perform a deleting action, we want to delete an inserted faculty member, **Mhamed Jones**, which was inserted into the Faculty table in our sample database in Section 6.4.1.3 in Chapter 6. Select that faculty from the **Faculty Name** combo box and choose either the **TableAdapter DBDirect** or the **TableAdapter.Update** method from the Query Method combo box and then click on the **Delete** button. A MessageBox is displayed to ask you to confirm this deletion. Click on **Yes** if you want to delete it. Then you can validate that deletion by clicking on the **Select** button to try to retrieve that deleted record. What happened after you clicked on the **Select** button? A message "**No matched faculty found**" is displayed to indicate that that faculty record has been deleted from the database.

One point to be noted is that after you update the faculty name by changing the content of the Faculty Name textbox, be sure that you go to the Faculty Name combo box to select the modified

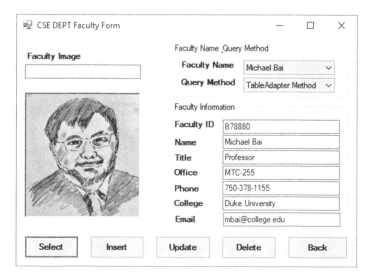

Figure 7.11 The updated faculty record. *Source:* Microsoft Visual Studio.

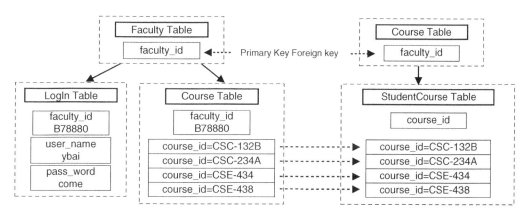

Figure 7.12 The relationships among tables.

faculty name to perform the data validation. You need to perform the same operations if you want to delete that record from the database. The key is that the content of the faculty name textbox may differ with the content of the Faculty Name combo box, and the former is an updated faculty name and the latter is an old faculty name if the faculty name is updated.

If you want to delete any faculty member from our original Faculty table (not new inserted), for example, delete the faculty **Ying Bai** from the Faculty table, it is highly recommended to recover the deleted faculty member since we want to keep our database neat and complete.

An import issue for this data recovery is the order of recovering these deleted records. Figure 7.12 shows the relationships between the Faculty table and other tables in our sample database CSE_DEPT. Based on this relationship, you should

- First recover the records in the parent table (Faculty and Course tables),
- Then recover the records in the child tables (LogIn and StudentCourse tables).

Follow the table order in Figure 7.12 and refer to Tables 7.3~7.6 to complete these records recovery.

Table 7.3   The data to be recovered in the Faculty table.

faculty_id	faculty_name	title	office	phone	college	email	fimage
B78880	Ying Bai	Associate Professor	MTC-211	750-378-1148	Florida Atlantic University	ybai@college.edu	NULL

Table 7.4   The data to be recovered in the LogIn table.

user_name	pass_word	faculty_id	student_id
ybai	come	B78880	NULL

Table 7.5   The data to be recovered in the Course table.

course_id	course	credit	classroom	schedule	enrollment	faculty_id
CSC-132B	Introduction to Programming	3	TC-302	T-H: 1:00-2:25 PM	21	B78880
CSC-234A	Data Structure & Algorithms	3	TC-302	M-W-F: 9:00-9:55 AM	25	B78880
CSE-434	Advanced Electronics Systems	3	TC-213	M-W-F: 1:00-1:55 PM	26	B78880
CSE-438	Advd Logic & Microprocessor	3	TC-213	M-W-F: 11:00-11:55 AM	35	B78880

Table 7.6   The data to be recovered in the StudentCourse table.

s_course_id	student_id	course_id	credit	major
1005	T77896	CSC-234A	3	CS/IS
1009	A78835	CSE-434	3	CE
1014	A78835	CSE-438	3	CE
1016	A97850	CSC-132B	3	ISE
1017	A97850	CSC-234A	3	ISE

You can access the sample database via the Server Explorer window to perform this recovery process. A complete project `UpdateDeleteWizard Project` can be found from the folder `Class DB Projects\Chapter 7\UpdateDeleteWizard Solution` that is located at the Wiley ftp site under the `Students` folder (refer to Figure 1.2 in Chapter 1).

Part II: Data Updating and Deleting with Runtime Objects

Updating or deleting data against the database using the run time objects method is a flexible and professional way to perform the data modification jobs in Visual Basic.NET environment. Compared with the method we discussed in Part I, in which Visual Studio.NET Design Tools and Wizards are utilized to update or delete data against the database, the run time objects method provides more sophisticated techniques to do this job efficiently and conveniently although a more complicated coding job is needed.

Relatively speaking, the methods we discussed in the first part are easy to learn and coding, but some limitations are existed for those methods. First, each TableAdapter can only access the associated data table to perform data actions such as updating or deleting data against that table only. Second, each query function built by using the TableAdapter Query Configuration Wizard can only perform a single query such as data updating or deleting. Third, after the query function is built, no modifications can be made to that function dynamically, which means that the only times when you can modify that query function are either before the project runs or after the project runs. In other words, you cannot modify that query function during the project runs.

To overcome those shortcomings, we will discuss how to update or delete data using the run time object method in this part.

Basically, you need to use the TableAdapter to perform data actions again the database if you develop your applications using the Visual Studio.NET Design Tools and Wizards in the design time. But you should use the DataAdapter to make those data manipulations if you develop your project using the run time objects method.

7.3 The Run Time Objects Method

We have provided a very detailed introduction and discussion about the run time objects method in Section 5.5 in Chapter 5. Refer to that section for more detailed information about this method. For your convenience, we highlight some important points and general methodology of this method as well as some keynotes in using this method to perform the data updating and deleting again the databases.

As you know, ADO.NET provides different classes to help users to develop professional data-driven applications by using the different methods to perform specific data actions such as updating data and deleting data. Among them, two popular methods are widely applied:

1) Update or delete records from the desired data table in the DataSet and then call the `DataAdapter.Update()` method to update the updated or deleted records from the table in the DataSet to the table in the database.
2) Build the update or delete command using the Command object and then call the command's method `ExecuteNonQuery()` to update or delete records against the database. Or you can assign the built command object to the UpdateCommand or DeleteCommand properties of the DataAdapter and call the `ExecuteNonQuery()` method from the UpdateCommand or DeleteCommand property.

The first method is to use the so-called DataSet-DataAdapter method to build a data-driven application. DataSet and DataTable classes can have different roles when they are implemented in a real application. Multiple DataTables can be embedded into a DataSet, and each table can be filled, inserted, updated, and deleted by using the different properties of a DataAdapter such as the SelectCommand, InsertCommand, UpdateCommand, or DeleteCommand when the DataAdapter's `Update()` method is executed. The DataAdapter will perform the associated operations based on the modifications you made for each table in the DataSet. For example, if you deleted rows from a table in the DataSet, and then you call this DataAdapter's `Update()` method. This method will perform a DeleteCommand based on your modifications. This method is relative simple since you do not need to call some specific methods such as the `ExecuteNonQuery()` to complete these data queries. But this simplicity brings some limitations for your applications. For instance, you cannot access different data tables individually to perform multiple data-specific operations. This method is very similar to the second method we discussed in Part I, so we will not continue to provide any discussion for this method in this part.

The second method is to allow you to use each object individually, which means that you do not have to use the DataAdapter to access the Command object, or use the DataTable with DataSet together. This provides more flexibility. In this method, no DataAdapter or DataSet is needed and you only need to create a new Command object with a new Connection object and then build a query statement and attach some useful parameter into that query for the new created Command object. You can update or delete data against any data table by calling the `ExecuteNonQuery()` method that belongs to the Command class. We will concentrate on this method in this part.

In this section, we provide a sample project named `OracleUpdataDeleteRTObject Project`, to illustrate how to update or delete records against the Oracle database using the run time object method.

In addition to the sample project, we will also discuss the data updating and deleting against our sample databases using the LINQ to DataSet query method. A sample project `LINQUpdateDelete Project` will be developed in this Chapter to discuss how to build an actual data-driven project to update and delete data against our sample databases using the LINQ to DataSet query method.

7.4 Update and Delete Data for Oracle Database Using the Run Time Objects

Now let us first develop the sample project `OracleUpdataDeleteRTObject Project` to update and delete data against the Oracle database using the run time object method. Recall in Sections 5.6.5~5.6.7 in Chapter 5, we discussed how to select data for the Faculty, Course, and Student Form windows using the run time object method. For the Faculty Form, a regular run time selecting query is performed, and for the Course Form, a run time joined table selecting query is developed. For the Student table, the stored procedures are used to perform the run time data query.

Similarly in this part, we divide this discussion into two sections:

1) Update and delete data against the Faculty table via the Faculty Form window using the run time object method.
2) Update and delete data against the Faculty table via the Faculty Form using the run time stored procedure method.

In order to avoid the duplication on the coding process, we will modify an existing project `OracleInsertRTObject Project` we developed in Chapter 6 to create our new project `OracleUpdataDeleteRTObject Project` used in this section.

Open the Windows Explorer and create a new folder such as `Class DB Projects\ Chapter 7` at your root drive and then browse to the folder `Class DB Projects\`Chapter 6 that is located at the Wiley ftp site under the `Students` folder (refer to Figure 1.2 in Chapter 1). Copy the entire solution `OracleInsertRTObject Solution` and project `OracleInsert-RTObject Project` to the new folder `Class DB Projects\Chapter 7` we just created. Change the names of the solution and project folder from `OracleInsertRTObject` to `OracleUpdataDeleteRTObject`. Also change the project name from `OracleInsert-RTObject Project.vbproj` to `OracleUpdateDeleteRTObject Project.vbproj`, from

`OracleInsertRTObject Project.vbproj.user` to `OracleUpdateDeleteRTObject Project.vbproj.user`. Then double click on the `OracleUpdataDeleteRTObject Project.vbproj` to open this project.

On the opened project, perform the following modifications to get our desired project:

- Go to `Project|OracleUpdataDeleteRTObject Project Properties` menu item to open the project's property window. Change the `Assembly name` and the `Root namespace` from `OracleInsertRTObject Project` to `OracleUpdataDeleteRTObject Project`, respectively.
- Click on the `Assembly Information` button to open the Assembly Information wizard. Change the `Title` and the `Product` to `OracleUpdataDeleteRTObject Project`. Click on the `OK` button to close this wizard.

Go to the `File|Save All` to save those modifications. Now we are ready to develop our graphic user interfaces based on our new project `OracleUpdataDeleteRTObject Project`.

7.4.1 Update Data Against the Faculty Table in the Oracle Database

Let us first discuss updating data against the Faculty table for the Oracle database. To update data against the Faculty data table, we do not need to add any new Windows Form and we can use the Faculty Form as the user interface. We need to perform the following two steps to complete this data updating action:

1) Develop codes to update the faculty data
2) Validate the data updating

First, let us develop the codes for our data updating action.

7.4.1.1 Develop Codes to Update the Faculty Data

Open the `Update` button's Click event procedure on the Faculty form window by double clicking on the `Update` button from the Faculty Form window and enter the codes that are shown in the top of Figure 7.13 into this event procedure.

Let's take a closer look at this piece of codes to see how it works.

A) The Update query string is defined first at the beginning of this procedure. Seven columns (except the column `FACULTY_ID`) in the Faculty table are input parameters. The dynamic parameter `:fid` represents the `FACULTY_ID`, which works as the query qualification and should not be updated.

B) Some data components and local variables are declared here such as the Command object and `intUpdate`. The `intUpdate` is used to hold the returned data value from calling of the `ExecuteNonQuery()` method.

C) The Command object is initialized and built using the connection object and the parameter object.

D) A user-defined subroutine `UpdateParameters()` is called to add all updated parameters into the Command object.

E) Then the `ExecuteNonQuery()` method of the Command class is executed to update the faculty table. The running result of this method is returned and stored in the local variable `intUpdate`.

F) The Command object is released after this data updating.

Figure 7.13 The codes for the data updating operation.

G) The updated faculty name is added into the **Faculty Name** combo box, and this name is used for the validation purpose later.

H) The returned value from calling the **ExecuteNonQuery()** method is equal to the number of rows that have been updated in the Faculty table. A zero means that no row has been updated, an error message is displayed and the procedure is exited if this situation occurred.

I) The detailed codes for the user defined subroutine procedure **UpdateParameters()** are shown in the lower part in Figure 7.13. Seven pieces of updated faculty information, including the updated faculty image, and the query qualification **FACULTY_ID** are assigned to the associated columns in the Faculty table.

At this point, we finished the coding process for the data updating operation for the Faculty table. Next let us take care of the data validation after this data updating to confirm that our data updating is successful.

7.4.1.2 Validate the Data Updating

We do not need to add any new window form to perform this data validation, but instead we can use the Faculty Form to perform this job. By selecting the updated faculty name from the **Faculty Name** combo box and clicking on the **Select** button on the Faculty Form window, we can perform the selection query to retrieve the updated faculty record from the database and display it on the Faculty Form.

Before we can run the project to test the data updating function, we want to complete the coding process for the data deleting operation.

7.4.2 Delete Data From the Faculty Table in the Oracle Database

As we mentioned in the previous section, to delete a faculty record from our database, we have to follow two steps listed below:

1) First, delete records from the child tables (LogIn and Course tables)
2) Second, delete record from the parent table (Faculty table)

The data deleting function can be performed by using the **Delete** button's Click event procedure in the Faculty Form window. Therefore, the main coding job for this function is performed inside that procedure.

7.4.2.1 Develop Codes to Delete Data

Open the **Delete** button's Click event procedure by double clicking on the **Delete** button from the Faculty Form window and enter the codes that are shown in Figure 7.14 into this event procedure.

Let's have a closer look at this piece of codes to see how it works.

A) The deleting query string is declared first at the beginning of this procedure. The only parameter is the faculty name. Although the primary key of the Faculty table is FACULTY_ID, but in order to make it convenient to the user, the faculty name is used as the criterion for this data deleting query. A potential problem of using the name as criterion in this query is that no duplicated faculty name can be used in the Faculty table for this application. In other words, each

```
btn Delete                                              Click

   Private Sub btnDelete_Click(ByVal sender As System.Object, ByVal e As System.EventArgs) Handles btnDelete.Click
A     Dim cmdString As String = "DELETE FROM Faculty WHERE (faculty_name = :fname)"
B     Dim vbButton As MessageBoxButtons = MessageBoxButtons.YesNo
C     Dim oraCommand As New OracleCommand
      Dim Answer As DialogResult
      Dim intDelete As Integer

D     Answer = MessageBox.Show("Are you sure  to delete this record?", "Delete", vbButton)

E     If Answer = System.Windows.Forms.DialogResult.Yes Then
         oraCommand.Connection = oraConnection
         oraCommand.CommandType = CommandType.Text
         oraCommand.CommandText = cmdString
F        oraCommand.Parameters.Add(":fname", OracleDbType.Char).Value = ComboName.Text
G        intDelete = oraCommand.ExecuteNonQuery()
H        oraCommand.Dispose()
         oraCommand = Nothing

I        If intDelete = 0 Then
            MessageBox.Show("The data Deleting is failed")
            Exit Sub
         End If

J        For intDelete = 0 To 6               'Clean up the Faculty textbox array
            FacultyTextBox(intDelete).Text = String.Empty
         Next intDelete
      End If
   End Sub
```

Figure 7.14 The codes for the data deleting query.

faculty name must be unique in the Faculty table. A solution to this problem is that we can use the FACULTY_ID as this query criterion in the future.

B) A MessageBoxs button's object is created, and this object is used to display both buttons in the MessageBox, **Yes** and **No**, when the project runs.

C) Some useful components and local variables are declared here. The data type of the variable **Answer** is DialogResult, but one can use an integer to replace it.

D) As the **Delete** button is clicked when the project runs, first a MessageBox is displayed to confirm that the user wants to delete the selected data from the Faculty table.

E) If the user's answer to the MessageBox is **Yes**, then the deleting operation begins to be processed. The Command object is initialized and built by using the Connection object and the command string we defined at the beginning of this procedure.

F) The dynamic parameter **:fname** is replaced by the real parameter, the faculty name stored in the **Faculty Name** combo box. A key point to be noted is that you must use the faculty name stored in the combo box control, which is an old faculty name, and you cannot use the faculty name stored in the Faculty Name textbox since that is an updated faculty name.

G) The **ExecuteNonQuery()** method of the Command class is called to execute the data deleting query to the Faculty table. The running result of calling this method is stored in the local variable **intDelete**.

H) The Command object is released after this data deleting action.

I) The returned value from calling of the **ExecuteNonQuery()** method is equal to the number of rows that have been successfully deleted from the Faculty table. If a zero returns, which means that no row has been deleted from the Faculty table and this data deleting has failed. An error message is displayed and the procedure is exited if that situation occurred.

J) After the data deleting is done, all pieces of faculty information stored in seven textboxes should be cleaned up. A **For** loop is used to finish this cleaning job.

Finally, let us take care of the coding process to validate the data deleting query.

7.4.2.2 Validate the Data Deleting

As we did for the validation for the data updating in the last section, we do not need to create any new window form to do this validation, instead we can use the Faculty Form to perform this data validation. Now let us run the project to test both data updating and deleting operations.

Since we do not want to do a fully recovery job for a deleted faculty, thus we selected a faculty member **Mhamed Jones** that was inserted into the Faculty table in our sample database in Section 6.4.1.3 in Chapter 6. That insertion is only related a new faculty member without any related courses and login information. Also we want to update a faculty **Michael Bai** to recover it back to the original faculty member **Ying Bai**.

Now click on the Start Debugging button to start our project, complete the login process, and open the Faculty Form window. First let us perform a query to get a faculty record and display it in this form.

On the opened Faculty Form window, select the faculty member **Michael Bai** from the **Faculty Name** combo box. Then update this faculty record by entering the following data to the associated textbox as an updated faculty record:

- **Ying Bai**   Faculty Name textbox
- **Associate Professor**   Title textbox
- **MTC-211**   Office textbox
- **750-378-1148**   Phone textbox

Figure 7.15 The updated faculty information window. *Source:* Microsoft Visual Studio.

- **Florida Atlantic University**   College textbox
- **ybai@college.edu**   Email textbox
- **Bai.jpg**   Faculty Image textbox

Then click on the **Update** button to update this record in the Faculty table.

To confirm this data updating, go to the **Faculty Name** combo box control and try to find the updated faculty name from this combo box in terms of the name. Immediately, you can find this updated faculty name. However, in order to test this data updating, first let us select another faculty name from this box and click on the **Select** button to show all pieces of information for that faculty. Then select our updated faculty, **Ying Bai**, from the box and click on the **Select** button to retrieve that updated faculty record. Immediately you can find that all pieces of updated information related to that faculty are displayed in this form. This means that our data updating is successful. Your updated faculty information window should match one that is shown in Figure 7.15.

Now let us test the data deleting functionality by selecting the faculty member **Mhamed Jones** from the **Faculty Name** combo box and clicking on the **Delete** button to try to delete this faculty record from the Faculty table. Click on the **Yes** to the message box and all pieces of related faculty information stored in seven textboxes are gone.

To confirm this deletion, one can use the codes in the **Select** button's Click event procedure to query back that deleted faculty. However, before one can do that, some modifications are needed for some codes in that event procedure. Follow the steps below to complete these modifications (refer to Figure 7.16):

A) Add one more Form level Boolean variable **findFaculty** and set it to **False**. This flag will be used to indicate whether a faculty member has been found or not from our sample database, and furthermore to decide if the **ShowFaculty()** subroutine should be called or not to display the queried faculty image later.

B) For the TableAdapter Method, if the desired faculty member is retrieved from our database, the flag **findFaculty** is set to True to indicate this, which is used later to call the **ShowFaculty()** to display the e faculty image.

Figure 7.16 Modified codes for the btnSelect button's Click event procedure.

C) For the DataReader Method, if a valid row that contains a record of the selected faculty member, this flag is also set to True to indicate this situation to make it ready to call the **ShowFaculty()** subroutine later to show the selected faculty image.

D) Similarly for the LINQ To DataSet Method, if the item `facultyinfo.Count() > 0`, which means that at least one valid DataRow has been retrieved from the sample database, each field can be obtained by using a For Each loop.

E) Otherwise, no matched faculty can be found from the database, a message box will be displayed to indicate this situation.

F) Now we need to check whether the flag `findFaculty` is set to `True`. If it is, which means that a valid faculty record has been retrieved, and therefore the subroutine `ShowFaculty()` should be called to display the image for that selected faculty.

G) The `findFaulty` flag needs to be reset and some cleaning jobs are performed.

Now you can use this modified `Select` button's Click event procedure to confirm our data deletion operation. Just select the deleted faculty name, `Mhamed Jones`, from the Faculty Name combo box, and click on the Select button to try to retrieve back this faculty's record. A message box with a warning message: `No matched faculty found!` is displayed, which means that the selected faculty member has been deleted from our database successfully.

If one prefers to delete some faculty members from our original database (not new inserted), it is highly recommended to recover the deleted faculty record that is not new inserted into this table for our sample database. To do that recovery, you need to follow the operational order listed below:

- First recover the deleted faculty record from the parent table (Faculty and Course tables).
- Then recover the deleted faculty record in the child tables (LogIn and the StudentCourse tables).

Refer to Figure 7.12 and Tables 7.3~7.6 in this chapter to complete this data recovery job. You can access and recover each table in our sample database via the Server Explorer window to perform this recovery process.

A completed project `OracleUpdateDeleteRTObject Project` can be found from the folder `Class DB Projects\Chapter 7` that is located at the Wiley ftp site under the `Students` folder (refer to Figure 1.2 in Chapter 1).

7.5 Update and Delete Data against Oracle Database Using Stored Procedures

Updating and deleting data via stored procedures developed in the Oracle database are very similar to the updating and deleting queries we performed in the last section. With a small modification to the existing project `OracleUpdateDeleteRTObject`, we can easily create our new project `OracleUpdateDeleteSP` to perform the data updating and deleting by calling stored procedures developed in the Oracle database.

To develop our new project in this section, we divide it into three sections:

1) Modify the existing project `OracleUpdateDeleteRTObject Project` to create our new project `OracleUpdateDeleteSP Project`.

2) Develop the data updating and deleting stored procedures with the Oracle SQL Developer.

3) Call the stored procedures to perform the data updating and deleting for the `COURSE` table using the Course Form window.

Now let us start with the first step.

7.5.1   Modify the Existing Project to Create Our New Project

Open the Windows Explorer and create a new folder `Class DB Projects\Chapter 7` if you have not and then browse to the folder `Class DB Projects\Chapter 7` that is located at the Wiley ftp site under the `Students` folder (refer to Figure 1.2 in Chapter 1). Copy the solution `OracleUpdateDeleteRTObject Solution` to the new folder `C:\Class DB Projects\Chapter 7` in your computer. Change the names of the solution and the project folders from `OracleUpdateDeleteRTObject Solution` to `OracleUpdateDeleteSP Solution`, and from `Oracle-UpdateDeleteRTObject Project` to `OracleUpdateDeleteSP Project`. Also change the name of the project file `OracleUpdateDeleteRTObject.vbproj` to `OracleUpdateDeleteSP.vbproj` and from `OracleUpdateDeleteRTObject.vbproj.user` to `OracleUpdateDeleteSP.vbproj.user`. Then double click on the project `OracleUpdateDeleteSP Project.vbproj` to open this new project.

On the opened project, perform the following modifications to get our desired project:

- Select a form window, such as the `LogIn Form.vb`, from the Solution Explorer window. Then go to `Project|OracleUpdateDeleteSP Project Properties` menu item to open the project's property wizard. Change the `Assembly name` and the `Root namespace` to `OracleUpdateDeleteSP Project` and `OracleUpdateDeleteSP_Project`.
- Click on the `Assembly Information` button to open the Assembly Information wizard. Change the `Title` and the `Product` to `OracleUpdateDeleteSP Project`. Click on the `OK` button to close this dialog box.

Go to the `File|Save All` to save those modifications and click `Yes` on the popup Message Box to overwrite the original solution file. Now we are ready to modify the codes based on our new project `OracleUpdateDeleteSP Project`.

7.5.2   Create the Codes to Update and Delete Data from the Course Table

The code creations and modifications include the following parts:

1) Modify the codes in the Course Form Load event procedure, `CourseForm_Load()`, to retrieve all current faculty members and display them in the Faculty Name combo box, `ComboName`.
2) Develop the query string in the `Update` button's Click event procedure in the Course Form with the name of the data updating stored procedure that will be developed in the next section to allow the procedure to call the related stored procedure to perform the data updating action.
3) Develop the query string in the `Delete` button's Click event procedure in the Course Form with the name of the data deleting stored procedure that will be developed in the next section to allow the procedure to call the related stored procedure to perform the data deleting action.

Regularly, the `COURSE_ID` should not be updated if a course record need to be updated since a new course with a new `COURSE_ID` can be inserted into the database and the old course can be deleted if it is not needed. Therefore, in this project, we update all pieces of information for a course record except its `COURSE_ID`. The input dynamic parameters to stored procedures include both `COURSE_ID` and related `FACULTY_ID`.

Regularly, the last two developments should be performed after the stored procedure has been created since we need some information from the created stored procedure to execute these developments, such as the name of the stored procedure and the names of the input parameters to the stored procedure. Because of the similarity between this project and the last one, we assumed that

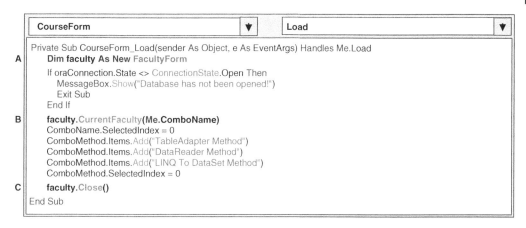

Figure 7.17 The modified codes in the CourseForm_Load() event procedure.

we have known those pieces of information and we can put those pieces of information into these two event procedures in advance.

First let us modify the codes inside the **CourseForm_Load()** event procedure to get all current faculty members and display them in the Faculty Name combo box. Open this event procedure and add the codes shown in Figure 7.17 into this procedure. The new added codes have been highlighted in bold.

Let's have a closer look at this piece of codes to see how it works.

A) First, a **FacultyForm** object, **faculty**, is generated since a user-defined subroutine **CurrentFaculty()** was defined in the Faculty Form, and we want to use that subroutine. Thus, we need first to declare an object to access that Form.

B) The subroutine **CurrentFaculty()** is called with the **Faculty Name** combo box, **ComboName**, as an argument that will be filled by retrieved faculty members. The prefix **Me** represents the current Form, Course Form, and the subroutine must be prefixed by the object **faculty**, in which the subroutine is included.

C) When all faculty members have been added into the combo box, the object faculty is released.

Now let us handle the coding process inside two event procedures to perform the data updating and deleting actions. The assumed known information includes the following:

A) For the Course Data Updating:
1) The name of the data updating stored procedure – **UpdateCourseSP**.
2) The names of the input updating parameters – identical with the columns' names in the Course table in our sample database.
3) The names of the input dynamic parameters – **:FacultyName** and Course ID **:CourseID**.

B) For the Course Data Deleting:
1) The name of the data deleting stored procedure – **DeleteCourseSP**.
2) The names of the deleting input parameters – identical with the columns' names in the Course table in our sample database.
3) The name of the input dynamic parameter – Course ID **:CourseID**

Based on these assumptions, we can first build our codes in the **Update** button's Click event procedure. The key point is that we need to remember the names of these parameters and the name of the stored procedure and put them into our stored procedure later when we developed it in the next section.

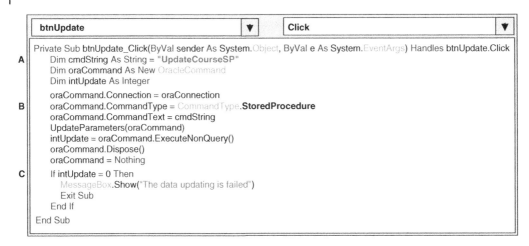

Figure 7.18 The codes for the Update button's event procedure.

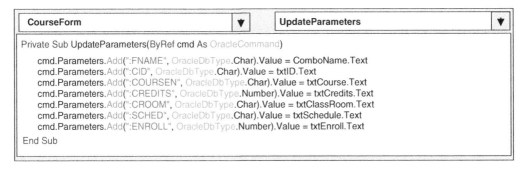

Figure 7.19 The codes for the user defined procedure UpdateParameters().

Open the **Update** button' Click event procedure in the Course Form and perform the coding developments. Your finished codes to this event procedure should match those codes that are shown in Figure 7.18.

Let us have a closer look at this piece of modified codes to see how it works.

A) The content of the query string now should be equal to the name of the stored procedure, **UpdateCourseSP**, which will be built later.

B) The CommandType property of the Command object should be set to **StoredProcedure** to tell the project that a stored procedure should be called as the project runs to perform the data updating job.

C) If the **ExecuteNonQuery()** method returned a zero, which means that this data updating is failed and no any record has been updated, a warning message is displayed to indicate this situation and the subroutine is exited.

The codes for the user defined subroutine procedure **UpdateParameters()** are shown in Figure 7.19. These nominal parameters' symbols starting with: must be identical with the names of those input parameters to the stored procedure **UpdateCourseSP** that will be built later. Otherwise, some possible errors or bugs may be encountered as the project runs since the compiler cannot find the matched input parameters for the stored procedure.

```
btn Delete                           ▼     Click

Private Sub btnDelete_Click(ByVal sender As System.Object, ByVal e As System.EventArgs) Handles btnDelete.Click
A       Dim cmdString As String = "DeleteCourseSP"
        Dim vbButton As MessageBoxButtons = MessageBoxButtons.YesNo
        Dim oraCommand As New OracleCommand
        Dim Answer As DialogResult
        Dim intDelete As Integer

        Answer = MessageBox.Show("Are you sure to delete this record?", "Delete", vbButton)

        If Answer = System.Windows.Forms.DialogResult.Yes Then
            oraCommand.Connection = oraConnection
B           oraCommand.CommandType = CommandType.StoredProcedure
            oraCommand.CommandText = cmdString
C           oraCommand.Parameters.Add(":CourseID", OracleDbType.Char).Value = txtID.Text
            intDelete = oraCommand.ExecuteNonQuery()
            oraCommand.Dispose()
            oraCommand = Nothing

            If intDelete = 0 Then
                MessageBox.Show("The data Deleting is failed")
                Exit Sub
            End If

D           txtID.Text = String.Empty                 'Clean up the Course textbox array
            txtCourse.Text = String.Empty
            txtSchedule.Text = ""
            txtClassroom.Text = String.Empty
            txtCredits.Text = ""
            txtEnroll.Text = String.Empty
        End If
End Sub
```

Figure 7.20   The codes for the Delete button's event procedure.

Next let's build the codes in the **Delete** button' Click event procedure. Open this event procedure and put the codes shown in Figure 7.20 to this procedure.

Let's have a closer look at this piece of modified codes to see how it works.

A) The content of the query string now should be equal to the name of the stored procedure, **DeleteCourseSP**, which will be built later.

B) The CommandType property of the Command object should be set to **StoredProcedure** to tell the project that a stored procedure should be called as the project runs to perform the data updating job.

C) The input dynamic parameter to the stored procedure is **:CourseID,** and this will work as a query qualification for this action.

D) After this deletion operation, all textboxes stored the selected course information are cleared.

Now we have finished all codes' modifications in Visual Basic.NET environment. Let us start to create our stored procedures with Oracle SQL Developer.

7.5.2.1   Develop Two Stored Procedures with Oracle SQL Developer

Open the Oracle SQL Developer and finish the login process by entering the system password and expand the **CSE_DEPT** server and the **Other Users** folder, and furthermore to expand our sample database folder CSE_DEPT. Then right click on the **Procedures** folder and select the item **New Procedure** to open the Create Procedure wizard, as shown in Figure 7.21. Perform the following operational steps to build this procedure:

1) Enter the name of the stored procedure, **UpdateCourseSP**, which should be identical with the name of the stored procedure we used in our codes in the last section, to the **Name** box.

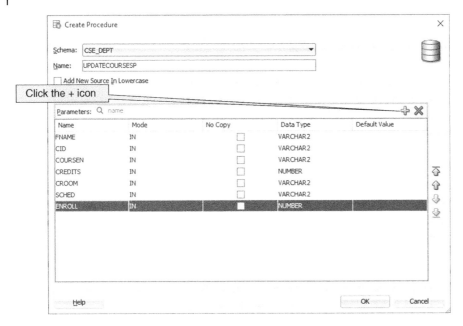

Figure 7.21   The opened Create Procedure wizard. *Source:* Microsoft Visual Studio.

```
CREATE OR REPLACE PROCEDURE UPDATECOURSESP
(
  FNAME IN VARCHAR2
, CID IN VARCHAR2
, COURSEN IN VARCHAR2
, CREDITS IN NUMBER
, CROOM IN VARCHAR2
, SCHED IN VARCHAR2
, ENROLL IN NUMBER
) AS
BEGIN
  DECLARE FID VARCHAR2(20);
  BEGIN SELECT faculty_id INTO FID FROM FACULTY
  WHERE faculty_name = FNAME;
  UPDATE CSE_DEPT.course
  SET course=COURSEN, credit=CREDITS, classroom=CROOM, schedule=SCHED,  enrollment=ENROLL,
    faculty_id=FID WHERE course_id=CID;
  END;
END UPDATECOURSESP;
```

Figure 7.22   The created stored procedure UpdateCourseSP().

2) Click on the green color + icon to add all input parameters one by one. Your finished parameter list should match one that is shown in Figure 7.21. One point to be noted is the order and the names of these input parameters, and they must be identical with those used in our codes built in the **Update** button's click event procedure in the last section. Click on the **OK** button to continue.

3) On the opened code wizard, enter the codes shown in Figure 7.22 into this code window as the body of this procedure.

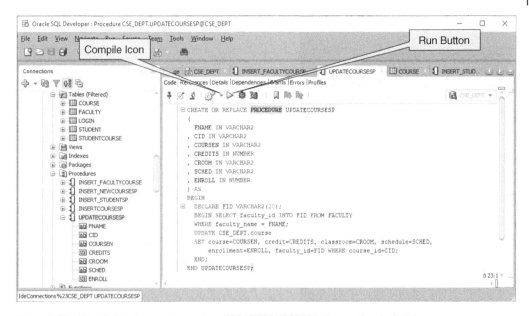

Figure 7.23 The finished stored procedure UPDATECOURSESP(). *Source:* Oracle Database.

4) Click on the **Compile** icon (Figure 7.23) to compile this procedure. A Compiled statement should be displayed in the **Message** window if everything is fine.

Your finished stored procedure should match one that is shown in Figure 7.23.

You can even test this stored procedure inside this Developer. To do that, click on the green color arrow on the top to run this procedure. Enter the following sample updated information into each field on the **Value** column of this wizard:

- Faculty Name   `Ying Bai`
- Course ID   `CSE-438`
- Course   `Artificial Controls`
- Credit   `4`
- Classroom   `MTC-313`
- Schedule   `T-H: 1:30 – 2:45 PM`
- Enrollment   `28`

Your finished information wizard should match one that is shown in Figure 7.24.

Click on the **OK** button to run this stored procedure. You may need to reenter your system password to run this procedure. A running sequence is displayed in the Running window if everything is success.

To confirm this data updating action, you can open the **COURSE** table in this Oracle SQL Developer to check it. Go to the **COURSE** table that is located under the **Tables** folder in our sample database **CSE_DEPT** in this Developer, expand the **Tables** folder, and click on the **COURSE** table to open it. You may need to refresh this table by clicking on the **Refresh** icon on the upper-left corner that is shown in Figure 7.25. Then you can find that the course **CSE-438** has been updated, which has been highlighted as shown in Figure 7.25.

In order to keep our database neat, we prefer to recover this updated course record back to the original one. To do that, you can rerun this stored procedure and enter the original data into the **Input Value** column shown in Figure 7.24.

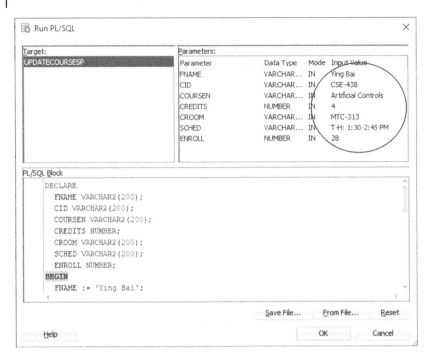

Figure 7.24 The finished information wizard. *Source:* Oracle Database.

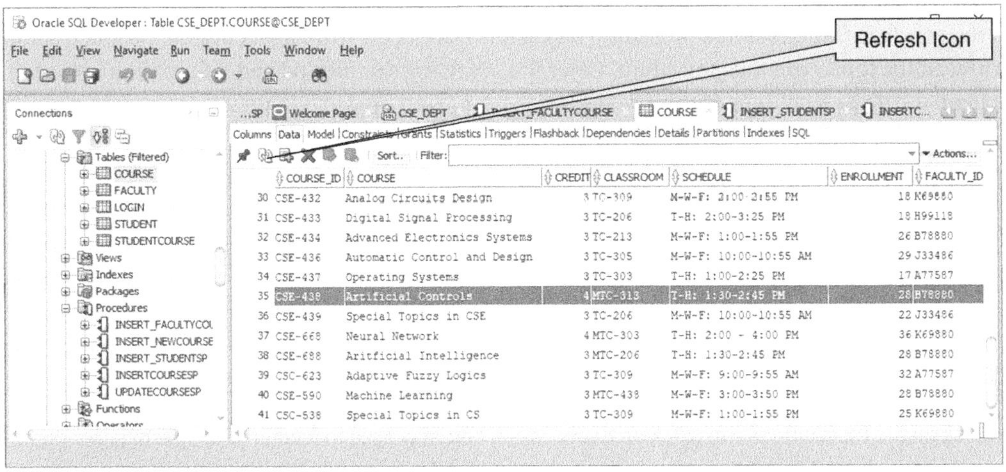

Figure 7.25 The updated Faculty table. *Source:* Oracle Database.

Next let us create our data deleting stored procedure **DeleteCourseSP** in the Oracle SQL Developer environment.

Open the Oracle SQL Developer and finished the login process by entering the system password and expand the **CSE_DEPT** server and the **Other Users** folder, and furthermore to expand our sample database folder **CSE_DEPT**. Then right click on **Procedures** folder and select the item **New Procedure** to open the Create Procedure wizard, as shown in Figure 7.26. Perform the following operational steps to build this procedure:

Figure 7.26 The finished Create Procedure wizard. *Source:* Microsoft Visual Studio.

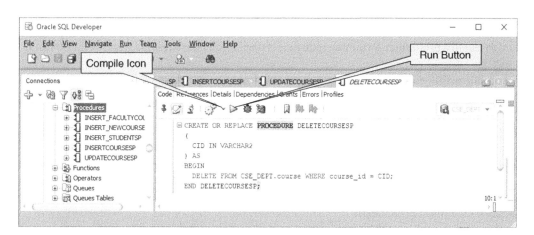

Figure 7.27 The created data deleting stored procedure. *Source:* Oracle Database.

1) Enter the name of the stored procedure, **DeleteCourseSP**, which should be identical with the name of the stored procedure we used in our codes in the last section, to the **Name** box.
2) Click on the green color + icon to add only one input parameter, **COURSE_ID** or **CID**, as shown in Figure 7.26. Click on the **OK** button to continue.
3) On the opened code wizard, enter the codes shown in Figure 7.27 into this code window as the body of this procedure.
4) Click on the **Compile** icon (Figure 7.27) to compile this procedure. A Compiled statement should be displayed in the **Message** window if everything is fine.

Your finished stored procedure should match one that is shown in Figure 7.27.

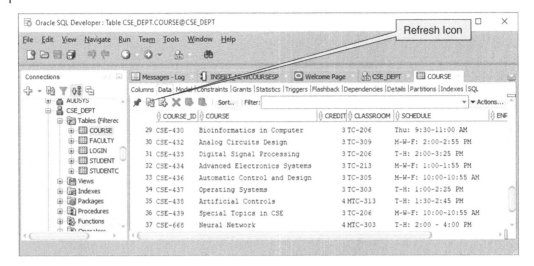

Figure 7.28 The opened COURSE table in our sample database. *Source:* Oracle Database.

You can even test this stored procedure inside this Developer. To do that, click on the green color arrow on the top to run this procedure and enter the following sample deleting information into the **Input Value** column of this wizard:

Course ID   CSC-538

Click on the **OK** button to run this stored procedure. You may need to reenter your system password to run this procedure. A running sequence is displayed in the Running window if everything is success.

To confirm this data updating action, you can open the **COURSE** table in this Oracle SQL Developer to check it. Go to the **COURSE** table that is located under the **Tables** folder in our sample database **CSE_DEPT** in this Developer, expand the **Tables** folder, and click on the **COURSE** table to open it. You may need to refresh this table by clicking on the **Refresh** icon on the upper-left corner, as shown in Figure 7.28. Then you can find that the course **CSC-538** has been deleted from this table (Figure 7.28).

To confirm the correct execution of these stored procedures, we can call them from our Visual Basic.NET project, **OracleUpdateDeleteSP Project**, to execute the updating and deleting actions from our sample database in the next section.

7.5.2.2 Call the Stored Procedures to Perform the Data Updating and Deleting

Start to run our project **OracleUpdateDeleteSP Project**, finish the login process, and open the Course Form window by selecting **Course Information** from the Selection Form. Select the faculty member **Ying Bai** from the **Faculty Name** combo box,click on the **CSE-438** from the Course List box, and enter the following information into the related textbox:

- Course ID   CSE-438
- Course   Advd Logic & Microprocessor
- Schedule   M-W-F: 11:00 - 11:55 AM
- Classroom   MTC-213
- Credit   3
- Enrollment   35

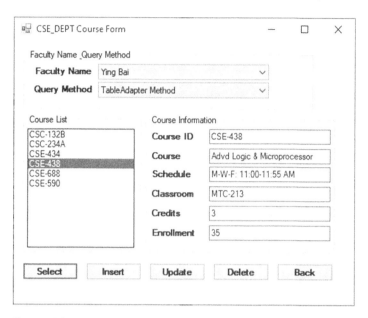

Figure 7.29 The recovered course CSE-438. *Source:* Microsoft Visual Studio.

The reason we enter the original course record for this course CSE-438 is because we updated this course in the Oracle SQL Developer when we built this stored procedure in the last section. Thus, now we can perform another updating to make this course record back to the original one.

Now click on the **Update** button to start this course updating action.

To validate this updating action, first select another course, such as **CSE-434**, from the **CourseList** box to display detailed information for that course. Then click on the updated course, **CSE-438**, again to get detailed information for this course. Now you can find that the course has been updated, as shown in Figure 7.29.

Now let's test our data deletion function by calling our stored procedure **DeleteCourseSP** we built in the last section.

As the project **OracleUpdateDeleteSP Project** is running, complete the login process and open the Course Form window by selecting the **Course Information** from the Selection Form, then click on the **Select** button to retrieve and display all courses taught by the faculty member **Ying Bai**. Now we try to delete this course, **CSE-438**, taught by this faculty member from the **COURSE** table in our sample database. Select this **COURSE_ID**, **CSE-438**, from the CourseList box and click on the **Delete** button.

Immediately one can find that all information related to that course is removed from all related textboxes. Now click the **Select** button again to try to retrieve all courses taught by the faculty member **Ying Bai**, one can find that the course (**COURSE_ID**) **CSE-438** has been removed from the CourseList box.

To check this deletion action, go to the Server Explorer window. Then right click on the **COURSE** table and select **Retrieve Data** item from the popup menu to open the **COURSE** table. You can find that the course **CSE-438** has been deleted from this table because you cannot find it from this table now.

In order to keep our database neat, we prefer to recover this deleted course record with the original data. Recall in Section 2.9.8.5 in Chapter 2, when a course record is deleted from the **COURSE** table (parent table), all records related to that course in the **COURSE** and **STUDENTCOURSE** table

Table 7.7 The data to be recovered in the **COURSE** table.

course_id	course	credit	classroom	schedule	enrollment	faculty_id
CSE-438	Advd Logic & Microprocessor	3	MTC-213	M-W-F: 11:00-11:55 AM	35	B78880

Table 7.8 The data to be recovered in the **STUDENTCOURSE** table.

s_course_id	student_id	course_id	credit	major
1014	A78835	CSE-438	3	CE

(child tables) will also be deleted. Therefore, totally two (2) records in our sample database have been deleted from two tables:

- One course record **CSE-438** from the **COURSE** table (parent table)
- One student course record **CSE-438** from the **STUDENTCOURSE** table (child table)

Open those tables in the Server Explorer window and add those deleted records back to each associated table one by one. Tables 7.7 and 7.8 shown those original course records in both tables. You can perform a copy and paste function to first copy each row from each table (Tables 7.7 or 7.8) and then paste it to the end of each table in our sample database.

Another important point in recovering these deleted records is the order in which you performed that copy and paste action. You must first recover the course deleted from the parent table, **COURSE** table, and then you can recover all other related records in all other child tables. The reason for this is that the **COURSE** is a parent table with the **COURSE_ID** as a primary key, and you cannot recover any other record in any child table without first recovering the deleted record from the parent table. Click on the **File|Save All** menu item when you finished these recoveries to save those recovered records.

7.5.3 Update and Delete Data Using the LINQ to DataSet Query

As we discussed in Chapter 4, LINQ can be used for different components to help to improve performances for database queries. Some most popular LINQ techniques include the following:

1) LINQ to Objects
2) LINQ to ADO.NET (LINQ to DataSet, LINQ to SQL, and LINQ to Entities)
3) LINQ to XML

Among these applications, the LINQ to ADO.NET is the most popular technique and widely implemented in database and DataSet queries.

LINQ to DataSet technique can only be implemented for DataSet, not database. In other words, this method can only be used to select, insert, update, and delete records from tables in the DataSet, but these actions or queries cannot be reflected to the related database. This means that the records located at tables inside the database cannot be modified even the related records located at the tables in the DataSet have been modified.

LINQ to SQL is the only technique developed by Microsoft, and it can only be used to modify records in both DataSet and database, but this method can only be implemented in

SQL Server database, not for other database, such as Oracle database. By using this technique, a Context object must be created to map a model to a database with related references or constraints.

Some exceptions are a few of third party products, such as **LinqConnect** by Devart, which is equivalent to LINQ to Oracle, and Oracle Data Access Components (ODAC) by Oracle, which provides an interface between Oracle database and Visual Studio.NET. An issue related to implementing these tools is the availability and compatibility to the updated version of Visual Studio.NET. The **LinqConnect** developed by Devart provides the updated software and compatible to the current version of Visual Studio.NET.

LINQ to Entity is similar to LINQ to SQL and an Entity model is needed to provide a connection between your Visual Basic.NET project and the Oracle database.

LINQ to DataSet queries can perform not only the data selections but also the data insertion, updating, and deletion. The standard LINQ to DataSet queries include:

- Select
- Insert
- Update
- Delete

To perform update and delete records by using LINQ to DataSet method, we need to perform two operational steps: first create a DataSet to fill it with our database and then build LINQ to DataSet query to perform either updating or deleting actions against our DataSet. Refer to Section 4.5.1.5 in Chapter 4 to get more details about the LINQ to Typed DataSet.

Now we use a sample project **LINQStudent** to illustrate how to use LINQ to DataSet method to update some student records in the **STUDENT** table in our DataSet object.

7.5.3.1 Update Data Using LINQ to DataSet for Student Table

In this section, we want to create a **Console App (.NET Framework)** project **LINQStudent Project** to perform updating actions against our **STUDENT** table in our sample database using the LINQ to DataSet query with our Student Form. Now let us perform the following steps to create our new project **LINQStudent**:

1) Open Visual Studio.NET 2019 and go to **File|New Project** menu item.
2) Select **Console App (.NET Framework) – Visual Basic** item and then click on the **Next** button.
3) Enter **LINQStudent** into the Project name box as the name for this project and browse to the folder **C:\Class DB Projects\Chapter 7** as the **Location** to save this project. Click on the **Create** button to create this Console App project.
4) On the opened project code window, change the Module name from **Module1** to **LINQStudent** in the first coding line and from the object **Module1.vb** to **LINQStudent.vb** in the Solution Explorer window.
5) Right click on our new project in the Solution Explorer window and select **Add|Reference** item to open the **Reference Manager** wizard.
6) Select the **Extensons** item from the left pane under the Assemblies and choose the items **Devart.Data** and **Devart.Data.Oracle** by checking them and click on the **OK** button to add them to this project.
7) Type **Imports Devart.Data.Oracle** into the top line on the code window.

Your finished project code window should match one that is shown in Figure 7.30.

Figure 7.30 The codes for the LINQStudent Console project.

Enter the codes shown in Figure 7.30 into this code window as the code body for this project. Let us have a closer look at this piece of codes to see how it works.

A) A directive or a reference for **Devart.Data.Oracle** is added into this project to provide the namespace used by the Oracle drive.

B) The query string and some query objects are declared here. This query is used to pick up all students from the **STUDENT** table from our database.

C) The Oracle Connection string is generated with the server, schema, UserID, and Password involved.

D) An Oracle database connection is executed with the connection string and the **Open()** command.

```
C:\Book17 - OracleDBVB\Oracle DB Programming\Students\Class DB Projects\Chapter 7\LINQStudent\LINQStudent\bin\Debug\LINQStudent.exe    —    □    ×
Andrew Woods, 3.26, 108, Computer Science, Senior, awoods@college.edu
Ashly Jade, 3.57, 116, Information System Engineering, Junior, ajade@college.edu
Blue Valley, 3.52, 102, Computer Science, Senior, bvalley@college.edu
Holes Smith, 3.87, 78, Computer Engineering, Sophomore, hsmith@college.edu
Tom Erica, 3.95, 127, Computer Science, Senior, terica@college.edu
Jones Case, 3.86, 118, Information Systems, Senior, jcase@college.edu
Aversion Wang, 3.38, 35, Computer Science, Freshman, awang@college.edu

Press any key to continue...
```

Figure 7.31 The running result of project LINQStudent. *Source*: LINQ.

E) The Oracle Command object is initialized with different properties. The `SelectCommand` property is assigned with the configured Oracle Command object to perform a select query to get a desired student based on the user's selection from the Student Name combo box later.

F) The `Fill()` method is executed to fill the `STUDENT` table in our DataSet with all records in the `STUDENT` table in our sample database.

G) A new data table is generated and initialized with our filled `STUDENT` table.

H) The LINQ query is created and initialized with three clauses, `From`, `Where`, and `Select`, to retrieve a single row based on the query standard or a student named **James Stevenson**. The range variable `si` is selected from the Student entity in our sample database. A selected student row based on the (`student_name`) will be read back using the `Select` clause.

I) The data updating action begins here and all six pieces of new information related to the selected student are updated with the `SetField()` method.

J) To make these updating actions effective, the `AcceptChanges()` method related to the `STUDENT` table in our DataSet is executed and also the entire table is updated by calling the `Update()` method of the DataAdapter.

K) All records, including the updated record, in the entire `STUDENT` table are displayed with the `Console.WriteLine()` method to check and confirm this updating.

L) Some cleaning jobs are performed here to release all used objects.

M) The `Console.WriteLine()` method is used again to provide an exit way for this project.

Now go to `Build|Build LINQStudent` menu item to build the project. Then run the project by clicking on the `Start` button. The running result is shown in Figure 7.31. It can be found that the original student **James Stevenson**, who is listed as the sixth student, has been updated to a new student named **Jones Case** with the updated information.

7.6 Chapter Summary

Data updating and deleting queries are discussed in this Chapter with Oracle XE 18c database.

Five popular data updating and deleting methods are discussed and analyzed with four real project examples:

1) Using TableAdapter DBDirect methods such as `TableAdapter.Update()` and `TableAdapter.Delete()` to update and delete data directly against the databases.

2) Using `TableAdapter.Update()` method to update and execute the associated TableAdapter's properties, such as UpdateCommand or DeleteCommand, to save changes made for the table in the DataSet to the table in the database.

3) Using the run time object method to develop and execute the Command's method ExecuteNonQuery() to update or delete data against the database directly.

4) Using the stored procedures to update or delete data against the database directly.

5) Using LINQ to DataSet query method to update and delete data in our DataSet.

Both methods 1 and 2 need to use Visual Studio.NET Design Tools and Wizards to create and configure suitable TableAdapters, build the associated queries using the Query Builder, and call those queries from Visual Basic.NET applications. The difference between methods 1 and 2 is that method 1 can be used to directly access the database to perform the data updating and deleting in a single step, but method 2 needs two steps to finish the data updating or deleting. First, the data updating or deleting are performed to the associated tables in the DataSet, and then those updated or deleted data are updated to the tables in the database by executing the `TableAdapter.Update()` method.

This Chapter is divided into two parts: Part I provides discussions on data updating and deleting using methods 1 and 2, or in other words, using the `TableAdapter.Update()` and `TableAdapter.Delete()` methods provided by Visual Studio.NET Design Tools and Wizards. Part II presents the data updating and deleting by using the run time object method to develop command objects to execute the `ExecuteNonQuery()` method dynamically. Updating and deleting data against our sample database using the stored procedures and the LINQ to DataSet query methods are also discussed in the second part.

Four (4) real sample projects are provided in this Chapter to help readers to understand and design the professional data-driven applications to update or delete data against the Oracle database. The stored procedures and LINQ To DataSet methods are discussed in the last section to help readers to perform the data updating or deleting more efficiently and conveniently.

Homework

I. True/False Selections

_____ 1 Three popular data updating methods are the TableAdapter DBDirect method, TableAdapter.Update() method, and ExecuteNonQuery() method of the Command class.

_____ 2 Unlike the Fill() method, a valid database connection must be set before any data can be updated in the database.

_____ 3 One can directly update data or delete records against the database using the TableAdapter.Update() method.

_____ 4 When executing an UPDATE query, the order of the input parameters in the SET list can be different with the order of the data columns in the database.

_____ 5 To update data against an Oracle database using stored procedures, the CommandType property must be set to StoredProcedure.

_____ 6 One can directly delete records from the database using the TableAdapter DBDirect method such as TableAdapter.Delete() method.

_____7 When performing the data updating, the same data can be updated in the database multiple times.

_____8 To delete data from the database using the TableAdapter.Update() method, the data should be first deleted from the table in the DataSet, and then the Update() method is executed to update that deletion to the table in the database.

_____9 To update data in the Oracle database using the stored procedures, one can create and test the new stored procedure in the Oracle SQL Developer.

_____ 10 To call stored procedures to update data against a database, the parameters' names and the order must be identical with those names and the order of the input parameters defined in the stored procedures.

II. Multiple Choices

1 To update data in a database using the TableAdapter.Update() method, one needs to use the _____ to build the _____.
 A Data Source, Qury Builder
 B TableAdapter Query Configuration Wizard, Update query
 C Runtime object, Insert query
 D Server Explorer, Data Source

2 To delete data from the database using the TableAdapter.Update() method, one needs first to delete data from the _____ and then update that data into the database.
 A Data table
 B Data table in the database
 C DataSet
 D Data table in the DataSet

3 To delete data from the database using the TableAdapter.Update() method, one can delete _____
 A One data row only
 B Multiple data rows
 C The whole data table
 D Either of above

4 Because the ADO.NET provides a disconnected mode to the database, to update or delete a record against the database, a valid _____ must be established.
 A DataSet
 B TableAdapter
 C Connection
 D Command

5 The _____ operator should be used in front of all input parameters for stored procedures to be called by Visual Basic.NET project.

A =:

B LIKE

C =

D @

6 To save a stored procedure built in the Oracle SQL Developer for an Oracle database, one can click the _____.

A File|Save menu item

B File|Save As menu item

C File|Save All menu item

D Update item

7 To test the stored procedure built in the Oracle SQL Developer for the Oracle XE 18c database, one can _____ the stored procedure to make sure it works.

A Build

B Execute

C Debug

D Compile

8 To recover some deleted records from an Oracle database, one should first recover data in the _____ and then the data in the _____.

A Child tables, Parent tables

B Data Source, Server Explorer

C Parent table, child table

D Primary keys, foreign keys

9 To update data using stored procedures, the CommandType property of the Command object must be equal to _____.

A CommandType.InsertCommand

B CommandType.StoredProcedure

C CommandType.Text

D CommandType.Insert

10 To update data using stored procedures, the CommandText property of the Command object must be equal to _____.

A The content of the CommandType.InsetCommand

B The content of the CommandType.Text

C The name of the Insert command

D The name of the stored procedure

III. Exercises

1   Develop a stored procedure **UpdateStudentSP** for our sample Oracle database. Please build
    this stored procedure in the Oracle SQL Developer.
    A Point is: The GPA column will not be involved in this updating action, thus do not include
    this column as input parameter for this updating query. It is still 3.95 with no change after this
    updating action is done.

2   Develop a piece of codes in Visual Basic.NET to call the stored procedure above to update a
    record in the STUDENT table in our sample database. One can use the Student Form in the
    project OracleUpdateDeleteSP **Project** we built in this chapter. Place your codes in the
    btnUpdate button's Click event procedure to call that stored procedure to update a student
    record.
    When running this project, one can use the following updated information to update the stu-
    dent **Tom Erica**:

    - Student ID   T77896
    - Student Name   **Toney Black**
    - Credits   85
    - Major   **Info System Engineering**
    - SchoolYear   **Junior**
    - Email   **tblack@college.edu**
    - sImage   **Default.jpg** (located at the folder **Students\Images\Students**
                       at Wiley ftp site, save this image to your **C:\Images** folder)

    One can open the **STUDENT** table in the Server Explorer to confirm this updating. It is highly
    recommended to recover this student to the original one by running this project again to do
    another updating action to recover this record.

3   Using the Runtime objects to complete the updating query for the Student Form by using the
    project OracleUpdateDeleteRTObject **Project**. The project file can be found at the folder
    Class DB **Projects\Chapter** **7** that is located at the Wiley ftp site under the **Students**
    folder (refer to Figure 1.2 in Chapter 1).
    Place your codes in the **btnUpdate** button's Click event procedure to call an updating query
    to update a student record. When running this project, one can use the following updated
    information to update the student **Andrew Woods**:

    - Student ID   A78835
    - Student Name   **Arlington David**
    - GPA   3.86
    - Credits   48
    - Major   **Computer Engineering**
    - SchoolYear   **Sophomore**
    - Email   **adavid@college.edu**
    - sImage   **David.jpg** (located at the folder **Students\Images\Students** at
                       Wiley ftp site, save this image to your **C:\Images** folder)

Table 7.9 Student table.

student_id	student_name	gpa	credits	major	schoolYear	email	simage
A78835	Andrew Woods	3.26	108	Computer Science	Senior	awoods@college.edu	Woods.jpg

It is highly recommended to recover this updated record to the original one. You can run this project again to do another updating action to do this recovering job. Follow the original record shown in Table 7.9 to recover this updated student record.

4 Build a stored procedure DeleteStudentSP with Oracle SQL Developer to complete the data-deleting query via the Student Form to the STUDENT table by using the project OracleUpdateDeleteSP **Project**. The project file can be found at the folder **Class** DB **Projects\Chapter 7** that is located at the Wiley ftp site under the **Students** folder (refer to Figure 1.2 in Chapter 1).

When building the stored procedure, the only input parameter is a **student_name**, but you need first to perform a query from the **STUDENT** table to get a related **student_id**, and then to perform the **DELETE** query with that **student_id**.

It is highly recommended to recover those deleted records after they are deleted. The best way to do this deleting action is to delete some new inserted student record, such as the new student, **Aversion Wang**, which was inserted in Exercise 5 at home work in Chapter 6. In this way, you do not need to recover that deleted student.

Hints: If you delete an original student record from the database (not a new inserted student), the student record in the parent table, **STUDENT** table, will be deleted. Also all related records to that student in the child tables, such as the **LOGIN**, **COURSE**, and **STUDENTCOURSE**, will be deleted, too. When you recover those records, you should first recover the record in the parent table and then those related records in the child tables.

8

Accessing Data in ASP.NET

We have provided a very detailed discussion on database programming with Visual Basic.NET using the Windows-based applications in the previous chapters. Starting from this chapter, we will concentrate on the database programming with Visual Basic.NET using the Web-based applications. To develop the Web-based application and allow users to access the database through the Internet, you need to understand an important component: Active Server Page.NET or ASP.NET.

Essentially, ASP.NET allows users to write software to access databases through a Web browser rather than a separate program installed on computers. With the help of ASP.NET, the users can easily create and develop an ASP.NET Web application and run it on a server as a server-side project. The user can then send requests to the server to download any Web page, to access the database to retrieve, display, and manipulate data, via the Web browser. The actual language used in the communications between a client and a server is so-called Hypertext Markup Language (HTML).

When finished this chapter, you will be able to

- Understand the structure and components of ASP.NET Web applications.
- Understand the structure and components of .NET Framework.
- Select data from the database and display data in a Web page.
- Understand the Application state structure and implement it to store global variables.
- Understand the AutoPostBack property and implement it to communicate with the server effectively.
- Insert, Update, and Delete data from the database through a Web page.
- Use the stored procedure to perform the data actions against the database via a Web application.
- Use LINQ to Oracle query to perform the data actions against the database via a Web application.
- Perform client-side data validation in Web pages.

To help readers to successfully complete this chapter, first we need to provide a detailed discussion about the ASP.NET. The prerequisite to understand the ASP.NET is the .NET Framework because the ASP.NET is a part of .NET Framework, or in other words, the .NET Framework is a foundation of the ASP.NET. So, we first need to provide a detailed discussion about the .NET Framework.

8.1 What Is .NET Framework?

The .NET Framework is a model that provides a foundation to develop and execute different applications at an integrated environment such as Visual Studio.NET. In other words, the .NET Framework can be considered as a system to integrate and develop multiple applications such as Windows applications, Web applications, or XML Web Services by using a common set of tools and codes such as Visual Basic.NET or Visual C#.NET.

The .NET Framework consists of the following components:

- The Common Language Runtime (CLR) (called runtime). The runtime handles runtime services such as language integration, security, and memory management. During the development stage, the runtime provides features that are needed to simplify the development.
- Class Libraries. Class libraries provide reusable codes for most common tasks such as data access, XML Web service development, Web and Windows forms.

The main goal to develop the .NET Framework is to overcome several limitations on Web applications since different clients may provide different client browsers. To solve these limitations, .NET Framework provides a common language called Microsoft Intermediate Language (MSIL) which is language-independent and platform-independent and allows all programs developed in any .NET-based language to be converted into this MSIL. The MSIL can be recognized by the CLR, and the CLR can compile and execute the MSIL codes by using the Just-In-Time compiler.

You can access the .NET Framework by using the class libraries provided by the .NET Framework, and you can implement the .NET Framework by using the tools such as Visual Studio.NET provided by the .NET Framework, too. All class libraries provided by the .NET Framework are located at the different namespaces. All .NET-based languages access the same libraries.

A typical .NET Framework model is shown in Figure 8.1.

The .NET Framework supports three types of user interfaces:

- Windows Forms that run on Windows 32 client computers. All projects we developed in the previous chapters used this kind of user interface.
- Web Forms that run on Server computers through ASP.NET and the Hypertext Transfer Protocol (HTTP).
- The Command Console.

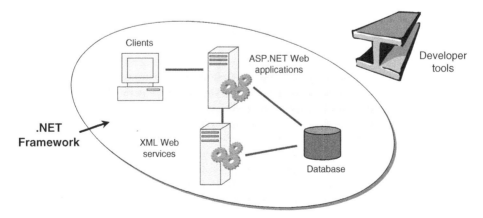

Figure 8.1   The .NET Framework model.

Summarily, the advantages of using the .NET Framework to develop Windows-based and Web-based applications include, but no limited to:

- The .NET Framework is based on Web standards and practices, and it fully supports Internet technologies, including the HTML, HTTP, XML, Simple Object Access Protocol (SOAP), XML Path Language (XPath), and other Web standards.
- The .NET Framework is designed using unified application models, so the functionality of any class provided by the .NET Framework is available to any .NET-compatible language or programming model. The same piece of code can be implemented in Windows applications, Web applications, and XML Web services.
- The .NET Framework is easy for developers to use since the code in the .NET Framework is organized into hierarchical namespaces and classes. The .NET Framework provides a common type system, which is called the unified type system, and it can be used by any .NET-compatible language. In the unified type system, all language elements are objects that can be used by any .NET application written in any .NET-based language.

Now let us have a closer look at the ASP.NET.

8.2   What Is ASP.NET?

ASP.NET is a programming framework built on the .NET Framework, and it is used to build Web applications. Developing ASP.NET Web applications in the .NET Framework is very similar to develop Windows applications. An ASP.NET Web application is composed of many different parts and components, but the fundamental component of ASP.NET is the Web Form. A Web Form is the Web page that users view in a browser, and an ASP.NET Web application can contain one or more Web Forms. A Web Form is a dynamic page that can access server resources.

A completed structure of an ASP.NET Web application is shown in Figure 8.2.

Unlike the traditional Web page that can run scripts on the client, an ASP.NET Web Form can also run server-side codes to access databases, to create additional Web Forms, or to take advantage of built-in security of the server. In addition, since an ASP.NET Web Form does not rely on client-side

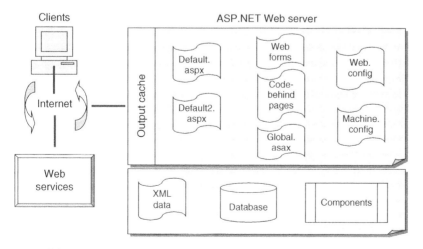

Figure 8.2   The structure of an ASP.NET Web application.

scripts, it is independent on the client's browser type or operating system. This independence allows users to develop a single Web Form that can be viewed on any device that has Internet access and a Web browser.

Because ASP.NET is part of the .NET Framework, the ASP.NET Web application can be developed in any .NET-based language.

The ASP.NET technology also supports XML Web services. XML Web services are distributed applications that use XML for transferring information between clients, applications, and other XML Web services.

The main parts of an ASP.NET Web application include:

- Web Forms or **Default.aspx** pages. The Web Forms or **Deafult.aspx** pages provide the user interface for the Web application, and they are very similar to the Windows Forms in the Windows-based application. The Web Forms files are indicated with an extension of **.aspx.**
- Code-behind pages. The so-called code-behind pages are related to the Web Forms and contain the server-side codes for the Web Form. This code-behind page is very similar to the code window for the Windows Forms in a Windows-based application we discussed in the previous chapters. Most event procedures or handlers associated with controls on the Web Forms are located in this code-behind page. The code-behind pages are indicated with an extension of **.aspx.vb.**
- Web Services or **.asmx** pages. Web services are used when you create dynamic sites that will be accessed by other programs or computers. ASP.NET Web services may be supported by a code-behind page that is designed by the extension of **.asmx.vb.**
- Configuration files. The Configuration files are XML files that define the default settings for the Web application and the Web server. Each Web application has one **Web.config** configuration file, and each Web server has one **machine.config** file.
- **Global .asax** file. The **Global.asax** file, also known as the ASP.NET application file, is an optional file that contains code for responding to application-level events that are raised by ASP. NET or by HttpModules. At runtime, **Global.asax** is parsed and compiled into a dynamically generated .NET Framework class that is derived from the HttpApplication base class. This dynamic class is very similar to the Application class or main thread in Visual C++, and this class can be accessed by any other objects in the Web application.
- XML Web service links. These links are used to allow the Web application to send and receive data from an XML Web service.
- Database connectivity. The Database connectivity allows the Web application to transfer data to and from database sources. Generally, it is not recommended to allow users to access the database from the server directly because of the security issues, instead, in most industrial and commercial applications; the database can be accessed through the application layer to strengthen the security of the databases.
- Caching. Caching allows the Web application to return Web Forms and data more quickly after the first request.

8.2.1 ASP.NET Web Application File Structure

When you create an ASP.NET Web application, Visual Studio.NET creates two folders to hold the files that are related to the application. When the project is compiled, a third folder is created to store the terminal dynamic linked library (dll) file. In other words, the final or terminal file of an ASP.NET Web application is a dll file.

Figure 8.3 shows the typical file structure of an ASP.NET Web application.

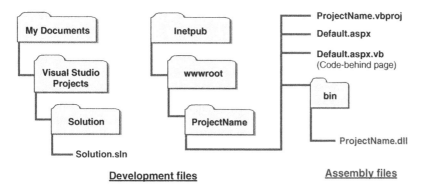

Figure 8.3 ASP.NET Web application file structure.

Those folders listed on the left side in Figure 8.3 are very familiar to us since they are created by the Windows-based applications. But the folders created on the right-hand side are new to us, and the functionalities of those folders are:

- The **Inetpub** folder contains another folder named **wwwroot,** and it is used to hold the root address of the Web project whose name is defined as **ProjectName**. The project file **ProjectName.vbproj** is an XML file that contains references to all project items, such as forms and classes.
- The **bin** folder contains the assembly file or the terminal file of the project with the name of ProjectName.dll. All ASP.NET Web applications will be finally converted to a dll file and stored in the server's memory.

8.2.2 ASP.NET Execution Model

When you finished an ASP.NET Web application, the Web project is compiled and two terminal files are created:

1) **Project Assembly files** (.dll). All code-behind pages (.aspx.vb) in the project are compiled into a single assembly file that is stored as **ProjectName.dll**. This project assembly file is placed in the **\bin** directory of the Web site and will be executed by the Web server when a request is received from the client at the running time.
2) **AssemblyInfo.vb file**. This file is used to write the general information, especially assembly version and assembly attributes, about the assembly.

When the Web project runs and the client requests a Web page for the first time, the following events occur:

1) The client browser issues a GET HTTP request to the server.
2) The ASP.NET parser interprets the course code.
3) Based on the interpreting result, ASP.NET will direct the request to the associated assembly file (.dll) if the code has been compiled into the dll files. Otherwise, the ASP.NET invokes the compiler to convert the code into dll format.
4) Runtime loads and executes the MSIL code and send back the required Web page to the client in the HTML file format.

For the second time when the user requests the same Web page, no compiling process is needed and the ASP.NET can directly call the dll file and execute the MSIL code to speed up this request.

From this execution sequence, it looks like the execution or running of a Web application is easy and straightforward, but in practice, a lot of data round trips occurred between the client and the server. To make it clear, let us make a little more analysis to see what happened between the client and the server when a Web application is executed.

8.2.3 What Is Really Happened When a Web Application Is Executed?

The key point is that a Web Form is built and runs on the Web server. When the user sends a request from the user's client browser to request that Web page, the server needs to build that form and sends it back to the user's browser in the HTML format. Once the Web page is received by the client's browser, the connection between the client and the server is terminated. If the user wants to request any other page or information from the server, additional requests must be submitted.

To make this issue more clear, we can use our LogIn form as an example. When the first time the user sends a request to the server to ask to start a logon process, the server builds the LogIn form and sends it back to the client in the HTML format. After that, the connection between the client and the server is gone. After the user received the LogIn Web page and entered the necessary logon information such as the username and password to the LogIn form, the user needs to send another request to the server to ask the server to process those pieces of logon information. If, after the server received and processed the logon information, the server found that the logon information is invalid, the server needs to re-build the LogIn form and re-send it back to the client with some warning message. So you can see how many round trips occurred between the client and the server when a Web application is executed.

A good solution to try to reduce those round trips is to make sure that all information entered from the client side should be as correct as possible. In other words, try to make as much validation as possible in the client side to reduce the burden of the server.

Now, we have finished the discussion about the .NET Framework and ASP.NET as well as the ASP.NET Web applications. Next, we will create and develop some actual Web projects using the ASP.NET Web Forms to illustrate how to access the database through the Web browser to select, display, and manipulate data on Web pages.

8.2.4 The Requirements to Test and Run the Web Project

Before we can start to create our real Web project using the ASP.NET, we need the following requirements to test and run our Web project:

1) Web server: To test and run our Web project, you need a Web server either on your local computer or on your network. By default, if you installed the Internet Information Services (IIS) on your local computer before the .NET Framework is installed on your computer, the FrontPage Server Extension 2002 may have been installed on your local computer. This software allows your Web development tools such as Visual Studio.NET to connect to the server to upload or download pages from the server.
2) To make our Web project simple and easy, we always use our local computer as a local server. In other words, we always use the `localhost`, which is the IP name of our local computer, as our Web server to communicate with our browser to perform the data accessing and manipulating.

Refer to Appendix H to install the FrontPage Server Extensions 2002 for Windows 10 on your computer if you have not installed this tool.

As we know, the .NET Framework includes two Data Providers for accessing enterprise databases: the .NET Framework Data Provider for OLE DB and the .NET Framework Data Provider for SQL Server. Because both the SQL Server and the Oracle database belong to the server database, in this Chapter, we only use the Oracle database as our target database to illustrate how to select, display, and manipulate data from the database through the Web pages.

This chapter is organized in the following ways:

1) Develop ASP.NET Web application to select and display data from the Oracle XE 18c database.
2) Develop ASP.NET Web application to insert data into the Oracle XE 18c database.
3) Develop ASP.NET Web application to update and delete data against the Oracle XE 18c database.
4) Develop ASP.NET Web application to select and manipulate data against the Oracle XE 18c database using LINQ to Oracle query.

Let us start from the first one to create and build our ASP.NET Web application.

8.3   Develop ASP.NET Web Application to Select Data from Oracle Databases

Let us start a new ASP.NET Web application project `OracleWebSelect` to illustrate how to access and select data from the database via the Internet. Open the Visual Studio.NET and click on the `File|New Project` to create a new ASP.NET Web application project. On the opened New Project wizard, which is shown in Figure 8.4, click on the `ASP.NET Web Application (.NET Framework)` item from the right pane. Click on the Next button to open the project configuration wizard.

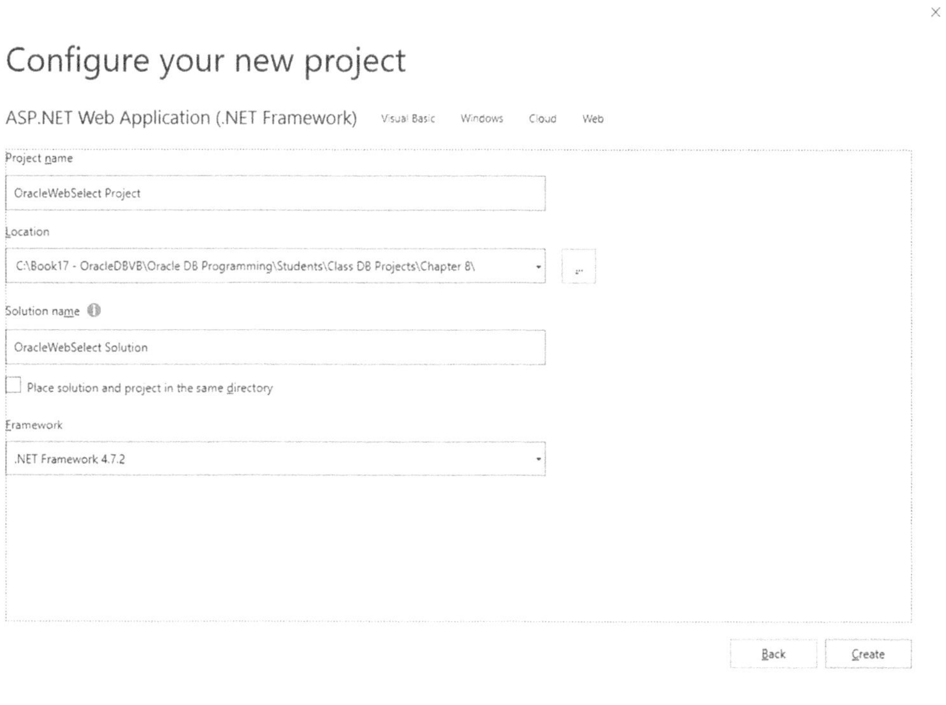

Figure 8.4   The opened Template wizard. *Source:* Used with permission from Microsoft.

On the opened configuration wizard, enter `OracleWebSelect Project` into the Project name and `OracleWebSelect Solution` into the Solution name boxes. Then, click on the `Browse` button to browse to any location or folder where you want to save this project to. In our case, we place it in our folder: `C:\Class DB Projects\Chapter 8`. Browse to that folder and click on the `Select Folder` button. Your finished New Web Site wizard is shown in Figure 8.4. Click on the `Create` button to continue. In the next wizard, select the `Web Forms` item and click the `Create` button again to create this new Web application project.

On the opened new project, the default Web Form is named `Default.aspx` and it is located at the Solution Explorer window. This is the Web Form that works as a user interface in the server-side. Now let us perform some modifications to this form to make it as our LogIn form.

8.3.1 Create the User Interface – LogIn Form

Right click on the `Default.aspx` item and rename it to `LogIn.aspx`. Then perform the following modifications to the Source file to make it as our LogIn Form page:

1) Open the Source file window by right clicking on the `LogIn.aspx` page and select the `Open` from the popup menu. Move the cursor to the end of the top or the first line and change from `Inherits = "OracleWebSelect_Project._Default"` to `Inherits = "OracleWebSelect_Project._LogIn"` (do not worry if a blue underscore appears and we can fix this in the next step).
2) Double click on the `LogIn.aspx.vb` from the Solution Explorer window to open the code-behind page. Change the class name from `_Default` to `_LogIn`. You need to click on the `Show All Files` button on the Solution Explorer top bar if you cannot find this `LogIn.aspx.vb` file, which should be located under the `LogIn.aspx` file.
3) Go to `Build|Rebuild OracleWebSelect Project` menu item to build our project.

The Source file basically is an HTML file that contains the related codes for all controls you added into this Web form in the HTML format. Compared with the codes in the code-behind page, the difference between them is that the Source file is used to describe all controls you added into the Web form in HTML format, but the code-behind page is used to describe all controls you added into the Web form in Visual Basic.NET code format with a default `Page_Load()` event procedure.

Now right click on the `LogIn.aspx` from the Solution Explorer window and select the `View Designer` item from the popup menu to open the Design view of the `LogIn` page.

Unlike Windows-based applications, by default the user interface in a Web-based application has no background color. You can modify the Web form by adding another Style Sheet and format the form as you like. Also if you want to make this style such as the header and footer of the form apply to all of your pages, you can add a Master Page to do that. But in this project, we prefer to use the default window as our user interface and each page in our project has different style.

We need to remove all default contents from this page and add the controls shown in Table 8.1 into our LogIn user interface or Web page. One point to be noticed is that there is no `Name` property available for any control in the Web form object, instead the property `ID` is used to replace the `Name` property and it works a unique identifier for each control you added into the Web form.

Another difference with the Windows-based form is that when you add these controls into our Web form, first you must locate a position for the control to be added using the `Space` key and the `Enter` key on your keyboard in the Web form, and then pick up a control from the Toolbox window and drag it to that location. You cannot pick and drag a control to a random location as you want in this Web form, and this is a significant difference between the Windows-based form and the Web-based form windows.

Table 8.1 Controls for the LogIn form.

Type	ID	Text	TabIndex	BackColor	TextMode	Font
Label	Label1	Welcome to CSE DEPT	0	#E0E0E0		Bold/large
Label	Label2	User Name	1			Bold/small
Textbox	txtUserName		2			
Label	Label3	Pass Word	3			Bold/small
Textbox	txtPassWord		4		Password	
Button	cmdLogIn	LogIn	5			Bold/medium
Button	cmdCancel	Cancel	6			Bold/medium

Figure 8.5 The finished LogIn Web form. *Source:* Used with permission from Microsoft.

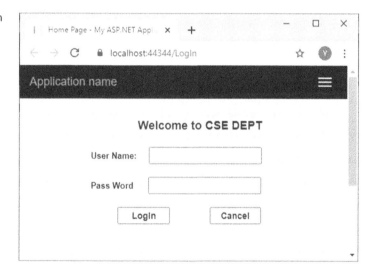

Your finished user interface should match the one that is shown in Figure 8.5.

Before we can add the codes into the code-behind page to response to the controls to perform the logon process, first we must run the project to allow the **Web.config** file to recognize those controls we have added into the Web form. Click on the **IIS Express** button on the toolbar to run our project. Click the **Yes** buttons for the next two Message Boxes to install a default license and add a **Web.config** file if you encountered these as the project runs.

Your running Web page should match the one that is shown in Figure 8.5. Click on the **Close** button that is located at the upper-right corner of the form to close this page.

Now let us develop the codes to access the database to perform the logon process.

8.3.2 Develop the Codes to Access and Select Data from the Database

Open the code-behind page by right clicking on the **LogIn.aspx.vb** from the Solution Explorer window, and select the **View Code** item from the popup menu. First, we need to add some data driver references to use our Oracle data driver provided by Devart. To do that, right click on our Web project **OracleWebSelect Project** from the Solution Explorer window and select the

Add | Reference item to open the **Reference Manager** wizard. Then click on the **Extensions** item from the left pane and check both items, **Devart.Data** and **Devart.Data.Oracle**, from the mid-pane. Click on the **OK** button to add these references to our project.

Now add two imports commands to the top of this code window to import the namespace of the Oracle Data Provider:

```
Imports Devart.Data
Imports Devart.Data.Oracle
```

Next, we need to create a global variable, **oraConnection**, for our connection object. Enter the following code under the class header:

```
Public oraConnection As OracleConnection
```

This connection object will be used by all Web forms in this project.

Now, we need to develop the codes for the **Page_Load()** event procedure, which is similar to the **Form_Load()** event procedure in the Windows-based application. Enter the codes that are shown in Figure 8.6 into this event procedure.

Let us have a closer look at this piece of codes to see how it works.

A) First, the namespaces for the Oracle Data Provider are imported since we need to use some components defined in those namespaces to perform data actions in this page.

B) A global connection object **oraConnection** is declared first, and this object will be used by all Web forms in this project later to connect to the database.

C) As we did for the **Form_Load()** event procedure in the Windows-based applications, we need to perform the database connection in this event procedure. A connection string is created with the database server or source name, database name, and security mode.

D) A new database connection object is created with the connection string as the argument.

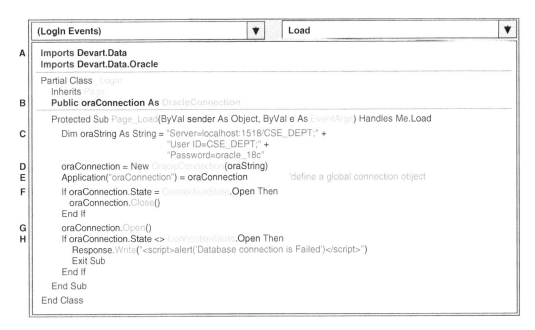

Figure 8.6 The codes for the Page_Load event procedure.

E) The global connection object `oraConnection` is added into the **Application state** function, and this object can be used by any pages in this application by accessing this Application state function later. Unlike global variables defined in the Windows-based applications, one cannot access a global variable by prefixing the form's name before the global variable declared in that form from other pages. In the Web-based application, the Application state function is a good place to store any global variable. In ASP.NET Web application, Application state is stored in an instance of the `HttpApplicationState` class that can be accessed through the Application property of the `HttpContext` class in the server side and is faster than storing and retrieving information in a database.

F) First, we need to check whether this database connection has been done. If it is, we first need to disconnect this connection by using the `Close()` method.

G) Then, we can call the `Open()` method to set up a valid database connection.

H) By checking the database connection state property, we can confirm whether the connection is successful or not. If the connection state is not equal to `Open`, which means that the database connection is failed, a warning message is displayed and the procedure is exited.

One significant difference in using something like a Message box to display some debug information in the Web form is that you cannot use a Message box as you did in the Windows-based applications. In the Web form development, no Message box object available and you can only use the Javascript `alert()` method to display a Message in ASP.NET.

Two popular objects are widely utilized in the ASP.NET Web applications: The `Request` and the `Response` objects.

The ASP Request object is used to get information from the user, and the ASP Response object is used to send output to the user from the server. The `Write()` method of the Response object is used to display the message sent by the server. You must add the script tag `<script>......</script>` to indicate that the content is written in Javascript language.

Now let us develop the codes for the `LogIn` button's Click event procedure. The function of this piece of codes is to access the LogIn table located in our sample Oracle database based on the username and password entered by the user to try to find the matched logon information. Currently, we have not created our next page – `Selection page`, so we just display a Message to confirm the success of the logon process if it is.

Right click on the `LogIn.aspx.vb` from the Solution Explorer and select the `View Designer` item from the popup menu to open the Web page view. Then double click on the `LogIn` button to open its event procedure. Enter the codes shown in Figure 8.7 into this event procedure. Let us have a closer look at this piece of codes to see how it works.

A) An Oracle query statement is declared first since we need to use this query statement to retrieve the matched username and password from the LogIn table. Since this query statement is too long, so we split it into two sub-strings. You can use the concatenating operator '&' to make these two strings as one if you like.

B) Some data objects are created here such as the Command object, DataReader object, and Parameter objects.

C) Then, two parameter objects are initialized with the parameter's name and value properties. The Command object is built by assigning it with the Connection object, `commandType` and `Parameters` collection properties of the Command class.

D) The `Add()` method is utilized to add two actual parameters to the Parameters collection of the Command class.

E) The `ExecuteReader()` method of the Command class is executed to access the database, retrieve the matched username and password, and return them to the DataReader object.

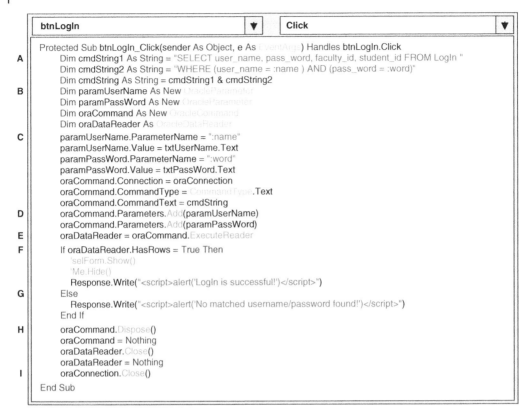

```
btnLogIn                                    ▼    Click                                              ▼

    Protected Sub btnLogIn_Click(sender As Object, e As EventArgs) Handles btnLogIn.Click
A       Dim cmdString1 As String = "SELECT user_name, pass_word, faculty_id, student_id FROM LogIn "
        Dim cmdString2 As String = "WHERE (user_name = :name ) AND (pass_word = :word)"
        Dim cmdString As String = cmdString1 & cmdString2
B       Dim paramUserName As New OracleParameter
        Dim paramPassWord As New OracleParameter
        Dim oraCommand As New OracleCommand
        Dim oraDataReader As OracleDataReader
C       paramUserName.ParameterName = ":name"
        paramUserName.Value = txtUserName.Text
        paramPassWord.ParameterName = ":word"
        paramPassWord.Value = txtPassWord.Text
        oraCommand.Connection = oraConnection
        oraCommand.CommandType = CommandType.Text
        oraCommand.CommandText = cmdString
D       oraCommand.Parameters.Add(paramUserName)
        oraCommand.Parameters.Add(paramPassWord)
E       oraDataReader = oraCommand.ExecuteReader
F       If oraDataReader.HasRows = True Then
            'selForm.Show()
            'Me.Hide()
            Response.Write("<script>alert('LogIn is successful!')</script>")
G       Else
            Response.Write("<script>alert('No matched username/password found!')</script>")
        End If
H       oraCommand.Dispose()
        oraCommand = Nothing
        oraDataReader.Close()
        oraDataReader = Nothing
I       oraConnection.Close()
    End Sub
```

Figure 8.7 The codes for the LogIn button's Click event procedure.

F) If the **HasRows** property of the DataReader is **True**, which means that at least one matched username and password has been found and retrieved from the database. A successful message is created and sent back from the server to the client to display in the client browser.

G) Otherwise, no matched username or password found from the database, and a warning message is created and sent back to the client and displayed in the client browser.

H) The used objects such as the Command and the DataReader are released.

I) In all Web-based application projects, we prefer to close the database connection after each data access to our database. The advantage of using this disconnection function is based on a fact that some components, such as OracleCommand and OracleDataReader, are closely dependent on the connection, and they cannot be closed until the database connection is closed.

Next let us develop the codes for the **Cancel** button's Click event procedure.

The function of this event procedure is to close the current Web page if this **Cancel** button is clicked, which means that the user wants to terminate the ASP.NET Web application. Double click on the **Cancel** button from the Design View of the LogIn form to open this event procedure and enter the codes shown in Figure 8.8 into this procedure.

A) First, we need to check whether the database is still connected to our Web form. If it is, we need to close this connection before we can terminate our Web application.

B) The server sends back a command with the Response object's method **Write()** to issue a Javascript statement **window.close()** to close the Web application.

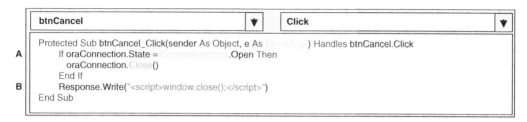

```
btnCancel              ▼        Click                                    ▼

    Protected Sub btnCancel_Click(sender As Object, e As          ) Handles btnCancel.Click
A       If oraConnection.State =             .Open Then
            oraConnection.Close()
        End If
B       Response.Write("<script>window.close();</script>")
    End Sub
```

Figure 8.8 The codes for the Cancel button's event procedure.

 A key point is the browser you are using for this kind of ASP.NET project. You must set the Internet Explorer as your running browser by selecting IIS Express (Internet Explorer) on the top of your page, otherwise you cannot close your page if some other browser, such as Google Chrome or Microsoft Edge, is used. Because both browsers do not recognize and execute the script instructions.

At this point, we have finished developing the codes for the LogIn Web form. Before we can run the project to test our Web page, we need to add some data validation functions in the client side to reduce the burden of the server.

8.3.3   Validate the Data in the Client Side

To reduce the burden on the server, we should make every effort to perform the data validation in the client side. In other words, before we can send requests to the server, we need to make sure that our information to be sent to the server should be as correct as possible. ASP.NET provides some tools to help us to complete this data validation. These tools include five validation controls that are shown in Table 8.2.

Table 8.2   Validation Controls.

Validation Control	Functionality
RequiredFieldValidator	Validate whether the required field has valid data (not blank).
RangeValidator	Validate whether a value is within a given numeric range. The range is defined by the MaximumValue and MinimumValue properties provided by users.
CompareValidator	Validate whether a value fits a given expression by using the different Operator property such as 'equal', 'greater than', 'less than', and the type of the value, which is set by the Type property.
CustomValidator	Validate a given expression using a script function. This method provides the maximum flexibility in data validation, but one needs to add a function to the Web page and sends it to the server to get the feedback from it.
RegularExpressionValidator	Validate whether a value fits a given regular expression by using the ValidationExpression property, which should be provided by the user.

All of these five controls are located at the **Validation** tab in the Toolbox window in Visual Studio.NET environment.

We want to use one control, **RequiredFieldValidator**, to validate our two textboxes, **txtUserName** and **txtPassWord** in the LogIn page to make sure that both of them are not empty when the **LogIn** button is clicked by the user as the project runs.

Open the Design View of the LogIn Web form, go to the Toolbox window, and expand the **Validation** tab. Drag the **RequiredFieldValidator** control from the Toolbox window and place it next to the **UserName** textbox. Set the following properties to this control in the property window:

- ErrorMessage: **UserName is Required**
- ControlToValidate: **txtUserName**

Perform a similar dragging and placing operations to locate the second **RequiredFieldValidator** just next to the PassWord textbox. Set the following properties for this control in the property window:

- ErrorMessage: **PassWord is Required**
- ControlToValidate: **txtPassWord**

Your finished LogIn Web form should match the one that is shown in Figure 8.9.

Now run our project to test this data validation by clicking on the IIS Express button. Without entering any data into two textboxes, and directly click on the **LogIn** button. Immediately two error messages, which are created by the **RequiredFieldValidators**, are displayed to ask users to enter these two pieces of information. After entering the username and password, click on the **LogIn** button again, a successful login message is displayed. So you can see how the **RequiredFieldValidator** works to reduce the processing load for the server.

One good thing always brings some bad thing, which is true to our project, too. After the **RequiredFieldValidator** is added into our Web page, the user cannot close the page by clicking on the **Cancel** button if both UserName and PassWord textboxes are empty. This is because the **RequiredFieldValidator** is performing the validation checking and no further action can be taken by the Web page until both textboxes are filled with some valid data. Therefore, if you want to close the Web page now, you have to enter a valid username and password, and then you can close the page by clicking on the **Cancel** button.

Another point is that you have to use the Internet Explorer browser to run the project.

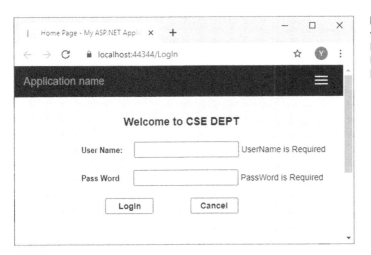

Figure 8.9 Adding the data validation – RequiredFieldValidator. *Source:* Used with permission from Microsoft.

8.3.4 Create the Second User Interface – Selection Page

Now let us continue to develop our Web application by adding another Web page, the `Selection` page. As we did in the previous chapters, after the logon process, the next step is to allow users to select different functions from the Selection form to perform the associated database actions.

The function of this Selection page is to allow users to visit different pages to perform different database actions such as selecting, inserting, updating, or deleting data against the database via the different tables by selecting the different items. So, this Selection page needs to perform the following jobs:

1) Provide and display all available selections to allow users to select them.
2) Open the associated page based on the users' selection.

Now let us build this page. To do that, we need to add a new Web page.

Right click on the project `OracleWebSelect` from the Solution Explorer window and select the `Add New Item` from the popup menu. On the opened window, keep the default Template `Web Form` selected, and enter `Selection.aspx` into the `Name` box as the name for this new page, and then click on the `Add` button to add this page into our project.

On the opened Web form, add the controls shown in Table 8.3 into this page.

As we mentioned in the last section, before you pick up any control from the Toolbox window and drag them into the page, you must first use the `Space` or the `Enter` keys from the keyboard to locate the positions on the page for those controls. Your finished Selection page should match the one that is shown in Figure 8.10.

Next let us create the codes for this Selection page to allow users to select the different sub-pages to perform the associated data actions.

8.3.5 Develop the Codes to Open the Other Page

First let us run the Selection page to build the Web configuration file. Click on the `IIS Express (Internet Explorer)` button to run this page, and then click on the `Close` button that is located on the upper-right corner of the page to close it. You can use `Project|Set As Start Page` to set this page as a start page to run it.

Right click on the `Selection.aspx.vb` from the Solution Explorer window and click on the `View Code` item from the popup menu to open the code page. First add two Imports commands to the top of this page to provide the namespace for the Oracle Provider:

Table 8.3 Controls on the Selection form.

Type	ID	Text	TabIndex	BackColor	Font
Label	Label1	Make Your Selection:	0	#E0E0E0	Bold/Large
DropDownList	ComboSelection		1		
Button	btnSelect	Select	2		Bold/Medium
Button	btnExit	Exit	3		Bold/Medium

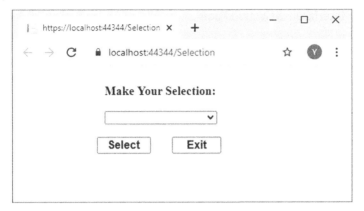

Figure 8.10 The finished Selection page. *Source:* Used with permission from Microsoft.

(Selection Events) ▼	Load ▼

```
Protected Sub Page_Load(ByVal sender As Object, ByVal e As System.EventArgs) Handles Me.Load

        ComboSelection.Items.Add("Faculty Information")
        ComboSelection.Items.Add("Course Information")
        ComboSelection.Items.Add("Student Information")
        'ComboSelection.SelectedIndex = 0

End Sub
```

Figure 8.11 The codes for the Page_Load event procedure of the Selection page.

btnSelect ▼	Click ▼

```
Protected Sub btnSelect_Click(sender As Object, e As EventArgs) Handles btnSelect.Click
        If ComboSelection.Text = "Faculty Information" Then
            Response.Redirect("Faculty.aspx")
        ElseIf ComboSelection.Text = "Student Information" Then
            Response.Redirect("Student.aspx")
        ElseIf ComboSelection.Text = "Course Information" Then
            Response.Redirect("Course.aspx")
        End If
End Sub
```

Figure 8.12 The codes for the Select button's event procedure.

```
Imports Devart.Data
Imports Devart.Data.Oracle
```

Then select the **(Selection Events)** from the Class Name combo box and select the **Load** item from the Method Name combo box to open the Page_Load event procedure. Enter codes that are shown in Figure 8.11 into this event procedure.

The function of this piece of codes is straightforward. Three pieces of information are added into the combo box **ComboSelection** by using the **Add()** method, and these pieces of information will be selected by the user as the project runs.

Next, we need to create the codes for two buttons' Click event procedures. First let us develop the codes for the **Select** button. Open the Designer View for the Selection Web form, and then double click on the **Select** button to open its event procedure. Enter the codes that are shown in Figure 8.12 into this event procedure.

Figure 8.13 The codes for the Exit button's Click event procedure.

The function of this piece of codes is easy. Based on the information selected by the user, the related Web page is opened by using the server's Response object, exactly by using the `Redirect()` method of the server's Response object. All of these three pages will be created and discussed in the following sections.

Finally, let us take care of the coding process for the **Exit** button's Click event procedure. The function of this piece of codes is to close the database connection and close the Web application. Double click on the **Exit** button from the Design View of the Selection page to open this event procedure. Enter the codes that are shown in Figure 8.13 into this event procedure.

First, we need to check if the database is still connected to our application. If it is, the global connection object stored in the Application state is activated with the `Close()` method to close the database connection. Then, the `Write()` method of the server Response object is called to close the Web application.

8.3.6 Modify Codes in the LogIn Page to Transfer to the Selection Page

Now, we have finished the coding process for the Selection page. Before we can run the project to test this page, we need to do some modifications to the codes in the **LogIn** button's Click event procedure in the LogIn page to allow the application to switch from the LogIn page to the Selection page as the login process is successful.

Open the LogIn page and the **LogIn** button's Click event procedure, replace the code line that is located inside the **If** block:

```
Response.Write("<script>alert('LogIn is successful!')</script>")
```

with the following code line:

```
Response.Redirect("Selection.aspx")
```

Also remove the last code line `oraConnection.Close()` from this event procedure since we need this connection opened during our project runs.

In this way, as long as the login process is successful, the next page, Selection page, will be opened by executing the `Redirect()` method of the server Response object. The argument of this method is the URL of the Selection page. Since the Selection page is located at the same application as the LogIn page does, so a direct page name is used.

Now, let us run the application to test these two pages. Make sure that the LogIn page is the starting page for our application. To do that, right click on the **LogIn.aspx** from the Solution Explorer window and select the item **Set As Start Page** from the popup menu. Click on the **IIS Express** button to run our project.

Enter the suitable username and password such as **jhenry** and **test** into the username and password boxes, and click on the **LogIn** button. The Selection page is displayed if this login pro-

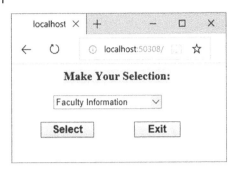

Figure 8.14 The running status of the second page – Selection page. *Source:* Used with permission from Microsoft.

cess is successful, as shown in Figure 8.14. Click on the **Exit** button to close the application. Now let us begin to develop our next page, Faculty page.

8.3.7 Create the Third User Interface – Faculty Page

Right click on our project `OracleWebSelect Project` from the Solution Explorer window and select the **Add|New Item** from the popup menu. On the opened wizard, select the template **Web Form** and enter `Faculty.aspx` into the **Name** box as the name for this new page, and then click on the **Add** button to add this new page into our project.

On the opened Web form, add the controls that are shown in Table 8.4 into this page.

As we mentioned in the last section, before you pick up those controls from the Toolbox window and drag them into the page, you must first use the Space or the Enter keys from the keyboard to locate the positions on the page for those controls. You cannot place a control in a random position on the form as you did in the Windows-based applications since the Web-based applications have the special layout requirements.

Now, you can enlarge the **Image** control **PhotoBox** and place it in the left on this page by dragging it to that position. Two points to be noted when building this page are:

1) After dragging and placing the **Image** control into this page, go to the **Properties** window and set the **ImageAlign** property to **Left**. Select **Solid** for the **BorderStyle** property.
2) Click on any place in this page and go to the **Properties** window. Select the **Style** property and click on the expansion button to open the **Modify Style** wizard. Click on the **Position** item from the left pane and select the **absolute** item from the **position:** combo box in the right pane.
3) Click on the **OK** button to complete these setups.

An easy way to build this page is to use an existing **Faculty.aspx** page, which can be found in a folder **VB Forms/Web** that is located under the **Students** folder at the Wiley ftp site (refer to Figure 1.2 in Chapter 1). To do that, right click on our project **OracleWeb-Select Project** from the Solution Explorer window and select the **Add|Existing item** from the popup menu, and browse to that folder and select one item, **Faculty.aspx**, by checking it, and click on the **Add** button to add it into our project.

Your finished Faculty page should match the one that is shown in Figure 8.15.

Although we added five buttons into this Faculty page, in this section, we only use the **Select** and the **Back** button since we want to discuss how to retrieve data based on the query command entered by the user from the database and display the retrieved result in this Faculty page. The other buttons will be used in the following sections later.

Now, let us begin to develop the codes for the Faculty page to perform data query from the Faculty table in our sample database.

Table 8.4 Controls on the Faculty form.

Type	ID	Text	TabIndex	BackColor	Font
Label	Label1	CSE_DEPT Faculty Page	0	#E0E0E0	Bold/Large
FileUpload	FileUploadImage		1		
Label	Label3	Faculty Name	2		Bold/Small
DropDownList	ComboName		3		
Image	PhotoBox		23		
Label	Label4	Faculty ID	4		Bold/Small
TextBox	txtID		5		
Label	Label5	Name	6		Bold/Small
TextBox	txtName		7		
Label	Label6	Title	8		Bold/Small
TextBox	txtTitle		19		
Label	Label7	Office	10		Bold/Small
TextBox	txtOffice		11		
Label	Label8	Phone	12		Bold/Small
TextBox	txtPhone		13		
Label	Label9	College	14		Bold/Small
TextBox	txtCollege		15		
Label	Label10	Email	16		Bold/Small
TextBox	txtEmail		17		
Button	btnSelect	Select	18		Bold/Small
Button	btnInsert	Insert	19		Bold/Small
Button	btnUpdate	Update	20		Bold/Small
Button	btnDelete	Delete	21		Bold/Small
Button	btnBack	Back	22		Bold/Small

8.3.8 Develop the Codes to Select the Desired Faculty Information

First, let us run the project to build the configuration file `Web.config` to configure all controls we just added into the Faculty page. Set the `LogIn.aspx` page as the `Start Page` and click on the `IIS Express` button to run the project, enter the suitable username and password to open the Selection page. Select the `Faculty Information` item from this page to open the Faculty page. Click on the `Close` button that is located at the upper-right corner of this page to close the project.

Open the code page of the Faculty page by double clicking on the `Faculty.aspx.vb` from the Solution Explorer window, and add two Imports commands to the top of this code page:

```
Imports Devart.Data
Imports Devart.Data.Oracle
```

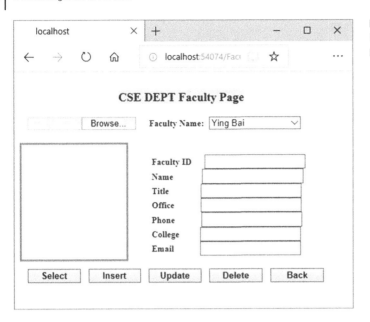

The codes for this page can be divided into three parts: Coding for the **Page_Load()** event procedure, coding for the **Select** button's Click event procedure, and coding for other procedures. First, let us take care of the coding for the **Page_Load()** event procedure.

8.3.8.1 Develop the Codes for the Page_Load Event Procedure

In the opened code page, open the **Page_Load()** event procedure by selecting the item (**Faculty Events**) from the Class Name combo box and the item **Load** from the Method Name combo box. Enter the codes that are shown in Figure 8.16 into this event procedure.

Let us have a closer look at this piece of codes to see how it works.

A) A form-level textbox array is created first since we need this array to hold eight pieces of faculty information and display them in textboxes and PhotoBox later.

B) Before we can perform the data actions against the database, we need to make sure that a valid database connection is set to allow us to transfer data between our project and the database. An Application state, which is used to hold our global connection object variable, is utilized to perform this checking and connecting to our database if it has not been connected.

C) As the project runs, each time as the user clicks the **Select** button to perform a data query, a request is sent to the database server and the Web server (they can be the same server). Then, the Web server will post back a refreshed Faculty page to the client when it received this request (**IsPostBack = True**). When this happened, the **Page_Load()** event procedure will be activated and the duplicated eight faculty members are attached to the end of the Faculty Name combo box control again. To avoid this duplication, we need to check the **IsPostBack** property of the page and add eight faculty members into the Faculty Name combo box control only one time when the project starts (**IsPostBack = False**). Refer to Section 8.3.9.1 for more detailed discussions about the **AutoPostBack** property.

Next, we need to develop the codes for the **Select** button's Click event procedure to perform the data query against the database.

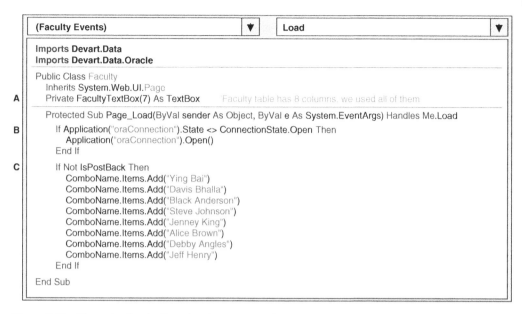

| (Faculty Events) | ▼ | Load | ▼ |

```
Imports Devart.Data
Imports Devart.Data.Oracle

Public Class Faculty
    Inherits System.Web.UI.Page
    Private FacultyTextBox(7) As TextBox        Faculty table has 8 columns, we used all of them

    Protected Sub Page_Load(ByVal sender As Object, ByVal e As System.EventArgs) Handles Me.Load
        If Application("oraConnection").State <> ConnectionState.Open Then
            Application("oraConnection").Open()
        End If

        If Not IsPostBack Then
            ComboName.Items.Add("Ying Bai")
            ComboName.Items.Add("Davis Bhalla")
            ComboName.Items.Add("Black Anderson")
            ComboName.Items.Add("Steve Johnson")
            ComboName.Items.Add("Jenney King")
            ComboName.Items.Add("Alice Brown")
            ComboName.Items.Add("Debby Angles")
            ComboName.Items.Add("Jeff Henry")
        End If
    End Sub
```

A (row label alongside the Private FacultyTextBox line)
B (row label alongside the If Application... block)
C (row label alongside the If Not IsPostBack block)

Figure 8.16   The codes for the Page_Load event procedure.

8.3.8.2   Develop the Codes for the Select Button Click Event Procedure

The function of this procedure is to make a query to the database to retrieve the faculty information based on the selected faculty member by the user from the Faculty Name combo box control, and display those pieces of retrieved information in seven textbox controls and faculty image on the Faculty page.

Open this **Select** button's Click event procedure by double clicking on this button from the Design View of the Faculty form, and enter the codes that are shown in Figure 8.17 into this event procedure.

Let us take a closer look at this piece of codes to see how it works.

A) The query string that contains a **SELECT** statement is declared here since we need to use this as our command text. The dynamic parameter of this query is **facultyName** defined in the **WHERE** clause.

B) Some data components such as the Command, Parameter, and DataReader objects are declared here since we need to use them to perform the data query later.

C) The Parameter object is initialized by assigning the dynamic parameter's name and value to it.

D) The Command object is initialized by assigning the associated components to it. These components include the global Connection object that is stored in the Application state, the Parameters collection object, and the CommandType as well as the CommandText properties.

E) The **ExecuteReader()** method of the Command object is called to execute the query command to retrieve the selected faculty information, and assign it to the DataReader object.

F) By checking the **HasRows** property of the DataReader, it can determine whether this query is successful or not. If this property is greater than zero, which means that at least one row is retrieved from the Faculty table in the database and thus the query is successful, a user-defined subroutine **FillFacultyReader()** is called to fill seven textboxes and the faculty image on the Faculty page with the retrieved faculty information.

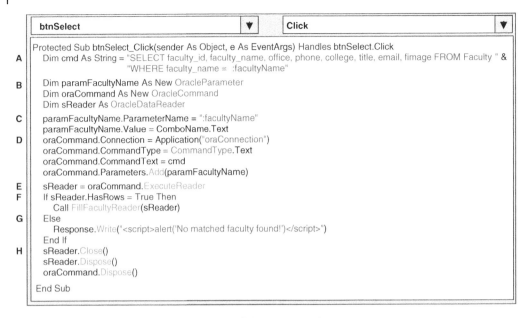

Figure 8.17 The codes for the Select button's Click event procedure.

G) Otherwise if the **HasRows** property is equal to zero, which means that no row has been retrieved from the database and the query is failed. A warning message is displayed in the client by calling the **Write()** method of the server Response object.

H) All data components used for this data query are released after this query.

At this point, we finished the codes for the **Select** button's Click event procedure.

8.3.8.3 Develop the Codes for Other Procedures

Next, let us take care of the coding process for other procedures in this Faculty page, this includes the coding process for the following procedures:

1) The User-defined subroutine procedure **FillFacultyReader()**.
2) The User-defined subroutine procedure **MapFacultyTable()**.
3) The **Back** button's Click event procedure.

The second user-defined subroutine procedure **MapFacultyTable()** is used and called by the first subroutine **FillFacultyReader()** in our project. Now let us discuss the coding process for these subroutines one by one.

The first user-defined subroutine is **FillFacultyReader()**. Open the code page of the Faculty Web form, and then type the codes that are shown in Figure 8.18 to create this subroutine procedure inside the Faculty class.

The function of this subroutine is to pick up each data column from the retrieved data that is stored in the DataReader and assign it to the associated textbox on the Faculty page to display it. Let us have a closer look at this piece of codes to see how it works.

A) A loop counter **intIndex** is declared first.

B) Seven instances of the textbox array are created and initialized. These seven objects are mapped to seven columns in the Faculty table in the database.

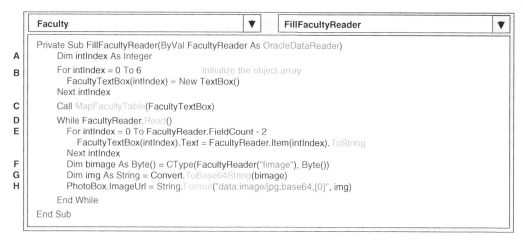

Faculty ▼	**FillFacultyReader** ▼

```
     Private Sub FillFacultyReader(ByVal FacultyReader As OracleDataReader)
A        Dim intIndex As Integer

B        For intIndex = 0 To 6                    'Initialize the object array
            FacultyTextBox(intIndex) = New TextBox()
         Next intIndex

C        Call MapFacultyTable(FacultyTextBox)

D        While FacultyReader.Read()
E           For intIndex = 0 To FacultyReader.FieldCount - 2
                FacultyTextBox(intIndex).Text = FacultyReader.Item(intIndex).ToString
            Next intIndex
F           Dim bimage As Byte() = CType(FacultyReader("fimage"), Byte())
G           Dim img As String = Convert.ToBase64String(bimage)
H           PhotoBox.ImageUrl = String.Format("data:image/jpg;base64,{0}", img)
         End While
     End Sub
```

Figure 8.18 The codes for the subroutine FillFacultyReader().

C) Another user-defined subroutine **MapFacultyTable()** is called to set up the correct mapping between the seven textbox controls on the Faculty page window and seven columns in the query string **cmdString**.

D) A **While** loop is executed as long as the loop condition, **Read()** method, is True, this means that a valid data is read out from the DataReader. This method will return a False if no any valid data can be read out from the DataReader, which means that all data has been read out. In this application, in fact, this **While** loop is only executed one time since we have only one row (one record) read out from the DataReader.

E) A **For...Next** loop is utilized to pick up each data read out from the DataReader object, and assign each of them to the associated textbox control on the Faculty page window. The **Item** property with the index is used here to identify each from the DataReader. The terminal column number is equal to **FieldCount − 2** since the last column (7) in the Faculty table is faculty image, **fimage**, which is an image object and it cannot be counted as a text. Thus, the 7 columns contained the text information for a faculty are in column 0~column 6 (**FieldCount = 8**).

F) Since the faculty image is stored in the last column with a format of binary data, therefore we need to get and convert it to a **Byte()** array.

G) Because there is no **PictureBox** object available in a Web page, thus we need to convert that image from a **Byte()** array to a 64-bit String and assign it to the **ImageUrl** property of the Image object in the Faculty page, **PhotoBox**, in step **H**.

Now let us develop the codes for the subroutine **MapFacultyTable()**.

The function of this subroutine, as we mentioned, is to set up a correct mapping relationship between seven textboxes in the textbox array on the Faculty page and the seven data columns in the query string. The reason for that is because the order of the textboxes distributed in the Faculty page may not be identical with the order of the data columns in the query string **cmdString** we created at the beginning of the **Select** button's Click event procedure.

Open the code page of the Faculty Web Form, type the codes that are shown in Figure 8.19 to create this subroutine inside the Faculty class.

The order of seven textboxes on the right-hand side of the equal operator should be equal to the order of the queried columns in the query string – **cmdString**. By performing this assignment, the seven textbox controls on the Faculty page window have a correct one-to-one mapping relation with the queried columns in the query string **cmdString**.

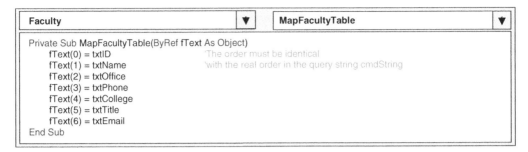

```
Faculty                          ▼   MapFacultyTable                    ▼

Private Sub MapFacultyTable(ByRef fText As Object)
    fText(0) = txtID                 'The order must be identical
    fText(1) = txtName               'with the real order in the query string cmdString
    fText(2) = txtOffice
    fText(3) = txtPhone
    fText(4) = txtCollege
    fText(5) = txtTitle
    fText(6) = txtEmail
End Sub
```

Figure 8.19 The codes for the subroutine MapFacultyTable().

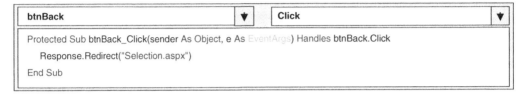

```
btnBack                          ▼   Click                              ▼

Protected Sub btnBack_Click(sender As Object, e As EventArgs) Handles btnBack.Click
    Response.Redirect("Selection.aspx")
End Sub
```

Figure 8.20 The codes for the Back button's Click event procedure.

Finally let us take care of the coding process for the **Back** button's Click event procedure. The function of this piece of codes is to return to the Selection page as this button is clicked. Double click on the **Back** button from the Faculty page window to open this event procedure and enter the code lines shown in Figure 8.20 into this procedure.

This piece of codes is straightforward and easy to be understood. The **Redirect()** method of the server Response object is executed to direct the client from the current Faculty page back to the Selection page when this button is clicked by the user. Exactly, the server re-sends the Selection page to the client when this button is clicked and a request is sent to the server.

We have finished all coding development for the Faculty page. It is the time for us to run the project to test our pages.

Now click on the IIS Express button to run our project. Enter the suitable username and password such as **jhenry** and **test** to the LogIn page, select the **Faculty Information** from the Selection page to open the Faculty page. Select one faculty member from the Faculty Name combo box such as **Ying Bai**, and then click on the **Select** button to retrieve the selected faculty information from the database. All pieces of information related to that selected faculty are retrieved and displayed in this Faculty page, as shown in Figure 8.21.

Click on the **Back** button to return to the Selection page, and then click on the **Exit** button to terminate our project. So far, our Web application is successful.

Next, we need to create our last Web page, Course page, and add it into our project to select and display all courses taught by the selected faculty member.

8.3.9 Create the Fourth User Interface – Course Page

To create a new Web page and add it into our project, go to the Solution Explorer window and right click on our project **OracleWebSelect Project**, then select **Add|New Item** from the popup menu to open the Add New Item wizard. On the opened wizard, select the template **Web Form** from the mid-pane. Then, enter **Course.aspx** into the **Name** box as the name for our new page and click on the **Add** button to add it into our project.

Figure 8.21 The running status of the Faculty page. *Source:* Used with permission from Microsoft.

On the opened Web form, add the controls that are shown in Table 8.5 into this page.

As we mentioned before, you cannot place a control in any position on the Web form as you like. You must first use the Space and the Enter keys from the keyboard to locate the positions on the page for those controls. You cannot place a control in a random position on the form as you did in the Windows-based applications since the Web-based applications have the special layout requirements.

An easy way to build this Course page is to add an existing Course page **Course.aspx** that can be found from the folder **VB Forms\Web** in the Wiley ftp site under the **Students** folder (refer to Figure 1.2 in Chapter 1). Perform the following operations to add this existing Course page into our project:

1) Right click on our current project **OracleWebSelect Project** from the Solution Explorer window, and select the **Add|Existing Item** from the popup menu.
2) Browse to the folder **Students\VB Forms\Web** in the Wiley ftp site and select the item, **Course.aspx**, and then click on the **Add** button to add it into our project. You can also save this page into a temporary folder in your computer and then perform this adding action.

Your finished Course page should match the one that is shown in Figure 8.22.

Before we can continue to develop our codes, we must emphasize one key point for the list box control used in the Web-based applications. There is a significant different process for the list box control used in the Windows-based and Web-based applications.

8.3.9.1 The AutoPostBack Property of the List Box Control

One important property is the **AutoPostBack** for the list box control **CourseList** in this page. Unlike the list box control used in the Windows-based applications, a **SelectedIndexChanged** event will not be created in the server side if the user clicked and selected an item from the list box. The reason for that is because the default value for the **AutoPostBack** property of a list box

Table 8.5 Controls on the Course form.

Type	ID	Text	TabIndex	BackColor	Font	AutoPostBack
Panel	Panel1		16	#C0C0FF		
Label	Label1	Faculty Name	0		Bold/Smaller	
DropDownList	ComboName		1			
ListBox	CourseList		17		Bold/Medium	True
Panel	Panel2		18	#C0C0FF		
Label	Label2	Course ID	2		Bold/Smaller	
TextBox	txtID		3			
Label	Label3	Course	4		Bold/Smaller	
TextBox	txtCourse		5			
Label	Label4	Schedule	6		Bold/Smaller	
TextBox	txtSchedule		7			
Label	Label5	Classroom	8		Bold/Smaller	
TextBox	txtClassroom		9			
Label	Label6	Credit	10		Bold/Smaller	
TextBox	txtCredit		11			
Label	Label7	Enrollment	12		Bold/Smaller	
TextBox	txtEnroll		13			
Button	btnSelect	Select	14		Bold/Medium	
Button	btnInsert	Insert	15		Bold/Medium	
Button	btnUpdate	Update	16		Bold/Medium	
Button	btnDelete	Delete	17		Bold/Medium	
Button	btnBack	Back	18		Bold/Medium	

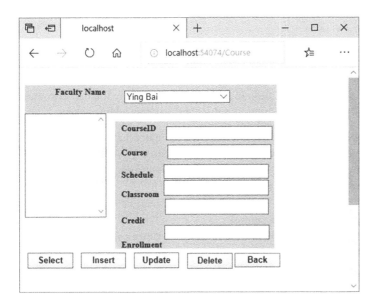

Figure 8.22 The finished Course Web page. *Source:* Used with permission from Microsoft.

control is reset to **False** when you add a new list box to your Web form. This means that even the user clicked and changed the item from a list box, a **SelectedIndexChanged** event can only be created in the client side and it cannot be sent to the server. As you know, all controls including the list box are running at the server side when your project runs. So no matter how many times you clicked and changed the items from the list box, no any event can be sent to the server side. Thus, it looks like that your clicking on the list box cannot be responded by your project.

However, in this project, we need to use this **SelectedIndexChanged** event to trigger our event procedure to perform the course information query. In order to solve this problem, the **AutoPostBack** property should be set to **True**. In this way, each time when you click on an item to select it from the list box, this **AutoPostBack** property will set a value to post back to the server to indicate that the user has triggered this control.

In this section, we only discuss the coding development for the **Select** and the **Back** buttons' Click event procedures to perform the course data query. The coding process for other buttons, such as **Insert, Update,** and **Delete**, will be discussed later in the following sections when we perform the data inserting, updating, or deleting actions against the database using the Web pages.

Now let us develop the codes for the **Select** and the **Back** buttons' Click event procedures to pick up the course data from the database using the Course Web page.

8.3.10   Develop the Codes to Select the Desired Course Information

The functions of the Course page include:

1) When users selected the desired faculty member from the Faculty Name combo box control and clicks on the **Select** button, all IDs of the courses taught by the selected faculty should be retrieved from the database and displayed in the list box control **CourseList** on the Course page.
2) When the user clicks on any **COURSE_ID** from the list box control **CourseList**, the detailed course information related to the selected **COURSE_ID** in the list box will be retrieved from the database and displayed in six textboxes on the Course page.

Based on the function analysis above, we need to concentrate our coding process on two event procedures; the **Select** button's Click event procedure and the **CourseList** box's **SelectedIndexChanged** event procedure. The first piece of codes is used to retrieve and display all **COURSE_ID** related to courses taught by the selected faculty in the list box control **CourseList**, and the second coding is to retrieve and display the detailed course information, such as the course title, schedule, classroom, credit, and enrollment, related to the selected **COURSE_ID** from the **CourseList** control.

The above coding jobs can be divided into four parts:

1) Coding for the Course page loading and ending event procedures. These procedures include the Page_Load() and the **Back** button's Click event procedure.
2) Coding for the **Select** button's click event procedure.
3) Coding for the **SelectedIndexChanged** event procedure of the list box control **CourseList**.
4) Coding for other user-defined subroutine procedures.

Before we can take care of the first coding job, we need to add two Imports commands to the top of the Course page. Open the code window of the Course page and enter two Imports commands to the top of that page:

```
Imports Devart.Data
Imports Devart.Data.Oracle
```

Now let us start our coding process from the first part.

8.3.10.1 Coding for the Course Page Loading and Ending Event Procedures

Open the Page_Load event procedure by selecting **(Page Events)** from the Class Name combo box and **Load** from the Method Name combo box from the code window. Enter the codes that are shown in Figure 8.23 into this event procedure.

Let us take a closer look at this piece of codes to see how it works.

A) This coding fragment is similar to the one we did for the Faculty form. Six textbox controls are used to display the detailed course information that is related to the selected faculty from the Faculty Name combo box. The Course table has seven columns, but we only need six of them, so the size of this TextBox array is 5 and each element or each TextBox control in this array is indexed from 0 to 5.

B) The function of this code segment is: Before we can perform any data query, we need to check whether a valid connection is available. Since we created a global connection instance in the LogIn page and stored it in the Application state, now we need to check this connection object and re-connect it to the database if our application has not been connected to the database.

C) These codes are used to initialize the Faculty Name combo box, and an **Add()** method is used to add all faculty members into this combo box to allow users to select one to get the course information as the project runs. Here, a potential bug is existed for this piece of codes. An **AutoPostBack** property will be set to **True** whenever the user clicked and selected an item from the list box control, and this property will be sent to the server to indicate that an action has been taken by the user to this list box. After the server received this property, it will send back a refreshed Course page to the client; therefore, the Page_Load event procedure of the Course page will be triggered and run again as a refreshed Course page is sent back. The result of execution of this Page_Load procedure is to attach another copy of all faculty members to the end of those faculty members that have been already added into the Faculty Name combo box when the Course page is displayed in the first time. As the number of your clicking on an item in the **CourseList** box increases, the number of copies of all faculty members will also

Figure 8.23 The codes for the Page_Load() event procedure.

be increased and displayed in the Faculty Name combo box. To avoid these duplications, we need to add all faculty members in the first time as the Course page is displayed, but do nothing if an **AutoPostBack** property occurred.

The codes for the **Back** button's Click event procedure are simple. When this button is clicked, the Course page is back to the Selection page. The **Redirect()** method of the server Response object is used to fulfill this switching function. Double click on the **Back** button from the Course page window and enter the following codes into this procedure:

```
Response.Redirect("Selection.aspx")
```

8.3.10.2 Coding for the Select Button's Click Event Procedure

As we mentioned at the beginning of this section, the function of this event procedure is: when the user selected the desired faculty member from the Faculty Name combo box control and clicks on the **Select** button, all **COURSE_ID** related to courses taught by the selected faculty should be retrieved from the database and displayed in the list box control **CourseList** in the Course page.

Double click on the **Select** button from the Course page window to open this event procedure, and enter the codes that are shown in Figure 8.24 into this procedure.

Let us have a closer look at this piece of codes to see how it works.

A) The joined table query string is declared at the beginning of this event procedure. Here, two columns are queried. The first one is the **COURSE_ID,** and the second is the course name. The reason for this is that we need to use the **COURSE_ID**, not course name, as the identifier to pick up each course' detailed information from the Course table when the user clicked and selected the **COURSE_ID** from the **CourseList** box. We use the **COURSE_ID** with the course name together in this joined table query, and we will use that **COURSE_ID** later. The assignment operator is used for the criteria in the **ON** clause in the query string, and this is required by Oracle database operation. For a more detailed discussion about the joined table query, refer to Section 5.6.6.1 in Chapter 5.

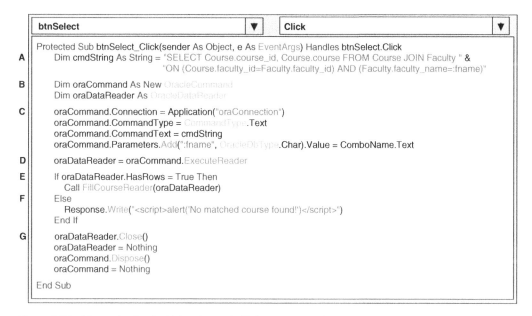

```
btnSelect                                          ▼    Click                                          ▼

      Protected Sub btnSelect_Click(sender As Object, e As EventArgs) Handles btnSelect.Click
A         Dim cmdString As String = "SELECT Course.course_id, Course.course FROM Course JOIN Faculty " &
                           "ON (Course.faculty_id=Faculty.faculty_id) AND (Faculty.faculty_name=:fname)"

B         Dim oraCommand As New OracleCommand
          Dim oraDataReader As OracleDataReader

C         oraCommand.Connection = Application("oraConnection")
          oraCommand.CommandType = CommandType.Text
          oraCommand.CommandText = cmdString
          oraCommand.Parameters.Add(":fname", OracleDbType.Char).Value = ComboName.Text

D         oraDataReader = oraCommand.ExecuteReader

E         If oraDataReader.HasRows = True Then
             Call FillCourseReader(oraDataReader)
F         Else
             Response.Write("<script>alert('No matched course found!')</script>")
          End If

G         oraDataReader.Close()
          oraDataReader = Nothing
          oraCommand.Dispose()
          oraCommand = Nothing

      End Sub
```

Figure 8.24 The codes for the Select button's Click event procedure.

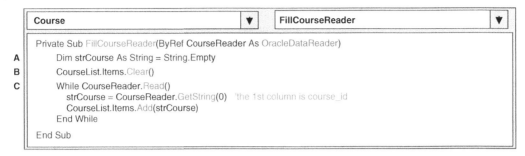

Course	▼	FillCourseReader	▼

```
      Private Sub FillCourseReader(ByRef CourseReader As OracleDataReader)
A        Dim strCourse As String = String.Empty
B        CourseList.Items.Clear()
C        While CourseReader.Read()
             strCourse = CourseReader.GetString(0)   'the 1st column is course_id
             CourseList.Items.Add(strCourse)
         End While
      End Sub
```

Figure 8.25 The codes for the subroutine FillCourseReader().

B) Some Oracle data objects such as the Command and DataReader are created here. All of these objects should be prefixed by the keyword **ora** to indicate that all those components are related to the Oracle Data Provider.

C) The **oraCommand** object is initialized with the connection string, command type, command text, and command parameter. The parameter's name must be identical to the dynamic parameter **:fname**, which is defined in the query string and it is exactly located after the = comparator in the **ON** clause. The parameter's value is the content of the Faculty Name combo box, which should be selected by the user as the project runs.

D) The ExecuteReader() method of the Command class is executed to read back all courses (**COURSE_ID**) taught by the selected faculty and assign them to the DataReader object.

E) If the **HasRows** property of the DataReader is **True**, which means that at least one row data has been retrieved from the database, the subroutine **FillCourseReader()** is called to fill the **COURSE_ID** into the **CourseList** box.

F) Otherwise, this joined query is failed and a warning message is displayed.

G) Finally some cleaning jobs are preformed to release objects used for this query.

Now let us develop the codes for the user-defined subroutine **FillCourseReader()**, which is shown in Figure 8.25. Open the code page of the Course Web form and enter the codes that are shown in Figure 8.25 to create this procedure inside the Course class.

Let us see how this piece of codes works.

A) A local string variable **strCourse** is created, and this variable can be considered as an intermediate variable that is used to temporarily hold the queried data from the Course table.

B) We need to clean up the **CourseList** box before it can be filled.

C) A **While** loop is utilized to retrieve each first column's data (**GetString(0)**) whose column index is 0, and the data value is the **COURSE_ID**. The queried data first is assigned to the intermediate variable **strCourse**, and then it is added into the **CourseList** box by using the **Add()** method.

Now let us start to develop the codes for the **SelectedIndexChanged** event procedure of the list box control **CourseList**. The function of this event procedure is: when the user clicks any **COURSE_ID** from the list box control **CourseList**, the detailed course information related to the selected **COURSE_ID**, such as the course title, schedule, credit, classroom, and enrollment, will be retrieved from the database and displayed in six textboxes on the Course page form.

8.3.10.3 Coding for the SelectedIndexChanged Event Procedure of the CourseList Box

Open the CourseList's **SelectedIndexChanged** event procedure by selecting **CourseList** from the Class Name combo box and **SelectedIndexChanged** item from the Method Name combo box, and enter the codes that are shown in Figure 8.26 into this procedure.

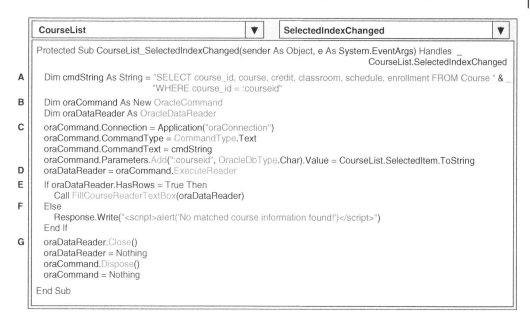

Figure 8.26 The codes for the SelectedIndexChanged event procedure.

Let us take a closer look at this piece of codes to see how it works.

A) The query string is created with six queried columns. The query criterion is **COURSE_ID**, which is obtained from the **CourseList** box control.

B) Two Oracle data objects are created, and these objects are used to perform the data operations between the database and our project. All of these objects should be prefixed by the keyword **ora** since in this project we used an Oracle Data Provider.

C) The **oraCommand** object is initialized with the connection object, command type, command text, and command parameter. The parameter's name must be identical to the dynamic nominal name **:courseid**, which is defined in the query string, exactly after the = comparator in the **WHERE** clause. The parameter's value is the **COURSE_ID** selected by the user from the **CourseList** box.

D) The ExecuteReader() method is executed to read back the detailed information for the selected course and assign it to the DataReader object.

E) If the **HasRows** property of the DataReader is **True**, which means that at least one row data has been retrieved from the database, the user-defined subroutine procedure **FillCourseReaderTextBox()** is called to fill detailed course information into six textboxes.

F) Otherwise, this query is failed, and a warning message is displayed.

G) Finally, some cleaning jobs are preformed to release objects used for this query.

The coding for other user-defined subroutine procedures includes the coding for the user-defined subroutine procedures **FillCourseReaderTextBox()** and **MapCourseTable()**.

8.3.10.4 Coding for Other User-Defined Subroutine Procedures

First let us develop the codes for the subroutine **FillCourseReaderTextBox()**. On the opened code page of the Course Web form, enter the codes that are shown in Figure 8.27 into the Course class to create this user-defined subroutine procedure.

Figure 8.27 The codes for the subroutine FillCourseReaderTextBox().

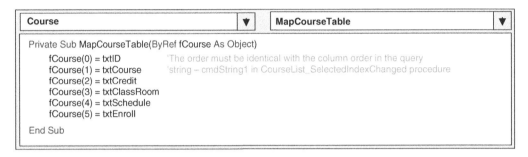

Figure 8.28 The codes for the subroutine MapCourseTable().

Let us take a closer look at this piece of codes to see how it works.

A) A loop counter **`intIndex`** is first created, and it is used for the loop of creation of the textbox object array and the loop of retrieving data from the DataReader later.

B) The first loop is used to create the textbox object array and perform the initialization for those objects.

C) The user-defined subroutine **`MapCourseTable()`** is executed to set up a one-to-one relationship between each textbox control in the Course page and each queried column in the query string. This step is necessary since the distribution order of six textbox controls in the Course page may be different with the column order in the query string.

D) A **`While`** and a **`For...Next`** loop are used to pick up all six pieces of course-related information from the DataReader one by one. The **`Read()`** method is used as the **`While`** loop condition. A returned **`True`** means that a valid data is read out from the DataReader, and a returned **`False`** means that no any valid data has been read out from the DataReader; in other words, no more data is available and all data has been read out. The **`For...Next`** loop uses the **`FieldCount - 1`** as the termination condition since the index of the first data field is 0, not 1, in the DataReader object. Each read-out data is converted to a string and assigned to the associated textbox control in the textbox object array.

The codes for the subroutine **`MapCourseTable()`** are shown in Figure 8.28.

The function of this piece of codes is straightforward with no trick. The order of the textboxes on the right-hand side of the equal operator is the column order in the query string – **`cmdString`**.

Figure 8.29 The running status of the Course page. *Source:* Used with permission from Microsoft.

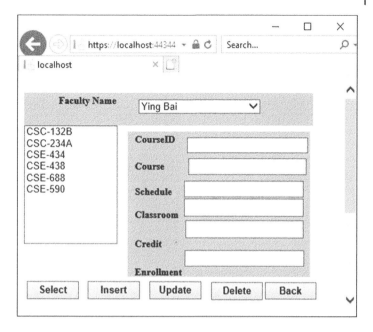

By assigning each column of required data to each of its partner, the textbox in the textbox object array in this order, a one-to-one relationship between each column of queried data and the associated textbox control in the Course page is built and the data retrieved from the DataReader can be mapped exactly to the associated textbox control in the Course page and can be displayed in there.

Now let us run the project to test the function of this form. Click on the **IIS Express (Internet Explorer)** button to run the project. Enter the suitable username and password such as **jhenry** and **test** to the LogIn page and select the **Course Information** item from the Selection page to open the Course page.

On the opened Course page, select a faculty member from the Faculty Name combo box control and click on the **Select** button to retrieve all courses (**COURSE_ID**) taught by that selected faculty. Immediately all courses (**COURSE_ID**) are retrieved and displayed in the CourseList box. Your running result should match the one that is shown in Figure 8.29.

Click on any **COURSE_ID** from the **CourseList** box to select it, immediately the detailed course information related to that selected **COURSE_ID** is displayed in six textboxes, which is shown in Figure 8.30.

Click on the **Back** button to return to the Selection page, and you can click on any other item from the Selection page to perform the associated information query or you can click on the **Exit** button to terminate the application.

Our Web application is successful.

A complete Web application project **OracleWebSelect Project**, which is used for data query from the Oracle database, can be found from a folder **Class DBProjects\Chapter 8** that is located under the **Students** folder at the Wiley ftp site (refer to Figure 1.2 in Chapter 1).

Next let us discuss how to insert data into our sample database via Web applications.

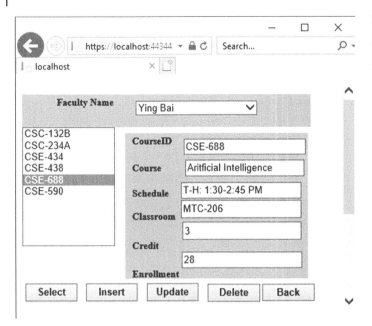

Figure 8.30 The detailed course information. *Source:* Used with permission from Microsoft.

8.4 Develop ASP.NET Web Application to Insert Data into Oracle Databases

In this section, we discuss how to insert a new faculty record into the Oracle database from the Web page. To do that, we do not need to create any new Web application; instead, we can modify an existing Web project `OracleWebSelect Project` we built in the last section to make it as our new Web application `OracleWebInsert Project`. Perform the following operations to create this new Web application project `OracleWebInsert Project`:

1) Open the Windows Explorer and create a new folder `C:\Chapter 8` in your computer if you have not done that.
2) Copy the entire Solution `OracleWebSelect Solution` from the folder `Students\Class DB Projects\Chapter 8` that is located at the Wiley ftp site (refer to Figure 1.2 in Chapter 1), and paste it to our new folder `C:\Chapter 8`.
3) Rename this Solution and Project on the primary and the nested folders to `OracleWebInsert Solution`, `OracleWebInsert Project.vbproj`, and `OracleWebInseret Project.vbproj.user`.
4) Open the renamed project `OracleWebInsert Project.vbproj` with Visual Basic.NET and perform the following modifications:

   a) Change the project name from `OracleWebSelect Project` to `OracleWebInsert Project` in the Solution Explorer window, and go to `File|Save All` to save modified project. Click on `Yes` and `Overwrite` buttons for this saving.
   b) Go to `Project|OracleWebInsert Project Properties` to open its Properties window.
   c) Change both `Assembly name` and `Root namespace` to `OracleWebInsert Project` and `OracleWebInsert_Project`.
   d) Click on the `Assembly Information` button, change both `Title` and `Product` to `OracleWebInsert Project`. Click on the `OK` button to close that wizard.
   e) Go to `Build|Rebuild OracleWebInsert Project` item to rebuild the entire project.

Recall that we built five buttons on the Faculty page in the project **OracleWebSelect Project**. In this section, we will concentrate on the coding development for the **Insert** button on the Faculty page to perform faculty data insertions to our sample database.

8.4.1 Develop the Codes to Perform the Data Insertion Function

These code developments can be divided into three parts: (i) the code modifications in the **Page_Load()** event procedure, (ii) the insert coding process built inside the **Insert** button's Click event procedure, and (iii) the codes development for the pre-check insertion function. Let us do these parts one by one in the following sections.

The reason we need to modify codes inside the **Page_Load()** event procedure is due to the changing of the faculty members in our **FACULTY** table after this insertion action. Thus, we cannot still use the codes in that event procedure as the faculty selection action did.

In order to get the current faculty members from the **FACULTY** table in our sample database. We need to add one more user-defined subroutine **CurrentFaculty()** and call this subroutine inside the **Page_Load()** event procedure, and to fill all current faculty members into the Faculty Name combo box, **ComboName**, to display them.

Open the **Page_Load()** event procedure in the Faculty page and enter the codes shown in Figure 8.31 into this procedure. Let us have a closer look at this piece of codes.

A) First, we need to make sure that this subroutine **CurrentFaculty()** can be only called in one time as the page is loaded to avoid multiple duplications for these faculty members to be added into the Faculty Name combo box.
B) Inside the subroutine, a temporary connection object, **oraConn**, is declared and it is assigned with our global connection object stored in the Application state function. This is because we do not want to create any new connection object and like to use an existing object.

Figure 8.31   The modified codes in the Page_Load() event procedure.

C) An Oracle DataReader object `oraReader` and a Command object `oraCommand` are created since we need them to perform faculty name query function to get all current faculty members from the **FACULTY** table in our database.

D) The Faculty Name combo box, `ComboName`, is cleaned up prior to being filled. This step is necessary; otherwise, more duplicated faculty members would be added into this combo box.

E) The `ExecuteReader()` method is called to retrieve and fill all current faculty members into this Data Reader.

F) A `While` loop is sued to repeatedly retrieve each faculty member and add it to the Faculty Name combo box. The loop condition is the `Read()` function. A new faculty record would be read and added into the combo box out as long as this function returns a True.

G) Some cleaning jobs are performed to remove all used objects.

The function of this `Insert` button's Click event procedure is:

1) To insert a new faculty record into the database, you need to enter seven pieces of new information into seven textboxes in the Faculty page. The information includes **FACULTY_ID**, **FACULTY_NAME, TITLE, OFFICE, PHONE, COLLEGE,** and **EMAIL**.

2) The Faculty Image PhotoBox is optional, which means that you can either enter a new faculty photo with this new record or leave it blank. If you leave it blank, a default faculty image will be adopted and displayed as this new record is validated.

3) After all pieces of information have been filled into all textboxes, you can click on the **Insert** button to insert this new record into the Faculty table in our database via the Web page.

Now let us start creating the codes for this `Insert` button's Click event procedure.

8.4.2 Develop the Codes for the Insert Button Click Event Procedure

Open the `Insert` button's Click event procedure by double clicking on the `Insert` button from the Faculty Web form, and enter the codes that are shown in Figure 8.32 into this event procedure. Let us have a closer look at this piece of codes to see how it works.

A) The insert query string is declared first, and it contains eight pieces of information that is related to eight columns in the Faculty table in the database.

B) The data components and local variables used in the procedure are declared here. The local integer variable `intInsert` is used to hold the returned running result from the execution of the data insertion command.

C) The Command object is initialized by assigning it with the connection object stored in the Application state, the command type, and the command text objects.

D) The user-defined subroutine `InsertParameters()` is executed to assign all eight input parameters to the Parameters collection of the command object.

E) The `ExecuteNonQuery()` method of the command object is called to run the insert query to perform this data insertion.

F) A cleaning job is performed to release all objects used in the procedure.

G) The `ExecuteNonQuery()` method will return an integer to indicate whether this data insertion is successful or not. The value of this returned data equals to the number of rows that have been successfully inserted into the Faculty table in the database. If a zero returned, which means that no any row has been inserted into the database, a warning message is displayed to indicate this situation and the procedure is exited. Otherwise, the data insertion is successful.

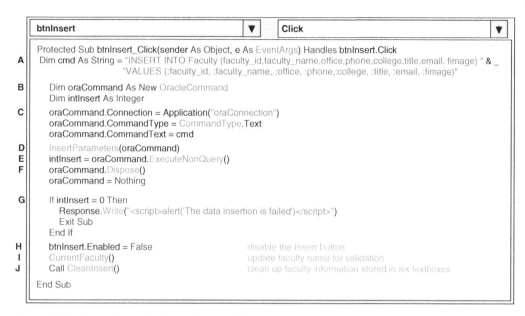

Figure 8.32 The codes for the Insert button's Click event procedure.

H) The **Insert** button is disabled after the current record is inserted into the database. This is to avoid the multiple insertions of the same record into the database. The Insert button will be enabled again when the content of the Faculty ID textbox is changed, which means that a new different faculty record will be inserted.

I) The new inserted faculty name is added into the Faculty Name combo box by calling the user-defined subroutine **CurrentFaculty()**, and this faculty name will be used later for the validation purpose.

J) Another user-defined subroutine procedure **CleanInsert()** is executed to clean up six textboxes in the Faculty page (except the Faculty ID textbox).

When the content of the **faculty_id** textbox is changed (a TextChanged event of the **faculty_id** textbox will be triggered), which means that a new faculty record should be inserted, we need to enable the **Insert** button if this situation happened. To do this piece of codes, double click on the **faculty_id** textbox from the Faculty page to open its TextChanged event procedure and enter **btnInsert.Enabled = True** into this procedure.

The detailed codes for the user-defined subroutine **InsertParameters()** are shown in Figure 8.33. Let us have a closer look at this piece of codes to see how it works.

A) A Byte() type variable **bImage** is generated, and it is used to retrieve and hold a selected faculty photo by calling a user-defined subroutine **getFacultyImage()**.

B) Each piece of new faculty information is assigned to the associated input parameter by using the **Add()** method of the Parameters collection of the command object.

The codes for the user-defined function **GetFacultyImage()** are shown in Figure 8.34.

As you may remember, in Section 8.3.7 when we created our Faculty Web page, a **FileUpload** component (represented by a combo box with a **Browse** button) is added into this page. The purpose of this **FileUpload** is to allow users to browse and select a faculty image file from your computer as a new faculty image to be inserted into the database.

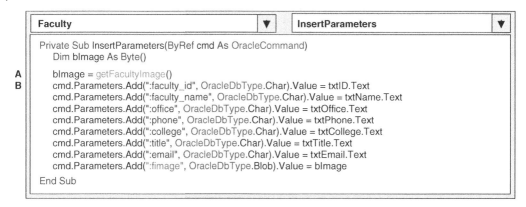

| Faculty | ▼ | InsertParameters | ▼ |

```
Private Sub InsertParameters(ByRef cmd As OracleCommand)
    Dim bImage As Byte()

A   bImage = getFacultyImage()
B   cmd.Parameters.Add(":faculty_id", OracleDbType.Char).Value = txtID.Text
    cmd.Parameters.Add(":faculty_name", OracleDbType.Char).Value = txtName.Text
    cmd.Parameters.Add(":office", OracleDbType.Char).Value = txtOffice.Text
    cmd.Parameters.Add(":phone", OracleDbType.Char).Value = txtPhone.Text
    cmd.Parameters.Add(":college", OracleDbType.Char).Value = txtCollege.Text
    cmd.Parameters.Add(":title", OracleDbType.Char).Value = txtTitle.Text
    cmd.Parameters.Add(":email", OracleDbType.Char).Value = txtEmail.Text
    cmd.Parameters.Add(":fimage", OracleDbType.Blob).Value = bImage
End Sub
```

Figure 8.33 The codes for the subroutine InsertParameters().

| Faculty | ▼ | GetFacultyImage | ▼ |

```
Private Function getFacultyImage() As Byte()
A       Dim path As String
        Dim length As Integer

B       path = Server.MapPath("/FacultyImage/")
C       FileUploadImage.SaveAs(path & FileUploadImage.FileName)
D       PhotoBox.ImageUrl = "/FacultyImage/" & FileUploadImage.FileName
E       length = FileUploadImage.PostedFile.ContentLength
        Dim img(length) As Byte
F       FileUploadImage.PostedFile.InputStream.Read(img, 0, length)

G       Return img
End Function
```

Figure 8.34 The codes for the subroutine getFacultyImage().

For this application, we prefer to create a new folder **FacultyImage** under the project folder **OracleWebInsert Project** and save all faculty image files into this folder. Before this project can be executed, make sure to copy all faculty image files that are located at the folder **Students | Images | Faculty** on the Wiley Web site (refer to Figure 1.2) and paste them into this folder **FacultyImage**.

Let us have a closer look at this piece of codes to see how it works.

A) Some local variables, **path** and **length**, are declared first, and they are used to hold the physical path for the selected faculty image and the length of the image file.

B) In Web applications, instead of using any physical or real file path, a virtual file path is used and issued by the server. Therefore, a server map function **MapPath()** is used to convert the relative virtual path to a physical path for the selected image file. In this case, the virtual path is **/FacultyImage/**, and this folder should have already been created with all faculty image files involved. The converted physical path is assigned to the variable **path** to be used later.

C) The **FileUpload** control allows users to select and send a file, including an image file, from users' computer to a Web server. The file to be uploaded is submitted to the server as part of the browser request during Postback. The **SaveAs()** method of the **FileUpload** control is used to upload this image file to the server. After the file has completed uploading, you can manage the file in the code behind page.

Figure 8.35 The codes for the subroutine CleanInsert().

D) To display this uploaded image in the image control **PhotoBox**, the virtual path with the selected image file's name is assigned to the **ImagUrl** property of the PhotoBox control.
E) The codes between steps **E** and **F** are used to convert the folder or the address of the image to the **Byte()** array, and insert it into our database. First, the length of the uploaded image file is retrieved by using the **ContentLength** property. Then, a Byte() array variable **img** is declared.
F) The folder or the address of the image file is converted from a String to a Byte() array **img** by executing the **InputStream.Read()** method in the **FileUpload** control.
G) The converted Byte() array **img** is returned to the calling function.

The codes for the user-defined subroutine **CleanInsert()** are shown in Figure 8.35.

The function of this piece of codes is to clean up contents of six textboxes and the Image control PhotoBox, except the **faculty_id** textbox. The reason for that is: the **Insert** button would be enabled if the content of the **faculty_id** textbox is cleaned up (changed) since a **TextChanged** event will be triggered. However, this cleaning up action has nothing to do with inserting a new record. Therefore, to avoid this confusing operation, we will not clean up the **faculty_id** textbox.

At this point, it looks like that we have completed all coding processes for this faculty insertion operation. Wait moment! We have some other things to do to make this insertion more complete and perfect. The following jobs are needed to perform to make this action perfect:

1) Add codes into the **Insert** button's Click event procedure to pre-check all textboxes and the **FileUpload** control **FileUploadImage** to make sure that all faculty information has been entered into the related textbox and a valid faculty image has been selected.
2) Build related user-defined function or subroutine to assist that pre-check functions shown above.

Now open the **Insert** button's Click event procedure and add the codes shown in Figure 8.36 (highlighted) into this event procedure.

Let us have a closer look at these codes to see how they work.

A) A local integer variable **ret** is declared and reset to 0. This variable is used to retrieve and hold the returning value from calling a user-defined function **CheckFaculty()** to make sure that all pieces of faculty information have been entered into related textbox and a valid faculty image has been selected.
B) The user-defined function **CheckFaculty()** is executed to do these checks. If 0 is returned, which means that some pieces of faculty information are missed, and a warning message is displayed to remind the users to enter missed information.

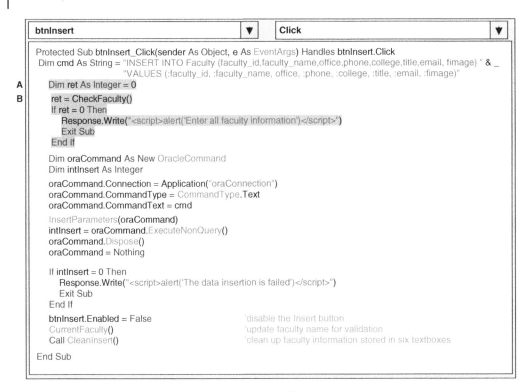

```
btnInsert ▼                                          Click ▼

Protected Sub btnInsert_Click(sender As Object, e As EventArgs) Handles btnInsert.Click
  Dim cmd As String = "INSERT INTO Faculty (faculty_id,faculty_name,office,phone,college,title,email, fimage) " & _
                      "VALUES (:faculty_id, :faculty_name, office, :phone, :college, :title, :email, :fimage)"
A   Dim ret As Integer = 0
B   ret = CheckFaculty()
    If ret = 0 Then
      Response.Write("<script>alert('Enter all faculty information')</script>")
      Exit Sub
    End If

    Dim oraCommand As New OracleCommand
    Dim intInsert As Integer

    oraCommand.Connection = Application("oraConnection")
    oraCommand.CommandType = CommandType.Text
    oraCommand.CommandText = cmd

    InsertParameters(oraCommand)
    intInsert = oraCommand.ExecuteNonQuery()
    oraCommand.Dispose()
    oraCommand = Nothing

    If intInsert = 0 Then
      Response.Write("<script>alert('The data insertion is failed')</script>")
      Exit Sub
    End If

    btnInsert.Enabled = False                    'disable the Insert button
    CurrentFaculty()                             'update faculty name for validation
    Call CleanInsert()                           'clean up faculty information stored in six textboxes

End Sub
```

Figure 8.36   The completed codes for the Insert button's Click event procedure.

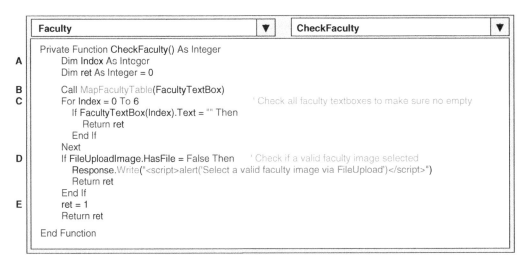

```
Faculty ▼                                          CheckFaculty ▼

A   Private Function CheckFaculty() As Integer
        Dim Index As Integer
        Dim ret As Integer = 0

B       Call MapFacultyTable(FacultyTextBox)
C       For Index = 0 To 6                        ' Check all faculty textboxes to make sure no empty
          If FacultyTextBox(Index).Text = "" Then
            Return ret
          End If
        Next
D       If FileUploadImage.HasFile = False Then   ' Check if a valid faculty image selected
          Response.Write("<script>alert('Select a valid faculty image via FileUpload')</script>")
          Return ret
        End If
E       ret = 1
        Return ret

    End Function
```

Figure 8.37   The codes for the function CheckFaculty().

Next let us take care of related user-defined function or subroutine. The codes for the function **CheckFaculty()** are shown in Figure 8.37. Let us have a closer look at this piece of codes to see how it works.

A) Some local integer variables are declared first, **Index** and **ret**. The former is used to work as a loop counter and the latter works as a returning variable.

B) Another user-defined subroutine **MapFacultyTable()** is executed to set up an one-to-one map between each member of **FacultyTextbox** and related TextBox in the Faculty Designer page.

C) A loop is used to check each **FacultyTextbox** to make sure that each of them has a valid piece of faculty information entered. If any of them is empty, a warning message is displayed to remind the user to enter the missed information. Also, a zero is returned to the calling function to indicate this situation.

D) If all textboxes are filled by related faculty information, the **FileUpload** control, **FileUploadImage**, is checked to inspect whether a valid faculty image has been selected. If the property **HasFile** is False, which means that no any faculty image file has been selected, a warning message is displayed to remind the users to do that selection. Zero is returned to the calling function to indicate this error.

E) Finally if nothing is wrong, or all pieces of faculty information, including a valid faculty image, have been entered into the page, a non-zero value is returned to indicate that this checking is successful.

Now, we have finished all coding development for this data insertion action, and we can run the project to test the data insertion function via the Web page. However, before we can start the project, make sure that all faculty image files, including a default faculty photo file named **Default. jpg**, have been stored in our default folder **FacultyImage** that is located under our current project folder. Also make sure that the start page is **LogIn** page by right clicking on the **LogIn. aspx** page from the Solution Explorer window and selecting the item **Set As Start Page**.

Click on the **IIS Express** button to run the project. Enter the suitable username and password such as **jhenry** and **test** to the LogIn page, and select the **Faculty Information** item from the Selection page to open the Faculty page. Enter the following data as the information for a new faculty record (Figure 8.38):

- **W28577** — Faculty ID textbox
- **Peter Wang** — Name textbox
- **Professor** — Title textbox
- **MTC-322** — Office textbox
- **750-330-2255** — Phone textbox
- **University of Dallas** — College textbox
- **pwang@college.edu** — Email textbox
- **Wang.jpg** — Faculty Image file name

Your finished new faculty information page is shown in Figure 8.38.

You need to use FileUpload control to select the faculty image file **Wang.jpg**.

Click on the **Insert** button to insert this new record into the database. The **Insert** button is immediately disabled, and the associated six textboxes and the faculty image box are cleaned up.

8.4.3 Validate the Data Insertion

To confirm and validate this faculty record insertion, go to the Faculty Name combo box control and you can find that the new inserted faculty name **Peter Wang** has already been there. Click on this name to select this faculty and then click on the **Select** button to retrieve this new inserted record from the database and display it in this page. The inserted record is displayed in this page, which is shown in Figure 8.39.

Figure 8.38 The running status of the Faculty page. *Source:* Used with permission from Microsoft.

Figure 8.39 The data validation process. *Source:* Used with permission from Microsoft.

Click on the **Back** button and then the **Exit** button to close our project.

A complete Web application project **OracleWebInsert Project** can be found from the folder **Class DB Projects\Chapter 8** that is located under the **Students** folder at the Wiley ftp site (refer to Figure 1.2 in Chapter 1).

8.5 Develop Web Applications to Update and Delete Data in Oracle Databases

Updating or deleting data against the relational databases is a challenging topic. We have provided a very detailed discussion and analysis for this topic in Section 7.1.1. Refer to that section to get more detailed discussion for these data actions. Here, we want to emphasize some important points related to the data updating and deleting.

1) When updating or deleting data against related tables in a DataSet, it is important to update or delete data in the proper sequence to reduce the chance of violating referential integrity constraints. The order of command execution will also follow the indices of the DataRowCollection in the data set. To prevent data integrity errors from being raised, the best practice is to update or delete data against the database in the following sequence:
   a) Child table: delete records.
   b) Parent table: insert, update, and delete records.
   c) Child table: insert and update records.
2) To update an existing data against the database, generally it is unnecessary to update the primary key for that record. It is much better to insert a new record with a new primary key into the database than only updating the primary key for an existing record because of the complicated tables operations listed above. It is very rare to update a primary key for an existing record against the database in real applications. So in this section, we concentrate our discussion on updating an existing record by modifying all data columns except the primary key column.
3) To delete a record from a relational database, the normal operation sequence listed above must be followed. For example, to delete a record from the **FACULTY** table in our application, one must first delete those records, which are related to the data to be deleted in the Faculty table, from the child table such as the **LOGIN** and **COURSE** tables, and then one can delete the record from the **FACULTY** table. The reason for this deleting sequence is because the **FACULTY_ID** is a foreign key in the **LOGIN** and the **COURSE** tables, but it is a primary key in the **FACULTY** table. One must first delete data with the foreign keys and then delete the data with the primary key from the database.

Keep these three points we discussed above in mind, now let us begin our project.

We need to modify one our existing project **OracleWebInsert Project** and make it as our new project **OracleWebUpdateDelete Project**. To do that, open the Windows Explorer and create a new folder **C:\Chapter 8** if you have not done that. Then copy the entire solution **OracleWebInsert Solution** from the folder **Class DB Projects\Chapter 8** that is located under the **Students** folder at the Wiley ftp site (refer to Figure 1.2 in Chapter 1) and paste it to our folder **C:\Chapter 8**. Rename this solution to **OracleWebUpdateDelete Solution**. Refer to Section 8.4 to complete this project renaming process.

To update or delete an existing record against our sample database, we do not need any new Web page as our user interface and we can use the Faculty page as our user interface to perform those data actions. To meet our data actions' requirements, we need to perform some modifications to the codes in the Faculty page.

First, let us handle the data updating action to the Faculty table in our sample database via the Faculty page. Now let us develop the codes for the **Update** button's click event procedure.

8.5.1 Develop the Codes for the Update Button Click Event Procedure

Open this event procedure by double clicking on the **Update** button from the Faculty Web form window and enter the codes that are shown in Figure 8.40 into this procedure.

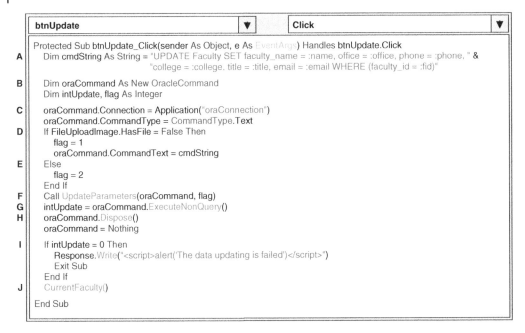

```
btnUpdate                                          ▼    Click                                              ▼

    Protected Sub btnUpdate_Click(sender As Object, e As EventArgs) Handles btnUpdate.Click
A       Dim cmdString As String = "UPDATE Faculty SET faculty_name = :name, office = :office, phone = :phone, " &
                                  "college = :college, title = :title, email = :email WHERE (faculty_id = :fid)"
B       Dim oraCommand As New OracleCommand
        Dim intUpdate, flag As Integer
C       oraCommand.Connection = Application("oraConnection")
        oraCommand.CommandType = CommandType.Text
D       If FileUploadImage.HasFile = False Then
            flag = 1
            oraCommand.CommandText = cmdString
E       Else
            flag = 2
        End If
F       Call UpdateParameters(oraCommand, flag)
G       intUpdate = oraCommand.ExecuteNonQuery()
H       oraCommand.Dispose()
        oraCommand = Nothing

I       If intUpdate = 0 Then
            Response.Write("<script>alert('The data updating is failed')</script>")
            Exit Sub
        End If
J       CurrentFaculty()

    End Sub
```

Figure 8.40 The codes for the Update button's click event procedure.

Let us take a closer look at this piece of codes to see how it works.

A) An updating query string is declared first with the **fid** as the name of the dynamic parameter. This is because we want to update all other columns in the Faculty table based on the **FACULTY_ID** that will be kept unchanged.

B) All data objects used in this procedure are created here, and a local integer variable **intUpdate** is also created, which is used as a value holder to keep the returned data from the executing the **ExecutNonQuery()** method.

C) The Command object is initialized with the connection object, command type, and command text.

D) By checking the content of the **FileUpload** control, **FileUploadImage**, we can determine whether an updated faculty image will be inserted into the database with this data updating operation. If no any faculty image has been selected, which means that the faculty image would not be updated, the flag signal **flag** is set to 1 to indicate this situation. Also, the **CommandText** property is assigned with the default query string, **cmdString**, in which no faculty image will be updated.

E) Otherwise if a faculty image has been selected and the content of the **FileUpload** control is not empty, which means that a valid faculty image has been selected and the faculty image will also be updated with this data updating. The flag signal **flag** is set to 2 to indicate this case.

F) The user-defined subroutine **UpdateParameters()**, whose detailed codes are shown below, is called to assign all input parameters to the command object.

G) The **ExecuteNonQuery()** method of the command class is called to execute the data updating operation. This method returns a feedback data to indicate whether this data updating is successful or not, and this returned data is stored to the local integer variable **intUpdate**.

H) A cleaning job is performed to release all data objects used in this procedure.

I) The data value returned from calling the **ExecuteNonQuery()** is exactly equal to the number of rows that have been successfully updated in the database. If this value is zero, which means that no any row has been updated and this data updating is failed, a warning message is displayed and the procedure is exited. Otherwise if this value is non-zero, which means that this data updating is successful.

J) Finally, the user-defined subroutine **CurrentFaculty()** is called to get the updated faculty names and fill them into the Faculty Name combo box, **ComboName**.

The detailed codes for the subroutine **UpdateParameters()** are shown in Figure 8.41. Let us have a closer look at this subroutine to see how it works.

A) Another query string that contains updating the faculty image is declared first, and this query is for updating a complete record, including a faculty image.

B) The default seven input parameters are assigned to the Parameters collection property of the command object using the **Add()** method. One point for this parameter assignment is the last input parameter **:fid**. Since we want to update all other columns in the Faculty table except this **FACULTY_ID**, therefore we will use the original **FACULTY_ID** without any modification.

C) Now, we need to check whether a complete faculty record updating is requested. If it is (**flag = 2**), the complete query string **cs**, which is declared first in this event procedure, will be assigned to the CommandText property.

D) Also by calling the user-defined function **getFacultyImage()**, a selected faculty image file that has been converted to a Byte() array is returned.

E) The returned faculty image with a Byte() array format is added into the Parameter property of the Command object.

At this point, we have finished all coding jobs for the data updating actions against the Oracle database in the Faculty page. Before we can run the project to test this data updating function, make sure that the starting page is the LogIn page and all faculty image files, including a default faculty image file **Default.jpg**, have been stored in our default folder, **FacultyImage**, which is under our current project folder **OracleUpdateDelete Project**. To check the starting page, perform the following operations:

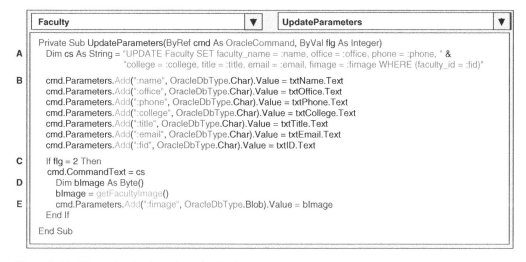

Figure 8.41 The codes for the subroutine UpdateParameters().

1) Right click on our project `OracleWebUpdateDelete Project` icon from the Solution Explorer window, and select the `Properties` item from the popup menu to open the Project Properties wizard.
2) Then select the `Web` tab on the left panel.
3) Then check on the `Specific Page` radio button and make sure that the `LogIn.aspx` page is selected. If not, click on the expansion button to open the `Select Page to Start` wizard to select it.
4) Click on the `OK` button to close this starting page setup.

Now let us run the project to test the data updating actions. Click on the `IIS Express` button to run the project. Enter the suitable username and password to the LogIn page, and select the `Faculty Information` item from the Selection page to open the Faculty page. Select the default faculty name `Ying Bai` from the Faculty Name combo box, and click on the `Select` button to retrieve the information for this selected faculty from the database and display it in this page.

Now let us test the data updating actions by entering the following data into the associated textboxes to update this faculty record:

- `Susan Bai`   Name textbox
- `Professor`   Title textbox
- `MTC-353`   Office textbox
- `750-378-3300`   Phone textbox
- `Duke University`   College textbox
- `sbai@college.edu`   Email textbox
- `White.jpg`   Faculty Image textbox

One needs to use the `FileUpload` control, `FileUploadImage`, to select the faculty image file, `White.jpg`, prior to clicking on the `Update` button to perform this updating. To use this image file, first one needs to find and copy this faculty image file from the folder `Students\Images\Faculty`, which is located at the Wiley site (refer to Figure 1.2 in Chapter 1) and paste it to our default folder `FacultyImage` under our current project, exactly it is `OracleWebUpdateDelete Solution\OracleUpdateDelete Project\FacultyImage`.

Click on the `Update` button to perform this data updating. To confirm this data updating, go to Faculty Name combo box and you can find that the updated faculty `Susan Bai` has been there. Click on it to choose this faculty and click on the `Select` button to retrieve and display this updated faculty record. You can see that the selected faculty information has been updated, which is shown in Figure 8.42.

It is highly recommended to recover this updated faculty record to the original one. Refer to original faculty record shown in Table 8.6 to complete this recovery job by using this `Update` function. Our data updating action is very successful. Click on the `Back` and then the `Exit` button to terminate our project.

Next let us take care of the data deleting action against the Oracle database.

8.5.2 Develop the Codes for the Delete Button Click Event Procedure

Since deleting a record from a relational database is a complex issue, we have provided a detailed discussion about this data action in Section 8.5. Refer to that part to get more detailed information for this data action. In this section, we divide this data deleting action discussion into the following five sections:

1) Relationships between five tables in our sample database
2) Data deleting sequence
3) Use the Cascade deleting option to simplify the data deleting

Figure 8.42 The data updating and validation process. *Source:* Used with permission from Microsoft.

Table 8.6 The original data for the faculty member Ying Bai in the Faculty table.

faculty_id	faculty_name	office	phone	college	title	email	fimage
B78880	Ying Bai	MTC-211	750-378-1148	Florida Atlantic University	Associate Professor	ybai@college.edu	Bai.jpg

4) Create a stored procedure to perform the data deleting
5) Call the stored procedure to perform the data deleting action

8.5.2.1 Relationships Between Five Tables in Our Sample Database

As we discussed in Section 8.5, to delete a record from a relational database, one must follow the correct sequence. In other words, one must first delete the records that are related to the record to be deleted in the parent table from the child tables. In our sample database, five tables are related together by using the primary and foreign keys. In order to make these relationships clear, we re-draw Figure 2.5, which is Figure 8.43 in this section, to illustrate this issue.

If you want to delete a record from the **FACULTY** table, you must first delete the related records from the **LOGIN**, **COURSE**, **STUDENTCOURSE,** and **STUDENT** tables, and then you can delete the desired record from the **FACULTY** table. The reason for that is because the relationships are existed between five tables.

For example, if one wants to delete a faculty record from the **FACULTY** table, one must perform the following deleting jobs:

● The **FACULTY_ID** is a primary key in the **FACULTY** table, but it is a foreign key in the **LOGIN** and the **COURSE** table. Therefore, the **FACULTY** table is a parent table and the **LOGIN** and the **COURSE** are child tables. Before one can delete any record from the **FACULTY** table, one must first delete records that have the **FACULTY_ID** as the foreign key from the child tables. In other words, one must first delete those records that use the **FACULTY_ID** as a foreign key from the **LOGIN** and the **COURSE** tables.

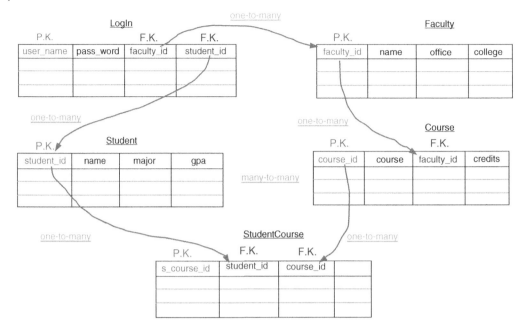

Figure 8.43 The relationships between five tables.

- When deleting records that use the **FACULTY_ID** as a foreign key from the **COURSE** table, the related **COURSE_ID** that is a primary key in the **COURSE** table will also be deleted. The **COURSE** table now is a parent table relative to the **STUDENTCOURSE** table since the **COURSE_ID** is a primary key in the **COURSE** table but a foreign key in the **STUDENTCOURSE** table. As we mentioned, to delete any record from a parent table, one must first delete the related records from the child tables. Now the **STUDENTCOURSE** table is a child table for the **COURSE** table, so the records that use the **COURSE_ID** as a foreign key in the **STUDENTCOURSE** table should be deleted first.
- After those related records in the child tables have been deleted, finally the faculty member can be deleted from the parent table, **FACULTY** table.

8.5.2.2 Data Deleting Sequence

Summarily, to delete a record from the Faculty table, one needs to perform the following deleting jobs in the **sequence** shown below:

1) Delete all records that use the **COURSE_ID** as the foreign key from the **STUDENTCOURSE** table.
2) Delete all records that use the **FACULTY_ID** as the foreign key from the **LOGIN** table.
3) Delete all records that use the **FACULTY_ID** as the foreign key from the **COURSE** table.
4) Delete the desired faculty member from the **FACULTY** table.

You can see how complicated it is in these operations to delete one record from the relational database from this example.

8.5.2.3 Use the Cascade Deleting Option to Simplify the Data Deleting

To simplify the data deleting operations, we can use the cascade deleting option provided by the Oracle XE 18c database engine.

Recall that when we created and built the relationship between our five tables, the following five **relationships** are built between tables:

1) A relationship between the LogIn and the Faculty tables is set up using the **FACULTY_ID** as a foreign key FK_LogIn_Faculty in the LogIn table.
2) A relationship between the LogIn and the Student tables is set up using the **STUDENT_ID** as a foreign key FK_LogIn_Student in the LogIn table.
3) A relationship between the Course and the Faculty tables is set up using the **FACULTY_ID** as a foreign key FK_Course_Faculty in the Course table.
4) A relationship between the StudentCourse and the Course table is set up using the **COURSE_ID** as a foreign key FK_StudentCourse_Course in the StudentCourse table.
5) A relationship between the StudentCourse and the Student table is set up using the **STUDENT_ID** as a foreign key FK_StudentCourse_Student in the StudentCourse table.

Refer to the data deleting sequence listed in Section 8.5.2.2, to delete a record from the Faculty table, one needs to perform four deleting operations in that sequence. Compared with all four deleting operations, the first one is the most difficult and the reason for that is:

- To perform the first data deleting, one must first find all **COURSE_ID** that use the **FACULTY_ID** as the foreign key from the Course table, and then based on those **COURSE_ID**, one needs to delete all records that use those **COURSE_ID** as the foreign keys from the StudentCourse table. For deleting operations in sequences 3 and 4, they are easy and each deleting operation only needs one deleting query. The conclusion for this discussion is: how to find an easy way to complete the deleting operation in sequence 1?
- A good solution to this question is to use the Cascade option for the data deleting and updating setup dialog provided by the Oracle XE 18c database engine. This Cascade option allows the Oracle XE 18c database engine to perform that deleting operation in sequence 1 as long as a Cascade option is selected for relationships 4 and 5 listed above.

Now let us use a real example to illustrate how to use this Cascade option to simplify the data deleting operations, especially for the first data deleting in that sequence.

Open the Oracle SQL Developer and complete the system login process. Then expand the **Other Users** folder and our sample database **CSE_DEPT**. Click on the plus icon (+) on the left of the **Tables** folder to expand display all five tables. Since we only have our interest on relationships 4 and 5, so open the **STUDENTCOURSE** table and click on the **Constraints** tab to display all **Keys**. Click on the first key, **STUDENTCOURSE_COURSE_FK**, to highlight it, which is shown in Figure 8.44.

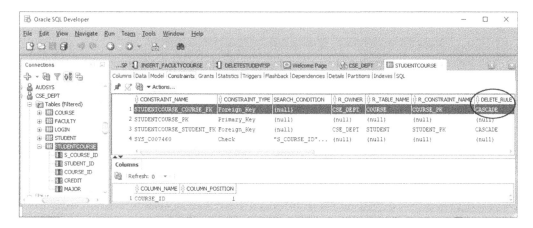

Figure 8.44 The Foreign Key Relationship wizard. *Source:* Oracle Corporation.

Go to the column **DELETE_RULE**, which is the last column in this screen shot, and you can find that a **CASCADE** keyword has been set up for this **DELETE RULE**, which means each time when you want to delete any record that used the **COURSE_ID** or the **STUDENT_ID** as the foreign keys in the **STUDENTCOURSE** table, the Oracle XE 18c engine will perform those cascaded data deleting operations automatically for you. So now you can see how easy it is to perform the data deleting in sequence 1.

After the first data deleting operation listed in the deleting sequence in Section 8.5.2.2 is performed, we can do the following three operations by executing three deleting queries. But we want to integrate those three queries into a single stored procedure to perform this data deleting operation.

Well, wait a moment before we can start to create our stored procedure. One question is that is it possible for us to set up Cascade options for relationships 1, 2, and 3 to allow the Oracle XE 18c engine to help us to perform those data deleting operations? If it is, can we only use one query to directly delete the faculty member from the **FACULTY** table? The answer is Yes! We prefer to leave this as homework to allow students to handle this issue themselves. Now let us create our stored procedure for this data deleting operation.

8.5.2.4 Create the Stored Procedure to Perform the Data Deleting

This stored procedure contains three deleting queries that can be mapped to three sequences listed in Section 8.5.2.2, which are sequences 2, 3 and 4.

Open the Oracle SQL Developer, finish the system login process, connect and expand our database **CSE_DEPT** and right click on the **Procedures** folder. Select the **New Procedure** item from the popup menu, and enter the procedure name **DELETEFACULTY_SP** and input parameter **FNAME**, which are shown in Figure 8.45, into this new stored procedure.

Click on the **OK** button to create this procedure.

Then enter the codes shown in Figure 8.46 into this procedure as the body for this procedure. Let us take a closer look at this piece of codes to see how it works.

Figure 8.45 The stored procedure DeleteFaculty_SP(). *Source:* Oracle Corporation.

```
     CREATE OR REPLACE PROCEDURE DELETEFACULTY_SP
     (
A      FNAME IN VARCHAR2
     ) AS
     BEGIN
B      DECLARE FID VARCHAR2 (20);
C      BEGIN SELECT faculty_id INTO FID FROM FACULTY
       WHERE faculty_name = FNAME;
D      DELETE FROM CSE_DEPT.login WHERE faculty_id = FID;
       DELETE FROM CSE_DEPT.course WHERE faculty_id = FID;
       DELETE FROM CSE_DEPT.faculty WHERE faculty_id = FID;
       END;
     END DELETEFACULTY_SP;
```

Figure 8.46   The code body for the stored procedure DeleteFaculty_SP().

A) This stored procedure has only one input parameter, which is the faculty name. So a nominal input parameter **FNAME** is defined in the input/output parameter list at the beginning of this stored procedure.

B) A local variable **FID** is declared, and it is used to hold the returned **FACULTY_ID** from the execution of the data query to the **FACULTY** table in step **C**.

C) The first data query is executed to pick up a matched **FACULTY_ID** from the **FACULTY** table based on the input parameter **FNAME**.

D) After the **FACULTY_ID** is obtained from the data query, three deleting queries are executed in the order that is shown in Figure 8.43 to perform three deleting operations. The order is: first one must delete all records that use the **FACULTY_ID** as the foreign keys from the child tables, such as the **LOGIN** and the **COURSE**. Then, one can delete the record that uses the **FACULTY_ID** as the primary key from the parent table, such as the **FACULTY** table.

Now click on the drop-down arrow on the Compile icon and select the **Compile** item by checking on it to compile and save our new created stored procedure. A successful compilation message should be displayed in the Messages box (**Compiled**). Your finished stored procedure is shown in Figure 8.47.

Now let us test this stored procedure in the Oracle SQL Developer environment to make sure that it works fine.

Click on the green-color **Run** button, as shown in Figure 8.47, to run this stored procedure. To make this deleting operation simple, here we just try to delete a new inserted faculty member, **Peter Wang**, which was inserted into our **FACULTY** table in Section 8.4.2 in this chapter. The reason we selected to delete this faculty member is that this deleting action only delete one single faculty member from a single table **FACULTY** without any related records in any child tables in our database since we only insert this member without adding any related course and login records in those tables. In this way, we do not need to do any recovery jobs and simplify this deleting action.

Now in the opened **Run PL/SQL** wizard, as shown in Figure 8.48, enter the faculty name, **Peter Wang**, into the Input Value box, and click on the **OK** button to run this stored procedure. You may need to perform another system login process to perform this deleting action.

The running sequence and result are displayed in the **Running** window, which is shown in Figure 8.49.

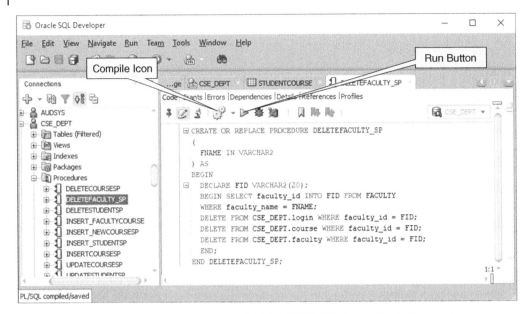

Figure 8.47 The completed stored procedure DELETEFACULTY_SP(). *Source:* Oracle Corporation.

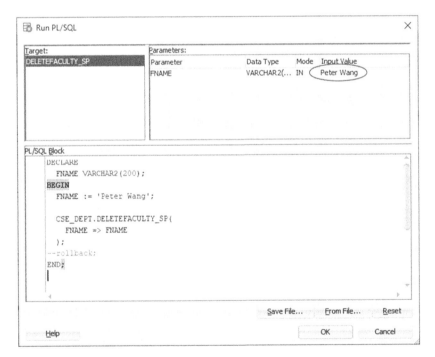

Figure 8.48 The Running status of the procedure wizard. *Source:* Oracle Corporation.

To confirm this data deleting, we can open the **FACULTY** table in this Oracle SQL Developer. Open this table by right clicking on the **FACULTY** table and select the **Open** item from the popup menu, and click on the **Data** tab on the top. You may need to click on the **Refresh** icon to get the correct updated deleting result. You can find that the faculty member, **Peter Wang**, cannot be

Figure 8.49 The running result of the stored procedure. *Source:* Oracle Corporation.

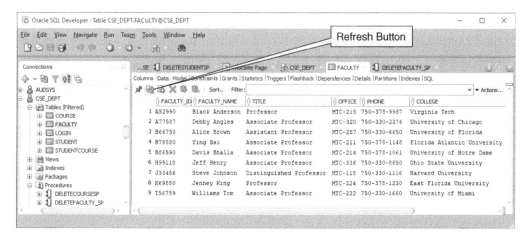

Figure 8.50 The updated FACULTY table after the deleting action. *Source:* Oracle Corporation.

found from this table since it has been deleted. The updated **FACULTY** table after this deleting action is shown in Figure 8.50.

8.5.2.5 Develop the Codes to Call the Stored Procedure to Perform the Data Deleting

On the opened Visual Studio.NET, go to `File|Open Project` menu item to open our Web application project `OracleWebUpdateDelete Project`. Then open the `Delete` button's Click event procedure and enter the codes that are shown in Figure 8.51 into this event procedure. Let us take a closer look at this piece of codes to see how it works.

A) The content of the query string now is equal to the name of the stored procedure we developed in the Oracle SQL Developer. This query string will be assigned to the CommandText property of the Command object later to inform it that a stored procedure needs to be executed to perform this data deleting action. Here, the name assigned to the query string must be exactly identical to the name of the stored procedure we developed in the last section, otherwise an

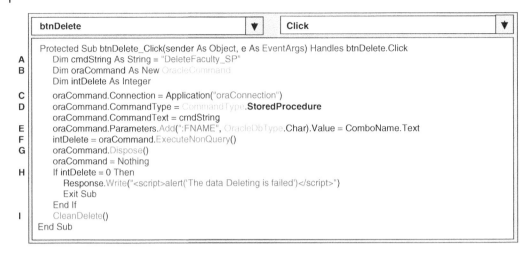

btnDelete ▼	Click ▼

```
Protected Sub btnDelete_Click(sender As Object, e As EventArgs) Handles btnDelete.Click
    Dim cmdString As String = "DeleteFaculty_SP"
    Dim oraCommand As New OracleCommand
    Dim intDelete As Integer

    oraCommand.Connection = Application("oraConnection")
    oraCommand.CommandType = CommandType.StoredProcedure
    oraCommand.CommandText = cmdString
    oraCommand.Parameters.Add(":FNAME", OracleDbType.Char).Value = ComboName.Text
    intDelete = oraCommand.ExecuteNonQuery()
    oraCommand.Dispose()
    oraCommand = Nothing
    If intDelete = 0 Then
        Response.Write("<script>alert('The data Deleting is failed')</script>")
        Exit Sub
    End If
    CleanDelete()
End Sub
```

Figure 8.51 The codes for the Delete button's Click event procedure.

error would be encountered as the project runs since the page cannot identify the stored procedure if no matched name can be found.

B) The data object and local variable used in this procedure are declared here. The integer variable **intDelete** is used to hold the returned value from calling of the **ExecuteNonQuery()** method of the Command class later.

C) The Command object is initialized by assigning the connection object that is a global variable and stored in the Application state to the Connection property.

D) The CommandType property must be assigned to the **StoredProcedure** to inform the Command object that a stored procedure needs to be called when this Command object is executed. This is very important and should be distinguished with the general query text string.

E) The input parameter, **:FNAME**, which is the only input to the stored procedure, is assigned with the real value that is the faculty name stored in the Faculty Name combo box in the Faculty page. Similarly, the name of this input parameter must be identical to the name of the input parameter used in the stored procedure we built earlier.

F) After the Command object is initialized, the **ExecuteNonQuery()** method of the Command class is called to run the stored procedure to perform the data deleting actions. This method will return an integer value and assign it to the local variable **intDelete**.

G) A cleaning job is performed to release all objects used in this procedure.

H) The returned value from calling the **ExecuteNonQuery()** method is exactly equal to the number of rows that have been successfully deleted from our sample database. If this value is zero, which means that no row has been deleted or affected from our database and this data deleting is failed, a warning message is displayed and the procedure is exited. Otherwise if a non-zero value returned, which means that at least one row in our database has been deleted (all related rows should be also deleted) from our database and this deleting is successful.

I) A user-defined subroutine **CleanDelete()**, whose detailed codes are shown below, is executed to clean up the contents of all textboxes that stored the deleted faculty information.

The codes for the subroutine **CleanDelete()** are shown in Figure 8.52.

This piece of codes is easy to be understood. All textboxes and the faculty image box are cleaned up by assigning an empty string or **Nothing** property to their **Text** property.

Figure 8.52 The codes for the subroutine CleanFaculty().

At this point, we finished all coding jobs for deleting data against the Oracle database using the stored procedure. Before we can run the project to test this deleting function, make sure that the starting page is the LogIn page.

After the project runs, enter the suitable username and password to complete the LogIn process, open the Faculty page and keep the default faculty name **Ying Bai** selected from the Faculty Name combo box and click on the **Select** button to retrieve and display this faculty's record. Click on the **Delete** button to run the stored procedure **DeleteFaculty_SP** to delete this faculty record from our database. Immediately all pieces of information stored in seven textboxes are deleted.

To confirm this data deleting, click on the **Select** button to try to retrieve the deleted record for the faculty member **Ying Bai** from the database. Immediately, a warning message "**No matched faculty found**" is displayed to indicate that the selected faculty record has been deleted. Click on the **OK**, then **Back,** and **Exit** buttons to exit the project.

Another way to confirm this deletion is to open either the Server Explorer or the Oracle SQL Developer and our sample database. You can find that all records related to that deleted faculty member, **Ying Bai**, have been deleted from our database. Yes, our data deleting is successful.

It can be found that all records listed in the Rows Affected in Table 8.7 have been deleted from the associated tables.

Table 8.7 The total number of rows affected or deleted.

Table	Rows Affected	Number of Rows Affected
LogIn	user_name = ybai (faculty_id = B78880)	1
Course	course_id = CSC-132B (faculty_id = B78880)	4
	course_id = CSC-234A (faculty_id = B78880)	
	course_id = CSE-434 (faculty_id = B78880)	
	course_id = CSE-438 (faculty_id = B78880	
StudentCourse	s_course_id = 1005 (course_id = CSC-234A)	5
	s_course_id = 1009 (course_id = CSE-434)	
	s_course_id = 1014 (course_id = CSE-438)	
	s_course_id = 1016 (course_id = CSC-132B)	
	s_course_id = 1017 (course_id = CSC-234A)	
Faculty	faculty_id = B78880	1

Another point to be noted is that we do not have to put all of three **DELETE** queries in this stored procedure to perform these data deleting actions, instead, we can use only one query: **DELETE FROM CSE_DEPT.faculty WHERE faculty_id = :FID**, to do the same function as these three queries did. The Oracle XE 18c engine can handle the data deleting actions from the child tables because of the cascaded deleting mode we have built for these tables in Chapter 2. Just for the illustration purpose, here we provide a complete picture with these deleting queries to show readers the details of this deleting function.

It is highly recommended to recover all deleted records in the associated tables. Refer to Tables 8.8~8.11 to recover those records in the associated tables. An easy to do this recovery job is:

1) Use the **Insert** button in this Faculty page to reinsert a new record for the faculty member **Ying Bai** into the **FACULTY** table in our sample database based on data columns shown in Table 8.8.
2) For all other recovery jobs, one can use either the Sever Explorer or Oracle SQL Developer to open the related tables and add those deleted records one by one manually. These recoveries include one record in the **LOGIN** table, four records in the **COURSE** table, and five records in the **STUDENTCOURSE** table. Refer to Tables 8.9~8.11 to complete these recovery jobs. One can use copy and paste function to do this job one by one. One can copy all rows from Tables 8.9~8.11 and paste them into the last line of the associated tables.

After these recovery jobs are done, save these changes to the database by going to **File | Save All** menu item.

A complete Web application project **OracleWebUpdateDelete Project** can be found from the folder **Class DB Projects\Chapter 8** that is located under the **Students** folder at the Wiley ftp site (refer to Figure 1.2 in Chapter 1).

Table 8.8 The data to be added into the Faculty table.

faculty_id	faculty_name	office	phone	college	title	email	fimage
B78880	Ying Bai	MTC-211	750-378-1148	Florida Atlantic University	Associate Professor	ybai@ college.edu	Bai.jpg

Table 8.9 The data to be added into the LogIn table.

user_name	pass_word	faculty_id	student_id
ybai	come	B78880	NULL

Table 8.10 The data to be added into the Course table.

course_id	course	credit	classroom	schedule	enrollment	faculty_id
CSC-132B	Introduction to Programming	3	TC-302	T-H: 1:00-2:25 PM	21	B78880
CSC-234A	Data Structure & Algorithms	3	TC-302	M-W-F: 9:00-9:55 AM	25	B78880
CSE-434	Advanced Electronics Systems	3	TC-213	M-W-F: 1:00-1:55 PM	26	B78880
CSE-438	Advd Logic & Microprocessor	3	TC-213	M-W-F: 11:00-11:55 AM	35	B78880

Table 8.11 The data to be added into the StudentCourse table.

s_course_id	student_id	course_id	credit	major
1005	T77896	CSC-234A	3	CS/IS
1009	A78835	CSE-434	3	CE
1014	A78835	CSE-438	3	CE
1016	A97850	CSC-132B	3	ISE
1017	A97850	CSC-234A	3	ISE

8.6 Develop ASP.NET Web Applications with LINQ to Oracle Query

As we discussed in Chapter 4, LINQ provides some popular tools to help users to build and develop various projects to access and manipulate records in databases. Some popular tools include LINQ to Objects, LINQ to DataSet, LINQ to SQL, and LINQ to Entities. Among them, only LINQ to SQL and LINQ to Entities allow users to access the real database to perform data actions. Also the LINQ to SQL and LINQ to Entities can only work for SQL databases. Thus to use LINQ to Oracle, we need to use some third party products, such as LINQ to Oracle (`LinqConnect`) provided by Devart and Oracle Data Access Components (`ODAC`) provided by Oracle, to build our LINQ to Oracle project to access and manipulate our sample Oracle database.

In this section, we use the LINQ to Oracle and Entity Data Model provided by the Devart as a tool to provide a fundamental end-to-end LINQ to Oracle scenario for selecting, adding, modifying, and deleting data against our sample database via Web pages. As you know, LINQ to Oracle queries can perform not only the data selection but also the data insertion, updating, and deletion actions. The standard LINQ to Oracle queries include,

- Select
- Insert
- Update
- Delete

To perform any of these operations or queries, we need to use entity classes and DataContext object we discussed in Section 4.6.1 in Chapter 4 to do LINQ to Oracle actions against our sample database. Let us first create our new Web Application project `LINQWebOracle` and then add the Faculty page and our Entity Model into this project to perform this LINQ to Oracle data query operations.

8.6.1 Generate a New Web Project LINQWebOracle and a New LinqConnect Model

Let us perform the following steps to create our new Web project `LINQWebOracle`:

1) Open the Visual Studio.NET 2019 and create a new **ASP.NET Web Application (.NET Framework)** project `LINQWebOracle Project` with a Solution `LINQWebOracle Solution` under the folder `C:\Chapter 8`. Select the **Web Forms** item and click on the **Create** button to generate these components.

2) Add an existing Web form page, **Faculty.aspx**, by selecting it from the folder **VB Forms\Web** that is located under the **Students** folder at the Wiley ftp site (refer to Figure 1.2 in Chapter 1).

3) Open the Source file for the **Faculty.aspx** page by right clicking on it and select the **View Markup** item, and go to the end of the first coding line. Change the last item to **Inherits="LINQWebOracle_Project.Faculty" %>**.

4) Remove the **Default.aspx** page from the project since we do not need it.

5) Save these newly added components by going to **File | Save All** menu item.

6) Build the entire project by going to **Build | Rebuild LINQWebOracle** item.

7) Right click on our new page **Faculty.aspx** from the Solution Explorer window and select **Set As Start Page** item to make this page as the starting page for our project.

Now perform the following operational steps to add a new LINQ to Oracle ED Model into our new application project:

1) Right click on our new Web project **LINQWebOracle Project** from the Solution Explorer and select **Add | New Item** to open the **Add New Item** wizard.

2) Click on the **Visual Basic** template under the Installed category and select the installed **Devart LinqConnect Model** and change the model name to **CSE_DEPT.lqml**, as shown in Figure 8.53, and click on the **Add** button to add it to our Web project.

3) Click on the **Next** button to go the next wizard, which is shown in Figure 8.54. This wizard allows you to select the mode of this model. Keep the default mode, **Database First**, with no change and this is identical with our situation.

4) On the next wizard, Database Connection wizard, enter server name, user ID, and password, as shown in Figure 8.55, where

    a) Server: **localhost:1518/CSE_DEPT**
    b) User Id: **CSE_DEPT**
    c) Password: **oracle_18c**

You can click on the **Test Connection** button to test this connection. A successful connection message should be displayed if everything is fine. Click on the **Next** button to continue.

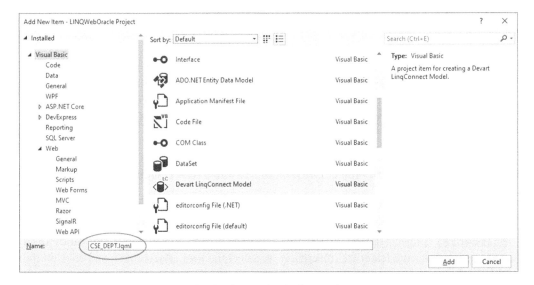

Figure 8.53 Add a new LinqConnect Model. *Source:* Oracle Corporation.

Figure 8.54 The opened model selection wizard. *Source:* Entity Developer.

Figure 8.55 The opened database connection wizard. *Source:* Entity Developer.

5) On the next wizard, keep the default selection, **Generate From Database**, unchanged since we want to create this model based on our sample database. Click on the **Next** button to continue.

6) The next wizard, as shown in Figure 8.56, shows all connected database components, including our five tables, stored procedures and packages we built in our previous projects. Uncheck all components under the **Procedures** and **Packages**, and only keep the top five tables checked, and then click on the **Next** button since this LinqConnect software we are using is an Express version and it only allows us to create and use up to five (5) entities.

7) In the next wizard, it is used to set up the naming rules. Keep all default settings and click on the **Next** button to continue.

8) The Model Properties wizard is opened, as shown in Figure 8.57. This wizard allows you to change the representation format for all data-related components. Just change the last connection setting string to **CSEDEPTConnectionString** to make it shorter. Click on the **Next** button to continue.

9) On the next wizard, keep the default selection, **All Entities**, since we may use different tables for this integrated entity, and click on the **Next** button to continue.

10) Click on the **Next** button for the next wizard to keep the default template.

11) Click on the **Finish** button for the final wizard, which indicates that the model is successfully generated.

12) A model diagram is immediately displayed after this model is generated in the Visual Studio environment, as shown in Figure 8.58.

At this point, we have finished adding a LinqConnect Model into our project. However, before we can begin our coding process, we need to make some small modifications to the added LinqConnect Model, exactly to the **CSE_DEPT.Designer.vb** file, which is just located under the Model, **CSE_DEPT.lqml**, in the Solution Explorer window.

Figure 8.56 The opened database objects selection wizard. *Source:* Entity Developer.

Figure 8.57 The opened Model Properties wizard. *Source:* Entity Developer.

Figure 8.58 The generated model diagram for our LinqConnect model. *Source:* Oracle Corporation.

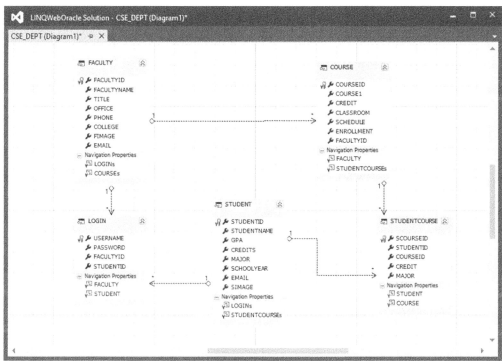

```
Private Shared Function GetConnectionString(ConnectionStringName As String) As String
  Dim Settings As New System.Configuration.ConnectionStringSettings
  Settings.ConnectionString = "User Id=CSE_DEPT;Password=oracle_18c;Server=localhost:1518/CSE_DEPT;
                               Persist Security Info=True"
  'Settings = System.Configuration.ConfigurationManager.ConnectionStrings.Item(connectionStringName)
  'If (Settings Is Nothing) Then
  'Throw new InvalidOperationException("Connection string """ + connectionStringName +""" could not be found in
  the configuration file.")
  'End If
  Return Settings.ConnectionString
End Function
```

Figure 8.59 The modified codes in the function GetConnectionString()

The reason we need to do this modification is because we used two third party tools, **dotCon-nect for Oracle Express** and **LinqConnect Express** (LINQ to Oracle), both are free-charged products of Devart. Installing both tools in a single project may have some conflict effects during the project running time, or called runtime issues. To avoid those effects and make our project work, it is necessary to make these modifications.

Open the **CSE_DEPT.Designer.vb** file by double clicking on it from the Solution Explorer window, and browse to the **Shared Function GetConnectionString()**, as shown in Figure 8.59. Make the modifications as shown in Figure 8.59 and comment out original five coding lines, and the modification result should match the one that is shown in Figure 8.59. The new added line has been highlighted with the gray background color.

The possible issue may be some configuration files, such as **app.config** and **Web.config**, and the runtime cannot identify and select the suitable configuration file to use as the project runs. After this modification, the related components added into our project can be correctly implemented and applied, and to make our project work fine.

8.6.2 Develop the Codes for Our Web Project LINQWebOracle

Now let us begin the coding process for this project. Since we need to use the **Select** button's Click event procedure to validate our data insertion, data updating, and deleting actions, we need to divide our coding process into the following five parts:

A) Create a new object of the DataContext class and do some initialization coding processes in the **Page_Load()** event procedure, Back (**btnBack**) button click event procedure, and related user-defined subroutine **CurrentFaculty()**.
B) Develop the codes for the **Select** button's Click event procedure to retrieve the selected faculty information using the LINQ to Oracle query.
C) Develop the codes for the **Insert** button's Click event procedure to insert new faculty members using the LINQ to Oracle query.
D) Develop the codes for the **Update** button's Click event procedure to update the selected faculty member using the LINQ to Oracle query.
E) Develop the codes for the **Delete** button's Click event procedure to delete the selected faculty member using the LINQ to Oracle query.

Now let us start our coding process for this page. First let us handle creating a new object of the DataContext class and initialization processes in our project.

8.6.2.1 Create a New Object of the DataContext Class with Initialization Processes

We need to create this new object of the DataContext class since we need to use this object to connect to our sample database to perform data queries. We have connected this DataContext class to our sample database **CSE_DEPT** in the last section, and a connection string has been added into our **app.config** file when this connection is done. However, regularly this connection string should be added into our Web Configuration file **Web.config**. Because we installed and used multiple third-party tools, such as **dotConnect for Oracle Express** and **LinqConnect Express** (LINQ to Oracle), this may result in some conflicts between different tools as the project runs. This is the reason why we made some modifications to the codes in the **CSE_DEPT. Designer.vb** in the last section.

Some initialization codes include retrieving all current faculty members from the Faculty table in our sample database using the LINQ to Oracle query and displaying them in the Faculty Name combo box.

Open the code window and the **Page_Load()** event procedure of the Faculty Web page, and enter the codes that are shown in Figure 8.60 into this procedure.

Let us have a closer look at this piece of codes to see how it works.

A) A new form-level object of the DataContext class, **cse_dept**, is generated since we need to use this object to perform some LINQ related data queries later.

B) By checking the **Not IsPostBack** poperty, we can confirm that this is not a PostBack page and we can initialize our Faculty Name combo box, **ComboName**, by calling our user-defined subroutine **CurrentFaculty()** to get all updated faculty members from our sample database and fill them into that combo box.

C) The **SelectedIndex** is reset to 0 to make the **ComboName** to display the first faculty.

Now let us take a look at codes inside the user-defined subroutine **CurrentFaculty()**.

D) Before we can update the Faculty Name combo box control by adding the current faculty members into this control, a cleaning job is performed to avoid the multiple adding and displaying of those faculty members.

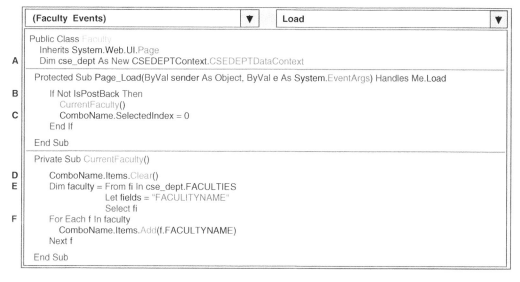

Figure 8.60 Initialization codes for the Faculty Web page.

```
btnBack                              ▼    Click                              ▼
Protected Sub btnBack_Click(sender As Object, e As EventArgs) HandlesbtnBackClick
        cse_dept.Dispose()
        Response.Write("<script>window.close()</script>")
End Sub
```

Figure 8.61 The codes for the Back button Click event procedure.

E) The LINQ query is created and initialized with three clauses, **From, Let,** and **Select**. The range variable **fi** is selected from the **FACULTIES** entity in our sample database. All current faculty members (**FACULTYNAME**) will be read back using the **Let** clause and assigned to the query variable **faculty**.

F) The LINQ query is executed to pick up all queried faculty members and add them into the Faculty Name combo box control in the Faculty Form.

Some readers may have found an issue for this query, which is the column names, and some column names have been changed. Refer to Figure 8.58 for our Entity Model Diagram, you may be able to understand the reason for this issue. One of the reasons is that the underscore for all columns has been removed when we setup our entity model.

The codes for the **Back** button's Click event procedure are shown in Figure 8.61.

The function of this piece of codes is to close the entity object and the Web project.

8.6.2.2 Develop the Codes for the Data Selection Query

Double click on the **Select** button to open its Click event procedure and enter the codes that are shown in Figure 8.62 into this procedure. The function of this piece of codes is to retrieve detailed information for the selected faculty member from the Faculty table in our sample database and display them in seven textboxes and an image control in the Faculty Form page as this **Select** button is clicked by the user.

Let us have a closer look at this piece of codes to see how it works.

```
     btnSelect                           ▼    Click                           ▼
        Protected Sub btnSelect_Click(sender As Object, e As EventArgs) Handles btnSelect.Click
A           Dim bimage As Byte() = Nothing
B           Dim faculty = From fi In cse_dept.FACULTIES
                          Where fi.FACULTYNAME = ComboName.Text
                          Select fi
C           For Each f In faculty
                txtID.Text = f.FACULTYID
                txtName.Text = f.FACULTYNAME
                txtTitle.Text = f.TITLE
                txtOffice.Text = f.OFFICE
                txtPhone.Text = f.PHONE
                txtCollege.Text = f.COLLEGE
                txtEmail.Text = f.EMAIL
D               bimage = f.FIMAGE.ToArray
            Next f
E           Dim img As String = Convert.ToBase64String(bimage)
            PhotoBox.ImageUrl = String.Format("data:image/jpg;base64,{0}", img)
        End Sub
```

Figure 8.62 The codes for the Select button Click event procedure.

A) A local **Byte()** variable **bimage** is declared first, and it is used to get and hold the converted faculty image file. To avoid some possible NULL results returned by this **Byte()** object, it has to be initialized to **Nothing**.

B) The LINQ query is created and initialized with three clauses, **From, Where,** and **Select.** The range variable **fi** is selected from the **FACULTIES** entity in our sample database based on a matched faculty members (**FACULTYNAME**).

C) The LINQ query is executed to pick up all columns for the selected faculty member and display them in the associated textbox in the Faculty Form page.

D) The only exception is how to get and display the faculty image in the Faculty table in our database. The faculty image stored in the fimage column is a Binary Large Object (**BLOB**), and it needs to be converted to a **Byte()** array. Thus, the property **ToArray** is used to do this conversion.

E) Then, the image file in the **Byte()** format is converted to a String or the address of that image file and assigned to the **ImageUrl** property of the Image control PhotoBox to display that faculty image.

Next, let us build the codes for the data insertion function via LINQ to Oracle query.

8.6.2.3 Develop the Codes for the Data Insertion Query

Double click on the **Insert** button from our Faculty Form page to open its Click event procedure and enter the codes that are shown in Figure 8.63 into this procedure.

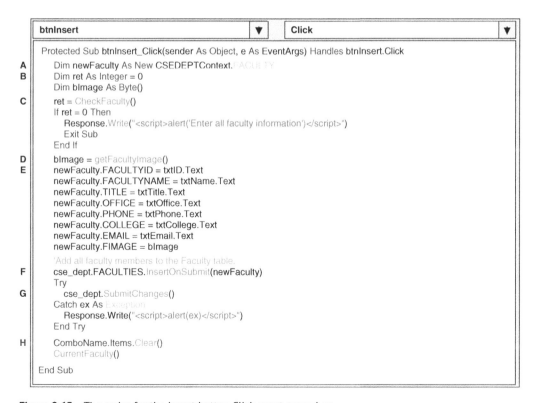

Figure 8.63 The codes for the Insert button Click event procedure.

Let us have a closer look at this piece of codes to see how it works.

A) A new instance of the **FACULTY** entity class is created since we need to add a new record into the Faculty table in our sample database.

B) Some local variables, **ret** and **bImage**, are declared here. The former is used to get and hold the checking result for all faculty textboxes to make sure that all faculty information has been filled, and the latter is used to retrieve and hold a valid faculty image file to be inserted into the database.

C) The user-defined function **CheckFaculty()** is called to check and make sure that all faculty textboxes have been filled with required new faculty information. A returned value of zero indicates that this checking is failed, and a warning message is displayed to remind users to enter all required information.

D) Another user-defined function **getFacultyImage()** is executed to get and display the selected and inserted faculty image.

E) All eight pieces of new faculty information, including a selected new faculty image, are assigned to the related column in the **newFaculty** instance.

F) A system method **InsertOnSubmit()** is executed to insert our completed **newFaculty** instance into our Faculty table via the DataContext class.

G) Another system method **SubmitChanges()** is executed to perform this data insertion. The point is that this method must be included in a **Try...Catch** block to avoid some possible unnecessary exceptions during the execution of this method.

H) After a new record has been inserted into our database, we need to update our Faculty Name combo box control to reflect that insertion. First, we need to clean up all original contents from this control to avoid multiple updating. Then, the user-defined subroutine **CurrentFaculty()** is called to complete this faculty data updating.

Two user-defined functions, **CheckFaculty()** and **getFacultyImage()**, and one subroutine **MapFacultyTable()**, have been built in previous sections in this chapter. Here, we just show them again in Figures 8.64~8.66 to make them convenient to users without illustrations. Only one exception is the coding line **A** in the **CheckFaculty()** function, where a local textbox array **FacultyTextBox()**, instead of a class-level array, is generated to meet the needs of subroutine **MapFacultyTable()** to check all faculty information in related textbox.

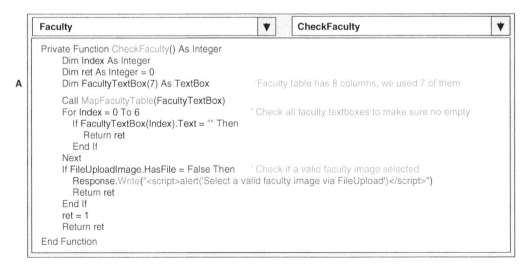

```
Faculty                        ▼    CheckFaculty                      ▼

      Private Function CheckFaculty() As Integer
          Dim Index As Integer
          Dim ret As Integer = 0
A         Dim FacultyTextBox(7) As TextBox          'Faculty table has 8 columns, we used 7 of them

          Call MapFacultyTable(FacultyTextBox)
          For Index = 0 To 6                        ' Check all faculty textboxes to make sure no empty
            If FacultyTextBox(Index).Text = "" Then
              Return ret
            End If
          Next
          If FileUploadImage.HasFile = False Then   ' Check if a valid faculty image selected
            Response.Write("<script>alert('Select a valid faculty image via FileUpload')</script>")
            Return ret
          End If
          ret = 1
          Return ret
      End Function
```

Figure 8.64 The codes for the function CheckFaculty().

Figure 8.65 The codes for the subroutine getFacultyImage().

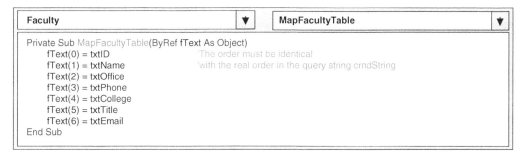

Figure 8.66 The codes for the subroutine MapFacultyTable.

One point to be noted is that to make this data insertion to work, one must make sure that all faculty image files, including a default faculty photo file named **Default.jpg**, have been stored in a default folder **FacultyImage** that should be located under our current project folder, **LINQWebOracle Solution|LINQWebOracle Project**; otherwise, the data insertion may encounter an error since it cannot find this virtual path for the faculty image file to be inserted into the database.

Make sure to create this folder **FacultyImage**, add all faculty image files into this folder, and save this folder under our current project folder **LINQWebOracle Project** before one can run this project to perform the data insertion action. All faculty image files can be found at the folder **Students\Images\Faculty** in the Wiley site (refer to Figure 1.2 in Chapter 1).

Now let us begin the coding development for our data updating and deleting actions.

8.6.2.4 Develop the Codes for the Data Updating and Deleting Queries

First let us build the codes for the data updating actions to the Faculty table in our sample database. Double click on the **Update** button from our Faculty page window to open its Click event procedure and enter the codes that are shown in Figure 8.67 into this procedure.

Let us have a closer look at this piece of codes to see how it works.

A) A LINQ selection query is executed using the Standard Query Operator method with the **FACULTYNAME** as the query criterion. The **First()** method is used to return only the first matched record. This method does not have any affection to our case since we have only one record that is matched to this specified **FACULTYNAME**.

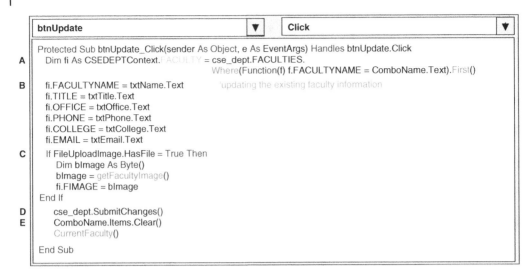

| btnUpdate ▼ | Click ▼ |

```
Protected Sub btnUpdate_Click(sender As Object, e As EventArgs) Handles btnUpdate.Click
A    Dim fi As CSEDEPTContext.FACULTY = cse_dept.FACULTIES.
                              Where(Function(f) f.FACULTYNAME = ComboName.Text).First()

B    fi.FACULTYNAME = txtName.Text           'updating the existing faculty information
     fi.TITLE = txtTitle.Text
     fi.OFFICE = txtOffice.Text
     fi.PHONE = txtPhone.Text
     fi.COLLEGE = txtCollege.Text
     fi.EMAIL = txtEmail.Text

C    If FileUploadImage.HasFile = True Then
         Dim bImage As Byte()
         bImage = getFacultyImage()
         fi.FIMAGE = bImage
     End If

D    cse_dept.SubmitChanges()
E    ComboName.Items.Clear()
     CurrentFaculty()

     End Sub
```

Figure 8.67 The codes for the Update button Click event procedure.

B) All six columns, except the **FACULTYID**, for the selected faculty member are updated by assigning the current value stored in the associated textbox to each column in the Faculty instance **fi** in our DataContext class object **cse_dept**.

C) If the faculty image is also to be updated, the updated faculty image file should have been selected by using the **FileUpload** control **FileUploadImage** and its **HasFile** property should contain a valid faculty image file. The selected faculty image can be obtained by calling the user-defined function **getFacultyImage()** and assigned to the **FIMAGE** column in the Faculty table.

D) This data updating can be really performed only after a system method **SubmitChanges()** is executed.

E) The Faculty Name combo box is cleaned up to make it ready to be updated, and the user-defined subroutine **CurrentFaculty()** is executed to refresh the current faculty members stored in the Faculty Name combo box control.

Before we can run our Web project to test these data actions, let us complete the last coding development for our data deleting action.

Double click on the **Delete** button from our Faculty page window to open its Click event procedure and enter the codes that are shown in Figure 8.68 into this procedure.

Let us have a closer look at this piece of codes to see how it works.

A) A LINQ selection query is first executed to pick up the faculty member to be deleted. This query is initialized with three clauses, **From, Where,** and **Select**. The range variable **fi** is selected from the **FACULTIES**, which is exactly an instance of our entity class Faculty and the column **FACULTYNAME** works as the query criterion for this query. All pieces of information related to the selected faculty member (**FACULTYNAME**) will be retrieved and stored in the query variable **faculty**. The **Single()** method means that only a single or the first record is queried.

B) The system method **DeleteOnSubmit()** is executed to issue a deleting action to the faculty instance, **FACULTIES**, in our DataContext class object **cse_dept**.

C) A **Try...Catch** block is used to execute another system method **SubmitChanges()** to exactly perform this deleting action against the data table in our sample database. The point is that this method must be included in this block to avoid some unnecessary exceptions during

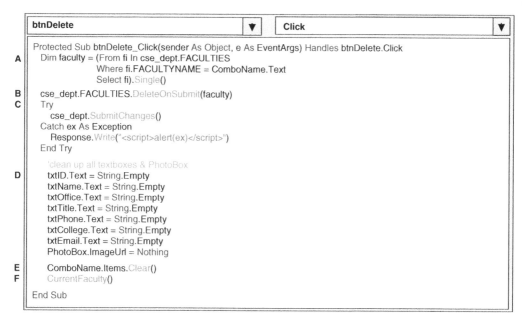

| btnDelete | ▼ | Click | ▼ |

```
    Protected Sub btnDelete_Click(sender As Object, e As EventArgs) Handles btnDelete.Click
A     Dim faculty = (From fi In cse_dept.FACULTIES
                     Where fi.FACULTYNAME = ComboName.Text
                     Select fi).Single()
B     cse_dept.FACULTIES.DeleteOnSubmit(faculty)
C     Try
          cse_dept.SubmitChanges()
      Catch ex As Exception
          Response.Write("<script>alert(ex)</script>")
      End Try

      'clean up all textboxes & PhotoBox
D     txtID.Text = String.Empty
      txtName.Text = String.Empty
      txtOffice.Text = String.Empty
      txtTitle.Text = String.Empty
      txtPhone.Text = String.Empty
      txtCollege.Text = String.Empty
      txtEmail.Text = String.Empty
      PhotoBox.ImageUrl = Nothing

E     ComboName.Items.Clear()
F     CurrentFaculty()

    End Sub
```

Figure 8.68 The codes for the Delete button Click event procedure.

the execution of this method. Only after this method is executed, the selected faculty record can be deleted from our database.

D) All textboxes that stored the selected faculty information and the PhotoBox that stored the faculty image are cleaned up after this deletion action.

E) The Faculty Name combo box is cleaned up to make it ready to be updated.

F) The user-defined subroutine **CurrentFaculty()** is executed to reflect this faculty record deleting for all faculty members stored in the Faculty Name combo box.

Now, we can build and run our Web project to test the data actions against our sample database. One point to be noted is that before running the project, one must make sure that all faculty image files should have been stored in a virtual folder, **FacultyImage**, which is located under our Web project **LINQWebOracle Project** foler. In this application, it should be: **C:\Chapter 8\LINQWebOracle Solution\LINQWebOracle Project**. You can find all faculty and student image files from the folders **Students\Images\Faculty** and **Students\Images\Students** that are located at the Wiley ftp site (refer to Figure 1.2 in Chapter 1). Also setup the **Faculty.aspx** page as a Start Page.

Click on the **IIS Express** button to run the project. On the opened Faculty page, click on the **Select** button to test the faculty data query function.

Now let us test the data insertion by entering following eight pieces of information into eight textboxes as a new faculty record:

- **W28577**   Faculty ID textbox
- **Peter Wang**   Name textbox
- **Professor**   Title textbox
- **MTC-322**   Office textbox
- **750-330-2255**   Phone textbox
- **University of Dallas**   College textbox
- **pwang@college.edu**   Email textbox
- **Wang.jpg**   Faculty Image file name

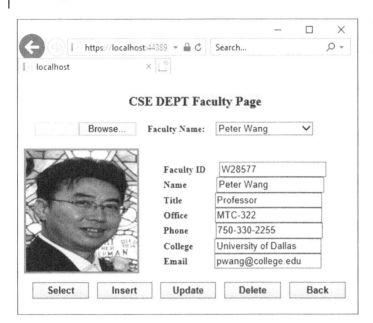

Figure 8.69 The testing status of the data insertion action. *Source:* Used with permission from Microsoft.

Using the FileUpload control, `FileUploadImage`, to select the desired faculty image file, `Wang.jpg`. Then click on the `Insert` button to perform this data insertion.

To confirm this data action, first select another faculty member from the Faculty Name combo box and click on the `Select` button to retrieve and display that faculty's record. Then select the new inserted faculty `Peter Wang` from the Faculty Name combo box, and click on the `Select` button to try to retrieve this new inserted faculty's record and display it in this page. Your data insertion confirmation page should match the one that is shown in Figure 8.69.

Now let us test the Updating action against the Faculty table in our sample database. Keep this new inserted faculty information with no change, but only change the faculty image file to `Default.jpg` by using the FileUpload control, `FileUploadImage`. Then click on the `Update` button to try to update this faculty record in our sample database.

To confirm this updating action, first select another faculty name from the combo box and click on the `Select` button to retrieve and show that record. Then select the updated faculty member, `Peter Wang`, from the combo box with the `Select` button clicked to get his record. Immediately one can find that his record is really updated with the `Default.jpg` image file. One can perform another updating to get the original image back if you like.

To test the data deleting function for this project, just keep the current updated faculty record with no change and click on the `Delete` button to delete this faculty record. One can confirm this deletion by checking the faculty member in the `Faculty Name` combo box. Since this is a new inserted faculty record with no any related data in any other tables in our sample database, thus no any columns are affected and therefore one does not need to recover any related data. However, if an original faculty record, such as `Ying Bai`, is deleted, one had better recover all faculty related records, including the columns in the child tables and parent table. Refer to Tables 8.8~8.11 in Section 8.5.2.5 in this chapter to recover the deleted records in our sample database. You can do this recovery job for all child tables with either the Server Explorer or the Oracle SQL Developer.

A complete Web page application project `LINQWebOracle Project` can be found from the folder `Class DB Projects\Chapter 8` that is located under the `Students` folder at the Wiley ftp site (refer to Figure 1.2 in Chapter 1).

8.7   Chapter Summary

A detailed and completed introduction to the ASP.NET and the .NET Framework is provided at the beginning of this chapter. This part is especially useful and important to readers or students who do not have any knowledge or background in the Web application project developments and implementations.

Following the introduction section, a detailed discussion about how to install and configure the environment to develop the ASP.NET Web applications is provided. Some essential tools such as the Web server, IIS and FrontPage Server Extension 2000, as well as the installation process of these tools are also introduced and discussed in details.

Starting from Section 8.3, the detailed development and building process of ASP.NET Web applications to access databases are discussed with four (4) real Web application projects. One popular database, Oracle XE 18c, is utilized as the target database. Four real ASP.NET Web application projects include:

1) Develop ASP.NET Web application to select and display data from the Oracle XE 18c database.
2) Develop ASP.NET Web application to insert data into the Oracle XE 18c database.
3) Develop ASP.NET Web application to update and delete data against the Oracle XE 18c database.
4) Develop ASP.NET Web application project to access and manipulate data against Oracle XE 18c database using LINQ To Oracle query method.

The stored procedures are utilized in some projects to help readers or students to perform the data updating and deleting actions against the Oracle XE 18c database more efficiently and conveniently. The detailed discussion on the data deleting order is provided to help readers to understand the integrity constraint built in the relational database. It is a tough topic to update or delete data from related tables in a relational database, and a clear and deep discussion on this topic will significantly benefit the readers and improve their knowledge and hands-on experience on these issues.

Homework

I.   True/False Selections

_____ **1** The actual language used in the communications between the client and the server is HTML.

_____ **2** ASP.NET and .NET Framework are two different models that provide the development environments to the Web programming.

_____ **3** The .NET Framework is composed of the Common Language Runtime (called runtime) and a collection of class libraries.

_____ **4** You can access the .NET Framework by using the class libraries provided by the .NET Framework, and you can implement the .NET Framework by using the tools such as Visual Studio.NET provided by the .NET Framework, too.

_____ **5** ASP.NET is a programming framework built on the .NET Framework, and it is used to build Web applications.

_____ **6** The fundamental component of ASP.NET is the Web Form. A Web Form is a Web page that users view in a browser, and an ASP.NET Web application can contain one or more Web Forms.

_____ **7** A Web Form is a dynamic page that runs on the server side, and it can access server resources when it is viewed by users via the client browser.

_____ **8** Similar to traditional Web pages, an ASP.NET Web page can only run scripts on the client side.

_____ **9** The controls you added to the Web Form will run on the Web server side when this Web page is requested by the user through a client browser.

_____ **10** To allow a List Box control to response to a user click as the Web page runs, the AutoPostBack property of that List Box must be set to False.

II. Multiple Choices

1 When users send a request from the users' client browser to request a Web page, the server needs to build that form and sends it back to the user's browser in the _____ language format.
   A ASP.NET
   B .NET Framework
   C XML
   D HTML

2 Once a requested Web page is received by the client's browser, the connection between the client and the server is _____.
   A Still active
   B Terminated
   C Not active
   D Either active or inactive

3 As a Web application runs, the programs developed in any .NET-based language are converted into the _____ codes that can be recognized by the CLR, and the CLR can compile and execute the MSIL codes by using the Just-In-Time compiler.
   A Visual Studio.NET
   B Visual Basic.NET
   C Microsoft Intermediate Language (MSIL)
   D C#

4 The terminal file of an ASP.NET Web application is a _____ file.
   A Dynamic Linked Library (dll)
   B MSIL
   C XML
   D HTML

5 Because Web pages are frequently refreshed by the server, one must use the _____ to store the global variable.
  A Global.asax file
  B Defaulty.aspx file
  C Config file
  D Application state

6 One needs to use the _____ method to display a message box in Web applications.
  A MessageBox.Show()
  B MessageBox.Display
  C Java script alert()
  D Response.Write()

7 Unlike the Windows-based applications that use the Form_Load as the first event procedure, a Web-based application uses the _____ as the first event procedure.
  A Start_Page
  B Page_Load
  C First_Page
  D Web_Start

8 To delete data from a relational database, one must first delete the data from the _____ tables, and then one can delete the target data from the _____ table.
  A Major, minor
  B Parent, child
  C Parent, parent
  D Child, parent

9 To allow an Oracle database engine to delete all related records from the child tables, the Delete Rule item in the UPDATE And DELETE Specifications box of the Foreign Key Relationship dialog box must be set to _____.
  A No action
  B Cascade
  C Set default
  D Set Null

10 To display any message on a running Web page, one must use the _____ method.
  A MessageBox.Show()
  B Response()
  C Response.Redirect()
  D Response.Write()

III. Exercises

1 Write a paragraph to answer and explain the following questions:
  A What is ASP.NET?
  B What is the main component of the ASP.NET Web application?
  C How an ASP.NET Web application is executed?

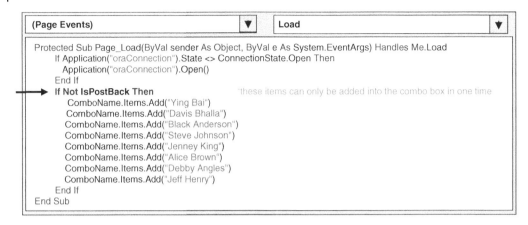

Figure 8.70 The codes for the Page_Load() event procedure.

2 Suppose we want to delete one record from the **STUDENT** table in our sample database **CSE_DEPT** based on one **STUDENT_ID = H10210**. List all deleting steps and deleting queries including the data deleting from the child and the parent tables.

3 Figure 8.70 shows a piece of codes developed in the Page_Load() event procedure. Explain the function of the statement **If Not IsPostBack Then** block.

4 Create a new ASP.NET Web Application project WebSelectStudent **Project** and add a Web page **Student.aspx** to develop the codes for the **Select** button's Click event procedure to perform the data query from our sample database **CSE_DEPT** for the Student page. You can copy the project OracleWebUpdateDelete **Project** and change its name to WebSelectStudent **Project**. The project file OracleWebUpdateDelete **Project** can be found from the folder **Class** DB **Projects\Chapter 8** that is located at the Wiley ftp site under the **Students** folder (refer to Figure 1.2 in Chapter 1).
Hint1: One can build the **Student.aspx** page by adding an existing page **Student.aspx** that is located at a folder **Students\VB Forms\Web** on the Wiley ftp site.

5 In the Web page **Student.aspx**, develop the codes for the **Insert** button's Click event procedure to perform the data insertion into our sample database **CSE_DEPT** with a new project WebInsertStudent **Project**. You can copy the OracleWebUpdateDelete **Project** and change its name to WebInsertStudent **Project**. The project file OracleWebUpdateDelete **Project** can be found from the folder **Class** DB **Projects\Chapter 8** that is located at the Wiley ftp site under the **Students** folder (refer to Figure 1.2 in Chapter 1).
Hint1: See Hint1 in Exercise 4.
Hint2: Prior to running and testing the project, make sure to save all student image files into a virtual folder **StudentImage**, and this folder should be located under your project folder, **WebInsertStudent Project**, in your computer.
Hint3: Also modify your codes inside the user-defined function **getStudentImage()** to change the path from **FacultyImage** to **StudentImage**.

6 Create a new ASP.NET Web Application project WebUpdateStudent **Project** and develop the codes for the **Update** button's Click event procedure in the Web page **Student.aspx** to perform the data updating function. You can copy the project OracleWebUpdateDelete **Project** and change its name to WebUpdateStudent **Project**. The project file OracleWebUpdateDelete **Project** can be found from the folder **Class** DB **Projects\ Chapter 8** that is located at the Wiley ftp site under the **Students** folder (refer to Figure 1.2 in Chapter 1).

Hint1: See Hint1 in Exercise 4.

Hint2: Prior to running and testing the project, make sure to save all student image files into a virtual folder **StudentImage**, and this folder should be located under your project folder, **WebUpdateStudent Project**, in your computer.

Hint3: Also modify your codes inside the user-defined function **getStudentImage()** to change the path from **FacultyImage** to **StudentImage**.

It is highly recommended to recover the updated student's information back to the original information by using the **Update** button's Click event procedure again.

7 Using the Cascade options for relationships 1, 2, and 3 listed in Section 8.5.2.2 in this chapter to create a stored procedure **DELETE_STUDENT** with only one deleting query to delete a student member (**Holes Smith** with **STUDENT_ID = **H10210) from the STUDENT table in our sample database (refer to Section 8.5.2.2 to get a detailed discussion for this issue). One needs to create a new ASP.NET Web project WebDeleteStudent **Project** and build codes for Delete button's click event procedure to perform this deleting action. One can copy and modify the project OracleWebUpdateDelete **Project** to make it as a new project. The project file OracleWebUpdateDelete **Project** is located at the folder **Class** DB **Projects\Chapter 8** that is located at the Wiley ftp site under the **Students** folder (refer to Figure 1.2 in Chapter 1). Exactly one can use the **Delete** button's Click event procedure to call this stored procedure to this deleting action.

Hint1: See Hint1 in Exercise 4.

Hint2: The only input parameter to the stored procedure is the student name, one needs to perform 2 queries to do this deleting action; (i) query **STUDENT** table to get related **STUDENT_ ID** based on the input student name, and (ii) perform the deleting query via stored procedure.

It is highly recommended to recover the deleted student record by using the **Insert** button's Click event procedure in the Student Web Form for the **STUDENT** table (parent table), and then recover other records in **LOGIN** and **STUDENTCOURSE** tables (child tables) with either Server Explorer or Oracle SQL Developer. Refer to Exercise 2 and **STUDENT**, **LOGIN**, and **STUDENTCOURSE** tables in Chapter 2 to recover those deleted records for the deleted student (**STUDENT_ID = **H10210).

9

ASP.NET Web Services

We provided a very detailed discussion about the ASP.NET Web applications in the last chapter. In this chapter, we will concentrate on another ASP.NET related topic – ASP.NET Web Services.

Unlike the ASP.NET Web applications in which the user needs to access the Web server through the client browser by sending requests to the server to obtain the desired information, the ASP.NET Web Services provide an automatic way to search, identify, and return the desired information required by the user through a set of methods installed in the Web server, and those methods can be accessed by a computer program, not the user, via the Internet. Another important difference between the ASP.NET Web applications and ASP.NET Web Services is that the latter does not provide any graphic user interfaces (GUIs) and the users need to create those GUIs themselves to access the Web services via the Internet.

When finished this chapter, you will be able to:

- Understand the structure and components of ASP.NET Web services, such as Simple Object Access Protocol (SOAP), Web Services Description Language (WSDL), and Universal Description, Discovery, and Integration (UDDI).
- Create correct SOAP namespaces for the Web Services to make used names and identifiers unique in the user's document.
- Create suitable security components to protect the Web methods.
- Build the professional ASP.NET Web Service projects to access our sample database to obtain required information.
- Build client applications to provide GUIs to consume a Web Service.
- Build the professional ASP.NET Web Service projects to insert new records into our sample database.
- Build the professional ASP.NET Web Service projects to update and delete data against our sample database.

In order to help readers to successfully complete this chapter, first we need to provide a detailed introduction about the ASP.NET Web Services and their components.

Oracle Database Programming with Visual Basic.NET: Concepts, Designs, and Implementations, First Edition. Ying Bai.
© 2021 The Institute of Electrical and Electronics Engineers, Inc. Published 2021 by John Wiley & Sons, Inc.
Companion website: www.wiley.com/go/bai-VB-Oracle

9.1   What Are Web Services and Their Components?

Essentially, the Web services can be considered as a set of methods installed in a Web server and can be called by computer programs installed on the clients through the Internet. Those methods can be used to locate and return the target information required by the computer programs. Web services do not require the use of browsers or HTML, and therefore Web services are sometimes called *application services.*

To effectively find, identify, and return the target information required by computer programs, a Web service needs the following components:

1) XML (Extensible Markup Language).
2) SOAP (Simple Object Access Protocol).
3) UDDI (Universal Description, Discovery, and Integration).
4) WSDL (Web Services Description Language).

The function of each component is listed below:

XML is a text-based data storage language and it uses a series of tags to define and store data. Exactly, the so-called tags are used to `mark up` data to be exchanged between applications. The `marked up` data then can be recognized and used by different applications without any problem. As you know, the Web services platform is XML + HTTP (Hypertext Transfer Protocol) and the HTTP protocol is the most popular Internet protocol. But the XML provides a kind of language that can be used between different platforms and programming languages to express complex messages and functions. In order to make the codes used in the Web services to be recognized by applications developed in different platforms and programming languages, the XML is used for the coding in the Web services to make them up line by line.

SOAP is a communication protocol used for communications between applications. Essentially, SOAP is a simple XML-based protocol to help applications developed in different platforms and languages to exchange information over HTTP. Therefore, SOAP is a platform-independent and language-independent protocol, which means that it can run at any operating systems with any programming languages. Exactly, the SOAP works as a carrier to transfer data or requests between applications. Whenever a request is made to the Web server to request a Web Service, this request is first wrapped into a SOAP message and sent over the Internet to the Web server. Similarly, as the Web service returns the target information to the client, the returned information is also wrapped into a SOAP message and sent over the Internet to the client browser.

WSDL is an XML-based language for describing Web services and how to access them. In WSDL terminology, each Web service is defined as an abstract endpoint or a Port and each Web method is defined as an abstract operation. Each operation or method can contain some SOAP messages to be transferred between applications. Each message is constructed using the SOAP protocol as a request is made from the client. WSDL defines two styles for how a Web service method can be formatted in a SOAP message: Remote Procedure Call (RPC) and Document. Both RPC- and Document-style message can be used to communicate with a Web Service using a RPC.

A single endpoint can contain a group of Web methods and that group of methods can be defined as an abstract set of operations called a Port Type. Therefore, WSDL is an XML format for describing network services as a set of endpoints operating on SOAP messages containing either document-oriented or procedure-oriented information. The operations and messages are described abstractly and then bound to a concrete network protocol and message format to define an endpoint.

UDDI is an XML-based directory for businesses to list themselves on the Internet, and the goal of this directory is to enable companies to find one another on the Web and make their systems

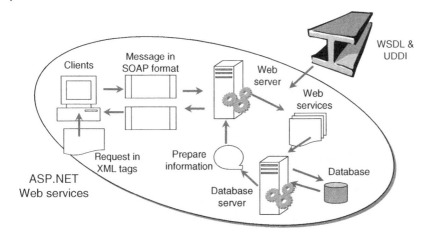

Figure 9.1 A typical process of a Web Service.

interoperable for e-commerce. UDDI is often considered as a telephone book's yellow and white pages. Using those pages, it allows businesses to list themselves by name, products, locations, or the Web services they offer.

Summarily, based on these components and their roles discussed above, we can conclude:

- The XML is used to tag the data to be transferred between applications.
- SOAP is used to wrap and pack the data tagged in the XML format into the messages represented in the SOAP protocol.
- WSDL is used to map a concrete network protocol and message format to an abstract endpoint and describe the Web services available in a WSDL document format.
- UDDI is used to list all Web services that are available to users and businesses.

Figure 9.1 shows a diagram to illustrate these components and their roles in an ASP.NET Web service process.

By now, we have obtained the fundamental knowledge about the ASP.NET Web services and their components, next let's see how to build a Web service.

9.2   Procedures to Build a Web Service

Different methods and languages can be used to develop different Web services such as the C# Web services, Java Web services, and Perl Web services. In this section, we only concentrate on developing the ASP.NET Web services using the Visual Basic.NET. Before we can start to build a real Web service project, let's first take a closer look at the structure of a Web service project.

9.2.1   The Structure of a Typical Web Service Project

A typical Web service project contains the following components:

1) As a new Web service project is created, two page files and two folders are created under this new project. The folder **App_Code** contains the code-behind page that has all real codes for a simple default Web service and the Web service to be created. The folder **App_Data** is used to store all project data.

2) The code-behind page `Service.vb`. This page contains the real Visual Basic.NET codes for a simple Web service. Visual Web Developer includes three default declarations to help users to develop Web services on the top of this page, which are

```
Imports System.Web
Imports System.Web.Services
Imports System.Web.Services.Protocols
```

By default, a new code-behind file contains a class named `Service` that is defined with the `WebService` and `WebServiceBinding` attributes. This class defined a default Web method named HelloWorld that is a placeholder and you can replace it with your own method or methods later when you develop your own Web service project.

3) The main Web Service page file is `Service.asmx`. This page is used to display information about the Web service's methods and provide access to the Web service's WSDL information. The extension `.asmx` means that this is an Active Service Method file, and the letter **x** is just a rotation of the attached symbol + after the keyword ASP, since the ASP.NET was called ASP+ in the early day. If you open the ASMX file on disk, you will see that it actually contains only one command line:

```
<%@ WebService Language="vb" CodeBehind="~/App_Code/Service.
vb" Class="Service" %>
```

It indicates the programming language in which the Web service's code-behind file is written, the code-behind file's location, and the class that defines the Web service. When you request the ASMX page through IIS, ASP.NET uses this information to generate the content displayed in the Web browser.

4) The configuration file `Web.config`, which is XML-based file, is used to set up a configuration for the new created Web service project, such as the namespaces for all kinds of Web components, Connection string, and default authentication mode. Each Web service project has its own configuration file.

Of all files and folders discussed above, the code-behind page is the most important file since all Visual Basic.NET codes related to build a Web service are located in this page and our major coding development will be concentrated on this page, too.

9.2.2 Some Real Considerations When Building a Web Service Project

Based on the structure of a typical Web service project, some issues related to build an actual Web service project are emphasized here, and these issues are very important and should be followed carefully to successfully create a Web service project in Visual Studio.NET environment.

As a request is made and sent from a Windows or Web form client over the Internet to the server, the request is packed into a SOAP message and sent to the Internet Information Services (**IIS**) on the client computer, which works as a pseudo-server. Then the **IIS** will pass the request to the ASP.NET to get it processed in terms of the extension `.asmx` of the main service page. ASP.NET checks the page to make sure that the code-behind page contains the necessary codes to power the Web Service, exactly to trigger the associated Web methods to search, find, and retrieve the information required by the client, pack it to the SOAP message, and return it to the client.

During this process, the following detailed procedures must be performed:

1) When ASP.NET checks the received request represented in a SOAP message, the ASP.NET will make sure that the names and identifiers used in the SOAP message must be unique, in other

words, those names and identifiers cannot be conflicted with any other name and identifier used by any other message. To make names and identifiers unique, we need to use our specific namespace to place and hold our SOAP message.

2) Generally, a request contains a set of information, not a single piece of information. To request those pieces of information, we need to create a Web service proxy class to consume Web services. In other words, we do not want to develop separate Web method to query each piece of information, and that will make our project's size terribly large if we need a lot of information. A good solution is to instantiate an object based on that class and to integrate those pieces of information into that object. All pieces of information can be embedded into that object and returned if that object returns. Another choice is to design a Web method to make it return a DataSet, and it is a convenient way to return all data.

3) As a professional application, we need to handle the exceptions to make our Web service as prefect as possible. In that case, we need to create a base class to hold some error-checking codes to protect our real class that will be instantiated to an object that contains all pieces of information we need, so this real class should be a child class inherited from the base class.

4) Since any Web services did not provide any GUI, so we need to develop some GUIs in either Windows-based or Web-based applications to interface to the Web services to display returned information on GUIs.

Starting from .NET Frameworks 4.0, a good platform, Windows Communication Foundation (WCF), is provided to support to build professional Web Services projects. First, let' have a basic understanding about this new tool.

9.2.3 Introduction to Windows Communication Foundation (WCF)

As the advanced development of the service-oriented communications, the software development has been significantly changed. Whether the message is done with SOAP or in some other ways, applications that interact through services have become the normal. For Windows developers, this change is made possible using the WCF. This is first released as part of the .NET Framework 3.0 in 2006, then updated in the .NET Framework 3.5, and the most recent version of this technology is included in the .NET Framework 4.7. For a substantial share of new software built on .NET, WCF is the right foundation.

9.2.3.1 What is the WCF?

WCF is a framework for building service-oriented applications. Using WCF, you can send data as asynchronous messages from one service endpoint to another. A service endpoint can be part of a continuously available service hosted by IIS, or it can be a service hosted in an application. An endpoint can be a client of a service that requests data from a service endpoint.

WCF is a unified framework for creating secure, reliable, transacted, and interoperable distributed applications. In earlier versions of Visual Studio, there were several technologies that could be used for communicating between applications.

If you wanted to share information in a way that enabled it to be accessed from any platform, you would use a Web service (also known as an ASMX Web service). If you wanted to just move data between a client and server that are running on the Windows operating system, you would use .NET Remoting. If you wanted transacted communications, you would use Enterprise Services (DCOM), or if you wanted a queued model you would use Message Queuing (also known as MSMQ).

WCF brings together the functionality of all those technologies under a unified programming model. This simplifies the experience of developing distributed applications.

In fact, WCF is implemented primarily as a set of classes on the top of the .NET Framework's Common Language Runtime (CLR). This allows .NET developers build service-oriented applications in an easy way. Also, WCF allows creating clients that access services in a mutual way, which means that both the client and the service can run in pretty much same way as any Windows process did. WCF does not define a required host. Wherever they run, clients and services can interact via SOAP, via a WCF-specific binary protocol, and in other ways.

9.2.3.2 WCF Data Services

WCF Data Services, formerly known as ADO.NET Data Services, is a component of the .NET Framework that enables you to create services that use the Open Data Protocol (OData) to expose and consume data over the Web or intranet using the semantics of representational state transfer (REST). OData exposes data as resources that are addressable by URIs. Data are accessed and changed using standard HTTP verbs of GET, PUT, POST, and DELETE. OData uses the entity-relationship conventions of the Entity Data Model to expose resources as sets of entities that are related by associations.

WCF Data Services uses the OData protocol for addressing and updating resources. In this way, you can access these services from any client that supports OData. OData enables you to request and write data to resources using well-known transfer formats: atom, a set of standards for exchanging and updating data as XML, and JavaScript Object Notation (JSON), a text-based data exchange format used extensively in AJAX application.

WCF Data Services can expose data that originate from various sources as OData feeds. Visual Studio tools make it easier for you to create an OData-based service by using an ADO.NET Entity Framework data model. You can also create OData feeds based on CLR classes and even late-bound or untyped data.

WCF Data Services also includes a set of client libraries, one for general .NET Framework client applications and another specifically for Silverlight-based applications.

These client libraries provide an object-based programming model when you access an OData feed from environments such as the .NET Framework and Silverlight.

9.2.3.3 WCF Services

A WCF service is based on an interface that defines a contract between the service and the client. It is marked with a **ServiceContractAttribute** attribute, as shown in the codes shown in Figure 9.2.

You define functions or methods that are exposed by a WCF service by marking them with an **OperationContractAttribute** attribute. In addition, you can expose serialized data by marking a composite type with a **DataContractAttribute** attribute. This enables data binding in a client.

After an interface and its methods are defined, they are encapsulated in a class that implements the interface. A single WCF service class can implement multiple service contracts.

```
<ServiceContract()>
Public Interface IService1
<OperationContract()>
Function GetData(ByVal value As String) As String
```

Figure 9.2 The service interface and contract.

A WCF service is exposed for consumption through what is known as an **endpoint**. The endpoint provides the only way to communicate with the service; you cannot access the service through a direct reference as you would with other classes.

An endpoint consists of an address, a binding, and a contract. The address defines where the service is located; this could be a URL, an FTP address, or a network or local path. A binding defines the way that you communicate with the service. WCF bindings provide a versatile model for specifying a protocol such as HTTP or FTP, a security mechanism such as Windows Authentication or user names and passwords, and much more. A contract includes the operations that are exposed by the WCF service class.

Multiple endpoints can be exposed for a single WCF service. This enables different clients to communicate with the same service in different ways. For example, a banking service might provide one endpoint for employees and another for external customers, each using a different address, binding, and/or contract.

9.2.3.4 WCF Clients

A WCF client consists of a **proxy** that enables an application to communicate with a WCF service, and an endpoint that matches an endpoint defined for the service. The proxy is generated on the client side in the **app.config** file and includes information about the types and methods that are exposed by the service. For services that expose multiple endpoints, the client can select the one that best fits its needs, for example, to communicate over HTTP and use Windows Authentication.

After a WCF client has been created, you reference the service in your code just as

what you could do for any other object. For example, to call the **GetData()** method shown in Figure 9.2, you would write the codes shown in Figure 9.3.

In most cases, you need to create a proxy to set up a reference to the server in the client to access the operations defined in the server.

9.2.3.5 WCF Hosting

From a developer perspective, WCF provides two alternatives for hosting services, which are both mostly identical under the covers. The easier of the two alternatives is to host services inside an ASP.NET application, and the more flexible and more explicit alternative is to host services yourself and in whichever application process you choose.

Hosting WCF services in ASP.NET is very simple and straightforward and very similar to the ASMX model. You can either place your entire service implementation in a ***.svc** file just as with ASP.NET Web services ***.asmx** files or you can reference a service implementation residing in a code-behind file or some other assembly. With respect to how the service implementation class is

```
Private Sub Button1_Click(ByVal sender As System.Object, _
                          ByVal e As System.EventArgs) Handles Button1.Click

    Dim client As New ServiceReference1.Service1Client
    Dim returnString As String

    returnString = client.GetData(TextBox1.Text)
    Label1.Text = returnString

End Sub
```

Figure 9.3   The codes in the client side to call the operation GetData() in the server.

located (and possibly compiled), none of these options differ much from how you would typically create an ASMX Web service, even the attributes of the **@Service** directive are the same as those for the **@WebService** directive.

The important difference between WCF and ASMX is that the WCF service will not do anything until you specify precisely how it shall be exposed to the outside world. An ASMX service will happily start talking to the world once you place the ***.asmx** file into an IIS virtual directory. A WCF service will not talk to anybody until you tell it to do so, and how to do so.

9.2.3.6 WCF Visual Studio Templates

Visual Studio.NET provides a set of WCF templates to help developers to build different Web services and applications. In fact, WCF Visual Studio templates are predefined project and item templates you can use in Visual Studio to quickly build WCF services and surrounding applications.

WCF Visual Studio templates provide a basic class structure for service development. Specifically, these templates provide the basic definitions for service contract, data contract, service implementation, and configuration. You can use these templates to create a simple service with minimal code interaction, as well as a building block for more advanced services.

Two popular templates are **WCF Service Application** template and **WCF Service Library** template. Both are located under the **New Project\Visual Basic\WCF** command folder.

9.2.3.6.1 WCF Web Service Application Template   When you create a new Visual Basic.NET project using the **WCF Web Service Application** template, the project includes the following three major files:

1) Service Contract File (**IService1.vb**). The service contract file is an interface that has WCF service attributes applied. This file provides a definition of a simple service to show you how to define your services and includes parameter-based operations and a simple data contract sample. This is the default file displayed in the code editor after creating a WCF service project.
2) Service implements file (**Service1.svc**). This file is an implement file for the class **IService1** interface file, and it implements the contract defined in the service contract file.
3) Web Configuration File (**Web.config**). The configuration file provides the basic elements of a WCF service model with a secure HTTP binding. It also includes an endpoint for the service and enables metadata exchange.

The template automatically creates a Web site that will be deployed to a virtual directory and hosts a service in it.

9.2.3.6.2 WCF Service Library Project Template   When you create a new Visual Basic.NET project using the **WCF Service Library** template, the new project automatically includes the following three files:

1) Service Contract File (**IService.vb**).
2) Service Implementation File (**Service.vb**).
3) Application Configuration File (**App.config**).

Now let's start to build our Web service project using the WCF template. We prefer to use the **WCF Web Service Application** template and include our Web service in our ASP.NET application project.

9.2.4 Procedures to Build an ASP.NET Web Service

The advantages of using the WCF templates to build our Web services are obvious, for instance, the protocols of the interface and contract have been predefined. However, you must follow up those protocols to fill your codes such as operations and methods. An easy way to do these is to directly add our Web service with our operations in our ways. In the following sections, we will not use the protocols provided by WCF and directly create our Web services and place them into an ASP.NET Web services `*.asmx` file.

Web service is basically composed of a set of Web methods that can be called by the computer programs in the client side. To build those methods, generally one needs to perform the following steps:

1) Create a new WCF Web Service project.
2) Add a new ASP.NET Web Service project.
3) Create a base class to handle the error checking to protect our real class.
4) Create our real Web service class to hold all Web methods and codes to response to requests.
5) Add all Web methods into our Web service class.
6) Develop the detail codes for those Web methods to perform the Web services.
7) Build a Windows-based or Web-based project to consume the Web service to pick up and display the required information on the GUI.
8) Store our ASP.NET Web service project files in a safe location.

In this chapter, we try to develop the following projects to illustrate the building and implementation process of Web services project:

- Build a professional ASP.NET Web Service project to access the Oracle database to obtain required information.
- Build client applications to provide GUIs to consume a Web Service.
- Build a professional ASP.NET Web Service project to insert new records into the Oracle database.
- Build client applications (Windows-based and Web-based) with GUIs to insert data to our sample database via Web Services.
- Build a professional ASP.NET Web Service project to update and delete data against the Oracle database.
- Build client applications (Windows-based and Web-based) with GUIs to update and delete data to our sample database via Web Services.

Based on procedures discussed above, we can start to build our first Web service project `WebServiceOracleSelect Project`. However, before we can create this project, we need first to install WCF via Visual Studio Installer, since this tool is no longer a default installation component since Visual Studio.NET 2019.

9.2.5 Install WCF Component with Visual Studio Installer

You can use any way to open this Visual Studio Installer, but an easy way is to go to `Start|All Programs` and you can find this by scrolling down on the component list. Another way is to create a new project with Visual Studio.NET 2019 by going to `File|New Project` menu item, scroll down all templates until the bottom, and click on `Install more tools and features` link.

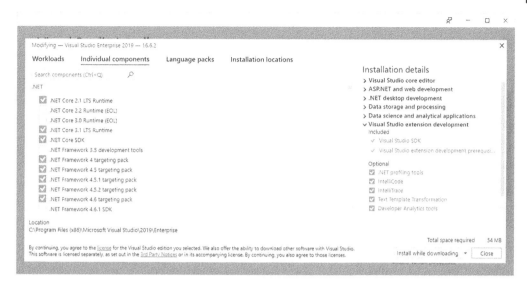

Figure 9.4 The opened individual components view. *Source:* Used with permission from Microsoft.

You may need to complete the updating function for your Visual Studio.NET first and then perform the following steps to add this WCF into the Visual Studio.NET 2019:

1) On the opened Visual Studio Installer, click on the **Modify** button to open and display all components available to be installed.
2) Then click on the **Individual Components** on the top to show all components, including the installed and uninstalled components, in an individual view, as shown in Figure 9.4.
3) On the Search components box, enter **WCF** and press the Enter key from your keyboard, then you can find the **Windows Communication Foundation** component. Check the checkbox on the left of this component, keep the default mode on the **Install while downloading** combo box, and click on the **Modify** button to begin this downloading and installing process.
4) Click on the **Continue** button on the popup message box if you open this Installer from the Visual Studio.NET by creating a new project to enable the Installer to process. The installation process starts, as shown in Figure 9.5.
5) As the downloading and installation process is completed, it will automatically launch the Visual Studio.NET 2019. Then click on the **Close** button on the upper-right corner of the Installer to close it.

Now, we are ready to create our new WCF Service Application project using the installed WCF Service component.

9.3 Build ASP.NET Web Service Project to Access Oracle Database

To create a new ASP.NET Web Service project, perform the following operations:

1) Open the Windows Explorer to create a new folder **C:\Chapter 9**.
2) Open the Visual Studio.NET and go to **File|New Project** item.

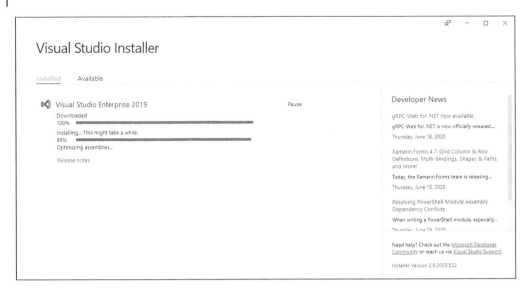

Figure 9.5 The installation process. *Source:* Used with permission from Microsoft.

3) On the opened New Project wizard, select the **WCF Service Application** template with **Visual Basic** (located under the WCF Service Application) from the right pane, and click on the **Next** button to create our WCF project.
4) Enter **WebServiceOracleSelect Project** into the **Project name** box, and **WebService-OracleSelect Solution** into the **Solution name** box. Select **C:\ Chapter 9** for the **Location** for this project, which is shown in Figure 9.6, and click on the **Create** button to create this new project.

9.3.1 Files and Items Created in the New Web Service Project

After this new WCF Web service project is created, four items are produced in the Solution Explorer window, which are shown in Figure 9.7. These components include

1) Additional connected service files (**Connected Services**)
2) Service contract file (**IService1.vb**).
3) Service implements file (**Service1.svc**).
4) Web configuration file (**Web.config**).

The files 2 and 3 are used to provide some default functions to get some system data. Since we want to build our Web service in our customer way, thus perform the following operations to add a new Web main service into our project:

1) Right-click on our new project **WebServiceOracleSelect Project** from the Solution Explorer window and select the **Add|New Item**.
2) On the opened wizard, select **Web Service (ASMX)** from the Template list, and enter **WebServiceOracleSelect.asmx** into the **Name** box.
3) Click on the **Add** button to complete this item addition operation.

The modified Web service project is shown in Figure 9.8.

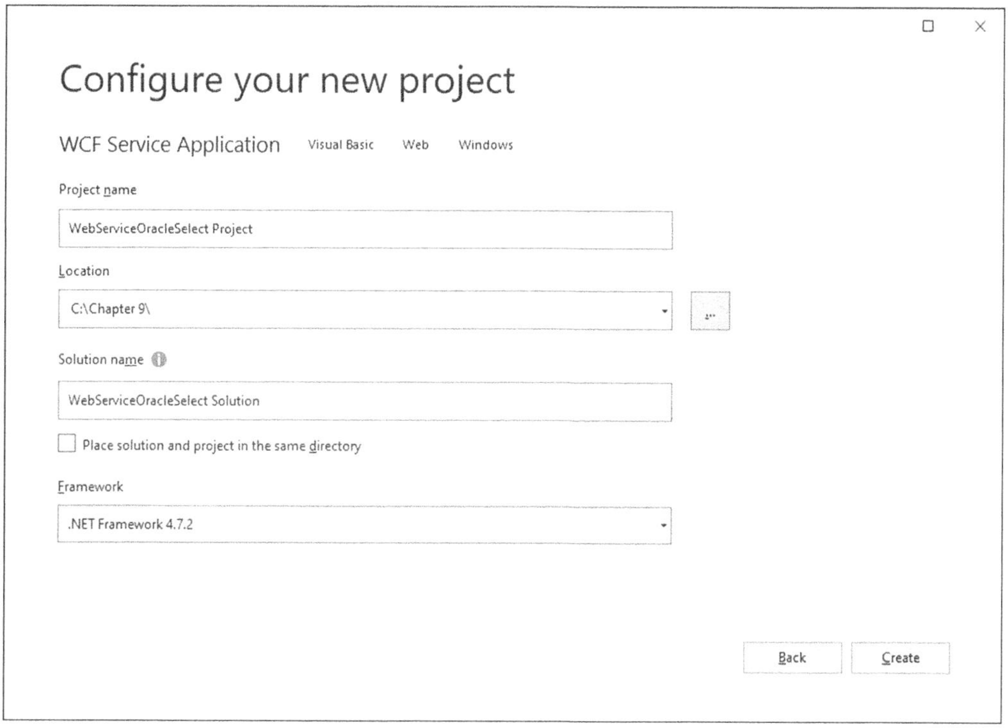

Configure your new project

WCF Service Application   Visual Basic   Web   Windows

Project name

WebServiceOracleSelect Project

Location

C:\Chapter 9\

Solution name ⓘ

WebServiceOracleSelect Solution

☐ Place solution and project in the same directory

Framework

.NET Framework 4.7.2

Back   Create

Figure 9.6   Create a new WCF Web Service project. *Source:* Used with permission from Microsoft.

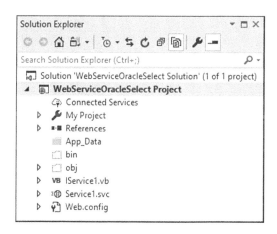

Figure 9.7   New created items for a WCF Web service project. *Source:* Used with permission from Microsoft.

The main Web service file, **WebServiceOracleSelect.asmx**, is a code-behind page and it is the place where we need to create and develop the codes for our Web services. This page contains a default class that is derived from the base class **WebService**. The class defined a default Web method **HelloWorld** that is a placeholder and we can replace it with our own method or methods later on based on the requirement of our Web service project. This file is also used to display information about the Web service's methods and provide access to the Web service's WSDL information.

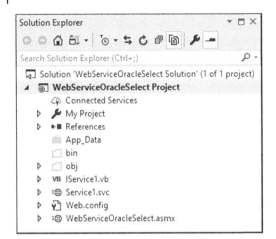

Figure 9.8   The modified Web Service project.

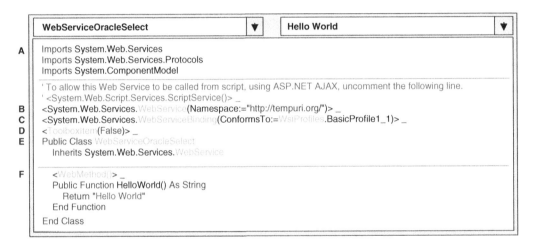

Figure 9.9   The default codes for the code-behind page WebServiceOracleSelect.vb.

The configuration file **Web.config** is used to set up a configuration for our new Web service project, such as the namespaces for all kinds of Web components, connection strings for data components, and Web services and Windows Authentication mode. All of these components are automatically created and added into our new project. More important, the page file **WebServiceOracleSelect.asmx** is designed to automatically create extensible WSDL, dispatch Web methods, serialize and de-serialize parameters, and provide hooks for message interception within our applications. But now, the default file **WebServiceOracleSelect.asmx** only contains a compile directive when a new Web service project is created and opened from the File System.

Now double-click on the code-behind page **WebServiceOracleSelect.asmx** to open this file that is shown in Figure 9.9, and let's have a closer look at the codes in this page.

A) The Web services-related namespaces that contain the Web service components are imported first to allow us to access and use those components to build our Web service project. A detailed description about those namespaces and their functionalities is shown in Table 9.1.

Table 9.1 The Web Service Namespaces.

Namespace	Functionality
System.Web.Services	Enable creations of XML Web services using ASP.NET
System.Web.Services. Protocols	Define the protocol used to transmit data across the wire during the communication between the Web Service clients and servers
System. ComponentModel	Provide classes used to implement the runtime and design-time behavior of components and controls. It includes the base classes and interfaces for implementing attributes and type converters, binding to data sources, and licensing components.

B) Some WebService attributes are defined in this part. Generally, WebService attributes are used to identify additional descriptive information about deployed Web services. The namespace attribute is one of the examples. As we discussed in the last section, we need to use our own namespace to store and hold names and identifiers used in our SOAP messages to distinguish them with any other SOAP messages used by other Web services. Here in this new project, Microsoft used a default namespace **http://tempuri.org,** which is a temporary system-defined namespace to identify all Web Services code generated by the .NET Framework, to store this default Web method. We need to use our own namespace to store our Web methods later when we deploy our Web services in a real application.

C) This Web Service Binding attribute indicates that the current Web service complies with the Web Services Interoperability Organization (WS-I.org) Basic Provide 1.1. Here exactly a binding is equivalent to an interface in which it defines a set of concrete operations.

D) This attribute indicates that a base implementation of a toolbox item class.

E) Our Web service class **WebServiceOracleSelect** is a child class that is derived from the parent class **WebService** located in the namespace **System.Web.Services**.

F) The default Web method HelloWorld is defined as a global function and this function returns a string "**Hello World**" when it is returned to the client.

Now, let's run the default HelloWorld Web service method to get a feeling about what it looks like and how it works.

Click on the **IIS Express** button to run the default HelloWorld project.

9.3.2   A Feeling of the Hello World Web Service Project as it Runs

Our **WebServiceOracleSelect.asmx** page should be the starting page and the following IE page is displayed as shown in Figure 9.10.

This page displays the Web service class name **WebServiceSQLSelect** and all Web methods or operations developed in this project. By default, only one method HelloWorld is created and used in this project.

Below the method, the default namespace in which the current method or operation is located is shown up, and a recommendation that suggests us to create our own namespace to store our Web service project is displayed. Following this recommendation, some example namespaces used in C#, Visual Basic, and C++ are listed.

Now let's access our Web service by clicking on the **HelloWorld** method. The test method page is shown up, which is shown in Figure 9.11.

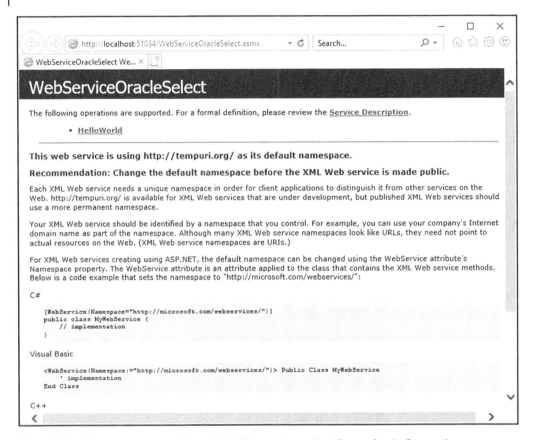

Figure 9.10 The running status of the default Web service project. *Source:* Oracle Corporation.

The **Invoke** button is used to test our HelloWorld method using the HTTP protocol. Below the **Invoke** button, some message examples that are created using different protocols are displayed. These include the requesting message and responding message created in SOAP 1.1, SOAP 1.2, and HTTP Post. The placeholder that is the default namespace **http://tempuri.org/** should be replaced by the actual namespace when this project is modified to a real application.

Now click on the **Invoke** button to run and test the default method HelloWorld.

As the **Invoke** button is clicked, an URL that contains the default namespace and the default HelloWorld method's name is activated, and a new browser window that is shown in Figure 9.12 is displayed. When the default method HelloWorld is executed, the main service page **WebServiceOracleSelect.asmx** sends a request to the IIS, and furthermore, the IIS sends it to the ASP.NET runtime to process this request based on that URL.

The ASP.NET runtime will execute the HelloWorld method, pack the returned data as a SOAP message, and send it back to the client. The returned message contains only a string object, exactly a string of **"Hello World"** for this default method.

In this returned result, the version and the encoding of the used XML code are indicated first. The **xmlns** attribute is used to indicate the namespace used by this String object that contains only a string of "Hello World."

As we discussed in the previous section, ASP.NET Web service did not provide any GUI, so the running result of this default project is represented using the XML codes in some Web interfaces we have

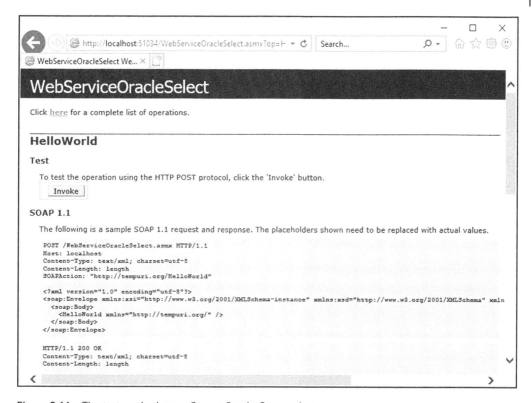

Figure 9.11 The test method page. *Source:* Oracle Corporation.

Figure 9.12 The running status of the default method. *Source:* Oracle Corporation.

seen. This is because those Web interfaces are only provided and used for the testing purpose for the default Web service. In a real application, no such Web interface will be provided and displayed.

Click on the **Close** button that is located on the upper-right corner of the browser to close two browser pages. You may also click on the **Stop** button to stop this project.

At this point, we should have a basic understanding and feeling about a typical Web service project and its structure as well as its operation process. Next, we will build our own Web service project by developing the codes to perform the request to our sample database, exactly to the **FACULTY** table, to get the desired faculty information.

We will develop our Web service project in the following sequence:

1) Modify the default namespace to create our own Web service namespace.
2) Create a customer base class to handle error-checking codes to protect our real Web service class.

3) Create a customer returned class to hold all required and retrieved faculty information. This class is a derived class based on the base class above.
4) Add Web methods to our Web main service class to access our sample database.
5) Develop the detailed codes for those Web methods to perform the Web services.
6) Build a Windows-based and a Web-based project to consume the Web service to pick up and display the required information on the GUI.
7) Deploy our completed Web service to IIS.

9.3.3 Modify the Default Namespace

First, let's modify the default Web service namespace to create our own namespace to store our Web service project.

Open the main service page **WebServiceOracleSelect.asmx** by double-clicking on it from the Solution Explorer window and perform the modifications that are shown in Figure 9.13 to this page.

Let's have a closer look at this piece of modified codes to see how it works.

A. We need to use our own namespace to replace the default namespace used by the Microsoft to tell the ASP.NET runtime the location from which our Web service is loaded as it runs. This specific namespace is unique because it is the home page of the Wiley appended with a book's ISBN number. In fact, you can use any unique location as your specific namespace to store your Web service project.

Now click on the **IIS Express** button to run our new Web service project, a default Web interface is displayed with our project name, as shown in Figure 9.14.

If you click on the default method **HelloWorld** and then **Invoke** button to test that method, you can find that the namespace has been updated to our new specific namespace, **http://www. wiley.com/9780521712354**.

A point to be noted is that you must set the service file **WebServiceOracleSelect.asmx** as the start page before you can run our service project since this file is the entry point of our Web service project.

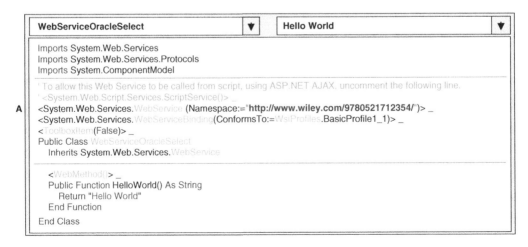

Figure 9.13 The modified main service page.

Figure 9.14 The running status of the modified Web service project. *Source:* Oracle Corporation.

9.3.4 Create a Base Class to Handle Error Checking for Our Web Service

In this section, we want to create a parent class or a base class and use it to handle some possible errors or exceptions as our project runs. It is possible for some reasons that our requests cannot be processed and returned properly. One of the most possible reasons for that is the security issue. To report any errors or problems occurred in the processing of requests, a parent or base class is a good candidate to perform those jobs. We name this base class as `OracleSelectBase` and it has two member data:

- `OrcleRequestOK As Boolean`: True if the request is fine, otherwise a False is set.
- `OracleRequestError As String`: A string used to report the errors or problems.

To create a new base class in our new project, right-click on our new service project `WebServiceOracleSelect` from the Solution Explorer window. Then select the `Add|New Item` from the popup menu. On the opened wizard, select the `Class` item from the `Visual Basic` Template and enter `OracleSelectBase.vb` into the `Name` box as our new class name. Then click on the `Add` button to add this new class into our project.

Now double-click on this new added class and enter the codes that are shown in Figure 9.15 into this class as the class member data.

Two public class member data, `OracleRequestOK` and `OracleRequestError`, are added into this new base class. These two data will work together to report possible errors or problems during the request processing.

9.3.5 Create a Customer Returned Class to Hold all Retrieved Data

Now, we need to create our returned Web service class that will be instantiated and returned to us with our required information as the project runs. This class should be a child class of our base class `OracleSelectBase` we just created. We name this class as `OracleSelectResult`.

```
| OracleSelectBase                    ▼ | (Declarations)                    ▼ |

'Imports Microsoft.VisualBasic

Public Class OracleSelectBase
    'class member data
    Public OracleRequestOK As Boolean
    Public OracleRequestError As String
End Class
```

Figure 9.15 The OracleSelectBase class member data.

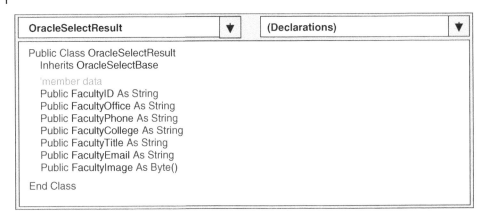

Figure 9.16 The member data for the class OracleSelectResult.

Right-click on our new Web service project **WebServiceOracleSelect Project** from the Solution Explorer window and select the **Add | New Item** from the popup menu. On the opened Add New Item wizard, select the **Class** item from the Template list. Then enter **OracleSelectResult.vb** into the **Name** box as the name for this new class and then click on the **Add** button to add this new class into our project.

Double-click on this new added class and enter the codes that are shown in Figure 9.16 into this class as the member data to this class.

Since this class will be instantiated to an object that will be returned with our desired faculty information to us as the Web method is called, so all desired faculty information should be added into this class as the member data. When we make a request to this Web service project, and furthermore, to our sample database, the following desired faculty data should be included and returned (exclude the **FACULTY_NAME** since it will be input to a related Web method later to be called to get all of these pieces of faculty information):

- Faculty_id
- Faculty office
- Faculty phone
- Faculty college
- Faculty title
- Faculty email
- Faculty image

All of these pieces of information, which can be exactly mapped to all columns in the **FACULTY** table in our sample database, are needed to be added into this class as the member data. This does not look like a professional schema, yes that is true. Another better option is that we do not need to create any class that will be instantiated to an object to hold these pieces of information, instead we can use a DataSet to hold those pieces of information and allow the Web method to return that DataSet as a whole package for those pieces of faculty information. But that better option is relatively complicated compared with our current class. So right now we prefer to start our project with an easier way, and later on we will discuss how to use the DataSet to return our desired information in the following sections.

As we mentioned before, this class is a child class of our base class **OracleSelectBase**, in other words, this class is inherited from that base class. Seven pieces of faculty information without **FACULTY_NAME** are declared here as the member data for this class.

Next, we need to take care of our Web method that will response to our request and return our desired faculty information to us as this method is called.

9.3.6 Visual Basic System Class and Web Service Class

Before we can add a Web method to our project and perform the coding process for it, we want to emphasize an important point that is easy to be confused by users, which is the Web service class and those classes we just created in the last section.

The Web service class `WebServiceOracleSelect.asmx` is a system class and it is used to contain all codes we need to access the Web service and Web methods to execute our requests. The base class `OracleSelectBase` and the child class `OracleSelectResult` are created by us and they belong to application classes. These application classes will be instantiated to the associated objects that will be used by the Web methods developed in the system class `WebServiceOracleSelect.asmx` to return the requested information as the project runs. Keep this difference in mind and this will help you to understand them better as you develop a new Web service project.

We can modify the default method `HelloWorld` and make it as our new Web method in our system class `WebServiceOracleSelect.asmx`. This method will use an object instantiated from the application class `SOracleSelectResult` we created in the previous section to hold and return the faculty information we requested.

9.3.7 Add and Build Web Method GetOracleSelect() to the Web Services

The name of this Web method is `GetOracleSelect()`, and it contains an input parameter Faculty Name with the following functions as this method is called:

1) Set up a valid connection to our sample database.
2) Create all required data objects and local variables to perform the necessary data operations.
3) Instantiate a new object from the application class `OracleSelectResult` and use it as the returned object that contains all required faculty data.
4) Execute the associated data object's method to perform the data query to the **FACULTY** table based on the input parameter, Faculty Name.
5) Assign each piece of acquired information obtained from the **FACULTY** table to the associated class member data defined in the class `OracleSelectResult`.
6) Release and clean up all data objects used.
7) Return the object to the client.

9.3.7.1 Web Service Connection Strings

Among above seven functions, function 1 is one of the most challenging tasks. There are two ways to perform this database connection in Web service applications. One way is to directly use the connection string and connection object in the Web service class as we did in the previous projects. Another way is to define the connection string in the `Web.config` file. The second way is better since the `Web.config` file provides an attribute `<connectionStrings/>` for this purpose and ASP.NET 4.0 recommends to store the data components' connection string in the `Web.config` file.

In this project, we will use the second way to store our connection string. To do that, open the `Web.config` file by double-clicking on it and enter the following codes into this configuration file (just above the configuration ending tag `</configuration>`):

```
<connectionStrings>
  <add name="ora_conn" connectionString="Server=localhost:1518/CSE_DEPT; _
  User ID=CSE_DEPT; Password=oracle_18c"/>
</connectionStrings>
```

The following important points should be noted while creating this connection string:

1) This `connectionStrings` attribute must be written in a **single line** in the `Web.config` file. However, because of the space limitation, here we used two lines to represent this attribute. But in your real codes, you must place this attribute in a single line in your `Web.config` file; otherwise, a grammar problem will be encountered.

2) Web services that require a database connection in this project use Oracle XE 18c authentication with a login ID and password for a user account. Thus, we attached our user ID and password with this connection string.

Before we can test this connection string, first let's add some Oracle database drive directives into our project by adding related references with the following steps:

1) Right-click on our Web Service project `WebServiceOracleSelect  Project` in the Solution Explorer and select **Add | Reference** item from the popup menu.

2) Click on the **Extensions** item from the left pane and check two items, `Devart.Data` and `Devart.Data.Oracle`, from the right pane and click on the **OK** button to add them into our project.

To test and confirm this `connectionString`, we can develop some codes and modify the codes in the default `HelloWorld` Web method in the main service page to do that. Close the `Web.config` file and open the main service page `WebServiceOracleSelect.asmx` by double-clicking on it from the Solution Explorer window and enter the codes shown in Figure 9.17 into this page.

All modified codes have been highlighted with the bold words, and let's see how this piece of codes works when testing our connection string defined in the `Web.config` file.

A) The namespace that contains the Oracle Data Provider is added into this page using the `Imports` command since we need to use this database driver to access our sample database to perform related data actions to our Oracle database.

B) The `ConnectionStrings` property of the `ConfigurationManager` class is used to pick up the connection string we defined in the `Web.config` file, which can be considered as a default connection configuration. The connection name `ora_conn` that works as an argument for this property must be identical with the name we used for the connection name in the `Web.config` file. When this property is used, it returns a `ConnectionStringSettingsCollection` object containing the contents of the `ConnectionStringsSection` object for the current application's default configuration, and a `ConnectionStringsSection` object contains the contents of the configuration file's `connectionStrings` section.

C) A new Oracle Connection object is created and initialized with the connection string we obtained above.

D) The `Open()` method of the Oracle Connection object is executed to try to open our sample database and set up a valid connection.

E) By checking the `State` property of the Connection object, we can determine whether this connection is successful or not. If the `State` property is not equal to the `ConnectionState.`

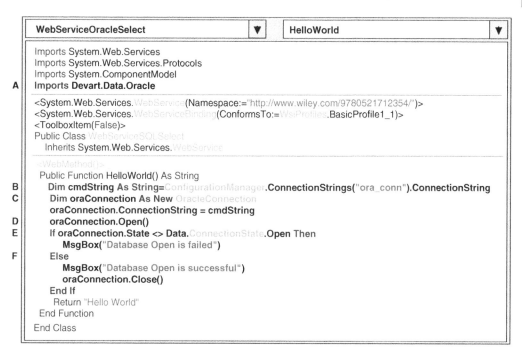

```
WebServiceOracleSelect  ▼        HelloWorld  ▼

      Imports System.Web.Services
      Imports System.Web.Services.Protocols
      Imports System.ComponentModel
 A    Imports Devart.Data.Oracle

      <System.Web.Services.WebService(Namespace:="http://www.wiley.com/9780521712354/")>
      <System.Web.Services.WebServiceBinding(ConformsTo:=WsiProfiles.BasicProfile1_1)>
      <ToolboxItem(False)>
      Public Class WebServiceSQLSelect
          Inherits System.Web.Services.WebService

          <WebMethod()>
          Public Function HelloWorld() As String
 B            Dim cmdString As String=ConfigurationManager.ConnectionStrings("ora_conn").ConnectionString
 C            Dim oraConnection As New OracleConnection
              oraConnection.ConnectionString = cmdString
 D            oraConnection.Open()
 E            If oraConnection.State <> Data.ConnectionState.Open Then
                 MsgBox("Database Open is failed")
 F            Else
                 MsgBox("Database Open is successful")
                 oraConnection.Close()
              End If
               Return "Hello World"
          End Function
      End Class
```

Figure 9.17 The modified codes to test the connection string.

Open, which means that a valid database connection has not been established, a warning message is displayed.

F) Otherwise the connection is successful, a successful message is displayed and the connection is closed.

Now you can run the project by clicking on the **IIS Express** button. Click on the **HelloWorld** method from the built-in Web interface and then click on the **Invoke** button to execute that method to test our database connection.

A successful message should be displayed if this connection is fine. Click on the **OK** button on the message box and you can get the returned result from the execution of the method **HelloWorld**.

An issue is that when you run this project, it may take a little while to complete this database connection. The reason for that is because the **MsgBox()** is being executed and it may be displayed behind the current Web page when it is activated. You need to move the current page by dragging it down and then you can find that MsgBox. Click on the **OK** button on that MsgBox and the project will be continued and the running result will be displayed.

Another issue is that this piece of codes is only used for the testing purpose and we will modify this piece of codes and place it into a user-defined function **OracleConn()** later when we develop our real project.

9.3.7.2 Modify the Existing HelloWorld Web Method

Now let's start to take care of our Web methods. In this project, we want to modify the default method **HelloWorld** as our first Web method and develop codes for this method to complete those functions (2~7) listed at the beginning of Section 9.3.7.

Open the Web main service page **WebServiceOracleSelect.asmx** if it is not opened and make the following modifications:

1) Change the Web method's name from **HelloWorld** to **GetOracleSelect**.
2) Change the data type of the returned object of this method from **String** to **OracleSelectResult** that is our child application class we developed before.
3) Add a new input parameter **FacultyName** as an argument to this method using Passing-By-Value format.
4) Create a new object based on our child application class **OracleSelectResult** and name this object as **OracleResult**.
5) Create the following data components used in this method:
   a) Oracle Command Object **oraCommand**.
   b) Oracle Data Reader Object **oraReader**.
6) Replace the default returned object in the method from "Hello World" string to the new created object **OracleResult**.
7) Move the connection testing codes we developed in this section into a user-defined function **OracleConn()**.

Your finished Web method **GetOracleSelect()** is shown in Figure 9.18. Let's take a closer look at this piece of modified codes to see how it works.

A) Modification steps 1, 2, and 3 listed above are performed at this line. The method's name and the returned data type are modified to **GetOracleSelect** and **OracleSelectResult**, respectively. Also an input parameter **FacultyName** is added into this method as an argument.
B) Modification step 4 is performed at this line, and an instance of the application class **OracleSelectResult** is created here.
C) Modification step 5 is performed at this line and two Oracle data objects are created: **oraCommand** and **oraReader**, respectively.
D) Modification step 6 is performed at this line, and the original returned data are updated to the current object **OracleResult**.
E) Modification step 7 is performed here and a new user-defined function **OracleConn()** is created with the codes we developed to test the connection string above.

Figure 9.18 The modified Web method – GetOracleSelect().

F) If this connection is failed, a warning message is displayed and the returned connection object is assigned with **Nothing**. Otherwise, a successful connection object is assigned to the returned connection object **conn**.

G) The connection object is returned to the Web method.

Next, we need to develop the codes to execute the associated data object's method to perform the data query to the **FACULTY** table based on the input parameter, Faculty Name.

9.3.7.3 Develop the Codes to Perform the Database Queries

To perform the database query via our Web service project, we need to perform the following coding developments:

- Add the major codes into our Web method to perform the data query.
- Create a user-defined subroutine **FillFacultyReader()** to handle the data assignments to our returned object.
- Create an error or exception-processing subroutine **ReportError()** to report any errors encountered during the project runs.

Now let's first concentrate on adding the codes to perform the data query to our sample database **CSE_DEPT**.

Open our main service page and add the codes that are shown in Figure 9.19 into our Web method. The codes we developed in the previous sections have been highlighted with the gray color as the background.

Let's take a closer look at these new added codes to see how they work:

A) The query string is declared at the beginning of this method. One point you may have already noted is that a **+** symbol is used here to replace the concatenated operator **&** that is used in our Visual Basic.NET project before. The Web service page allows us to use this one as the concatenating operator.

B) Initially, we assume that our Web method works fine by setting the Boolean variable **OracleRequestOK**, which we defined in our base class **OracleSelectBase**, to **True**. This variable will keep this value until an error or exception is encountered.

C) The user-defined function **OracleConn()**, whose detailed codes are shown in Figure 9.18, is called to perform the database connection. This function will return a connection object if the connection is successful. Otherwise, the function will return a **Nothing** object.

D) If a **Nothing** is returned from calling the function **OracleConn()**, which means that the database connection has something wrong, a warning message is displayed and the user-defined subroutine **ReportError()**, whose codes are shown in Figure 9.21, is executed to report the encountered error.

E) The Command object is initialized with the connection object that is obtained from the function **OracleConn()**, command type and command text. Also the input parameter **:facultyName** is assigned with the real input parameter **FacultyName** that is an input parameter to the Web method.

F) The ExecuteReader() method of the Command class is called to invoke the DataReader to perform the data query from our **FACULTY** table.

G) By checking the **HasRows** property of the DataReader, we can determine whether this query is successful or not. If this property is **True**, which means that at least one row has been returned and the query is successful, the user-defined subroutine **FillFacultyReader()** is called to assign all queried data columns to the associated member data we created in our child class

WebServiceOracleSelect	▼	GetOracleSelect	▼

```
Imports System.Web
Imports System.Web.Services
Imports System.Web.Services.Protocols
Imports Devart.Data.Oracle

' To allow this Web Service to be called from script, using ASP.NET AJAX, uncomment the following line.
' <System.Web.Script.Services.ScriptService()> _
<WebService(Namespace:="http://www.wiley.com/9780521712354/")> _
<WebServiceBinding(ConformsTo:=WsiProfiles.BasicProfile1_1)> _
<Global.Microsoft.VisualBasic.CompilerServices.DesignerGenerated()> _
Public Class WebServiceOracleSelect
    Inherits System.Web.Services.WebService

    <WebMethod()> _
    Public Function GetOracleSelect(ByVal FacultyName As String) As OracleSelectResult
A       Dim cmdString As String = "SELECT faculty_id, office, phone, college, title, email, fimage FROM Faculty " + _
                                  "WHERE faculty_name = :facultyName"
        Dim oraConnection As New OracleConnection
        Dim OracleResult As New OracleSelectResult()
        Dim oraCommand As New OracleCommand
        Dim oraReader As OracleDataReader
B       OracleResult.OracleRequestOK = True
C       oraConnection = OracleConn()
D       If oraConnection Is Nothing Then
            OracleResult.OracleRequestError = "Database connection is failed"
            ReportError(OracleResult)
            Return Nothing
        End If
E       oraCommand.Connection = oraConnection
        oraCommand.CommandType = CommandType.Text
        oraCommand.CommandText = cmdString
        oraCommand.Parameters.Add(":facultyName", OracleDbType.NVarChar).Value = FacultyName
F       oraReader = oraCommand.ExecuteReader
G       If oraReader.HasRows = True Then
            Call FillFacultyReader(OracleResult, oraReader)
H       Else
            OracleResult.OracleRequestError = "No matched faculty found"
            ReportError(OracleResult)
        End If
I       If Not oraReader Is Nothing Then oraReader.Close()
        oraReader = Nothing
        If Not oraConnection Is Nothing Then oraConnection.Close()
        oraConnection = Nothing
J       Return OracleResult
    End Function
```

Figure 9.19 The modified codes for the Web method.

OracleSelectResult. Two arguments, **OracleResult** that is our returning object and **oraReader** that is our DataReader object, are passed into that subroutine. The difference between these two arguments is the passing mode; the returning object **OracleResult** is passed using a passing-by-reference mode, which means that an address of that object is passed into the subroutine and all assigned data columns to that object can be brought back to the calling procedure. This is very similar to a returned object from calling a function. But the DataReader **oraReader** is passed using a passing-by-value mode, which means that only a copy of that object is passed into the subroutine and any modification to that object is temporary.

H) If the **HasRows** property returns **False**, it means that the data query is failed. An error message is assigned to the member data **OracleRequestError** defined in our base class **OracleSelectBase**, and our **ReportError()** subroutine is called to report this error.

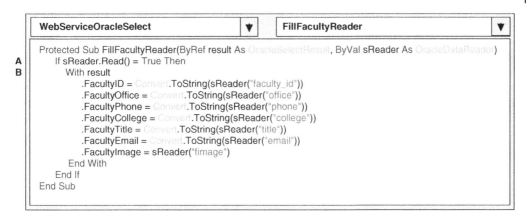

Figure 9.20   The codes for the subroutine FillFacultyReader().

Figure 9.21   The codes for the subroutine ReportError().

I)   A cleaning job is performed to release all data objects used in this method.

J)   The object **OracleResult** is returned as the query result to our Web service.

Next, let's take care of developing the codes for our two user-defined subroutine procedures: **FillFacultyReader()** and **ReportError()**.

9.3.7.4   Develop the Codes for Subroutines Used in the Web Method

The codes for the subroutine **FillFacultyReader()** are shown in Figure 9.20. Let's have a closer look at this piece of codes in this subroutine to see how it works:

A. The **Read()** method of the DataReader is executed to read out the queried data row, in our case, only one row that is matched to the input faculty name is read out and feed into the DataReader object **sReader**.

B. A **With …End With** block is utilized here to simplify the assignment operations. The object **result** that is our returning object is attached after the keyword **With**, and all member data of that object can be represented using the dot (**.**) operator without needing the prefix of that object. Each data column in the **FACULTY** table can be identified using its name from the DataReader object **sReader**, converted to a string using the **Convert** class method **ToString()**, and finally assigned to the associated member data in our returning object. The format of the faculty image column **fimage** itself is **Image**, thus no any conversion is needed.

Optionally you can use the **GetString()** method to retrieve each data column from the DataReader **sReader** if you like. An index that is matched to the position of each column in the query string **cmdString** must be used to locate each data if this method is used.

The key point for this subroutine is the passing mode for the first argument. A passing-by-reference mode is used for our returning object and this is equivalent to return an object from a function.

The detailed codes for the subroutine **ReportError()** are shown in Figure 9.21.

The input parameter to this subroutine is our returning object. A **False** is assigned to the **SQLRequestOK** member data and the error message is assigned to the **SQLRequestError** string variable defined in our base class **SQLSelectBase**. Since our returning object is instantiated from our child class **SQLSelectResult** that is inherited from our base class, so our returning object can access and use those member data defined in the base class.

At this point, we finished all coding jobs for our Web service project. Now let's run our project to test the data query functionality. Click on the **IIS Express** button to run the project and the built-in Web interface is displayed, which is shown in Figure 9.22.

Click on our Web method **GetOracleSelect** to open the built-in Web interface for our Web method, which is shown in Figure 9.23. Enter the faculty name **Ying Bai** into the **FacultyName** box as an input Value and then click on the **Invoke** button to execute the Web method to trigger the ASP.NET runtime to perform our data query.

The running result is returned and displayed in the XML format, which is shown in Figure 9.24.

Each returned data is enclosed by a pair of XML tags to indicate or mark up its facility. For example, the **B78880**, which is the queried **faculty_id**, is enclosed by the tag **<FacultyID>...</FacultyID>**, and the name of this tag is defined in our child class **OracleSelectResult**. Our first Web service method is very successful.

Figure 9.22 The running status of the Web service. *Source:* Oracle Corporation.

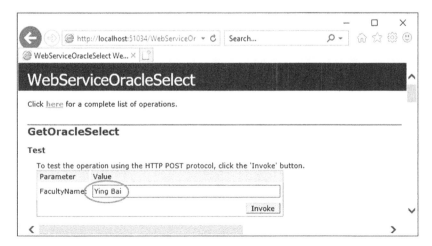

Figure 9.23 The running status of our Web method. *Source:* Oracle Corporation.

Figure 9.24 The running result of our Web service project. *Source:* Oracle Corporation.

As we mentioned before, a Web service did not provide any user interface and users need to develop some user interfaces to consume the Web service if one wants to display those pieces of information obtained from the Web services. Here, a built-in Web interface is provided by Microsoft to help users to display queried information from the Web services. In most real applications, users need to develop user interfaces themselves to perform these data displaying or other data operations.

Click on the **Close** button that is located at the upper-right corner of the page to close our Web service project.

9.3.8 Develop the Stored Procedure to Perform the Data Query

An optional and better way to perform the data query via Web service is to use the stored procedures. The advantage of using this method is that the coding process can be greatly simplified and most query jobs can be performed in the database side. Therefore, the query execution speed can be improved. The query efficiency can also be improved and the query operations can be integrated into a single group or block of code body to strengthen the integrity of the query.

9.3.8.1 Develop an Oracle Package and Add a Stored Procedure

As we discussed in Section 5.6.7.3 in Chapter 5, in order to query records to get returned data from an Oracle database using stored procedures, an Oracle package must be generated and the stored procedure must be attached with that package to enable stored procedures return records.

Now let's first develop our package and then add a stored procedure into the package to perform this query action in the Oracle SQL Developer environment.

Perform the following operational steps to build this package and stored procedure:

1) Open the Oracle SQL Developer, connect to our server **CSE_DEPT**, and expand the **Other Users** folder and our database **CSE_DEPT**. Then right-click on the **Packages** folder and select the item **New Package** from the popup menu to open a new package.
2) Enter **WEB_FACULTYINFO** as the name for this package, as shown in Figure 9.25, into **Name** box. Click on the **OK** button to generate this package.
3) In the opened package file, enter the codes that have been circled and shown in Figure 9.26 into this package as the declaration for our stored procedure. The **CURSOR** is a special data type in Oracle and it is used to return a group of data to the calling function. This stored procedure

Figure 9.25 The package WEB_FACULTYINFO. *Source*: Oracle Corporation.

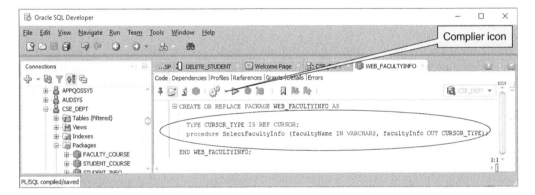

Figure 9.26 The opened Package Definition wizard. *Source:* Oracle Corporation.

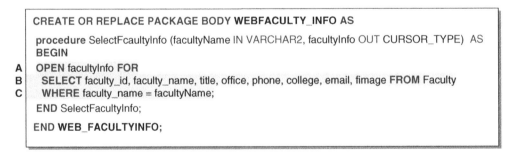

Figure 9.27 The finished Package Body wizard.

contains two arguments, one input `facultyName` and one output `facultyInfo`, which has a `CURSOR` data type.

4) Click on the drop-down arrow and select `Compile` item to compile and save this package. A `Compiled` message should be displayed in the Message-Log window if this compiling is successful.
5) Now right-click on our new created package, `WEB_FACULTYINFO`, under the `Packages` folder from the left pane and select the `Create Body` item to add codes into this package.
6) On the opened `Package Body` wizard, enter the codes that are highlighted and shown in Figure 9.27 into this body wizard.

7) Click on the drop-down arrow, select **Compile** item to compile, and save this Package Body. A **Compiled** message should be displayed in the Message-Log window if this compiling is successful.

Your finished package, **WEB_FACULTYINFO**, is shown in Figure 9.28.
Let's have a closer look at this piece of codes to see how it works:

A) The **OPEN facultyInfo FOR** command is used to assign the returned data columns from the following query to the cursor variable **facultyInfo**.
B) The **SELECT** query is executed to get all columns from the **FACULTY** table in our sample database **CSE_DEPT**.
C) The input argument, **facultyName**, is assigned to the **FACULTY_NAME** column as a query criterion for this package.

Now we can test this package in this Oracle SQL Developer environment to confirm its correctness. Click on the green arrow (**Run**) button on the task bar, as shown in Figure 9.28, to run this package. The opened Run PL/SQL wizard is shown in Figure 9.29.

Enter a faculty's name, such as **Ying Bai**, into the **Input Value** box (Figure 9.29) and click on the **OK** button to run this package. You may need to reenter the system password to run this package.

To check the running result, click on the **Output Variables** tab at the lower-right corner, and all eight selected columns related to the faculty named **Ying Bai** on the **FACULTY** table are displayed under the **Value** tab, as shown in Figure 9.30.

9.3.8.2 Add Another Web Method to Call the Stored Procedure

To distinguish with the first Web method we developed in the previous section, we had better add another Web method to perform this data query by calling the stored procedure.

To do that, highlight and select the whole coding body of our first Web method **GetOracleSelect()**, including both the method header and the code body. Then copy this whole coding body and paste it to the bottom of our code-behind page (must be inside our Web service class). Perform the modifications shown in Figure 9.31 to this copied Web method to make it as our second Web method **GetOracleSelectSP()**. The modified parts have been highlighted in bold.

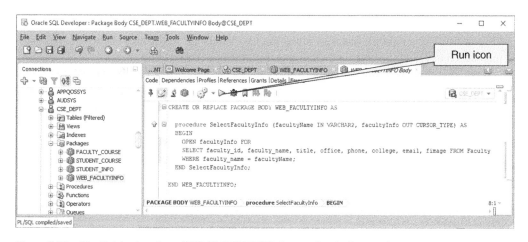

Figure 9.28 The finished package WEB_FACULTYINFO. *Source:* Oracle Corporation.

Figure 9.29 The opened Run PL/SQL wizard. *Source:* Oracle Corporation.

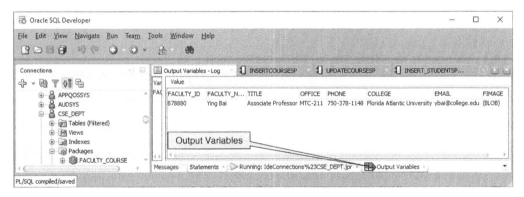

Figure 9.30 The running result of the stored procedure. *Source:* Oracle Corporation.

A) Change the Web method's name by attaching two letters **SP** to the end of the original Web method's name, and the new method's name becomes **GetOracleSelectSP**.

B) Change the content of the query string **cmdString** to "**WEB_FACULTYINFO.Select-FacultyInfo**". To call a stored procedure from a Web service project, the content of the query string must be exactly equal to the name of the package and the stored procedure we developed in the last section. Otherwise, a running error may be encountered during the project runs because the project cannot find the desired stored procedure.

C) Change the CommandType property of the Command object from the **CommandType.Text** to the **CommandType.StoredProcedure**. This changing is very important since we need to call a stored procedure to perform the data query. Therefore, we must tell the ASP.NET runtime that a stored procedure should be called when the command object is executed.

Now you can run the project to test this new Web method. Click on the second Web method **GetOracleSelectSP** as the project runs, enter a desired faculty member such as **Ying Bai**

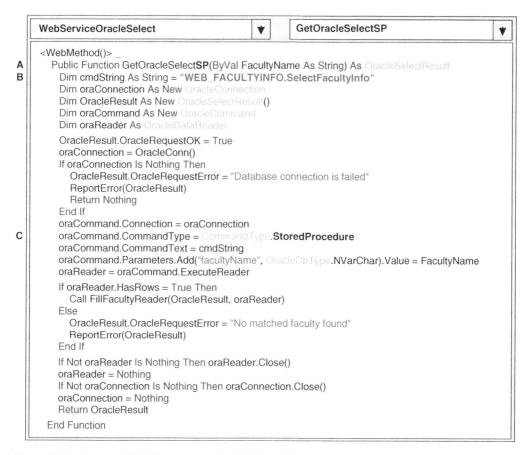

```
WebServiceOracleSelect  ▼        GetOracleSelectSP  ▼

     <WebMethod()> _
A       Public Function GetOracleSelectSP(ByVal FacultyName As String) As OracleSelectResult
B         Dim cmdString As String = "WEB_FACULTYINFO.SelectFacultyInfo"
          Dim oraConnection As New OracleConnection
          Dim OracleResult As New OracleSelectResult()
          Dim oraCommand As New OracleCommand
          Dim oraReader As OracleDataReader

          OracleResult.OracleRequestOK = True
          oraConnection = OracleConn()
          If oraConnection Is Nothing Then
             OracleResult.OracleRequestError = "Database connection is failed"
             ReportError(OracleResult)
             Return Nothing
          End If
          oraCommand.Connection = oraConnection
C         oraCommand.CommandType = CommandType.StoredProcedure
          oraCommand.CommandText = cmdString
          oraCommand.Parameters.Add("facultyName", OracleDbType.NVarChar).Value = FacultyName
          oraReader = oraCommand.ExecuteReader

          If oraReader.HasRows = True Then
             Call FillFacultyReader(OracleResult, oraReader)
          Else
             OracleResult.OracleRequestError = "No matched faculty found"
             ReportError(OracleResult)
          End If

          If Not oraReader Is Nothing Then oraReader.Close()
          oraReader = Nothing
          If Not oraConnection Is Nothing Then oraConnection.Close()
          oraConnection = Nothing
          Return OracleResult
        End Function
```

Figure 9.31 The modified Web method – GetSQLSelectSP().

into the **FacultyName** box, and click on the **Invoke** button to run it. The same running result as we got from the last project can be obtained.

You can see how easy it is to develop codes to perform the data query by calling the package and stored procedure in the Web service project.

Next, we will discuss how to use a DataSet as a returning object to contain all pieces of queried information we need from running a Web service project.

9.3.9   Use DataSet as the Returning Object for the Web Method

The advantage of using a DataSet as a returning object for a Web method is that we do not need to create any application class to instantiate a returning object. Another advantage is that a DataSet can contain multiple records coming from the different tables, and we do not need to create multiple member data in our application class to hold those data items. Finally, the size of our coding body could be greatly reduced when a DataSet is used, especially for a large block of data that are queried via the Web service project.

To distinguish with those Web methods we developed in the previous sections, we can create another new Web method **GetOracleSelectDataSet()** and add it into our Web service project. To do that, open our code-behind page if it is not opened, highlight and select the whole coding body of our first Web method `GetOracleSelect()`, including the method header and coding body. Copy and paste it to the bottom of our page (must be inside our Web service class). Perform the modifications as shown in Figure 9.32 to this copied Web method to make it as our third Web method. The modified codes have been highlighted in bold.

Let's have a closer look at this modified Web method to see how it works:

A) The Web method's name is modified by attaching the `DataSet` to the end of the original method name. Also the data type of the returning object is the `DataSet`, which means that this Web method will return a DataSet.

B) Two new data objects, `FacultyAdapter` and `dsFaculty`, are created. The first object works as a DataAdapter and the second works as a DataSet, respectively. A local integer variable `intResult` is also created and it will be used to hold the returning value from calling the Fill() method of the DataAdapter to perform the data query later.

C) The initialized Command object is assigned to the SelectCommand property of the DataAdapter class. This Command object will be executed when the `Fill()` method is called to perform the data query, exactly to fill the faculty table in the DataSet `dsFaculty`.

D) The `Fill()` method of the DataAdapter class is executed to fill the Faculty table in our DataSet. This method will return an integer value stored in the local integer variable `intResult` to indicate whether this calling is successful or not.

Figure 9.32 The modified Web method – GetOracleSelectDataSet().

E) If the returned value is zero, which means that no any row has been retrieved from the Faculty table in our sample database and no any row has been filled into our Faculty table in our DataSet **dsFaculty**. Therefore, this data query is failed. An error message will be sent back via our member data in our base class and that error will be reported using the subroutine **ReportError()**.

F) Otherwise if the returned value is nonzero, which means that at least one row has been retrieved and filled into the **FACULTY** table in our DataSet, a cleaning job is performed to release all objects used for this Web method. Typically, this returned value is equal to the number of rows that have been successfully retrieved from the Faculty table in our database and filled into the **FACULTY** table in our DataSet. In our application, this value should be equal to one since only one record is returned from the **FACULTY** table in our sample database and filled into the DataSet.

G) Finally the filled DataSet, **dsFaculty**, exactly the filled **FACULTY** table in this DataSet, is returned to the Web service.

Now we can run the project to test this returned DataSet functionality. Click on the **IIS Express** button to run the project. By now we have three Web methods available in this Web service, which is shown in Figure 9.33.

Click on the second Web method **GetOracleSelectDataSet** from the built-in Web interface window and enter the faculty name **Ying Bai** into the **Value** box as our desired faculty member. Then click on the **Invoke** button to call this Web method to perform the data query. The running result is returned and is shown in Figure 9.34.

A new DataSet is created since we used a non-typed DataSet in this application and all six pieces of faculty information related to the desired faculty member **Ying Bai** are retrieved and filled into the Faculty table in our DataSet. Also these pieces of information are returned to our Web service project and displayed in the built-in Web interface window, as shown in Figure 9.34. Do not worry about the top part codes on this running result since those are XML codes used to configure and initialize this new DataSet.

At this point, we have finished all codes developing jobs in our Web service project in the server side. A complete Web service project **WebServiceOracleSelect Project** that contains all three Web methods can be found from the folder **Class DB Projects\Chapter 9** that is located under the **Students** folder at the Wiley ftp site (refer to Figure 1.2 in Chapter 1).

Next, we need to develop some professional Windows-based or Web-based applications with beautiful GUIs to use or consume our Web service project. Those Windows-based or Web-based applications can be considered as Web service clients.

Figure 9.33   Three Web methods in built-in Web interface window. *Source:* Oracle Corporation.

Figure 9.34 The running result of the Web method GetOracleSelectDataSet(). *Source:* Oracle Corporation.

9.3.10 Build Windows-based Web Service Clients to Consume the Web Services

To use or consume a Web service, first we need to create a Web service proxy class in our Windows-based or Web-based applications. Then we can create a new instance of that Web service proxy class and execute the desired Web methods located in that Web service class. The process of creating a Web service proxy class is equivalent to add a

Web reference to our Windows-based or Web-based applications.

9.3.10.1 Create a Web Service Proxy Class

Basically, adding a Web reference to our Windows-based or Web-based applications is to execute a searching process. During this process, Visual Studio.NET 2019 will try to find all Web services available to our applications. The following operations will be performed by Visual Studio.NET 2019 during this process:

1) When looking for Web services from the local computers, Visual Studio.NET will check all files that include a Web service main page with an **.asmx** extension, a WSDL file with a **.wsdl** extension or a Discovery file with a **.disco** extension.
2) When searching for Web services from the Internet, Visual Studio.NET 2019 will try to find a UDDI file that contains all registered Web services with their associated Discovery documents.
3) When all available Web services are found, either from your local computer or from the Internet, you can select your desired Web services from them by adding them into the Web client project as Web references. Also you can open each of them to take a look at the detail description for each Web service and its Web methods. Once you selected the desired Web services, you can modify the names of the selected Web services as you want. The point is that even the name of the Web service is changed in the Web client side, the ASP.NET runtime can remember and still use the original name of that Web service as it is consumed.
4) As those Web services have been referenced to the client project, a group of necessary files or documents are also created by Visual Studio.NET 2019. These files include
    a) A Discovery Map file that provides the necessary SOAP interfaces for communications between the client project and the Web services.
    b) A Discovery file that contains all available XML Web services on a Web server, and these Web services are obtained through a process called XML Web services Discovery.
    c) A WSDL file that provides a detailed description and definition about those Web services in an abstract manner.

To add a Web reference to our client project, we need first to create a client project.

Open Visual Studio.NET 2019 in the Administrator mode, create a new Visual Basic Windows Forms App (.NET Framework), name it as **WinClientOracleSelect Project**, and save it in the folder **C:\Chapter 9**. Now let's add a Web reference to our new project.

There are two ways to select the desired Web services and add it as a reference to our client project: one way is to use the **Browser** provided by the Visual Studio.NET to find the desired Web service and another way is to copy and paste the desired Web service URL to the URL box located in this Add Web Reference wizard. In order to use the second way, you need first to run the Web service and then copy its URL and paste it to the URL box in this wizard if you have not deployed that Web service to IIS. If you did deploy that Web service, you can directly type that URL into the **Address** box in that wizard.

Because we developed and built our Web service on our local computer, but we have not deployed our Web service to IIS, thus we should use the second way to find our Web service. Perform the following operations to find and add this Web reference:

1) Open Visual Studio.NET 2019 and our Web service project **WebServiceOracleSelect Project** and click on the **IIS Express** button to run it. Then copy the URL from the **Address** bar in the running Web service project.
2) Then open another Visual Studio.NET 2019 in the Administrator mode and open our client project **WinClientOracleSelect Project**.
3) Right-click on our client project **WinClientOracleSelect Project** from the Solution Explorer window and select the item **Add|Service Reference** from the popup menu to open the Add Service Reference wizard.
4) Click on the **Advanced** button located at the lower-left corner on this wizard to open the **Service Reference Settings** wizard.
5) Click on the **Add Web Reference** button in the lower-left corner to open the **Add Web Reference** wizard, which is shown in Figure 9.35.
6) Paste that URL we copied from step 1 into the URL box in the Add Web Reference wizard and click on the blue color **Arrow** button to enable the Visual Studio.NET to begin to search this reference.
7) When the Web service is found, the name of our Web service is displayed in the right pane, which is shown in Figure 9.35.
8) Alternately you can change the name for this Web reference from **localhost** to any meaningful name, such as **WS_OracleSelect** in our case. Click on the **Add Reference** button to add this Web service as a reference to our new client project.
9) Click on the **Close** button from our Web service built-in Web interface window to terminate our Web service project.

Immediately you can find that the Web service **WS_OracleSelect**, which is under the folder **Web References**, has been added into the Solution Explorer window in our client project. This reference is the so-called Web service proxy class.

Next, let's develop the GUI by adding useful controls to interface to our Web service and display the queried faculty information.

9.3.10.2 Develop the Graphic User Interface for the Windows-based Client Project
Perform the following modifications to our new project:

1) Rename the Form File object from the default name **Form1.vb** to our desired name **WinClient Form.vb**.

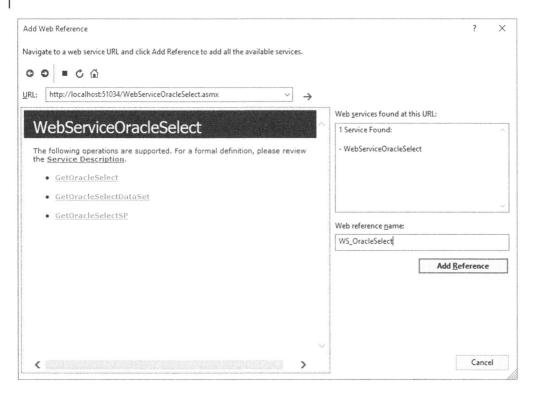

Figure 9.35 The Add Web Reference wizard. *Source*: Oracle Corporation.

2) Rename the Window Form object from the default name **Form1** to our desired name **FacultyForm** by modifying the **Name** property of the form window.
3) Rename the form title from the default title **Form1** to **CSE_DEPT Faculty Form** by modifying the **Text** property of the form.

To save time and space, we can use the GUI located in the project **OracleUpdateDeleteRTObject Project** we developed in Chapter 7. Open that project from the folder **Class DB Projects\ Chapter 7** that is located under the **Students** folder at the Wiley ftp site (refer to Figure 1.2 in Chapter 1). Then open the Faculty form window and select all controls from that form by going to the menu item **Edit | Select All**, and then **Edit | Copy** menu item to copy all controls selected from this form window.

Return to our new Windows-based Web service client project **WinClientOracleSelect Project**, open our form window and paste those controls to this form window.

The purpose of the combo box control **Query Method** is to select one of three different query methods developed in our Web service project to get the desired faculty information:

1) Method 1: Uses an object to return our queried information.
2) Method 2: Uses a stored procedure to return our queried information.
3) Method 3: Uses a DataSet to return our queried information.

The Faculty Name combo box control is used to select a desired faculty member as the input parameter for the Web method to pick up the desired faculty information. In this project, only the **Select** and **Back** buttons are used.

The function of this project is: when the project runs, as the desired method and the faculty name have been selected from the associated controls, the `Select` button will be clicked by the user. Our client project will be connected to our Web service based on the Web reference we provided, and the selected method will be called based on the method chosen from the Query Method combo box control, to perform the data query to retrieve the desired faculty record from our sample database and display it in this GUI.

Now let's take care of the coding process for this project to connect to our Web service using the Web reference we developed in the last section.

9.3.10.3 Develop the Code to Consume the Web Service

The coding job can be divided into four parts:

1) The coding development for the Form_Load event procedure to initialize the Query Method and the Faculty Name combo box controls. The first initialization is to set up three Web methods that can be selected by the user to perform the data query from the Web service. The second one is to set up a default list of faculty members that can be selected by the user to perform the associated faculty information query.
2) The coding process for the `Back` button's click event procedure, which is used to terminate the project.
3) The coding development for the `Select` button's click event procedure.
4) The coding process for some user-defined subroutine procedures, such as `ProcessObject()`, `FillFacultyObject()` and `FillFacultyDataSet()`.

The main coding job is performed inside the `Select` button's click event procedure. As we discussed, as this button is clicked by the user, a connection to our Web service should be established using the Web reference we set up in the previous section. So we need first to create an object based on that Web reference or instantiate that Web service to get an instance, then we can access the different Web methods to perform our data query. This process is called instantiating the proxy class and invokes the Web methods. The protocol to instantiate a proxy class is

```
Dim newInstanceName As New WebReferenceName.WebServiceName
```

After this new instance is created, a connection between our client project and our Web service can be set up using this instance. The pseudocodes for this event procedure are listed below:

A) A new Web service instance `wsOracleSelect` is created using the protocol given above.
B) A new object `wsOracleResult` is also created and it can be used as a mapping to the real object `OracleSelectResult` developed in the Web service. We can easily access the related Web method to perform our data query and pick up the result from that returning object by assigning it to the mapping object.
C) A new DataSet object is created and it is used to call the Web method that returns a DataSet.
D) Based on the method selected by the user from the Query Method combo box control, different Web method can be called to perform the related data query.
E) The returned data that are stored in the real object are assigned to our mapping object, and each piece of information can be retrieved from this object and displayed in our GUI in the client side.
F) If a DataSet method is used, the returned DataSet object is assigned to our mapping DataSet and the subroutine `FillFacultyDataSet()` is called to fill the textboxes in the Client Form with the information picked up from the DataSet.

Let's start our coding process from the Form_Load() event procedure.

9.3.10.3.1 Develop the Codes for the Form_Load Event Procedure Now let's begin to develop the codes for the Form_Load event procedure to complete the initialization jobs listed in step 1 above.

Open the Form_Load event procedure by selecting the **(FacultyForm Events)** item from the Class Name combo box and **Load** item from the Method Name combo box from the code window of the **FacultyForm**. Enter the codes that are shown in Figure 9.36 into this event procedure.

Let's take a closer look at this piece of codes to see how it works:

A) Eight default faculty members are added into the Faculty Name combo box control using the **Add()** method. This will allow users to select one desired faculty from this combo box control to perform the data query as the project runs. The default faculty is the first one by setting the SelectedIndex property to zero.

B) Three Web query methods are also added into the Query Method combo box control to allow users to select one of them to perform the associated data query via our Web service. The default method is selected as the first one.

The codes for the **Back** button's click event procedure are very simple. Open this event procedure and enter **Me.Close()** into this event procedure, which means that the project will be terminated as soon as the user clicks on this button as the project runs. The **Close()** method tells Visual Basic.NET to terminate the current project.

Next let's build the codes for the **Select** button's Click event procedure.

9.3.10.3.2 Develop the Codes for the Select Button's Click Event Procedure Open the **Select** button's Click event procedure and enter the codes that are shown in Figure 9.37 into this procedure. Let's have a closer look at this piece of codes to see how it works:

A) Some data objects are created at the beginning of this event procedure, which include a new Web service instance **wsOracleSelect** that is created using the protocol given above, a new object **wsOracleResult** that can be used as a mapping to the real object **OracleSelectResult** developed in the Web service. We can easily access the Web method

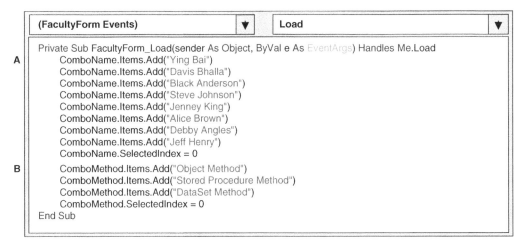

Figure 9.36 The codes for the Form_Load() event procedure.

to perform our data query and pick up the result from that returning object by assigning it to this mapping object later. Also a new DataSet object is declared and it is used to call the Web method that returns a DataSet.

B) If the user selected the **Object Method** from the Query Method combo box control, a **Try...** **Catch** block is used to call the associated Web method **GetOracleSelect()**, which is developed in our Web service, through the instantiated reference class to perform the data query. The selected faculty that is located in the Faculty Name combo box control is passed as a parameter for this calling.

C) The **Catch** statement is used to collect any possible exceptions if any error occurred for this calling, and the error message is displayed using a message box.

D) If no exception occurred, the user-defined subroutine **ProcessObject()** is executed to pick up all pieces of retrieved information from the returned object and displays them in this form window.

E) If the user selected the **Stored   Procedure   Method**, the associated Web method **GetOracleSelectSP()**, which is developed in our Web service, is called via the instance of the Web referenced class to perform the data query.

F) The **Catch** statement is used to collect any possible exceptions if any error occurred for this calling, and the error message is displayed using a message box.

G) The user-defined subroutine **ProcessObject()** is executed to pick up all pieces of retrieved information from the returned object and displays them in this form.

Figure 9.37   The codes for the Select button's click event procedure.

H) If users selected the **DataSet Method**, the Web method **GetOracleSelectDataSet()** is called through the instance of the Web referenced class, and the method returns a DataSet that contains our desired faculty record.

I) The **Catch** statement is used to collect any possible exceptions if any error occurred for this calling, and the error message is displayed using a message box.

J) The subroutine **FillFacultyDataSet()** is called to pick up all pieces of retrieved information from the returned DataSet and displays them in this form window.

9.3.10.3.3 Develop Codes for User-Defined Subroutine Procedures The codes for the user-defined subroutines **ProcessObject()** and **FillFacultyObject()** are shown in Figure 9.38. Both subroutines use our child class **OracleSelectResult** as the data type of the passed argument since our returned object is an instance of this class. The function of this piece of codes is

A) If the member data **OracleRequestOK** that is stored in the instance of our child class or returned object is set to **True**, which means that our Web method is executed successfully, the user-defined subroutine **FillFacultyObject()** is called and executed. This subroutine picks up each piece of information from the queried object **wsResult** and displays it in this form window.

B) Otherwise, some exceptions were occurred and a warning message is displayed with a message box.

C) As the subroutine **FillFacultyObject()** is called, all six pieces of faculty information stored in the returned object are picked up and assigned to the associated textbox in this form to be displayed. The faculty name can be obtained directly from the Faculty Name combo box control from this form window.

The codes for the subroutine **FillFacultyDataSet()** are shown in Figure 9.39. The argument passed into this subroutine is an instance of DataSet we created in the **Select** button's click event procedure. Let's take a look at this piece of codes to see how it works:

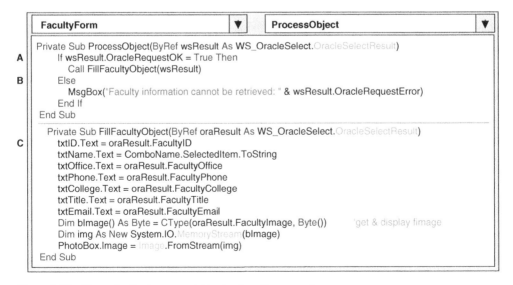

```
 FacultyForm                    ▼    ProcessObject                           ▼

    Private Sub ProcessObject(ByRef wsResult As WS_OracleSelect.OracleSelectResult)
A      If wsResult.OracleRequestOK = True Then
          Call FillFacultyObject(wsResult)
B      Else
          MsgBox("Faculty information cannot be retrieved: " & wsResult.OracleRequestError)
       End If
    End Sub

    Private Sub FillFacultyObject(ByRef oraResult As WS_OracleSelect.OracleSelectResult)
C      txtID.Text = oraResult.FacultyID
       txtName.Text = ComboName.SelectedItem.ToString
       txtOffice.Text = oraResult.FacultyOffice
       txtPhone.Text = oraResult.FacultyPhone
       txtCollege.Text = oraResult.FacultyCollege
       txtTitle.Text = oraResult.FacultyTitle
       txtEmail.Text = oraResult.FacultyEmail
       Dim bImage() As Byte = CType(oraResult.FacultyImage, Byte())    'get & display fimage
       Dim img As New System.IO.MemoryStream(bImage)
       PhotoBox.Image = Image.FromStream(img)
    End Sub
```

Figure 9.38 The codes for two user-defined subroutine procedures.

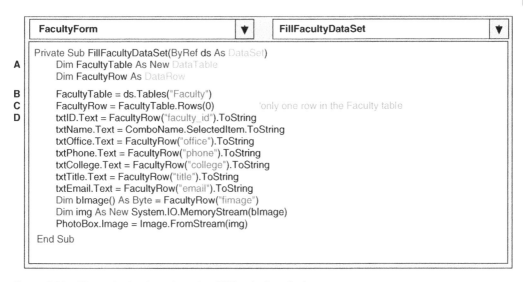

FacultyForm ▼	FillFacultyDataSet ▼

```
     Private Sub FillFacultyDataSet(ByRef ds As DataSet)
A        Dim FacultyTable As New DataTable
         Dim FacultyRow As DataRow

B        FacultyTable = ds.Tables("Faculty")
C        FacultyRow = FacultyTable.Rows(0)          'only one row in the Faculty table
D        txtID.Text = FacultyRow("faculty_id").ToString
         txtName.Text = ComboName.SelectedItem.ToString
         txtOffice.Text = FacultyRow("office").ToString
         txtPhone.Text = FacultyRow("phone").ToString
         txtCollege.Text = FacultyRow("college").ToString
         txtTitle.Text = FacultyRow("title").ToString
         txtEmail.Text = FacultyRow("email").ToString
         Dim bImage() As Byte = FacultyRow("fimage")
         Dim img As New System.IO.MemoryStream(bImage)
         PhotoBox.Image = Image.FromStream(img)
     End Sub
```

Figure 9.39   The codes for the subroutine FillFacultyDataSet().

A) Two data objects, FacultyTable that is a new object of the DataTable class and FacultyRow that is a new instance of the DataRow class, are created first since we need to use these two objects to access the DataSet to pick up all requested faculty information later.

B) The returned Faculty table that is embedded in our returned DataSet is assigned to our new created object **FacultyTable**. Because the DataSet we created in the **Select** button's click event procedure is an untyped DataSet, the table name must be clearly indicated with a string **"Faculty."** For typed DataSet, you can directly use the table name to access the desired table without needing any string.

C) Since we only request one record or one row from the Faculty table, so the returned Faculty table contains only one row information that is located at the top with an index of zero. This one row information is assigned to our **FacultyRow** object we created above.

D) We can access each column from returned one row data using the column name represented by a string with a class method **ToString()**. As we mentioned, the DataSet we are using is an untyped DataSet; therefore, the column name must be indicated with a string and the value of that column must be converted to a string using the **ToString()** method. If a typed DataSet is used, you can directly use the column name to access that column without needing to use the **ToString()** method. Each piece of information returned is assigned to the associated textbox, and it will be displayed there.

At this point, we have finished all coding development for this Windows-based Web service client project. Now we can start to run this client project to interface to our Web service and furthermore to access and use the Web methods to perform our data query.

Wait a moment! There is one import issue you need to note before you can run this project, which is that you must run our Web service project **WebServiceOracleSelect Project** first to allow our Web service available to all clients. Otherwise, you may encounter some running exceptions (such as the Web service or remote computer cannot be found) during your client project runs.

Open Visual Studio.NET and our Web Service project **WebServiceOracleSelect Project**, and click on the **IIS Express** button to run it. One point is that our Web service project must be kept in the running status (even the page has been closed) in order to allow our client project to access and interface to it. An exception will be encountered if you stop our Web service when you try to access it using our client project.

Make sure that our Web service has been run once and it is in the running status, which can be identified by a small Web service running icon in the task bar on the bottom of your screen. You may need to click on the **Show hidden icons** item on the bottom task bar to find this **IIS Express** icon. Then open it by right-clicking on this icon and select **Show All Applications** item. The opened running status of this Web service project is shown in Figure 9.40.

Then start our client project by clicking on the Start Debugging button from the project **WinClientOracleSelect Project**. The running status is shown in Figure 9.41.

Select any Web method and the faculty name **Jenney King** and click on the **Select** button to call the associated Web method to retrieve the desired faculty record. The returned faculty data are displayed in the associated textboxes with the faculty photo, which is shown in Figure 9.41.

You can try to select any other Web method, either the **Stored Procedure** or the **DataSet** method, and other faculty members to perform this data query. The running result confirmed that both our Web service and our Windows-based Web service client projects are very successful. Click on the **Back** button to terminate our project.

A complete Windows-based Web service client project **WinClientOracleSelect Project** can be found from the folder **Class DB Projects\Chapter 9** that is located under the **Students** folder at the Wiley ftp site (refer to Figure 1.2 in Chapter 1). You need to load both our client and our Web service projects from that site and install them in your computer if you want to run and test this client project. Also you must run our Web service project one time to make sure that our Web service is ready to be consumed by that client project.

Next we want to develop a Web-based project to consume our Web service by retrieving the desired faculty information.

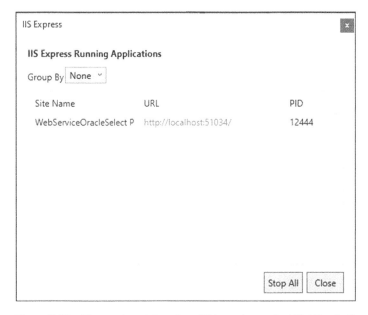

Figure 9.40 The running status of our Web service project WebServiceOracleSelect. *Source:* Used with permission from Microsoft.

Figure 9.41 The running status of our client project. *Source*: Used with permission from Microsoft.

9.3.11 Build Web-based Web Service Clients to Consume the Web Service

Develop a Web-based client application to consume a Web service is very similar to develop a Windows-based client project to reference and access a Web service as we did in the last section. As long as a Web service is referenced by the Web-based client project, one can access and call any Web method developed in that Web service to perform the desired data queries via the Web-based client project without problem. Visual Studio.NET will create the same document files such as the Discovery Map file, the WDSL file, and the DISCO file for the client project no matter this Web service is consumed by a Windows-based or a Web-based client application.

To save time and space, we can modify an existing ASP.NET Web Application **OracleWebSelect Project** we developed in Chapter 8 to make it as our new Web-based Web service client project **WebClientOracleSelect Project**. In fact, we can copy and rename that entire project as our new Web-based client project. However, we prefer to create a new ASP.NET Web site application project and only copy and modify the Faculty page.

The developing process in this section can be divided into the following parts:

1) Create a new ASP.NET Web Application (.NET Framework) for Visual Basic project **WebClientOracleSelect Project** and add the existing Web pages related to **Faculty.aspx** from the project **OracleWebSelect Project** into our new project.
2) Add a Web service reference to our new project and modify the Web page window of the **Faculty.aspx** to meet our data query requirements.
3) Modify the GUI and codes in the related event procedures of the **Fcaulty.aspx.vb** file to call the associated Web method to perform our data query. These modifications include the following sections:
   a) Add a **DropDownList** control to the Designer to enable users to select different methods to consume the Web service to perform data query.
   b) Modify the codes in the Page_Load event procedure.
   c) Modify the codes in the **Select** button's click event procedure.

d) Add three user-defined subroutines: `ProcessObject()`, `FillFacultyObject()`, and `FillFacultyDataSet()`. These three subroutines are basically identical with those we developed in the last Windows-based Web service client project `WinClientOracleSelect Project`. One can copy and paste them into our new project. The only modification is for the subroutine `ProcessObject()`.

e) Modify the codes in the `Back` button's click event procedure.

Now let's start with the first building part listed above.

9.3.11.1 Create a New Web Project and Add an Existing Web Page

Open Visual Studio.NET and go to the `File|New Project` menu item to create a new ASP.NET Web Application project. Enter `WebClientOracleSelect Project` and `WebClientOracleSelect Solution` into the `Project name` and the `Solution name` box, and `C:\Chapter 9` into the `Location` box. Click the `Create` button to create this new Web project. Then select the `Web Forms` item and click on the `Create` button to continue.

Perform the following operations to add all existing Web page files related to `Faculty.aspx` into our new Web site project:

1) Right-click on our new project `WebClientOracleSelect Project` from the Solution Explorer window and select the item `Add|Existing Item` from the popup menu.
2) Browse to our Web project `OracleWebSelect Project` that can be found from the folder `Class DB Projects\Chapter 8` that is located under the `Students` folder at the Wiley ftp site (refer to Figure 1.2 in Chapter 1). Select the Web page file, `Faculty.aspx`, from the list and click on the `Add` button to add this Web page file into our new Web client project.
3) Open the Source file of the `Faculty.aspx`, go to the last tag in the first line, and change it to `Inherits="WebClientOracleSelect_Project.Faculty" %>`.

Now let's handle to add a Web reference to our project to access the Web service we built in the previous section.

9.3.11.2 Add a Web Service Reference and Modify the Web Form Window

Perform the following operations to add this Web reference:

1) Run our Web service project `WebServiceOracleSelect Project` first.
2) Copy the URL from the `Address` bar in our running Web service project.
3) Then open our Web client project `WebClientOracleSelect Project`.
4) Right-click on our client project `WebClientOracleSelect Project` from the Solution Explorer window and select the item `Add|Web Reference` from the popup menu to open the Add Web Reference wizard, which is shown in Figure 9.42.
5) Paste that URL we copied from step 2 into the URL box in the `Add Web Reference` wizard and click on the blue color `Arrow` button to search our Web Service.
6) When the Web service is found, the name of our Web service is displayed in the right pane, which is shown in Figure 9.42.
7) Change the name for this Web reference from `localhost` to any meaningful name, such as `WS_OracleSelect` in our case. Click on the `Add Reference` button to add this Web service as a reference to our new client project.
8) Click on the `Close` button from our Web service built-in Web interface window to stop our Web service page.

Figure 9.42 Add a Web reference. *Source:* Oracle Corporation.

Immediately you can find that the following two files are created in the Solution Explorer window under the folder of the new added Web reference (you may need to click on the **Show All Files** icon on the Solution Explorer window bar to see them):

- WebServiceOracleSelect.disco
- WebServiceOracleSelect.wsdl

This reference is the so-called Web service proxy class.

Next, let's begin the code modification process to build the codes for this project.

9.3.11.3 Modify the Designer and Coding for the Related Event Procedures

The first modification is to add a combo box control **Query Method** to the **Faculty.aspx** page to enable users to select one of three query methods to perform the related data query operation.

9.3.11.3.1 Add a Combo Box Control Query Method to the Faculty Page
Open the **Faculty.aspx** page and add one more DropDownList control **ComboMethod** and an associated label **Query Method** just under the Faculty Name combo box control in this page. Your modified **Faculty. aspx** page is shown in Figure 9.43.

The second modification is to change the codes in the Page_Load event procedure and some global variables.

9.3.11.3.2 Modify the Codes in the Page_Load Event Procedure
Perform the following changes to complete this modification:

1) Remove two Imports, **Imports Devart.Data** and **Imports Devart.Data.Oracle**, from the top of this page since we do not need them in this application.

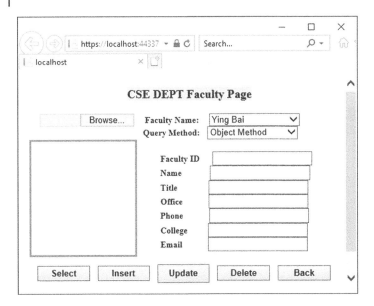

Figure 9.43 The modified Faculty.aspx page. *Source:* Used with permission from Microsoft.

2) Remove the form-level variable **FacultyTextBox(7)** that is a textbox array.
3) Remove the global connection string and **If** block inside the Page_Load event procedure and the associated connection object stored in the Application state **Application("oraConnection")**.
4) Add the codes (highlighted) to display three Web query methods in the **Query Method** DropDownList control.

Your finished codes for the Page_Load event procedure should match one that is shown in Figure 9.44. The new added codes have been highlighted in bold.

The next modification is to change the codes inside the **Select** button's click event procedure.

9.3.11.3.3 Modify the Codes in the Select Button's Event Procedure Replace all codes in this event procedure with the modified codes shown in Figure 9.45. This replacement includes

A) Create the following three new instances:
   1) **wsOracleSelect** for the proxy class of our Web service
   2) **wsOracleResult** for the child class of our Web service
   3) **wsDataSet** for the DataSet class
B) Create a local string variable **errMsg** and it is used to store the possible error message.
C) If the user selected the Web Object method, a **Try…Catch** block is used to call the first Web method **GetOracleSelect()** that we developed in our Web service project with the selected faculty name as the input parameter. The returned object that contains our queried faculty information is assigned to our local mapping object **wsOracleResult** if this calling is successful. Otherwise, an error message is displayed using the **Write()** method of the Response object of the server.
D) The subroutine **ProcessObject()** is executed to assign the retrieved faculty information to the associated textbox in our Web page to display each of them.
E) If the user selected the **Stored Procedure Method**, the associated Web method **GetOracleSelectSP()**, which is developed in our Web service, is called via the instance of

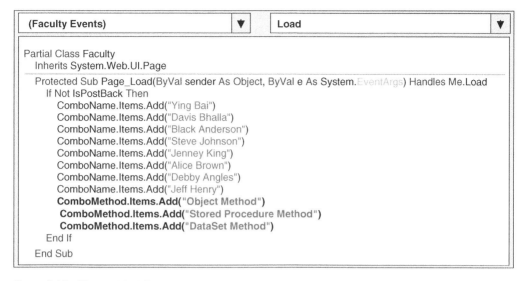

Figure 9.44   The modified Page_Load event procedure.

Figure 9.45   The modified codes for the Select button's Click event procedure.

the Web referenced class to perform the data query. The `Catch` statement is used to collect any possible exceptions if any error occurred for this calling, and the error message is displayed using the `Write()` method of the Response object of the server. The subroutine `ProcessObject()` is executed to pick up all pieces of retrieved information from the returned object and displays them in this page.

F) If users selected the `DataSet Method`, the Web method `GetOracleSelectDataSet()` is called through the instance of the Web referenced class, and the method returns a DataSet that contains the queried faculty information. The `Catch` statement is used to collect possible exceptions if any error occurred, and the error message is displayed using the `Write()` method of the Response object of the server.

G) The subroutine `FillFacultyDataSet()` is called to pick up all pieces of retrieved information from the returned DataSet and displays them in this page.

9.3.11.3.4 Add Three User-Defined Subroutine Procedures
We need to add three user-defined subroutines: `ProcessObject()`, `FillFacultyObject()`, and `FillFacultyDataSet()`, into this project. The codes for these three subroutines are basically identical with those we developed in the last Windows-based Web service client project `WinClientSQLSelect`, and one can copy and paste them into our new project with a little modification.

Open our Windows-based Web service client project `WinClientOracleSelect Project`, copy these three subroutines from that project and paste them into the code page of our current Faculty page. Perform the following modifications to make those window-based subroutines to meet the needs of our Web-based subroutines:

A) The first modification is for the `MsgBox()` method in the subroutine `ProcessObject()`. As you know, in the Web site project, we need to use the `Write()` method provided by the Response object of the server class to replace the Windows-based method `MsgBox()` to display an error message. Create a local string variable `errmsg` for this subroutine to hold the possible error message. Your modified codes for this subroutine should match those that are shown in Figure 9.46. The modified parts have been highlighted in bold.

B) The modifications to the subroutines `FillFacultyObject()` and `FillFacultyDataSet()` are similar, in which the faculty image is converted to the address or a string of that image and assigned to the `ImagUrl` property of the faculty image control `PhotoBox`.

Both modifications are shown in Figures 9.47 and 9.48 and have been highlighted with bold style.

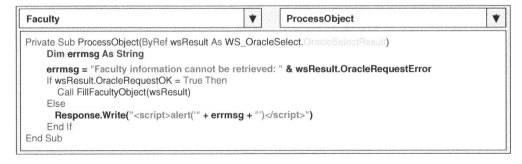

Figure 9.46 The modified codes for the subroutine procedure ProcessObject().

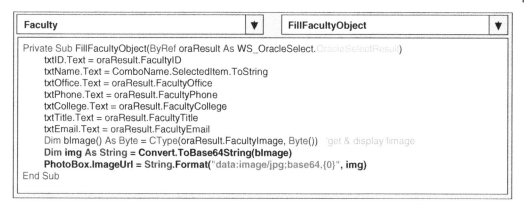

Figure 9.47 The modified codes for the subroutine FillFacultyObject().

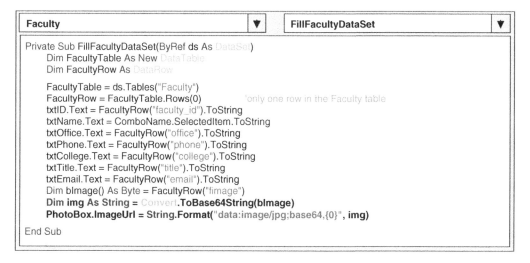

Figure 9.48 The modified codes for the subroutine FillFacultyDataSet().

9.3.11.3.5 Modify the Codes for the Back Button's Event Procedure

The modification to the **Back** button's click event procedure is to use the Web-based **Response.Write()** method to terminate our Web client page project. The modified **Back** button's click event procedure is shown in Figure 9.49.

Before we can run our project, we need to remove two unused user-defined subroutine procedures, **FillFacultyReader()** and **MapFacultyTable()**, from this project since both of them were built in the previous project and we will not use them in this project.

Now it is the time for us to run our Web-based Web service client project to test the functions of our data query for our Web service. However, before we can run our project, we need to make sure that the following two things have been done:

1) Make sure that the starting page is our **Faculty.aspx** page as the project runs. To confirm that, right-click our **Faculty.aspx** page from the Solution Explorer window and select the item **Set As Start Page** from the popup menu.

2) Make sure that our Web service **WebServiceOracleSelect Project** has been run at least one time and that Web service status is running. This can be identified by a small white icon located in the task bar at the bottom of the screen.

```
btnBack                    ▼    Click                              ▼
Protected Sub btnBack_Click(sender As Object, e As EventArgs) Handles btnBack.Click
    Response.Write("<script>window.close()</script>")
End Sub
```

Figure 9.49 The modified codes for the Back button's event procedure.

Figure 9.50 The running status of our Web-based client project. *Source:* Used with permission from Microsoft.

Now click on the **IIS Express** button to run our project. The Faculty page is displayed and it is shown in Figure 9.50.

Keep the default Web query method, **Object Method**, in the Query Method combo box control selected and the faculty name in the Faculty Name combo box unchanged. Then click on the **Select** button to call the associated Web method developed in our Web service to retrieve the selected faculty information from our sample database via the Web server. The query result is shown in Figure 9.50.

You can try to select different Web query methods with different faculty members to test this project. Our Web-based Web service client project is very successful.

A complete Web-based Web service client project **WebClientOracleSelect Project** can be found from the folder **Class DB Projects\Chapter 9** that is located under the **Students** folder at the Wiley ftp site (refer to Figure 1.2 in Chapter 1).

9.3.12 Deploy the Completed Web Service to Production Servers

When finished developing and testing our Web service in our local machine, we need to deploy it to the .NET SDK or an IIS 5 or higher virtual directory to allow users to access and use it via a production server. We may discuss this topic in the early section when we finished developing our Web service project. The reason we delay this discussion until this section is that we do not have to perform this Web service deployment if we running our Web service and accessing it using a client project in our local computer (development server). However, we must deploy our Web service to IIS if we want to run it in a formal Web server (production server).

Basically, we have two ways to do this deployment; one way is to copy our Web service files to a server running the IIS 5 or higher, or to the folder that is or contains our virtual directory. Another way is to use the Builder provided by Visual Studio.NET to pre-compile the Web pages and copy the compiled files to our virtual directory. The so-called virtual directory is a default directory that can be recognized and accessed by a Web server such as IIS to run our Web services. In both ways, we need a virtual directory to store our Web service files and allow Web server to pick up and run our Web service from that virtual directory. Now let's see how to create an IIS virtual directory.

The following steps describe how to add a target Web service and create an IIS virtual directory using the IIS Manager:

1) First create a folder to save our virtual directory's files. Typically we need to create this folder under the default Web service root folder `C:\Inetpub\wwwroot`. In our case, create a new folder named `WSOracleSelect` and place it under the root folder `C:\Inetpub\wwwroot`.
2) Open the IIS Manager by double-clicking on the `Administrative Tools` icon from the Control Panel. On the opened wizard, double-click on the icon `Computer Management`, then expand the item `Services and Applications` from the opened wizard, and click the item `Internet Information Services (IIS) Manager`. Now click the `Current View` tab on the bottom of this wizard. Two items are listed under this icon: `Application Pools` and `Sites`.
3) Right-click on the item `Sites` and select `Add Website` item to open this wizard, as shown in Figure 9.51.
4) Enter `WebServiceOracleSelect Project` into the `Site name` box as the name for this site, and click on the expansion button on the right of the `Physical path` to browse to the location of our Web service project located, in this case, it is `C:\Oracle DB Programming\Students\Class DB Projects\Chapter 9\WebServiceOracleSelect Solution\WebServiceOracleSelect Project`. But in your case, it should be `C:\Chapter 9\WebServiceOracleSelect Solution\WebServiceOracleSelect Project`. In our case, enter the server name `YBSMART` into the Host name box. However, you need to enter your server name into this box. Then click on the `Test Settings` button to test the Pass-through authentication of this service.
5) Click on the `OK` button to complete this adding operation.

After our Web service is added into the IIS, next we can deploy our Web service by either copying files to this virtual directory or performing a pre-compile process. Starting from Visual Studio.NET 2017, Microsoft provides an easy way to help users to build, configure, perform settings, and deploy the Web service on the IIS with a Publish tool.

Next we will discuss how to publish a Web service to the production server using the Publish tool.

9.3.12.1 Publish the Desired Web Service

Perform the following steps to complete this publish process for our Web service:

1) Open our Web service project `WebServiceOracleSelect Project` as the Administrator mode (must be in this mode, otherwise the service cannot be published).
2) Right-click on our opened project and select `Publish` item from the popup menu.

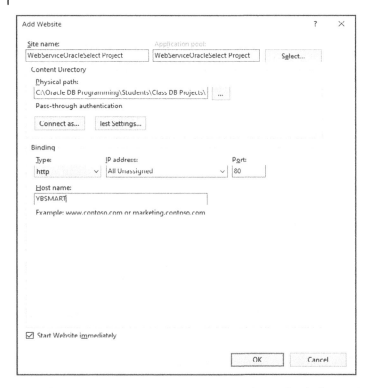

Figure 9.51 The completed Add Website wizard. *Source:* Oracle Corporation.

3) Click on the **Start** button to begin this process.
4) Keep the default **Create New** radio button in the mid-pane selected and select **IIS, FTP, etc,** item from the left pane. Then click on the **Publish** button to open the customer profile wizard for this publish process. Select the **Web Server (IIS)** item and click on the **Next** button.
5) Select the **Web Deploy** item and click on the **Next** button to continue.
6) On the opened wizard shown in Figure 9.52, Enter the server name into the **Server** box, in our case, it is our computer name, **YBSMART**.
7) Enter the site name into the **Site name** box. In our case, it is **WebServiceOracleSelect Project** (refer to step 4 in the last section when we add the Web site to the IIS).
8) Enter our target URL, http://localhost:51034\WebServiceOracleSelect.asmx, into the **Destination URL** box (refer to Add Web Service Reference in Section 9.3.11.2 for this URL).
9) Now click the **Finish** button to complete these setup processes.
10) On the next wizard, first run our Web service project **WebServiceOracleSelect Project** by clicking on the **IIS Express** button and then click on the **Publish** button to publish our Web Service.

The Visual Studio.NET begins the building and publishing process. If everything is fine, our Web site will be published successfully, which is shown in Figure 9.53.

If for some reasons, your Web service cannot be deployed or published successfully, you may need to go to site https://www.microsoft.com/web/downloads/platform.aspx to download and install Web Platform Installer 5.0 (WebPI 5.0) provided by Microsoft to make sure that a valid and updated IIS is installed in your computer.

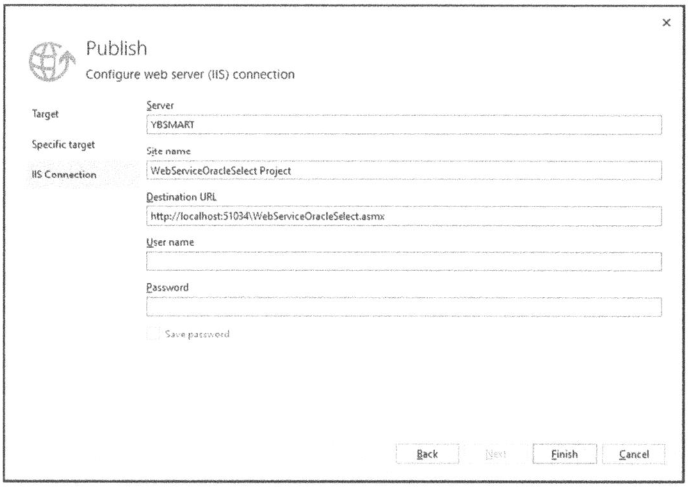

Figure 9.52 The Customer Profile setup wizard. *Source:* Used with permission from Microsoft.

Figure 9.53 The Web site Publishing result. *Source:* Used with permission from Microsoft.

At this point, we have finished discussion about how to create and consume a Web service using a Windows-based and a Web-based Web service client project. In the following sections, we will expand these discussions to perform the data insertion, and data updating and deleting actions against the database via the Web services.

9.4 Build ASP.NET Web Service Project to Insert Data Into Oracle Databases

In this section, we will discuss how to insert data into our sample database through a Web service developed in Visual Studio.NET. The data table we try to use for this data action is the **COURSE** table. In other words, we want to insert a new course record for the selected faculty into the **COURSE** table via a Web service project.

9.4.1 Create a New Web Service Project WebServiceOracleInsert

First let's create a new folder such as `C:\Chapter 9` in your root directory using the Windows Explorer. Then create a new **WCF Service Application** for Visual Basic project **WebServiceOracleInsert Project** and place it into our new created folder `C:\Chapter 9`.

Perform the following operations to add a new Web main service into our project:

1) Right-click on our new project `WebServiceOracleInsert Project` from the Solution Explorer window and select the **Add|New Item**.
2) On the **Add New Item** wizard, select **Web Service (ASMX)** from the Template list.
3) Enter `WebServiceOracleInsert.asmx` into the **Name** box.
4) Click on the **Add** button to complete this item addition operation.

Based on Section 9.3.2 in this Chapter, the complete procedure to build this Web service project can be summarized as:

1) Modify the default namespace to make it our own Web service namespace.
2) Add a new database connection string into the Web configuration file `Web.config`.
3) Create a customer base class to handle error-checking codes.
4) Create a customer returned class to hold all required course information. This class is a derived class based on the base class above.
5) Add Web methods to our Web main service class to access our sample database.
6) Develop the detail codes for those Web methods to perform the Web services.

Let's perform these procedures one by one in the following sequence:

1) Add two References, `Devart.Data` and `Devart.Data.Oracle`, into this service project.
2) Refer to Section 9.3.3 to modify the default namespace to make it our Web service namespace, http://www.wiley.com/9780521712354.
3) Refer to Section 9.3.7.1 to add a new database connection string into the Web configuration file `Web.config` as below:

```
<connectionStrings>
    <add name="ora_conn" connectionString="Server=localhost:1518/CSE_DEPT; _
    User ID=CSE_DEPT; Password=oracle_18c"/>
</connectionStrings>
```

4) Create a customer base class `OracleInsertBase.vb` with the following member data:
   - `Public OracleInsertOK As Boolean`
   - `Public OracleInsertError As String`
5) Create a customer derived class `OracleInsertResult.vb` based on the `OracleInsertBase` class with the following seven member data:
   - `Public FacultyID As String`
   - `Public CourseID(10) As String`
   - `Public Course As String`
   - `Public Schedule As String`
   - `Public Classroom As String`
   - `Public Credit As Integer`
   - `Public Enrollment As Integer`

Go to the **File|Save All** menu item to save above modifications.

Next let's take care of creating the different Web methods with detailed codes to perform the course record insertion actions.

9.4.2 Develop Four Web Service Methods

We try to develop four Web methods in this Web service project, two of them are used to insert the desired course information into our sample database and two of them are used to retrieve the new inserted course information from the database to test the data insertion. One of Web methods is used to retrieve the detailed course information based on the `COURSE_ID`. The functions of these methods are described below:

1) Develop a Web method `SetOracleInsertSP()` to call a stored procedure to perform a new course insertion.
2) Develop a Web method `GetOracleInsert()` to retrieve the new inserted course information from the database using a joined table query.
3) Develop a Web method `OracleInsertDataSet()` to perform a data insertion using multi-query and return a DataSet that contains the updated `COURSE` table.
4) Develop a Web method `GetOracleInsertCourse()` to retrieve the detailed course information based on the input `COURSE_ID`.

The reason we use two different methods (1 and 3) to perform this data insertion is to try to compare them. As you know, there is no faculty name column in the Course table and each course is related to an associated `faculty_id`. In order to insert a new course into the Course table, one must first perform a query to the Faculty table to get the desired `faculty_id` based on the selected faculty name, and then one can perform an insertion query to insert a new course based on that `faculty_id` obtained from the first query. The first method combines those queries into a stored procedure and the third method uses a DataSet to return the whole Course table to make this data insertion more convenient.

The major code developments are performed inside our main service page file `WebServiceOracleInsert.asmx`.

9.4.2.1 Develop Codes for the First Web Method SetOracleInsertSP()

Open our new project `WebServiceOracleInsert Project` if it has not been opened. Open the code window of our main service page `WebServiceOracleInsert.asmx` and enter the codes shown in Figure 9.54 to replace the default Web method, `HelloWorld()`, with our first new Web method `SetOracleInsertSP()`.

This Web method uses a stored procedure to perform the data insertion. Recall that in Section 6.5.1.1 in Chapter 6, we developed a stored procedure `INSERT_FACULTYCOURSE` in the Oracle SQL Developer and used it to insert a new course into the Course table. We will use this stored procedure again in this Web method to reduce our coding load. Refer to that section to get more detailed information about how to develop this stored procedure. Seven input parameters are used for this stored procedure, `:FacultyName`, `:CourseID`, `:Course`, `:Schedule`, `:Classroom`, `:Credit,` and `:Enroll`. All of these parameters will be input by the user as this Web service project runs.

Let's take a closer look at the codes for this Web method to see how they work:

A) The `Devart.Data` and `Devart.Data.Oracle` data driver is imported first since we need to use this driver to access and query to our Oracle database.
B) The Web method name is also changed to `SetOracleInsertSP()`, which means that this Web method will call a stored procedure to perform the data insertion action. Seven input parameters are passed into this method as a new course record to be inserted into the Course table. The returned object should be an instance of our modified base class `OracleInsertBase`.
C) The content of the query string must be equal to the name of the stored procedure we developed in Section 6.5.1.1 in Chapter 6. Otherwise a possible running error may be encountered as this Web service is executed since the stored procedure is identified by its name when it is called.

WebServiceOracleInsert ▼	SetOracleInsertSP ▼

```
        Imports System.Web.Services
        Imports System.Web.Services.Protocols
        Imports System.ComponentModel
        Imports Devart.Data
A       Imports Devart.Data.Oracle

        <System.Web.Services.WebService(Namespace:="http://www.wiley.com/9780521712354/")>
        <System.Web.Services.WebServiceBinding(ConformsTo:=WsiProfiles.BasicProfile1_1)>
        <ToolboxItem(False)>
        Public Class WebServiceOracleInsert
            Inherits System.Web.Services.WebService

        <WebMethod()> _
B       Public Function SetOracleInsertSP(ByVal FacultyName As String, ByVal CourseID As String, ByVal Course As String, _
            ByVal Schedule As String, ByVal Classroom As String, ByVal Credit As Integer, ByVal Enroll As Integer) As _
                                                                                                    OracleInsertBase
C           Dim cmdString As String = "INSERT_FACULTYCOURSE"
            Dim oraConnection As New OracleConnection
D           Dim SetOracleResult As New OracleInsertBase
            Dim oraCommand As New OracleCommand
E           Dim intInsert As Integer

F           SetOracleResult.OracleInsertOK = True
            oraConnection = OracleConn()

G           If oraConnection Is Nothing Then
               SetOracleResult.OracleInsertError = "Database connection is failed"
               ReportError(SetOracleResult)
               Return Nothing
            End If

            oraCommand.Connection = oraConnection
H           oraCommand.CommandType = CommandType.StoredProcedure
            oraCommand.CommandText = cmdString
I           oraCommand.Parameters.Add(":FacultyName", OracleDbType.Char).Value = FacultyName
            oraCommand.Parameters.Add(":CourseID", OracleDbType.Char).Value = CourseID
            oraCommand.Parameters.Add(":Course", OracleDbType.Char).Value = Course
            oraCommand.Parameters.Add(":Credit", OracleDbType.Number).Value = Credit
            oraCommand.Parameters.Add(":Classroom", OracleDbType.Char).Value = Classroom
            oraCommand.Parameters.Add(":Schedule", OracleDbType.Char).Value = Schedule
            oraCommand.Parameters.Add(":Enroll", OracleDbType.Number).Value = Enroll
J           intInsert = oraCommand.ExecuteNonQuery()
K           oraCommand.Dispose()
            oraCommand = Nothing
            If Not oraConnection Is Nothing Then oraConnection.Close()
            oraConnection = Nothing

L           If intInsert = 0 Then
               SetOracleResult.OracleInsertError = "Data insertion is failed"
               ReportError(SetOracleResult)
            End If
M           Return SetOracleResult
        End Function
```

Figure 9.54 Modifications to the first Web method.

D) A returned object **SetOracleResult** is created based on our customer base class **OracleInsertBase**. Exactly, there is no any data supposed to be returned for the data insertion action. However, in order to enable our client project to get a clear feedback from execution of this Web service, we prefer to return an object that contains the information indicating whether this Web service is successful or not.

E) A local integer variable **intInsert** is declared and this variable is used to hold the returned value from calling of the ExecuteNonQuery() method of the Command class, and that method will call the stored procedure to perform the data insertion action. This returned value is equal to the number of rows that have been successfully inserted into our database.

F) Initially, we set the member data `OracleInsertOK` that is located in our customer base class `OracleInsertBase` to `True` to indicate that our Web service running status is good. Then we call the `OracleConn()` function to connect to our database.

G) If the connection to our sample database is failed, which is indicated by a returned Connection object contained `Nothing`, an error message is assigned to another member data `OracleInsertError` that is also located in our customer base class `OracleInsertBase` to log on this error. The user-defined subroutine `ReportError()` is called to report this error.

H) The property value `CommandType.StoredProcedure` must be assigned to the CommandType property of the Command object to tell the project that a stored procedure should be called as this command object is executed.

I) Seven input parameters are assigned to the Parameters collection property of the Command object, and the last six parameters work as a new course record to be inserted into the Course table. One important point to be noted is that these input parameters' names must be identical with those names defined in the stored procedure `INSERT_FACULTYCOURSE` developed in Section 6.5.1.1 in Chapter 6. Refer to that section to get a detailed description of those parameters' names defined in: that stored procedure.

J) The ExecuteNonQuery() method is executed to call the stored procedure to perform this data insertion. This method returns an integer that is stored in our local variable `intInsert`.

K) A cleaning job is performed to release data objects used in this method.

L) The returned value from calling of the ExecuteNonQuery() method, which is stored in the variable `intInsert`, is equal to the number of rows that have been successfully inserted into the Course table. If this value is zero, which means that no any row has been inserted into our database and this data insertion is failed, a warning message is assigned to the member data `OracleInsertError` that will be reported using our user-defined subroutine procedure `ReportError()`.

M) Finally, the instance of our derived class, `SetOracleResult`, is returned to the calling procedure to indicate the running result of this Web method.

9.4.2.2 Develop Codes for User-Defined Functions and Subroutine Procedures

Refer to Figure 9.18 in Section 9.3.7.2 and Figure 9.21 in Section 9.3.7.4 to get more details about these user-defined function and subroutine procedure. For you convenience, the detailed codes are shown in Figure 9.55 again.

At this point, we have finished the coding development and modification to this Web method. Now we can run this Web service project to insert a new course record into our sample database via this Web service. Click on the `IIS Express` button to run the project. The built-in Web interface is shown in Figure 9.56.

Click on the Web method `SetOracleInsertSP` to open another built-in Web interface to display the input parameters window, which is shown in Figure 9.57.

Enter the following parameters as a new course record into this Web method:

- FacultyName: `Ying Bai`
- CourseID: `CSE-556`
- Course: `Advanced Fuzzy Systems`
- Schedule: `M-W-F: 1:00-1:55 PM`
- Classroom: `MTC-315`
- Credit: `3`
- Enroll: `28`

WebServiceOracleInsert	▼	OracleConn	▼

```
Protected Function OracleConn() As OracleConnection
    Dim cmdString As String = ConfigurationManager.ConnectionStrings("ora_conn").ConnectionString
    Dim conn As New OracleConnection

    conn.ConnectionString = cmdString
    conn.Open()
    If conn.State <> Data.ConnectionState.Open Then
       MsgBox("Database Open is failed")
       conn = Nothing
    End If
    Return conn
End Function

Protected Sub ReportError(ByVal ErrSource As OracleInsertResult)
    ErrSource.OracleInsertOK = False
    MsgBox(ErrSource.OracleInsertError)
End Sub
```

Figure 9.55 Detailed codes for the user-defined function and subroutine.

Figure 9.56 The running status of the built-in Web interface. *Source:* Oracle Corporation.

Figure 9.57 The input parameter interface. *Source:* Oracle Corporation.

Figure 9.58 The running result of the first Web method. *Source:* Oracle Corporation.

Click on the **Invoke** button to run this Web method to call the stored procedure to perform this data insertion. The running result is displayed in the built-in Web interface, which is shown in Figure 9.58.

Based on the returned member data **OracleInsertOK = True**, it indicates that our data insertion is successful. To confirm this, first click on the **Close** button that is located at the upper-right corner of this Web interface to terminate our Web service project. Then open the **COURSE** table in our sample database **CSE_DEPT** using either the Sever Explorer or the Oracle SQL Developer to check this new inserted course.

One can find that the new inserted course record with **COURSE_ID = CSE-556** has been inserted into our Course table with a **FACULTY_ID = B78880**. This confirmed that our data insertion is successful.

9.4.2.3 Develop the Second Web Method GetOracleInsert()
The function of this Web method is to retrieve all **COURSE_ID**, which includes the original and the new inserted **COURSE_ID**, from the Course table based on the input faculty name. This Web method will be called or consumed by a client project later to get back and display all **COURSE_ID** in a ListBox control in the client project.

Recall that in Section 5.6.6.1 in Chapter 5, we developed a joined-table query to perform the data query from the Course table to get all **COURSE_ID** based on the faculty name. The reason for that is because there is no faculty name column available in the Course table, and each course or **COURSE_ID** is related to a **FACULTY_ID** in the Course table. In order to get the **FACULTY_ID** that is associated with the selected faculty name, one must first perform a query from the Faculty table to obtain it. In this situation, a join query is a desired method to complete this function.

We will use the same strategy to perform this data query in this section.

Open the code window of our main service page **WebServiceOracleInsert.asmx** and enter the codes that are shown in Figure 9.59 into this page to create our new Web method **GetOracleInsert()**.

Let's have a closer look at the codes in this Web method to see how they work:

A) The returning data type for this Web method is our modified base class **OracleInsertBase**, and an entire course record is stored in the different member data in this class. The input parameter to this Web method is a selected faculty name.
B) The joined-table query string is defined here and an ANSI92 standard that is an up-to-date standard is used for the syntax of this query string. The ANSI 89, which is an out-of-date syntax standard, can still be used for this query string definition. But the up-to-date standard is recommended. Refer to Section 5.6.6.1 in Chapter 5 to get more detailed descriptions for this topic. The nominal name of the input dynamic parameter to this query is **: fname**.

```
  WebServiceOracleInsert                    ▼      GetOracleInsert                              ▼

    < WebMethod()> _
A     Public Function GetOracleInsert( ByVal FacultyName As String) As OracleInsertResult
B         Dim cmdString As String =  "SELECT Course.course_id FROM Course JOIN Faculty"+ _
                                     "ON (Course.faculty_id = Faculty.faculty_id) AND (Faculty.faculty_name = : fname)"
C         Dim oraConnection As New OracleConnection
          Dim GetOracleResult As New OracleInsertResult
          Dim oraCommand As New OracleCommand
          Dim oraReader As OracleDataReader
D         GetOracleResult.OracleInsertOK = True
E         oraConnection = OracleConn()
          If oraConnection Is Nothing Then
             GetOracleResult.OracleInsertError = "Database connection is failed"
             ReportError(GetOracleResult)
             Return Nothing
          End If
F         oraCommand.Connection = oraConnection
          oraCommand.CommandType = CommandType.Text
          oraCommand.CommandText = cmdString
G         oraCommand.Parameters.Add(":fname", OracleDbType.NVarChar).Value = FacultyName
H         oraReader = oraCommand.ExecuteReader()
I         If oraReader.HasRows =True Then
             Call FillCourseReader(GetOracleResult, oraReader)
J         Else
             GetOracleResult.OracleInsertError = "No matched course found"
             ReportError(GetOracleResult)
          End If
K         If Not oraReader Is Nothing Then oraReader.Close()
          oraReader = Nothing
          If Not oraConnection Is Nothing Then oraConnection.Close()
          oraConnection = Nothing
          oraCommand.Dispose()
L         Return GetOracleResult
      End Function
```

Figure 9.59   The codes for our second Web method GetOracleInsert().

C)   All used data objects are declared here, such as the Connection, Command, and DataReader objects. A returned object **GetOracleResult** that is instantiated from our base class **OracleInsertBase** is also created and it will be returned to the calling procedure with the queried course information.

D)   Initially, we set the running status of our Web method to ok.

E)   The user-defined function **OracleConn()** is called to connect to our sample database. A warning message is assigned to the member data in our returned object and the user-defined subroutine **ReportError()** is executed to report any exception occurred during this connection. The Web method is exited if an error occurs for this connection.

F)   The Command object is initialized with appropriate properties such as the Connection object, command type, and command text.

G)   The real input parameter **FacultyName** is assigned to the dynamic parameter **:fname** using the **Add()** method.

H)   The ExecuteReader() method is called to trigger the DataReader and perform the data query. This method is a read-only method and the returned reading result is assigned to the DataReader object **oraReader**.

I)   By checking the **HasRows** property of the DataReader, we can determine whether this reading is successful or not. If this reading is successful (**HasRows=True**), the user-defined subroutine **FillCourseReader()**, whose detailed codes will be discussed below, is called to assign the returned **COURSE_ID** to each associated member data in our returned object **GetOracleResult**.

J) Otherwise if this reading is failed, a warning message is assigned to our member data **OracleInsertError** in our returned object and this error is reported by calling the subroutine **ReportError()**.

K) A cleaning job is performed to release all data objects used in this Web method.

L) The returned object that contains all queried **COURSE_ID** is returned to the calling procedure.

The detailed codes for our user-defined subroutine **FillCourseReader()** are shown in Figure 9.60.

The function of this piece of codes is straightforward without tricks. A **While** loop is used to continuously pick up each **COURSE_ID** whose column index is zero from the Course table, convert it to a string, and assign it to the **CourseID()** string array defined in our base class **OracleInsertBase**.

Now let's test this Web method by running this project. Click on the **IIS Express** button to run our project and the built-in Web interface is displayed, which is shown in Figure 9.61.

Click on the first Web method **GetOracleInsert** and enter the faculty name **Ying Bai** into the **FacultyName** box in the next built-in Web interface, which is shown in Figure 9.62.

Click on the **Invoke** button to execute this Web method. The running result of this method is shown in Figure 9.63.

It can be seen that all courses (exactly all **COURSE_ID**), including our new inserted course **CSE-556**, taught by the selected faculty **Ying Bai**, are listed in an XML format.

Our second Web method is successful. Click on the **Close** button that is located at the upper-right corner of this page to terminate our Web service project. Then go to **File | Save All** to save all methods we have developed.

Figure 9.60 The codes for the subroutine FillCourseReader().

Figure 9.61 The running status of our Web service project. *Source:* Oracle Corporation.

Figure 9.62 The input parameter for the Web method GetOracleInsert(). *Source:* Oracle Corporation.

Figure 9.63 The running result of our Web method GetOracleInsert(). *Source:* Oracle Corporation.

Next let's take care of building our third Web method `OracleInsertDataSet()` to insert data into the Course table using the DataSet method.

9.4.2.4 Develop the Third Web Method OracleInsertDataSet()

The function of this Web method is similar to that of the first Web method, which is to insert a new course record into the **COURSE** table based on the selected faculty member. The difference is that this Web method uses multi-query to insert a new course record into the **COURSE** table and uses a DataSet as the returned object. Furthermore, the returned DataSet contains the updated **COURSE** table that includes the new inserted course record. The advantages of using a DataSet as the returned object are

1) Unlike Web methods 1 and 2, which are a pair of methods and the first one is used to insert data into the database and the second one is used to retrieve the new inserted data from the database

to confirm the data insertion, Web method 3 contains both data insertion and retrieving functions. Later when a client project is developed to consume this Web service, methods 1 and 2 must be called together from that client project to perform both data insertion and data validation jobs. However, method 3 has both data insertion and data validation functions, so it can be called independently.

2) Because a DataSet is returned, we do not need to create any new instance for our customer class as the returned object. However, in order to report or log on any exception encountered during the project runs, we still need to create and use an instance of our customer class to handle those error-processing issues.

Create a new Web method `OracleInsertDataSet()` and enter the codes that are shown in Figure 9.64 into this method.

Let's have a closer look at the codes in this Web method to see how they work.

A) The name of the Web method is `OracleInsertDataSet()`. Seven input parameters are passed into this method as a new inserted record, and this method returns a DataSet, thus the returned data type is DataSet.

B) The data insertion query string is declared here. In fact, totally we have three query strings in this method. The first two queries are used to perform the data insertion and the third one is used to retrieve the new inserted data from the database to validate the data insertion. For the data insertion, first we need to perform a query to the **FACULTY** table to get the matched **FACULTY_ID** based on the input faculty name since there is no faculty name column available in the **COURSE** table. Second we can insert a new course record into the **COURSE** table by executing another query based on the **FACULTY_ID** obtained from the first query. The query string declared here is the second query string.

C) All data objects and variables used in this Web method are declared here, which include the Connection, Commands, DataAdapter, DataSet, and an instance of our customer class `OracleInsertResult`. The integer variable `intResult` is used to hold the returned value from calling the ExecuteNonQuery() method. The string variable `FacultyID` is used to reserve the **FACULTY_ID** that is obtained from the first query. Here three `OracleCommand` objects, `oraCmd0`, `oraCmd1`, and `oraCmd2`, are declared since we need to perform thee different query operations. According to Microsoft ADO.NET regulations, different Command objects must be used if more than one Command object is utilized in one subroutine or function. Otherwise, a single Command object cannot be used to handle different query operations with same Connection object.

D) The member data `OracleInsertOK` is initialized to the normal case.

E) The user-defined subroutine procedure `OracleConn()` is called to perform the database connection. A warning message will be displayed and reported using the subroutine `ReportError()` if this connection encountered any error.

F) The first Command object `oraCmd0` is initialized to perform the first query and get **FACULTY_ID** from the **FACULTY** table based on the input faculty name.

G) The first query string is assigned to the CommandText property.

H) The dynamic parameter `:fname` is assigned with the actual input parameter `FacultyName`.

I) The ExecuteScalar() method of the Command object is called to perform the first query to pick up the **FACULTY_ID** and assign it to the local string variable `FacultyID`. One point to be noted is the data type that the ExecuteScalar() method returned. An `Object` type is returned from calling of this method in the normal case, but it can be automatically converted to a `String` type by Visual Basic.NET if it is assigned to a variable with the `String` type.

```
  WebServiceOracleInsert          ▼      OracleInsertDataSet          ▼

A   <WebMethod()> _
    Public Function OracleInsertDataSet(ByVal FacultyName As String, ByVal CourseID As String, _
              ByVal Course As String, ByVal Schedule As String, ByVal Classroom As String, ByVal Credit As Integer, _
              ByVal Enroll As Integer) As DataSet
B   Dim cmdString As String = "INSERT INTO Course (course_id, course, credit, classroom, schedule, enrollment, " +
                  " faculty_id)  VALUES  (:course_id, :course, :credit, :classroom, :schedule, :enrollment, :faculty_id)"
C   Dim oraConnection As New OracleConnection
    Dim SetOracleResult As New OracleInsertResult
    Dim oraCmd0, oraCmd1, oraCmd2 As New OracleCommand

    Dim CourseAdapter As New OracleDataAdapter
    Dim dsCourse As New DataSet
    Dim intResult As Integer
    Dim FacultyID As String
D   SetOracleResult.OracleInsertOK = True
E   oraConnection = OracleConn()
    If oraConnection Is Nothing Then
       SetOracleResult.OracleInsertError = "Database connection is failed"
       ReportError(SetOracleResult)
       Return Nothing
    End If
F   oraCmd0.Connection = oraConnection
    oraCmd0.CommandType = CommandType.Text
G   oraCmd0.CommandText = "SELECT faculty_id FROM Faculty WHERE faculty_name = :fname"
H   oraCmd0.Parameters.Add(":fname", OracleDbType.VarChar).Value = FacultyName
I   FacultyID = oraCmd0.ExecuteScalar()
J   oraCmd1.Connection = oraConnection
K   oraCmd1.CommandType = CommandType.Text
    oraCmd1.CommandText = cmdString
    oraCmd1.Parameters.Clear()
    oraCmd1.Parameters.Add(":course_id", OracleDbType.Char).Value = CourseID
    oraCmd1.Parameters.Add(":course", OracleDbType.Char).Value = Course
    oraCmd1.Parameters.Add(":credit", OracleDbType.Number).Value = Credit
    oraCmd1.Parameters.Add(":classroom", OracleDbType.Char).Value = Classroom
    oraCmd1.Parameters.Add(":schedule", OracleDbType.Char).Value = Schedule
    oraCmd1.Parameters.Add(":enrollment", OracleDbType.Number).Value = Enroll
    oraCmd1.Parameters.Add(":faculty_id", OracleDbType.VarChar).Value = FacultyID
L   CourseAdapter.InsertCommand = oraCmd1
M   intResult = CourseAdapter.InsertCommand.ExecuteNonQuery()
N   If intResult = 0 Then
       SetOracleResult.OracleInsertError = "No matched course found"
       ReportError(SetOracleResult)
    End If
O   oraCmd2.Connection = oraConnection
    oraCmd2.CommandType = CommandType.Text
    oraCmd2.CommandText = "SELECT * FROM Course WHERE faculty_id = :FacultyID"
P   oraCmd2.Parameters.Add(":FacultyID", OracleDbType.VarChar).Value = FacultyID
Q   CourseAdapter.SelectCommand = oraCmd2
R   CourseAdapter.Fill(dsCourse, "Course")
S   CourseAdapter.Dispose()
    CourseAdapter = Nothing
    If oraConnection IsNot Nothing Then oraConnection.Close()
    oraConnection = Nothing
    oraCmd0.Dispose()
    oraCmd1.Dispose()
    oraCmd2.Dispose()
T   Return dsCourse
    End Function
```

Figure 9.64   The codes for the Web method OracleInsertDataSet().

J) The second query string is assigned to the CommandText property of the second Command object `oraCmd1` to make it ready to perform the second query – insert a new course record into the `COURSE` table.

K) All seven input parameters to the `INSERT` command are initialized by assigning them with the actual input values. The point to be noted is the data types of two parameters, `credit` and `enrollment`. Both are integers, so the `OracleDbType.Number` is used for both of them.

L) The initialized Command object `oraCmd1` is assigned to the InsertCommand property of the DataAdapter.

M) The ExecuteNonQuery() method is called to perform this data insertion query to insert a new course record into the `COURSE` table in our sample database. This method will return an integer to indicate the number of rows that have been successfully inserted into the database.

N) If this returned integer is zero, which means that no row has been inserted into the database and this insertion is failed, a warning message is assigned to the member data `OracleInsertError` and our subroutine `ReportError()` is called to report this error.

O) The third query string, which is used to retrieve all courses, including the new inserted course, from the database based on the input `FACULTY_ID`, is assigned to the CommandText property of the third Command object `oraCmd2`.

P) The dynamic parameter `FacultyID` is initialized with the actual `FACULTY_ID` obtained from the first query as we did above.

Q) The third Command object, `oraCmd2`, is assigned to the SelectCommand property of the DataAdapter.

R) The `Fill()` method of the DataAdapter is executed to retrieve all courses, including the new inserted courses, from the database and add them into the DataSet `dsCourse`.

S) A cleaning job is performed to release all objects used in this Web method.

T) Finally, the DataSet that contains the updated course information is returned to the calling procedure.

Compare with the first Web method, it looks like that more codes are involved in this method. Yes it is true. However, this method has two functionalities with three queries: inserting data into the database and validating the inserted data from the database. In order to validate the data insertion for the first method, the second Web method must be executed. Therefore, from the point of view of data insertion and data validation process, the third Web method has less code compared with the first one.

Now let's run our Web service project to test this Web method using the built-in Web interface. Click on the `IIS Express` button to run the project and click on our third Web method `OracleInsertDataSet` from the built-in Web interface to start it. The parameters wizard is displayed, which is shown in Figure 9.65. Enter the following parameters into each associated `Value` box as the data of a new course:

- FacultyName: `Ying Bai`
- CourseID: `CSE-688`
- Course: `Advanced Deep Learning`
- Schedule: `T-H: 9:30-10:45 AM`
- Classroom: `MTC-109`
- Credit: `3`
- Enroll: `35`

Your finished parameter wizard should match one that is shown in Figure 9.65.

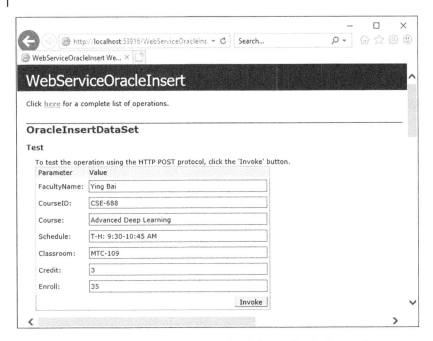

Figure 9.65 The finished input parameter wizard. *Source:* Oracle Corporation.

Figure 9.66 The running result of the third Web method. *Source:* Oracle Corporation.

Click on the **Invoke** button to run this Web method to perform this new course insertion. The running result is shown in Figure 9.66.

All six courses, including the sixth course **CSE-688** that is the new inserted course, are displayed in the XML format or tags in this running result interface.

A point to be noted is that you can only insert this new course record into the database one time. Another point is that when you use multiple Command objects for a single subroutine or function with multi-query, you must create multiple Command objects, and you cannot use only one Command object to handle multiple queries since this is required by Microsoft ADO.NET regulations.

Click on the **Close** button that is located at the upper-right corner of this Web interface to terminate our service. A complete Web service project **WebServiceOracleInsert Project** can be found from the folder Class **DB Projects\Chapter 9** that is located under the **Students** folder at the Wiley ftp site (refer to Figure 1.2 in Chapter 1).

Next let's develop our fourth Web method.

9.4.2.5 Develop the Fourth Web Method GetOracleInsertCourse()

The function of this method is to retrieve the detailed course information from the database based on the input **COURSE_ID**. This method can be consumed by a client project when users want to get the detailed course information such as the course name, credit, schedule, classroom, enrollment, and **FACULTY_ID** when a **COURSE_ID** is selected from the **CourseList** ListBox control.

Because this query is a single query, you can use either a normal query, or a stored procedure if you want to reduce the coding load for this method. Relatively speaking, a stored procedure is more efficient compared with a normal query, so we prefer to use a stored procedure to perform this query.

Now let's first create our stored procedure **WEB_SELECTCOURSESP()**.

9.4.2.5.1 *Create an Oracle Package and Add a Stored Procedure*   As we discussed in Section 5.6.7.3 in Chapter 5, in order to retrieve any data item from an Oracle database via a stored procedure, one must create an Oracle Package and embed a stored procedure into that Package. Thus, let's first create our Oracle Package **WEB_SELCOURSEPKG** and then embed a stored procedure **WEB_SELECTCOURSESP** into it.

Open the Oracle SQL Developer and connect to our sample database folder **CSE_DEPT**. Then expand the **Other Users** and our database schema **CSE_DEPT** folder, right-click on the **Packages** folder, and select the **New Package** item to open the Create Package wizard.

1) Enter **WEB_SELCOURSEPKG** into the **Name** box and click on the **OK** button to continue.
2) On the opened Package Definition wizard, enter the codes shown in Figure 9.67 into this Package Body as our procedure declaration part. Click on the **Compile** item to build and save this declaration section.

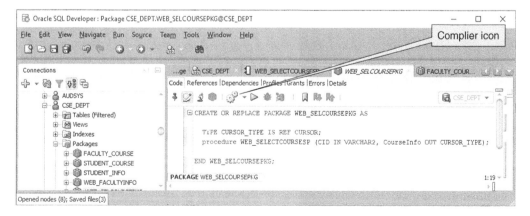

Figure 9.67 The declaration codes for the package and stored procedure. *Source:* Oracle Corporation.

3) Now right-click on our new created package, **WEB_SELCOURSEPKG**, under the **Packages** folder and select the **Create Body** item to add Package Body into this package.
4) On the opened **Package Body** wizard, enter the codes that are highlighted and shown in Figure 9.68 into this body wizard.
5) Click on the drop-down arrow and select **Compile** item to compile this Package Body. A **Compiled** message should be displayed in the Message-Log window if this compiling is successful.
6) Your finished package, **WEB_SELCOURSEPKG**, is shown in Figure 9.69.

Let's have a closer look at this piece of codes to see how it works (Figure 9.68).

A) The **OPEN CourseInfo FOR** command is used to assign the returned data columns from the following query to the cursor variable **CourseInfo**.
B) The **SELECT** query is executed to get all columns from the **COURSE** table.
C) The input argument, **CID**, is assigned to the **COURSE_ID** column as a query criterion for this package.

To test this package in this Oracle SQL Developer environment, click on the green arrow (**Run**) icon on the task bar, as shown in Figure 9.69, to run this package. The opened Run PL/SQL wizard is displayed to allow users to enter a valid **COURSE_ID** to retrieve back all detailed course information for this course.

```
CREATE OR REPLACE PACKAGE BODY WEB_SELCOURSEPKG AS

procedure WEB_SELECTCOURSESP (CID IN VARCHAR2, CourseInfo OUT CURSOR_TYPE) AS
BEGIN
A    OPEN CourseInfo FOR
B      SELECT course, credit, classroom, schedule, enrollment, faculty_id FROM CSE_DEPT.course
C      WHERE course_id = CID;
     END WEB_SELECTCOURSESP;

END WEB_SELCOURSEPKG;
```

Figure 9.68 The finished Package Body wizard.

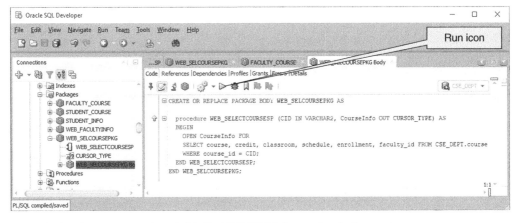

Figure 9.69 The finished package WEB_SELCOURSEPKG. *Source:* Oracle Corporation.

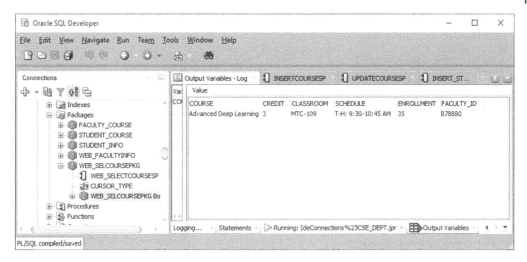

Figure 9.70 The running result of package WEB_SELCOURSEPKG. *Source:* Oracle Corporation.

Enter **CSE-688** into the **Value** box in this wizard as the input **COURSE_ID** and click on the **OK** button to run this stored procedure. You may need to redo the system login process to perform this query.

The running result is displayed in the **Ourput Variables** window, which is shown in Figure 9.70. All queried six columns, which include detailed information for the selected course, are retrieved from our sample database, exactly from the Course table, and displayed in this window. Our stored procedure works fine. Go to **File | Save All** in the Oracle SQL Developer to save our package and procedure. Then you can close this Developer by clicking on the Close button on the upper-right corner of this tool.

9.4.2.5.2 Develop Codes to Call the Stored Procedure WEB_SELECTCOURSESP
Now let's develop the codes for our fourth Web method **GetOracleInsertCourse()** to call our stored procedure to perform the detailed course information query.

Open the main service page **WebServiceOracleInsert.asmx** and add the codes that are shown in Figure 9.71 into this page to create this Web method.

Let's take a look at the codes in this Web method to see how they work.

A) The name of the Web method is **GetOracleInsertCourse** and it returns an instance of our returned class **OracleInsertResult**. The returned instance contains the detailed course information.

B) The content of the query string is the name of the package and the stored procedure we developed in the last section. This is required if a stored procedure is used and called to perform a data query. This name must be exactly identical with the name of the package and the stored procedure we developed, otherwise a running error may be encountered. The format of this name must be in the form of **package_name.stored_procedure_name**.

C) Some data objects such as the Connection and the DataReader are created here. Also a returned instance of our derived class is also created.

D) The subroutine **OracleConn()** is called to perform the database connection. A warning message is displayed and reported using the subroutine **ReportError()** if any error is encountered during the database connection process.

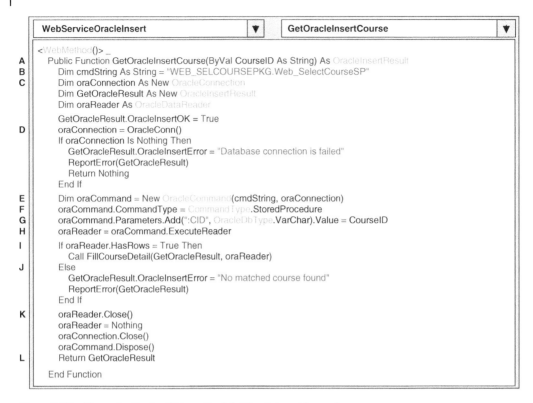

Figure 9.71 The codes for the Web method GetOracleInsertCourse().

E) The Command object is created with two arguments: query string and connection object. The coding load can be reduced but the working load cannot when creating a Command object in this way. As you know, the Command class has four kinds of constructors and we used the third one here.

F) The CommandType property of the Command object must be set to the value of **StoredProcedure** since we need to call a stored procedure to perform this course information query in this method.

G) The dynamic parameter **:CID** is assigned with the actual parameter **CourseID** that will be entered as an input parameter by the user as the project runs. One point to be noted is that the nominal name of this dynamic parameter must be identical with the name of input parameter defined in the stored procedure we developed in the last section.

H) After the Command object is initialized, the ExecuteReader() method is called to trigger the DataReader and to run the stored procedure to perform the course information query. The returned course information is stored to the DataReader.

I) By checking the **HasRows** property of the DataReader, we can determine whether the course information query is successful or not. If this property is **True**, which means that at least one row has been found and returned from our database, the subroutine **FillCourseDetail()**, whose detailed codes are shown in Figure 9.72, is executed to assign each piece of course information to the associated member data defined in our derived class, and an instance of this class will be returned as this method is done.

J) Otherwise if this property returns **False**, which means that no row has been selected and returned from our database, a warning message is displayed and reported using the subroutine **ReportError()**.

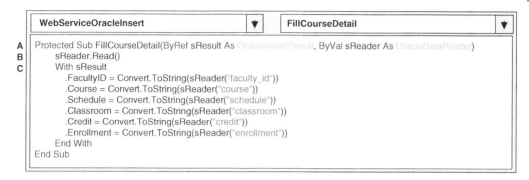

Figure 9.72 The codes for the subroutine FillCourseDetail().

K) A cleaning job is performed to release all data objects used in this Web method.
L) Finally, an instance of our returned class OracleInsertResult, **GetOracleResult** that contains the queried course detailed information, is returned to the calling procedure.

The detailed codes for the subroutine **FillCourseDetail()** are shown in Figure 9.72. Let's have a closer look at this piece of codes to see how it works.

A) Two arguments are passed into this subroutine: the first one is our returned object that contains all member data and the second one is the DataReader that contains queried course information. The point is that the passing mode for the first argument is passing-by-reference, which means that an address of our returned object is passed into this subroutine. In this way, all modified member data that contain the course information in this returned object can be returned to the calling procedure from our Web method – **GetOracleInsertCourse()**. From this point of view, this subroutine works just as a function and our object can be returned as this subroutine is completed.
B) The **Read()** method of the DataReader is executed to read course record from the DataReader.
C) A **With...End With** block is executed to assign each column of queried course record to the associated member data in our derived class. A **Convert.ToString()** class method is used to convert all data to strings before this assignment.

Now let's run our project to test this Web method. Click on the **IIS Express** button to run the project. Select our Web method **GetOracleInsertCourse** from the built-in Web interface and enter **CSE-688** as the **COURSE_ID** into the **Value** box. Then click on the **Invoke** button to run this Web method. The running result is shown in Figure 9.73.

Six pieces of course information are displayed in XML tags except the **COURSE_ID**. We defined this member data as a string array with a dimension of 11. Keep in mind that the index of an array starts from 0, not 1. Therefore, the size of our array **CourseID(10)** is 11. This member data is used for our second Web method, **GetOracleInsert()**, which returns an array contains all retrieved **COURSE_ID**. Since we did not use it in this method, eleven elements of this **CourseID** array are set to **true** and displayed in this resulting file.

Click on the **Close** button that is located at the upper-right corner of this Web interface to terminate our service. A complete Web service project **WebServiceOracleInsert Project** that contains all of those four Web methods can be found from the folder **Class DB Projects\Chapter 9** that is located under the **Students** folder at the Wiley ftp site (refer to Figure 1.2 in Chapter 1).

At this point, we have finished all code developing jobs in our Web service project in the server side. Next, we need to develop some professional Windows-based and Web-based application

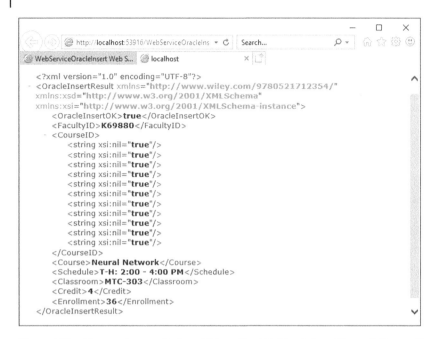

Figure 9.73 The running result of our Web method GetOracleInsertCourse(). *Source*: Oracle Corporation.

projects with beautiful GUIs to use or to consume the Web service we built in this Web service project `WebServiceOracleLInsert Project`. Those Windows-based and Web-based applications can be considered as Web service clients.

However, before we can continue, we need to handle some possible error, `ORA-28001: Password expired`, for our Oracle XE 18c database as we run our projects. Because the password set for our sample database `CSE_DEPT` needs to be updated periodically according to the regulations managed by the Oracle XE Database engine.

9.4.2.5.3 *Solve the Password Expired Error – ORA 28001*

To solve this error, we need to open and use Oracle SQL Developer to change our password periodically. Follow steps below to complete this password change process:

1) Open the Oracle SQL Developer and complete the login process for the Oracle XE 18c database system.
2) Expand the system database `CSE_DEPT` and `Other Users` folders and select our sample database schema, `CSE_DEPT`.
3) Right-click on our schema `CSE_DEPT` and select the `Edit User` item to open the `Edit User` wizard, which is shown in Figure 9.74.
4) You can see that our password has expired and this has been indicated by a check in the `Password Expired` checkbox.
5) Enter the new password into both the `New Password` and the `Confirm Password` boxes, as shown in Figure 9.74. In our case, we used `oracle18c` as our new password. Uncheck the `Password Expired` checkbox to remove this indication.
6) Press the `Apply` button to complete this password changing process.
7) A successful message is displayed to indicate this password changing process.

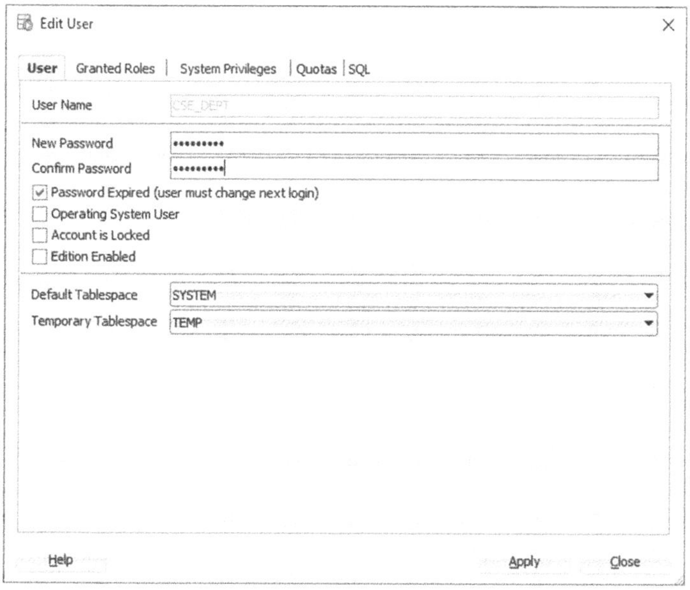

Figure 9.74 The opened Edit User wizard. *Source:* Oracle Corporation.

Wait a moment, the changing process has not been done! You also need to change this password you set up in the `ConnectionString` in the `Web.config` file. Otherwise, a running login error may be encountered if this step were not performed.

While this error can be fixed by changing the password setup in our sample database, but this changing brought a lot of inconveniences to us since we have to change all passwords we used in our previous projects and it is very time-consuming to do these modifications. Is there any other way to solve this issue? The answer is Yes. How? We may be able to redo this password changing to get the original password `oracle_18c` back and continue to use it in all our projects. Just try to do this, and you would find that it is working! and we do not need to do any change to our password in all our projects.

Now we can continue to build our project and use our sample database.

9.4.3 Build Windows-based Web Service Clients to Consume the Web Services

To use or consume a Web service, first we need to create a Web service proxy class in our Windows-based or Web-based applications. Then we can create a new instance of the Web service proxy class and execute the desired Web methods located in that Web service class. The process of creating a Web service proxy class is equivalent to add a Web reference to our Windows-based or Web-based applications.

9.4.3.1 Create a Windows-Based Consume Project and a Web Service Proxy Class

Basically, adding a Web reference to our Windows-based or Web-based applications is to execute a searching process. During this process, Visual Studio.NET 2019 will try to find all Web services available to our applications.

Open Visual Studio.NET 2019 in the Administrator mode and create a new Visual Basic Windows Forms App(.NET Framework) or Windows-based project and name it as `WinClientOracleInsert Project` and a Solution `WinClientOracleInsert Solution`, save them in the folder `C:\ Chapter 9`. Now let's add a Web reference to our new project.

As we mentioned in Section 9.3.10.1, there are two ways to select the desired Web service and add it as a reference to our client project. We can use the second way to find our Web service. Perform the following operations to add this Web reference:

1) Open our Web service project `WebServiceOracleInsert Project` and click on the `IIS Express` button to run it.
2) Copy the URL from the `Address` bar in our running Web service project.
3) Then open our Windows-based client project `WinClientOracleInsert Project`.
4) Right-click on our client project `WinClientOracleInsert Project` from the Solution Explorer window and select the item `Add│Service Reference` from the popup menu to open the Add Service Reference wizard.
5) Click on the `Advanced` button located at the lower-left corner on this wizard to open the Service Reference Settings wizard.
6) Click on the `Add Web Reference` button to open the Add Web Reference wizard, which is shown in Figure 9.75.
7) Paste that URL we copied in step 2 into the URL box in the Add Web Reference wizard and click on the `Arrow` button to enable the Visual Studio.NET to begin to search it.
8) When the Web service is found, the name of our Web service is displayed in the right pane, which is shown in Figure 9.75.
9) Alternately you can change the name for this Web reference from `localhost` to any meaningful name such as `WS_OracleInsert` in our case. Click on the `Add Reference` button to add this Web service as a reference to our new client project.
10) Click on the `Close` button from our Web service built-in Web interface window to terminate our Web service project.

Figure 9.75 The finished Add Web Reference wizard. *Source:* Oracle Corporation.

Immediately you can find that the Web service **WS_OracleInsert**, which is under the folder **Web References**, has been added into the Solution Explorer window in our client project. This reference is the so-called Web service proxy class.

Next let's develop the GUI by adding useful controls to interface to our Web service and to display the queried course information.

9.4.3.2 Develop the Graphic User Interface for the Client Project

Perform the following modifications to our new client project:

1) Rename the Form File object from the default name **Form1.vb** to our desired name **WinClient Form.vb**.
2) Rename the Window Form object from the default name **Form1** to our desired name **CourseForm** by modifying the **Name** property of the form window.
3) Rename the form title from the default title **Form1** to **CSE_DEPT Course Form** by modifying the **Text** property of the form.
4) Change the **StartPosition** property of the form window to **CenterScreen**.

To save the time and the space, we can use the Course Form located in the project **OracleUpdateDeleteRTObject Project** we developed in Chapter 7 as our GUI. You can find this project from the folder **Class DB Projects\Chapter 7** that is located under the **Students** folder at the Wiley ftp site (refer to Figure 1.2 in Chapter 1). Perform the following operations to add this Course Form into our new client project:

1) Open the project **OracleUpdateDeleteRTObject Project** and the Course Form window from the above Wiley ftp site.
2) Select all controls from that form by going to the item **Edit|Select All** and go to **Edit|Copy** menu item to copy all controls selected from this form window.
3) Return to our Windows-based Web service client project **WinClientOracleInsert Project**, open our form window **CourseForm**, and paste those controls we copied from step 2 into this form.

Your finished GUI is shown in Figure 9.76.

The purpose of the **Query Method** combo box control is used to select two different methods developed in our Web service project to get our desired course information:

1) **Stored Procedure Method** that uses a stored procedure to insert a new course record into the database.
2) **DataSet Method** that uses three queries to insert a new course record into the database and return a DataSet that contains the detailed course information.

The Faculty Name combo box control is used to select a desired faculty member as the input parameter to the Web methods to insert and pick up the desired course record.

In this application, only the **Insert**, **Select**, and **Back** buttons are used. The **Insert** button is used to trigger a data insertion action, the **Select** button is to trigger a data validation action to confirm that data insertion, and the **Back** button is used to terminate our project.

The detailed functions of this project are

1) **Insert Data Using the Stored Procedure Method**: when the project runs, as this method and a faculty name as well as a new course record that is stored in six textboxes have been selected and entered, and then the **Insert** button is clicked by the user. Our client project

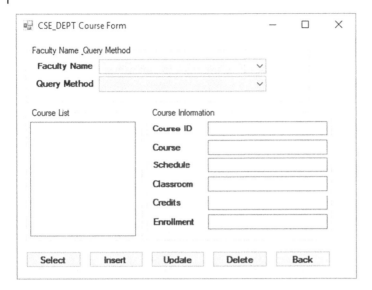

Figure 9.76 The finished graphic user interface. *Source:* Used with permission from Microsoft.

will be connected to our Web service via the Web reference we provided, and the selected Web method `SetOracleInsertSP()` will be called to run the stored procedure to insert that new course record into our sample database.

2) **`Insert Data Using the DataSet Method`**: if this method is selected, the Web method `OracleInsertDataSet()` developed in our Web service will be called to execute two queries to perform this new course insertion. Also all courses, which include the new inserted course, taught by the selected faculty that works as an input to this method will be retrieved and stored into a DataSet by another query, and that DataSet will be returned to our client project.

3) **`Validate Data Insertion Using the Stored Procedure Method`**: to confirm this data insertion, the `Select` button, exactly the `Select` button's click event procedure we will develop below, is used to validate that data insertion. If the `Stored Procedure Method` is selected, the Web method `GetOracleInsert()` is called to perform a joined-table query to retrieve all `COURSE_ID`, which include the new inserted `COURSE_ID`, from the database and stored them into an instance of our returned class `OracleInsertResult` in our Web service. This instance will be returned to our client project and all `COURSE_ID` stored in that instance will be taken out and displayed in the list box control `CourseList` in our client form window.

4) **`Validate Data Insertion Using the DataSet Method`**: if this method is selected and the `Select` button is clicked, the `Select` button's click event procedure we will develop below is executed to pick up all `COURSE_ID` from a DataSet that is returned in step 2 above. Also all `COURSE_ID` will be displayed in the list box control `CourseList` in our client form window.

5) **`Get Detailed Course Information for a Specific Course`**: when this method is selected and a `COURSE_ID` in the list box control `CourseList` is selected, the Web method `GetOracleInsertCourse()` in our Web service will be called to run a stored procedure to retrieve all six pieces of information related to that selected `COURSE_ID` and store them into an instance of our returned class `OracleInsertResult` in our Web service. This instance will be returned to our client project and all six pieces of course information stored in that instance will be taken out and displayed in six textbox controls in our client form window.

Now let's take care of the coding development for this project to connect to our Web service using the Web reference we developed in the last section to call the associated Web methods to perform the different data actions.

9.4.3.3 Develop the Code to Consume the Web Service

The coding development can be divided into the following four parts:

1) Initialize and terminate the client project.
2) Insert a new course record into the database using both methods.
3) Validate the data insertion using both methods.
4) Get the detailed information for a specific course using both methods.

Now let's start our coding process based on these four steps.

9.4.3.3.1 Develop the Codes to Initialize and Terminate the Client Project
This coding process includes the developing codes for the Form_Load event procedure, the **Back** button's click event procedure, and some other initializations such as some form-level variables.

Open our client project **WinClientOracleInsert Project** if it has not been opened. Then open the code window of this client project by clicking on the View Code button from the Solution Explorer window and enter the codes that are shown in Figure 9.77 into this code window. Let's have a closer look at this piece of codes to see how it works:

A) Four form-level variables are created here. The first one is a Boolean variable **dsFlag** and it is used to set a flag to indicate whether the **OracleInsertDataSet** Web method has been executed or not. Because this Web method performs both data insertion and data retrieving function, it can only be called once from the **Insert** button's click event procedure without

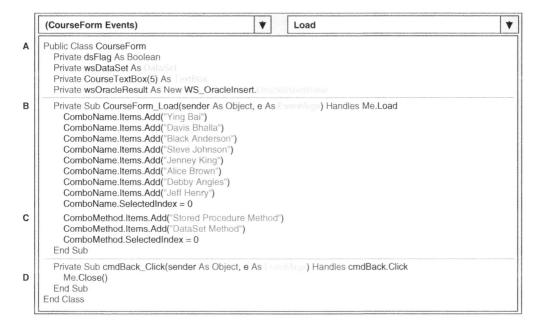

Figure 9.77 The codes of the Form_Load and Back button's event procedures.

needing to perform the data retrieving from the `Select` button's click event procedure. The second is a DataSet object since we need to use this DataSet in multiple event procedures and multiple processes in this project. The third one is a textbox array `CourseTextBox()` and it is used to hold all six pieces of course information to be inserted into our database later. The fourth one is an instance of the returned class `OracleInsertResult` developed in our Web service project, and this instance is generated from our base class and it is used to receive the returned instance from calling the first Web method `SetOracleInsertSP()` when perform a data insertion.

B) In the Form_Load event procedure, eight default faculty members are added into the Faculty Name combo box control using the `Add()` method. These faculty members will be displayed and selected by the user as an input parameter to call different Web methods to perform either data insertion or data validation operation as the project runs. The first faculty member is selected as the default one by setting the SelectedIndex property to zero.

C) Two Web methods, `Stored Procedure Method` and `DataSet Method`, are added into the Query Method combo box control, and these methods can be selected by the user to call the associated Web method to perform the desired data operation as the project runs. Similarly, the first method, the `Stored Procedure Method`, is selected as the default one.

D) The codes for the `Back` button's click event procedure are very simple. The system method `Me.Close()` is called to terminate our client project.

The first coding job is done and let's continue to perform the next coding process.

9.4.3.3.2 Develop the Codes to Insert a New Course Record into the Database
This coding development can be divided into two parts based on two methods: the `Stored Procedure Method` and the `DataSet Method`. Because of the similarity between the codes in these two methods, we combine them together.

To insert a new course record into the database via our Web service, the following three jobs should have been completed before the `Insert` button can be clicked:

1) The Web method has been selected from the Query Method combo box control.
2) The faculty name has been selected from the Faculty Name combo box control.
3) Six textboxes have been filled with six pieces of information related to a new course to be inserted.

Besides those conditions, one more important requirement for this data insertion is that any new course record can only be inserted into the database by one time. In other words, no duplicated record can be inserted into the database. This duplication can be identified by checking the content of the textbox `Course ID`, or the column `COURSE_ID` in the Course table in the database. As you know, the `COURSE_ID` is the primary key in the Course table and each record is identified using this primary key. As long as the `COURSE_ID` is different, no duplication could be occurred. Based on this analysis, in order to avoid the duplicated insertion occurs, the `Insert` button should be disabled after a new course record is inserted into the database and it should be disabled until a different or a new `COURSE_ID` is entered into the `Course ID` textbox, which means that a new record is ready to be inserted into the database.

Keep this in mind and now let's start to develop the codes for the `Insert` button's click event procedure. Double-click on the `Insert` button from the Design View of our client project to open the `Insert` button's click event procedure. Then enter the codes that are shown in Figure 9.78 into this event procedure.

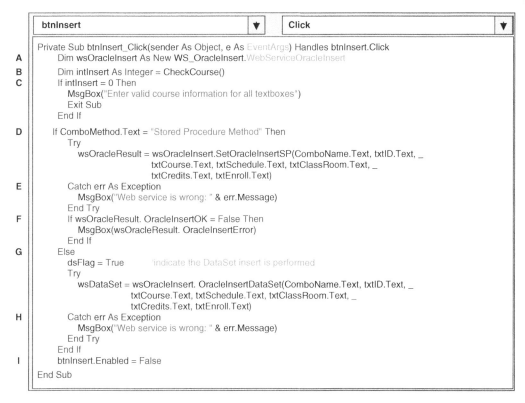

Figure 9.78 The codes for the Insert button's click event procedure.

Let's have a closer look at this piece of codes to see how it works:

A) An instance of the Web reference to our Web service or our proxy class is created here, since we need it to access our Web methods to perform different data actions. This instance works as a bridge between our client project and Web methods developed in our Web service project.

B) A user-defined function **CheckCourse()** is called to check whether all course-related textboxes have been filled with all pieces of course information.

C) If the returned value from calling that function is 0, which means that not all course information has been entered, a warning message is displayed to remind the user to fill all required course information to all textboxes.

D) If users selected the **Stored Procedure Method** to perform the data insertion, a **Try…Catch** block is used to call the Web method **SetOracleInsertSP()** with seven pieces of new course information as arguments to insert a new course record into the database. The calling result is returned and assigned to our form-level variable **wsOracleResult** that will be checked later.

E) If any error is encountered, the error message is displayed.

F) Besides those errors checking performed by the **Catch** statement, we also need to check the member data defined in our returned class to make sure that the running status of our Web method is fine. One of member data, **OracleInsertOK**, is used to store this running status. If this status is **False**, which means that something is wrong during the execution of this Web method, the error message is displayed using another member data **OracleInsertError** that stored the error source.

G) If users selected the **DataSet Method**, first the Boolean variable **dsFlag** is set to **True** to indicate that the Web method **OracleInsertDataSet()** has been executed once. This flag should be reset to **False** if users want to only retrieve the course information from the database using the **Select** button's event procedure, but they have not called this Web method to first insert a new course record. If this happened, a message is displayed to direct the users to first execute this Web method to insert a new record into the database. Another **Try...Catch** block is used to call the Web method **OracleInsertDataSet()** with seven pieces of new course information as arguments to insert a new course record into the database. In addition to performing the new course insertion, this Web method also performed a data query to retrieve all courses, including the new inserted course, from the database and assign them to the DataSet that will be returned to our client project.

H) If any system error is detected, the error message is displayed.

I) Finally, the **Insert** button is disabled to avoid multiple insertions of the same record into the database.

The codes for the user-defined function **CheckCourse()** are shown in Figure 9.79.

A) All six pieces of course information are assigned to six course-related textboxes that are integrated in an array.

B) A loop is executed to check whether any textbox is empty. If it is, the returned variable **ret** is returned with a default value of 0.

C) Otherwise, a successful value of 1 is returned to indicate that this checking is fine.

Another coding development is for the **Course ID** textbox, exactly to the **TextChanged** event procedure of the **Course ID** textbox and the Combo box, **ComboMethod**, exactly to the **SelectedIndexChanged** event. As we mentioned, the **Insert** button should be disabled after one course record has been inserted into the database to avoid the multi-insertion of the same data. However, this button should be enabled when a new different course record is ready to be inserted into the database. As soon as the content of the **Course ID** textbox is changed or the insert method is changed, which means that a new record is ready and the **Insert** button should be

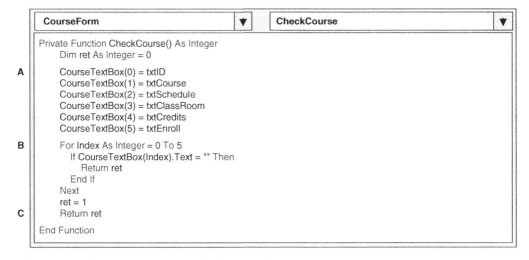

Figure 9.79 The codes for the user-defined function CheckCourse().

enabled. To do these codes, double-click on the textbox `Course ID` and Combo box `ComboMethod` from the Design View of our client project window to open both `TextChanged` and `SelectedIndexChanged` event procedures. Enter the following codes into these two event procedure:

```
btnInsert.Enabled = True
```

At this point, we have finished all coding developments for the data insertion process. Before we can continue to develop the rest of our project, we prefer to first run the client project to test this data insertion functionality.

The prerequisite to run our client project is to make sure that our Web service is in the running status in this local computer. To check and confirm that, open our Web service project `WebServiceOracleInsert Project` and click on the `IIS Express` button to run it. Then you may hide our Web service page by clicking on the `Minimize` button (make sure that our Web service is still in the running status even the page is hidden).

Now you should find that a small white icon has been added into the status bar on the bottom of the screen. This small white icon means that our Web service is in the running status and any client can access and use it now. The reason we hide our Web service page is that we do not need to keep our Web service page on the screen, but instead we need it in the background running status.

Also make sure that our `CourseForm` is the Startup Form by checking this from the Project Property Window.

Now run our Windows-based client project `WinClientOracleInsert Project` by clicking on the Start Debugging button. As the `CourseForm` window is displayed, perform the following two insertions using two Web methods with the following operations and parameters:

1) Insert the first new course record shown in Table 9.2 using the `Stored Procedure Method`. Click on the `Insert` button to finish this data insertion.
2) Insert the second new course record shown in Table 9.3 using the `DataSet Method`.

Click on the `Insert` button to finish these data insertion functions. Now click on the `Back` button to terminate our client project.

To confirm these two data insertions, open the Server Explorer or Oracle SQL Developer. Then open our sample database `CSE_DEPT` and our `Course` table. You can find that these two records have been added into our Course table in the last two rows.

Table 9.2 The first course record to be inserted.

Controls	Input Parameters
Method:	Stored Procedure Method
Faculty Name:	Ying Bai
Course ID:	CSE-678
Course Name:	Introduction to Neural Networks
Schedule:	T-H: 9:30-10:45 PM
Classroom:	MTC-348
Credits:	3
Enrollment:	30

Table 9.3 The second course record to be inserted.

Controls	Input Parameters
Method:	DataSet Method
Faculty Name:	Ying Bai
Course ID:	CSE-526
Course Name:	Embedded Microcontrollers
Schedule:	M-W-F: 9:00-9:55 AM
Classroom:	MTC-308
Credits:	3
Enrollment:	32

It is highly recommended to delete these two new records from our Course table after this checking since we may need to perform the same data insertions when we confirm these data insertions programmably in the following section.

9.4.3.3.3 Develop the Codes to Perform the Inserted Data Validation
To confirm or validate the data insertion, we can open our database and data table to check it. However, a professional way to do this confirmation is to use codes to perform this validation. In this section, we discuss how to perform this validation by developing the codes in the `Select` button's click event procedure in our client project.

As we mentioned in the previous sections, as this `Select` button is clicked after a new course insertion, all `COURSE_ID`, including the new inserted `COURSE_ID`, will be retrieved from the database and displayed in a ListBox control in this `CourseForm` window. This data validation is also divided into two parts according to the method adopted by the user: either the `Stored Procedure Method` or the `DataSet Method`. Different processes will be performed based on these two methods. Because of the codes similarity between these two methods, we combine these codes together and put them into this `Select` button's click event procedure.

Now double-click on the `Select` button from the Design View of our client project `WinClientOracleInsert Project` to open this event procedure and enter the codes that are shown in Figure 9.80 into this event procedure.

Let's take a closer look at this piece of codes to see how it works:

A) An instance of our Web service reference or proxy class is created and this instance works as a bridge to connect our client project with the Web methods developed in our Web service together.

B) If the `Stored Procedure Method` has been selected by the user, a `Try….Catch` block is used to call our Web method `GetSQLInsert()` with the selected faculty name as the input to retrieve all `COURSE_ID` from the database. This method returns an instance of our returned class defined in the Web service and this instance, which contains all `COURSE_ID` retrieved from the database, is assigned to our local variable `wsOracleResult` to be processed later. An error message is displayed if any error was encountered during the execution of this Web method.

C) In addition to the error checking performed by the system in the `Catch` statement, we also need to do our error checking by inspecting the status of the member data `OracleInsertOK`. The error source will be displayed if any error is occurred.

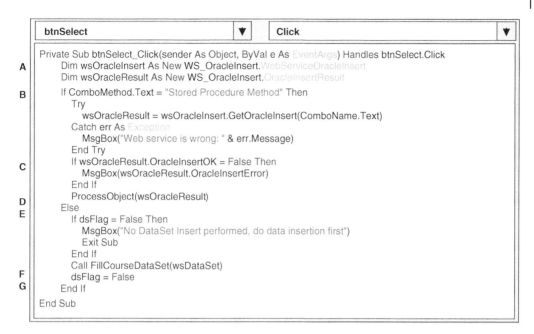

btnSelect	▼	Click	▼

```
     Private Sub btnSelect_Click(sender As Object, ByVal e As EventArgs) Handles btnSelect.Click
A       Dim wsOracleInsert As New WS_OracleInsert.WebServiceOracleInsert
        Dim wsOracleResult As New WS_OracleInsert.OracleInsertResult

B       If ComboMethod.Text = "Stored Procedure Method" Then
          Try
            wsOracleResult = wsOracleInsert.GetOracleInsert(ComboName.Text)
          Catch err As Exception
            MsgBox("Web service is wrong: " & err.Message)
          End Try
          If wsOracleResult.OracleInsertOK = False Then
C           MsgBox(wsOracleResult.OracleInsertError)
          End If
          ProcessObject(wsOracleResult)
D       Else
E         If dsFlag = False Then
            MsgBox("No DataSet Insert performed, do data insertion first")
            Exit Sub
          End If
          Call FillCourseDataSet(wsDataSet)
F         dsFlag = False
G       End If
     End Sub
```

Figure 9.80 The codes for the Select button's click event procedure.

D) If this Web method works fine, a user-defined subroutine **ProcessObject()**, whose detailed codes are shown in Figure 9.81 is called to extract all course columns from that returned instance **wsOracleResult** and add them into the **CourseList** box.

E) If the user selected the **DataSet Method**, first we need to check whether the Web method **OracleInsertDataSet()** has been executed or not by checking the status of the form-level variable **dsFlag**. Because when users use this method to retrieve the course information from the database, this method must have been executed once from the **Insert** button's click event procedure. The reason for that is because this method performs both data insertion and data retrieving action. An error may be encountered if you use this method to retrieve the course information from the **Select** button's click event procedure without first performing the data insertion from the **Insert** button's click event procedure since nothing has been inserted. Therefore, nothing can be obtained from the returned DataSet. If this **dsFlag** is **False**, which means that nothing has been inserted, a warning message is displayed to ask you to first perform the data insertion.

F) If the Web method **OracleInsertDataSet()** has been executed, a user-defined subroutine **FillCourseDataSet()**, whose detailed codes are shown in Figure 9.82, is called to fill the list box control with all retrieved **COURSE_ID**.

G) Finally, the **dsFlag** is reset to **False**.

The detailed codes for the subroutines **ProcessObject()** and **FillCourseListBox()** are shown in Figure 9.81.

Let's have a look at the codes in these two subroutines to see how they work:

A) First, we need to check the member data **OracleInsertOK** to make sure that the Web method is executed successfully. If it is, the subroutine **FillCourseListBox()** is called to fill all **COURSE_ID** contained in the returned instance to the list box control in our client form.

Figure 9.81 The codes for the subroutines ProcessObject() and FillCourseListBox().

B) Otherwise, a warning message is displayed if any error was encountered during the execution of that Web method.

C) In the subroutine `FillCourseListBox()`, a local integer variable `index` is created and it works as a loop number for a `For` loop to continuously pick up all `COURSE_ID` from the returned instance and add them into the list box control.

D) The course list box control is cleaned up first before any `COURSE_ID` can be added into it. This process is very important in displaying all `COURSE_ID`, otherwise all new `COURSE_ID` will be attached to the end of the original `COURSE_ID` in this control and the displaying result is messy.

E) A `For` loop is used to continuously pick up all `COURSE_ID` from the `CourseID()` array defined in our returned class `OracleInsertResult`. One point to be noted is the upper bound and the length of this array. The length or the size of this array is 11 but the upper bound of this array is 10 since the index of this array starts from 0, not 1. Therefore, the upper bound of this array is equal to the length of this array minus by 1. As long as the content of the `CourseID(index)` is not Null, the current selected `COURSE_ID` is added into the list box control using the `Add()` method.

The codes for the subroutine `FillCourseDataSet()` is shown in Figure 9.82. Let's have a look at the codes in this subroutine to see how they work:

A) Two objects, a DataTable and a DataRow, are declared at the beginning of this subroutine since we need to use them to perform the data extraction from the returned instance and add them into the list box control.

B) The list box control is first cleaned up to avoid messy displaying of multiple `COURSE_ID`.

C) The `CourseTable` object is initialized by assigning a new data table named "`Course`" embedded in a DataSet object `ds`.

D) A `For Each…In` loop is used to continuously pick up the first column that is the `COURSE_ID` column from all returned rows and add each of them into the list box control. One point to be noted is that the first column has an index value of 0, not 1, since the index starts from 0.

At this point, we finished all coding process for the `Select` button's click event procedure. In other words, all codes related to the data validation are done.

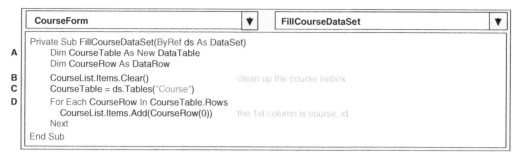

| CourseForm | ▼ | FillCourseDataSet | ▼ |

```
     Private Sub FillCourseDataSet(ByRef ds As DataSet)
A       Dim CourseTable As New DataTable
        Dim CourseRow As DataRow
B       CourseList.Items.Clear()                    'clean up the course listbox
C       CourseTable = ds.Tables("Course")
D       For Each CourseRow In CourseTable.Rows
           CourseList.Items.Add(CourseRow(0))       'the 1st column is course_id
        Next
     End Sub
```

Figure 9.82   The codes for the subroutine FillCourseDataSet().

Now let's run our client project to perform the data validation after the data insertion process. Before we can start to run the project, make sure that the following two conditions are met:

1) Our Web service is in the running status and this can be checked by locating a small white icon on the status bar on the bottom of the screen. If you cannot find this icon, open our Web service project **WebServiceOracleInsert Project** and click on the **IIS Express** button to run it. After the Web service starts to run, you can minimize the Web page but make sure that it is still in the running status.
2) Two new course records shown in Tables 9.2 and 9.3, which we inserted before by testing the **Insert** button's click event procedure, have been deleted from the Course table in our sample database since we want to insert the same course records in the following test.

Now click on the Start Debugging button to run our client project. Enter the same input parameters as shown in Table 9.2 and click on the **Insert** button to finish this data insertion using the **Stored Procedure Method**. Next, enter the same input parameters as shown in Table 9.3 and click on the **Insert** button to finish this data insertion using the **DataSet Method**.

To check or validate these data insertions, make sure that the selected method in the Query Method combo box is still the **DataSet Method** and the Faculty Name is **Ying Bai**.

Then click on the **Select** button to retrieve all **COURSE_ID** from the database. It can be found that all six courses taught by the selected faculty are listed in the list box control with the **COURSE_ID** as the identifier for each course.

To test the **Stored Procedure Method**, make sure that the **Stored Procedure Method** is selected from the Query Method combo box. Now you can select another faculty from the Faculty Name combo box control and click on the **Select** button to pick up all **COURSE_ID** taught by the that faculty. Then reselect the default Faculty Name **Ying Bai** and then click on the **Select** button to try to retrieve all **COURSE_ID** taught by the selected faculty. You can find that the same results as we obtained from using the **DataSet Method** are displayed in the list box control.

The running result or the data validation is shown in Figure 9.83. It can be found that our new inserted two courses, **CSE-668** and **CSE-526**, have been added and displayed in the list box control and our data insertion is successful. Click on the **Back** button to terminate our project.

Next, let's concentrate on the coding development to display the detailed course information for a selected **COURSE_ID** from the list box control.

9.4.3.3.4   *Develop the Codes to Get the Detailed Information for a Specific Course*   The function of this piece of codes is that the detailed course information, such as the course name, schedule, classroom, credit, and enrollment, will be displayed in the associated textbox control as the user clicked and

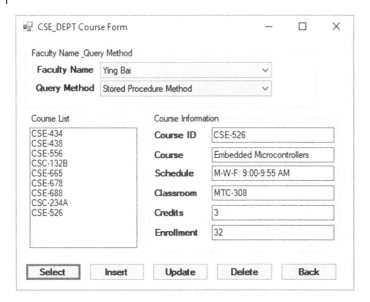

Figure 9.83 The running result of the data validation. *Source:* Used with permission from Microsoft.

selected one **COURSE_ID** from the list box control. Exactly the main coding job is performed inside the **SelectedIndexChanged** event procedure of the list box control **CourseList**. Because when user clicks or selects a **COURSE_ID** from the list box control, a SelectedIndexChanged event is issued and this event is passed to the associated SelectedIndexChanged event procedure to be processed.

To pick up the detailed course information for a selected **COURSE_ID**, the Web method **GetOracleInsertCourse()** in our Web service project **WebServiceOracleInsert Project** is called.

This method returns an instance of the returned class **OracleInsertResult** to our client project. The detailed course information is stored in that returned instance.

Double-click on the list box control **CourseList** from the Design View of our client project window to open the SelectedIndexChanged event procedure of the list box control and enter the codes that are shown in Figure 9.84 into this event procedure.

Let's take a closer look at this piece of codes to see how it works:

A) An instance of our Web service reference or the proxy class **wsOracleInsert** is created here. This instance works as a bridge between our client project and the Web methods developed in the Web service project.
B) A **Try…Catch** block is used to call the Web method **GetOracleInsertCourse()** with the selected **COURSE_ID** from the list box control as the argument to perform this course information retrieving. The selected **COURSE_ID** is stored in the **Text** property of the **CourseList** control.
C) An exception message is displayed if any error was encountered during the execution of this Web method and catched by the system method **Catch**.
D) In addition to the error checking performed by the system, we also need to perform our exception checking by inspecting the member data **OracleInsertOK** in the returned class **OracleInsertResult**. If this data value is **False**, which means that an application error was occurred during the running of this Web method, an error message is displayed and the subroutine is exited.

Figure 9.84   The codes for the SelectedIndexChanged() event procedure.

E) If everything is fine, a user-defined subroutine `FillCourseDetail()` is executed to extract the detailed course information from the returned instance and assign it to each associated textbox control in our client Window Form.

F) The codes for the subroutine `FillCourseDetail()` are simple. The `COURSE_ID` can be directly obtained from the list box control and all other pieces of information can be extracted from the returned instance and assigned to the associated textbox.

When performing this function to get the detailed course information from the database, no difference is existed between the `Stored Procedure Method` and the `DataSet Method`. Both methods use the same process.

At this point, we have finished all coding jobs for our Windows-based client project. Now we can run the client project to test all functions of this project as well as the functions of our Web service project. Before we can do this, make sure that the following jobs have been performed:

1) Our Web service is in the running status and this can be checked by locating a small white icon on the status bar on the bottom of the screen. If you cannot find this icon, run our Web service project `WebServiceOracleInsert Project` first.

2) Two new course records shown in Tables 9.2 and 9.3, which we inserted before by testing the `Insert` button's click event procedure, should have been deleted from the Course table in our sample database since we want to insert the same course records in this test.

Now click on the Start Debugging button to run our client project. Insert two new courses by entering parameters listed in Tables 9.2 with `Stored Procedure Method` and 9.3 with `Data Set Method`. Make sure that the `Stored Procedure Method` is selected and then perform the data validation by clicking on the `Select` button. To get the detailed course information for the selected `COURSE_ID` from the list box control, click one `COURSE_ID`, and immediately the detailed information about the selected `COURSE_ID` is displayed in those associated textboxes, which is shown in Figure 9.85.

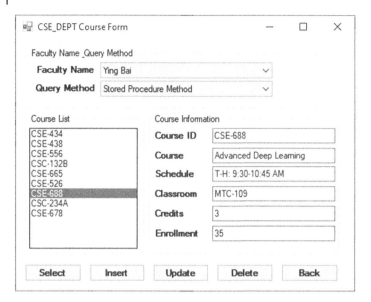

Figure 9.85 The running status of getting the detailed course information. *Source:* Used with permission from Microsoft.

Click on the **Back** button to terminate our client project.

A complete Windows-based Web service client project **WinClientOracleInsert Project** can be found from the folder **Class DB Projects\Chapter 9** that is located under the **Students** folder at the Wiley ftp site (refer to Figure 1.2 in Chapter 1).

9.4.4 Build Web-based Web Service Clients to Consume the Web Services

As we did in Section 9.3.11, it can be found that there is no significant difference between developing a Web-based client application and a Windows-based client project to consume a Web service. As long as the Web service is referenced by the Web-based client project, one can access and call any Web method developed in that Web service to perform the desired data queries via the Web-based client project. Visual Studio.NET will create the same document files, such as the Discovery Map file and the WDSL file, for the client project no matter this Web service is consumed by a Windows-based or a Web-based client application.

To save time and space, we can modify an existing ASP.NET Web Application **OracleWebInsert Project** we developed in Chapter 8 to make it as our new Web-based Web service client project **WebClientOracleInsert Project**. In fact, we can copy and rename that entire project as our new Web-based client project, but we prefer to create a new ASP.NET Web site project and only copy and modify the Course page.

This section can be developed in the following sequences:

1) Create a new ASP.NET Web Application (.NET Framework) for Visual Basic project **WebClientOracleInsert Project** and a Solution **WebClientOracleInsert Solution**, and add an existing Web page **Course.aspx** from the project **OracleWebInsert Project** into our new project.

2) Add a Web service reference to our new project and modify the Web form page **Course.aspx** to meet our data insertion requirements.

3) Modify the codes in the related event procedures of the `Course.aspx.vb` file to call the associated Web method to perform our data insertion. The code modifications include the following sections:
   a) Modify the codes in the Page_Load event procedure.
   b) Develop the codes for the `Insert` button's click event procedure.
   c) Develop the codes for the TextChanged event procedure of the Course ID textbox.
   d) Modify the codes in the `Select` button's click event procedure. Also add four user-defined subroutines: `ProcessObject()`, `FillCourseListBox()`, `FillCourseDataSet()`, and `FillCourseDetail()`. These four subroutines are basically identical with those we developed in the last Windows-based Web service client project `WinClientOracleInsert Project`. One can copy and paste them into our new project with a few modifications.
   e) Modify the codes in the SelectedIndexChanged event procedure.
   f) Modify the codes in the `Back` button's click event procedure.

Now let's start with the first step listed above.

9.4.4.1   Create a New Web Project and Add an Existing Web Page
Open Visual Studio.NET and create a new ASP.NET Web Application project. Enter `WebClientOracleInsert Project` and `WebClientOracleInsert Solution` into the `Project Name` and the `Solution Name` box, and `C:\Chapter 9` into the `Location` box, and click on the `Create` button to continue. Click on the `Web Forms` item and then the `Create` button to create this ASP.NET Application project.

On the opened new project, right-click on our new project `WebClientOracleInsert Project` from the Solution Explorer window and select the item **Add|Existing Item** from the popup menu to open the Add Existing Item wizard. Browse to our Web project `OracleWebInsert Project` folder that can be found from the folder `Class DB Projects\Chapter 8` that is located under the `Students` folder at the Wiley ftp site (refer to Figure 1.2 in Chapter 1), select one item `Course.aspx` by checking it from the list, and click on the `Add` button to add this page into our new Web application project.

9.4.4.2   Add a Web Service Reference and Modify the Web Form Window
Refer to Section 9.4.3.1 to complete this Web reference adding process. Also change this Web service reference name to `WS_OracleInsert`.

The modifications to the Web page of the `Course.aspx` include three steps:

1) Open the Source file for the `Course.aspx` page by right-clicking on the `Course.aspx` page and select the item `View Markup`. Then go to the end of the top line and change the last tab to `Inherits="WebClientOracleInsert_Project.Course" %>`.
2) Open the Designer View and set the `AutoPostBack` property of the Course ID textbox to True. **This is very important** since when the content of this textbox is changed during the project runs, a TextChanged event occurs. However, this event only occurs in the client side, not the server side. Our Web-based client project is running is a Web server or server side, so this event cannot be responded by the server. Therefore, the command inside this event procedure cannot be executed (the `Insert` button cannot be enabled) even the content of the Course ID textbox is changed when the project runs. To solve this problem, we must set the `AutoPostBack` property of this textbox to `True` to allow the server to send back a TextChanged event to the client automatically as the content of this textbox is changed.

3) Add one more DropDownList control and the associated label to the left of the Faculty Name combo box control. Name this DropDownList as `ComboMethod` and the label with the `Text` property as `Method`. This DropDownList control is used to store two Web methods developed in our Web service and allow users to select one of them to perform the associated data insertion as the project runs.
4) Change the `ID` property of the Credit textbox from `txtCredit` to `txtCredits`.
5) Set the Course page as a start-up page by right-clicking on the `Course.aspx` from the Solution Explorer and select the `Set As Start Page` item.

Your modified `Course.aspx` Web form window is shown in Figure 9.86.
Go to the `File|Save All` menu item to save these modifications.

9.4.4.3 Modify the Codes for the Related Event Procedures
The first modification is to change the codes in the Page_Load event procedure and some global variables.

9.4.4.3.1 Modify the Codes in the Page_Load Event Procedure Use the codes shown in Figure 9.87 to replace all original codes in the Page_Load event procedure and some global variables. The main changes are some declarations for three form-level or class-level variables:

```
Private dsFlag As Boolean
Private wsDataSet As New DataSet
Private wsOracleResult As New WS_OracleInsert.OracleInsertBase
```

Your finished codes for the Page_Load event procedure should match one that is shown in Figure 9.87. The new added codes have been highlighted in bold.

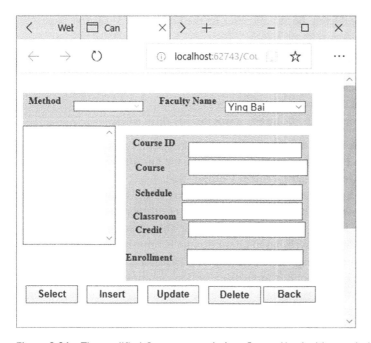

Figure 9.86 The modified Course page window. *Source:* Used with permission from Microsoft.

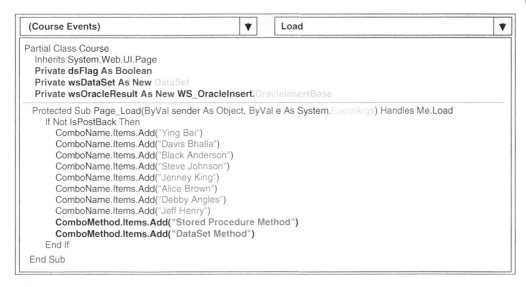

Figure 9.87 The modified Page_Load() event procedure.

The next step is to develop the codes for the **Insert** button's click event procedure.

9.4.4.3.2 Develop Codes for the Insert Button's Event Procedure The function of this piece of codes is to insert a new course record that is stored in six textboxes in the Web page into the database as this **Insert** button is clicked. This piece of codes is basically identical with those in the same event procedure of the Windows-based client project we developed in the last section. Therefore, we can copy those codes from that event procedure and paste them into our current procedure with a few modifications.

Open the Windows-based client project **WinClientOracleInsert Project** from the folder **Class DB Projects\Chapter 9** that is located under the **Students** folder at the Wiley ftp site (refer to Figure 1.2 in Chapter 1). Copy all codes from the **Insert** button's Click event procedure and paste them into the **Insert** button's click event procedure in our current Web-based client project **WebClientOracleInsert Project**.

The only modification is to add one more String variable **errMsg** that is used to store the returned error information from calling different Web methods. Also all message box functions **MsgBox()** should be replaced by the **Write()** method of the Response object of the server class since the **MsgBox()** can only be used in the client side.

Your finished codes for the **Insert** button's click event procedure should match one that is shown in Figure 9.88. The modification parts have been highlighted in bold.

Let's have a quick review for this piece of codes to see how it works:

A) First, we need to call a user-defined function **CheckCourse()** to make sure that all textboxes related to this new inserted course record have been filled.
B) If the user selected the **Stored Procedure Method** to perform this data insertion, the Web method **SetOracleInsertSP()** in the Web service is executed to call the associated stored procedure to insert a new course record into our sample database.
C) If the user chosen the **DataSet Method** to perform this data insertion, we need to set a flag to tell the project that a DataSet data insertion has been performed.

D) This flag is stored in a global variable using the Application state. The reason is that the Web method `OracleInsertDataSet()` has two functions: insert and retrieve data from the database. In order to perform the data retrieving using this method, first one must insert data using this method. Otherwise, no data can be retrieved. The reason we use an Application state to store this flag is that our Web client project will run on a Web server and the server will send back a refreshed page to the client each time a request is sent to the server, thus all global variables' values will also be refreshed when a refreshed page is sent back. But the Application state is never changed no matter how many times our client page is refreshed.

E) The associated Web method `OracleInsertDataSet()` is called to insert this new course record into the database.

F) The returned DataSet object `wsDataSet` that contains all `COURSE_ID` is a form-level variable. Because of the same reason as we discussed in step **D**, we need to use an Application state to store this DataSet since we need to pick up all `COURSE_ID` from it when we perform the validation process later by clicking on the `Select` button. Otherwise, the content of this DataSet will be refreshed each time when a refreshed Course page is sent back by the server.

G) Finally, the `Insert` button is disabled to avoid multi-insertion to the database.

The codes for the user-defined function `CheckCourse()` are shown in Figure 9.89.

Figure 9.88 The codes for the Insert button's Click event procedure.

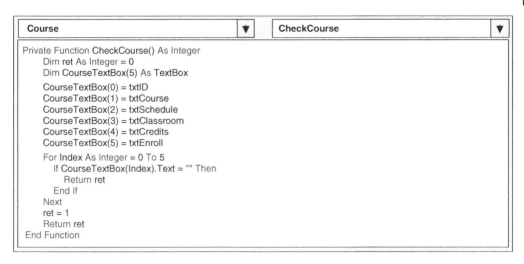

Figure 9.89 The detailed codes for the user-defined function CheckCourse().

9.4.4.3.3 Develop Codes for the CourseID TextChanged Event Procedure The `Insert` button should be enabled either as the content of the `COURSE_ID` textbox is changed or when the content of the `ComboMethod` DropDownList is changed. In either case, it indicates that a new course record is ready to be inserted into the database. The events related to these two cases are `TextChanged` for `COURSE_ID` textbox and the `SelectedIndexChanged` for `ComboMethod` control. Open these two event procedures by double-clicking them from the Web page window and enter the following code into these event procedures:

```
btnInsert.Enabled = True
```

As we mentioned, after a new course record has been inserted into the database, the `Insert` button must be disabled to avoid the possible multi-insertion of the same record into the database. But as another new course record is ready to be inserted into the database, this `Insert` button should be enabled. To distinguish between the existed and a new course record, the content of the Course ID textbox is a good candidate since it is a primary key in our Course data table. Each `COURSE_ID` is a unique identifier for each course record, and therefore as long as the content of this Course ID textbox changed, which means that a new course record is ready to be inserted, the `Insert` button should be enabled. Similar situation is true for the `ComboMethod` DropDownList control.

Another important point is that making sure that the `AutoPostBack` property of this Course ID textbox is set to `True` to allow the server to send back a TextChanged event to the client when its content is changed.

9.4.4.3.4 Modify the Codes in the Select Button's Click Event Procedure The codes in this event procedure are similar to those codes we developed in the same event procedure in our Windows-based client project `WinClientOracleInsert Project`. So we can copy those codes and paste them into our current `Select` button's click event procedure with a few modifications. Open the `Select` button's click event procedure from our Windows-based client project `WinClientOracleInsert Project` and copy those codes and paste them into our `Select` button's click event procedure. The only modifications to this piece of copied codes are to change the Windows-based message box function `MsgBox()` to the Web-based message box function.

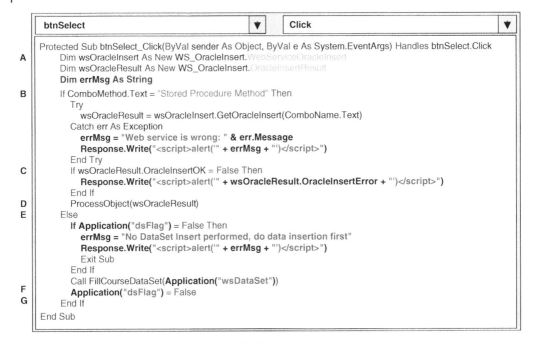

Figure 9.90 The codes for the Select button's Click event procedure.

Your finished codes for this event procedure are shown in Figure 9.90. The modified parts have been highlighted in bold.

Let's take a quick review for this piece of codes to see how it works:

A) An instance of our Web service reference **WebServiceOracleInsert** is created first and this instance works as a bridge to connect this client project with the associated Web methods built in the Web service together. Also an **errMsg** string variable is created and it is used to store the error message to be displayed and reported later.

B) If the **Stored Procedure Method** is selected by the user, the associated Web method **GetOracleInsert()** is executed to call the stored procedure to pick up all **COURSE_ID** taught by the selected faculty based on the input faculty name. If any error were occurred during the execution of this Web method, the error source is reported and displayed with an **alert()** script method.

C) Besides the system error checking, we also need to inspect any application error, and this can be performed by checking the status of the member data **OracleInsertOK** that is defined in the base class **OracleInsertBase** in our Web service project.

D) If no error is detected, the user-defined subroutine **ProcessObject()**, whose detailed codes are shown in Figure 9.91, is called to extract all retrieved **COURSE_ID** from the returned instance and add them into the list box control.

E) If user selected the **DataSet Method**, first we need to check the **dsFlag** stored in an Application state to make sure that the Web method **OracleInsertDataSet()** has been executed once since our current data query needs to extract all **COURSE_ID** from the DataSet that is returned from the last execution of the Web method **OracleInsertDataSet()**. If this **dsFlag** is **False**, which means that this Web method has not been called and executed; therefore, we do not have any returned DataSet available. A warning message is displayed and the procedure is exited if that situation occurred.

F) If the **dsFlag** is **True**, which means that the Web method **OracleInsertDataSet()** has been executed and a returned DataSet that contains all **COURSE_ID** is available. A user-defined subroutine **FillCourseDataSet()** is executed to extract all **COURSE_ID** from that returned DataSet and add them into the list box control in our client page window. The global DataSet object **wsDataSet** that is stored in an Application state is passed as an argument for this subroutine calling.

G) Finally, the **dsFlag** stored in an Application state is reset to **False**.

The detailed codes for the subroutines **ProcessObject()** and **FillCourseListBox()** are shown in Figure 9.91. Let's have a closer look at this piece of codes to see how it works.

A) A local string variable **errMsg** is declared and it is used to hold any error message to be displayed and reported later.

B) First, we need to check the member data **OracleInsertOK** to make sure that the Web method is executed successfully. If it is, a user-defined subroutine procedure **FillCourseListBox()** is called to fill all **COURSE_ID** contained in the returned instance to the list box control in our client page.

C) A warning message is displayed if any error was encountered during the execution of that Web method.

D) In the subroutine **FillCourseListBox()**, first a local integer variable **index** is created and it works as a loop number for a **For** loop to continuously pick up all **COURSE_ID** from the returned instance and add them into the list box control.

E) The course list box control is cleaned up first before any **COURSE_ID** can be added into it. This process is very important in displaying all **COURSE_ID**, otherwise all new **COURSE_ID** will be attached to the end of the original **COURSE_ID** in this control and the displaying result is messy.

F) A **For** loop is used to continuously pick up all **COURSE_ID** from the **CourseID()** array defined in our returned class **OracleInsertResult**. One point to be noted is the upper bound and the length of this array. The length or the size of this array is 11, but the upper bound of this array is 10 since the index of this array starts from 0, not 1. Therefore, the upper

```
| Course                                    ▼ | ProcessObject                              ▼ |

   Private Sub ProcessObject(ByRef wsResult As WS_OracleInsert.OracleInsertResult)
A      Dim errMsg As String
B      If wsResult.OracleInsertOK = True Then
          Call FillCourseListBox(wsResult)
C      Else
          errMsg = "Course information cannot be retrieved: " & wsResult.OracleInsertError
          Response.Write("<script>alert('" + errMsg + "')</script>")
       End If
   End Sub

   Private Sub FillCourseListBox(ByRef oraResult As WS_OracleInsert.OracleInsertResult)
D      Dim index As Integer
E      CourseList.Items.Clear()                            'clean up the course listbox
F      For index = 0 To oraResult.CourseID.Length - 1
          If oraResult.CourseID(index) <> vbNullString Then
             CourseList.Items.Add(oraResult.CourseID(index))
          End If
       Next index
   End Sub
```

Figure 9.91 The codes for subroutines ProcessObject() and FillCourseListBox().

bound of this array is equal to the length of this array minus by 1. As long as the content of the `CourseID(index)` is not Null, a valid `COURSE_ID` is added into the list box control using the `Add()` method.

The codes for the subroutine `FillCourseDataSet()` are shown in Figure 9.92. This piece of codes is identical with that in the same subroutine we developed in our Windows-based client project `WinClientOracleInsert Project`. You can copy it from that Windows-based project and paste it into our current project.

Let's have a look at the codes in this subroutine to see how they work:

A) Two objects, a DataTable and a DataRow, are declared at the beginning of this subroutine since we need to use them to perform the data extraction from the returned instance and the data addition to the list box control.
B) The list box control is first cleaned up to avoid messy displaying of multiple `COURSE_ID`.
C) The `CourseTable` object is initialized by assigning a new data table named **"Course"** that is embedded to the DataSet object **ds**.
D) A `For Each…In` loop is used to continuously pick up the first column that is the `COURSE_ID` column from all returned rows and add each of them into the list box control. One point to be noted is that the first column has an index value of 0, not 1, since the index starts from 0.

Next, we need to modify the codes in the `SelectedIndexChanged` event procedure for the `CourseList` box and add the fourth subroutine `FillCourseDetail()`. Before we can continue to do these jobs, first we need to delete the following procedures and subroutines from our current project:

- `FillCourseReader()`
- `FillCourseReaderTextBox()`
- `MapCourseTable()`

Now let's modify the codes in the `SelectedIndexChanged` event procedure for the `CourseList` box and add the fourth user-defined subroutine procedure `FillCourseDetail()`.

9.4.4.3.5 Modify the Codes in the SelectedIndexChanged Event Procedure The function of this piece of codes is that the detailed course information, such as the course name, schedule, classroom, credit, and enrollment, will be displayed in the associated textbox controls as the user clicked and selected one `COURSE_ID` from the list box control. In fact, the main coding job is performed inside the SelectedIndexChanged event procedure of the list box control `CourseList`. Because when

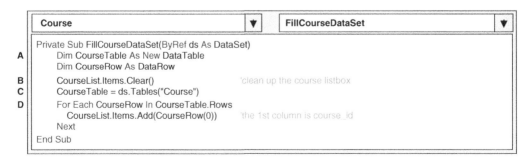

Figure 9.92 The codes for the subroutine FillCourseDataSet().

user clicks or selects a **COURSE_ID** from the list box control, a SelectedIndexChanged event is issued and this event is passed to the associated SelectedIndexChanged event procedure.

To pick up the detailed course information for the selected **COURSE_ID**, the Web method **GetOracleInsertCourse()** in our Web service project **WebServiceOracleInsert Project** is called, and this method returns an instance of the returned class **OracleInsertResult** to our client project. The detailed course information is stored in that returned instance.

The codes in this event procedure are identical with those we did for the same event procedure in our Windows-based client project **WinClientOracleInsert Project**. So we can copy those codes from that event procedure and paste them into our current project with a few modifications.

Double-click on the list box control **CourseList** from our client page window to open the SelectedIndexChanged event procedure of the list box control. Copy and paste those codes into our current Web-based project. The only modification is to change the Windows-based **MsgBox()** method to the Web-based script message method **alert()**. Your finished **SelectedIndexChanged** event procedure should match one that is shown in Figure 9.93. The modified parts have been highlighted in bold.

Let's take a closer look at this piece of codes to see how it works:

A) An instance of our Web service reference or the proxy class **wsOracleInsert** is created here. Another instance of our derived class **OracleInsertResult** is declared here, too. This instance is used to hold all queried **COURSE_ID**. Also a local string variable **errMsg** is declared and it is used to hold the error message to be displayed and reported later.

B) A **Try…Catch** block is used to call the Web method **GetOracleInsertCourse()** with the selected **COURSE_ID** from the list box control as the argument to perform this course information retrieving. The selected **COURSE_ID** is stored in the **Text** property of the **CourseList** control. An exception message is displayed if any error was encountered during the execution of this Web method and catched by the system method **Catch**.

C) In addition to the error checking performed by the system, we also need to perform our exception checking by inspecting the member data **OracleInsertOK** in the base class **OracleInsertBase**. If this data value is **False**, which means that an application error was occurred during the running of this Web method. A related error message is displayed and the subroutine is exited.

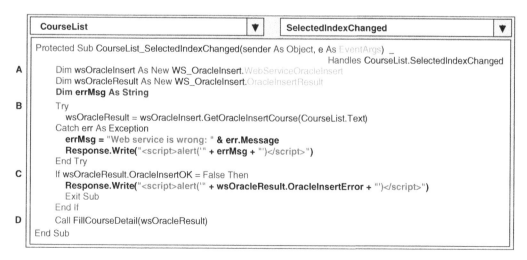

Figure 9.93 The modified codes for the SelectedIndexChanged() event procedure.

D) If everything is fine, the user-defined subroutine `FillCourseDetail()` is executed to extract the detailed course information from the returned instance and assign it to each associated textbox control in our client page form.

The detailed codes for the subroutine `FillCourseDetail()` is shown in Figure 9.94.

This piece of codes is identical with that we developed in the same subroutine in our Windows-based client project `WinClientOracleInsert Project`. You can copy it from that project and paste it in this project.

The function of this piece of codes is straightforward without tricks. Each piece of course information is extracted from the returned instance and assigned to the associated textbox control in our client page window.

9.4.4.3.6 Modify the Codes in the Back Button's Click Event Procedure
The final modification is the codes in the `Back` button's Click event procedure. When this button is clicked by the user, our client project is terminated. Open this event procedure and replace the original codes with the following codes:

```
Response.Write("<script>window.close();</script>")
```

In this way, our client page will be terminated when the script command `close()` is executed.

At this point, we have finished all coding jobs for this Web-based client project. Before we can run this project to test the data insertion and validation functionalities, make sure that the following tasks have been performed:

- Our main Web page `Course.aspx` has been set as the starting page. This can be done by right-clicking on our main Web page and select the item `Set As Start Page` from the popup menu.
- Our Web service `WebServiceOracleInsert Project` is in the running status and this can be checked by locating a small white icon on the status bar on the bottom of the screen. If you cannot find this icon, open our Web service project and click on the `IIS Express` button to run it.
- Two new course records, `CSE-678` and `CSE-526`, which are shown in Tables 9.2 and 9.3 and are inserted before using the `Insert` button's click event procedure, should have been deleted from the Course table in our sample database since we want to insert the same course records in this test.
- Two database provider imports directives at the top, `Imports Devart.Data` and `Imports Devart.Data.Oracle`, have been removed from this page code window.

Now click on the `IIS Express` button to run our Web client project. First, let's test the data insertion function. Select the `Stored Procedure Method` from the `Method` combo box control. Then select the default faculty `Ying Bai` from the `Faculty Name` combo box control, enter the first new course record (shown in Table 9.2 in Section 9.4.3.3.2) into the associated textboxes,

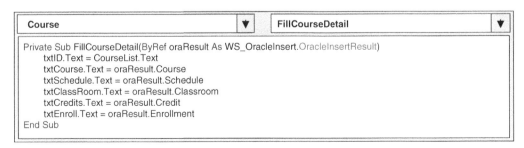

Figure 9.94 The codes for the subroutine FillCourseDetail().

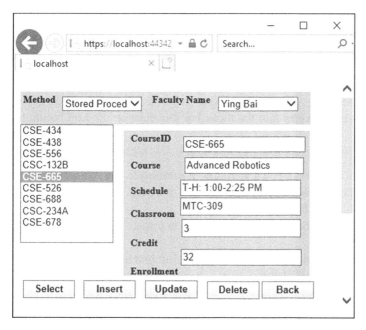

Figure 9.95 The running status of getting the detailed course information. *Source:* Used with permission from Microsoft.

and then click on the **Insert** button. Perform the similar operation to insert the second new course record (shown in Table 9.3 in Section 9.4.3.3.2) with the **DataSet Method** selected.

To validate these data insertions, click on the **Select** button for **DataSet Method** and then the **Stored Procedure Method**.

You can find that our two new inserted courses, **CSE-678** and **CSE-526**, have been added into and retrieved from our database and displayed in the list box control.

To get detailed course information for a specific course, click a desired **COURSE_ID** from the list box control. Immediately, the detailed course information for the selected **COURSE_ID** is displayed on each associated textbox, which is shown in Figure 9.95.

You can try to get the detailed information for different course by selecting different **COURSE_ID** from the list box control via either DataSet or Stored Procedure method. Click on the **Back** button to terminate our Web client project.

A completed Web-based Web service client project **WebClientOracleInsert Project** can be found from the folder **Class DB Projects\Chapter 9** that is located under the **Students** folder at the Wiley ftp site (refer to Figure 1.2 in Chapter 1).

Next, we need to take care of updating and deleting data via Web services.

9.5 Build ASP.NET Web Service to Update and Delete Data for Oracle Database

In this section, we discuss how to update and delete a record against the **Student** table in our sample database via the Web services. Two major Web methods are developed in this Web service project: **OracleUpdateSP()** and **OracleDeleteSP()**, both methods call the associated stored procedure to perform the data updating and deleting operations.

Open Visual Studio.NET 2019 and create a new WCF Service Application project `WebServiceOracleUpdateDelete Project` and a `WebServiceOracleUpdateDelete Solution` in the location at the folder `C:\Chapter 9`.

Then right-click on the new created project from the Solution Explorer window and select `Add|New Item` to open the `Add New Item` wizard. Select the `Web` template from the left pane and the `Web Service (ASMX) Visual Basic` from the mid pane. Then enter `WebServicOracleUpdateDelete.asmx` into the `Name` box and click on the `Add` button to add this page into our project.

As we did in Section 9.3.2, perform the following operations to build this service:

1) Modify the default namespace to create our own Web service namespace.
2) Add a Reference for Oracle data drives and two data provider directives to import the Oracle data provider namespaces where the data drives are located.
3) Create a customer base class to handle error-checking codes to protect our real Web service class.
4) Create a customer returned class to hold all required or updated student information. This class is a derived class based on the base class above.
5) Add Web methods to our Web main service class to access our sample database.
6) Develop the detail codes for those Web methods to perform the Web services.

Let's start our jobs based on this sequence now.

9.5.1 Modify the Default Namespace and Add Database Connection String

Open the main service page `WebServiceOracleUpdateDelete.asmx` by double-clicking on it from the Solution Explorer window and change the default namespace to our special one that is shown in Figure 9.96.

We need to use our own namespace to replace the default namespace used by the Microsoft to tell the ASP.NET runtime the location from which our Web service is loaded as it runs. This specific namespace is unique because it is the home page of the Wiley appended with the book's ISBN

Figure 9.96 The modified namespace.

number. In fact, you can use any unique location as your specific namespace to store your Web service project if you like.

Now perform the following operational steps to add a reference to our project:

1) Right-click on our project `WebServiceOracleUpdateDelete Project` from the Solution Explorer and select `Add | Reference` item to open the Reference Manager wizard.
2) Select the `Extensions` item under the `Assemblies` at the left pane, check two items from the right pane, `Devart.Data` and `Devart.Data.Oracle`, and click on the `OK` button to add them into our project.
3) Add two directives, `Imports Devart.Data` and `Imports Devart.Data.Oracle`, to the top on our main page, as shown in step **A** in Figure 9.96.

Now as we did before, open the configuration file `Web.config` and add the database connection string by entering the following tabs into this file:

```
<connectionStrings>
    <add name="ora_conn" connectionString="Server=localhost:1518/CSE_DEPT; _
    User ID=CSE_DEPT; Password=oracle_18c"/>
</connectionStrings>
```

Make sure that this `<add name=...>` tag is a completed one-line code without any break-connection symbol in it. Here, we used a break-connection symbol to make this line looks better.

One can add this connection string tab at any location inside this configuration file, such as by the end of this file or just before the end tag </configuration>.

9.5.2   Create Our Customer-Built Base and Returned Classes

Right-click on new our project in the Solution Explorer and select `Add | New Item` to add a Visual Basic class `OracleBase.vb` with two member data:

1) `Public OracleOK As Boolean`
2) `Public OracleError As String`

In a similar way to create another class `OracleResult.vb`, which is a derived class based on the `OracleBase` class with two members, as shown in Figure 9.97.

The member data `StudentName(20)` is a text string array used to hold all `student_name` columns in the `STUDENT` table in our sample database. Some `student_name` columns may be changed after the data updating operations, thus we need to get the updated student names and display them in the `Student Name` combo box to reflect the current students and to enable users

Figure 9.97   The member data for the class OracleResult.

to select them to perform the validation for the data updating actions. The member data `StudentIndex` is an index used to hold the upper-bound index value for the text string `StudentName(20)`.

The purpose we set up this derived class is to enable users to retrieve back the updated students' names from the `STUDENT` table after the data updating operations, and those current students' names can be collected and used by the consuming projects to perform the updating validation process.

Go to the `File|Save All` menu item to save these operations.

9.5.3   Create a Web Method to Call Stored Procedure to Update Student Records

The function of this Web method `OracleUpdateSP()` is to call an Oracle stored procedure `Web_UpdateStudentSP()` that will be developed in Section 9.5.5 to perform the data updating for a student record based on a student's name.

Regularly, we do not need to update the primary key for a record to be updated because it is better to insert a new record with a new primary key than to updating that record with a new primary key. Another reason for this issue is that it would be very complicated if one wants to update a primary key in a parent table since that primary key may be used as foreign keys in many other child tables. Therefore, one has to update those foreign keys first in child tables before the primary key can be updated in the parent table. In this application, we concentrate on updating all other columns for a student record without touching the primary key `STUDENT_ID`.

Now we just assume that our stored procedure is available and let's first to build our Web method `OracleUpdateSP()`.

Open our Web service project `WebServiceOracleUpdateDelete Project` and use the Web method `OracleUpdateSP()`, whose codes are shown in Figure 9.98, to replace the default method `HelloWorld`. Let's have a closer look at these codes to see how they work:

A) The name of this Web method is `OracleUpdateSP` with eight pieces of updated student information. A point to be noted is that the data type for the student image is `Byte()`, which is compatible with the data type used in the stored procedure. Also the returned data type is our returned class `OracleResult`.

B) The content of the query string is equal to the name of the stored procedure that will be developed in Section 9.5.5. Keep in mind that this name must be identical with the name of the stored procedure to be developed later.

C) Some local variables are declared first at this method, including an instance of our returned class `OracleResult`, Connection and Command objects. The local variable `intUpdate` is used to hold the returned value from calling the ExecuteNonQuery() method later.

D) First, we preset a good running status of this Web method to the member data `OracleOK` to indicate that so far our Web method is running fine. A database connection is established by calling a user-defined function `OracleConn()`.

E) If any error is encountered during the database connection process, the error information is stored into the member data `OracleError` and reported using a user-defined subroutine `ReportError()`.

F) The Command object is initialized with related data objects such as connection object, command text, and command type. One point to be noted is that the command type must be set to the `StoredProcedure` since this method will call a stored procedure to perform the data updating. The next initialization process for the Command object is to assign all input or updating parameters to the associated dynamic parameter in the `UPDATE` statement.

G) The `ExecuteNonQuery()` method is executed to call the stored procedure to perform the data updating. An integer value will be returned from this method and this value is the number of rows that have been updated in our **STUDENT** table.

H) A cleaning job is performed to release all objects used in this method.

I) If the returned value from calling of the `ExecuteNonQuery()` method is zero, which means that no any row has been updated in our **STUDENT** table and this data updating is failed. An error message is sent to the member data `OracleError` and reported using the subroutine `ReportError()`.

J) Finally, the instance `OracleResult` that contains the running status of this Web method is returned to the calling procedure.

Go to `File|Save All` menu item to save these modifications.

The codes for the user-defined function `OracleConn()` and user-defined subroutine `ReportError()` are identical with those function and subroutine we built in our previous projects, such as `WebServiceOracleInsert Project`. You can open that project to copy and

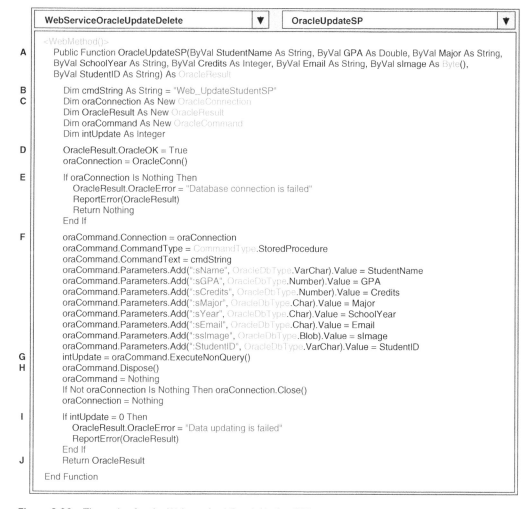

Figure 9.98 The codes for the Web method OracleUpdateSP().

paste them into this project. The only modifications for the subroutine `ReportError()` include to change the data type of the argument `ErrSource` to `OracleResult`, as shown in step **A** in Figure 9.99, and remove the word `Insert` for two member data to make them as `OracleOK` and `OracleError`, as shown in step **B** in Figure 9.99. Next, let's build our Web method `OracleDeleteSP` to call a stored procedure to delete a student record.

9.5.4 Create a Web Method to Call Stored Procedure to Delete Student Records

As we discussed in Section 7.1.1 in Chapter 7, to delete a record from a relational database, one needs to follow the operational steps listed below:

1) Delete records that are related to the parent table using the foreign keys from the child tables.
2) Delete records that are defined as primary keys from the parent table.

In other words, to delete one record from the parent table, all records that are related to that record as foreign keys and located at different child tables must be deleted first. In our case, in order to delete a record using the `STUDENT_ID` as the primary key from the Student table (parent table), one must first delete those records using the `STUDENT_ID` as a foreign key from the LogIn and the StudentCourse table (child tables). Refer to Section 2.5 and Figure 2.5 in Chapter 2 to get a clear relationship description among different data tables in our sample database.

From this discussion, it can be found that to delete a student record from our sample database, two deleting queries need to be performed: the first query is used to delete the related records from the child tables, LogIn and StudentCourse tables, and the second query is used to delete the target record from the parent table or the Student table. However, because we selected the Cascaded Delete function when we built all tables in our sample database, thus we do not need to take care of those child tables, and the database engine can handle those deleting actions for us automatically.

A point to be noted is that our dynamic input parameter to this deleting query is a student name, but we need a `STUDENT_ID` to perform a deleting action. Thus, two queries are needed for this deleting function; first, we need to get a `STUDENT_ID` based on the input parameter student name and then perform a cascaded deleting to that student record based on the `STUDENT_ID`.

Figure 9.99   The codes for the user-defined function and subroutine.

To save the time and the space as well as the efficiency, we place these two queries into a stored procedure **Web_DeleteStudentSP()** that will be developed in the following section. A single input parameter **sName** (student name) is passed into this stored procedure. At this moment, we just assume that we have already developed that stored procedure and will use it in this Web method.

Open our main service page **WebServiceOracleUpdateDelete.asmx** and create this Web method **OracleDeleteSP()**, which is shown in Figure 9.100.

Let's take a closer look at this piece of codes to see how it works:

A) The name of this Web method is **OracleDeleteSP** and the returned data type is our customer returned class **OracleResult**.
B) The content of the query string is equal to the name of the stored procedure we will develop soon. The point is that the name used in this query string must be identical with the name used in our stored procedure. Otherwise, a running error may be encountered since the stored procedure is identified by its name as the project runs.
C) An instance of our returned class, **OracleResult**, is created. This instance contains the running status of this Web method and will be returned to the calling procedure when this method is done. A local integer variable **intDelete** is declared and this variable is used to hold the returned value from calling the **ExecuteNonQuery()** method after this method runs.
D) First, we preset a good running status of this Web method to the member data **OracleOK** to indicate that so far our Web method is running fine.

```
┌─────────────────────────────────────────┬───┬─────────────────────────────┬───┐
│ WebServiceOracleUpdateDelete             │ ▼ │ OracleDeleteSP              │ ▼ │
├─────────────────────────────────────────┴───┴─────────────────────────────┴───┤
```

```vb
      <WebMethod()> _
A       Public Function OracleDeleteSP(ByVal sName As String) As OracleResult
B         Dim cmdString As String = "Web_DeleteStudentSP"
          Dim oraConnection As New OracleConnection
C         Dim OracleResult As New OracleResult
          Dim intDelete As Integer
D         OracleResult.OracleOK = True
          oraConnection = OracleConn()
E         If oraConnection Is Nothing Then
              OracleResult.OracleOK = False
              OracleResult.OracleError = "Database connection is failed"
              ReportError(OracleResult)
              Return Nothing
          End If
F         Dim oraCommand = New OracleCommand(cmdString, oraConnection)
          oraCommand.CommandType = CommandType.StoredProcedure
G         oraCommand.Parameters.Add(":sName", OracleDbType.VarChar).Value = sName
H         intDelete = oraCommand.ExecuteNonQuery()
I         If intDelete = 0 Then
              OracleResult.OracleError = "Data deleting is failed"
              ReportError(OracleResult)
          End If
J         oraConnection.Close()
          oraCommand.Dispose()
          oraCommand = Nothing
K         Return OracleResult
        End Function
```

Figure 9.100 The codes for the Web method OracleDeleteSP().

E) If any error is encountered during the database connection process, the error information is stored into the member data **OracleError** and reported using the subroutine **ReportError()**.

F) The Command object is created with a constructor that includes two arguments: Command string and Connection object. Then the Command object is initialized with associated data objects and properties such as Command Type. The point is that the Command Type property must be set to the value of **StoredProcedure** since this command object will call a stored procedure to perform this data deleting.

G) Also the dynamic parameter **:sName** is assigned with the actual **sName** that is an input parameter to this Web method.

H) The **ExecuteNonQuery()** method is executed to call our stored procedure to perform this data deleting action. This method returns an integer to indicate the running status of this method, and the returned value is assigned to the local integer variable **intDelete**.

I) The value returned from execution of the **ExecuteNonQuery()** method is equal to the number of rows that have been successfully deleted from the **STUDENT** table. If this returned value is zero, which means that no any row has been deleted from the **STUDENT** table, an error message is displayed and reported using the subroutine **ReportError()**.

J) A cleaning job is performed to release all objects used in this method.

K) Finally, the instance containing the running status of this Web method is returned to the calling procedure.

Next, let's create our third Web method to collect the current student members from our updated **STUDENT** table in our sample database.

9.5.5 Create a Web Method to Collect the Current Student Members

As we mentioned, we want to validate this data updating action after a student's record is updated by retrieving back all updated student members (**student_name** column) from our sample database. In fact, we can do this retrieving function in our consuming projects later by accessing to our sample database directly from the consuming projects. However, in order to provide a more complete and complicated data retrieving actions, we prefer to do this retrieving function via our Web project, exactly via this Web method.

Open our main service page **WebServiceOracleUpdateDelete.asmx** and create this Web method **CurrentStudents()**, which is shown in Figure 9.101.

Let's take a closer look at this piece of codes to see how it works:

A) The name of this Web method is **CurrentStudents()** with no argument, but this method needs to return an object, **Result**, from our derived class **OracleResult**.

B) Some local objects and variables are declared at the beginning of this method, including our derived object, OracleCommand, OracleDataReader, and OracleConnection objects.

C) First, we need to set the running status of his method as **True** via the **OracleOK** member data. This step is very important since this status of this variable is initialized to **False** by Visual Basic.NET after this member data is created.

D) The user-defined function **OracleConn()** is executed to connect to our sample database, and this function will return an OracleConnection object if this connection is successfully made.

E) Otherwise, if this function returned a built-in constant, **Nothing**, which means that this connection is failed and a warning message is displayed to indicate this situation and the Web method is exited.

Figure 9.101 The codes for the Web method CurrentStudents().

F) If the database connection is fine, the OracleCommand object is initialized with appropriate parameters. Here, to simplify this query, a query string is directly assigned to the CommandText property to retrieve back all current students.

G) Then the **ExecuteReader()** method is executed to try to read all students' names and assign them to the OracleDataReader object, **oraReader**.

H) If the property of the OracleDataReader, **HasRows**, is set up to **True**, which means that the reading operation is successful, then another user-defined subroutine procedure, **FillStudentReader()**, is called to collect all queried students' names.

I) Otherwise, if a **False** is returned by the property **HasRows**, which means that the data reading operation is failed, and a message is displayed to indicate this case.

J) Some cleaning jobs are performed here to release all objects used in this method.

K) Finally, the collected students' names are returned via the **Result** object.

The codes for the user-defined subroutine **FillStudentReader()** are shown in Figure 9.102. Let's have a quick look at this piece of codes to see how they work:

A) A local integer variable **num** is declared first and it is used as a loop number later.

B) A **While** loop is utilized to repeatedly retrieve all student names with a loop condition, **Read()**, which is a method of the OracleDataReader. As long as this method returns a True, which means a valid student name is read out, the **GetString(0)** method is executed to get column 0 (**student_name**) and is assigned to the member data **StudentName(num)** in our OracleResult object, **ret**.

C) The final loop number **num** is assigned to the member data **StudentIndex**.

Figure 9.102 The codes for the user-defined subroutine FillStudentReader().

A point to be noted is the data type of the second argument, **ret**, to this subroutine, which is a Reference (**ByRef**). This means that an address of this object is passed into this subroutine, and any modification for this object is permanent and it will be attached with this object when the object is returned to the calling program.

At this point, we have finished all coding jobs for our Web service project. Next, let's begin to develop our two stored procedures.

9.5.6 Develop Two Oracle Stored Procedures with Oracle SQL Developer

Both stored procedures can be developed in the Oracle SQL Developer environment.

9.5.6.1 Develop the Stored Procedure Web_UpdateStudentSP

Open the Oracle SQL Developer, connect and expand our sample Oracle database **CSE_DEPT** and the Other Users folder, and then expand our database schema **CSE_DEPT** to find the **Procedures** folder. Right-click on this folder and select the item **New Procedure** from the popup menu to open the Create Procedure wizard.

Perform the following operational steps to generate this stored procedure:

1) Enter **WEB_UPDATESTUDENTSP** into the **Name** box and add eight input parameters that are shown in Figure 9.103 into this procedure. Click on the **OK** button to create this stored procedure.
2) On the opened procedure body, enter the codes that are shown in Figure 9.104 into this procedure to make it as our new stored procedure.
3) Click on the **Compile** item to save and build this new stored procedure.

Now we can test this stored procedure in the Oracle SQL Developer environment. To do that, click on the green color **Run** button to execute this stored procedure. On the opened **Run PL/SQL** wizard, enter eight input parameters into the **Input Value** column, as shown in Figure 9.105. A trick for this update query is that the email column, **SEMAIL**, shown in the bottom pane (it is highlighted) cannot be converted and assigned as a string variable to that column, and you must add single quotation marks manually on both ends of this column to make it a string variable, as shown in Figure 9.105. Now you can click on the **OK** button to run this stored procedure. You may need to redo system login to perform this data updating action. The updating parameters used for this test are shown in Table 9.4 and the original record is a student member named **Tom David**.

As we know, the student **Tom David** is inserted by us in some previous project, but it is not the original student member in our sample database. Therefore, this student has no any related record in any other tables. This is good for us to perform a deleting action for this student later to avoid any cascaded deletion action.

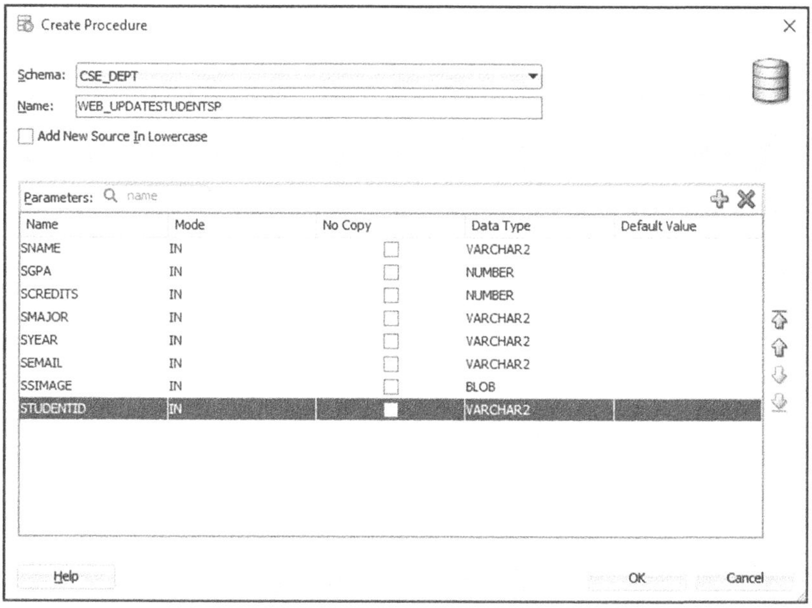

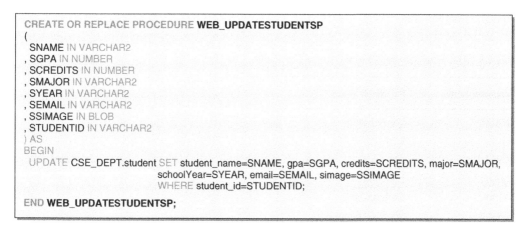

Figure 9.103 The arguments for the stored procedure Web_UpdateStudentSP(). *Source:* Used with permission from Microsoft.

```
CREATE OR REPLACE PROCEDURE WEB_UPDATESTUDENTSP
(
  SNAME IN VARCHAR2
, SGPA IN NUMBER
, SCREDITS IN NUMBER
, SMAJOR IN VARCHAR2
, SYEAR IN VARCHAR2
, SEMAIL IN VARCHAR2
, SSIMAGE IN BLOB
, STUDENTID IN VARCHAR2
) AS
BEGIN
  UPDATE CSE_DEPT.student SET student_name=SNAME, gpa=SGPA, credits=SCREDITS, major=SMAJOR,
                    schoolYear=SYEAR, email=SEMAIL, simage=SSIMAGE
                    WHERE student_id=STUDENTID;
END WEB_UPDATESTUDENTSP;
```

Figure 9.104 The detailed codes for the procedure WEB_UPDATESTUDENTSP.

To check and confirm this record updating action, we can open the **STUDENT** table in the Oracle SQL Developer. Expand the **Tables** folder under our sample database schema **CSE_DEPT** and click on the **STUDENT** table to open it. Sometimes you need to refresh this table by clicking on the **Refresh** icon shown in Figure 9.106 to see the updated result. You can find that the student **Tom David** has been updated to **Toney David** with six pieces of updated information in the **STUDENT** table, as shown in Figure 9.106.

Next let's build the second stored procedure **WEB_DELETESTUDENTSP()**.

9.5.6.2 Develop the Stored Procedure Web_DeleteStudentSP
Open Oracle SQL Developer if it is not opened, login, connect, and expand our sample database **CSE_DEPT**, then expand the **Other Users** folder and our database schema **CSE_DEPT**, and

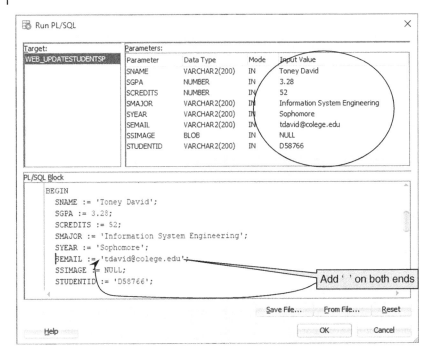

Figure 9.105 The input parameters to stored procedure Web_UpdateStudentSP(). *Source:* Used with permission from Microsoft.

Table 9.4 The input parameters to the stored procedure.

Parameter Name	Parameter Value
SNAME	Toney David
SGPA	3.28
SCREDITS	152
SMAJOR	Information System Engineering
SYEAR	Sophomore
SEMAIL	tdavid@college.edu
SSIMAGE	NULL
STUDENTID	D58766

right-click on the **Procedures** folder and select the item **New Procedure** from the popup menu to open the **Create Procedure** wizard, as shown in Figure 9.107.

Perform the following operational steps to generate this stored procedure:

1) Enter **WEB_DELETESTUDENTSP** into the **Name** box and add only one input parameter, **SNAME** that are shown in Figure 9.107 into this procedure. Click on the **OK** button to create this stored procedure.
2) On the opened procedure body, enter the codes that are shown in Figure 9.108 into this procedure to make it as our new stored procedure.
3) Click on the **Compile** item to save and build this new stored procedure.

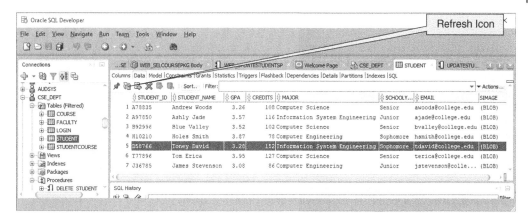

Figure 9.106 The running result of the stored procedure Web_UpdateStudentSP(). *Source:* Oracle Corporation.

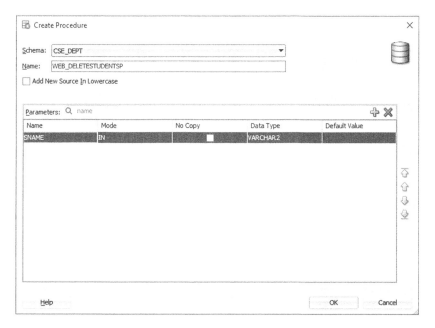

Figure 9.107 The opened Create Procedure wizard. *Source*: Used with permission from Microsoft.

One input parameter **SNAME** is listed in the parameter section with the related data type. A point to be noted is that the name of this input parameter must be identical with one we used inside our Web method **OracleDeleteSp()**, exactly in step **G** in Figure 9.100.

Two queries are included in this procedure. The first one is used to get the desired **STUDENT_ID** based on the input student's name, and the second query is used to delete the target student record based on the retrieved **STUDENT_ID** obtained from the first query.

Click on the **Compile** item to build and save this stored procedure.

To test this stored procedure, we can run it in the Oracle SQL Developer environment. Click on the green color **Run** button to run our procedure. On the opened **Run PL/SQL** wizard, which is shown in Figure 9.109, enter a student's name, **Toney David**, in the **Input Value** column and

```
CREATE OR REPLACE PROCEDURE   WEB_DELETESTUDENTSP
(
  SNAME IN VARCHAR2
) AS
BEGIN
  DECLARE SID VARCHAR2 (20);
  BEGIN SELECT  student_id INTO SID FROM STUDENT
  WHERE student_name = SNAME;
  DELETE FROM  CSE_DEPT.student WHERE student_id = SID;
  END;

END DELETESTUDENTSP;
```

Figure 9.108   The codes for the stored procedure WEB_DELETESTUDENTSP().

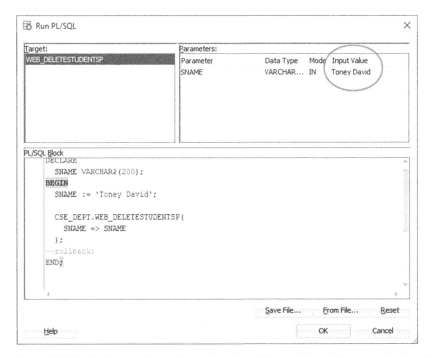

Figure 9.109   The Execute Stored Procedure wizard. *Source*: Used with permission from Microsoft.

click on the **OK** button to try to delete this student record. You may need to redo the system login process to perform this data deletion.

To confirm this deleting action, open our **STUDENT** table in the Oracle SQL Developer, One can find that the student named **Toney David** has been deleted or removed from that table. Sometimes you need to refresh this table by clicking on the **Refresh** icon to get the updated students' records.

As we mentioned, the student **Toney David** is a new inserted record and it is not the original student member in our sample database. Therefore, this student has no any related record in any other tables. This is good for us to perform a deleting action for this student to avoid any cascaded deletion action.

However, if you delete an original student record, which means that this record is not inserted by us in any of our previous project, instead it is generated with our sample database and contained some other records in the child tables, such as **LOGIN** and **STUDENTCOURSE** tables, you may need to spend a lot of time and energy to recover that record from both the parent and the child tables when a recovery job is needed.

For example, if you deleted an original student named **Tom Erica** from the **STUDENT** table, you have not only deleted this student record from the parent table, the **STUDENT** table, but also you deleted one record from the **LOGIN** table and six records from the **STUDENTCOURSE** table, and the latter two tables are called child tables.

Now if you open these two child tables related to this deleted student, such as **LOGIN** and **STUDENTCOURSE** tables, you can find that all records related to that student in those tables have also been deleted. These deleted records used **STUDENT_ID** as a foreign key in those tables, and all of those deleted records are shown in Table 9.5.

It is highly recommended to recover those deleted records from all tables since we may need to delete this record again when we test our Web service project later. One can use Server Explorer or Oracle SQL Developer to recover those deleted records one by one based on data shown in Tables 9.6–9.8.

An issue is the order to do that data recovery. One must first do recovery job for the deleted student in the **STUDENT** table (parent table) as shown in Table 9.8 and then recover other deleted data in other tables (child tables) since the **STUDENT_ID** is a primary key in the **STUDENT** table. For the student image column, **sImage**, just left it as **NULL** at this moment and we can handle that later when we test this service project by calling it from a consume application project.

Now go to **File|Save All** in the Oracle SQL Developer to save our two built stored procedures and close this tool by clicking on the **Close** button located at the upper-right corner on this wizard.

We have finished the development for this Web service project, and next let's build some client projects to consume our Web service project to update and delete some student records from our sample database.

Table 9.5 The deleted records for student Toney Black in all tables.

Table Name	Column Name	Column Value
LogIn Table	user_name	terica
	pass_word	excellent
	student_id	T77896
StudentCourse Table	s_course_id	1002
	s_course_id	1005
	s_course_id	1010
	s_course_id	1015
	s_course_id	1020
	s_course_id	1024

Table 9.6 Deleted data in LogIn table.

user_name	pass_word	faculty_id	student_id
Terica	excellent	NULL	T77896

Table 9.7 Deleted data in StudentCourse table.

s_course_id	student_id	course_id	credit	major
1002	T77896	CSC-335	3	CS/IS
1005	T77896	CSC-234A	3	CS/IS
1010	T77896	CSC-439	3	CS/IS
1015	T77896	CSC-432	3	CS/IS
1020	T77896	CSE-439	3	CS/IS
1024	T77896	CSC-333A	3	CS/IS

Table 9.8 Deleted data in Student table.

student_id	student_name	gpa	credits	major	schoolYear	email	simage
T77896	Tom Erica	3.95	127	Computer Science	Senior	terica@college.edu	NULL

9.6 Build Windows-Based Web Service Clients to Consume the Web Services

To save time and space, we do not need to create any new project and perform a full development for this project. Instead, we can copy and modify an existing Windows-based project `OracleUpdateDeleteSP Project` we developed in Section 7.5 in Chapter 7. Copy this project from the folder `Class DB Projects\Chapter 7` that is located under the `Students` folder at the Wiley ftp site (refer to Figure 1.2 in Chapter 1) and paste it into our new folder `C:\Chpater 9`.

Now let's perform the necessary modifications to this project to make it as our new project. The modifications can be divided into three parts:

1) Add a new Web reference to our new client project.
2) Modify the `Form_Load` event procedure in the Student Form.
3) Build the codes for two buttons, `Update` and `Delete`, exactly to these two buttons' click event procedures in the code window.

First, let's perform the first part to add a Web Service reference to our client project.

9.6.1 Add a Web Service Reference to Our Client Project

To consume or use the Web service `WebServiceOracleUpdateDelete Project` we developed in the last section, we need first to set up a Web reference to connect to that Web service with our client project together.

Refer to Section 9.4.3.1 to complete this Web reference adding process. Also change this Web service reference name from `localhost` to `WS_OracleUpdateDelete`.

Next let's build and modify the codes in the related event procedures and user-defined subroutines to call our Web service to perform the desired data actions.

9.6.2 Modify the Codes in the Form_Load Event Procedure

The reason we need to modify the codes inside this event procedure is that the student records may be updated after any updating action to our sample database, and these changes include the updating on **STUDENT_NAME**, **GPA**, **CREDITS** and other pieces of related information for the updated student's record. Thus, we need also to update all students' names in the **Student Name** combo box to enable users to select the updated student from this box to perform the related data actions, especially for the data updating validations.

Open this event procedure and enter the codes shown in Figure 9.110 into this event procedure to replace all original codes.

Let's have a closer look at this piece of codes to see how they work:

A) The only modification is to use a user-defined subroutine **CurrentStudent()** to replace the original six **Add()** methods under the **Student Name** combo box control, **ComboName**, and those methods are used to add six students' names into this combo box. Now we try to use this **CurrentStudent()** subroutine to replace those six **Add()** methods to directly access to our sample database to retrieve back the actual or current student members in real time.

The detailed codes for this subroutine **CurrentStudent()** are shown in Figure 9.111. Let's have a closer look at these codes to see how they work:

A) First, some objects and variables used for this subroutine are declared, which include the Web Reference or proxy class object **wsOracleUpDt**, our derived class object **oraResult** and a local integer variable **index**, which will be used as a loop number later.

B) A **Try - Catch** block is used to call our Web method **CurrentStudents()** via our Web Reference to collect all current students' names from our sample database and assign them to our derived class object **oraResult**.

C) By checking the member data **OracleOk** in our base class, we can determine whether this execution of the Web method is successful or not. A warning message is displayed if this operation is failed.

D) The **Student Name** combo box (**ComboName**) is cleared before it can be filled.

E) A **For** loop is utilized to repeatedly retrieve all students' names from the member data **StudentName(index)** and add them into the **ComboName** combo box one by one until the last student name in the **StudentName()** array is retrieved (**Length-1**).

F) The property **SelectedIndex** of the **ComboName** combo box is initialized to 0 to make the first student name selected and displayed.

Figure 9.110 The modified codes for the Form_Load event procedure.

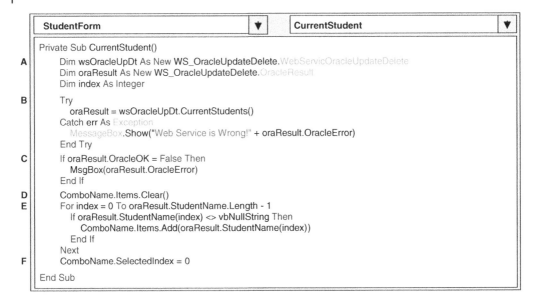

Figure 9.111 The detailed codes for the subroutine CurrentStudent().

```
btnUpdate                    ▼    Click                                        ▼

A   Private Sub btnUpdate_Click(sender As Object, e As EventArgs) Handles btnUpdate.Click
        Dim wsOracleUpDt As New WS_OracleUpdateDelete.WebServiceOracleUpdateDelete
        Dim oraResult As New WS_OracleUpdateDelete.OracleResult
B       Dim bImage As Byte()

        bImage = getStudentImage()

        Try
C           oraResult = wsOracleUpDt.OracleUpdateSP(txtName.Text, txtGPA.Text, txtMajor.Text, txtSchoolYear.Text,
                                        txtCredits.Text, txtEmail.Text, bImage, txtID.Text)

        Catch err As Exception
            MsgBox("Web service is wrong: " & err.Message)
        End Try
D       If oraResult.OracleOK = False Then
            MsgBox(oraResult.OracleError)
        End If

E       CurrentStudent()
    End Sub
```

Figure 9.112 Detailed codes for the Update button's Click event procedure.

Next let's build the codes for our two buttons, **Update** and **Delete** buttons' click event procedures.

9.6.3 Build the Codes to the Update Button's Click Event Procedure

Open this event procedure and add the codes shown in Figure 9.112 into this event procedure. Let's take a closer look at this piece of codes to see how it works:

A) A local reference object **wsOracleUpDt** is declared and it is used to access to our Web service project via this reference. An instance of our derived class OracleResult, **oraResult**, is also declared since we need to use this instance to access our member data defined inside that class later.

B) An image object **bImage** is declared and this is a byte array used to hold the updated student image file. The user-defined function **getStudentImage()** is called to get the desired student's image to be updated in our sample database.

C) Our Web method **OracleUpdateSP()** is executed via our Web reference object **wsOracle-UpDt** with eight pieces of updated student's information.

D) If this data updating action is failed, the returned error code should be located in the **OracleError** member, and this error is displayed via a **MsgBox()** function.

E) Finally, the user-defined subroutine **CurrentStudent()** is called to get all updated students' names and add them into the **Student Name** combo box control to enable users to perform a validation for this data updating later.

The codes for the user-defined function **getStudentImage()** are shown in Figure 9.113. We have discussed these codes in our previous projects.

Next let's build the codes for the **Delete** button's click event procedure.

9.6.4   Build the Codes to the Delete Button's Click Event Procedure

The function of this event procedure is to call our Web method **OracleDeleteSP()** in our Web service project with a student's name to delete the selected student's record from our sample database.

Open this event procedure and add the codes that are shown in Figure 9.114 into this event procedure. Let's have a closer look at this piece of codes to see how it works:

A) A local reference object **wsOracleUpDt** is declared and it is used to access to our Web service project via this reference.

B) Some local variables are declared first, which include a MessageBox buttons protocol object **vbButton** and a feedback variable **Answer**. The former is used to set up the button's format and the latter is used to hold the feedback value of calling the MessageBox() function.

```
StudentForm                          ▼        getStudentImage                      ▼

Private Function getStudentImage() As Byte()

    Dim ms As New System.IO.MemoryStream()
    Dim dlg As New OpenFileDialog()
    Dim bimage As Byte()

    dlg.Filter = "JPG Files (*.jpg)|*.jpg|All Files (*.*)|*.*"
    dlg.Title = "Select the Faculty Image"

    If (dlg.ShowDialog() = DialogResult.OK) Then
        PhotoBox.Image = Image.FromFile(dlg.FileName)
        PhotoBox.Image.Save(ms, PhotoBox.Image.RawFormat)
        bimage = ms.ToArray()
    Else
        PhotoBox.Image = Image.FromFile("C:\Images\Default.jpg")
        PhotoBox.Image.Save(ms, PhotoBox.Image.RawFormat)
        bimage = ms.ToArray()
    End If

    Return bimage
End Function
```

Figure 9.113   The detailed codes for the function getStudentImage().

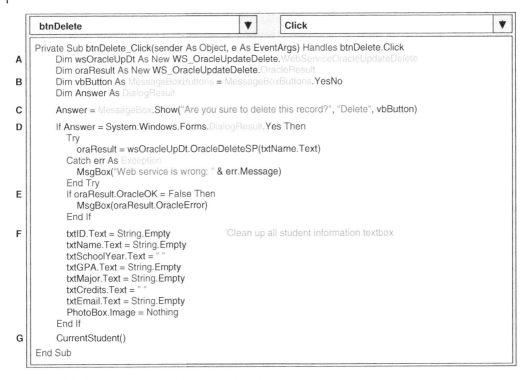

Figure 9.114 The codes for the Delete button's click event procedure.

C) The MessageBox() function is called with a warning message and two buttons.
D) If the feedback value is **Yes**, which means that the user wants to delete this record, our Web method **OracleDeleteSP()** is called to perform this data deleting action via our Web service. A warning message would be displayed if any error is encountered during this data deleting action.
E) In addition to the system exception error checking, we also need to check our Web method to make sure that it is running fine. If a **False** is returned from our returned class, exactly from the member data **OracleOK**, which means that something is wrong for executing of this Web method, a warning message is also displayed via the **MsgBox()** function.
F) All eight pieces of deleted student's information stored in seven textboxes and the student image box are cleared.
G) The user-defined subroutine **CurrentStudent()** is called to get all updated students' names and update them in the **Student Name** combo box, **ComboName**.

Go to **File | Save All** menu item to save these modifications and developments.

At this point, we have finished all modifications to this client project and now it is the time for us to run this project to access our Web service to perform the data updating and deleting actions. However, before we can run this project, make sure that our Web service project **WebServiceOracleUpdateDelete Project** is in the running status. This can be identified by a small white icon located in the status bar on the bottom of the screen. If you cannot find this icon, open our Web service project **WebServiceOracleUpdateDelete Project** and click on the **IIS Express** button to run it.

Now click on the Start Debugging button from our client project to run it. Enter valid `user_name` and `pass_word` for the `LogIn` Form and select `Student Information` to open the Student Form. First, let's test the data updating function by updating a student record `Tom Erica`. First click on the `Select` button to get all pieces of information about the student `Tom Erica`. Let's update this student record by entering data shown in Table 9.9 into related textbox and student image box `PhotoBox`.

Click on the `Update` button to call the Web method `OracleUpdateSP()` in our Web service to update this student record. On the opened Find-File wizard, browse to the student image folder and select the student image file `David.jpg`. One can find all student image files at the Folder `Images|Students` located at the `Students` folder in the Wiley ftp site (refer to Figure 1.2 in Chapter 1). One can copy those files and paste them to a special folder on your computer.

When this data updating is completed, the updated student image is displayed with all seven pieces of updated information shown in related textboxes, as shown in Figure 9.115.

Table 9.9 The updated record for the student Tom Erica.

Record Name	Record Value
student_id	T77896
student_name	Toney David
gpa	3.28
credits	52
major	Information System Engineering
schoolYear	Sophomore
email	tdavid@college.edu
sImage	David.jpg

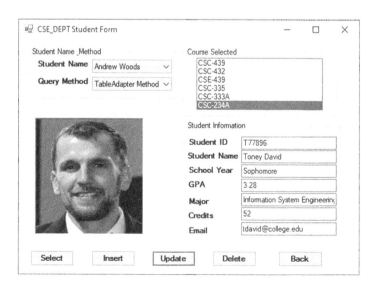

Figure 9.115 The running status of the student updating process. *Source:* Used with permission from Microsoft.

To confirm this data updating, go to the `ComboName` combo box and you can find that the original student, `Tom Erica`, has been replaced by an updated student named `Toney David`. You can select some other student with the `Select` button being clicked to retrieve the information for that student and then select the updated student `Toney David` and click on the Select button to confirm this data updating action.

You can find that all information related to that student has been updated and displayed in this form. Our data updating action is successful!

To test the deleting function, keep the current updated student `Toney David` selected and click on the `Delete` button to try to delete this record from the Student table. Click on the `Yes` button to the popup MessageBox to confirm this deletion action. If this deletion action is successful, all pieces of information related to this student would be deleted from both our sample database and this Student Form window.

To confirm this data deleting action, one can go to the `Student Name` combo box to try to find the deleted student. However, one cannot find that student from this `ComboName` combo box since that student has been deleted from our sample database.

Click on the `Back` and `Exit` buttons to terminate our client project.

However, the story is not finished. It is highly recommended to recover that deleted student record, `Tom Erica`, for our Student table since we want to keep our database neat and complete. You can recover this record by following the order shown below:

1) Insert the student, `Tom Erica`, as a new student record with the image using the `Insert` button's click event procedure on the Student Form or Student page into the `STUDENT` table in our sample database based on Table 9.9 in Section 9.5.6.2.
2) Using the Server Explorer or Oracle SQL Developer to open our sample database `CSE_DEPT` and our `LOGIN` and `STUDENTCOURSE` tables and add the original records shown in Tables 9.7 and 9.8 in Section 9.5.6.2 into these two tables manually.

To perform recovery job (1) listed above, one may need to use any previous homework exercise projects:

1) Project `OracleInsertRTObjectSP Project` or `OracleInsertRTObject Project`, which are Exercises 4 and 5 on Chapter 6, if you completed any of them.
2) Project `WebInsertStudent Project`, which is Exercise 5 on Chapter 8.

The recover order is: first recover the deleted record in the `STUDENT` table since the `STUDENT_ID` is a primary key in that table and then do recovery jobs for other child tables.

A complete Windows-based Web service client project `OracleUpdateDeleteSP Project` can be found from the folder `Class DB Projects\Chapter 9` that is located under the `Students` folder at the Wiley ftp site (refer to Figure 1.2 in Chapter 1).

9.7 Build Web-Based Web Service Clients to Consume the Web Services

It is no significant difference between building a Windows-based and a Web-based client project to consume a Web service. To save the time and the space, we can create a new ASP.NET Web Application project and then add and modify a `Student` page to consume our Web service project.

This section can be developed in the following sequences:

1) Create a new ASP.NET Web Application project `WebClientOracleUpdateDelete Project` and add an existing Web page `Student.aspx` from the folder `VB Forms|Web` that is located at the Wiley ftp site under the `Student` folder (refer to Figure 1.2 in Chapter 1) into our new project.
2) Add a Web service reference to our new project.
3) Add and modify codes in the related event procedures on the `Student.aspx.vb` file to call the associated Web method to perform our data updating and deleting. The code additions and modifications include the following sections:

   a) Develop the codes for the `Page_Load()` event procedure.
   b) Build the codes inside the `Back` button's click event procedure.
   c) Develop the codes for the `Update` button's click event procedure.
   d) Develop the codes for the `Delete` button's click event procedure.
   e) Develop the codes for the `Select` button's click event procedure.

Now let's start with the first step listed above.

9.7.1 Create a New ASP.NET Web Project and Add an Existing Web Page

Open Visual Studio.NET and go to the `File|New Project` menu item to create a new ASP.NET Web Application project. Enter `WebClientOracleUpdateDelete Project` and `WebClientOracleUpdateDelete Solution` into the `Project Name` and `Solution Name` box, and `C:\Chapter 9` into Location box, and click on the `Create` button to create this new project. Select the `Web Forms` as the template for this project.

On the opened new project Solution Explorer window, right-click on our new project icon `WebClientOracleUpdateDelete Project` and select the item `Add|Existing Item` from the popup menu to open the Add Existing Item wizard. Browse to the folder `VB Forms|Web` that is located under the `Students` folder at the Wiley ftp site (refer to Figure 1.2 in Chapter 1). Select the item `Student.aspx` by checking it and click on the `Add` button to add these items into our new Web site project.

Perform the following operations to make the `Student.aspx` page as the main page:

1) Open the `Source` file for the `Student.aspx` page and go to the end of the top line, change the last tag to `Inherits="WebClientOracleUpdateDelete_Project.Student`.
2) Right-click on the `Student.aspx` page from the Solution Explorer window and select the item `Set As Start Page` from the popup menu to set it as a start page.
3) Go to `File|Save All` to save all changes.
4) Go to `Build|Rebuild WebClientOracleUpdateDelete Project` to build the entire project.

9.7.2 Add a Web Service Reference and Modify the Web Form Window

Refer to Section 9.4.3.1 to complete this Web reference adding process. Also change this Web service reference name to `WS_UpdateDelete`. Your finished Add Web reference wizard should match one that is shown in Figure 9.116.

Click on the `Add Reference` button to finish this adding Web reference process.

Now let's take care of creations and modifications to the codes in the related event procedures and subroutines in the `Student.aspx` page.

Figure 9.116 The finished Add Web Reference wizard. *Source:* Used with permission from Microsoft.

9.7.3 Develop the Codes for the Page_Load() Event Procedure

The major function of this event procedure is to retrieve all current students' names and add them into the **Student Name** combo box to enable users to select any student member from that combo box to perform related data actions. In this project, the popular data actions include the student record updating and deleting actions.

As we know, a Web Method named **CurrentStudents()** is provided in our Web service project **WebServiceOracleUpdateDelete Project**, thus we can call that method to perform this students' names updating function. We can generate a user-defined subroutine named **CurrentStudent()** to call that Web method to perform these functions, so just enter one coding line into this event procedure to retrieve and load all students' names and display them in the **ComboName** combo box.

```
If Not IsPostBack Then CurrentStudent() End If
```

Now let's build and develop the codes for this user-defined subroutine. Enter the codes shown in Figure 9.117 into this subroutine, and let's have a closer look at this piece of codes to see how it works:

A) First, some objects and variables used for this subroutine are declared, which include the Web Reference or proxy class object **wsOracleUpDt**, our derived class object **oraResult**, and a local integer variable **index**, which will be used as a loop number later.

B) A **Try – Catch** block is used to call our Web method **CurrentStudents()** via our Web Reference to collect all current students' names from our sample database and assign them to our derived class object **oraResult**.

C) By checking the member data **OracleOk** in our base class, we can determine whether this execution of the Web method is successful or not. A warning message is displayed if this operation is failed.

D) The **Student Name** combo box (**ComboName**) is cleared before it can be filled.

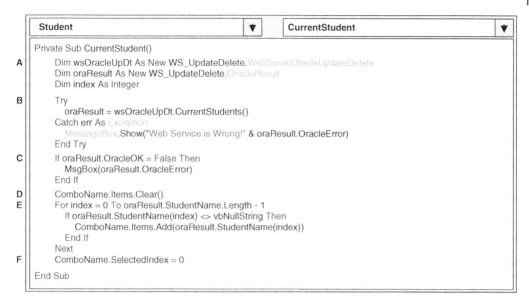

Student	▼	CurrentStudent	▼

```
Private Sub CurrentStudent()
A       Dim wsOracleUpDt As New WS_UpdateDelete.WebServicOracleUpdateDelete
        Dim oraResult As New WS_UpdateDelete.OracleResult
        Dim index As Integer

B       Try
            oraResult = wsOracleUpDt.CurrentStudents()
        Catch err As Exception
            MessageBox.Show("Web Service is Wrong!" & oraResult.OracleError)
        End Try

C       If oraResult.OracleOK = False Then
            MsgBox(oraResult.OracleError)
        End If

D       ComboName.Items.Clear()
E       For index = 0 To oraResult.StudentName.Length - 1
            If oraResult.StudentName(index) <> vbNullString Then
                ComboName.Items.Add(oraResult.StudentName(index))
            End If
        Next
F       ComboName.SelectedIndex = 0

End Sub
```

Figure 9.117   The detailed codes for the subroutine CurrentStudent().

E) A **For** loop is utilized to repeatedly retrieve all students' names from the member data **StudentName(index)** and add them into the **ComboName** combo box one by one until the last student name in the **StudentName()** array is retrieved (**Length-1**).

F) The property **SelectedIndex** of the **ComboName** combo box is initialized to 0 to make the first student name selected and displayed.

Next, let's build the codes for the **Back** buttons' click event procedures.

9.7.4   Build the Codes Inside the Back Button's Click Event Procedure

The purpose of this piece of codes is to terminate our project as this **Back** button is clicked by the user. Thus, just enter the following code line into this event procedure:

Response.Write("<script>window.close();</script>")

Next, let's take care of creating codes for the Update button's click event procedure.

9.7.5   Add the Codes to the Update Button's Click Event Procedure

This coding job is to add the codes to the **Update** button's click event procedure to perform the student record updating operations, exactly it is to call one of our Web methods, **OracleUpdateSP()** built in our Web service project, to perform this data updating action. Open this event procedure and enter the codes shown in Figure 9.118 into this procedure. Let's take a closer look at this piece of codes to see how it works:

A) A new instance of our Web proxy class WS_UpdateDelete, **wsOracleUpDt**, is created and this instance is used to access the Web method **OracleUpdateSP()** we developed in our Web service class **WebServiceOracleUpdateDelete Project** to perform this data updating operation.

B) An instance of our customer returned class OracleResult, **oraResult**, is also created and it is used to hold the running status of executing our Web method and updated students' names.

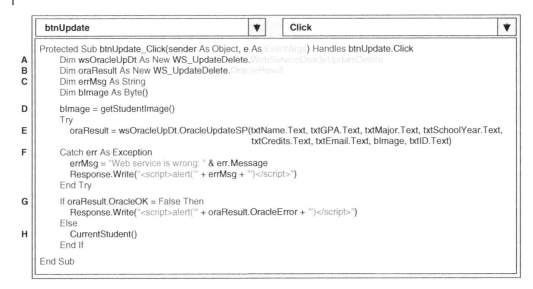

Figure 9.118 The codes for the Update button's Click event procedure.

C) A local string variable **errMsg** is also created and it is used to reserve the error source that will be displayed as a part of an error message later. A **Byte()** array, **bImage**, is declared and it is used to hold an updated student image file.

D) Prior to performing this data updating, a user-defined function **getStudentImage()** is called to pick up a selected student image file to be updated later.

E) A **Try...Catch** block is used to call the Web method **OracleUpdateSP()** with eight pieces of updated student information to execute a stored procedure **Web_UpdateStudentSP()** to perform this student record updating action against our sample database.

F) An error message will be displayed if any error is encountered during that data updating action. A point to be noted is that the displaying format of this error message. To displayed a string variable in a message box in the client side, one must use the Java script function **alert()** with the input string variable as an argument that is enclosed and representcd by **' "** + **input_string + "'**.

G) Besides the system error-checking process, we also need to check the member data **OracleOK** that is defined in our returned class in the Web service project to make sure that this data updating is error-free. A returned **False** indicates that this data updating encountered some application error and the error source stored in another member data **OracleError** is displayed using the Java script function **alert()**.

H) If this data updating is successful, all updated students' names are retrieved back from the updated **STUDENT** table in our sample database and added into our **Student Name** combo box to enable users to verify this data updating later.

The codes for the user-defined function **getStudentImage()** are shown in Figure 9.119. This function is basically identical with another user-defined function **getFacultyImage()** we built in Figure 8.65 at Section 8.6.2.3 in Chapter 8. The only differences are the function name (**getFacultyImage** and **getStudentImage**) and the virtual folder (**FacultyImage** and **StudentImage**) used to hold all students' image files. Both differences have been highlighted in bold.

A point to be noted is that prior running this project, one must store all students' image files into this virtual folder **StudentImage**, and this folder must be located under the current project

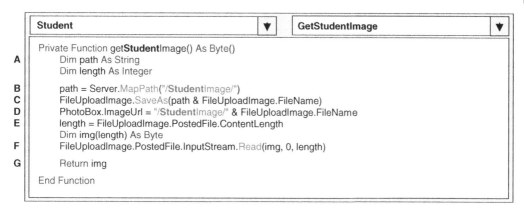

| Student | ▼ | GetStudentImage | ▼ |

```
     Private Function getStudentImage() As Byte()
A        Dim path As String
         Dim length As Integer

B        path = Server.MapPath("/StudentImage/")
C        FileUploadImage.SaveAs(path & FileUploadImage.FileName)
D        PhotoBox.ImageUrl = "/StudentImage/" & FileUploadImage.FileName
E        length = FileUploadImage.PostedFile.ContentLength
         Dim img(length) As Byte
F        FileUploadImage.PostedFile.InputStream.Read(img, 0, length)

G        Return img
     End Function
```

Figure 9.119 The codes for the subroutine GetStudentImage().

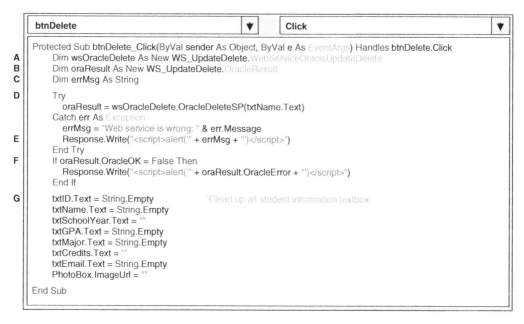

| btnDelete | ▼ | Click | ▼ |

```
     Protected Sub btnDelete_Click(ByVal sender As Object, ByVal e As EventArgs) Handles btnDelete.Click
A        Dim wsOracleDelete As New WS_UpdateDelete.WebServiceOracleUpdateDelete
B        Dim oraResult As New WS_UpdateDelete.OracleResult
C        Dim errMsg As String

D        Try
             oraResult = wsOracleDelete.OracleDeleteSP(txtName.Text)
         Catch err As Exception
             errMsg = "Web service is wrong: " & err.Message
E            Response.Write("<script>alert('" + errMsg + "')</script>")
         End Try
F        If oraResult.OracleOK = False Then
             Response.Write("<script>alert('" + oraResult.OracleError + "')</script>")
         End If

G        txtID.Text = String.Empty              'Clean up all student information textbox
         txtName.Text = String.Empty
         txtSchoolYear.Text = ""
         txtGPA.Text = String.Empty
         txtMajor.Text = String.Empty
         txtCredits.Text = ""
         txtEmail.Text = String.Empty
         PhotoBox.ImageUrl = ""
     End Sub
```

Figure 9.120 The codes for the Delete button Click event procedure.

folder **WebClientOracleUpdateDelete Project** to make this project executable. Otherwise, one may encounter some runtime error for this folder.

Next, let's develop the codes for the **Delete** button's click event procedure to perform the data deleting actions against our sample database.

9.7.6 Develop Codes for the Delete Button's Click Event Procedure

Double-click on the **Delete** button from our client page window to open the **Delete** button's click event procedure and enter the codes that are shown in Figure 9.120 into this event procedure. Let's take a closer look at this piece of codes to see how it works:

A) A new instance of our Web proxy class, **wsOracleDelete**, is created and this instance is used to access the Web method **OracleDeleteSP()** we developed in our Web service class **WebServiceOracleUpdateDelete Project** to perform the data deleting action.

B) An instance of our customer returned class OracleResult, `oraResult`, is created and it is used to hold the returned running status of executing our Web method and updated students' names.

C) A local string variable `errMsg` is also created and it is used to reserve the error source that will be displayed as a part of an error message later.

D) A `Try...Catch` block is used to call the Web method `OracleDeleteSP()` with one student's name, `txtName.Text` that works as an identifier, to run a stored procedure `Web_DeleteStudentSP()` to perform this deleting action against our sample database.

E) An error message will be displayed if any error is encountered during that data deleting action. A point to be noted is that the displaying format of this error message. To displayed a string variable in a message box in the client side, one must use the Java script function `alert()` with the input string variable as an argument that is enclosed and represented by `'"  +  input_string  + "'`.

F) Besides the system error-checking methods, we also need to check the member data `OracleOK` that is defined in our returned class in the Web service project to make sure that this data deleting is error-free. A returned `False` value of this member data indicates that this data deleting encountered some application error and the error source stored in another member data `OracleError` is displayed.

G) Finally, a cleaning job is performed to empty all pieces of information related to the deleted student from all textboxes and the student image box.

Go to `File | Save All` menu item to save these modifications and developments.

9.7.7 Develop Codes for the Select Button's Click Event Procedure

The reason we need to build the codes for this event procedure is that we want to use it to confirm both data updating and deleting actions we developed. By selecting and retrieving back all current students with their information from our sample database, we can conveniently check and validate our data updating and deleting actions.

The codes to be built for this event procedure include

1) Adding two references, `Devart.Data` and `Devart.Data.Oracle`, into our project by right-clicking on our project `WebClientOracleUpdateDelete Project` in the Solution Explorer and select `Add | Reference` item. In the opened Reference Manager, you need to select the `Extensions` item under the `Assemblies` to select desired references.

2) Adding one database drive directive, `Imports Devart.Data.Oracle`, into the top of the Student coding page (highlighted in step **A** in Figure 9.121).

3) Adding the query-related codes for this event procedure and two user-defined subroutines. Exactly these codes have been already included in some homework exercises in Chapters 6 and 8, thus here we only show these codes without any explanations, and you can try to understand them yourself.

The codes for the `Select` button's click event procedure are shown in Figure 9.121. Figure 9.122 shows the codes for two related user-defined subroutines.

Now we have completed all developments for the data updating and deleting actions in our client side. Before one can run this client project to access to our Web service to perform data actions for any student record, one needs to create and add a new folder `StudentImage` under our current project folder `C:\Chapter  9\WebClientOracleUpdateDelete  Solution\ WebClientOracleUpdateDelete Project` and copy all student image files from the folder

Figure 9.121 The codes for the Select button Click event procedure.

Figure 9.122 The codes for the user-defined subroutine procedures.

`Images\Students` located at the Wiley ftp site under the `Student` folder (refer to Figure 1.2 in Chapter 1) and paste them to this `StudentImage` folder. The reason for that is because we will use a virtual folder or path to save those student images for this Web client project to enable them to be found during the project runs.

Now let's run our projects to test the data updating function first.

First run our Web service project `WebServiceOracleUpdateDelete Project` and then run our Web client project `WebClientOracleUpdateDelete Project` by clicking on the `IIS Express` button. The running status of our client project is shown in Figure 9.123.

As we did before, to test this data updating, first click the `Select` button to retrieve back the information for the default student, `Tom Erica`. Then updating this student record by entering the following pieces of updated information to the related textbox:

- Name: `Toney David`
- GPA: `3.28`
- Credits: `52`
- Major: `Information System Engineering`
- SchoolYear: `Sophomore`
- Email: `tdavid@college.edu`

Then go to the `FileUploadImage` control and click on the `Browse` button to browse to the virtual folder or path where all student image files are located, which is `StudentImage`, and select the updated student image file, `David.jpg`, and click on the `Open` button to select this image file. Now click on the `Update` button to perform this data updating action.

To confirm this updating action, first select some other student, such as `Blue Valley`, from the `Student Name` combo box and click on the `Select` button to show that student's information. Then select our updated student's name, `Toney David`, from the combo box and click on the `Select` button. The information for the original student named `Tom Erica` has been successfully updated, as shown in Figure 9.123.

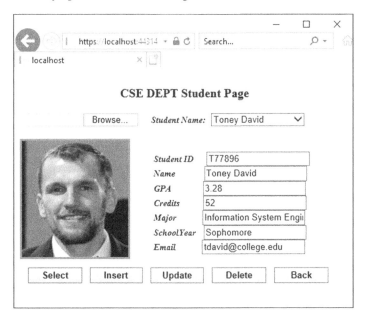

Figure 9.123 Running result of updating a student record. *Source*: Used with permission from Microsoft.

It is highly recommended to recover the updated student back to the original student record for the default student, **Tom Erica**. Refer to Table 9.10 in this section to perform another Updating operation to recover that student record.

Now let's test the data deleting actions.

To simplify this data deleting operation, we try to avoid or not to delete any original student record that was generated with our sample database, instead we prefer to delete an inserted student record to avoid complicated recovery jobs. One student, **James Stevenson**, was inserted into the **STUDENT** table in our sample database in Exercise 4 in our homework on Chapter 6. Thus, we can delete this student since no any login and course records have been set up for this student. In this way, we can avoid the complicated recover process if an original student record were deleted. Select this student from the **Student Name** combo box and click on the **Delete** button to call the Web method **OracleDeleteSP()** defined our Web service to try to delete that student record from our sample database. One can find that all pieces of information related to the updated student have been removed from this Form window.

To confirm this data deleting action, one can click on the **Select** button to try to retrieve back this deleted student's information. Immediately you will get a warning message to indicate that no matched student can be found from our sample database, which means that the selected student record has been deleted.

One can also confirm this deleting by opening the **STUDENT** table in our sample database from either the Server Explorer or the Oracle SQL Developer.

Click on the **Back** button to terminate our client project. Our client project is very successful.

However, the story is not finished. If you deleted an original student record, such as **Tom Erica**, it is highly recommended to recover that deleted student **Tom Erica** and related information from three tables; **STUDENT**, **LOGIN**, and **STUDENTCOURSE** in our sample database. One can do this recovery job in the following sequence:

1) First run a Web project **WebInsertStudent Projct**, which was built in Exercise 5 at Chapter 8 and use the **Insert** button's click event procedure to insert the deleted student record in the **STUDENT** table based on data shown in Table 9.10 for the original data of that student.
2) Then use the Server Explorer or Oracle SQL Developer to open the **LOGIN** and the **STUDENTCOURSE** tables. Refer to Tables 9.11 and 9.12 to add those original data into those two child tables. You can copy those records and paste them to the bottom of the related tables.

Table 9.10 Deleted data in Student table.

student_id	student_name	gpa	credits	major	schoolYear	email	simage
T77896	Tom Erica	3.95	127	Computer Science	Senior	terica@college.edu	Erica.jpg

Table 9.11 Deleted data in LogIn table.

user_name	pass_word	faculty_id	student_id
terica	excellent	NULL	T77896

Table 9.12   Deleted data in StudentCourse table.

s_course_id	student_id	course_id	credit	major
1002	T77896	CSC-335	3	CS/IS
1005	T77896	CSC-234A	3	CS/IS
1010	T77896	CSC-439	3	CS/IS
1015	T77896	CSC-432	3	CS/IS
1020	T77896	CSE-439	3	CS/IS
1024	T77896	CSC-333A	3	CS/IS

A complete Web-based Web service client project `WebClientOracleUpdateDelete Project` can be found from the folder `Class DB Projects\Chapter 9` that is located under the `Students` folder at the Wiley ftp site (refer to Figure 1.2 in Chapter 1).

At this point, we have finished the discussion about how to access and manipulate data against the Oracle database via ASP.NET Web services.

9.8   Chapter Summary

A detailed discussion and analysis about the structure and components of the Web services is provided in this chapter. Unlike the ASP.NET Web Applications in which the user needs to access the Web server through the client browser by sending requests to the server to obtain the desired information, the ASP.NET Web Services provide an automatic way to search, identify, and return the desired information required by the user through a set of methods installed in the Web server, and those methods can be accessed by a computer program, not the user, via the Internet. Another important difference between the ASP.NET Web Applications and ASP.NET Web services is that the latter do not provide any GUIs, and users need to create those GUIs themselves to access the Web Services via the Internet.

One of the most popular databases, Oracle database, is discussed and used for three example Web service projects, which include

- `WebServiceOracleSelect Project`.
- `WebServiceOracleInsert Project`.
- `WebServiceOracleUpdateDelete Project`.

Each Web service contains different Web methods that can be used to access different databases and perform the desired data actions such as `Select`, `Insert`, `Update`, and `Delete` via the Internet.

To consume those Web services, different Web service client projects are also developed in this chapter. Both Windows-based and Web-based Web service client projects are discussed and built for each kind of Web service listed above. Totally, nine projects, including the Web service projects and the associated Web service client projects, are developed in this chapter. All projects have been debugged and tested and can be run in any Windows compatible operating systems such as Windows XP, Windows 7, and Windows 10.

Homework

I. True/False Selections

_____ **1** Web services can be considered as a set of methods installed in a Web server and can be called by computer programs installed on the clients through the Internet.

_____ **2** Web services do not require the use of browsers or HTML, and therefore Web services are sometimes called *application services.*

_____ **3** XML is a text-based data storage language and it uses a series of tags to define and store data.

_____ **4** SOAP is an XML-based communication protocol used for communications between different applications. Therefore, SOAP is a platform-dependent and language-dependent protocol.

_____ **5** WSDL is an XML-based language for describing Web services and how to access them. In WSDL terminology, each Web service is defined as an abstract endpoint or a Port and each Web method is defined as an abstract operation.

_____ **6** UDDI is an XML-based directory for businesses to list themselves on the Internet and the goal of this directory is to enable companies to find one another on the Web and make their systems interoperable for e-commerce.

_____ **7** The main service page is the most important file in a Web service since all Visual Basic.NET codes related to build a Web service are located in this page and our major coding development will be concentrated on this page.

_____ **8** The names and identifiers used in the SOAP message can be identical, in other words, those names and identifiers can be the same name and identifier used by any other message.

_____ **9** A single Web service can contain multiple different Web methods.

_____ **10** You do not need to deploy a Web service to the development server if you use that service locally in your computer, but you must deploy it to a production server if you want other users to access your Web service from the Internet.

II. Multiple Choices

1 A Web service is used to effectively _____ the target information required by computer programs.
   A Find
   B Find, identify, and return
   C Identify
   D Return

2 Four fundamental components of a Web service are _____.
  A IIS, Internet, Client, and Server
  B Endpoint, Port, Operation, and types
  C .asmx, web.config, .asmx.vb, and Web_Reference
  D XML, SOAP, WSDL, and UDDI

3 The XML is used to _____ the data to be transferred between applications.
  A Tag
  B Re-build
  C Receive
  D Interpreter

4 SOAP is used to _____ the data tagged in the XML format into the messages represented in the SOAP protocol.
  A Organize
  B Build
  C Wrap and pack
  D Send

5 WSDL is used to map a concrete network protocol and message format to an abstract endpoint, and _____ the Web services available in a WSDL document format.
  A Illustrate
  B Describe
  C Provide
  D Check

6 UDDI is used to _____ all Web services that are available to users and businesses.
  A List
  B Display
  C Both a and b
  D None of the above

7 Unlike Web-based applications, a Web service project does not provide a _____.
  A Start Page
  B Configuration file
  C Code-behind page
  D Graphic User Interface

8 Each Web service must be located at a unique _____ in order to allow users to access it.
  A Computer
  B Server
  C SOAP file in a server
  D Namespace in a server

9 To consume a Web service by either a Windows-based or a Web-based client project, the prerequisite job is to add a _____ into the client project.
  A Connection

    B Web Reference

    C Reference

    D Proxy class

10 **The running result of a Web service is represented by a(n) _____ format since each Web service does not provide a Graphic User Interface (GUI).**

    A XML

    B HTTP

    C HTML

    D Java scripts

III. Exercises

1 Write a paragraph to answer and explain the following questions:

    A What is ASP.NET Web service?

    B What are main components of the ASP.NET Web service?

    C How an ASP.NET Web service is executed?

2 Suppose we have a Web service project and the main service page contains the following statement:

```
<%@ WebService Language="vb" CodeBehind="~/App_Code/testWeb.
vb" Class="testWeb" %>
```

Answer the following questions:

    A What is the name of this Web service?

    B What are the name and the location of the code-behind page of this Web service?

    C Is the content of this page related to the WSDL file of this Web service?

3 Suppose we have developed a Web service named WebServiceOracleSelect with a Web method GetStudent() that has an input parameter student_name and returns seven pieces of student information, such as student_id, gpa, credits, major, schoolYear, email, and sImage. Please list steps to develop a Windows-based client project to consume that Web service.

4 Add a Web method GetStudent() shown in question 3 into our Web service project WebServiceOracleSelect Project and develop the codes to that method to perform the data query for the Student via our sample Oracle database CSE_DEPT. The project file can be found from the folder Class DB Projects\Chapter 9 that is located at the Wiley ftp site for Students folder (refer to Figure 1.2 in Chapter 1).

Hint1: One needs to add another derived class OracleSelectStudent.vb as the returned class based on the derived class OracleSelectResult.vb to hold all eight columns retrieved from the STUDENT table.

Hint2: One can modify a user-defined subroutine FillFacultyReader() to make it as FillStudentReader() subroutine and use it to fill the queried student record to the returned instance for the derived class OracleSelectStudent.vb.

5 Develop a Windows-based Web service client project to consume the Web service developed in question 4, exactly to consume the new Web method GetStudent().

Hint1: One can use project WinClientOracleSelect Project that can be found from the folder Class DB Projects\Chapter 9 that is located under the Students folder at the Wiley ftp site (refer to Figure 1.2 in Chapter 1). You need to add a Student Form as a GUI to that project and coding the Select button's click event procedure on the Student Form window. Set that Student Form as the start Form.

Hint2: A completed Student Form window can be found at the folder VB Forms\ Window that is located under the Students folder at the Wiley ftp site (refer to Figure 1.2 in Chapter 1). You can use Add|Exiting Item to do this Student Form addition.

Hint3: One also needs to re-add service reference to our Web service since a new method GetStudent() has been added. To do that, (1) delete the original Web Reference WS_OracleSelect under the Web References folder and then delete this Web References folder in the Solution Explorer. (2) Add this Web Reference again into our project.

6 Similar to Exercise 4, add another Web method GetStudentCourse() into our Web service project WebServiceOracleSelect Project and develop the codes to that method to perform the course query for the selected student via our sample Oracle database CSE_DEPT. The project file can be found from the folder Class DB Projects\Chapter 9 that is located under the Students folder at the Wiley ftp site (refer to Figure 1.2 in Chapter 1).

Also consume that Web method in our client project WinClientOracleSelect Project in the Select button's click event procedure in the Student Form window.

Hint1: One can use a stored procedure STUDENT_COURSE.SelectStudentCourse() built in Section 5.6.7.4 in Chapter 5 to perform this course query action inside that Web method. One also needs to add a member data Public CourseID(10) As String into the derived class OracleSelectStudent.vb.

Hint2: One may refer to a subroutine FillCourseReader() built in Figure 9.60 in Section 9.4.2.3, modify, and use it in the Web service project to collect all course_id and assign them to the member data CourseID(10) in the class OracleSelectStudent.vb.

Hint3: One may refer to a subroutine FillCourseListBox() built in Figure 9.81 in Section 9.4.3.3.3, modify, and use it in the Window client project WinClientOracleSelect Project to consume the Web method GetStudentCourse().

Hint4: One needs to re-add the Web Reference WS_OracleSelect into this project since a new Web method GetStudentCourse() has been added into that Web service project.

7 Develop a Web-based Web service client project to consume the Web service developed in Exercise 4, exactly to consume the new Web method GetStudent().

Hint1: Refer to project WebClientOracleSelect Project that can be found from the folder Class DB Projects\Chapter 9 that is located at the Wiley ftp site under the Students category (refer to Figure 1.2 in Chapter 1). In fact, you need to add a Student page, Student.aspx into this project. One can find this page file from a folder VB Forms\Web in the Wiley ftp site under the Students folder (refer to Figure 1.2 in Chapter 1). Do the codes to the Select button's click event procedure in the Student page in that project to complete this assignment.

Hint2: One needs to re-add the Web Reference using the Web service project WebServiceOracleSelect Project built in Exercise 4 since a new Web method GetStudent() was added into this service project.

Hint3: After adding the Student page, one needs to open the Source file for that page by right-clicking on the Student.aspx from the Solution Explorer and select View Markup item, then gototheendofthetopcodingline,andchangethelasttagto**Inherits="WebClientOracleSelect_ Project.Student"** %>. Then go to Build|Rebuild WebClientOracleSelect Project menu item to rebuild the project.

Hint4: One can refer to the codes in the Facuty.aspx.vb page to build the codes for this Student page. Also set up the Student page as Start Page.

Hint5: One needs to remove the database drive directive Imports Devart.Data.Oracle from the top of the Student page.

8 Add and develop a Web method Update_CourseSP() in our Web service project WebServiceOracleUpdateDelete Project to perform course updating function. This method will call a stored procedure UpdateCourseSP() built in Section 7.5.2.1 in Chapter 7 to do this course updating action. Test this Web method when it is done and confirm its correctness by checking the COURSE table in our sample database. The service project WebServiceOracleUpdateDelete Project can be found from the folder Class DB Projects\Chapter 9 that is located at the Wiley ftp site under the Students folder (refer to Figure 1.2 in Chapter 1).

Hint: One can refer to the codes in the Web method OracleUpdateSP() in the project WebServiceOracleUpdateDelete Project to build this Web method. Refer to Section 7.5.2.1 in Chapter 7 to get more details for input parameters used for this method.

9 Replace and create new codes in the Update button's click event procedure in the Course Form window located at the project OracleUpdateDeleteSP Project to consume the Web method Update_CourseSP() built in Exercise 8. Confirm this updating action using the Select button's click event procedure. The project OracleUpdateDeleteSP Project can be found from the folder Class DB Projects\Chapter 9 that is located at the Wiley ftp site under the Students folder (refer to Figure 1.2 in Chapter 1).

Hint: One needs to re-add the Web Reference WS_OracleUpdateDelete into this new project since a new Web method Update_CourseSP() has been added into that Web Service project WebServiceOracleUpdateDelete Project.

10 Develop a Web-based project to consume the Web method Update_CourseSP() built in Exercise 8.

One can use the Update button's click event procedure in the Course page in a Web-based project WebClientOracleUpdateDelete Project that can be found from the folder Class DB Projects\Chapter 9 in the Wiley ftp site under the Students folder (refer to Figure 1.2 in Chapter 1). One may need to develop some initialization codes to display all faculty members in the Faculty Name combo box control and place those codes in the Page_Load() event procedure in the Course page. Also needs to code for the Back button's click event procedure to close the project. Set the Course page as the Start page to test this project.

Hint1: One needs to re-add the Web Reference WebServiceOracleUpdateDelete into this project since a new Web method Update_CourseSP() is added.

Hint2: One needs to add an existing Course page into this project, and that page can be found from the folder VB Forms\Web under the Students folder in the Wiley ftp site (refer to Figure 1.2 in Chapter 1).

Hint3: Open the Source file for the added Course page, go to the end of the top coding line, and change the last tag to: Inherits="WebClientOracleUpdateDelete_Project.Course" %>.

<u>Hint4:</u> Refer to the codes in the CourseForm_Load() event procedure in the project OracleUpdateDeleteRTObject Project built in Chapter 7 to develop the codes for the Page_ Load() event procedure in this Course page.

<u>Hint5:</u> Refer to the codes in the Select button's click event procedure in the project OracleUpdateDeleteRTObject Project built in Chapter 7 to develop the codes for the Select button's click event procedure in this Course page.

<u>Hint6:</u> Refer to the codes in the CourseList_SelectedIndexChanged event procedure in the Course Form at the project OracleUpdateDeleteRTObject Project built in Chapter 7 to develop the codes for the CourseList_SelectedIndexChanged event procedure in this Course page.

<u>Hint7:</u> One can refer to the codes in the Update button's click event procedure in the Student page to build this Update event procedure in the Course page.

Appendix A

Download and Install Oracle Database XE 18c

Similar to Oracle Database 11g XE, for most applications, you only need to download and install the Oracle Database 18c XE Server component if you want to use it as a standard product since it provides both an Oracle database and tools for managing Oracle database.

The Oracle Database XE also provides a Client component. However, regularly you do not need to install it unless you want to perform remote database connections for remote clients located at different sites. For most applications, you need only to download and install Oracle Database 18c XE server on your computer, which can connect to the database from the same computer on which you installed the Server, and then administer the database and develop Visual Studio.NET applications.

A.1 Download the Oracle Database 18c XE

Go to: https://www.oracle.com/database/technologies/xe-downloads.html to begin this downloading process. Perform the following operations to complete this downloading and installation process:

1) Click on the second link Oracle Database 18c Express Edition for Windows x64 to begin this process, as shown in Figure A.1.
2) On the next widget, click on the checkbox: `I accept the Oracle License Agreement`, and click on the `Download OracleXE184_Win64.zip` button to download it.
3) In the next sign-in page, you need to create a new login account in the Oracle Technology Network (OTN). Enter your confirmed username and password, click on the Sign in button to complete this `sign-in` process. The downloading process starts (be patient and it may take a while to complete this process).
4) Double click on the downloaded zip file `OracleXE184_Win64.zip` located at the lower-left corner to unzip it as this downloading process is done.

A.2 Install the Oracle Database 18c XE

1) Double click on the `Setup` application file under the `Download` folder to begin this installation process, as shown in Figure A.2.
2) Click on the `Next` button on the `InstallShield Wizard` to start the installation.

Oracle Database Programming with Visual Basic.NET: Concepts, Designs, and Implementations, First Edition. Ying Bai.
© 2021 The Institute of Electrical and Electronics Engineers, Inc. Published 2021 by John Wiley & Sons, Inc.
Companion website: www.wiley.com/go/bai-VB-Oracle

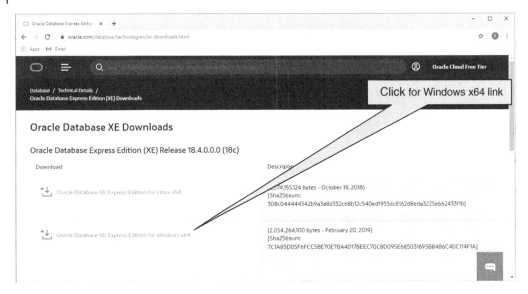

Figure A.1 The opened Download wizard.

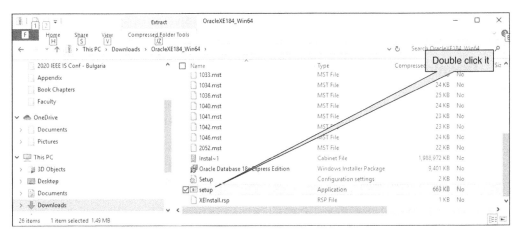

Figure A.2 The downloaded Oracle Database 18c Express Edition.

3) Click the radio button: `I accept the terms in the license agreement,` and `Next` button to continue.
4) On the next wizard, one can select the desired destination for this installation by clicking on the `Change` button if you like. Otherwise, just click on the `Next` button to use the default location, as shown in Figure A.3.
5) On the next wizard, one can enter a desired password, and then click the `Next` button to continue.
6) Click on the `Install` button on the next wizard to begin the preinstallation and installation process, as shown in Figure A.4.
7) When the installation process completes, as shown in Figure A.5, click on the `Finish` button to close this process.
8) Now you can check some important documents related to this installation. One of the most important documents is the `tnsnames.ora` file, which is located at the `C:\app\yingb\`

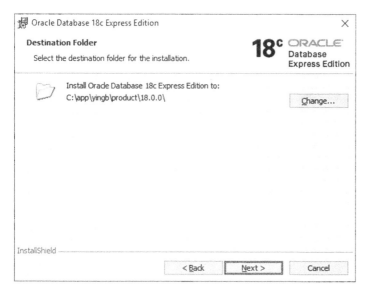

Figure A.3 Select the desired location for this installation.

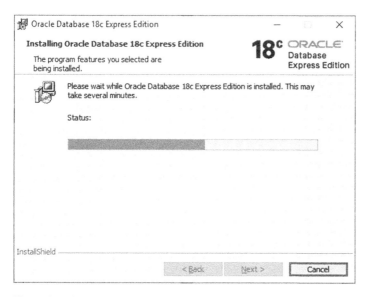

Figure A.4 The installation process starts.

`product\18.0.0\dbhomeXE\NETWORK\ADMIN` in my case. The path after `C:\app,` `yingb,` is the user name on the author's computer, and it should be replaced by your user name in your computer. Open this file using the Notepad, and you can find some important parameters for this Oracle Database 18c XE, as shown in Figure A.6.

The following important parameters can be found from this file:

A) The full address of this Oracle Database 18c XE in my computer, which is `TCP\YBSMART\1251,` represents the `protocol\host\port`. The `YBSMART` is the author's computer's name, and it should be replaced by your computer's name.
B) The installed Oracle database server name, which is `XE`.

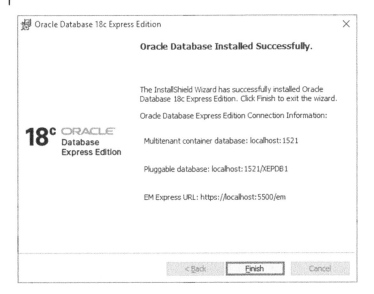

Figure A.5 The installation process completes.

```
# tnsnames.ora Network Configuration File: C:\app\yingb\product\18.0.0\dbhomeXE\NETWORK\ADMIN\tnsnames.ora
# Generated by Oracle configuration tools.

XE =
  (DESCRIPTION =
    (ADDRESS = (PROTOCOL = TCP)(HOST = YBSMART)(PORT = 1521))
    (CONNECT_DATA =
      (SERVER = DEDICATED)
      (SERVICE_NAME = XE)
    )
  )

LISTENER_XE =
  (ADDRESS = (PROTOCOL = TCP)(HOST = YBSMART)(PORT = 1521))


ORACLR_CONNECTION_DATA =
  (DESCRIPTION =
    (ADDRESS_LIST =
      (ADDRESS = (PROTOCOL = IPC)(KEY = EXTPROC1521))
    )
    (CONNECT_DATA =
      (SID = CLRExtProc)
      (PRESENTATION = RO)
    )
  )
```

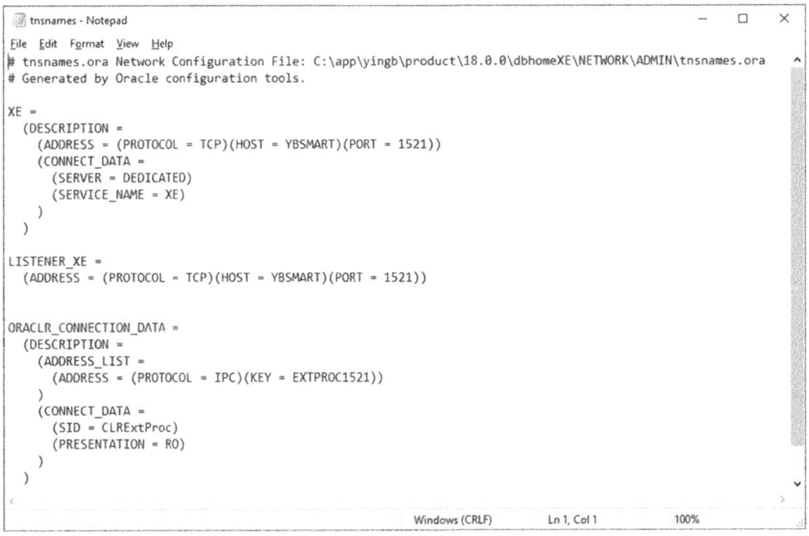

Figure A.6 The opened tnsnames.ora file.

These parameters are important since we need to use them to create and connect an Oracle data source to our applications later.

Now we can open a tool named **`Oracle Database Configuration Assistant`** to create a new Oracle Database 18c XE database or modify an existing one from our computer by going to **`Start\All Programs\Database Configuration Assistant.`** The opened assistant is shown in Figure A.7.

It looks totally different from Oracle Database 11g XE. Yes, starting from 18c, many new functions have been added into the Oracle database server and tools. Different tabs have the different purposes.

Most newly added tabs are used for the Web and network database controls and operations. You can go through the entire workspace to get a full understanding about this new product by clicking

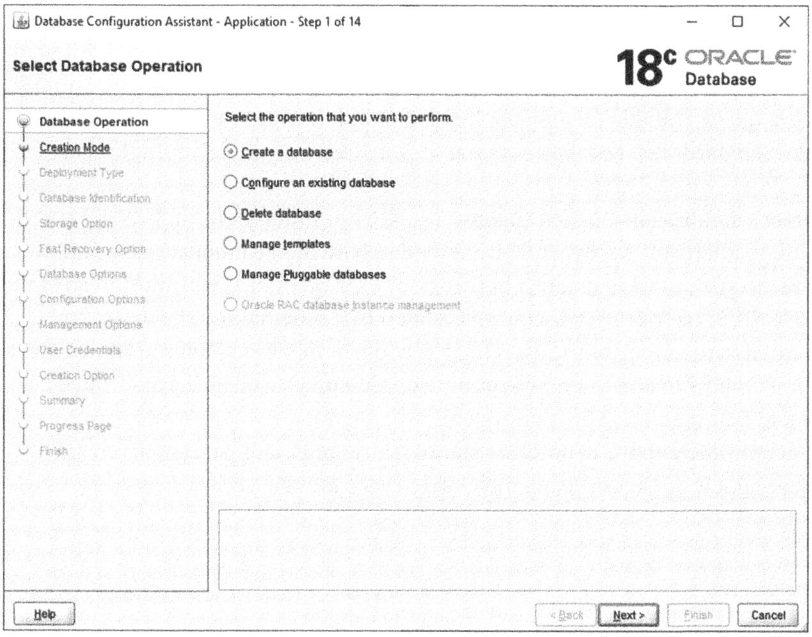

Figure A.7 The home page of the Oracle Database 18c XE.

Figure A.8 The configuration page of the Oracle Database 18c XE.

and viewing each tab one by one. Click on the **Next** button to open the **Configuration** or **Creation Mode** page, as shown in Figure A.8.

This concludes our downloading and installation process for Oracle Database 18c XE. We will create and build our sample database **CSE_DEPT** using two different ways provided by 18c in Chapter 2 and Appendix G.

You need to note that the Oracle Database 18c Express Edition is a single- instance database, which means that only a single instance of your database can be created and utilized with your applications. You cannot create multiple instances of your database at a time. However, in most cases, single instance is good enough for our applications, and you can upgrade this Express Edition to the Oracle Standard 18c Database system if you like to handle multiple database instances later.

To create the customer's database in Oracle Database 18c XE, it is different from the ways to create a customer database in Microsoft Access or SQL Server database management system (MDBS). In Oracle Database 18c XE, you need to create a new user or user account if you want to create a new customer database. Each user or user account is related to a schema or a database, and the name of each user is equal to the name of the associated schema or database. Refer to Appendix D for detailed information on how to create a new user or user account as well as the associated customer database in Oracle Database 18c XE environment.

Go to https://bijoos.com/oraclenotes/2018/2246/ site to get more details on how to create and build different customer Oracle databases using the Oracle Database 18c XE.

Appendix B

Download and Install Oracle SQL Developer

1) Go to https://www.oracle.com/tools/downloads/sqldev-v192-downloads.html page.
2) Click on the **Download** button to start this process.
3) Select and click on the **Windows 64-bit with JDK 8 included** link, as shown in Figure B.1.
4) Click on the downloaded zip file **sqldeveloper-19.2.1.zip** on the lower-left corner as the download process is done to unzip this file.
5) Double click on the **sqldeveloper.exe** file from the unzipped folder to start the installation process.
6) Click on the **Extract all**, and then **Extract** buttons to extract all files, as shown in Figure B.2.
7) As this extraction process is done, return to the **sqldeveloper.exe** file and double click on it to begin the installation process, as shown in Figure B.3.
8) Click on the **OK** button to automatically report issues to Oracle.
9) When the installation process is completed, you can right click on the **sqldeveloper.exe** and select **Pin to taskbar** to save it to the task bar for further usages.

Oracle Database Programming with Visual Basic.NET: Concepts, Designs, and Implementations, First Edition. Ying Bai.
© 2021 The Institute of Electrical and Electronics Engineers, Inc. Published 2021 by John Wiley & Sons, Inc.
Companion website: www.wiley.com/go/bai-VB-Oracle

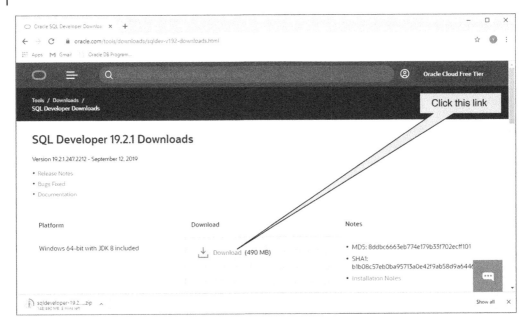

Figure B.1   The opened downloading page for Oracle SQL Developer.

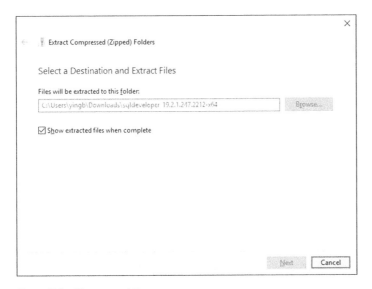

Figure B.2   The opened Extract page.

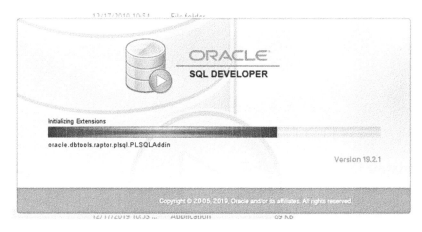

Figure B.3 The installation process.

Appendix C

Download and Install DevExpress WinForms

When building Faculty and Student tables, we need to store faculty and student images into the Oracle 18c XE database directly. Due to the updated property of Oracle 18c XE database, an image can be directly stored into the database column as an image object, in fact, it is a binary large object (`BLOB`) data type.

With the help of a product developed by Developer Express Incorporated, exactly a user interface component, DevExpress WinForms, we can directly insert an image into an Oracle 18c XE database's column via Microsoft Visual Studio.NET platform without any coding process.

In order to use this component, one needs to download this DevExpress WinForms. Perform the following operations to complete this download and installation process.

1) Go to **https://www.devexpress.com/#ui** site.
2) Click on `WinForms` icon as shown in Figure C.1 to open the 30-day free trial dialog.
3) Click on `FREE 30-DAY TRIAL` button to begin this downloading process. An executable file: `DevExpressUniversalTrialSetup-20190902.exe` is downloaded. Click on that .exe file to run this file.
4) Click on the `Trial Installation` button to start the installation process.
5) Click on the `WinForms Controls` icon (Figure C.2) and the **Next** button to install this component only.
6) Click on the `Accept & Continue` button for the next page to continue.
7) On next page, select either Yes or No, to participate in a customer experience program, and click the `Install` button to start this process.
8) The downloading and installation process starts, as shown in Figure C.3.
9) When the installation is completed, click on the `Finish` button.

Oracle Database Programming with Visual Basic.NET: Concepts, Designs, and Implementations, First Edition. Ying Bai.
© 2021 The Institute of Electrical and Electronics Engineers, Inc. Published 2021 by John Wiley & Sons, Inc.
Companion website: www.wiley.com/go/bai-VB-Oracle

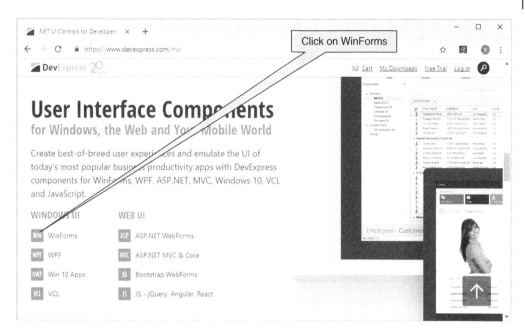

Figure C.1 The opened site for DevExpress WinForms component.

Figure C.2 Select WinForms Controls to install the DevExpress WinForms component.

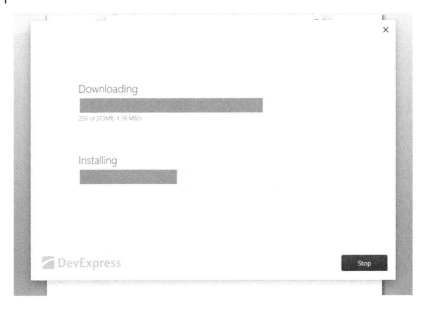

Figure C.3 The downloading and installation process starts.

Appendix D

How to Use the Sample Database

A completed Oracle sample database, **CSE_DEPT** that is used in this book, has been built and stored in a folder **Sample Database** under the **Students** folder at the Wiley ftp site (refer to Figure 1.2 in Chapter 1). The purpose of building this sample database is to make this database development process easy for the readers to save their time and energy to enable them to copy and duplicate it in their Oracle database environment.

To duplicate this sample database, users or readers can copy an exported database, **CSE_DEPT. sql**, from the **Sample Database** folder under the **Students** folder at the Wiley ftp site, and save it in any desired folder on the reader's local machine folder, such as **Documents** folder. Then follow the following steps to complete this database duplication process. It is assumed that the **CSE_DEPT.sql** has been pasted in the **Documents** folder in the user's local computer, as **Documents\CSE_DEPT.sql**.

1) Refer to Appendix A to complete the download and installation of the Oracle Database 18c XE.
2) Refer to Appendix B to complete the download and installation of Oracle SQL Developer.
3) Refer to Section 2.9 in Chapter 2, which includes Sections 2.9.1~2.9.4, to complete the creation of a new Oracle 18c XE Database and a new User Account **CSE_DEPT**.
4) Expand the newly created User Account **CSE_DEPT** under the **Other Users** folder in the Oracle SQL Developer, and click on the **Tables** folder to select it.
5) Then go to **File | Open** menu item to open the **Open** wizard, as shown in Figure D.1.

Figure D.1 The opened Open wizard.

Oracle Database Programming with Visual Basic.NET: Concepts, Designs, and Implementations, First Edition. Ying Bai.
© 2021 The Institute of Electrical and Electronics Engineers, Inc. Published 2021 by John Wiley & Sons, Inc.
Companion website: www.wiley.com/go/bai-VB-Oracle

6) Select the **Documents** folder on the left pane by clicking on it.
7) Then choose the pasted sample database **CSE_DEPT.sql** from the right pane, as shown in Figure D.1.
8) Click on the **Open** button to open this sample database. The opened sample database is shown in Figure D.2.
9) Click on the **Run Script** button, as shown in Figure D.2, to run this script file.
10) The running result is shown in Figure D.3.
11) Click on the **Refresh** button on the upper-left pane, as shown in Figure D.3, you can find that all five tables have been added into our sample database **CSE_DEPT**, as shown in Figure D.3.

Now you can check these duplicated tables by selecting each of them from the left pane, and click on the **Data** tab on the top of right pane one by one.

An example of data in one table, the **FACULTY** table, is shown in Figure D.4.

A point to be noted is that two image columns, **FIMAGE** and **SIMAGE**, in the **FACULTY** and STUDENT tables are NULL, which means that there are no image files that have been built and inserted into these columns. The reason for that is because we intentionally make those columns as blanks, and this will enable the users or readers to insert those images themselves later in Sections 2.9.9.1 and 2.9.9.2 in Chapter 2.

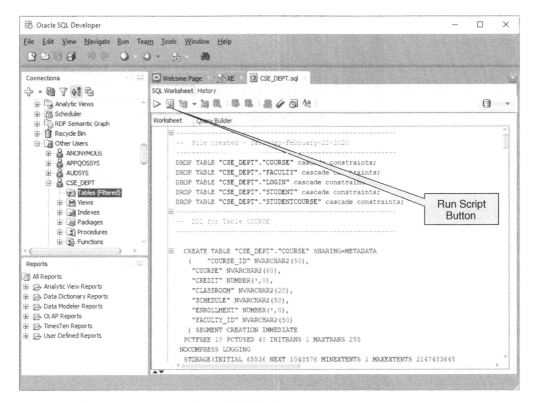

Figure D.2 The opened sample database CSE_DEPT.sql.

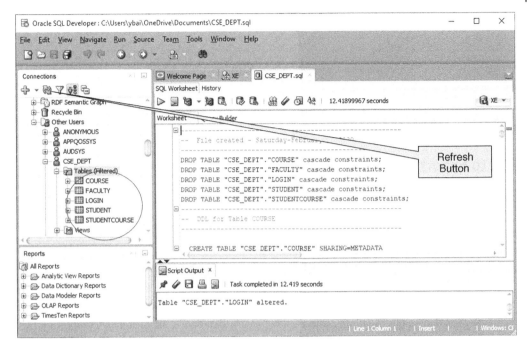

Figure D.3 The running result.

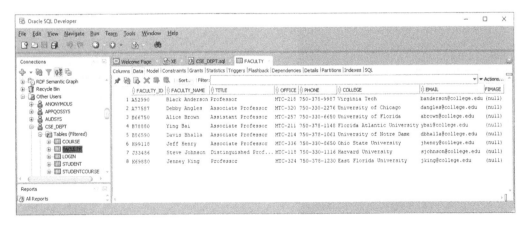

Figure D.4 Example data in the FACULTY table.

Appendix E

How to Export the Sample Database

In Appendix D, we introduced how to use our Oracle sample database, **CSE_DEPT**, which was built in Chapter 2 by using the Import method in the Oracle SQL Developer.

In this section, we will discuss how to export our sample database **CSE_DEPT** to enable some other users to import it to their blank database to simplify this database building process.

Suppose that we will export this sample database into a desired folder, such as Documents folder in users' local machine. Perform the following operational steps to complete this export process

1) Open the Oracle SQL Developer and connect to our database **CSE_DEPT** by completing the login process.
2) Expand the **Other Users** folder, our user account **CSE_DEPT** folder, and the **Tables** folder.
3) Select our all five tables, **COURSE, LOGIN, FACULTY, STUDENT**, and **STUDENTCOURSE**, by pressing and holding the **Ctrl** key and clicking on each of these tables.
4) Then right click on these selected tables and select the **Export** item from the popup menu to open the Export wizard, as shown in Figure E.1.

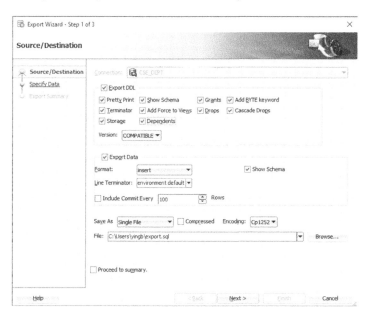

Figure E.1 The opened Export wizard.

Oracle Database Programming with Visual Basic.NET: Concepts, Designs, and Implementations, First Edition. Ying Bai.
© 2021 The Institute of Electrical and Electronics Engineers, Inc. Published 2021 by John Wiley & Sons, Inc.
Companion website: www.wiley.com/go/bai-VB-Oracle

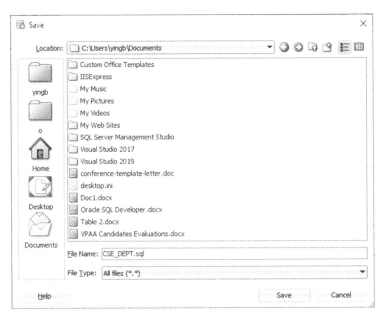

Figure E.2   The opened Save wizard.

5) Select all checkboxes under the **Export DDL** group by checking each of them, as shown in Figure E.1.
6) Click on the **Browse** button to open the **Save** wizard to select the location to save our exported database file, as shown in Figure E.2.
7) Click on the **Documents** icon on the left pane and enter the exported database file's name as **CSE_DEPT.sql** into the **File Name:** box, as shown in Figure E.2.
8) Then click on the **Save** button to close this **Save** wizard.
9) Your finished Export wizard should match one that is shown in Figure E.3.

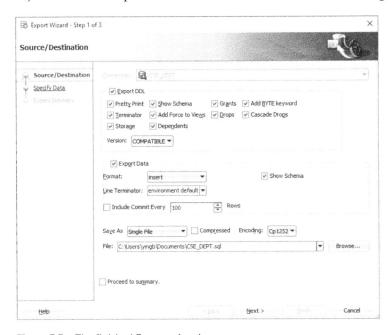

Figure E.3   The finished Export wizard.

Figure E.4 The second step of Export wizard.

10) Click on the **Next** button to open the second step of this Export wizard, as shown in Figure E.4.
11) Click on the **Next** button again to go to the next step since we do not want to do any modification for the location of storing this file.
12) On the next or the last step of this Export wizard, as shown in Figure E.5, click on the **Finish** button to complete this export operation.

Figure E.5 The third step of the Export wizard.

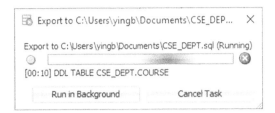

Figure E.6 The export building process.

13) The exporting process starts, as shown in Figure E.6.
14) The final exporting results are shown in Figure E.7.
15) Now if you open the **Documents** folder in your local machine, you can find this exported file **CSE_DEPT.sql.**
16) You can save this exported database file to any location for future importing usage.

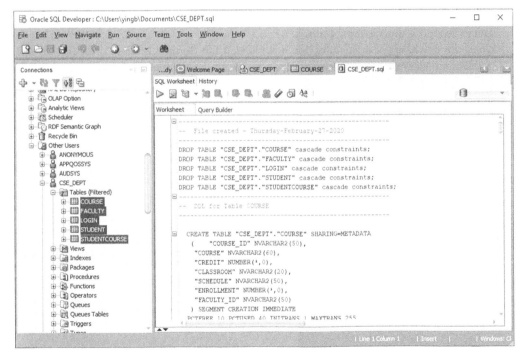

Figure E.7 The completed exporting results.

Appendix F

Download and Install dotConnect Express

Go to the site https://www.devart.com/dotconnect/oracle/compatibility.html site to download dot-Connect for Oracle 9.9 Express since this tool is free. The opened window is shown Figure F.1.

1) Click on the **DOWNLOAD** button that is under the **dotConnect for Oracle** label to start.
2) Click on the **DOWNLAOD** button on the right of **dotConnect for Oracle 9.9 Express** item to begin this downloading process.
3) When the download is done, click the downloaded file **dcoraclefree.exe** to start the installation. The installation wizard is shown in Figure F.2. Click on the **Next** button.
4) On the next wizard, License Agreement wizard, check **I accept the agreement** radio button, as shown in Figure F.3, and the **Next** button to continue.

Figure F.1 The setup starting wizard.

Oracle Database Programming with Visual Basic.NET: Concepts, Designs, and Implementations, First Edition. Ying Bai.
© 2021 The Institute of Electrical and Electronics Engineers, Inc. Published 2021 by John Wiley & Sons, Inc.
Companion website: www.wiley.com/go/bai-VB-Oracle

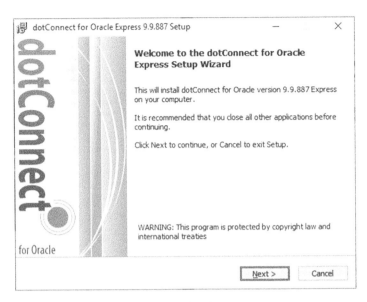

Figure F.2   The initial installation wizard.

Figure F.3   The license agreement wizard.

5) The destination to install this software is shown in the next wizard, as shown in Figure F.4, to enable you to select the desired folder to install this program tool. Keep the default location unchanged and click on the **Next** button to go to the next wizard.

6) The next wizard, the Select Components wizard, is used to enable you to select the desired elements to be installed. For our applications, we need to install all of components. Keep the default selection and click on the **Next** button to continue.

Figure F.4   The installation destination wizard.

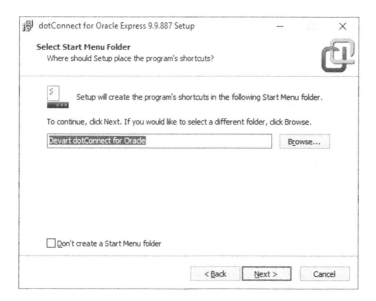

Figure F.5   The Select Start Menu Folder wizard.

7) In the opened Select the Start Menu wizard, as shown in Figure F.5, keep the default folder to save the start menu and click on the **Next** button.
8) The next wizard, **Additional Tasks**, allows you to install additional tasks. Keep the default setting and click on the **Next** button to continue.
9) Click on the **Install** button on the next wizard, **Ready to Install**, to begin this installation. The installation process starts, as shown in Figure F.6.
10) When the installation process is complete, as shown in Figure F.7, click on the Finish button to complete this process.

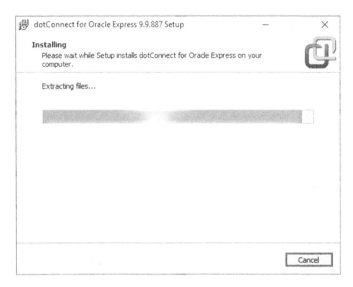

Figure F.6 The installing process starts.

Figure F.7 The option to add the documentation wizard.

Now you can open the Visual Studio.NET 2019 to check and confirm this installation as well as components installed by this installation. Perform the following operations to confirm and check components related to this installation:

1) First create a new Visual Basic.NET 2019 Windows Forms App (.NET Framework) project with any desired name, such as DotConnect `Project`.
2) Then open the Design View or the Form window of the newly created project and the `Toolbox` window. Browse through the `Oracle Data` sub folder, which is shown in Figure F.8. You can find that four new components related to Oracle data access have been added into this folder, they are:

- OracleConnection
- OracleCommand
- OracleCommandBuilder
- OracleDataAdapter

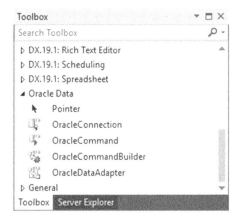

Figure F.8   Four newly added Oracle data components.

3) Right click on the newly created project, **DotConnect Project**, from the Solution Explorer window, and select the **Add|Reference** item to open the Add Reference wizard, which is shown in Figure F.9.

4) Expand the **Assemblies** icon and select the **Extensions** item. Then scroll down along the .NET Framework 4.7.2 window, and you can find that two Oracle-related libraries, **Devart.Data** and **Devart.Data.Oracle**, have been added into the reference library under the .NET Framework 4.7.2 tab.

5) Click on the **OK** button to add these two libraries into our project DotConnect Project.

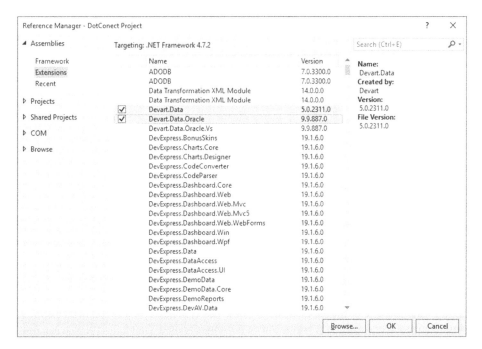

Figure F.9   The newly added reference libraries.

To confirm that both libraries have been added into our project, expand the **References** item under our project, **DotConnect Project**, in the Solution Explorer, and you can find these two libraries.

We need to add these two library references into our all projects later when we build our applications to access the Oracle database.

Appendix G

How to Use User-Defined Windows/Web Forms

In most Chapters of this book, such as Chapters 5~7, we discussed how to build a complete project by using some user-defined Windows Forms, such as `Faculty, Course`, and `Student` Forms, to save developer's time and efforts.

However, in order to correctly copy and add these Forms to your Visual Basic.NET project, certain operational steps with the correct orders are necessary; otherwise, some errors may be encountered and those Forms cannot be added into your projects and they may not work properly at all.

This is absolutely true if some Visual Basic.NET Design Tools and Wizards are used in your projects and a DataSet has been built to connect to your database.

In this Appendix, we try to use an example Form, `Faculty Form`, to illustrate how to add this Form to your project correctly and easily. We will use a sample project `SampleWizards Project` to discuss this addition function.

First, create a new blank solution `SampleWizards Solution` and then add a new **Windows Forms App (.NET Framework)** project `SampleWizards Project` into this solution.

Open the newly created project and remove the default Form, `Form1.vb`, from the Solution Explorer window. Now follow the operational steps listed further to add this Faculty Form to this new project.

1) Go to Solution Explorer window and right click on our newly created project, `SampleWizards Project`, and select **Add|Existin Item** from the popup menu.
2) Browse through the folder `Students\VB Forms\Window`, which is located at the Wiley ftp site (Refer to Figure 1.2 in Chapter 1), and select the `Faculty Form.vb` from the list by checking on it, and click on the **Add** button to add it into the project.
3) Now expand the added `Faculty Form.vb` from the Solution Explorer window and select the `FacultyForm`, which is just under the `Faculty Form.vb` folder, by clicking on it, as shown in Figure G.1a.
4) Then right click on the project `SampleWizards Project` from the Solution Explorer window, and select **Add|Existing Item** again to try to add another two objects related to this Faculty Form.
5) Still go to the folder `Students\VB Forms\Window`, which is located at the Wiley ftp site (Refer to Figure 1.2 in Chapter 1), and select the `Faculty Form.designer.vb` from the list be checking on it, and click on the **Add** button to add it into the project.
6) Click on the **Yes** button if a MessageBox is displayed.
7) In a similar way, add the third item, `Faculty Form.resx`, into the project.

Oracle Database Programming with Visual Basic.NET: Concepts, Designs, and Implementations, First Edition. Ying Bai.
© 2021 The Institute of Electrical and Electronics Engineers, Inc. Published 2021 by John Wiley & Sons, Inc.
Companion website: www.wiley.com/go/bai-VB-Oracle

(a)   (b)

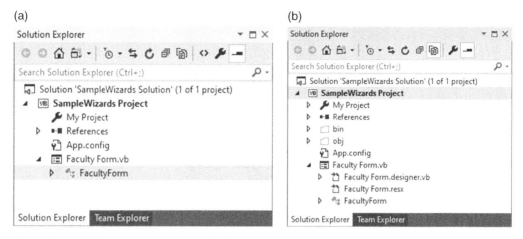

Figure G.1   (a, b) The opened and finished Solution Explorer window.

Your finished Solution Explorer window should match one that is shown in Figure G.1b.

Now you may have some errors displayed in the Error List window. Let's fix them one by one now. First let's build a DataSet **CSE_DEPTDataSet** to connect to our sample database to remove some errors.

1) Open the Data Sources window if it has not been opened by going to **View|Other Windows|Data Sources** item.
2) Then click on the **Add New Data Source** link to open the Data Source Configuration Wizard. Click on the **Next** button to keep the default **Database** item selected.
3) Click on the **Next** button again for the next wizard to keep the **Dataset** selected.
4) Click on the **New Connection** button to open the **Add Connection** wizard.
5) Click on the **Change** button for the Data source box to open the **Change Data Source** wizard, as shown in Figure G.2.

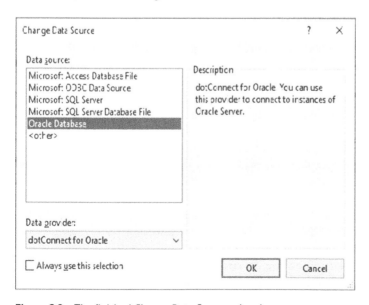

Figure G.2   The finished Change Data Source wizard.

(a)

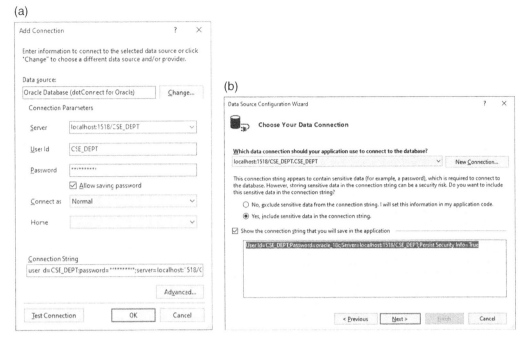

(b)

Figure G.3   (a, b) The finished Add Connection and Configuration wizards.

6) Then select the `Oracle Database` item from the list, as shown in Figure G.2. The data provider, `dotConnect for Oracle`, has been selected and displayed in the Data provider box at the bottom. Click on the `OK` button to continue.

7) On the opened `Add Connection` wizard, as shown in Figure G.3a, enter the following credentials into the related box:

8) `localhost:1518/CSE_DEPT` to the Server box.

9) `CSE_DEPT` to the User Id box

10) `oracle_18c` to the Password box

11) Check the Allow saving password checkbox.

12) Now you can click on the `Test Connection` button to test this connection now. Then click on the `OK` button to do this connection.

13) On the next wizard, check the `Yes` radio button to save sensitive data in the connection string and show the connection string by checking its checkbox. Your finished Configuration wizard should match one that is shown in Figure G.3b. Click on the `Next` button to continue.

14) Click on the `Next` button on the next wizard to connect to our sample database.

15) This may take a while of time. When everything is ready, check the `Tables` checkbox, and it is equivalent to checking and selecting all tables, as shown in Figure G.4. Also change the DataSet name to `CSE_DEPTDataSet` on the bottom.

16) Your finished connection wizard and created DataSet should match one that is shown in Figure G.4. Click on the `Finish` button to complete this database connection and DataSet creation process.

Now you can find this created DataSet `CSE_DEPTDataSet` from your Data Sources window by expanding it in your Visual Basic.NET windows environment, as shown in Figure G.5.

Now only four (4) errors are displayed in the Error List. Let's continue to remove these errors by solving them one by one.

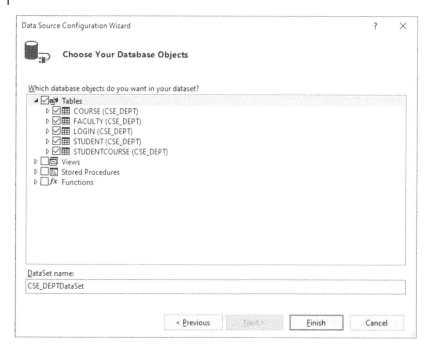

Figure G.4 The finished connection with created DataSet.

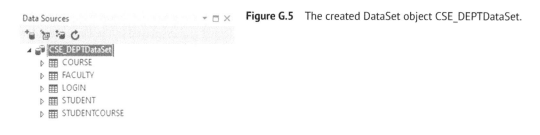

Figure G.5 The created DataSet object CSE_DEPTDataSet.

First, we need to fix the name of the DataSet to match our newly created DataSet. Double click on the first error, **Type "SelectWizard_Project.CSE_DEPTDataSet" is not defined**, in the Error List to open the location for this error, and replace the **SelectWizard_ Project** with **SampleWizards_Project** since our project name is different from the name of project in which the **Faculty Form.vb** is added with the original DataSet. After this fixing, the error in the second line is also fixed.

The next error indicated that a query function, **FillByFacultyName**, is not our Faculty TableAdapter. This makes sense since that query method was created with the Faculty Form on that project. To fix this error, we need to rebuild this query function in this project. Refer to Section 5.4.7 in Chapter 5 to finish this function building. This error would be removed as soon as this query function is built.

The last error is related **Form1.vb** since we removed this form but without making related changes on the codes.

To fix this error, first expand the **My Project** and then the **Application.myapp** folder in the Solution Explorer window, and double click on the **Application.Designer.vb** item to

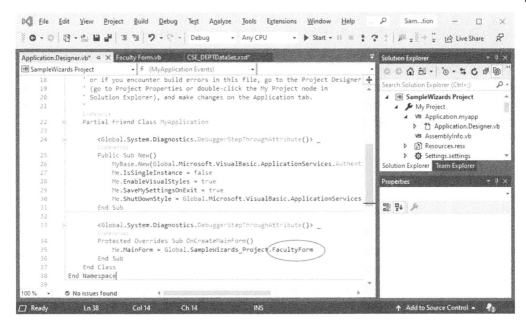

Figure G.6 The finished error-fixed window for the Form1.vb.

open its code window, as shown in Figure G.6. Replace the last object **Form1** with our **FacultyForm** object, as shown in Figure G.6.

The last job is to setup our FacultyForm as the startup Form as the project runs. To do this, double click on the My Project folder in the Solution Explorer window to open the SampleWizards Project Properties window, as shown in Figure G.7.

On the opened Properties window, go to Startup forms box and replace the original form Fom1 with our Faculty Form, FacultyForm, as shown in Figure G.7.

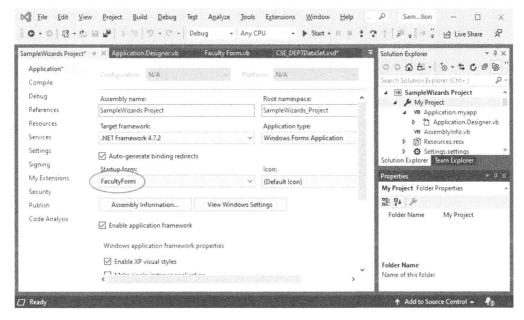

Figure G.7 The modified Startup form object.

Now go to **File|Save All** to save this modified project, and you can find that no error existed in this project now.

You can also go to **Build|Redulid SampleWizards Project** menu item to rebuild this project to make sure that this project is a zero-error project.

In a similar way, you can use all Web Pages built for any Web Application projects in this book. Just add each Web page by right clicking on the target project in the Solution Explorer, and select **Add|Existing Item** menu item, and go to **VB Forms/Web** folder that is located under the **Students** folder at the Wiley ftp site (refer to Figure 1.2 in Chapter 1 for more detailed information).

Appendix H

Download and Install FrontPage Server Extension for Windows 10

1) Go to link: http://www.rtr.com/fpse/Win2008R2/
2) Click on the link: **IIS 10:** Download the RTR FrontPage Server Extensions 2002 for IIS 10 on Windows Server 2016 and Windows 10 to download this software.
3) Double click on the downloaded file `fpse02_IIS10_rtwc_ENG.msi` in your `Downloads` folder to start this installation. You may need to reboot your computer to perform this installation.

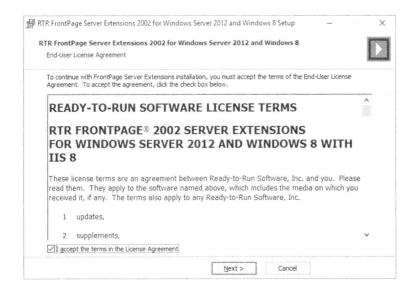

4) As the install start wizard opens, check and accept the agreement, click on the **Next** button.
5) Click on the **Next** button for the next wizard to install additional components for this IIS.
6) The next wizard displays some optional features provided by this IIS. Select the **Indexing Service** and **ASP** items since we need some of them in the next chapter. Then click on the **Next** button.

Oracle Database Programming with Visual Basic.NET: Concepts, Designs, and Implementations, First Edition. Ying Bai.
© 2021 The Institute of Electrical and Electronics Engineers, Inc. Published 2021 by John Wiley & Sons, Inc.
Companion website: www.wiley.com/go/bai-VB-Oracle

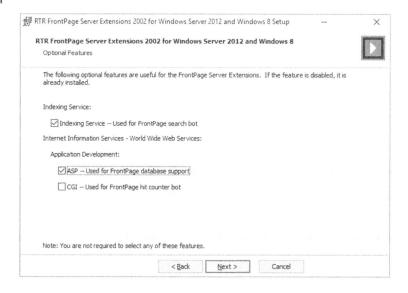

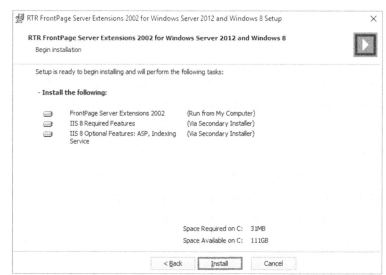

7) The installation summarization is displayed in the next wizard. Click on the **Install** button to begin this installation process. The installation process is starting.

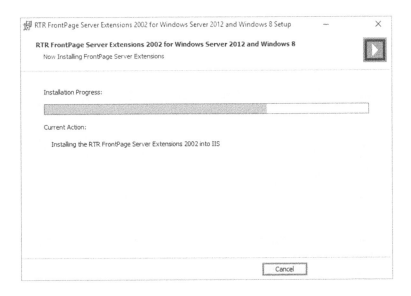

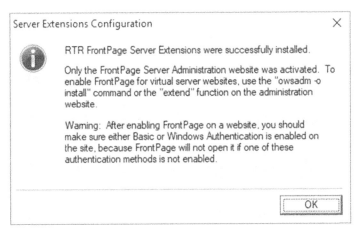

8) When the installation is done, a message box is displayed to indicate some important issues related to how to apply or use this Server. The administration authorization is needed to run this server.

The FrontPage Server Extensions 2002 for Windows 8 is installed as this process is done. This Server is also working for Windows 10.

One may need to get a license if this FrontPage Server Extensions is used for commercial purposes.

Appendix I

Download and Install LinqConnect Express

1) Go to the link https://www.devart.com/linqconnect/download.html to open the page and click on the **DOWNLOAD** button on the right of **LinqConnect 4.9 Express** to download this tool.
2) When download is completed, click on the **linqconnectfree.exe** item on the lower-left corner to run this software and begin this installation process.
3) Click on the **Continue to Install** if you encountered some warning message. The installation process started with the wizard shown as follows. Click on the **Next** button to continue.

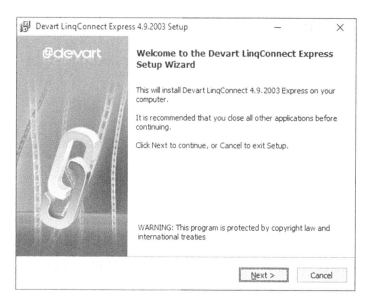

4) Check the radio button: **I accept the agreement** and click on the **Next** button.
5) On the next wizard, change the default installation folder to **C:\Program Files\Devart\LinqConnect**, as shown as follows. It is very important to select a different folder to install this tool if you have installed **doConnect for Oracle** in your computer.

Oracle Database Programming with Visual Basic.NET: Concepts, Designs, and Implementations, First Edition. Ying Bai.
© 2021 The Institute of Electrical and Electronics Engineers, Inc. Published 2021 by John Wiley & Sons, Inc.
Companion website: www.wiley.com/go/bai-VB-Oracle

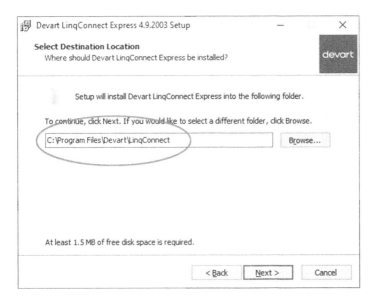

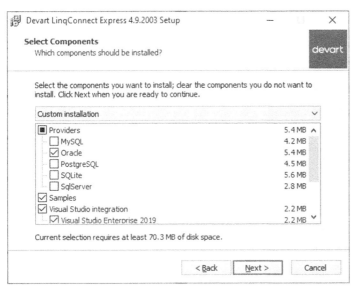

6) Click on the **Next** button to continue.

7) On the next wizard, uncheck all other data sources and only keep the **Oracle** data source under the **Providers** category, as shown above, since we only need this Oracle database as our target source. Click on the **Next** button to continue.

8) Click on the **Next** button for the next two wizards to keep the default shortcut and not install assemblies in the GAC.

9) Click on the **Install** button on the next wizard to begin the installation process, as shown as follows.

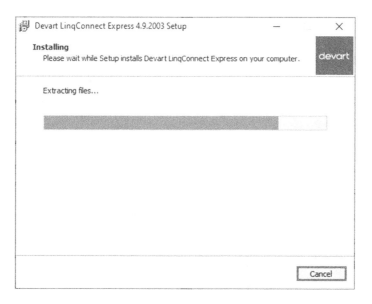

10) When the installation process is completed, click on the **Finish** button to complete this process.

Index

Oracle Database Programming with Visual Basic.NET: Concepts, Designs, and Implementations, First Edition. Ying Bai.
© 2021 The Institute of Electrical and Electronics Engineers, Inc. Published 2021 by John Wiley & Sons, Inc.
Companion website: www.wiley.com/go/bai-VB-Oracle